The
School
in
Society

The School in Society

Studies in the Sociology of Education

Edited by

SAM D. SIEBER and DAVID E. WILDER

THE FREE PRESS
A Division of Macmillan Publishing Co., Inc.
NEW YORK

Collier Macmillan Publishers
LONDON

To Ed Brunner and Bert Brim
who gave us our first chance
to be sociologists of education

Acknowledgments

We are pleased to acknowledge the assistance of Karen Seashore, who worked on the annotations, and Louis and Adair Lummis, who helped with library searches. We also wish to thank David Rogers for his valuable editorial advice. Finally, Gloria Nabors and Beth Hay should be cited for their reliable secretarial assistance.

The Free Press
A Division of Macmillan Publishing Co., Inc.
866 Third Avenue, New York, New York 10022

COLLIER-MACMILLAN CANADA LTD., TORONTO, ONTARIO

Library of Congress Catalog Card Number: 72-80079

Printed in the United States of America

Printing number
   2 3 4 5 6 7 8 9 10

Contents

WITHDRAWN

Overview

DURING RECENT YEARS, critics of American education have increasingly questioned the manner in which children are educated in our society. But despite mounting criticism and efforts to create new and innovative patterns of schooling, the vast majority of our youth continue to receive education according to well-established patterns. In this volume we attempt to bring together empirically based sociological knowledge about educational patterns in our society. We have deliberately focused on studies of the American school as an organization in its immediate social environment, and we have included only a few studies of international and comparative education. Our choice of this emphasis was guided by our belief that these latter, more macrosociological topics had been admirably covered in *Economy, Education, and Society*, published by The Free Press in 1961 and edited by A. H. Halsey, Jean Floud, and C. Arnold Anderson. Topics on a more microsociological level which relate to schools in American society, however, have never been adequately brought together in a single volume.

A second distinguishing characteristic of this collection grew out of what we regarded as a tendency among sociologists to favor the study of higher education while neglecting elementary and secondary education except as they relate to higher education. We believe there is need to bring together studies that concentrate on the schools as sociological entities in their own right. Consequently, there are no selections in the present volume devoted exclusively to the familiar problems of college aspirations and college attendance, or to demonstrating the well-established relationships between stratification and educational achievement in our society. There are, however, a number of selections about schools as formal and informal organizations and about the role behavior of their members and constituents.

A third consideration that guided our choice of selections was the belief that research should demonstrate how sociologists test their ideas through empirical inquiry. The earlier volume edited by Halsey, Floud and Anderson set an admirable precedent in this respect. Our attempts to find studies that illustrated this principle for all the topics in the present volume have not always been successful. The majority of selections are based on individual studies, but there are some important areas still relatively untouched by empirical research, and we have included theoretical selections in an attempt to fill these gaps. In addition, there are a few areas where research has been so abundant that we have included research reviews rather than attempting to locate single definitive studies.

The sociology of education has grown more rapidly in the past decade than most other major areas in sociology. Textbooks, journals, monographs, and sections of professional associations have proliferated at a rate which has made it difficult to keep abreast of scholarly developments. Moreover, the delineation of new problems and the efforts to follow up previous research have fostered the appearance of *sub*specialties—for example, educational organization, innovation, classroom socialization, and school-community relations. Thus, we feel that the sociology of education has passed beyond the stage of acquiring *legitimacy* and has entered a new phase of progressive *refinement* of major ideas. We hope that the next phase will entail the formulation of a comprehensive conceptual framework so that research needs can be identified and new work can be related to previous efforts in a more cumulative fashion. The following discussion of trends and deficiencies in the sociology of education, and our introductions to the separate sections of this volume, are directed toward this third stage of development.

There are also signs of increasing specialization in both the *macro*- and *micro*aspects of education, that is, education viewed as a social institution with relations to the family, economy, polity, and stratification system, versus education viewed as a relatively self-contained domain of human activity or "social system." The growing distinction between the interinstitutional and the social systems approaches seems to have been the result of the recent rapid development of the latter perspective, rather than to the splitting up of a formerly coherent outlook that gave weight to *both* perspectives. The interinstitutional approach was introduced by the founders of modern sociology (see Weber and Durkheim in Part I, Classical Perspectives) and consequently this emphasis mainly held the attention of succeeding generations of scholars. It is not surprising, then, that the first major collection of papers in the sociology of education to reflect the interests of contemporary sociology (i.e., Halsey, Floud and Anderson, 1961) focused on the interinstitutional aspects of education.

In the schools of education, there *was* a tendency to look at schools as self-contained systems. But lacking a theoretical framework that would have facilitated the accumulation of systematic knowledge about schools —a framework which the liberal arts sociologists might have contributed had their attention not been directed elsewhere—professional educators remained vulnerable to the demands of the profession for *services*, namely, teacher training, social bookkeeping, the solution of problems in the operation of schools, the definition of educational goals, and the like. The result was a strong *normative* emphasis in "educational sociology" as practiced in the departments of education. In the twenties, for example, courses in educational sociology were "a hodgepodge of subjects which instructors in sociology and education might put together for the training of teachers and others interested in education" (Brookover, 1949). And as late as 1948, a paper read at the meetings of the American Sociology Society argued that "Educational sociology cannot be a pure science; it must be applied to the control of education" (cited by Brookover, 1949). As a consequence of this normative orientation in schools of education, sociologists in the liberal arts developed a certain disrespect for the study of schools as social systems—an attitude which no doubt reinforced their early preoccupation with the interinstitutional aspects of education.

Several factors were probably responsible for overcoming the bias which prevented sociologists from studying schools as social systems. One was the publication of a few major works which derived from, and contributed to, the mainstream of academic sociology (e.g., *Explorations in Role Analysis*, by Gross et al.; *The Adolescent Society*, by Coleman; and *Sociology and the Field of Education*, by Brim). These writings tended to legitimize the investigation of schools as relatively self-contained communities. Another factor was the appearance of large amounts of money in the late fifties (primarily from the federal government) for research with an applied orientation. Not only did these newly available funds enable sociologists to test their ideas in educational settings, but the emphasis of the funding agencies on the solution of educational problems meant that the schools had to be studied as goal-oriented agencies, and therefore that the internal dynamics which hindered or facilitated the achievement of goals had to be taken into account. A supplemental trend was the growing interest in the application of sociology to problems of modern society. When joined with widespread public criticism of education in the fifties and sixties, this new concern in sociology for the application of knowledge may have been a potent instigator of greater interest in schools as social systems.

Allied with the earlier tendency to look at the relationships of education to the social order was the emphasis on the *selection and allocation* function. Not surprisingly, if one is chiefly concerned with the changes wrought in education by shifts in the occupational structure, or with the possible contribution of education to social mobility, for example, then the selection-allocation process will receive foremost attention. While this focus by no means precludes the investigation of the *internal* dynamics of schools as selecting and allocating agencies, the emphasis on interinstitutional analysis diverted the attention of sociologists from studying these internal processes. Instead, sociologists interested in selection and allocation have tended to address themselves to clarifying the relationships between *student inputs* (e.g., social class background, race, IQ, etc.) and *outputs* for the larger society (e.g., college attendance, earnings, occupational position, etc.). The intervening variables of guidance, tracking, role-modeling and the scaling down or encouragement of aspirations have been generally ignored. (A notable exception was *Elmtown's Youth* by Hollingshead, 1949, and more recently, *The Educational Decision-Makers* by Cicourel and Kitsuse, 1963). But perhaps the most striking outcome of the emphasis on the selection-allocation function was a deemphasis on the second major function of education—socialization and training.

Problems of socialization and training were occasionally addressed by "educational sociologists" in the departments of education. But the preemption of learning as a field of study by psychologists, and the pressures for service stemming from school practitioners, tended to undermine the study of socialization and training from a contemporary sociological perspective. Moreover, even when sociological interest was directed to this problem area by professors of education, scant attention was paid to the contribution of socialization in schools to society-at-large owing to the profession's concentration on the *micro*aspects of education, that is, the internal operation of schools. In short, professional educators also failed to answer the need for a full-scale attack on problems of socialization and training.

But it is not enough to say that education has only the two goals of socialization-training and selection-allocation. Because education is conducted by specially trained personnel working in highly complex organizations, the maintenance of this formal system also becomes an important goal. Thus, the recruitment and training of teachers, the sustaining of occupational commitment, the allocation of resources, and the security of the system in relation to its environment are goals which need to be examined in their own right. Without the fulfillment of these "maintenance" goals, the terminal goals of socialization-training and selection-allocation cannot be achieved. And, of course, the manner in which organizational problems are solved may *hinder* the attainment of the terminal goals of education. Yet it seems safe to say that until recently the issues related to organizational maintenance were even more neglected than the problems of socialization and allocation.

Perhaps the most neglected area of all, however, is the study of education as an *institutional complex*. By "institutional complex" we mean to draw attention to the elaborate arrangements which exist outside of local school systems for the purpose of supporting and directing the activities of these systems—for example, teacher training institutions, testing agencies, state education agencies, research and development organizations, accreditation bodies and textbook publishers. These "ancillary structures," as Wayland (1964) calls them, have virtually created a national education system despite the nominal local control of education in the United States. The influences of these structures on socialization-training, selection-allocation, and organizational maintenance have hardly begun to be assessed from the perspective of sociology.

In the foregoing discussion we have referred to several major foci of the sociology of education. We have remarked on the earlier concern with interinstitutional analysis, the more recent interest in social systems analysis and the still undeveloped field of education as an institutional complex. We have also mentioned three overarching goals: socialization-training, selection-allocation, and organizational maintenance. Thus, we have been dealing with two major dimensions, one concerned with the *level of analysis* and the other with the *goals* of the educational system. A simple diagram which combines these two dimensions shows that the sociology of education comprises nine principle domains of inquiry.

Table 1—The Sociology of Education

	Level of Analysis		
	SOCIAL SYSTEM		INTERINSTITUTIONAL
	Internal Dynamics of Schools	Institutional Complex	
SOCIALIZATION-TRAINING	1	2	3
SELECTION-ALLOCATION	4	5	6
ORGANIZATIONAL MAINTENANCE	7	8	9

Goals (at left, spanning the three goal rows)

Although each of these domains represents a distinct orientation subsuming a specific set of variables, our discussion should not be construed as advocating exclusive attention to one or another of these domains. Indeed, we feel that the future development of the sociology of education depends to a great extent on our success in illuminating the *interconnections* among these nine areas of substantive concentration.

Because of the limited amount of work in certain of these domains, and because sociologists often touch on more than one of the domains in a single work, we did not attempt to organize the selections in this volume according to this highly abstract scheme. All of the nine areas, however, are represented. The section on *Socialization and Learning* is mainly concerned with the first domain, socialization in the context of the internal dynamics of schools. Trow's paper on changes in the functions of secondary education and Coleman's paper on equality of opportunity, however, also touch on domains 3 and 6 (interinstitutional analysis of socialization goals and of selection). The articles in Part IV, The School As an Informal System, afford additional materials on domain 1, but also include analyses of informal aspects of educational agencies bearing on several other domains. Selection-allocation is a concern of Coleman inasmuch as he studies the effects of the students' status system on academic effort; and organizational maintenance is the chief interest of Gross et al. in their study of the superintendent's role conflicts. Part III, The School As a

Formal Organization, focuses on many aspects of organizational maintenance, but also contains implications for socialization and selection (see Wheeler, Corwin, and Jackson). Part V, Teaching As an Occupation, is also mainly relevant to organizational maintenance, but again crosses the boundaries into other domains (e.g., Charters' review of research on the influence of teachers' social class on values expressed in the classroom bears on socialization). And finally, Part VI, School-Community Relations, is concerned with socialization (Sieber and Wilder, and Fein), organizational maintenance (Kerr, and Litwak and Meyer), and selection-allocation (Crain and Street, and Fein).

As we noted at the outset, our interest has been mainly in the social system of education rather than in the relation of education to the economy, polity and stratification systems of society. Accordingly, we have emphasized materials on the internal dynamics of schools (domains 1, 4, and 7) and the institutional complex of education (domains 2, 5, and 8). We have nevertheless included certain writings that bear on broader societal issues (see Coleman on equality of education, Trow on historical shifts in education owing to occupational changes and other trends, and Fein on the theoretical significance of "community control" of schools). We are therefore reasonably confident that every major social aspect of education is dealt with at some point in the volume.

Overviews of the Field

Bidwell, Charles E. "The School as a Formal Organization." In *Handbook of Organizations*, edited by James G. March. Chicago: Rand-McNally, 1965.

Brim, Orville G., Jr. *Sociology and the Field of Education*. New York: Russell Sage Foundation, 1958.

Brookover, Wilbur B. "Sociology of Education: A Definition." *American Sociological Review*, 14 (June, 1949), pp. 407–415.

Clark, Burton R. "Sociology of Education." In *Handbook of Modern Sociology*, edited by Robert E. L. Faris, pp. 734–769. Chicago: Rand-McNally, 1964.

Gross, Neal. "The Sociology of Education." In *Sociology Today*, edited by R. K. Merton, L. Broom, and L. S. Cottrell, Jr., pp. 128–152. New York: Basic Books, 1959.

Hansen, Donald A. "The Uncomfortable Relation of Sociology and Education." In *On Education—Sociological Perspectives*, edited by Donald A. Hansen and Joel E. Gerstl, pp. 3–35. New York: Wiley, 1967.

Textbooks

Brookover, Wilbur B., and Gottlieb, David. *A Sociology of Education*. New York: American Book Co., 1964.

Corwin, Ronald G. *A Sociology of Education: Emerging Patterns of Class, Status and Power in the Public Schools*. New York: Appleton-Century-Crofts, 1965.

Havighurst, Robert J., and Neugarten, Bernice L. *Society and Education*. Boston: Allyn and Bacon, 1957.

Nelson, Jack L., and Besag, Frank. *Sociological Perspectives in Education: Models for Analysis*. New York: Pitman, 1970.

I

Classical Perspectives

Introduction

CLASSICAL WRITINGS disclose the assumptions on which a field of thought was founded; they enable us to gauge the distance that a field has traveled since its inception, and they pose questions for current study. The selections included here should be read from these three perspectives. With regard to the last purpose—the location of problems for current research and theory—there are two ways in which classical writings can be used. First, and most obviously, we sometimes encounter ideas which simply have escaped the attention of posterity. A good example can be found in Willard Waller's writings on the enduring conflict of interests between students and teachers. But there is a more subtle way in which classical writings can help us identify questions for contemporary research. When viewed from a modern perspective, certain early formulations are clearly inadequate. In order to take advantage of this fact, we should first formulate as precisely as possible the discrepancy between contemporary knowledge and past theory. Second, rather than discard past theory, we should try to make the necessary adjustments in it—for only in this way are we likely to contribute to the cumulative theoretical development of a field. The third step follows quite naturally; in attempting to adjust the theories of the past to take present knowledge into account, we often find that our knowledge leaves something to be desired. Thus, our attention is directed to *new* problems for current study.

Durkheim, for example, was concerned with sources of moral integration in modern society and he therefore viewed education solely from this standpoint. In essence, he stressed the *conservative* function of education for society. What he neglected to consider was the emergence of a second major function of education: selection for adult roles in a rapidly changing social order. When this task is added to that of value transmission, the question arises of how (and whether) education is able to avoid misfitting each new generation by indoctrination with values unsuited to the emerging system of adult roles. In short, the conservative, moral function of education and the task of selection and allocation to future roles must somehow be accommodated to one another. The extent in which the two functions are integrated, deserve the attention of contemporary sociology. One way in which they might be accommodated to each other is through the transmission of certain values that will enable graduates to perform in a broad spectrum of social positions. Assimilation of these values might therefore serve as criteria for *selection* within the school—a hypothetical solution which raises the question of the criteria used by school personnel for promotability. Alternatively, it could be the case that effective selection for adult roles is *sabotaged* by the conservative, moral function of education. In sum, by noting an inadequacy in Durkheim's theory, and then trying to recast his theory in the light of newer ideas, we discover that our knowledge about the selection-allocation function of educational systems is far from complete.

Let us take another example. Durkheim argues that inasmuch as education is necessary for the transmission of culture, which process is viewed as fundamental to the continued integration of society, education cannot be left in the hands of any special group, social institution, or subculture. This problem of insuring a universal socialization experience did not arise in simpler societies where moral consensus was presumably widespread. Modern society, therefore, instead of relying upon the authority of the family or church for educational directives, must have recourse to the State for the propagation of its "self-evident" values. The analysis is a functionalist one insofar as Durkheim explains the existence of public control of education by reference to the contribution (function) of education to the integration of society; and hence the necessity for a structural arrangement (State control) to facilitate that function. But Durkheim overlooked the vulnerability of the State to the power and influence of numerous interest groups, a situation that prevents the emergence of a set of universal precepts. In effect, there are *other* functional requirements of modern society which must be served, such as the political expression of competing subcultures. The diversity of interests to which the State is subjected undermines the assumption that the State is automatically qualified to dictate the substance of education.

The inadequacy of Durkheim's thinking on this point raises the intriguing question of how an educational system can serve two masters: general value consensus, as opposed to the special needs and interests of subgroups. Efforts to cope with this dual socialization goal are reflected today in recurrent curricular and organizational reforms (e.g., compensatory education and tracking), in controversies over the education of minority groups and community control of schools, and in the stresses and strains between governmental bodies and local school systems. Durkheim's lack of resolution on this point reminds us, therefore, that our own theoretical formulations have also skirted the question.

Another problem that emerges from Durkheim's writings concerns the relationship between the teacher and the student. Since Durkheim views the critical function of education as forming the "social being" rather than the "individual being," it becomes imperative that the teacher have a deep sense of the importance of his role as "the agent of a great moral person who surpasses him: . . . society." However, he also appreciates that the child must not submit blindly to the teacher's authority—on the contrary, according to Durkheim, the pupil must be instilled with "self-mastery." This implicit conflict between authoritarian and pupil-centered pedagogy has given rise to considerable controversy in our own day. But apart from such problems as those discussed here, it should be recognized that Durkheim's work establishes one important basis for the emergence of educational agencies in complex societies.

The selections from Weber, Dewey, and Waller furnish extensions of Durkheim's thought. Weber's historical perspective led him to study the broad stages of social development. His references to education therefore bear on the maintenance of a *particular* stage or social order, modern society being only one of these. Via this historical route, Weber was prompted to examine the relationship between education and the polity, economy, and stratification systems associated with three major types of social order. He derived these types from three kinds of authority systems: *charismatic*, *traditional* and *legal*. The charismatic system devolves upon the leader whose heroic or magical gifts instill confidence in his followers; traditional authority is based on the prerogatives of certain elite status groups, such as aristocracies; and legal authority (which is found in its most developed form in modern bureaucratic society) is based on functional competence and rationally created rules. Our selection from Weber briefly contrasts the different roles of education associated with each of these three typical structures of domination, with emphasis being placed on the modern system. And it is clear that Weber, unlike Durkheim, recognizes the selection-allocation function of education in contemporary society. Thus, in his discussion of the growth of examination systems, he writes: "Special examinations mean or appear to mean a 'selection' of those who qualify from all social strata rather than a rule by notables." In short, Weber opened the way for a comparative sociology of education; and it was precisely this comparative perspective that caused him to recognize the selective function of education in addition to that of value transmission.

Both Durkheim and Weber saw the need for rationally organized agencies of education; and both believed that the requirements of modern society dictated State control. But neither delved into the implications for socialization and selection of the way in which schools are organized and operated. Dewey was among the first to draw our attention to this matter inasmuch as he saw "conspicuous dangers attendant upon the transition from indirect to formal education." While the "social medium" of informal education is personal and vital, providing opportunities to learn through participation in everyday affairs, formal schooling "easily becomes remote and dead—abstract and bookish . . ." Consequently, there is danger that the child's motivation will be eroded. The school must therefore find means of providing for "conjoint activities in which those instructed take part, so that they may acquire a *social sense* of their own powers and of the materials and appliances used." In short, the principles which make informal social participation so effective a medium of socialization must be applied in the school as a formal agency. Clearly, Dewey resolved the dilemma between authoritarian and pupil-centered pedagogy in favor of the latter.

But Dewey's insight led him directly into matters of pedagogy, that is, of what instruction *ought* to entail to overcome the "artificiality" of formal education. He therefore shifted from an analytical to a normative posture without a detailed examination of the *social system* which emerges in the school in response to the school's formalized character. It is the latter issue that was raised by Waller, whose starting point was the conception of the school as a "social organism." Thus, Waller delves into numerous areas of school life that remain salient in contemporary sociology of education. (Indeed, Waller's viewpoint is so timely that we have included a selection from his work in Part IV, The School as an Informal System.) The present selection from Waller's work outlines a large domain of present-day sociology of education, including such topics as the vulnerability of schools to their environment, the formal and informal structures of authority, student peer culture, the social differentiation of students and of faculty, the effects of faculty interactions on student-teacher relationships, and the pervasive problem of social control. Waller, then, is the immediate forerunner of the topics and issues discussed in the remainder of this volume.

Definitions of Education—
Critical Examination

Education: Its Nature and Its Role

Emile Durkheim

Reprinted with permission of The Macmillan Company from Education and Sociology *by Emile Durkheim, pp. 61–76, 78–82, 83–85, and 87–90. Copyright © by The Free Press, a Corporation, 1956.*

THE WORD "education" has sometimes been used in a very broad sense to designate the totality of influences that nature or other men are able to exercise either on our intelligence or on our will. It includes, says John Stuart Mill, "all that we ourselves do and all that others do for us to the end of bringing us closer to the perfection of our nature. In its most widely accepted sense, it includes even indirect effects on the character and faculties of men produced by things having quite a different objective: by laws, by forms of government, the industrial arts, and even by physical phenomena, independent of human will, such as climate, soil, and locality." But this definition includes elements that are quite disparate, and that one cannot combine under a single heading without confusion. The influence of things on men is very different, in their processes and effects, from that which comes from men themselves; and the influence of peers on peers differs from that which adults exercise on youth. It is only the latter that concerns us here, and, therefore, it is this meaning that it is convenient to reserve for the word "education."

But what is the specific nature of this influence? Various answers have been given to this question; they can be divided into two main types.

Following Kant, "the end of education is to develop, in each individual, all the perfection of which he is capable." But what is meant by perfection? It is, as has often been said, the harmonious development of all the human faculties. To carry to the highest point that can be reached all the capacities that are in us, to realize them as completely as possible, without their interfering with one another, is not this an ideal beyond which there can be no other?

But if, to a degree, this harmonious development is indeed necessary and desirable, it is not wholly attainable; for it is in contradiction to another rule of human behavior which is no less cogent: that which has us concentrate on a specific, limited task. We cannot and we must not all be devoted to the same kind of life; we have, according to our aptitudes, different functions to fulfill, and we must adapt ourselves to what we must do. We are not all made for reflection; there is need for men of feeling and of action. Conversely, there is need of those whose job is thinking. Now, thought can develop only in detachment from action, only by turning in upon itself, only by turning its object entirely away from overt action. From this comes a first differentiation which is accompanied by a break of equilibrium. And behavior, in turn, as thought, can take a variety of different and specialized forms. Doubtless this specialization does not exclude a certain common base and, consequently, a certain balance of functions, organic and psychic alike, without which the health of the individual would be endangered, as well as social cohesion. We see, thus, that perfect harmony cannot be presented as the final end of conduct and of education.

Still less satisfactory is the utilitarian

11

definition, according to which the objective of education would be to "make the individual an instrument of happiness for himself and for his fellows" (James Mill); for happiness is an essentially subjective thing that each person appreciates in his own way. Such a formula, then, leaves the end of education undetermined and, therefore, education itself, since it is left to individual fancy. Spencer, to be sure, tried to define happiness objectively. For him, the conditions of happiness are those of life. Complete happiness is the complete life. But what is meant by life? If it is a matter of physical existence alone, one may well say: that without which it would be impossible; it implies, in effect, a certain equilibrium between the organism and its environment, and, since the two terms in relation are definable data, it must be the same with their relation. But one can express, in this way, only the most immediate vital necessities. Now, for man, and above all for the man of today, such a life is not life. We ask more of life than normal enough functioning of our organs. A cultivated mind prefers not to live rather than give up the joys of the intellect. Even from the material point of view alone, everything over and above what is strictly necessary cannot be exactly determined. The "standard of life," as the English say, the minimum below which it does not seem to us that we can consent to descend, varies infinitely according to conditions, milieux, and the times. What we found sufficient yesterday, today seems to us to be beneath the dignity of man, as we define it now, and everything leads us to believe that our needs in this connection grow increasingly.

We come here to the general criticism that all these definitions face. They assume that there is an ideal, perfect education, which applies to all men indiscriminately; and it is this education,

universal and unique, that the theorist tries to define. But first, if history is taken into consideration, one finds in it nothing to confirm such an hypothesis. Education has varied infinitely in time and place. In the cities of Greece and Rome, education trained the individual to subordinate himself blindly to the collectivity, to become the creature of society. Today, it tries to make of the individual an autonomous personality. In Athens, they sought to form cultivated souls, informed, subtle, full of measure and harmony, capable of enjoying beauty and the joys of pure speculation; in Rome, they wanted above all for children to become men of action, devoted to military glory, indifferent to letters and the arts. In the Middle Ages, education was above all Christian; in the Renaissance, it assumes a more lay and literary character; today science tends to assume the place in education formerly occupied by the arts. Can it be said, then, that the fact is not the ideal; that if education has varied, it is because men have mistaken what it should be? But if Roman education had been infused with an individualism comparable to ours, the Roman city would not have been able to maintain itself; Latin civilization would not have developed, nor, furthermore, our modern civilization, which is in part descended from it. The Christian societies of the Middle Ages would not have been able to survive if they had given to free inquiry the place that we give it today. There are, then, ineluctable necessities which it is impossible to disregard. Of what use is it to imagine a kind of education that would be fatal for the society that put it into practice?

This assumption, so doubtful, in itself rests on a more general mistake. If one begins by asking, thus, what an ideal education must be, abstracted from conditions of time and place, it is to admit implicitly that a system of education has no reality in itself. One does not see in education a collection of practices and institutions that have been organized slowly in the course of time, which are comparable with all the other social institutions and which express them, and which, therefore, can no more be changed at will than the structure of the society itself. But it seems that this would be a pure system of *a priori* concepts; under this heading it appears to be a logical construct. One imagines that men of each age organize it voluntarily to realize a determined end; that, if this organization is not everywhere the same, it is because mistakes have been made concerning either the end that it is to pursue or the means of attaining it. From this point of view, educational systems of the past appear as so many errors, total or partial. No attention need be paid to them, therefore; we do not have to associate ourselves with the faulty observation or logic of our predecessors; but we can and must pose the question without concerning ourselves with solutions that have been given, that is to say, leaving aside everything that has been, we have only to ask ourselves what should be. The lessons of history can, moreover, serve to prevent us from repeating the errors that have been committed.

In fact, however, each society, considered at a given stage of development, has a system of education which exercises an irresistible influence on individuals. It is idle to think that we can rear our children as we wish. There are customs to which we are bound to conform; if we flout them too severely, they take their vengeance on our children. The children, when they are adults, are unable to live with their peers, with whom they are not in accord. Whether they had been raised in accordance with ideas that were either obsolete or premature does not matter; in the one case as in the other, they are not of their time and, therefore, they are outside the conditions of normal life. There is, then, in each period, a prevailing type of education from which we cannot deviate without encountering that lively

resistance which restrains the fancies of dissent.

Now, it is not we as individuals who have created the customs and ideas that determine this type. They are the product of a common life, and they express its needs. They are, moreover, in large part the work of preceding generations. The entire human past has contributed to the formation of this totality of maxims that guide education today; our entire history has left its traces in it, and even the history of the peoples who have come before. It is thus that the higher organisms carry in themselves the reflection of the whole biological evolution of which they are the end product. Historical investigation of the formation and development of systems of education reveals that they depend upon religion, political organization, the degree of development of science, the state of industry, etc. If they are considered apart from all these historic causes, they become incomprehensible. Thus, how can the individual pretend to reconstruct, through his own private reflection, what is not a work of individual thought? He is not confronted with a *tabula rasa* on which he can write what he wants, but with existing realities which he cannot create, or destroy, or transform, at will. He can act on them only to the extent that he has learned to understand them, to know their nature and the conditions on which they depend; and he can understand them only if he studies them, only if he starts by observing them, as the physicist observes inanimate matter and the biologist, living bodies.

Besides, how else to proceed? When one wants to determine by dialectics alone what education should be, it is necessary to begin by asking what objectives it must have. But what is it that allows us to say that education has certain ends rather than others? We do not know *a priori* what is the function of respiration or of circulation in a living being. By what right would we be more well informed concerning the educational function? It will be said in reply that from all the evidence, its object is the training of children. But this is posing the problem in slightly different terms; it does not resolve it. It would be necessary to say of what this training consists, what its direction is, what human needs it satisfies. Now, one can answer these questions only by beginning with observation of what it has consisted of, what needs it has satisfied in the past. Thus, it appears that to establish the preliminary notion of education, to determine what is so called, historical observation is indispensable.

Definition of Education

To define education we must, then, consider, educational systems, present and past, put them together, and abstract the characteristics which are common to them. These characteristics will constitute the definition that we seek.

We have already determined, along the way, two elements. In order that there be education, there must be a generation of adults and one of youth, in interaction, and an influence exercised by the first on the second. It remains for us to define the nature of this influence.

There is, so to speak, no society in which the system of education does not present a twofold aspect: it is at the same time one and manifold.

It is manifold. Indeed, in one sense, it can be said that there are as many different kinds of education as there are different milieux in a given society. Is such a society formed of castes? Education varies from one caste to another; that of the patricians was not that of the plebeians; that of the Brahman was not that of the Sudra. Similarly, in the Middle Ages, what a difference between the culture that the young page received, instructed in all the arts of chivalry, and that of the villein, who learned in his parish school a smattering of arithmetic, song and grammar! Even today, do we not see education vary with social class, or even with locality? That of the city is not that of the country, that of the middle class is not that of the worker. Would one say that this organization is not morally justifiable, that one can see in it only a survival destined to disappear? This proposition is easy to defend. It is evident that the education of our children should not depend upon the chance of their having been born here or there, of some parents rather than others. But even though the moral conscience of our time would have received, on this point, the satisfaction that it expects, education would not, for all that, become more uniform. Even though the career of each child would, in large part, no longer be predetermined by a blind heredity, occupational specialization would not fail to result in a great pedagogical diversity. Each occupation, indeed, constitutes a milieu *sui generis* which requires particular aptitudes and specialized knowledge, in which certain ideas, certain practices, certain modes of viewing things, prevail; and as the child must be prepared for the function that he will be called upon to fulfill, education, beyond a certain age, can no longer remain the same for all those to whom it applies. That is why we see it, in all civilized countries, tending more and more to become diversified and specialized; and this specialization becomes more advanced daily. The heterogeneity which is thus created does not rest, as does that which we were just discussing, on unjust inequalities; but it is not less. To find an absolutely homogeneous and egalitarian education, it would be necessary to go back to prehistoric societies, in the

structure of which there is no differentiation; and yet these kinds of societies
represent hardly more than one logical
stage in the history of humanity.

But, whatever may be the importance
of these special educations, they are not
all of education. It may even be said that
they are not sufficient unto themselves;
everywhere that one observes them, they
vary from one another only beyond a
certain point, up to which they are not
differentiated. They all rest upon a
common base. There is no people among
whom there is not a certain number of
ideas, sentiments and practices which
education must inculcate in all children
indiscriminately, to whatever social category they belong. Even in a society which
is divided into closed castes, there is
always a religion common to all, and,
consequently, the principles of the religious culture, which is, then, fundamental,
are the same throughout the population.
If each caste, each family, has its special
gods, there are general divinities that are
recognized by everyone and which all
children learn to worship. And as these
divinities symbolize and personify certain
sentiments, certain ways of conceiving
the world and life, one cannot be
initiated into their cult without acquiring,
at the same time, all sorts of thought
patterns which go beyond the sphere of
the purely religious life. Similarly, in the
Middle Ages, serfs, villeins, burgers and
nobles received, equally, a common
Christian education. If it is thus in
societies where intellectual and moral
diversity reach this degree of contrast,
with how much more reason is it so
among more advanced peoples where
classes, while remaining distinct, are,
however, separated by a less profound
cleavage! Where these common elements
of all education are not expressed in the
form of religious symbols, they do not,
however, cease to exist. In the course of
our history, there has been established a
whole set of ideas on human nature, on
the respective importance of our different

faculties, on right and duty, on society,
on the individual, on progress, on science,
on art, etc., which are the very basis of
our national spirit; all education, that of
the rich as well as that of the poor, that
which leads to professional careers as
well as that which prepares for industrial
functions, has as its object to fix them in
our minds.

From these facts it follows that each
society sets up a certain idea of man, of
what he should be, as much from the
intellectual point of view as the physical
and moral; that this ideal is, to a degree,
the same for all the citizens; that beyond
a certain point it becomes differentiated
according to the particular milieux that
every society contains in its structure. It
is this ideal, at the same time one and
various, that is the focus of education. Its
function, then, is to arouse in the child:
(1) a certain number of physical and
mental states that the society to which he
belongs considers should not be lacking
in any of its members; (2) certain physical
and mental states that the particular
social group (caste, class, family, profession) considers, equally, ought to be
found among all those who make it up.
Thus, it is society as a whole and each
particular social milieu that determine
the ideal that education realizes. Society
can survive only if there exists among its
members a sufficient degree of homogeneity; education perpetuates and reinforces this homogeneity by fixing in the
child, from the beginning, the essential
similarities that collective life demands.
But on the other hand, without a certain
diversity all co-operation would be impossible; education assures the persistence of this necessary diversity by being
itself diversified and specialized. If the
society has reached a degree of development such that the old divisions into
castes and classes can no longer be
maintained, it will prescribe an education

more uniform at its base. If at the same time there is more division of labor, it will arouse among children, on the underlying basic set of common ideas and sentiments, a richer diversity of occupational aptitudes. If it lives in a state of war with the surrounding societies, it tries to shape people according to a strongly nationalistic model; if international competition takes a more peaceful form, the type that it tries to realize is more general and more humanistic. Education is, then, only the means by which society prepares, within the children, the essential conditions of its very existence. We shall see later how the individual himself has an interest in submitting to these requirements.

We come, then, to the following formula: *Education is the influence exercised by adult generations on those that are not yet ready for social life. Its object is to arouse and to develop in the child a certain number of physical, intellectual and moral states which are demanded of him by both the political society as a whole and the special milieu for which he is specifically destined....*

The Role of the State in Education

This definition of education provides for a ready solution of the controversial question of the duties and the rights of the State with respect to education.

... If, as we have tried to establish, education has a collective function above all, if its object is to adapt the child to the social milieu in which he is destined to live, it is impossible that society should be uninterested in such a procedure. How could society not have a part in it, since it is the reference point by which education must direct its action? It is, then, up to the State to remind the teacher constantly of the ideas, the sentiments that must be impressed upon the child to adjust him to the milieu in which he must live. If it were not always there to guarantee that pedagogical influence be exercised in a social way, the latter would necessarily be put to the service of private beliefs, and the whole nation would be divided and would break down into an incoherent multitude of little fragments in conflict with one another. One could not contradict more completely the fundamental end of all education. Choice is necessary: if one attaches some value to the existence of society—and we have just seen what it means to us—education must assure, among the citizens, a sufficient community of ideas and of sentiments, without which any society is impossible; and in order that it may be able to produce this result, it is also necessary that education not be completely abandoned to the arbitrariness of private individuals.

Since education is an essentially social function, the State cannot be indifferent to it. On the contrary, everything that pertains to education must in some degree be submitted to its influence. This is not to say, therefore, that it must necessarily monopolize instruction. The question is too complex to be able to be treated thus in passing; we shall discuss it later. One can believe that scholastic progress is easier and quicker where a certain margin is left for individual initiative; for the individual makes innovations more readily than the State. But from the fact that the State, in the public interest, must allow other schools to be opened than those for which it has a more direct responsibility, it does not follow that it must remain aloof from what is going on in them. On the contrary, the education given in them must remain under its control. It is not even admissible that the function of the educator can be fulfilled by anyone who does not offer special guarantees of which the State alone can be the judge. No doubt, the limits within which its intervention should be kept may be rather difficult to determine once and for all, but the principle of intervention could not be disputed. There is no school which can claim the right to give, with full freedom, an antisocial education.

It is nevertheless necessary to recognize that the state of division in which we now find ourselves, in our country, makes this duty of the State particularly delicate and at the same time more important. It is not, indeed, up to the State to create this community of ideas and sentiments without which there is no society; it must be established by itself, and the State can only consecrate it, maintain it, make individuals more aware of it. Now, it is unfortunately indisputable that among us, this moral unity is not at all points what it should be. We are divided by divergent and even sometimes contradictory conceptions. There is in these divergences a fact which it is impossible to deny, and which must be reckoned with. It is not a question of recognizing the right of the majority to impose its ideas on the children of the minority. The school should not be the thing of one party, and the teacher is remiss in his duties when he uses the authority at his disposal to influence his pupils in accordance with his own preconceived opinions, however justified they may appear to him. But in spite of all the differences of opinion, there are at present, at the basis of our civilization, a certain number of principles which, implicitly or explicitly, are common to all, that few indeed, in any case, dare to deny overtly and openly: respect for reason, for science, for ideas and sentiments which are at the base of democratic morality. The role of the State is to outline these essential principles, to have them taught in its schools, to see to it that nowhere are children left ignorant of them, that everywhere they should be spoken of with the respect which is due

them. There is in this connection an influence to exert which will perhaps be all the more efficacious when it will be less aggressive and less violent, and will know better how to be contained within wise limits. . . .

. . . Education must be essentially a matter of authority. This important proposition can, moreover, be established directly. Indeed, we have seen that the object of education is to superimpose, on the individual and asocial being that we are at birth, an entirely new being. It must bring us to overcome our initial nature; it is on this condition that the child will become a man. Now, we can raise ourselves above ourselves only by a more or less difficult effort. Nothing is so false and deceptive as the Epicurean conception of education, the conception of a Montaigne, for example, according to which man can be formed while enjoying himself and without any other spur than the attraction of pleasure. If there is nothing somber in life and if it is criminal artificially to make it so in the eyes of the child, it is, however, serious and important; and education, which prepares for life, should share this seriousness. To learn to contain his natural egoism, to subordinate himself to higher ends, to submit his desires to the control of his will, to confine them within proper limits, the child must exercise strong self-control. Now, we restrain ourselves, we limit ourselves, only for one or the other of the following two reasons: because it is necessary through some physical necessity, or because we must do it on moral grounds. But the child cannot feel the necessity that imposes these efforts on us physically, for he is not faced directly with the hard realities of life which make this attitude indispensable. He is not yet engaged in the struggle; whatever Spencer may have said about it, we cannot leave him exposed to these too harsh realities.

It is necessary, then, that he be already formed, in large part, when he really encounters them. One cannot, then, depend on their influence to make him bow his will and acquire the necessary mastery over himself.

Duty remains. The sense of duty is, indeed, for the child and even for the adult, the stimulus *par excellence* of effort. Self-respect itself presupposes it. For, to be properly affected by reward and punishment, one must already have a sense of his dignity and, consequently, of his duty. But the child can know his duty only through his teachers or his parents; he can know what it is only through the manner in which they reveal it to him through their language and through their conduct. They must be, then, for him, duty incarnate and personified. Thus moral authority is the dominant quality of the educator. For it is through the authority that is in him that duty is duty. What is his own special quality is the imperative tone with which he addresses consciences, the respect that he inspires in wills and which makes them yield to his judgment. Thus it is indispensable that such an impression emanate from the person of the teacher. . . .

. . . It is not from the outside that the teacher can hold his authority, it is from himself; it can come to him only from an inner faith. He must believe, not in himself, no doubt, not in the superior qualities of his intelligence or of his soul, but in his task and in the importance of his task. What makes for the authority which is so readily attached to the word of the priest, is the high idea that he has of his calling; for he speaks in the name of a god in whom he believes, to whom he feels himself closer than the crowd of the uninitiated. The lay teacher can and should have something of this feeling. He too is the agent of a great moral person who surpasses him: it is society. Just as the priest is the interpreter of his god, the teacher is the interpreter of the great moral ideas of his time and of his country. Let him be attached to these ideas, let him feel all their grandeur, and the authority which is in them, and of which he is aware, cannot fail to be communicated to his person and to everything that emanates from him. Into an authority which flows from such an impersonal source there could enter no pride, no vanity, no pedantry. It is made up entirely of the respect which he has for his functions and, if one may say so, for his office. It is this respect which, through word and gesture, passes from him to the child.

Liberty and authority have sometimes been opposed, as if these two factors of education contradicted and limited each other. But this opposition is factitious. In reality these two terms imply, rather than exclude, each other. Liberty is the daughter of authority properly understood. For to be free is not to do what one pleases; it is to be master of oneself, it is to know how to act with reason and to do one's duty. Now, it is precisely to endow the child with this self-mastery that the authority of the teacher should be employed. The authority of the teacher is only one aspect of the authority of duty and of reason. The child should, then, be trained to recognize it in the speech of the educator and to submit to its ascendancy; it is on this condition that he will know later how to find it again in his own conscience and to defer to it.

We CANNOT HERE analyze the far-reaching and general cultural effects that the advance of the rational bureaucratic structure of domination, as such, develops quite independently of the areas in which it takes hold. Naturally, bureaucracy promotes a "rationalist" way of life, but the concept of rationalism allows for widely differing contents. Quite generally, one can only say that the bureaucratization of all domination very strongly furthers the development of "rational matter-of-factness" and the personality type of the professional expert. This has far-reaching ramifications, but only one important element of the process can be briefly indicated here: its effect upon the nature of training and education.

Educational institutions on the European continent, especially the institutions of higher learning—the universities, as well as technical academies, business colleges, gymnasiums, and other middle schools—are dominated and influenced by the need for the kind of "education" that produces a system of special examinations and the trained expertness that is increasingly indispensable for modern bureaucracy.

The "special examination," in the present sense, was and is found also outside of bureaucratic structures proper; thus, today it is found in the "free" professions of medicine and law and in the guild-organized trades. Expert examinations are neither indispensable to nor concomitant phenomena of bureaucratization. The French, English, and American bureaucracies have for a long time foregone such examinations entirely or to a large extent, for training and service in party organizations have made up for them.

"Democracy" also takes an ambivalent stand in the face of specialized examinations, as it does in the face of all the phenomena of bureaucracy—although democracy itself promotes these developments. Special examinations, on the one hand, mean or appear to mean a "selec-

The "Rationalization" of Education and Training

Max Weber

From Max Weber: Essays in Sociology, *edited and translated by H. H. Gerth and C. Wright Mills,* pp. 240–243. Copyright 1946 by Oxford University Press, Inc. Reprinted by permission.

tion" of those who qualify from all social strata rather than a rule by notables. On the other hand, democracy fears that a merit system and educational certificates will result in a privileged "caste." Hence, democracy fights against the special-examination system.

The special examination is found even in pre-bureaucratic or semi-bureaucratic epochs. Indeed, the regular and earliest locus of special examinations is among prebendally organized dominions. Expectancies of prebends, first of church prebends—as in the Islamite Orient and in the Occidental Middle Ages—then, as was especially the case in China, secular prebends, are the typical prizes for which people study and are examined. These examinations, however, have in truth only a partially specialized and expert character.

The modern development of full bureaucratization brings the system of rational, specialized, and expert examinations irresistibly to the fore. The civil service reform gradually imports expert training and specialized examinations into the United States. In all other countries this system also advances, stemming from its main breeding place, Germany. The increasing bureaucratization of administration enhances the importance of the specialized examination in England. In China, the attempt to replace the semi-patrimonial and ancient bureaucracy by a modern bureaucracy brought the expert examination; it took the place of a former and quite differently structured system of examinations. The bureaucratization of capitalism, with its demand for expertly trained technicians, clerks, et cetera, carries such examinations all over the world. Above all, the development is greatly furthered by the social prestige of the educational certificates acquired through such specialized examinations. This is all the more the case as the educational patent is turned to economic advantage. Today, the certificate of education becomes what the test for ancestors has been in the past, at least where the nobility has remained powerful: a prerequisite for equality of birth, a qualification for a canonship, and for state office.

The development of the diploma from universities, and business and engineering colleges, and the universal clamor for the creation of educational certificates in all fields make for the formation of a privileged stratum in bureaus and in offices. Such certificates support their holders' claims for intermarriages with notable families (in business offices people naturally hope for preferment with regard to the chief's daughter), claims to be admitted into the circles that adhere to "codes of honor," claims for a "respectable" remuneration rather than remuneration for work done, claims for assured advancement and old-age insurance, and, above all, claims to monopolize socially and economically advantageous positions. When we hear from all sides the demand for an introduction of regular curricula and special examinations, the reason behind it is, of course, not a suddenly awakened "thirst for education" but the desire for restricting the supply for these positions and their monopolization by the owners of educational certificates. Today, the "examination" is the universal means of this monopolization, and therefore examinations irresistibly advance. As the education prerequisite to the acquisition of the educational certificate requires considerable expense and a period of waiting for full remuneration, this striving means a setback for talent (charisma) in favor of property. For the "intellectual" costs of educational certificates are always low, and with the increasing volume of such certificates, their intellectual costs do not increase, but rather decrease.

The requirement of a chivalrous style of life in the old qualification for fiefs in Germany is replaced by the necessity of participating in its present rudimental form as represented by the dueling corps of the universities which also distribute the educational certificates. In Anglo-Saxon countries, athletic and social clubs fulfil the same function. The bureaucracy, on the other hand, strives everywhere for a "right to the office" by the establishment of a regular disciplinary procedure and by removal of the completely arbitrary disposition of the "chief" over the subordinate official. The bureaucracy seeks to secure the official position, the orderly advancement, and the provision for old age. In this, the bureaucracy is supported by the "democratic" sentiment of the governed, which demands that domination be minimized. Those who hold this attitude believe themselves able to discern a weakening of the master's prerogatives in every weakening of the arbitrary disposition of the master over the officials. To this extent, bureaucracy, both in business offices and in public service, is a carrier of a specific "status" development, as have been the quite differently structured officeholders of the past. We have already pointed out that these status characteristics are usually also exploited, and that by their nature they contribute to the technical usefulness of the bureaucracy in fulfilling its specific tasks.

"Democracy" reacts precisely against the unavoidable "status" character of bureaucracy. Democracy seeks to put the election of officials for short terms in the place of appointed officials; it seeks to substitute the removal of officials by election for a regulated procedure of discipline. Thus, democracy seeks to replace the arbitrary disposition of the hierarchically superordinate "master" by the equally arbitrary disposition of the governed and the party chiefs dominating them.

Social prestige based upon the advantage of special education and training as such is by no means specific to bureaucracy. On the contrary! But educational prestige in other structures of domination rests upon substantially different foundations.

Expressed in slogan-like fashion, the "cultivated man," rather than the "specialist," has been the end sought by education and has formed the basis of social esteem in such various systems as the feudal, theocratic, and patrimonial structures of domination: in the English notable administration, in the old Chinese patrimonial bureaucracy, as well as under the rule of demagogues in the so-called Hellenic democracy.

The term "cultivated man" is used here in a completely value-neutral sense; it is understood to mean solely that the goal of education consists in the quality of a man's bearing in life which was *considered* "cultivated," rather than in a

specialized training for expertness. The "cultivated" personality formed the educational ideal, which was stamped by the structure of domination and by the social condition for membership in the ruling stratum. Such education aimed at a chivalrous or an ascetic type; or, at a literary type, as in China; a gymnastic-humanist type, as in Hellas; or it aimed at a conventional type, as in the case of the Anglo-Saxon gentleman. The qualification of the ruling stratum as such rested upon the possession of "more" cultural quality (in the absolutely changeable, value-neutral sense in which we use the term here), rather than upon "more" expert knowledge. Special military, theological, and juridicial ability was of course intensely practiced; but the point of gravity in Hellenic, in medieval, as well as in Chinese education, has rested upon educational elements that were entirely different from what was "useful" in one's specialty.

Behind all the present discussions of the foundations of the educational system, the struggle of the "specialist type of man" against the older type of "cultivated man" is hidden at some decisive point. This fight is determined by the irresistibly expanding bureaucratization of all public and private relations of authority and by the ever-increasing importance of expert and specialized knowledge. This fight intrudes into all intimate cultural questions.

The Typological Position of Confucian Education

Max Weber

From Max Weber: Essays in Sociology, edited and translated by H. H. Gerth and C. Wright Mills, pp. 426–428. Copyright 1946 by Oxford University Press, Inc. Reprinted by permission.

WE SHALL NOW discuss the position of this educational system among the great types of education. To be sure, we cannot here, in passing, give a sociological typology of pedagogical ends and means, but perhaps some comments may be in place.

Historically, the two polar opposites in the field of educational ends are: to awaken charisma, that is, heroic qualities or magical gifts; and, to impart specialized expert training. The first type corresponds to the charismatic structure of domination; the latter type corresponds to the *rational* and bureaucratic (modern) structure of domination. The two types do not stand opposed, with no connections or transitions between them. The warrior hero or the magician also needs special training, and the expert official is generally not trained exclusively for knowledge. However, they are polar opposites of types of education and they form the most radical contrasts. Between them are found all those types which aim at cultivating the pupil for a *conduct of life*, whether it is of a mundane or of a religious character. In either case, the life conduct is the conduct of a status group.

The charismatic procedure of ancient magical asceticism and the hero trials, which sorcerers and warrior heroes have applied to boys, tried to aid the novice to acquire a "new soul," in the animist sense, and hence, to be reborn. Expressed in our language, this means that they merely wished to *awaken* and to test a capacity which was considered a purely personal gift of grace. For one can neither teach nor train for charisma. Either it exists *in nuce*, or it is infiltrated through a miracle of magical rebirth—otherwise it cannot be attained.

Specialized and expert schooling attempts to *train* the pupil for practical usefulness for administrative purposes— in the organization of public authorities, business offices, workshops, scientific or industrial laboratories, disciplined armies. In principle, this can be accomplished with anybody, though to varying extent.

The pedagogy of cultivation, finally, attempts to *educate* a cultivated type of man, whose nature depends on the decisive stratum's respective ideal of cultivation. And this means to educate a man for a certain internal and external deportment in life. In principle this can be done with everybody, only the goal differs. If a separate stratum of warriors form the decisive status group—as in Japan—education will aim at making the pupil a stylized knight and courtier, who despises the pen-pushers as the Japanese Samurai have despised them. In particular cases, the stratum may display great variations of type. If a priestly stratum is decisive, it will aim at making the disciple a scribe, or at least an intellectual, likewise of greatly varying character. In reality, none of these types ever occurs in pure form. The numerous combinations and intermediary links cannot be discussed in this context. What is important here is to define the position of Chinese education in terms of these forms.

The holdovers of the primeval charismatic training for regeneration, the milk name, the previously discussed initiation rites of youth, the bridegroom's change of name, and so on, have for a long time in China been a formula (in the manner of the Protestant confirmation) standing beside the testing of educational qualifications. Such tests have been monopolized by the political authorities. The educational qualification, however, in view of the educational means employed, has been a "cultural" qualification, in the sense of a general education. It was of a similar, yet of a more specific nature than, for instance, the *humanist* educational qualification of the Occident.

In Germany, such an education, until recently and almost exclusively, was a prerequisite for the official career leading to positions of command in civil and military administration. At the same time this *humanist* education has stamped the pupils who were to be prepared for such careers as belonging socially to the *cultured* status group. In Germany, however—and this is a very important difference between China and the Occident—rational and specialized *expert* training has been added to, and in part has displaced, this educational status qualification.

The Chinese examinations did not test any special skills, as do our modern rational and bureaucratic examination regulations for jurists, medical doctors, or technicians. Nor did the Chinese examinations test the possession of charisma, as do the typical "trials" of magicians and bachelor leagues. To be sure, we shall presently see the qualifica-

tions which this statement requires. Yet it holds at least for the technique of the examinations.

The examinations of China tested whether or not the candidate's mind was thoroughly steeped in literature and whether or not he possessed the *ways of thought* suitable to a cultured man and resulting from cultivation in literature. These qualifications held far more specifically with China than with the German humanist gymnasium. Today one is used to justifying the gymnasium by pointing to the practical value of formal education through the study of Antiquity. As far as one may judge from the assignments given to the pupils of the lower grades in China, they were rather similar to the essay topics assigned to the top grades of a German gymnasium, or perhaps better still, to the select class of a German girls' college. All the grades were intended as tests in penmanship, style, mastery of classic writings, and finally—similar to our lessons in religion, history, and German—in conformity with the prescribed mental outlook. In our context it is decisive that this education was on the one hand purely secular in nature, but, on the other, was bound to the fixed norm of the orthodox interpretation of the classic authors. It was a highly exclusive and bookish literary education.

Education as a Necessity of Life

John Dewey

Renewal of Life by Transmission

SOCIETY EXISTS THROUGH a process of transmission quite as much as biological life. This transmission occurs by means of communication of habits of doing, thinking, and feeling from the older to the younger. Without this communication of ideals, hopes, expectations, standards, opinions, from those members of society who are passing out of the group life to those who are coming into it, social life could not survive. If the members who compose a society lived on continuously, they might educate the new-born members, but it would be a task directed by personal interest rather than social need. Now it is a work of necessity.

If a plague carried off the members of a society all at once, it is obvious that the group would be permanently done for. Yet the death of each of its constituent members is as certain as if an epidemic took them all at once. But the graded difference in age, the fact that some are born as some die, makes possible through transmission of ideas and practices the constant reweaving of the social fabric. Yet this renewal is not automatic. Unless pains are taken to see that genuine and thorough transmission takes place, the most civilized group will relapse into barbarism and then into savagery. In fact, the human young are so immature that if they were left to themselves without the guidance and succor of others, they could not acquire the rudimentary abilities necessary for physical existence. The young of human beings compare so poorly in original efficiency with the young of many of the lower animals, that even the powers needed for physical sustentation have to be acquired under tuition. How much more, then, is this the case with respect to all the technological, artistic, scientific, and moral achievements of humanity!

Education and Communication

So obvious, indeed, is the necessity of teaching and learning for the continued existence of a society that we may seem to be dwelling unduly on a truism. But justification is found in the fact that such emphasis is a means of getting us away from an unduly scholastic and formal notion of education. Schools are, indeed, one important method of the transmission which forms the dispositions of the immature; but it is only one means, and, compared with other agencies, a relatively superficial means. Only as we have grasped the necessity of more fundamental and persistent modes of tuition can we make sure of placing the scholastic methods in their true context. . . .

Not only is social life identical with communication, but all communication (and hence all genuine social life) is educative. To be a recipient of a communication is to have an enlarged and changed experience. One shares in what another has thought and felt and in so far, meagerly or amply, has his own attitude modified. Nor is the one who communicates left unaffected. Try the experiment of communicating, with fullness and accuracy, some experience to another, especially if it be somewhat complicated, and you will find your own attitude toward your experience changing; otherwise you resort to expletives and ejaculations. The experience has to be formulated in order to be communicated. To formulate requires getting outside of it, seeing it as another would see it, considering what points of contact it has with the life of another so that it may be got into such form that he can appreciate its meaning. Except in dealing with commonplaces and catch phrases one has to assimilate, imaginatively, something of another's experience in order to tell him intelligently of one's own experience. All communication is like art. It may fairly be said, therefore, that any social arrangement that remains vitally social, or vitally shared, is educative to those who participate in it. Only when it becomes cast in a mold and runs in a routine way does it lose its educative power.

In final account, then, not only does social life demand teaching and learning for its own permanence, but the very process of living together educates. It enlarges and enlightens experience; it stimulates and enriches imagination; it creates responsibility for accuracy and vividness of statement and thought. A man really living alone (alone mentally as well as physically) would have little or no occasion to reflect upon his past experience to extract its net meaning. The inequality of achievement between the mature and the immature not only necessitates teaching the young, but the necessity of this teaching gives an immense stimulus to reducing experience to that order and form which will render it most easily communicable and hence most usable.

The Place of Formal Education

There is, accordingly, a marked difference between the education which every one gets from living with others, as long as he really lives instead of just continuing to subsist, and the deliberate educating of the young. In the former case the education is incidental; it is natural and important, but it is not the express reason of the association. While it may be said, without exaggeration, that the measure of the worth of any social institution, economic, domestic, political, legal, religious, is its effect in enlarging and improving experience; yet this effect is not a part of its original motive, which is limited and more immediately practical. Religious associations began, for example, in the desire to secure the favor of overruling power and to ward off evil influences; family life in the desire to gratify appetites and secure family perpetuity; systematic labor, for the most part, because of enslavement to others, etc. Only gradually was the by-product of the institution, its effect upon the quality and extent of conscious life, noted, and only more gradually still was this effect considered as a directive factor in the conduct of the institution. Even today, in our industrial life, apart from certain values of industriousness and thrift, the intellectual and emotional reaction of the forms of human association under which the world's work is carried on receives little attention as compared with physical output.

But in dealing with the young, the fact of association itself as an immediate human fact, gains in importance. While it is easy to ignore in our contact with them the effect of our acts upon their disposition, or to subordinate that educative effect to some external and tangible result, it is not so easy as in dealing with adults. The need of training is too evident; the pressure to accomplish a change in their attitude and habits is too urgent to leave these consequences wholly out of account. Since our chief business with them is to enable them to share in a common life we cannot help considering whether or no we are forming the powers which will secure this ability. If humanity has made some headway in realizing that the ultimate value of every institution is its distinctively human effect —its effect upon conscious experience— we may well believe that this lesson has been learned largely through dealings with the young.

We are thus led to distinguish, within the broad educational process which we have been so far considering, a more formal kind of education—that of direct tuition or schooling. In undeveloped social groups, we find very little formal teaching and training. Savage groups mainly rely for instilling needed dispositions into the young upon the same sort of association which keeps adults loyal to their group. They have no special devices, material, or institutions for teaching save in connection with initiation ceremonies by which the youth are inducted into full social membership. For the most part, they depend upon children learning the customs of the adults, acquiring their emotional set and stock of ideas, by sharing in what the elders are doing. In part, this sharing is direct, taking part in the occupations of adults and thus serving an apprenticeship; in part, it is indirect, through the dramatic plays in which children reproduce the actions of grown-ups and thus learn to know what they are like. To savages it would seem preposterous to seek out a place where nothing but learning was going on in order that one might learn.

But as civilization advances, the gap between the capacities of the young and the concerns of adults widens. Learning by direct sharing in the pursuits of grown-ups becomes increasingly difficult except in the case of the less advanced occupations. Much of what adults do is so remote in space and in meaning that playful imitation is less and less adequate to reproduce its spirit. Ability to share effectively in adult activities thus depends upon a prior training given with this end in view. Intentional agencies—schools— and explicit material—studies—are devised. The task of teaching certain things is delegated to a special group of persons.

Without such formal education, it is not possible to transmit all the resources and achievements of a complex society. It also opens a way to a kind of experience which would not be accessible to the young, if they were left to pick up their training in informal association with others, since books and the symbols of knowledge are mastered.

But there are conspicuous dangers attendant upon the transition from indirect to formal education. Sharing in actual pursuit, whether directly or vicariously in play, is at least personal and vital. These qualities compensate, in some measure, for the narrowness of available opportunities. Formal instruction, on the contrary, easily becomes remote and dead—abstract and bookish, to use the ordinary words of depreciation. What accumulated knowledge exists in low grade societies is at least put into practice; it is transmuted into character; it exists with the depth of meaning that attaches to its coming within urgent daily interests.

But in an advanced culture much which has to be learned is stored in symbols. It is far from translation into familiar acts and objects. Such material is relatively technical and superficial. Taking the ordinary standard of reality as a measure, it is artificial. For this measure is connection with practical concerns. Such material exists in a world by itself, unassimilated to ordinary customs of thought and expression. There is the standing danger that the material of formal instruction will be merely the subject matter of the schools, isolated from the subject matter of life-experience. The permanent social interests are likely to be lost from view. Those which have not been carried over into the structure of social life, but which remain largely matters of technical information expressed in symbols, are made conspicuous in schools. Thus we reach the ordinary notion of education: the notion which ignores its social necessity and its identity with all human association that affects conscious life, and which identifies it with imparting information about remote matters and the conveying of learning through verbal signs: the acquisition of literacy.

Hence one of the weightiest problems with which the philosophy of education has to cope is the method of keeping a proper balance between the informal and the formal, the incidental and the inten-

tional, modes of education. When the acquiring of information and of technical intellectual skill do not influence the formation of a social disposition, ordinary vital experience fails to gain in meaning, while schooling, in so far, creates only "sharps" in learning—that is, egoistic specialists. To avoid a split between what men consciously know because they are aware of having learned it by a specific job of learning, and what they unconsciously know because they have absorbed it in the formation of their characters by intercourse with others, becomes an increasingly delicate task with every development of special schooling.

Education as a Social Function

John Dewey

Reprinted with permission of The Macmillan Company from Democracy and Education by John Dewey, pp. 10–14, 16–22, 23–24, and 39–40. Copyright 1916 by The Macmillan Company, renewed 1944 by John Dewey.

The Nature and Meaning of Environment

WE HAVE SEEN that a community or social group sustains itself through continuous self-renewal, and that this renewal takes place by means of the educational growth of the immature members of the group. By various agencies, unintentional and designed, a society transforms uninitiated and seemingly alien beings into robust trustees of its own resources and ideals. Education is thus a fostering, a nurturing, a cultivating, process. All of these words mean that it implies attention to the conditions of growth. We also speak of rearing, raising, bringing up—words which express the difference of level which education aims to cover. Etymologically, the word education means just a process of leading or bringing up. When we have the outcome of the process in mind, we speak of education as shaping, forming, molding activity—that is, a shaping into the standard form of social activity. In this chapter we are concerned with the general features of the *way* in which a social group brings up its immature members into its own social form.

Since what is required is a transformation of the quality of experience till it partakes in the interests, purposes, and ideas current in the social group, the problem is evidently not one of mere physical forming. Things can be physically transported in space; they may be bodily conveyed. Beliefs and aspirations cannot be physically extracted and inserted. How then are they communicated? Given the impossibility of direct contagion or literal inculcation, our problem is to discover the method by which the young assimilate the point of view of the old, or the older bring the young into likemindedness with themselves.

The answer, in general formulation, is: By means of the action of the environment in calling out certain responses. The required beliefs cannot be hammered in; the needed attitudes cannot be plastered on. But the particular medium in which an individual exists leads him to see and feel one thing rather than another; it leads him to have certain plans in order that he may act successfully with others: it strengthens some beliefs and weakens others as a condition of winning the approval of others. Thus it gradually produces in him a certain system of behavior, a certain disposition of action. The words "environment," "medium" denote something more than surroundings which encompass an individual. They denote the specific *continuity* of the surroundings with his own active tendencies. An inanimate being is, of course, continuous with its surroundings; but the environing circumstances do not, save metaphorically, constitute an environment. For the inorganic being is not *concerned* in the influences which affect it. On the other hand, some things which are remote in space and time from a living creature, especially a human creature, may form his environment even more truly than some of the things close to him. The things with which a man *varies* are his genuine environment. Thus the activities of the astronomer vary with the stars at which he gazes or about which he calculates. Of his immediate surroundings, his telescope is most intimately his environment. The environment of an antiquarian, as an antiquarian, consists of the remote epoch of human life with which he is concerned, and the relics, inscriptions, etc., by which he establishes connections with that period.

In brief, the environment consists of those conditions that promote or hinder, stimulate or inhibit, the *characteristic* activities of a living being. Water is the environment of a fish because it is necessary to the fish's activities—to its life. The north pole is a significant element in the environment of an arctic explorer, whether he succeeds in reaching it or not, because it defines his activities, makes them what they distinctively are. Just because life signifies not bare passive existence (supposing there is such a thing), but a way of acting, environment or medium signifies what enters into this activity as a sustaining or frustrating condition.

The Social Environment

A being whose activities are associated with others has a social environment. What he does and what he can do depend upon the expectations, demands, approvals, and condemnations of others. A being connected with other beings cannot perform his own activities without taking the activities of others into account. For they are the indispensable conditions of the realization of his tendencies. When he moves he stirs them and reciprocally. We might as well try to imagine a business man doing business, buying and selling, all by himself, as to conceive it possible to define the activities of an individual in terms of his isolated actions. The manufacturer moreover is as truly socially guided in his activities when he is laying plans in the privacy of his own countinghouse as when he is buying his raw material or selling his finished goods.

Thinking and feeling that have to do with action in association with others is as much a social mode of behavior as is the most overt coöperative or hostile act.

What we have more especially to indicate is how the social medium nurtures its immature members. There is no great difficulty in seeing how it shapes the external habits of action. Even dogs and horses have their actions modified by association with human beings; they form different habits because human beings are concerned with what they do. Human beings control animals by controlling the natural stimuli which influence them; by creating a certain environment in other words. Food, bits and bridles, noises, vehicles, are used to direct the ways in which the natural or instinctive responses of horses occur. By operating steadily to call out certain acts, habits are formed which function with the same uniformity as the original stimuli. If a rat is put in a maze and finds food only by making a given number of turns in a given sequence, his activity is gradually modified till he habitually takes that course rather than another when he is hungry.

Human actions are modified in a like fashion. A burnt child dreads the fire; if a parent arranged conditions so that every time a child touched a certain toy he got burned, the child would learn to avoid that toy as automatically as he avoids touching fire. So far, however, we are dealing with what may be called *training* in distinction from educative teaching. The changes considered are in outer action rather than in mental and emotional dispositions of behavior. The distinction is not, however, a sharp one. The child might conceivably generate in time a violent antipathy, not only to that particular toy, but to the class of toys resembling it. The aversion might even persist after he had forgotten about the original burns; later on he might even invent some reason to account for his seemingly irrational antipathy. In some cases, altering the external habit of action by changing the environment to affect the stimuli to action will also alter the mental disposition concerned in the action. Yet this does not always happen; a person trained to dodge a threatening blow, dodges automatically with no corresponding thought or emotion. We have to find, then, some differentia of training from education.

A clew may be found in the fact that the horse does not really share in the social use to which his action is put. Some one else uses the horse to secure a result which is advantageous by making it advantageous to the horse to perform the act—he gets food, etc. But the horse, presumably, does not get any new interest. He remains interested in food, not in the service he is rendering. He is not a partner in a shared activity. Were he to become a copartner, he would, in engaging in the conjoint activity, have the same interest in its accomplishment which others have. He would share their ideas and emotions.

Now in many cases—too many cases—the activity of the immature human being is simply played upon to secure habits which are useful. He is trained like an animal rather than educated like a human being. His instincts remain attached to their original objects of pain or pleasure. But to get happiness or to avoid the pain of failure he has to act in a way agreeable to others. In other cases, he really shares or participates in the common activity. In this case, his original impulse is modified. He not merely acts in a way agreeing with the actions of others, but, in so acting, the same ideas and emotions are aroused in him that animate the others. A tribe, let us say, is warlike. The successes for which it strives, the achievements upon which it sets store, are connected with fighting and victory. The presence of this medium incites bellicose exhibitions in a boy, first in games, then in fact when he is strong enough. As he fights he wins approval and advancement; as he refrains, he is disliked, ridiculed, shut out from favorable recognition. It is not surprising that his original belligerent tendencies and emotions are strengthened at the expense of others, and that his ideas turn to things connected with war. Only in this way can be become fully a recognized member of his group. Thus his mental habitudes are gradually assimilated to those of his group.

If we formulate the principle involved in this illustration, we shall perceive that the social medium neither implants certain desires and ideas directly, nor yet merely establishes certain purely muscular habits of action, like "instinctively" winking or dodging a blow. Setting up conditions which stimulate certain visible and tangible ways of acting is the first step. Making the individual a sharer or partner in the associated activity so that he feels its success as his success, its failure as his failure, is the completing step. As soon as he is possessed by the emotional attitude of the group, he will be alert to recognize the special ends at which it aims and the means employed to secure success. His beliefs and ideas, in other words, will take a form similar to those of others in the group. He will also achieve pretty much the same stock of knowledge since that knowledge is an ingredient of his habitual pursuits. . . .

After sounds have got meaning through connection with other things employed in a joint undertaking, they can be used in connection with other like sounds to develop new meanings, precisely as the things for which they stand are combined. Thus the words in which a child learns about, say, the Greek helmet originally got a meaning (or were understood) by use in an action having a common interest and end. They now arouse a new meaning by inciting the one who hears or reads to rehearse imaginatively the activities in which the helmet has its use. For the time being, the one who understands the words "Greek helmet" becomes mentally a partner with those who used the helmet. He engages, through his imagination, in a shared activity. It is not easy to get the *full* meaning of words. Most persons probably stop with the idea that "helmet" denotes a queer kind of headgear a people called the Greeks once wore. We conclude, accordingly, that the use of language to convey and acquire ideas is an extension and refinement of the principle that things gain meaning by being used in a shared experience or joint action; in no sense does it contravene that principle. When words do not enter as factors into a shared situation, either overtly or imaginatively, they operate as pure physical stimuli, not as having a meaning or intellectual value. They set activity running in a given groove, but there is no accompanying conscious purpose or meaning. Thus, for example, the plus sign may be a stimulus to perform the act of writing one number under another and adding the numbers, but the person performing the act will operate much as an automaton would unless he realizes the meaning of what he does.

The Social Medium As Educative

Our net result thus far is that social environment forms the mental and emotional disposition of behavior in individuals by engaging them in activities that arouse and strengthen certain impulses, that have certain purposes and entail certain consequences. A child growing up in a family of musicians will inevitably have whatever capacities he has in music stimulated, and, relatively, stimulated more than other impulses which might have been awakened in

another environment. Save as he takes an interest in music and gains a certain competency in it, he is "out of it"; he is unable to share in the life of the group to which he belongs. Some kinds of participation in the life of those with whom the individual is connected are inevitable; with respect to them, the social environment exercises an educative or formative influence unconsciously and apart from any set purpose.

In savage and barbarian communities, such direct participation (constituting the indirect or incidental education of which we have spoken) furnishes almost the sole influence for rearing the young into the practices and beliefs of the group. Even in present-day societies, it furnishes the basic nurture of even the most insistently schooled youth. In accord with the interests and occupations of the group, certain things become objects of high esteem; others of aversion. Association does not create impulses or affection and dislike, but it furnishes the objects to which they attach themselves. The way our group or class does things tends to determine the proper objects of attention, and thus to prescribe the directions and limits of observation and memory. What is strange or foreign (that is to say outside the activities of the groups) tends to be morally forbidden and intellectually suspect. It seems almost incredible to us, for example, that things which we know very well could have escaped recognition in past ages. We incline to account for it by attributing congenital stupidity to our forerunners and by assuming superior native intelligence on our own part. But the explanation is that their modes of life did not call for attention to such facts, but held their minds riveted to other things. Just as the senses require sensible objects to stimulate them, so our powers of observation, recollection, and imagination do not work spontaneously, but are set in motion by the demands set up by current social occupations. The main texture of disposition is formed, independently of schooling, by such influences. What conscious, deliberate teaching can do is at most to free the capacities thus formed for fuller exercise, to purge them of some of their grossness, and to furnish objects which make their activity more productive of meaning. . . .

The School As a Special Environment

. . . The only way in which adults consciously control the kind of education which the immature get is by controlling the environment in which they act, and hence think and feel. We never educate directly, but indirectly by means of the environment. Whether we permit chance environments to do the work, or whether we design environments for the purpose makes a great difference. And any environment is a chance environment so far as its educative influence is concerned unless it has been deliberately regulated with reference to its educative effect. An intelligent home differs from an unintelligent one chiefly in that the habits of life and intercourse which prevail are chosen, or at least colored, by the thought of their bearing upon the development of children. But schools remain, of course, the typical instance of environments framed with express reference to influencing the mental and moral disposition of their members.

Roughly speaking, they come into existence when social traditions are so complex that a considerable part of the social store is committed to writing and transmitted through written symbols. Written symbols are even more artificial or conventional than spoken; they cannot be picked up in accidental intercourse with others. In addition, the written form tends to select and record matters which are comparatively foreign to everyday life. The achievements accumulated from generation to generation are deposited in it even though some of them have fallen temporarily out of use. Consequently as soon as a community depends to any considerable extent upon what lies beyond its own territory and its own immediate generation, it must rely upon the set agency of schools to insure adequate transmission of all its resources. To take an obvious illustration: The life of the ancient Greeks and Romans has profoundly influenced our own, and yet the ways in which they affect us do not present themselves on the surface of our ordinary experiences. In similar fashion, peoples still existing, but remote in space, British, Germans, Italians, directly concern our own social affairs, but the nature of the interaction cannot be understood without explicit statement and attention. In precisely similar fashion, our daily associations cannot be trusted to make clear to the young the part played in our activities by remote physical energies, and by invisible structures. Hence a special mode of social intercourse is instituted, the school, to care for such matters.

This mode of association has three functions sufficiently specific, as compared with ordinary associations of life, to be noted. First, a complex civilization is too complex to be assimilated *in toto*. It has to be broken up into portions, as it were, and assimilated piecemeal, in a gradual and graded way. The relationships of our present social life are so numerous and so interwoven that a child placed in the most favorable position could not readily share in many of the most important of them. Not sharing in them, their meaning would not be communicated to him, would not become a part of his own mental disposition. There would be no seeing the trees because of the forest. Business, politics, art, science, religion, would make all at once a clamor for attention; confusion would be the outcome. The first office of the social organ we call the school is to provide a simplified environment. It selects the features which are fairly fundamental and capable of being responded to by the young. Then it establishes a progressive order, using the factors first acquired as means of gaining insight into what is more complicated.

In the second place, it is the business of the school environment to eliminate, so far as possible, the unworthy features of the existing environment from influence upon mental habitudes. It establishes a purified medium of action. Selection aims not only at simplifying but at weeding out what is undesirable. Every society gets encumbered with what is trivial, with dead wood from the past, and with what is positively perverse. The school has the duty of omitting such things from the environment which it supplies, and thereby doing what it can to counteract their influence in the ordinary social environment. By selecting the best for its exclusive use, it strives to reënforce the power of this best. As a society becomes more enlightened, it realizes that it is responsible *not* to transmit and conserve the whole of its existing achievements, but only such as make for a better future society. The school is its chief agency for the accomplishment of this end.

In the third place, it is the office of the school environment to balance the various elements in the social environment, and to see to it that each individual gets an opportunity to escape from the limitations of the social group in which he was born, and to come into living contact with a broader environment. Such words as "society" and "community" are likely to be misleading, for they have a tendency to make us think there is a single thing corresponding to the single word. As a matter of fact, a modern society is many societies more or less loosely connected. Each household with its immediate extension of friends makes a society; the village or street group of playmates is a community; each business group, each club, is another. Passing beyond these more intimate groups, there is in a country like our own a variety of races, religious affiliations, economic divisions. Inside the modern city, in spite of its nominal political unity, there are probably more communities, more differing customs, traditions, aspirations, and forms of government or control, than existed in an entire continent at an earlier epoch.

. . . While books and conversation can do much, these agencies are usually relied upon too exclusively. Schools require for their full efficiency more opportunity for conjoint activities in which those instructed take part, so that they may acquire a *social* sense of their own powers and of the materials and appliances used.

The School as a Social Organism

Willard Waller

Reprinted from The Sociology of Teaching (*New York:*
John Wiley & Sons, Inc., Science Editions, 1965),
pp. 6–13, by permission of the publisher.

THE SCHOOL IS a unity of interacting personalities. The personalities of all who meet in the school are bound together in an organic relation. The life of the whole is in all its parts, yet the whole could not exist without any of its parts. The school is a social organism;[1] it is this first and most general aspect of the social life of the schools which we propose to deal with in this chapter. As a social organism the school shows an organismic interdependence of its parts; it is not possible to affect a part of it without affecting the whole. As a social organism the school displays a differentiation of parts and a specialization of function. The organism as an entirety is nourished by the community.

Changing the figure slightly, the school is a closed system of social interaction. Without pedantry, we may point out that this fact is of importance, for if we are to study the school as a social entity, we must be able to distinguish clearly between school and not-school. The school is in fact clearly differentiated from its social milieu. The existence of a school is established by the emergence of a characteristic mode of social interaction. A school exists wherever and whenever teachers and students meet for the purpose of giving and receiving instruction. The instruction which is given is usually formal classroom instruc-

tion, but this need not be true. The giving and receiving of instruction constitutes the nucleus of the school as we now think of it. About this nucleus are clustered a great many less relevant activities.

When we analyze existing schools, we find that they have the following characteristics which enable us to set them apart and study them as social unities:

1. They have a definite population.
2. They have a clearly defined political structure, arising from the mode of social interaction characteristic of the school, and influenced by numerous minor processes of interaction.
3. They represent the nexus of a compact network of social relationships.
4. They are pervaded by a we-feeling.
5. They have a culture that is definitely their own.

Schools differ widely in the degree to which they show these traits and in the manner in which they are combined. Private boarding schools exemplify them all in the highest degree. They have a stable and homogeneous population; the original homogeneity, produced by economic and social selection, has been enhanced by intimate association and common experiences. They have a clear and explicit political organization, sometimes expressed in a book of rules and a long line of precedents. The persons of the school live very close to each other, and are bound each to each by an intricate maze of crisscrossing social relationships. Intimacy of association, stability of the group, the setting apart of the group by a distinctive dress and its isolation from other cultural influences, combine to make possible a strong feeling of unity in such a school; it has often been remarked that a private school has something of the solidarity of the family. The isolation of the school from the remainder of the community, and the richness of the life which its members lead in their close-packed association, make the culture developed in such a school pronounced and distinctive.

The private day school sometimes represents such a closed corporation, and shows up very clearly as a social unit. It may not, for the day school is sometimes nothing more than a painless substitute for public school for the children of wealthy parents. But in the ideal case the private day school may be a functioning unity much more clearly marked off from the rest of the world than is the public school.

The various kinds and conditions of public schools differ in the degree to which they are recognizable and delimitable social units. The one-room country school is obviously such a unit. So likewise is the great suburban high school, and the high school of the small city described in *Middletown*. Sometimes, however, the public school is so split into divergent social groups that the underlying unity is somewhat obscured. This is possible where the school population is drawn from several sources and where there is no school program capable of welding these groups together.

The school has, as we have said, a definite population, composed of those who are engaged in the giving or receiving of instruction, who "teach" or "are in school." It is a relatively stable population and one whose depletion and replacement occur slowly. Population movements go according to plan and can be predicted and charted in advance. A bimodal age distribution marks off teachers from students. This is the most significant cleavage in the school.

The young in the school population are likely to have been subjected to some sifting and sorting according to the economic status and social classification of their parents. The private schools select out a certain group, and there are specializations within the private schools, some being in fact reformatories for the children of the well-to-do, and some

being very exacting as to the character and scholastic qualifications of their students. The public schools of the exclusive residence district are usually peopled by students of a limited range of social types. Slum schools are for slum children. Country schools serve the children of farmers. In undifferentiated residence districts and in small towns which have but one school the student population is least homogeneous and most representative of the entire community.

The teaching population is probably less differentiated. In part, this is because the variation from the teacher type must be limited if one is to teach successfully. There is nevertheless considerable variation in the training and ability of teachers from one school to another and one part of the country to another. Teachers the country over and in all schools tend to be predominantly selected from the rural districts and from the sons and daughters of the lower middle classes. The teaching population is in some schools more permanent than the student population. There is nevertheless a large turnover among the teachers.

The characteristic mode of social interaction of the school, an interaction centered about the giving and receiving of instruction, determines the political order of the school. The instruction which is given consists largely of facts and skills and of other matter for which the spontaneous interests of students do not usually furnish a sufficient motivation. Yet teachers wish students to attain a certain mastery of these subjects, a much higher degree of mastery than they would attain, it is thought, if they were quite free in their choices. And teachers are responsible to the community for the mastery of these subjects by their students. The political organization of the school, therefore, is one which makes the teacher dominant, and it is the business of the teacher to use his dominance to further the process of teaching and learning which is central in the social interaction of the school.

Typically the school is organized on some variant of the autocratic principle. Details of organization show the greatest diversity, Intra-faculty relations greatly affect the relations between teachers and students. Where there is a favorable rapport between the teachers and the administrative authorities, this autocracy becomes an oligarchy with the teacher group as a solid and well-organized ruling class. It appears that the best practice extends the membership in this oligarchy as much as possible without making it unwieldy or losing control of it. In the most happily conducted institutions all the teachers and some of the leading students feel that they have a very real voice in the conduct of school affairs.

Where there is not a cordial rapport between school executives and teachers, control becomes more autocratic. A despotic system apparently becomes necessary when the teaching staff has increased in size beyond a certain limit. Weakness of the school executive may lead him to become arbitrary, or it may in the extreme case lead some other person to assume his authority. The relationship between students and teachers is in part determined by intra-faculty relationships; the social necessity of subordination as a condition of student achievement, and the general tradition governing the attitudes of students and teachers toward each other, set the limits of variation. But this variation is never sufficient to destroy the fact that the schools are organized on the authority principle, with power theoretically vested in the school superintendent and radiating from him down to the lowest substitute teacher in the

system. This authority which pervades the school furnishes the best practical means of distinguishing school from not-school. Where the authority of the faculty and school board extends is the school. If it covers children on the way to and from school, at school parties, and on trips, then those children are in school at such times.

The generalization that the schools have a despotic political structure seems to hold true for nearly all types of schools, and for all about equally, without very much difference in fact to correspond to radical differences in theory. Self-government is rarely real. Usually it is but a mask for the rule of the teacher oligarchy, in its most liberal form the rule of a student oligarchy carefully selected and supervised by the faculty. The experimental school which wishes to do away with authority continually finds that in order to maintain requisite standards of achievement in imparting certain basic skills it has to introduce some variant of the authority principle, or it finds that it must select and employ teachers who can be in fact despotic without seeming to be so. Experimental schools, too, have great difficulty in finding teachers who are quite free from the authoritarian bias of other schools and able to treat children as independent human beings. Military schools, standing apparently at the most rigid pole of authority, may learn to conceal their despotism, or, discipline established, may furnish moments of relaxation and intimate association between faculty and students, and they may delegate much power and responsibility to student officers; thus they may be not very much more arbitrary than schools quite differently organized, and sometimes they are very much less arbitrary than schools with a less rigid formal structure. The manifestations of the authority principle vary somewhat. The one-room country school must have a different social structure from the city high school with five thousand students, but the basic fact of authority, of dominance and subordination, remains a fact in both.

It is not enough to point out that the school is a despotism. It is a despotism in a state of perilous equilibrium. It is a despotism threatened from within and exposed to regulation and interference from without. It is a despotism capable of being overturned in a moment, exposed to the instant loss of its stability and its prestige. It is a despotism demanded by the community of parents, but specially limited to them as to the techniques which it may use for the maintenance of a stable social order. It is a despotism resting upon children, at once the most tractable and the most unstable members of the community.

There may be some who, seeing the solid brick of school buildings, the rows of nicely regimented children sitting stiff and well-behaved in the classroom or marching briskly through the halls, will doubt that the school is in a state of unstable equilibrium. A school may in fact maintain a high morale through a period of years, so that its record in the eyes of the community is marred by no untoward incident. But how many schools are there with a teaching body of more than—let us say—ten teachers, in which there is not one teacher who is in imminent danger of losing his position because of poor discipline? How many such schools in which no teacher's discipline has broken down within the last three years? How many school executives would dare to plan a great mass meeting of students at which no teachers would be present or easily available in case of disorder?

To understand the political structure of the school we must know that the school is organized on the authority principle and that that authority is constantly threatened. The authority of the school executives and the teachers is in unremitting danger from: (1) The students. (2) Parents. (3) The school board. (4) Each

other. (5) Hangers-on and marginal members of the group. (6) Alumni. The members of these groups, since they threaten his authority, are to some extent the natural enemies of the person who represents and lives by authority. The difficulties of the teacher or school executive in maintaining authority are greatly increased by the low social standing of the teaching profession and its general disrepute in the community at large. There is a constant interaction between the elements of the authoritative system; the school is continually threatened because it is autocratic, and it has to be autocratic because it is threatened. The antagonistic forces are balanced in that ever-fickle equilibrium which is discipline.

Within the larger political order of the school are many subsidiary institutions designed to supplement, correct, or support the parent institution, drawing their life from it and contributing in turn to its continued existence. These institutions are less definitely a part of the political structure, and they mitigate somewhat the rigidity of that structure by furnishing to students an opportunity for a freer sort of social expression. These ancillary institutions are organizations of extra-curricular activities, and comprise such groups as debating societies, glee clubs, choral societies, literary societies, theatrical groups, athletic teams, the staff of a school paper, social clubs, honorary societies, fraternities, etc. They are never entirely spontaneous social groupings but have rather the character of planned organizations for which the major impetus comes from the faculty, generally from some one member of the faculty delegated to act as "faculty adviser." These "activities" are part of that culture which springs up in the school from the life of students or is created by teachers for the edification of students. Such groups are often hardly less pervaded by faculty control than classroom activities, and there seems a tendency for the work of such institutions to be taken over by the larger social structure, made into courses and incorporated into the curriculum. Perhaps the worst that can happen to such organizations, if they are viewed as opportunities for the spontaneous self-expression of students, is that they shall be made into classes. But the school administrator often thinks differently; from his point of view, the worst that can happen to such groups is that they shall become live and spontaneous groups, for such groups have a way of declaring their independence, much to the detriment of school discipline.

The political order of the school is characterized by control on three levels. Roughly, these are:

1. Theoretical. The control of the school by the school board, board of trustees, etc.

2. Actual. The control of school affairs by school executives as exerted through the teaching force or directly.

3. Ultimate. The control of school affairs by students, government resting upon the consent, mostly silent, of the governed.

The school is the meeting-point of a large number of intertangled social relationships. These social relationships are the paths pursued by social interaction, the channels in which social influences run. The crisscrossing and interaction of these groups make the school what it is. The social relationships centering in the school may be analyzed in terms of the interacting groups in the school. The two most important groups are the teacher-group and the pupil-group, each of which has its own moral and ethical code and its customary attitudes toward members of the other groups. There is a marked tendency for these groups to turn into conflict groups. Within the teacher group are divisions according to rank and position, schismatic and conspiratorial groups, congenial groups, and cliques centering around different personalities. Within the student groups are various divisions representing groups in the larger community, unplanned primary groups stair-stepped according to age, cliques, political organizations, and specialized groups such as teams and gangs. The social influence of the school is a result of the action of such groups upon the individual and of the organization of individual lives out of the materials furnished by such groups.

A rough idea of some of the more important social relationships arising in the school may be derived from the following schema:

I. Community-School relationships.
  1. Relation of community to school in general. (Mediated through tradition and the political order of the community.)
  2. Relation of community to students individually and in groups. The parental relation and the general relation of the elders of the community to the young.
  3. Relation of community to teachers.
  4. Relation of special groups in the community to the school. (The school board, parent-teacher clubs, alumni, self-constituted advisory groups, etc.)
  5. Relation of special individuals to the school. (Patrons, ex-teachers, patriarchs, hangers-on, etc.)
II. Pupil to pupil relationships as not affected by the presence of teachers.
  1. Pupil to pupil relationships.
  2. Pupil to pupil-group relationships.
  3. Pupil-group to pupil-group relationships.
III. Teacher-pupil relationships. (Including also pupil to pupil relationships as affected by the presence of teachers.)

1. Teacher to pupil-group relationship. (The customary classroom situation.)
2. Teacher to pupil relationship.
3. Pupil to pupil relationship as affected by the presence of the teacher.

IV. Teacher to teacher relationships.
   1. Relation of teacher to teacher.
      a. Teacher to teacher relationship as not affected by the presence of students.
      b. Teacher to teacher relationship as as affected by the presence of students.
   2. Relation of teacher to teacher groups.
   3. Relation of teacher groups to teacher groups.
   4. Relation of teaching force to administrative officers.

NOTE: All these relationships are reciprocal.

The school is further marked off from the world that surrounds it by the spirit which pervades it. Feeling makes the school a social unity. The *we*-feeling of the school is in part a spontaneous creation in the minds of those who identify themselves with the school and in part a carefully nurtured and sensitive growth. In this latter aspect it is regarded as more or less the property of the department of athletics. Certainly the spirit of the group reaches its highest point in those ecstatic ceremonials which attend athletic spectacles. The group spirit extends itself also to parents and alumni.

A separate-culture, we have indicated, grows up within the school. This is a culture which is in part the creation of children of different age levels, arising from the breakdown of adult culture into simpler configurations or from the survival of an older culture in the play group of children, and in part devised by teachers in order to canalize the activities of children passing through certain ages. The whole complex set of ceremonies centering around the school may be considered a part of the culture indigenous to the school. "Activities," which many youngsters consider by far the most important part of school life, are culture patterns. The specialized culture of the young is very real and satisfying for those who live within it. And this specialized culture is perhaps the agency most effective in binding personalities together to form a school.

Note

[1] We do not, of course, subscribe to the organismic fallacy, which Ward and others have so ably refuted. We have adopted the analogy here simply as a device of exposition. The school is like an organism; it is not a true organism.

Part I
Auxiliary Readings

Jean Floud and A. H. Halsey. "The Sociology of Education." *Current Sociology*, 7 (1958), 165–193.

Beginning with a discussion of the historical development of the sociology of education since the late nineteenth century, the authors go on to relate past work to present theory and method. The main body of the paper is devoted to a review of the literature relating social structure to education and educational institutions. Works from Germany, France, and England are included, as well as from the United States. The emphasis on the limitations of much of the early work leads the authors to define major areas which have not been sufficiently treated. An extensive bibliography is included.

Jean Floud and A. H. Halsey, "Education and Social Structure: Theories and Methods." *Harvard Educational Review*, 29 (1959), pp. 288–296.

As in the preceding article, the authors take a critical approach to the theoretical formulations of classical writers in education, and conclude that for the most part these theories have retarded the development of a systematic and comprehensive approach to an institutional treatment of education. Of particular concern are the problems posed by viewing education primarily as a culture transmitting mechanism (Durkheim) or as a socialization mechanism (Weber). The authors believe that both of the approaches were inapplicable and simplistic in the context of "technological society" where the contribution of education to social persistence and development is difficult to determine. As an alternative perspective, they propose that modern sociologists take their lead from Dewey and emphasize the interrelationships between education and social change. This would result in an emphasis on institutional rather than "functional" or "psychologistic" aspects of education.

Charles E. Bidwell, "The Sociology of Education." In *Encyclopedia of Educational Research*, edited by Robert Ebel. New York: Macmillan Co., 1969.

Recent empirical findings in the sociology of education are related to earlier theoretical works, primarily Durkheim, Weber, and Waller. On the macrosociological level, the author discusses work on comparative and historical aspects of educational systems; the relationship of education to economic and political structures; and the interactions of class structure, mobility, and school performance. Microsociological areas covered include the social organization of schools and classrooms, subcultures within the educational system, historical effects on the social system of schools, and teaching as an occupation.

Karl Mannheim. *Freedom*, *Power and Democratic Planning*, ch. 10. New York: Oxford University Press, 1950.

Mannheim characterizes the schools not only as mechanisms for socialization, but also for social change and social integration. He believes that the scope of education should be redefined to include all age ranges, and that at every level it should stress problem-solving rather than transmission of facts. Particular emphasis is placed on the idea that the elite bias of higher education should be eliminated, and that the trend towards specialization should be countered with equal emphasis on a common educational background.

II

Socialization and Learning

Introduction

THE MOST obvious way in which contemporary sociologists differ from their predecessors is in their reliance on empirical research. Earlier writers were limited by the evidence on which they could base generalizations, and they tended to be concerned with general societal problems that were often quite abstract. Ideally, the work of modern sociologists would embody both empirical research and theory, but this is all too frequently not the case. Nevertheless, in the selections that follow there is considerable evidence that the problems associated with socialization identified by Durkheim, Weber, Dewey, and Waller remain concerns of empirical researchers today.

In the first selection, Martin Trow utilizes census statistics dating back to the post–Civil War period to remind us that the highly differentiated system of secondary education in the United States and the crises this system now faces have been slowly developing over the past century. Trow points out that secondary education in the latter part of the nineteenth century was largely charismatic, to use Weber's term, in that it was mainly confined to presocialization of college-bound "gentlemen." A shift to mass terminal secondary education occurred, however, during the first part of the twentieth century. This first transformation of the schools reflected changes in the occupational profile of the larger society, changes which required different socialization patterns for the majority of students, who were now expected to receive practical training from the secondary schools. Hence, new curricula had to be developed for terminal students, and these curricula were taught along with traditional college preparatory curricula in comprehensive schools. The upward spiral of occupational levels and of educational requirements were soon to force a *second* transformation of the secondary schools. Writing in 1961, Trow suggested that this second transformation might be far more problematic than the first, both in terms of organizational accommodations and in terms of adequately motivating the minority who remain terminal secondary students.

Robert Dreeben points out that the major effort of research on schools as socializing agencies has been to assess the cognitive-intellective outcomes of schooling. This effort, which reflects the strong emphasis placed by our society on the intellectual goals of education, has been made possible by the large number of standard instruments that regularly measure such outcomes in school systems. While Dreeben rejects the acquisition of cognitive skills as his own topic, he nevertheless selects another set of educational *outcomes*, the learning of norms. These norms are potentially researchable as dependent variables using the same general model that has been applied to cognitive skills. Thus, while he employs a conceptual-theoretical approach, both the selection of the topic and the framework in which he presents it reveal the debt of contemporary sociology of education to the precedents established by empirical research.

Dreeben begins by contrasting selected structural features of the home and the school which are encountered by children. He argues that specific structural characteristics of the school afford the necessary conditions for the inculcation of four norms that cannot be adequately presented within the structure of the family: independence, achievement, universalism, and specificity. Dreeben's formulations share with Waller a concern with the influence of the social organization of the school on socialization, and they share with Dewey a concern with the discontinuities between socialization processes outside and inside the school. Dreeben continues with a discussion of the problem of cheating in school as it contrasts with cooperative norms found in the society at large, and he touches upon the Durkheimian problem of moral integration again in the concluding section. In addition, the four norms are discussed in relation to the selection-allocation functions which concerned Weber. Thus, in the course of his analysis, Dreeben presents a synthesis of major ideas about socialization that can be traced to the writings of Durkheim, Weber, Dewey, and Waller.

The vastness of the research literature on the cognitive outcomes of education has led to the inclusion in Part II of two research reviews. In the first selection, David E. Lavin divides the available studies into two groups: those that analyze the effects of ecological and demographic variables on academic performance, and those that relate selected role relationships to academic performance. Next, Sarane S. Boocock focuses on the dimensions of the classroom that affect student performance. At first glance, the strong emphasis on academic outcomes suggests an overriding concern with assessing the rational efficiency of schools in performing selection-allocation functions. However, both Lavin and Boocock are able to identify and to illuminate a variety of sociological problems as they review the research literature, and they emphasize the fact that the determinants of performance cannot be adequately researched without more complex theoretical constructs and research designs than are usually found. It is still possible to recast many of the studies reviewed in terms of the perspectives of the classical writers, but the growing complexity of research suggests that the general problems identified in the past cannot be adequately answered by research without first undergoing conceptual reformulation and greater specificity. If, for example, we are able to identify variations in the dominant socialization patterns of mothers and teachers, and differing modes for organizing classrooms, how will different *combinations* of these modes affect the cognitive and affective responses of particular types of children? Edward L. McDill et al. further complicate this problem by adding the school to the general equation as a relevant unit of analysis, and by showing that there are school *climate* effects on both academic performance and level of aspiration that persist when relevant individual characteristics are controlled. Further, a set of role relationships not generally studied, but implied in the phrase "parental involvement and commitment to the school," are shown to be a major source of climate effects. Moreover, the contextual effects of parental involvement on mathematics achievement and on level of aspiration sharply reduces the contextual effects of four curriculum and facilities characteristics of schools on these same two dependent variables. This suggests that socialization by the school is most effective when parents are most directly involved in school activities. We shall return to this problem in the section on school-community relations.

No sociological study of American education has ever had as much publicity or aroused as much controversy as *Equality of Educational Opportunity*, commonly called the Coleman Report, and no study has ever made more obvious the complexity of studying the effectiveness of schools as socializing agencies. It must be assumed that any serious student of the sociology of education will familiarize himself with James S. Coleman's study and with the critical literature it has inspired. However, familiarity with the history of the concepts that Coleman set out to study cannot be assumed. The selection by Coleman that concludes Part II is an unusual example of how the process of designing empirical research led to the elaboration and specification of theoretical constructs. It is all the more remarkable because of the ease with which one can identify the attention that Coleman gives to each of the major problems of socialization discussed by Durkheim, Weber, Dewey, and Waller. For example, the mandate of the 1954 Supreme Court decision can be viewed as a Durkheimian problem in moral integration; the curriculum and tracking distinctions made within the schools can be seen both in terms of Waller's concern with the impact of school structure on socialization and Weber's concern with selection-allocation; and, of course, the serious attempt to educate all children regardless of social origins can be viewed in terms of Dewey's interest in the discontinuities found between socialization in the home and in the school.

Coleman reminds us that while the socialization goals set for the school vary over time and from one society to another, these goals have always been intimately connected with the stratification system and occupational structure. Historically, school structure and curriculum have been altered to accommodate these changing goals, and the concept of equality of educational opportunity has also changed. At the individual level, schools face a genuine dilemma in deciding the curriculum to which a child should be assigned, since curriculum is known to set limits on opportunity. At the societal level, Coleman points out that the 1954 Supreme Court decision implied that we should consider the *effects* of schooling in determining whether opportunity is equal. Hence even the Court has framed its decisions in a manner that requires the study of educational *outputs*. But, as Coleman demonstrates, regardless of whether we can measure output from schooling and the relative impact of a variety of factors on this output, we must still decide which set of findings would represent equality of educational opportunity. The limits of the responsibility of the school for producing similar *performance* from children with different social origins is clearly at issue here, and the refinement of research on educational outputs will no doubt continue to play a major role in this growing controversy during the coming years.

The Transformation of America

THE CIVIL WAR is the great watershed of American history. It stands midway between the Revolution and ourselves, and symbolically, but not just symbolically, separates the agrarian society of small farmers and small businessmen of the first half of the nineteenth century from the urbanized industrial society with its salaried employees that followed. And the mass public secondary school system as we know it has its roots in the transformation of the economy and society that took place after the Civil War.

In 1820, at least 7 out of every 10 Americans in the labor force were farmers or farm laborers. In 1870, farmers still comprised about half the labor force. By 1960, that figure was below 10 per cent. At the same time, the proportion of salaried white collar workers rose from less than 10 per cent in 1870 to nearly 40 per cent today.[1] The proportion of non-farm manual workers in the labor force rose until 1920, leveled off at about 40 per cent since then and has shown signs of falling over the past decade. Thus, there has been a large and rapid growth of a new salaried middle class, paralleled by a large and rapid decline in the proportion of the labor force in agriculture, with the proportions of manual workers rising till about 1920 but relatively constant over the past forty years.

These changes in the occupational structure have reflected tremendous changes in the economy and organization of work. Since the Civil War, and especially in the past fifty years, an economy based on thousands of small farms and businesses has been transformed into one based on large bureaucratized organizations characterized by centralized decision-making and administration carried out through coordinated managerial and clerical staffs.

When small organizations grow large,

The Second Transformation of American Secondary Education

Martin Trow

Reprinted, with omissions, from the International Journal of Comparative Sociology, 2 (1961), pp. 144–166, by permission of the author and the publisher, E. J. Brill.

papers replace verbal orders; papers replace rule of thumb calculations of price and profit; papers carry records of work flow and inventory that in a small operation can be seen at a glance on the shop floor and materials shed. And as organizations grew, people had to be trained to handle those papers—to prepare them, to type them, to file them, to process them, to assess and use them. The growth of the secondary school system after 1870 was in large part a response to the pull of the economy for a mass of white collar employees with more than an elementary school education.

The First Transformation of American Secondary Education

In 1870 there were roughly 80,000 students enrolled in high schools of all kinds in this country, and the bulk of these were in tuition academies. Public high schools were just beginning to grow in numbers—there were perhaps no more than 500 in the whole country, concentrated in the Northeast, and still greatly outnumbered by the tuition academies.[2]

The 16,000 high school graduates in that year comprised only about 2 per cent of the seventeen year olds in the country.[3] Moreover, a very large proportion of those who went to secondary school went on to college.[4]

The American secondary school system of 1870 offered a classical liberal education to a small number of middle and upper middle class boys.[5] Very few students went to secondary school, most who went graduated, and many who graduated went on to college. By 1910, there were over 1,100,000 high school students, nearly 90 per cent of them enrolled in the over 10,000 public high schools, and they comprised about 15 per cent of the 14–17 year age group.[6] But for the bulk of these students, high school was as far as they were going. By 1957, 90 per cent of the 14–17 year age group were in school, while 62 per cent of the 17 year old cohort were gaining high school diplomas. Before 1870, the small secondary school system offered a curriculum and maintained standards of scholarship geared to the admissions requirements of the colleges.[7] After 1870, the growing mass secondary system was largely terminal, providing a useful and increasingly vocational education for the new body of white collar workers.

The evidence for the connection between education and occupation that developed after the Civil War is embedded in the census reports. In 1950, at the end of the fifty year period that might be called "the age of the terminal high school" the median years of schooling completed by men and women 25 years and older in various occupational groups were as follows:[8]

professionals:	16+
managers, officials, and proprietors:	11.3
clerical and kindred:	11.4
sales workers:	11.2
craftsmen, foremen, and kindred:	8.3
operatives and kindred:	7.7
laborers, except mine and farm:	7.0
service workers:	7.8

Of course, changes in the occupational structure do not provide the whole explanation of the extraordinary growth of secondary and higher education in the United States. The changes in the occupational structure have raised the educational aspirations of large parts of the American population, and the educational system has been responsive to these higher aspirations. The role of public education in American thought and popular sentiment, and its perceived connection with the national welfare and individual achievement, have, at least until recently, been greater in America than in any other country. Other countries, Great Britain to name one, have had comparable revolutions in their economic structure without comparable educational transformations. The commitment of America to equality of opportunity, the immense importance attached to education throughout American history, the very great role of education as an avenue of mobility in a society where status ascribed at birth is felt to be an illegitimate barrier to advancement—all of these historical and social psychological forces are involved in the extraordinary American commitment to mass secondary and higher education. Moreover, there were forces involved in the growth of the high school —such as large scale immigration and urbanization, and the movement to abolish child labor[9]—which are not present in the growth of mass higher education, whereas transformations of the occupational structure are common to both educational movements.

Now, the creation of a system of mass secondary education that accompanied the growth of mass organizations after 1870 could not be simply the extension of the old elite secondary system; it would be different in function (terminal rather than preparatory) and in organization (public locally controlled rather than private tuition and endowed schools). Moreover, it needed its own curriculum and its own teacher-training programs and institutions. It needed its own teacher-training programs first because the sheer number of secondary teachers required by mass secondary education was far beyond the capacities of the traditional colleges to supply, as they had supplied the older tuition academies.[10] In the old academies, the principals and masters were products of the colleges, and often went on to teach in the colleges; there was no sharp break between the academies and the colleges since they taught roughly the same subjects to the same kinds of students.[11] This was no longer possible with the new terminal public high school; the students were different, the curriculum was not preparation for college, by and large, and new Departments of Education and State Teachers Colleges were created at least in part to train the staffs of these new high schools.[12] These centers of professional education were not identified with the older, elite traditions of higher education, but created their own traditions of education for life, for citizenship, for useful tasks, the traditions, that is, of the mass democratic terminal secondary system that came to full flower between 1910 and 1940. . . .[13]

In the fifty years between 1880 and 1930, the numbers of students in public high schools in the United States roughly doubled every decade, rising from 110,000 to nearly four and a half million. And the new secondary education was shaped both by the enormous increase in numbers of students, and by their social characteristics. Many of the new students were in school unwillingly, in obedience to the new or more stringent state compulsory education laws; many came from poor, culturally impoverished homes and had modest vocational goals; many of these were the sons and daughters of recent immigrants, and seemed to observers very much in need of "Americanization."[14] These new students posed new problems for secondary education; and these problems, and the answers which they engendered, transformed public secondary education, its philosophy and its curriculum. Commenting on the influential National Education Association Report of 1918 entitled *Cardinal Principles of Secondary Education*, a report strongly influenced by the writings of John Dewey, and responsive to the new demands of mass secondary education, James Conant observes:

> Confronted with a "heterogeneous high school population destined to enter all sorts of occupations," high school teachers and administrators and professors of education needed some justification for a complete overhauling of a high school curriculum originally designed for a homogeneous student body. The progressives with their emphasis on the child, "on learning by doing," on democracy and citizenship, and with their attack on the arguments used to support a classical curriculum were bringing up just the sort of *new* ideas that were sorely needed. After closing John Dewey's volume, *Democracy and Education*, I had the feeling that, like the Austro-Hungarian Empire of the nineteenth century, if John Dewey hadn't existed he would have had to be invented. In a sense perhaps he was, or at least his doctrines were shaped by school people with whom he talked and worked.[15]

The creation of a mass terminal system, with functions and orientations quite different from that of the traditional college preparatory system it succeeded, forced not merely certain changes in the curriculum, but a drastic shift in the basic assumptions underlying secondary education. Speaking of the writings of

G. Stanley Hall in support of the "child-centered school," Lawrence Cremin notes that they

> paved the way for a fundamental shift in the meaning of equal opportunity at the secondary level. Formerly, when the content and purpose of the secondary school had been fairly well defined, equal opportunity meant the right of all who might profit from secondary education as so defined to enjoy its benefits. Now, the "given" of the equation was no longer the school with its content and purposes, but the children with their background and needs. Equal opportunity now meant simply the right of all who came to be offered something of value, and it was the school's obligation to offer it. The magnitude of this shift cannot be overestimated; it was truly Copernican in character. And tied as it was to the fortunes of the child-study movement, it gained vast popularity during the first decade of the twentieth century.[16]

The Growth of Mass Higher Education in America

During the decades when the institutions, the curriculum, and the philosophies of mass terminal education were being created, the college population was rising very slowly.[17] As recently as 1940 the total number of students enrolled in college comprised only 15 per cent of the college age group (the 18 to 21 year olds). By 1954, that proportion was up to 30 per cent, and by 1960 it was around $37\frac{1}{2}$ per cent. Over both the longer 20 year period between 1940 and 1960 and the recent six year period, 1954–1960, the rate of increase in college enrollments as a proportion of the college age group has been about 1.3 per cent a year. If that rate of increase is maintained, and that is a conservative forecast, then by 1970 college enrollments will comprise about half of the college

age group.[18] The rapid rate of increase since 1940 is in marked contrast with the average rate of increase of only 0.35 per cent per annum between 1920, when college enrollments comprised 8 per cent of the college age group, and 1940, when that figure had risen to 15 per cent.

Figure 1 shows the phases in the parallel development of American secondary and higher education graphically. If we take, somewhat arbitrarily, an enrollment of 15 per cent of the age-grade as the beginning of the mass phase of an educational system, then secondary education passed this line around 1910, and higher education in 1940. The period 1870–1980 with which we are dealing falls naturally then into three phases. In Phase I secondary and higher education were by and large offering an academic education to an elite minority. Phase II, between roughly 1910 and 1940, saw the rapid growth of mass terminal education, with higher education still offered to a small but slowly growing minority.[19] Since 1940, or more precisely, since World War II, we are (in Phase III) seeing the rapid growth of mass higher education. With enrollments in higher education continuing to grow, and with secondary school enrollments (as a proportion of the 14–17 year old population) near saturation, the transformation of the terminal secondary system into a mass preparatory system is well under way.

It is interesting to compare rates of increase in college attendance during the first two decades of Phase III with the rate of increase in high school enrollments during the decades 1909–1939 (Phase II), the years of growth of the mass secondary system. In the last twenty years of Phase I, 1889–1909, the high school population (as a proportion of the 14–17 year olds) rose from 6.7 per cent to 15.4 per cent, an annual rate of increase of about 0.44 per cent. Over the next three decades, (Phase II), the rate increased from 15.4 per cent to 73.3 per cent, an annual rate of increase of about 1.9 per cent. While this is somewhat higher than the rate of increase of about 1.3 per cent annually in college attendance (as a proportion of the 18–21 year olds) thus far in Phase III, there is in both cases a marked increase in the rate of growth over the previous period. In the case of both secondary and higher education, the rate of increase has been about four times as great in the period of rapid growth as compared with the immediately preceding periods of slow growth. In both cases we see the rapid transformation of an education for a relatively small elite into a system of mass education. This process is about

completed for the secondary education (in 1958 the high school population comprised nearly 90 per cent of the high school age group), while we are in the middle of the expansion of opportunities for higher education. And as with secondary education, there is no reason to believe that the United States will stop short of providing opportunities and facilities for nearly universal experience of some kind in higher education.

The immediate force behind these trends in both secondary and higher education are changes in public senti-

Figure 1. Enrollment rates in secondary and higher education. United States, 1870–1980.

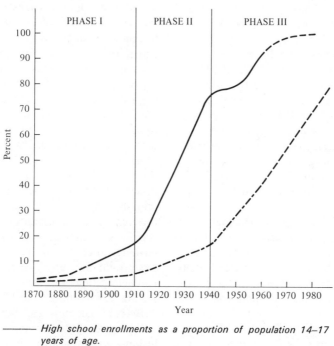

——— High school enrollments as a proportion of population 14–17 years of age.
— · — College and university enrollments as a proportion of population 18–21 years of age.
— — — Estimated.

Note: These curves are based on the figures at 10 year intervals, and do not show the enrollment rates during World War II and the Korean War.

Sources: Progress of Public Education in the United States, 1959–1960, op. cit. Historical Statistics, op. cit. Fact Book, op. cit. Bogue, The Population of the United States, op. cit.

ment—in people's ideas of what they want and expect for their children in the way of formal education. Where most Americans have come to see a high school education as the ordinary, expected thing for their children, they are now coming to think of at least some time in college in the same way.[20] Behind these changes in sentiment are other social forces, not least among which is another change in our occupational structure, parallel to the massive growth in the white collar population which underlay the growth of the public secondary school system. The current change is the immense growth of demand for more highly trained and educated people of all kinds. Between 1940 and 1950, the number of engineers in the country doubled; the number of research workers increased by 50 per cent. Even more striking, between 1950 and 1960 the total labor force increased by only 8 per cent; but the number of professional, technical, and kindred workers grew by 68 per cent[21]—and these, of course, are the occupations that call for at least some part of a college education. Moreover, it is estimated that the period 1957–1970 will see an increase of a further 60 per cent in this category of highly educated workers.[22] Where in the decades 1900–1930, clerical and kindred workers were the fastest growing occupational classification and by far, in the period 1950–1970 it has been and will be the professional and technical occupations.[23]

The Second Transformation of American Secondary Education

There are two major points to be made in summary here. First, much the same forces which made for the development of the mass secondary system in this country are now at work creating a system of mass higher education. And second, this development is rapidly changing the function of the secondary system. Secondary education in the United States began as an elite preparatory system; during its great years of growth it became a mass terminal system; and it is now having to make a second painful transition on its way to becoming a mass preparatory system. But this transition is a good deal more difficult than the first, because while the first involved the *creation* of the necessary institutions, the second is requiring the *transformation* of a huge existing institutional complex. It is almost always easier to create new institutions to perform a new function than it is to transform existing institutions to meet new functions. And as a further complication, during these long decades of transition, the secondary schools are going to have to continue to perform the old terminal education functions for very large if decreasing proportions of students who are not equipped, motivated, or oriented toward college. In the earlier transition, the old college preparatory schools continued to exist and to perform their preparatory functions, with much the same curriculum and kinds of personnel, thus permitting a rough division of function between the older and the newer schools. And where this was not possible, the number of preparatory students was shortly so small as compared with the terminal students that the schools did not have quite the same sense of equal but conflicting functions that secondary people are now coming to feel.[24]

By contrast, now and for the foreseeable future, both the preparatory and terminal functions will have to be performed by the same institutions and the same personnel. Of course, that has always been true to some extent—there have always been college-oriented students in our high schools, and provisions have been made for them. But by and large, they have been a minority in an institution created for the great mass of terminal students. The dominant philosophies and structure of the high school could be determined by its central function of providing a terminal secondary education for the mass of American youth. As preparatory students become an increasingly large proportion of all high school youth, and in more and more places a majority, they provide by their existence not just a demand for special provision, but a challenge to the basic structure and philosophy of the school. And this is the challenge that underlies the criticism of secondary education that flows from many sources. . . .

The High School and Its Changing Public

In the coming decades the high schools will be dealing not only with a different kind of student, but also with a different kind of parent. During the formative years of the mass terminal secondary system in the United States, the teachers and educators who were building the system were dealing by and large with parents who themselves had gone no further than grade school. These people, many of them immigrants or of rural origins, whose children were going no further than high school, had neither the competence nor the motivation to be greatly concerned with the high school curriculum. And the debates about secondary education were carried on largely over the heads of these parents, among the professionals themselves, and between the educators and sections of the academic community. But increasingly, secondary school people are dealing with educated parents of preparatory students, who possess both the competence and the direct motivation to be concerned with the character of their children's secondary education. As recently as 1940, three American adults in five had never been to high school, and only one in four had

completed high school.[25] By 1960 three in five had been to high school, and over 40 per cent were high school graduates.[26] By 1970 over 50 per cent will be high school graduates, and by 1980 it is estimated that figure will reach 60 per cent.[27] Parents who themselves have been through high school, and many of them through some years of college as well, feel themselves more competent to pass judgment on the secondary education of their children, and are less likely to accept passively and on faith the professional recommendations of school administrators, educators and counsellors. It is this rapidly growing group of educated parents whose children are going on to college which provides the audience and the support for the "academic" critics of the secondary school and its curriculum. There is every reason to believe that their interest will grow as their numbers increase, and as competition among their children for the better college places becomes sharper.

This development places a strain on the professional autonomy of educators, who paradoxically find that their professional expertise and judgment is increasingly challenged even while their professional standards and organizations are strengthened, and as the body of knowledge and theory on which their professional status rests is steadily enlarged. This paradox inevitably creates bewilderment and resentment among the professional educators. But it may be that as educators recognize that the very high success of their efforts to extend educational opportunities through high school and beyond creates a large body of parents who take a detailed and active interest in the education of their children, they may find some solace in what is probably a permanent condition of external scrutiny and criticism. Moreover, wistful and wholly misleading parallels with the enviable autonomy of doctors and lawyers only sharpen their bewilderment and resentment; they will neither reduce the volume of lay criticism nor account for its existence.[28] Professional educators in America will have to resign themselves to the fact that mass public education, especially at the secondary level, involves conflicts of values and interests which are independent of professional skills and knowledge, and which are increasingly less likely to be left solely to professional decision. And foremost among these is the relative weight and importance placed in each school and district on college preparation as over against a terminal "education for life."

Teachers for Mass Preparatory Secondary Education

The difficulties of strengthening secondary education for college preparatory students in public high schools are complicated by what is clearly a pattern of negative selection to teaching below the college level. And this pattern is especially marked for the recruitment of men, who comprise about half of all high school teachers.[29] Moreover, a recent nationwide study of beginning teachers conducted by the U.S. Office of Education shows that 70 per cent of the men and over 80 per cent of the women did not expect to continue teaching until retirement.[30] The bulk of the women said, as might be expected, that they hoped to leave teaching for homemaking. More significant for the college preparatory programs in high schools, over half of the men in the sample expected to leave teaching for some other job in education, chiefly administration, while fully 20 per cent were already planning to leave education entirely. And the evidence suggests that the men who remain in the classroom are by and large less able than those who move on to administration or out of education altogether.[31]

The much lower incomes of teachers, as compared with school administrators, with men who leave education, and with most other occupations requiring a comparable amount of education, account for much of this unfortunate pattern of recruitment and retention of male teachers.[32] Moreover, the relatively low status of teaching below the college level, which is both a cause and a consequence of the low salaries, also helps to explain why teaching attracts and holds too few of the most able men.[33] And while teachers' salaries are rising, it is unlikely that the gross differentials in pay and prestige between high school teaching and other occupations requiring a college education are likely to be significantly narrowed in the near future. On the contrary, there is reason to fear they may be widened. The continued extension of opportunities for higher education to able students— through public and private scholarships, the expansion of public higher education, and the like—is offering to able young college men a wider range of occupational alternatives, many of which carry greater prestige and higher incomes than does secondary teaching. In the past a career in teaching was often the only intellectual occupation (aside from the ministry) open to serious young boys from farms and small towns; and the local normal schools or state teachers college were often the only educational avenues of mobility open to such boys. There are proportionately fewer boys from farms and small towns today, and wider opportunities for them, as for the great mass of urban youth, in higher education. This, together with the continued growth of the "intellectual occupations" is almost certain to make the competition for able men sharper in the years to come. Our society's demands for scientists, engineers, technically trained people of all kinds appears insatiable, and the rewards for work in these fields are usually considerably more generous than for high school teaching. Of even greater importance, the very rapid expansion of higher education currently under way in this country, and the enormous demands for college teachers that it creates, constitutes perhaps the strongest set of competitive opportunities open to young men who want to teach. . . .[34]

Pressures for Reform of the Curriculum

The character and quality of high school teachers are especially important in view of the recent efforts to strengthen the preparatory aspects of the high school curriculum which are predicated on the existence of large numbers of teachers in the schools able to put the new curriculum into effect. The pressures for reform of the curriculum have been strongest in the areas of science and mathematics. The enormous expansion during and since World War II of scientific research and development, both in government and industry, has created a continuing demand for large numbers of highly trained technicians, and at the same time has generated very strong pressures for the reform of what was a manifestly inadequate curriculum in high school science and mathematics. And this in turn has involved many more academic scientists in efforts to reform the secondary school curriculum.[35] Largely on the initiative of the university scientists, a number of studies and programs have been initiated expressly to develop new secondary school courses in the sciences and mathematics, and to prepare textbooks and other materials for use in them. The first of these was the Physical Science Study Committee, begun at the Massachusetts Institute of Technology in 1956, followed closely by the School Mathematics Study Group (1958), the Biological Sciences Curriculum Study (1958), the Chemical Education Material Study (1959), and many others. There are movements afoot to extend these programs and studies aiming at the reform of the secondary school curriculum to the social studies and the humanities. Moreover, the Advanced Placement Program has introduced college level work directly into the high school by allowing students who have taken college level work in high school and who pass standard achievement tests in those fields to be admitted to a large number of colleges with advanced standing. This program is growing rapidly, as more and more able students, most with graduate and professional schools in mind, try for advanced placement both to improve their chances for admission to the better colleges and also as a way of saving time in the early stages of a lengthy higher education.[36]

All of these efforts to reform and strengthen the preparatory work offered by the high schools require teachers with both academic ability and training. The lack of preparation of many teachers in academic fields is real though reparable.[37] Extensive programs of summer training sessions and workshops, supported in large part by Federal funds, are now organized on a continuing basis to strengthen the high school teachers' own skills in the subjects they teach and to introduce them to more recent developments in their subjects.[38] A more serious question raised by the evidence cited earlier is that of the academic aptitudes and abilities of high school teachers; this question conditions every proposal for the reform of the curriculum. Of course, efforts can and should be made to recruit and retain highly competent teachers. Meanwhile, the reform of the curriculum calls for new ways to make the best use of the most able teachers already in the schools.

It may be that the matching of academically oriented and able teachers and students which already takes place informally will be encouraged and even formalized. But it is precisely such invidious distinctions that American public schools try hard to avoid. It is in the schools that the American value of equality is most deeply rooted, and it is in the doctrines of democratic education that we find the most determined equation and encouragement of all kinds of talents and abilities, with academic abilities only one kind among many. When college preparatory students were only a small minority of all students in high schools, they could be dealt with as "exceptions" without challenging the basic equalitarian ethos of the school which equated all students and all activities and interests.[39] But the transformation of the secondary schools into predominantly preparatory institutions profoundly challenges this ethos; the criteria of academic ability and achievement which are so much more important in higher education are increasingly relevant to and applied within the walls of the high school.[40]

Under pressures such as these, it is likely that both the philosophy and organization of American secondary education will change in the decades ahead. And the nature of these changes will in turn affect the kinds of people drawn to high school teaching, how they are trained,[41] and how they are used in the schools. The more emphasis placed on academic subject matter in the high school curriculum, and in the training and employment of teachers, the more likely people with academic interests will be attracted to teaching. This is certainly the direction of change in public secondary education's Phase III. But where does this leave the high school's remaining responsibility for terminal education?

The Impact of the Transformation on Terminal Education

The expansion of the college-going population fills the high schools with college preparatory students, and generates the pressures for a strengthening of the preparatory function that we have spoken of. But this development also affects the character of the terminal students, and of terminal education in high school, as well. When few students went on to college, there was no disgrace in not doing so; moreover, except for the professions, it was not so clear that occupational success was closely linked to academic achievement. The Horatio Alger myth, and the American folklore celebrating the successes of the self-made (and self-educated) man, served to define school achievement as only one among several legitimate avenues to success. But the rationalization of industry, and the increased importance of higher education for advancement beyond the lowest levels of the occupational structure, make educational achievement objectively more important for later success; the increased numbers of college-going students make this importance visible to high school students. The consequence of all this is to change the character of the students who do not go on to college when increasing majorities of students do so. Already in some localities, and increasingly in coming decades, the students not going on to college are being reduced to a hard core composed of two groups: children from ethnic and racial groups which do not place strong emphasis on high educational and occupational aspirations —for example, Negroes and Mexicans; and children of low intelligence who simply cannot handle college preparatory work.

The transformation of "not going to college" into "failure" has both social and psychological consequences. Among those who want to succeed in school but cannot, the effects of failure may be a loss of self-respect, with widespread if not highly visible and dramatic consequences for the social behaviors of those so affected. One English observer suggests that:

As a result of the close relationship between education and occupation a situation may soon be reached when the educational institutions legitimize social inequality by individualizing failure. Democratization of the means of education together with the internalizing of the achievement ethic by members of the working-class strata may lead to an individualizing of their failure, to a loss of self-respect which in turn modifies an individual's attitude both to his group and to the demands made upon him by his society.[42]

This problem of the motivated student of low ability may be more severe in England, and in other Western countries in the earlier stages of the democratization of education, than in the United States, where among our nearly 2,000 institutions of higher education there is a college somewhere for everybody.[43] Moreover, the elaborate student counselling programs in our mass public institutions are designed explicitly to help students of low academic ability accept their limitations, and direct their energies toward attainable educational and occupational goals without a sense of personal failure and resentment toward society.[44]

But while the emerging American educational system promises to make some provision for all those who accept its values, regardless of their academic ability, it is not so clear what it can do for those who deeply reject its values and purposes, along with many of the values and purposes of the larger society. The increasing extent and violence of juvenile delinquency in the United States may be closely linked to the extension of educa-tional opportunities to the conforming majority. Where educational achievement (in terms at least of years completed) becomes more widespread and thus more visible, and more important to even modest success in the occupational world, then educational failure *pari passu* becomes more devastating to one's hopes of achieving the advertised "good life" through legitimate channels. Failure in school for many is part of a familiar vicious cycle. Absence of encouragement or concern with school performance in the home (especially marked in certain ethnic and racial groups) leads to failure to acquire basic skills, such as reading, in the early grades, which ensures academic failure in higher grades. These repeated failures make school seem a punishing prison, from which the boy escapes as early as the law allows. But lacking education or training, it is unlikely that he can get any but the poorest jobs. And the habits and resentments generated at home, on the street, and in school make it unlikely that such a boy can move into better jobs. After repeated failures in school and a succession of poorly paid odd jobs, the rewards of membership in a gang, and of participation in its delinquent subculture are considerable. And the more the high school is organized around the college preparatory programs, the more it stresses academic achievement, the more punishing it will be for the non-achievers.[45] The delinquent subculture is a way of dealing with deprivations of status, very largely experienced in the schools, and as a response to these deprivations, "the gang offers an heroic rather than an economic [or intellectual] basis of self-respect."[46]

Special school programs may help meet the complex problems of low aspirations and juvenile delinquency, though children growing up in disorganized families, or in cultures cut off from the dominant American value systems, or exposed to the corrosive effects of racial prejudice, present problems that cannot be wholly dealt with in and by the schools. The point here is that the growth of educational opportunity threatens to make the greater part of terminal education in high schools coincidental with the social problems of juvenile delinquency. This is not to say that every classroom full of non-college going students is or will be a "blackboard jungle." It does mean that the hostility toward the school characteristic of the juvenile gangs, but much more widespread than their membership, will be an increasing part of the educational problem faced by schools and teachers dealing with terminal students. The clusters of values which characterize juvenile delinquency—"the search for kicks, the disdain of work. . . . and the acceptance of aggressive toughness as proof of masculinity"[47]—is incompatible with disciplined school work, either academic *or* vocational. Moreover, much of the serious vocational training the high schools have offered in the past is increasingly shifted to higher education, especially to the junior colleges.[48]

The terminal education of the future will not simply be the terminal education of the past offered to a decreasing proportion of students. The growth of the college-going population changes the character of the remaining terminal students, it changes the meaning of their terminal work, and it will force changes in the organization and curriculum of terminal secondary education. It may also call for teachers with special skills and training in dealing with the problems of the minority or "hard-core" of terminal students. But if the increasingly important preparatory programs claim the best resources of secondary education and command the most able teachers, then terminal education will indeed be a second-class program for second-class students. And they will know it, and that knowledge will feed their bitterness and resentment. Neither the old terminal education for life, nor the strengthened academic programs will meet their needs. If the terminal education of the future is not to be an educational slum, it will demand large resources and much intelligence. But these are always in short supply, and terminal education will be competing for both with the more attractive programs of preparatory education.

Conclusion

Universal secondary education in the United States was achieved through a system of comprehensive high schools, devoted primarily to the education of the great mass of its students for work and life, and secondarily to the preparation of a small minority for higher education. The present concern with the reform of the high school curriculum and teacher training reflects the rapid growth of the college-going population, and the increased importance of the preparatory function.

Nevertheless, it may have been possible to combine terminal education for a majority and preparatory education for a minority more successfully than it will be to combine preparatory education for a majority and terminal education for a minority under one roof. Moreover, the shortage of highly qualified and motivated teachers of academic subjects may require that they be used where their talents and interests are most productive —that is, in teaching the academically most talented fraction of the student body. Secondary education in America may have to accept a higher measure of division of labor and differentiation of function than it has in the past. As a terminal system, it could in its comprehensiveness and emphasis on "education for life" simply carry further the basic education of the elementary school of which it was an outgrowth. As it becomes increasingly a preparatory system, it may be forced to take on some of the characteristics of higher education for which it is preparing, and place greater emphasis on differences among both teachers and students in academic ability and intellectual and occupational interests.

American higher education deals with the diversity of student abilities and talents largely through the great diversity of institutions which compose it, institutions which vary greatly in their selectivity, and in the academic abilities of their students.[49] American comprehensive high schools contain all this diversity within themselves, providing different streams or tracks for students with different educational or vocational intentions, or, as Conant has urged, grouping by ability, subject by subject.[50] But these arrangements ignore the effects of the students on one another, and of the student "mix" on the intellectual climate of the school. In a school where the academically motivated students are in a minority, they cannot help but be affected by the predominantly anti-intellectual values (and behaviors) of the majority[51]; similarly, where the low-achieving terminal students are in the minority, it is hard for them not to be defined as second-class students by other students and teachers, with the effects on them discussed earlier. It may be that the period we are entering will call for a critical evaluation of the comprehensive high school, the institution created by and for mass terminal secondary education. . . .[52]

Notes

[1] Sources: U.S. Bureau of the Census, *Statistical Abstract of the United States: 1960* (81st ed., Washington, D.C.: 1960), Table 279, p. 216. Donald J. Bogue, *The Population of the United States* (New York; Free Press, 1959). Kurt Mayer, "Recent Changes in the Class Structure of the United States," *Transactions of the Third World Congress of Sociology* (Amsterdam: 1956), III, 66–80.

[2] Ellwood P. Cubberley, *Public Education in the United States* (New York: Houghton-Mifflin, 1934), pp. 255, 627.

[3] U.S. Bureau of the Census, *Historical Statistics of the United States, Colonial Times to 1957* (Washington, D.C.: 1960), p. 207.

[4] Compare the annual output of the secondary schools in 1870 (16,000 graduates) with the total college enrollment of 52,000 in that year. *Ibid.*

[5] On the academies in the nineteenth century, see E. E. Brown, *The Making of Our Middle Schools* (New York, Longmans, Green, 1903). While the early academies were not intended as preparatory schools, "the idea of liberal culture [was] the dominant note of both academy and college education in the nineteenth century." (*Ibid.*, p. 229.)

[6] U.S. Department of Health, Education, and Welfare, *Progress of Public Education in the United States, 1959–60* (Washington, D.C.: 1960), Table 2, p. 11. *Historical Statistics of the United States, Colonial Times to 1957*, p. 207.

[7] Brown, *op. cit.*, p. 231.

[8] Bogue, *op. cit.*, Table 17–11, p. 510. For over sixty years, the dominant stereotype of social class in America, based on solid reality but enshrined in folk-lore and mass fiction, has been that white collar people have been to high school, while manual workers by and large have not. These educational and class cleavages in America have also roughly coincided with religious and ethnic cleavages—between the older Protestant immigration from Northern and Western Europe and the later Catholic immigration from Southern and Eastern Europe. But the educational dimensions of this cleavage is now changing. See footnote 19.

[9] Although "the raising of the school-leaving age in many states followed the change in the pattern of school attendance of a majority of the youth." James Conant, *The Child, The Parent and The State* (Cam-

bridge: Harvard University Press, 1959), p. 95.

[10] The number of public high school teachers increased from about 20,000 in 1900 to over 200,000 in 1930. U.S. Office of Education, *Biennial Survey of Education, 1928–1930, Bulletin*, No. 20, Vol. II (1931), pp. 8, 222.

[11] "In 1872, 70 per cent of the students entering the eastern colleges were graduates of the academies." Cubberley, *op. cit.*, p. 260, footnote 1.

[12] On the upgrading of Normal Schools to the status of four year State Teachers Colleges, and the establishment of departments of education in other colleges and universities in the decades before 1920, see Benjamin W. Frazier, "History of the Professional Education of Teachers in the United States," and E. S. Evenden et al., "Summary and Interpretations," U.S. Office of Education, *National Survey of Education, Bulletin 1933*, No. 10, Vols. V and VI (1935).

[13] "During the first half of the present century, while many liberal arts colleges turned their backs on the problems of teacher education, legal requirements for certification were established in nearly all states. . . . [W]hile the liberal arts colleges were preoccupied with other things, while they ignored the problems of teacher education, a like-minded group of school administrators and other professional educators came to agreement among themselves on the necessity for professional preparation for teachers and transmitted their convictions into law. It was during this same period that the educators became imbued with a new philosophy of education, one far removed from the academic traditions of the liberal arts colleges." Paul Woodring, *New Directions in Teacher Education* (New York: The Fund for the Advancement of Education, 1957), p. 23. See also Merle L. Borrowman, *The Liberal and Technical in Teacher Education* (New York: Teachers College, Columbia University, 1956).

[14] During the twelve years immediately preceding World War I, an average of almost one million new immigrants a year arrived in America; they were predominantly from Southern and Eastern Europe, and settled chiefly in the big cities of the Midwest and the Eastern seabord.

[15] Conant, *op. cit.*, pp. 93–94.

[16] Lawrence A. Cremin, "The Revolution in American Secondary Education, 1893–1918," *Teachers College Record*, 56 (1955), p. 303.

[17] Data on enrollments in both high school and college drawn from *Historical Statistics of the United States, Colonial Times to 1957; Progress of Public Education in the United States, 1959–60;* Bogue, *op. cit.*; American Council on Education, *Fact Book on Higher Education* (Washington, D.C.: n.d.).

[18] Indeed, projections of the college age population of the United States reported in the *Fact Book* (*op. cit.*) coupled with U.S. Bureau of the Census estimates of college enrollments in 1970 (reported in Bogue, *op. cit.*, Table 26–10, p. 778), give a figure of 55 per cent of the 18–21 age group. And a recent Roper study of parental expectations regarding their children's education suggests that even this figure may be considerably low. (See "Why College Enrollments May Triple by 1970," *College Board Review*, 40 [Winter, 1960], pp. 18–19).

[19] But the social composition of this minority was changing during this phase. Already in 1920, when college enrollments comprised only 8 per cent of the 18–21 year old population, some 40 per cent of the college population, by one estimate, came from lower-middle and working class backgrounds. By 1940, at the end of Phase II, 60 per cent of college students came out of those classes. (R. J. Havighurst, *American Higher Education in the 1960s* (Columbus: Ohio State University Press, 1960), Table 7, p. 34).

[20] Compare the recent Roper study done in 1959 (*Parents' College Plans Study*, The Ford Foundation, New York: mimeographed, n.d.), which shows that nearly 70 per cent of children under 12 are expected by their parents to go to college, with the Roper study of a decade earlier. (*Higher Education*, a supplement to *Fortune*, September, 1949). The hopes of the earlier decade have become the expectations of today, and will probably be the enrollments of tomorrow. Of the latest Roper study, one observer noted that "it demonstrated that a college education has come to be widely regarded as the *sine qua non* of personal success, just as the high school diploma did earlier." (Philip Coombs, *College Board Review*, 40 [1960], p. 18).

[21] *Statistical Abstract of the United States, 1960*, p. 216.

²² Bureau of Labor Statistics estimates, reported in Newell Brown, "The Manpower Outlook for the 1960's: Its Implications for Higher Education," Office of Education, U.S. Department of Education, *Higher Education* (December, 1959), pp. 3–6. It is also estimated that the number of engineers will double during this period.

²³ Bogue, *op. cit.*, Table 17–2, p. 475 and *Fact Book, op cit.*, p. 146.

²⁴ For example, of those students entering high school in 1928, only 1 in 5 went on to college four years later, and only 2 in 5 of the high school graduates of 1932 went on to college. But in the coming decades the numbers of terminal and preparatory students in the high schools will be nearly equal. A third of the students entering high school in 1954 went on to college, and by 1958 half of the high school graduates in the United States were going on to some kind of higher education. (Computed from data in *Progress of Public Education, op. cit.*, Figure 1, p. 13). And in some parts of the country that proportion is very much higher.

These transformations can be shown in another way. In 1880, there were roughly the same number of students in American colleges and universities as in our public high schools. By 1940 there were nearly five times as many students in the public high schools as in institutions of higher education. But by 1960, the ratio of high school to college students had fallen to about three to one. (*Historical Statistics, op. cit.*, pp. 207 and 209, and for 1960, *Fact Book, op. cit.*, pp. 10 and 237).

²⁵ Bogue, Table 13–8, p. 343.

²⁶ Between 1940 and 1959, the average educational level of the whole adult population rose from 8.4 to 11.0 years of schooling completed (U.S. Bureau of the Census, *Current Population Reports*, Series P-20, No. 99 [1959], p. 5). Moreover, recent increases in educational opportunity are closing the historic gap in education between white collar people and manual workers. In 1940, at the end of Phase II, the broad white collar categories had on the average completed high school, while manual workers had on the average no more than an elementary schooling. (Mayer, Table 5, p. 76). By 1950, young men between 25 and 29 who were skilled workers and foremen already had an average of nearly 12 years of schooling—less than a year of schooling separated them as a group from young white collar people.

Even the semi-skilled and service workers among these young men had completed two or three years of high school on the average. (*Ibid.*). By 1959, semi-skilled and service workers of all ages had completed an average of two years of high school.

²⁷ Bogue, Table 26–11, p. 779.

²⁸ The relation of professional educators to their public resembles that of the organized medical profession, whose position on medical insurance is under widespread public criticism, more than it does that of the individual physician or hospital staff.

²⁹ The extensive studies done with national samples by the Educational Testing Service and others show that students who major in Education score lowest, on comprehensive tests of verbal and mathematical competence, as compared with majors in almost every other field. (Henry Chauncey, "The Use of the Selective Service College Qualification Test of the Deferment of College Students," *Science*, July 4, 1952, p. 75). See also Dael Wolfle and Toby Oxtoby, "Distribution of Ability of Students Specializing in Different Fields," *Science*, September 26, 1952, pp. 311–14, and Dael Wolfle, Director, *America's Resources of Specialized Talent*, The Report of the Commission on Human Resources and Advanced Training (New York: Harper, 1934), pp. 189–208. This finding is supported by a recent study on the campus of the University of California at Berkeley, which shows that the men who took the education courses had, on the average, poorer grades and less knowledge about public affairs than did men in other majors. They were also, as a group, both less informed and more illiberal on matters of political tolerance and academic freedom than men on the same campus in others areas of specialization. (H. C. Selvin and Warren O. Hagstrom, "Determinants of Support for Civil Liberties," *The British Journal of Sociology*, 11 [March, 1960], pp. 51–73).

³⁰ W. S. Mason, R. J. Dressel, and R. K. Bain, "Sex Role and Career Orientations of Beginning Teachers," *Harvard Educational Review*, 29 (Fall, 1959), pp. 370–84. A study done of men who entered education below the college level after World War II showed that by 1955 fewer than half of them (48 per cent) were still in the classroom, 23 per cent

had become educational administrators, and 29 per cent had left education entirely. R. L. Thorndike and Elizabeth Hagen, *Characteristics of Men Who Remained in and Left Teaching* (Teachers College, Columbia University, n. d.), Table 3, p. 19.

[31] The Study of Thorndike and Hagen (*op. cit.*) of a group of men who were aviation cadet candidates in World War II shows that of all those who went into public school teaching after the War, "those who were academically more capable and talented tended to drop out of teaching and that those who remained as classroom teachers in the elementary and secondary schools were the less intellectually able members of the original group" (p. 10). Both the men who remained in education as administrators, and those who had left education completely, showed more academic ability on the Air Force tests than did those who stayed in the classrooms.

[32] In the study by Thorndike and Hagen (*op. cit.*), fewer than one in ten of the men still in classroom teaching were earning more than $600 a month, while over half of both the school administrators and the men who had left education were earning more than that. The median earnings of the administrators and the ex-teachers exceeded that of the teachers by over 25 per cent. Two-thirds of the ex-teachers in this study mentioned "low pay" as one of the major reasons for their having left teaching.

[33] In addition, teaching in primary and secondary schools, by contrast both with school administration and with college teaching, is widely perceived as a woman's occupation. And "female occupations" are generally less well paid and give less status to the men in them than do comparable "male occupations."

[34] See M. A. Trow, "Reflections on Recruitment to College Teaching," in Halsey, Floud and Anderson, eds., *Education, Economy and Society* (New York: Free Press, 1961). Junior colleges, in particular, draw a substantial proportion of their faculties directly from the high schools, and in all likelihood the more academically oriented teachers at that. The continued expansion of the junior colleges cannot help but improverish the teaching staffs of the high schools.

[35] See Bentley Glass, "The Academic Scientist, 1940–1960," *AAUP Bulletin* (June, 1960), p. 153.

[36] See Richard Pearson, "Advanced Placement Programs: Opportunities Ahead," *College Board Review*, 39 (Fall, 1959), pp. 24–27.

[37] For example, a recent study by the U.S. Office of Education shows that 39 per cent of the teachers in the study who were teaching one or more courses in high school mathematics had not had the calculus or a more advanced course in mathematics, while 7 per cent had had no college mathematics at all. (K. E. Brown and E. S. Obourn, *Qualifications and Teaching Loads of Mathematics and Science Teachers in Maryland, New Jersey, and Virginia*, U.S. Department of Health, Education, and Welfare, Office of Education, Circular 575 [1959], Tables 20 and 22, p. 46). Similarly, a recent report of the National Council of Teachers of English observes that half of the nation's high school English teachers do not have a college major in English, and that because of deficiencies in preparation, 70 per cent of American colleges and universities must offer remedial work in English. (Reported in *Phi Delta Kappan*, 42 [March, 1961], p. 271).

[38] For example, the National Science Foundation through its Summer Institute Program during 1961 supported the attendance of about 20,000 high school and college teachers of science, mathematics, and engineering at some 400 Institutes around the country.

[39] See I. L. Kandel, *The Dilemma of Democracy* (Cambridge: Harvard University Press, 1934).

[40] But this will almost certainly continue to be the comprehensive high school. The resistance of most American educators to selective schools which "segregate" students of academic ability and interests is very great, despite the reputation and accomplishments of such academically "segregated" high schools as New York's High School of Music and Art, the Bronx High School of Science, and the late Townsend Harris High School. See I. L. Kandel, "Current Issues in Expanding Secondary Education," *International Review of Education*, 2 (1959), pp. 155–65.

[41] We cannot here discuss the controversies over teacher training, certification, and the like except to suggest that they also reflect the deep cleavage between the terminal and

preparatory functions of secondary education. In most other advanced countries, which have rather distinct terminal and preparatory school systems, the patterns of social recruitment and training of teachers for these systems also differ: Teachers in the terminal systems usually get their training in teacher training institutes, while teachers in the preparatory systems are educated in the universities for which they are preparing the best of their students. It is probably neither possible nor desirable to reintroduce this pattern into American education. Yes pressures for a reform in teacher education rise, in response to the changing function of the schools. For example, a bill introduced in the California legislature in 1961 would eliminate the "education major" in college by requiring all teachers to have a degree in some academic discipline.

[42] Basil Bernstein, "Some Sociological Determinants of Perception: An Enquiry Into Sub-cultural Differences," *The British Journal of Sociology*, 1 (June, 1958), p. 173.

[43] See T. R. McConnell and Paul Heist, "The Diverse College Student Population," in N. Sanford, ed., *The American College* (New York: Wiley, 1962).

[44] See Burton R. Clark, "The Cooling-Out Function in Higher Education," *American Journal of Sociology*, 65 (May, 1960).

[45] Speaking of this group "for whom adaptation to educational expectations at *any* level is difficult," Parsons notes: "As the acceptable minimum of educational qualifications rises, persons near and below the margin will tend to be pushed into an attitude of repudiation of these expectations. Truancy and delinquency are ways of expressing this repudiation. Thus the very *improvement* of educational standards in the society at large may well be a major factor in the failure of the educational process for a growing number at the lower end of the status and ability distribution." (Talcott Parsons, "The Social Class As a Social

System: Some of Its Functions in American Society," *Harvard Educational Review*, 4 [Fall, 1959], p. 313).

[46] Jackson Toby, "Hoodlum or Business Man: An American Dilemma," in Marshall Sklare, *The Jews* (New York: Free Press, 1958), p. 546. See also, R. K. Merton, *Social Theory and Social Structure* (rev. ed.; New York: Free Press, 1957), Chapter 4, "Social Structure and Anomie"; and Albert K. Cohen, *Delinquent Boys: The Culture of the Gang* (New York: Free Press, 1955), especially Chapter 5, "A Delinquent Solution."

[47] David Matza and Gresham Sykes, "Juvenile Delinquency and Subterranean Values," *American Sociological Review*, 26 (1961) pp. 712–19.

[48] See Burton R. Clark, *The Open Door College* (New York: McGraw-Hill, 1960).

[49] McConnell and Heist, *op. cit.*

[50] See his remarks on "ability grouping" in *The American High School Today* (New York: McGraw-Hill, 1959), pp. 49–50.

[51] See James S. Coleman, "Academic Achievement and the Structure of Competition," *Harvard Educational Review*, 29 (Fall, 1959), pp. 330–52. See also Alan B. Wilson, "Residential Segregation of Social Classes and Aspirations of High School Boys," *American Sociological Review*, 24 (December, 1959), pp. 836–45.

[52] One possibility, in the best experimental tradition of American education, would be to organize one or two academically selective high schools in each major city, where some of the gains and losses of institutional differentiation can be observed, and where experimental programs can be developed for later application in the comprehensive schools. The "hard-core" terminal students present a more difficult problem.

The Contribution of Schooling to the Learning of Norms

Robert Dreeben

I wish to thank Barrie D. Bortnick, Andrew Effrat, Michael B. Katz, Larry A. Weiss, and Charlene A. Worth f or their invaluable help The research and development reported herein was performed pursuant to a contract (OE 5-10-239) with the United States Department of Health, Education, and Welfare, Office of Education, under the provisions of the Cooperative Research Program, as a project of the Harvard University Center for Research and Development on Educational Differences, Copyright © 1967, Dreeben; reproduction in whole or in part permitted for any purposes by the United States Government.

This paper is adapted from Part IV of On What Is Learned in School (Reading, Mass.: Addison-Wesley, 1968).

Reprinted, with omissions, from the Harvard Educational Review, 37 (1967), pp. 211–37, by permission of the author and publisher. Copyright © 1967 by President and Fellows of Harvard College.

THIS PAPER IS CONCERNED with the familiar phenomenon known as schooling. It departs from the usual approaches to education in that the problems of instruction and its direct outcomes are of peripheral interest. The main argument is based on the observation that schools and the classrooms within them have a characteristic pattern of organizational properties different from those of other agencies in which socialization takes place and on the contention that what children learn derives as much from the nature of their experiences in the school setting as from what they are taught.

Traditional approaches to understanding the educational process usually deal with the explicit goals of schools as expressed in curriculum content: the cognitive skills involved in reading, arithmetic, and the like; subject matter content; national tradition; vocational skills; and a multitude of good things such as citizenship, self-discipline, tolerance, patriotism, cooperation, and benevolent attitudes of various kinds. They are also concerned with pedagogy: methods of instruction considered broadly enough to include motivation and quasi-therapeutic activities as well as didactics more narrowly conceived. One indication that curriculum and pedagogy occupy a central place in educational thinking is the existence of a massive literature reporting research devoted overwhelmingly to problems in these two areas and to evaluations of instructional effectiveness in bringing about curricular outcomes.[1]

There is no question but that schools are engaged in an instructional enterprise, but the preoccupation with instruction has been accompanied by the neglect of other equally important problems. It is my contention that the traditional conception of schooling as an instructional process, primarily cognitive in nature, is at best only partially tenable. That is, what pupils learn is in part some function of what is taught; but what *is* learned and from what experiences remain open questions. Doubtless, the dissemination of knowledge is high on the school's agenda; but does such dissemination represent its peculiar contribution?

Instruction and knowledge, even at a high level, are made available to children outside the school: through the family, the mass media, travel, museums, libraries, and personal contacts with a variety of people. Perhaps the inconclusiveness of research designed to measure the impact of teaching on learning is attributable in part to the fact that many social agencies other than schools contribute to the acquisition of similar knowledge generally thought to fall largely within the school's jurisdiction.

Even though other agencies may resemble schools in their instructional impact, schools do have structural characteristics that distinguish them sharply from other settings—most particularly the family—contributing to the socialization of children, characteristics whose obviousness and familiarity probably account for their neglect. For example:

1. Responsibility for the control of schools and for instruction in the classroom rests in the hands of adults who are not the kinsmen of pupils.
2. Children leave the household daily to attend school but return at the close of the day; that is, they continue their active membership and participation in the family.
3. Schools are distinguished structurally according to level; despite the similarities between elementary and secondary levels, there are conspicuous differences involving:
   a. variation in the heterogeneity of the student body related to school district size;
   b. degree of differentiation of the teaching staff based upon subject matter specialization;
   c. presence or absence of formal provision for tracking pupils based largely on past academic achievement;
   d. variation in the number of pupils that each teacher confronts daily.
4. Pupils progress through school grade-by-grade at yearly intervals, each time severing associations with one set of teachers and establishing associations with a new set (unlike the family where children's relationships with parents do not follow a sequential pattern of severance and re-establishment).
5. Pupils move through school as members of age-equal cohorts (unlike the family in which the age dispersion of children is characteristically larger than that of the classroom).
6. Classrooms, like families, consist of adult and non-adult positions, but the former have a much larger non-adult membership.

Whatever pupils learn from the didactic efforts of teachers, they also learn something from their participation in a social setting some of whose structural characteristics have been briefly identified. Implicit in this statement are the following assumptions: (a) the tasks, constraints, and opportunities available within social settings vary with the structural properties of those settings; (b) individuals who participate in them derive principles of conduct based on their experiences coping with those tasks, constraints, and opportunities; and (c) the content of the principles learned varies with the nature of the setting. To the question of what is learned in school, only a hypothetical answer can be offered at this point: pupils learn to accept social norms, or principles of conduct, and to act according to them.[2]

Social Norms

The concept of social norm has long been important in sociological thinking where it has been treated primarily as a determinant, a prior condition accounting in part for some pattern of behavior: a rule, expectation, sanction, or external constraint; an internal force, obligation, conviction, or internalized standard. Given some pattern of conduct or rate of behavior, sociologists characteristically ask, among other things, whether it represents conformity to or deviation from a norm or whether it is a phenomenon emerging from a situation in which several norms operate. Comparatively little attention has been paid to the question of how norms originate in social settings and how individuals learn them.

Norms are situationally specific standards for behavior: principles, premises, or expectations indicating how individuals in specifiable circumstances *ought* to act.

For example, pupils are expected to arrive at school on time. To say that they accept this norm means that: (a) there is such a standard whose existence can be determined independently of pupils' conduct (in this case, the hour they arrive at school); and (b) pupils adhere to the standard in the sense they consider that their actions should be governed by it. Acceptance, then, refers to a self-imposed, acknowledgeable obligation of variable intensity. The content of the norm must be in somebody's mind and communicable by gesture, spoken word, written rule, or sanction.

There are both logical and empirical problems in using the concept "norm."[3] First, norm and behavior must be distinguished analytically, for there is a logical circularity in inferring norms from behavior and then using them to account for variations in behavior. Second, norm acceptance and related behavior are empirically distinct; that is, there is a range of behavioral alternatives relative to any norm. Conduct varies, for example, relative both to a given norm and to prevailing conditions, and some norms explicitly acknowledge permissable variation in conduct.[4]

The Functions of Schooling

Schooling contributes to pupils' learning what the norms are, accepting them, and acting according to them; norm content, acceptance, and behavior can, however, all vary independently. This ostensibly straightforward assertion, however, conceals complexities behind obvious facts. Children leaving the household each day to attend school is an event so familiar that one tends to forget how problematic it is. Herskovits reminds us that "the significance of the distinction between 'schooling' and 'education' is to

be grasped when it is pointed out that while every people must train their young, the cultures in which any substantial part of this training is carried on outside the household are few indeed."[5] The separation of schooling from the household is most characteristic of industrial societies (though not restricted to them), where economic, political, and religious institutions also tend to be independent of the family—independent, that is, in the sense that dominant principles of conduct (social norms) governing relations among kin differ from those governing the conduct of persons in non-familial institutions.

Even though the norms of family life have an important and complex relationship to conduct in non-familial settings, I am concerned here not with that relationship but with aspects of the process by which individuals learn new norms; for when other social institutions in industrial societies have replaced the family as the predominant economic, political, and religious unit and differ from it structurally, principles of conduct appropriate among kin cannot be generalized to them. Since schooling follows a period of life when children are largely dependent on kin, and precedes the period of adulthood when individuals participate as economic producers and citizens, one naturally looks to the school to discover how the addition of new principles of behavior to the psychological repertoire takes place.

Four norms have particular relevance to economic and political participation in industrial societies; those of independence, achievement, universalism, and specificity. I have selected these, not because they form an exhaustive list, but because they are central to the dominant, non-familial activities of adults in American society.[6] In school, pupils participate in activities where they are expected to act as if they were conforming to these norms whether they actually accept them at a particular time or not. Through such participation, it is my belief, pupils will in time know their content,[7] accept them as binding upon themselves, and act in accordance with them in appropriate situations. How schooling contributes to the acquisition of these norms will be discussed in the following pages.

In speaking of independence, achievement, universalism, and specificity as norms, I mean that individuals accept the obligations, respectively: to act by themselves (unless collaborative effort is called for) and accept personal responsibility and accountability for their conduct and its consequences (independence); to perform tasks actively and master the environment according to standards of excellence (achievement); and to acknowledge the right of others to treat them as members of categories often based on a few discrete characteristics rather than on the full constellation of them representing the whole person (universalism and specificity).

In one sense, full adult status, at least for men, requires occupational employment; and one of the outcomes of schooling is employability. The ability to hold a job involves not only adequate physical capacities but the appropriate psychological skills to cope with the demands of work. The requirements of job-holding are multifarious; most occupations, for example, require among other things that individuals assume personal responsibility for the completion and quality of their work and individual accountability for its shortcomings and that they perform their tasks to the best of their ability. Public life, however, extends beyond occupational employment. Although people work in their occupational capacities and in association with others (as clients, patients, customers, parishioners, students, and so on in *their* occupational capacities), they also have non-occupational identities as voters, communicants, petitioners, depositors, applicants, and creditors, to name a few, in which people are classified similarly as members of the same cate-

gory based on a small number of specific characteristics irrespective of how they differ in other respects. . . .

In the early grades, a formal and prolonged process of separating children from the family begins. It does not involve severing or renouncing kinship ties nor relinquishing the normative principles of family life since most members of society, after all, remain part of some kinship unit throughout most of their lives. Schooling does, however, put demands on pupils to adopt principles of conduct different from those they have come to accept as family members— more precisely, to restrict the premises governing family life to conduct among kinsmen, and to learn new premises that apply to settings outside the family. It is a process in which children learn both to generalize principles of conduct from one setting to another and at the same time to specify what principles are appropriate to which setting.

The Structural Basis of Sanctions

Learning to accept norms and act according to them, like other forms of learning, requires the use of sanctions. In both family and school, patterns of action appropriate to each setting are encouraged and discouraged by rewards and punishments taking the form of both specific, momentary acts and more elaborate patterns of action over time.

I assume that in encouraging and discouraging enduring patterns of behavior, a sustained relationship between the parties involved must exist, one that involves more than the reward and punishment of specific acts on a *quid pro quo* basis. In the family, the basis for encouraging and discouraging children's behavior lies in their dependence on parents from earliest childhood and in mutual affection—in effect, the maintenance of a continuous and diffuse relationship based on goodwill. Although rewards for specific acts can replenish the bank of goodwill, it is maintained by gratuitous expressions of concern, friendliness, support, sympathy, encouragement, and the like, not simply as responses to specific acts, but as indications of a more enduring solidarity. Punishment, even if severe, will then mean one thing if administered in the context of sustained affection and another where such feeling is absent.

Problems of reward and punishment confront teachers as well as parents, but the problems differ. First, since children in classrooms outnumber those in families, teachers, because of the limitations on their time and energy, can neither attend to nor sanction each child in the same ways that parents can; they must control a class without sacrificing the school's agenda to the imperatives of keeping order. Second, pupils' school work is customarily sanctioned by means of grades based on the quality of assignments completed. Grades, however, are not inherently rewarding or punishing, at least not at the outset. One critical problem of early elementary schooling is for teachers to establish grades *as* sanctions; and to the extent that pupils do not learn to accept them as such, grades cannot serve to reward good performance and punish poor. Secondary schools operate on the assumption—not always correct—that pupils have already come to accept the sanctioning quality of grades.

Teaching in the early grades presents a classic problem in the creation of goodwill—finding some appropriate equivalent in the classroom of affection in the family. That is, gratuitous pleasure not tied to specific acts in a relationship of exchange must be created in order to develop in pupils a diffuse and positive attachment both to the teacher and to the school. But the problem of sanctioning does not end with the creation of goodwill and the assignment of grades. The demands of schooling, particularly in the early years, can prove difficult, taxing, and often alien when contrasted with the more protective and indulgent environment of the home. The school day is long; there is much sitting in one place, following orders, completing assigned and not necessarily enjoyable tasks on time; teachers devote less time and interest to each child than parents do—this despite whatever intrinsic pleasures children may find in the school environment. Yet the school must convey to the pupil that certain forms of conduct acceptable at home will be held unacceptable at school, that certain rights he may legitimately claim from the household will not be honored in the classroom, that however alien they may seem, the tasks that school presents must be confronted and will hopefully come to represent new courses of gratification. To effect such changes, the school must have more resources than grades and goodwill in its kit of sanctions.

Resources available for sanctioning derive initially from two structural characteristics of classrooms: the visibility of pupils and their homogeneity of age. Classrooms are public places in that their membership is collective and visible. Many activities are carried on out loud and in front of everybody (reports, recitations, replies to questions, discussions, praise, chastisement, laughter); pupils perform publicly and are judged openly by the teacher and by other members of the class.[8]

The similarity of pupils in age is important for at least three reasons. First, age represents an index (even if inexact) of developmental maturity, and by implication, of capacity;[9] and even though children of the same age vary greatly in what they can do, age is still used as a common shorthand to gauge the assignment of tasks, responsibilities, privileges, and the like. Second, it provides classrooms with a built-in standard for comparison, a fixed point indicative of the level of those capacities directly relevant to the activities in which pupils are engaged. Each pupil, then, can be compared and compare himself with all others because the comparisons can be anchored to the standard. Third, it allows each pupil the experience of finding himself in the same boat with others in terms of the characteristics of their local surroundings and in the way they are treated by teachers.

Since many classroom activities are in effect judged in public, the pupil is bombarded with messages telling him how well he has done and—with a short inferential leap—how good he is. If he doesn't take the teacher's word for it, he need only look at the performance of others of the same age and in the same circumstances. The school, in effect, plays on his self-respect. Each pupil is exposed and vulnerable to the judgments of adults in authority and of his equals—those who resemble him in many respects.[10] If the child at home wonders whether he is loved, the pupil in school wonders whether he is a worthwhile person. In both settings, he can find some kind of answer by observing how others treat him and what they think of him.

Given the standards for and the patterns of behavior that children learn from their family experiences, the schools, in preparing them for adult public life, must effect changes of considerable magnitude, changes that require giving up certain patterns of conduct found gratifying in other settings and adopting new patterns whose gratifications may at best take the form of promissory notes. If knowledge about other forms of socialization is applicable to schooling— and there is no reason in principle why it should not be—the sanctions required

must affect people's emotions deeply as is true in some of the most demanding and stressful social situations involving psychological change: psychotherapy, religious conversion, brain-washing, deracination. It is my contention that the emotions aroused in schooling derive from events in which the pupil's sense of self-respect is either supported or threatened, and that school classrooms, permitting the public exposure and judgment of performance against a reasonably fixed reference point (age-adapted tasks), are organized so that the pupil's sense of personal adequacy, or self-respect, becomes the leverage for sanctioning.

Not all sanctions employed in school settings have the potentiality for arousing intense emotions, nor are they similarly diffuse in character. Some, like grades, compliments, admonitions, and chastisements, are contingent upon desirable and undesirable conduct; others, like friendly greetings, gentleness, sympathy, sarcasm, bitchiness, and so on through the whole gamut of words and gestures indicating approval, disapproval, and general attitude are non-contingent. All represent resources at the teacher's disposal—used consciously or unconsciously—and influence whether or not pupils will find their early experiences at school enjoyable enough to act according to its standards.

As suggested earlier, the school provides constraints and opportunities related to its structural properties, the behavior of its members, and its resources available for sanctioning. I have argued that pupils infer principles of conduct on the basis of their experiences in school, that they learn principles underlying the alternative ways of coping with a social situation having a particular set of properties. Over a period of years, they discover which patterns of conduct permit them to cope with the school's constraints and opportunities; and, to the extent that they find that certain patterns of action lead to the successful accomplishment of tasks and bring gratifications, they adopt those patterns as the right ways to act— that is, they value them.[11]

The Learning of Social Norms

The social properties of schools are such that pupils, by coping with the sequence of classroom tasks and situations, are more likely to learn the principles—social norms—of independence, achievement, universalism, and specificity than if they had remained full-time members of the household.

INDEPENDENCE

Pupils learn to acknowledge that there are tasks to be done by them alone and to do them that way. Along with this self-imposed obligation goes the idea that others have a legitimate right to expect such independent behavior under certain circumstances.[12] Independence has a widely acknowledged though not unequivocal meaning. In using it here I refer to a cluster of meanings: doing things on one's own, being self-reliant, accepting personal responsibility for one's behavior, acting self-sufficiently;[13] and to a way of approaching tasks in whose accomplishment *under different circumstances* one can rightfully expect the help of others. The pupil, when in school, is separated from family members who have customarily provided help, support, and sustenance—persons on whom he has long been dependent.

A constellation of classroom characteristics and both teacher- and pupil-actions shape experiences in which the norm of independence is learned. In addition to the fact that school children

are removed from persons with whom they have already formed strong relationships of dependency, the sheer size of a classroom assemblage limits each pupil's claim to personal contact with the teacher, and more so at the secondary levels than at the elementary.[14] This numerical property of classrooms reduces pupils' opportunities for establishing new relationships of dependency with adults and for receiving help from them.

Parents expect their children to act independently in many situations but teachers are more systematic in expecting pupils to adhere to standards of independence in performing academic tasks. There are at least two additional aspects of classroom operation, however, that bear directly on learning the norm of independence: rules about cheating and formal testing. First, as to cheating. The word itself is condemnatory in its reference to illegal and immoral acts. Most commonly, attention turns to how much cheating occurs, who cheats, and why. But these questions are of no concern here (though obviously they are elsewhere). My interest is in a different problem: to what types of conduct is the pejorative "cheating" assigned?

In school, cheating usually refers to acts in which two or more parties participate when the unaided action of only one is expected and pertains primarily to instructional activities. Illegal and immoral acts such as stealing and vandalism, whether carried out by individuals or groups, are not considered cheating because they have no direct connection with the central academic core of school activities. Nor is joint participation categorically proscribed; joint effort is called cooperation or collusion depending upon the teacher's prior definition of the task. . . .

. . . In the case of homework, the school, in effect, attempts to redefine the relationship between parents and children by proscribing one form of parental support, unproblematic in other circumstances. The teacher has no direct control over parents, but tries to influence them at a distance by asking their adherence to a principle clothed in moral language whose violations are punishable. The line between legitimate parental support (encouraged when it takes the form of parents stressing the importance of school and urging their children to do well) and collusion is unclear; but by morally proscribing parental intervention beyond a certain point, the teacher attempts to limit the child's dependence upon family members in doing his school work. He expects the pupil, in other words, to work independently. The same argument applies to pupils and their friends: the teacher attempts to eliminate those parts of friendship that make it difficult or impossible for him to discover what a pupil can do on his own. In relationships with kin and friends, the customary sources of support in times of adversity, the school intervenes by restricting solidarity and, in the process, determines what the pupil can accomplish unaided. The pupil, for his part, discovers which of his actions he is held accountable for individually within the confines of tasks set by the school.

The comparison between schooling and occupational employment for which school is intended as preparation provides indirect support for this argument. The question here is the sense in which school experience is preparatory. Usually workers are not restricted in seeking help on problems confronting them; on the contrary, many occupations provide resources specifically intended to be helpful: arrangements for consultation, libraries, access to more experienced colleagues, and so on. Only in rare situations are people expected not to enlist the aid of family and friends in matters pertaining to work where that aid is appropriate. In other words, activities on the job analogous to school work do not carry comparable restrictions. Required, however, is that people

in their occupational activities accept individual responsibility and accountability for the performance of assigned and self-initiated tasks. To the extent that the school contributes to the development of independence, the preparation lies more in the development of a frame of mind to act independently than in a vocationalism consisting of the capacity to perform a certain range of tasks without help.

Second, as to testing, and particularly the use of achievement tests. Most important for independence are the social conditions designed for the *administration* of tests, not their content or format. By and large, pupils are tested under more or less rigorously controlled conditions. At one end of the spectrum, formal, standardized tests are administered most stringently: pupils are physically separated, and the testing room is patrolled by proctors whose job is to discover contraband and to guarantee that no communication occurs—these arrangements being designed so that each examination paper represents independent work. At the other end, some testing situations are more informal, less elaborately staged, although there is almost always some provision that each pupil's work represents the product of only his own efforts.[15]

Testing represents an approach to establishing the norm of independence different from the proscription against cheating even though both are designed to reduce the likelihood of joint effort. Whereas the rules against cheating are directed more toward delineating the form of appropriate behavior, the restrictions built into the testing situation provide physical constraints intended to guarantee that teachers will receive samples of work that pupils do unassited; the restrictions, that is, bear more on the product than on the motive.

Actually, unless they stimulate otherwise, teachers expect pupils to do most of their everyday work by themselves; daily assignments provide opportunities for and practice in independent work. Tests, because they occur at less frequent intervals than ordinary assignments, cannot provide comparably frequent opportunities; by the elaborate trappings of their administration, particularly with college entrance exams, and the anxiety they provoke, they symbolize the magnitude of the stakes. . . .

ACHIEVEMENT

Pupils come to accept the premise that they should perform their tasks the best they can, and act accordingly. The concept of achievement, like independence, has several referents. It usually denotes activity and mastery, making an impact on the environment rather than fatalistically accepting it, and competing against some standard of excellence. Analytically, the concept should be distinguished from independence since, among other differences, achievement criteria can apply to activities performed collectively.

Much of the recent literature treats achievement in the context of child-rearing within the family, as if achievement motivation were primarily a product of parental behavior.[16] Even though there is reason to believe that early childhood experiences in the family do contribute to its development, classroom experiences also contribute through teachers' use of resources beyond those ordinarily at the command of family members.

Classrooms are organized around a set of core activities in which a teacher assigns tasks to pupils and evaluates and compares the quality of their work. In the course of time, pupils differentiate themselves according to how well they perform a variety of tasks, most of which require the use of symbolic skills.

Achievement standards are not limited in applicability to the classroom nor is their content restricted to cognitive areas. Schools afford opportunities for participation in a variety of extra-curricular activities, most conspicuously, athletics, but also music, dramatics, and a bewildering array of club and small group activities appealing to individual interests and talents.

The direct relevance of classroom work to learning achievement standards is almost self-evident; the experience is built into the assignment-performance-evaluation sequence of the work. Less evident, however, is that classroom activities force pupils to cope with various degrees of success and failure both of which can be psychologically problematic. Consistently successful performance requires that pupils deal with the consequences of their own excellence in a context of peer-equality in non-academic areas. For example, they confront the dilemma inherent in surpassing their age-mates in some respects but depending on their friendship and support in others, particularly in out-of-school social activities. The classroom thus provides not only the achievement experience itself but by-products of it, taking the form of the dilemma just described.

Similarly, pupils whose work is consistently poor not only must participate in activities leading to their academic failure but also experience living with that failure. They adopt various modes of coping with this, most of which center around maintaining personal self-respect in the face of continuing assaults upon it. Probably a minority succeed or fail consistently; a large proportion, most likely, do neither one consistently, but nonetheless worry about not doing well. Schooling, then, affords most pupils the experiences of both winning and losing; and to the extent that they gain some modicum of gratification from academic activities they learn to accept the general expectation of approaching their work with an achievement frame of mind. At the same time, they learn how to cope in a variety of ways, and more or less well, with success and failure.

Failure is perhaps the more difficult because it requires acknowledgement that the premise of achievement, to which failure itself can be attributed in part, is a legitimate principle for governing one's actions. Yet, endemic to industrial societies in which many facets of public life are based on achievement principles are situations that constrain people to live with personal failure; political defeat and occupational non-promotion being two cases in point.

As already suggested, the school provides a broader range of experiences than those restricted to the classroom and academic in nature; these experiences are based similarly on achievement criteria but differ in several important respects. The availability of alternatives to academic performance means that a pupil can experience success in achievement-oriented activities even if he lacks the requisite talents for doing well in the classroom.

How these alternative activities differ from those of the classroom is as important as the fact that they do, as evidenced by the case of athletics. Competitive sports resemble classroom activities in that both provide participants with the chance to demonstrate individual excellence; however, the former—and this is more true of team than individual sports —permit collective responsibility for defeat whereas the latter by and large allow only individual responsibility for failure. That is to say, the chances of receiving personal gratification for success are at least as great in sports as in the classroom, while the assault on personal self-respect for failure is potentially less intense. Athletics should not be written off as a manifestation of mere adolescent non-intellectualism as several recent writers have so treated it.[17]

A similar contention holds for music and dramatics; both provide the potentiality for individual accomplishment and recognition but without the persistent, systematic, and potentially corrosive evaluation typical of the classroom. Finally, in various club activities based on interest and talent, a pupil can do the things he is good at in the company of others who share an appreciation for them. In all these situations, either the rigors of competition and judgment characteristic of the classroom are mitigated; or the activity in question has its own built-in sources of support and personal protection, not to the same extent as in the family, but more than is available in the crucible of the classroom. . . .

UNIVERSALISM AND SPECIFICITY

Unlike independence and achievement, universalism and specificity are not commonly regarded as good things. Parents and teachers admonish children to act independently and to do their work well; few of them support the idea that people should willingly acknowledge their similarity to others in specifically categorical terms while ignoring obvious differences—denying, in a sense, their own individuality.

Ideologically, social critics have deplored the impersonal, ostensibly dehumanizing aspects of categorization, a principle widely believed to lie at the heart of the problem of human alienation —the attachment of man to machine, the detachment of man from man. Often ignored, however, is the connection between this principle and the idea of fairness, or equity. Seen from this vantage point, categorization is widely regarded as a good thing, especially when contrasted to nepotism, favoritism, and arbitrariness. People resent the principle when they think they have a legitimate reason to receive special consideration, or when their individuality appears to vanish by being "processed." Yet, when a newcomer breaks into a long queue instead of proceeding to the end of the line, they usually condemn him for acting unfairly (for not following the standard rule for all newcomers to a line) and do *not* express any sense of their own alienation (for abiding by the same categorical principle). The contrasts between individuality and dehumanization, fairness and special privilege, are similarly predicated on universalism and specificity; they differ in the ideological posture of an observer, and, more cynically, in his conception of self-interest.

The concepts of universalism and specificity have been formulated most comprehensively by Parsons, though only part of his formulation pertains directly to this discussion. As part of his concern with social systems, Parsons views universalism as one horn of a dilemma—the other being particularism—in role definition; under what circumstances does the occupant of one social position govern his actions by adopting one standard or the other in dealing with the occupant of another position? My concern, however, is not with a selection among alternative, conflicting standards but with the conditions under which individuals learn to accept the obligation to impose the standards of universalism and specificity upon themselves and to act accordingly.

Defining the central theme of universalism raises problems because the term has various meanings, not all of them clear.[18] The relevant distinction here is whether individuals are treated as members of categories or as special cases. In one respect or another, an individual can always be viewed as a member of one or more categories; he is viewed particularistically if, notwithstanding his similarity to others in the same category or circumstances, he still receives special treatment.[19]

The norm of specificity is easily confused with universalism despite its distinctiveness. It refers to the scope of one person's interest in another; to the obligation to confine one's interest to a narrow range of characteristics and concerns, or to extend them to include a broad range.[20] Implicit is the notion of relevance; the characteristics and concerns that should be included in the range, whether broad or narrow, are those considered relevant in terms of the activities in which the persons in question are involved. Doctors and storekeepers, for example, differ in the scope of their interest in persons seeking their services, but the content of their interests also varies according to the nature of the needs and desires of those persons.

It is my contention that the school's contribution to children's accepting these norms that penetrate so many areas of public life is critical because children's preschool experience in the family is weighted heavily on the side of special treatment and parental consideration of the whole child.

To say that children learn the norm of universalism means that they come to accept being treated by others as members of categories (*in addition to* being treated as special cases, as in the family). Schools provide a number of experiences that families cannot readily provide because of limitations in their social composition and structure, one of which is the systematic establishment and demarcation of membership categories. First, by assigning all pupils in a classroom the same or similar tasks to perform, teachers in effect make them confront the same set of demands; and even if there are variations in task content, class members still confront the same teacher and the obligations he imposes. Second, parity of age creates a condition of homogeneity according to developmental stage, a rough equalization of pupil capacities making it possible for teachers to assign similar tasks. Third, through the process of yearly promotion from grade to grade, pupils cross the boundaries separating one age category from another. With successive boundary crossings comes the knowledge that each age-grade category is associated with particular circumstances (e.g., teachers, difficulty of tasks, subject matter studied); moreover, pupils learn the relationship between categories and how their present positions relate to past and future positions by virtue of having experienced the transitions between them. In these three ways, the grade—more specifically, the classroom within the grade—with its age-homogeneous membership and clearly demarcated boundaries provides a basis for categorical grouping that the family cannot readily duplicate. Most important, as a by-product of repeated boundary-crossing, pupils acquire a relativity of perspective, a capacity to view their own circumstances from other vantage points, having themselves occupied them. . . .[21]

The second school experience fostering the establishment of social categories is the re-equalization of pupils by means of the high-school track system after they have differentiated themselves through academic achievement in the lower grades, a mechanism that reduces the likelihood that teachers will have to deal with special cases.[22] Teachers with a variegated batch of pupils must adopt more individualized methods of instruction than those whose pupils are similar in their level of achievement, and who in so doing would partially recreate a kinship-type of relationship with pupils, treating segments of the class differently according to differences in capacity much as parents treat their children differently according to age-related capacities.

As far as level is concerned, the high school is a better place to learn the principle of universalism than the lower school levels because pupils within each tract, and therefore of roughly similar

capacity, move from classroom to classroom, in each one receiving instruction in a different subject area from a different teacher. They discover that over a range of activities they are treated alike and that relatively uniform demands and criteria of evaluation are applied to them. That is to say, by providing instruction from different teachers in different subject matter areas and by at the same time applying criteria for judging performance and task difficulty which remain roughly constant within each track and across subjects, the school makes it possible for pupils to learn which differences in experience are subordinated to the principle of categorization. The elementary classroom, oriented more to instruction in different subjects by a single teacher, does not provide the necessary variations in persons and subjects for a clear-cut demonstration of the categorical principle.

Although the idea of categorization is central to the norm of universalism, there are additional and derivative aspects of it. One is the crucial distinction, widely relevant in industrial society, between the person and the social position he occupies. A frequent demand made on individuals is to treat others and be treated by them according to the identity that their positions confer rather than according to who they are as people. Schooling contributes to the capacity to make the distinction (and the obligation to do so) by making it possible for pupils to discover that different individuals can occupy a single social position but act in ways that can be discovered as attached to the position rather than to the different persons filling it. . . .

Regarding the norm of specificity, again the school provides structural arrangements more conducive to its acquisition than does the family. First, since the number of persons and the ratio of non-adults to adults is much larger in classrooms than in the household, the school provides large social aggregates in which pupils can form many casual associations (in addition to their close friendships), in which they invest but a small portion of themselves. As both the size and heterogeneity of the student body increase at each successive level, the opportunities for these somewhat fragmented social contacts increase and diversify. The relative shallowness and transiency of these relationships increase the likelihood that pupils will have experiences in which the fullness of their individuality is *not* involved as it tends to be in their relationships among kin and close friends.

Second, upon leaving the elementary school and proceeding through the departmentalized secondary levels, pupils form associations with teachers who have a progressively narrowing and specialized interest in them. (This comes about both because of subject matter specialization itself and because the number of pupils each teacher faces in the course of a day also grows larger.) Although it is true that children, as they grow older, tend to form more specific relationships with their parents—symptomatically, this trend manifests itself in adolescents' complaints of parental invasions of privacy—the resources of the school in providing the social basis for establishing relationships in which only narrow segments of personality are invested far exceed those of the family.

A second facet of universalism is the principle of equity, or fairness (I use the terms interchangeably). . . . Among children in a family, age is critical in determining what is fair and unfair. In a sense, it is the clock by which we keep developmental time. . . . In school classrooms, the age of children is nearly constant; the problem of settling equity questions attributable to age variations found in families does not arise. . . .

The contrast between classroom and family is pronounced. Equity in the former is based by and large on how well pupils perform and how they are treated in a setting whose characteristics are alike for all. From the vantage point of an outside observer, objective conditions within the classroom are similar for each pupil as are the tasks assigned; pupils, in other words, find themselves in the same boat. Within the family, on the other hand, each child rides his own boat, and judgments about equity derive from that fact.

. . . Equity involves a comparative assessment of one's circumstances: gains and losses, rewards and punishments, rights and duties, privileges and responsibilities. To determine whether his circumstances in a given situation are equitable, an individual must learn to make comparisons by which he can discover whose circumstances resemble his own and whose do not, who is treated like him and who is not; he must also discover the relationships between his circumstances and the way he is treated.

Schooling, then, through the structural properties of classrooms at each school level and through teachers' treatment of pupils, provides opportunities for making the comparisons relevant for defining questions of equity far more effectively than does the family. The process is similar to that (above described) of learning the norm of universalism in general. Both within the classroom and within each grade, age and, to a lesser extent, other personal and social characteristics provide a basis for discovering both similarities and differences in categorical terms. The existence of grade levels, distinguished primarily by the demandingness of work and demarcated by the device of yearly promotion, and the progression of pupils through them year by year make it possible for children to learn that *within the context of the school* certain qualities that determine their uniqueness as persons become subordinated to those specific characteristics in which they are alike. Thus, fourth and fifth graders, despite their individuality, are judged according to specific criteria of achievement; and the content and difficulty of their assigned tasks are regulated according to the developmental considerations symbolized by grade. The fourth grader having completed the third grade can grasp the idea that he belongs to a category of persons whose circumstances differ from those of persons belonging to another.

Family relationships are not organized on a cohort basis nor do they entail anything comparable to the systematic, step-by-step progression of grades in which the boundaries between one category and another are clearly demarcated. Although a child knows the difference between family members and non-members and can distinguish even the categorical distinctions within his own family, his experiences in a kinship setting do not allow him to find as clear an answer to the question of whether his circumstances are uniquely his own or whether they are shared. In other words, these relationships are not structured in such a way as to form a basis for making the categorical comparisons basic to the universalistic norm. Specifically, they provide little or no basis for the repeated experience of crossing boundaries from one category to another so important for learning to make the comparisons involved in judgments of equity. Moreover, since parents treat their children more in terms of the full range of personal characteristics—that is, according to the norm of diffuseness rather than that of specificity—the family setting is more conducive to the special rather than the categorical treatment of each child (since the boundaries of a category are more clearly delineated if one characteristic, not many, constitutes the basis of categorization). . . .

Notes

[1] In one near-encyclopedic volume on educational research, the instructional emphases are most clearly illustrated. Nine of twenty-three long chapters are devoted to "Research on Teaching Various Grade Levels and Subject Matters." Six deal with measurement: both problems of measurement *per se*, and of measuring particular types of educational outcomes (cognitive and non-cognitive). Two deal with the characteristics of teachers, two with methods and media; one with social interaction in classrooms. The major preoccupations of educators and educational researchers are summarized in the following statement from Benjamin S. Bloom, "Testing Cognitive Ability and Achievement," in *Handbook of Research on Teaching*, ed. N. L. Gage (Chicago: Rand McNally, 1963), p. 379: "While it may or may not be true that the most important changes in the learner are those which may be described as cognitive, i.e., knowledge, problem-solving, higher mental processes, etc., it is true that these are the types of changes in students which most teachers do seek to bring about. These are the changes in learners which most teachers attempt to gauge in their own tests of progress and in their final examinations. These, also, are the changes in the learners which are emphasized in the materials of instruction, in the interaction between teachers and learners, and in the reward system which the teachers and the schools employ." There is a brief treatment of the characteristics of learning environments but with primary emphasis on teaching techniques in George G. Stern, "Measuring Non-cognitive Variables in Research on Teaching" (*ibid.*, pp. 425–33).

[2] Several questions pertaining to the connection between the acquisition of norms and the structural properties of social settings are beyond the scope of this paper, and so in places the argument must remain elliptical. For a more detailed discussion, see the writer's book: *On What Is Learned in School* (Reading, Mass.: Addison-Wesley).

[3] The empirical problems of identifying norms in a given situation are beyond the scope of this discussion. Suffice it to say that

identifying them requires that one consider at least the following: verbal statements, behavior, situation, and emotional expressions—none of which when taken alone is sufficient—and the connections among them.

⁴ A variety of conditions can affect the relationship between norm acceptance and behavior. (a) There may be disagreements among persons about what norm applies in a particular situation; behavior where consensus is lacking may not represent conformity to any of the conflicting norms. (b) Behavioral conformity may depend on the explicitly or implicitly conditional nature of norms. For example, although lying is proscribed in principle, there are widely acknowledged situations in which telling "white lies" is acceptable. (c) People vary in their desire to conform; they calculate the likelihood and severity of punishment if they do not; they judge the opportunities to conform or deviate; and they determine where their interests lie.

⁵ Melville J. Herkovits, *Man and His Works* (New York: Knopf, 1949), p. 311.

⁶ For technical discussions of the relevance of these norms to industrialism, see Talcott Parsons, *The Social System* (New York: Free Press, 1951) and S. N. Eisenstadt, *From Generation to Generation* (New York: Free Press, 1956).

⁷ I do not imply that accepting a norm as binding upon oneself implies the ability to formulate its underlying general principle verbally.

⁸ Formal grades, both for assigned work and for general evaluation of performance over several months' time, are customarily given in some degree of privacy; once pupils receive them, whatever confidentiality the teacher maintains in assigning grades usually tends to be short-lived. Pupils themselves turn private into public knowledge, and parents have been known to do the same.

⁹ Perhaps the social expectations for and beliefs about the capacities of similar-aged children are narrower than their actual capacities (however these are measured). If so, age is an exaggeratedly "good" index of equal capacity even if the "goodness" represents a self-fulfilling prophesy. There is some controversy about the usefulness of the term "capacity" among psychometricians, but for present purposes, it is beside the point since people often think in terms of children's capacities and act accordingly.

¹⁰ "Remember that you are as good as any man—and also that you are no better. . . . [But] the man who is as good as his neighbors is in a tough spot when he confronts all of his neighbors combined." Louis Hartz, *The Liberal Tradition in America* (New York: Harcourt, Brace, 1955), p. 56. The opinions of massed equals are not negligible.

¹¹ For empirical confirmation of the fact that experience in the performance of particular tasks can produce changes in preferences, beliefs, and most importantly in values (norms) and their generalization from one situation to another without verbal instruction in the content of those outcomes, see Paul E. Breer and Edwin A. Locke, *Task Experience as a Source of Attitudes* (Homewood: Dorsey Press, 1965), especially Chapter 6. A statement of the argument of how the actual performance of a task can effect changes in norms—how it *should* be performed—is beyond the scope of this paper.

¹² My emphasis here differs from Parsons' in that he views independence primarily as a personal resource: ". . . It may be said that the most important single predispositional factor with which the child enters the school is his level of independence" (Parsons, *op. cit.*, p. 300). Although independence is very likely such a predisposition—whether it is the most important single one is moot—it is part of the school's agenda to further the development of independence to a point beyond the level at which family resources become inadequate to do so.

¹³ Winterbottom, for example, lumps independence and mastery together; the indices she uses to measure them involve ostensibly distinct phenomena in that the mastery items refer to tendencies toward activity rather than independence. Marian R. Winterbottom, "The Relation of Need for Achievement to Learning Experiences in Independence and Mastery," in *Motives in Fantasy, Action, and Society*, ed. John T. Atkinson (Princeton: Van Nostrand, 1958), pp. 453–78. As a definitional guideline for this discussion, I have followed the usage of Bernard C. Rosen and Roy D'Andrade, "The Psychosocial Origins of Achievement Motivation," *Sociometry*, 22 (1959), 186, in their discussion of achievement training; also, David C. McClelland, A. Rindlisbacher, and Richard DeCharms, "Religious

and Other Sources of Parental Attitudes toward Independence Training," in *Studies in Motivation*, ed. David C. McClelland (New York: Appleton-Century-Crofts, 1955), pp. 389–97.

[14] Thus, the ratios of children per adult in households are 0.5, 1.0, 2.0, and 3.0 in one-, two-, four-, and six-child families, respectively, with two parents present; comparatively few families have more than six children. In classrooms, the ratios of different children per adult at the elementary and secondary levels are approximately 28.1 and 155.8 respectively; *The American Public School Teacher, 1960–61*, Research Monograph 1963–M2, Research Division, National Education Association, April, 1963, p. 51.

[15] By describing the conditions surrounding the administration of tests, I do not thereby attempt to justify these procedures; other means might accomplish the same ends.

[16] See, for example, Winterbottom, *op. cit.*, pp. 453–78; Rosen and D'Andrade, *op. cit.*, pp. 185–218; and Fred. L. Strodtbeck, "Family Interaction, Values, and Achievement," in *Talent and Society*, ed. David C. McClelland et al. (Princeton: Van Nostrand, 1958), pp. 135–91.

[17] For one attempt to treat athletics condescendingly as anti-intellectualism, see James S. Coleman, *The Adolescent Society* (New York: Free Press, 1961). I do not suggest that athletics has an as yet undiscovered intellectual richness; rather, that its contribution should not be viewed simply in terms of intellectuality.

[18] Although Parsons, in *The Social System*, p. 62, considers universalism and particularism to form a dichotomy, he distinguishes them on at least two dimensions: cognitive and cathetic: "The primacy of cognitive values may be said to imply a *universalistic* standard, while that of appreciative values implies a *particularistic* standard. In the former case the standard is derived from the validity of a set of existential ideas, or the

generality of a normative rule, in the latter from the particularity of the cathetic significance of an object or of the status of an object in a relational system."

[19] The treatment of others does not become more particularistic as an increasing number of categories is taken into account. If age, sex, religion, ethnicity, and the like—all examples of general categories—are considered, treatment is still categorical in nature because it is oriented to categorical similarities, even if they number more than one, and not to what is special or unique about the person or about a relationship in which he is involved.

[20] In the case of specificity, "the burden of proof rests on him who would suggest that ego has obligations vis-à-vis the object in question which transcend this specificity of relevance" (Parsons, *The Social System*, p. 65). In the case of diffuseness, "the burden of proof is on the side of the exclusion of an interest or mode of orientation as outside the range of obligations defined by the role-expectation" (*ibid.*, p. 66).

[21] For a discussion of relativity of perspective, empathy, and parochialism in the context of the economic and political development of nations, see Danier Lerner, *The Passing of Traditional Society* (New York: Free Press, 1958), pp. 43–75 and *passim*.

[22] The secondary school track system by which pupils are segregated according to academic achievement has conventionally been interpreted as a distributive device for directing pupils toward one or another broad segment of the occupational hierarchy. Although the distributive or allocative function of the track system has pre-empted most discussions, it should not be regarded as the only function; in fact, a very different view of it is taken here.

Sociological Determinants of Academic Performance

David E. Lavin

Chapter 6 of The Prediction of Academic Performance by David E. Lavin, copyright © 1965 by Russell Sage Foundation, New York.

THE SOCIOLOGICAL studies to be reviewed in this paper take two forms, both of which differ from the psychological studies. One type examines the effects of role relationships on academic achievement. An example would be a study of the student-teacher relationship in which the degree of congruence between student and teacher definitions of the student's role is measured. The association between congruence and level of academic performance would then be assessed. One might find that the more closely a student's definition of his role agrees with the teacher's definition, the more likely the student is to exhibit a high level of performance. This approach is distinguished from the personality studies because it asks whether characteristics of social settings have any general effects on performance irrespective of the personality of the individual.

A second type of sociological study assesses the effects of various ecological and demographic characteristics upon academic performance. These investigations examine variables such as socioeconomic status, sex of the student, religion, rural-urban background, and the like. As we shall see, these variables are related to performance because they symbolize certain uniformities of personality. That is, positions in the social structure such as socioeconomic status and sex tend to produce certain similarities in personality among the occupants of these positions. Some of these personality characteristics are, in turn, related to academic achievement. Studies of this type are thus related to the studies reviewed in the preceding chapter. What is distinctively sociological about them, however, is that they show that personality characteristics pertinent to achievement are not simply randomly distributed in the population; rather, they tend to be systematically associated with positions in the social structure.

This paper reviews and evaluates findings from both of these approaches. It begins with a review of the demographic and ecological findings; next it discusses the effects of specific role relationships; and finally it summarizes findings from both types of studies.

Effects of Demographic and Ecological Variables

SOCIOECONOMIC STATUS AS A DETERMINANT OF ACADEMIC PERFORMANCE

Of all the ecological and demographic factors to be discussed, the major variable in terms of the sheer quantity of research is socioeconomic status (SES). Most of the studies to be reviewed measure SES by some objective technique rather than by subjective ratings. The objective techniques all involve the combining or weighting of scores on variables such as occupation, education, income, attendance at private or public school, area of residence, and the like so as to produce an index of the position of the student's family in the status hierarchy.

We wish first to consider how such a

measure of SES can be predictive of school performance. The answer is that SES is a *derivative* or summarizing variable. Persons of different socio-economic status face different kinds of life situations, and in adapting to them, they may develop different sets of values and life styles.[1] In short, SES symbolizes a variety of values, attitudes, and motivations related to academic performance. There are two major factors symbolized by SES: one is intelligence; the other is what may be referred to as the "achievement syndrome."

SES and Intelligence. One factor positively associated with SES is intelligence. This finding is well documented,[2] but it raises a question concerning the degree to which SES and intelligence are independently related to academic performance. One study found that when SES is controlled, the correlation between intelligence and grades is not lowered.[3] On the other hand, when intelligence was controlled, correlations between SES and grades were lowered from a range of .37 to .47 to a range of .20 to .32. In another study, a traditional intelligence test and a "culture free" test were used to predict achievement test scores.[4] When SES was controlled, none of the correlations between intelligence and the criterion decreased very much. When intelligence was controlled, the original correlations between SES and the criterion were reduced from about .30 to .20.

If, as we have said, SES is a summarizing variable, it is to be expected that when any of the variables it summarizes (such as IQ) are controlled, relationships between SES and performance should be decreased. Since the relationship of SES to achievement was not totally erased when IQ was controlled, SES appears to summarize more than intelligence. In other words, if students are equated for intelligence, variations in social class are still associated with variations in achievement. Therefore, SES must also summarize other variables.

SES and the Achievement Syndrome. Another variable associated with SES is achievement motivation—or more appropriately perhaps, an achievement syndrome. Rosen found that achievement motivation is directly related to SES.[5] Students who exhibit high levels of motivation tend to come from higher status levels. Both achievement motivation and SES were directly related to the grades of high school students. However, when motivation was controlled, the relation between SES and grades was almost erased. This illustrates what was stated before; namely, that SES summarizes other variables.

Another aspect of the achievement syndrome is what may be called achievement values. They include, among others, these beliefs: (1) that it is possible to manipulate the environment; (2) that there is value in delaying immediate pleasure for the sake of long-run gratifications; and (3) that there is value in shedding affective ties to the family of orientation if these will interfere with mobility.[6] Students who adhere to these values tend to exhibit higher levels of career aspiration.

Evidence indicates that this set of beliefs is related to SES and is also associated with educational aspiration.[7] As with achievement motivation, when achievement values are controlled, the relation between SES and educational aspiration disappears. Strodtbeck found that achievement values were related to over- and under-achievement, and that they were independent of achievement motivation.[8] His findings suggest, therefore, that the use of achievement values and achievement motivation together may increase the efficiency of predicting academic performance. Schneider and Lysgaard showed that belief in the value of delayed gratification varies directly with SES.[9] Brim and Forer also demonstrated that the belief in the value of planning for the future is directly associated with SES.[10] Other studies find a direct association between SES and level of educational and occupational aspiration.[11] With the exception of the work by Rosen and by Strodtbeck, these investigations are not concerned with the prediction of academic performance. However, the achievement syndrome seems to be directly relevant to this question.

Research Findings. Of the research reviewed here, thirteen studies report that SES is directly related to academic performance.[12] That is, the higher one's social status, the higher his level of performance. This relationship holds for all educational levels.

Of special interest are six studies whose findings contrast with these results.[13] They find that SES is inversely related to performance.

The apparent contradiction in these studies needs to be resolved. It is important to note at the outset that the samples used in the studies that find SES to be directly related to performance are different in certain respects from the samples used in those that observe an inverse relationship. Of the latter, five of the six studies show inverse relationships when the college performance of public school graduates is compared with that of private school graduates. Furthermore, in four of these investigations, the subjects were males who attended some of the very top eastern Ivy League colleges,[14] where the preparatory school graduates (largely from the most prestigious eastern preparatory schools) were likely to come mainly from upper-class backgrounds, while the public school graduates were likely to be largely of middle- and upper-middle-class origins.

Since most of the research on SES and academic performance does not sample the upper-class segment of the SES range, we suggest that the inconsistency between the results of the various studies referred to at the outset can be accounted for by differences in the SES range sampled. The situation is probably as follows: The relationship between SES and academic performance is positive through most of the SES range, but at the upper SES levels, it is inverse. When the SES sample does not include this upper segment, positive relations will be found. When the sample does include the upper range and does not go below the middle class, inverse relations will be found.

The preceding explanation is, of course, a statistical one. There remains the question of the meaning of the discrepancy on a theoretical level. We turn now to this question.

Two studies of the performance of Princeton students found that public school graduates are superior academically to private school graduates during the freshman year and that this superiority is maintained during the sophomore year, even though the two groups do not differ with regard to ability.[15] It seems reasonable to assume, as have the authors in this research, that private school students tend to be of higher SES than public school students. Another writer, in discussing findings of this sort, also suggests that private school graduates represent mainly the upper classes.[16] In the Princeton studies the authors present a possible explanation for the findings. First, since the public school graduates are from somewhat lower SES, college is an important means of enhancing status; private school graduates, on the other hand, need only to maintain their status level. For the latter group, therefore, simply graduating from college may be more important than the academic record they establish. Thus, differential motivation may be operative.

A second interpretation would be that because private schools have a more directed regimen, their graduates encounter difficulty in adapting to the less structured college environment. If true, differences in college performance would be due to structural differences between private schools and public schools. At the present time, this remains an open question awaiting the results of additional research.

The first interpretation has received from McArthur,[17] who asserts that the eastern upper classes hold values that are not consistent with the American success orientation. Whereas this orientation stresses the future as the important time, the individual as the important person, and doing (achieving) as the important aspect of the person, among the upper-class group the important time is the past, the important persons are lineal ancestors, and "being" (a gentleman) is the most important aspect of the person. The latter is a portrayal of an aristocratic ideal in which behavior is oriented toward propriety in contrast to achievement. Presumably, the upper and middle classes differ in terms of these values.

These status groups also differ in terms of methods of child training. The parents of the middle-class public school group gear early training toward achievement and mobility; the parents of the upper-class private school group orient early training toward proper, gentlemanly behavior. These training and value differences may be reflected in the school achievement of the children. This probably constitutes the underlying theoretical meaning expressed in the earlier statistical explanation. In short, the inconsistency in the two sets of studies relating socioeconomic status to academic performance is more apparent than real. It can be resolved on both a statistical and a theoretical level.

Summary and Evaluation. The research shows that socioeconomic status is usually positively related to academic performance, but that on the college level the relationship is inverse when the range of SES runs from the upper to the middle

class. The apparent inconsistency is interpretable in terms of personality and value differences between social status categories.

SES is a significant variable in the study of performance because it summarizes systematic variations in attitudes, motivations, and value systems that are related to such performance. While two underlying factors have been pointed out (intelligence and the achievement syndrome), this is probably not an exhaustive list. What is needed is a thorough review of the differences in personality, value systems, and behavior that are related to SES. Such class-related variables can then be applied to the study of achievement in school.

Another neglected area of research concerns the question of sex differences in the relation of SES to academic performance. It might be that SES is directly related to performance for males, but not for females. In addition, the class-related personality characteristics that are predictive of academic performance might be qualitatively different for males and females. These possibilities have not yet been researched.

Social class differences may also partly determine the quality of student-teacher interaction. For example, one might ask how the interaction of middle-class teachers with lower-class students affects characteristics of the student-teacher relationship. Davidson and Lang found that children's perceptions of their teacher's favorability or unfavorability toward them were directly related to social class.[18] This suggests that SES-related behavioral characteristics may affect the treatment students receive from teachers.

In short, SES may summarize a number of other factors in addition to the ones noted earlier. Further research is needed.

SEX DIFFERENCES IN ACADEMIC PERFORMANCE

Throughout this review, sex has been used as one major point of reference for describing the research findings. However, most studies are not concerned with the study of sex differences. We now examine those studies that are concerned with this question.

The Findings. The studies that assess the relation between sex and academic performance show that females have higher academic performance than males.[19] The evidence ... also clearly suggests that the correlation between intelligence and performance is higher for females than for males; that is, the performance of females is more nearly in accord with their measured ability than is the case for males.

In addition, a few more specialized findings are of interest. In a longitudinal study on the elementary school level, Hughes found that when ability was controlled, the reading achievement of girls was superior to boys through the fourth grade; however, beyond this grade the sex differences were not significant and did not consistently favor the girls.[20]

In a most interesting study, Shaw and McCuen attempted to determine whether there is any specific academic level at which underachievement begins.[21] They used students in the top 25 per cent of the school population with regard to ability and classified them as achievers or underachievers on the basis of their cumulative grade-point averages in grades 9, 10, and 11. A student whose IQ was higher than 110 and whose grade-point average was below the mean for his class was classified as an underachiever,[22] one whose grade-point average was above his class mean and whose IQ was above 110 was classified as an achiever. By eliminating some students, the authors ensured that the comparison groups had equal means and variances in their intelligence scores. They also controlled for sex. After the groups were selected, the academic record of each student for grades 1 through 11 was obtained and the performance of each group at each grade level was computed. When the higher- and lower-achieving males were compared, the data showed a significant difference between the two groups beginning at the third grade and increasing at each grade level up to grade 10, where it began to decrease, though it remained statistically significant.

Comparison of higher- and lower-achieving females presents quite a different picture. Through grade 5 those females who are later to become low achievers tend to exceed the higher achievers in grade-point average. At grade 6 the higher achievers attain a higher grade-point average for the first time, and this difference increases every year until grade 10. It is interesting to note that the start of the drop for the lower-achieving group roughly coincides with the onset of puberty. In contrast, the low-achieving males show a predisposition toward lower performance very early in their elementary school careers.

Summary and Evaluation. The findings on sex differences indicate that the level of academic performance of females is higher than that of males. Second, they suggest that the development of underachievement may follow a different pattern for females than for males. In all likelihood the significance of these findings can be understood in terms of a variety of differences in attitudes and behavior which result from the fact that males and females are socialized differently. Each sex must learn to play a different role, and the attitudes and values associated with sex-role learning may help to explain sex differences in academic performance.

In the first place, academic success probably has different significance for males than for females. Within the context of the cultural definition of the male role, academic success is an instrumental goal having important implications for later career success. For females the instrumental aspect of academic performance may not be as important, since integration with the occupational system is less crucial for the female role. Because academic success for males is considered more significant in terms of later occupational success, family pressures on them to do well in school are probably stronger than they are for females. If academic success is more directly involved with the male's affective ties to his family, the school might be more likely to become an arena in which either compulsive conformity to, or rebelliousness from, parental expectations may occur. Compulsive conformity would lead to overachievement, and rebelliousness, to underachievement.

Another consideration is that female teachers far outnumber male teachers, especially in the elementary and high schools. This being the case, we might speculate that teacher definitions of the student role include more characteristics of the female sex role. That is, the model of a good student is a female model. If this is true, then for the male, deviation from the student role actually constitutes a confirmation of his masculinity. This point has been made by Parsons in an attempt to account for certain patterns of aggressive behavior.[23]

If these interpretations have any validity, they may help to explain why the phenomena of over- and underachievement are more often observed for males than for females.[24] While it is interesting to speculate about these sex differences, more research is required both to document this evidence further and to specify the sources of the differences. Particularly interesting are the questions raised by the longitudinal studies—such as why the development of underachievement for girls follows a different pattern than that for boys.

MISCELLANEOUS ECOLOGICAL AND DEMOGRAPHIC CHARACTERISTICS

The scattering of research on the relationship between academic performance and other ecological and demographic factors includes studies on religion, school size, age, geographic region, and academic load.

Religious Background. Some evidence suggests that with regard to religion, Jewish students outperform non-Jewish students. Strodtbeck found this to be true when he compared Jewish high school students with their Italian Catholic counterparts.[25] However, many of the differences between these two groups seemed attributable to the effects of socioeconomic status rather than religion. That is, while Jews were more likely to have characteristics related to high academic achievement, when SES was controlled, the effects of religion disappeared. One other study found that Jews were more likely to be high achievers than students of other religions.[26]

Because some evidence suggests the presence of differences in the value systems of different religious groups further study is warranted. The work to date indicates, for example, that relative to the Italian Catholic value system, the Jewish culture places greater emphasis on the value of education and confers more prestige upon the scholar. Presumably this emphasis upon scholarship fits into a value system which places great importance upon rationality, future time orientation, and the like. Whether such achievement-related values are unique to particular religious groups or are associated more generally with differences in socioeconomic status should be ascertained through further investigation.

Regional and Rural-Urban Variation. A few studies have looked at the effects of regional and community differences upon academic performance. In a summary of some of these findings, Rossi states that students in the South score lower on achievement tests than do students in the North.[27] He points out, however, that these studies do not hold intelligence constant. Therefore, the poorer achievement of southern students could be due to lower ability, to inferior schools, or perhaps to both.

Studies of rural-urban background find that students from urban areas have higher levels of academic performance than students from less populated areas.[28] However, the study by Washburne finds that the relation of urbanism to academic performance does not hold for the students who come from major metropolitan areas (500,000 or more), perhaps because of the greater heterogeneity of students from such areas. Another study found that while urban students were higher on aptitude than rural students, they were no different in academic performance.[29] However, the rural students tended to be registered in schools of agriculture, and urban students in business or arts and sciences colleges; consequently, it is difficult to interpret the results of these studies because the grades are not comparable.

While these findings indicate that northern students outperform southern students and that urban students outperform their rural counterparts, the meaning of such findings is ambiguous. A number of factors, either singly or in combination, could account for these results. Thus, urban students may obtain higher scores on intelligence tests. Moreover, they may come from higher SES levels and the urban schools may be educationally superior to rural schools. At present, the research findings do not allow us to assess these possibilities.

Age. Three studies of the effects of age on academic performance in the elementary school reach contradictory conclusions. One of these finds that under-age children have lower school achievement than children of normal age for the grade and equivalent ability.[30] Another finds that under-age children are somewhat superior in achievement,[31] and a third shows little effect of age.[32]

While no generalization can be made on the basis of these studies, on other educational levels—for example, on the high school level—one might expect that students who are older than the average would exhibit lower levels of academic performance, since academic difficulty may have slowed their progress. This could be the case even if ability were controlled.

High School Size. Two studies examine the relationship between size of high school and academic performance in college. One of these finds that graduates of smaller high schools tend to receive lower grades, even though they are not lower on intelligence.[33] The other study finds size to be unrelated to college performance.[34]

While these studies permit no generalization, it is suggested that if school size were found to have a consistent relation with college performance, this would probably be a result of differences in facilities, teacher salaries, and the like. Should this factor be systematically assessed, we would expect a curvilinear relationship between size and performance. Small high schools are probably found more frequently in rural areas, and their facilities and teacher salaries are likely to be inferior. At the other extreme, very large high schools are most likely to be found in congested urban areas where the schools suffer from overcrowding, inadequate facilities, and the presence of large proportions of economically and socially underprivileged youth. Medium-sized schools would be representative of communities able to provide facilities at a pace more or less in keeping with population increases.

Academic Load. Five studies find that academic load (number of courses carried) has little or no effect upon school performance.[35] For low-ability students, however, academic load is inversely related to grades. Because there is so little variability in load at any educational level, this probably cannot be considered to be an important factor.

Effects of Specific Role Relationships

This section is concerned with whether there are characteristics of a student's social relationships that affect his academic performance. To answer this question, research is presented on various characteristics of the student-to-student, student-to-teacher, and student-to-family relationships.

THE STUDENT-TO-STUDENT RELATIONSHIP

In studies of the student-to-student relationship the social acceptability of the student is the dimension that has received most attention. Many studies map the sociometric structure of the student peer group by assessing the network of friendship choices and by computing the number of choices that are received and reciprocated. The relationship between popularity and academic performance is then observed. In addition to the popularity dimension, other topics dealt with have been, for example, the effects of the value systems of peer group cliques upon individual performance.

The Findings. On the college level, Johnson studied the relationship of actual scholastic performance to peer ratings of popularity and peer ratings of performance.[36] He found that ratings of performance were directly related to both ratings of popularity and actual performance, and that ratings of popularity were also directly related to actual per-

formance. He did not control for sex or intelligence. If intelligence had been controlled, the relationship between popularity and performance might have disappeared.

Zumwinkle investigated factors associated with the compatibility of 85 pairs of female college roommates.[37] He hypothesized that compatible roommates are homogeneous with regard to a variety of characteristics—among them, grades. He found however, that compatability was not associated with homogeneity in grades. Although our concern is with the determinants of grades, not compatability, this study at least points to another variable (roommate interaction) that may be pertinent to the prediction of academic performance. Future research might consider the effects on grades of various characteristics of roommate interaction.

On the high school level, several studies have dealt with the relation of acceptability and popularity to academic performance. Edminston and Rhoades found that the best battery for the prediction of performance included a sociometric measure of social acceptance.[38] Ryan and Davie observed small positive relationships between social acceptability and grades.[39] However, this relationship was not consistent at different high schools, and popularity tended to be related to quantitative aptitude. The authors did not assess the relationship between popularity and grades with aptitude held constant. A third study used separate groups of males and females matched on intelligence but differing in school grades.[40] The different achievement groups within each sex were then compared on various trait ratings obtained from their classmates of the same sex. For boys, the data suggested that those with average grades were more likely to obtain trait ratings indicative of social acceptability—that is, students with average grades were better accepted than students with very high or very low grades. For girls, social acceptability trait ratings were directly related to grades: girls with higher grades had greater acceptability than girls with lower grades. However, girls with high grades were rated by their same-sex peers as being less acceptable to boys than girls with lower grades.

Coleman has shown how different aspects of the social structure of high schools can affect academic performance.[41] He found that among the criteria for membership in the "leading crowd" at different high schools in the Midwest, high scholarship ranks low compared to athletic ability. The members of the social elites in these high schools found it more undesirable to be seen as an intellectual than did nonmembers. And it was even less desirable for a girl to be perceived as an outstanding scholar than for a boy. Furthermore, at high schools where the peer culture placed a relatively low value on academic scholarship, the highest achieving students did not usually have the highest ability; but where the peer culture valued scholarly attainment more highly, the best students were more likely also to be the most intelligent. In short, the high-status cliques at many schools have explicit norms that tend to inhibit high levels of academic achievement. These are similar to norms among factory workers that have been found to restrict output.[42]

Coleman points out that the peer group rewards most highly excellence in areas in which a *group* represents the institution, such as athletics. Scholastic achievement, on the other hand, occurs on an individual basis. Coleman suggests that to raise the level of academic achievement, scholarly activity should be restructured so that outstanding individual achievement benefits the school as a whole. This could be done through interscholastic competition in debating, science projects, and the like. In short, he argues that the individualistic structure of competition for academic success needs to be shifted to a group basis so that the competitive context becomes intermural rather than intramural.

On the elementary school level, two studies find a positive relation between social acceptability and academic performance.[43] In both cases the relationship disappeared when intelligence was controlled.

Another elementary school investigation studied the relationship between students' liking or disliking for the classroom group and their own attitudes toward academic achievement.[44] The results showed that the attitudes toward academic performance of students who liked their group were similar to those they perceived the group as holding. The attitudes toward achievement of students who did not like their group were not related to those they perceived the group as holding. Although this study did not attempt to relate these findings to actual performance, it does illustrate the influence that perceived peer group standards can have upon individual students. Insofar as attitudes toward achievement are related to actual achievement, such findings become significant.

Summary and Evaluation. These studies show considerable variability in the relationships between sociometric measures of popularity and academic performance. The findings for the elementary school level suggest that the relationship between popularity and performance is positive, but the significance of the finding is open to question, since the relationship disappears when intelligence is controlled. This suggests that social acceptability may be a result rather than a determinant of academic performance. The rationale for this statement is that elementary school students may not be sufficiently autonomous to develop peer group norms independent of their teacher's attitudes. That is, peer norms regarding school achievement may be, in large part, reflections of teacher expectations. Thus, students who best meet these expectations (through high academic performance) may be the most popular among their peers. They may also be more likely to be the ones with the most ability.

On the high school level, the situation becomes more complicated because the findings are more variable. In one study popularity was independently related to performance, and in another it was not. A third suggested that the relationship between social acceptability and performance was positive for girls but curvilinear for boys. Perhaps the situation can be clarified by Coleman's findings which showed that the content of peer group norms influenced student attitudes toward academic achievement. For this reason the differences in findings might be attributed to variability in student value systems regarding achievement at various high schools. For example, a curvilinear relationship between popularity and performance for male students would suggest the presence of peer group norms that define the "gentleman's C" as the most desirable type of performance. A positive and direct relationship between popularity and performance might suggest the presence of peer group norms that value scholarly attainment.

At present one can do no more than speculate as to the reasons for differences in the findings. Further research along the lines illustrated by Coleman in which the attempt is made to understand status in the peer group in terms of the particular value systems defining peer group norms would be desirable. Most of the current research dealing with the social acceptability dimension pays insufficient attention to the content of the norms to which conformity is demanded.

The assessment of the normative structure of student subcultures should be accompanied by research on some related questions. For example, students are often members of several peer subgroups, and the possible effects of multiple group membership upon academic performance levels is one such question. Suppose, for example, that these different membership groups accord different priorities to scholarly attainment. What are the effects of such conflict on the individual student? Research on such questions promises to increase our understanding of the student-to-student relationship as a factor affecting academic performance.

THE STUDENT-TEACHER RELATIONSHIP

. . . One reason for the less-than-perfect correlations between ability and academic performance is what might be called teacher "error." . . . a grade is actually an index of summarizing certain characteristics of the student-teacher relationship. One indication of this lies in the fact that ability usually is more highly correlated with scores on achievement tests than with teacher grades.

Studies dealing with the effects of the student-teacher relationship upon academic performance can be divided into two classes. First are those that focus on the degree of consensus between students and teachers with regard to expectations defining their respective roles. The degree of consensus then is used as a variable for predicting school grades. Second are studies dealing with the relation between specific kinds of teacher behavior and specific types of student behavior that presumably constitute responses to the acts of the teacher.

Congruence of Student and Teacher Role Expectations. At the college level, Yourglich asked students and teachers to list spontaneously the characteristics of the ideal student and ideal teacher.[45] The data show that students and teachers are more likely to agree on the definition of the student role than on that of the teacher role. Furthermore, agreement about the student role tends to increase from the freshman to the senior year, but no such trend is evident with regard to the teacher role. Characteristics frequently mentioned as part of the ideal student role were "diligence," "maturity," "cooperative," "intelligent," "dependable," and "integrity." Characteristics frequently mentioned as part of the ideal teacher role were "understanding," "ability to communicate," "integrity," "maturity," and "stimulating." This study did not use the congruence between student and teacher role definitions to predict student grades. However, such measures of consensus could be used for this purpose.

Kelley attempted to assess the factors responsible for discrepancies in achievement as measured by instructor grades and common departmental term-end examination grades.[46] The students who received higher instructor grades than examination grades differed from the students in the reverse situation. The former tended to be more conforming, compulsive, and insecure. They were also lower in ability. This finding suggests that behavioral characteristics of students interact with teacher expectations so as to produce grades from teachers that are not closely related to achievement as measured by objective examinations.

On the high school level, Battle explored the effects on school grades of the degree of congruency in student-teacher value patterns.[47] He hypothesized that students whose value patterns were closer to the teacher's ideal would have higher grades than students whose patterns diverged more from the teacher's ideal. With age, sex, and aptitude controlled, the findings lent support to the

hypothesis. What is perhaps even more interesting is the implicit suggestion that some of the value dimensions need not be related to the instrumental aspects of the school situation in order to be predictive of school performance. Although one would normally expect that it is the task-relevant values such as diligence, integrity, and the like that are the important criteria used by the teacher in defining proper behavior for the student role and to which the successful student must conform, several of the value dimensions used in this study do not appear to have direct instrumental significance (among these are economic, political, and religious values). Thus, agreement with teacher values per se may be related to student achievement. In short, it may be that if the student shares the values of the teacher, he is more likely to do well in school even though such values are more or less irrelevant to explicitly defined criteria for the scholarship aspects of the student role. This is not to deny that the scholarship aspects are important; it is simply to point out that other considerations may also be involved.

A study by Carter also suggests that more than the scholarship aspects of the student role is involved in teacher grades.[48] He found that the sex of the student and the sex of the teacher interact to influence the degree of relationship between high school algebra grades and achievement test scores in algebra. Thus, when the teacher is a male, the correlation between algebra grades and scores on algebra achievement tests is higher for male students than for female students. When the teacher is a woman, there are no differences between male and female students in this correlation. However, for male teachers the *absolute* level of the correlations is higher for both male and female students. This indicates that the sex of the student has more influence on male instructors, but that beyond this, male teachers show greater objectivity in grading (assuming as we are that the achievement test score provides the truer measure of the student's learning). Female instructors are less objective, but the sex of the student is apparently not a factor influencing objectivity.

Two other studies deal with comparisons of perceptions of appropriate student conduct in high school situations by teachers, students, and parents. The first study showed that differences in perception between students on different grade levels were larger than differences among students, teachers, and parents.[49] The second study attempted to assess the relationships between students', teachers', and parents' definitions of the appropriate behavior for students in various situations.[50] Correlations on the order of .88 to .92 were observed among the perceptions of these three groups. Furthermore, there were certain sex differences in the perceptions: girls appeared to be more concerned with dimensions of student behavior involving etiquette, reputation, and appearance, and boys were more concerned with behavior involving the communication of ideas and efficiency. In short, the different perceptions of boys and girls seemed to be related to the performance of masculine and feminine roles. Neither study deals explicitly with the problem of predicting academic performance. Potentially, however, they could be applied to this question.

Getzels and Jackson, in their research on creativity, found that when students high in creativity but not correspondingly high in intelligence were compared with students high in intelligence but not correspondingly high in creativity, no differences in academic achievement appeared.[51] However, teachers preferred the latter group of students, perhaps because highly creative students are more difficult to deal with in class situations, since they are likely to think in terms that depart from a structured class agenda. This finding appears to contradict the finding of previously cited studies which suggest that teacher favorableness toward a student will result in higher grades, other things being equal. Perhaps these results can be reconciled by the interpretation that schools vary in breadth of definition of the student role. In some, the definition may be highly circumscribed, and in others, it may permit a wider range of behaviors, even though teachers may find certain kinds of class behavior preferable. In the latter type of school, there may be little relationship between student-teacher role congruence and academic performance. The Getzels and Jackson study might be illustrative of this.

On the elementary school level, Malpass administered a series of tests to eighth graders that were designed to measure student perceptions in five school areas: teachers, classmates, discipline, achievement, and school in general.[52] Responses were rated on a five-point scale of favorableness to each area. With ability controlled, correlations between these measures and two criteria of academic performance (grades and achievement test scores) were computed. It was found that favorable perceptions in the school areas were more highly related to grades than to achievement tests. In particular, favorable perceptions regarding teachers and achievement were most highly related to grades, the correlations ranging from .48 to .57. It is interesting that whereas most research finds that predictors correlate more highly with achievement test criteria than with grades, the findings of this study are the opposite. This suggests that favorable attitudes toward teachers and toward achievement result in better relations between student and teacher. The better relations may, in turn, lead to higher grades even though they may not objectively result in more learning, as measured by achievement tests.

Davidson and Lang studied children's perceptions of their teachers' feelings toward them in relation to their self-perceptions and their school achievements.[53] The measure of perception was a checklist of trait names. It was found that children's self-perceptions are similar to their perceptions of how their teacher feels toward them. Furthermore, favorableness of perceived feelings of the teacher was positively related to the teacher's actual rating of the child's school achievement. This relationship held true even when the social class background of the child was controlled. However, perceived favorability was directly related to social class, even when achievement rating was controlled. Thus, it appears that both social class and perceived favorableness are independently related to academic performance. A sex difference also appeared: girls perceived teachers as being more favorable than did boys. Furthermore, there was a slight tendency for girls to be rated higher in academic performance.[54] This suggests that the behavior of girls is more in line with teachers' definitions of the student role than is the behavior of boys. Perhaps this explains why a few studies have found that overachieving males tend to be higher on "femininity" scales.

A study by Baker and Doyle indicates that increasing teachers' knowledge of their elementary school pupils affects their grading behavior.[55] Teachers were provided with data on student achievement test scores, sociograms, student autobiographies, and anecdotal records. Thereafter, the correlations between ability and pupil grades decreased, suggesting that as teachers are provided with more information on students, their criteria for grading change. Perhaps increasing the teacher's awareness of individual differences leads him to adopt more flexible definitions of acceptable behavior within the student role.

Effects of Teacher Behavior on Student

Behavior. The major research in this area has been conducted by Ryans.[56] The primary emphasis was on the assessment of dimensions describing teacher behavior, but the characteristics of pupil behavior that are related to teacher behavior were also considered. These studies were carried out on both the elementary and high school levels. On the elementary level, Ryans finds that certain characteristics of teacher behavior are associated with particular characteristics of pupil behavior. Originality and adaptability are defined as one dimension of teacher behavior. Associated with this is pupil behavior characterized by responsibility and high levels of class participation. A second dimension of teacher behavior is defined as responsible, well-planned, and systematic classroom procedure. Associated with this are pupil behaviors labeled as constructive, responsible, cooperative, and controlled.

On the high school level, it is interesting to note that characteristics of teacher behavior appear to be unrelated to the classroom behavior of the students. Perhaps at the high school level students are more deeply involved in the peer group and with the norms that it defines, and these norms may determine classroom behavior to a greater extent than do teacher expectations for the students.

In these studies Ryans did not attempt to relate student-teacher interaction patterns to the more traditional measures of academic performance. However, his research could readily be extended to deal with this problem. Studies could be conducted to assess the effects of interaction patterns upon achievement levels.

Rosenfeld and Zander have shown that teacher behavior may affect student aspiration level.[57] Using a high school sample, they found that the type of influence attempt used by teachers in interaction with students affects the degree to which aspirations of the student are congruent with his perceived capacity. Congruence occurs when teacher influence attempts are perceived as rewarding and legitimate, and lack of congruence occurs when influence is viewed as coercive and indiscriminate.

On the elementary school level, Christensen found that vocabulary and arithmetic achievement among fifth-graders was significantly greater for students of teachers who were high on a "warmth" scale.[58] Stringer has shown that differences in academic progress are due in part to teacher behavior.[59]

Summary and Evaluation. This body of research suggests a number of generalizations. First, the degree of congruence in student-teacher values, attitudes, and expectations is directly related to the academic performance of the student. Furthermore, this generalization holds even when the student-teacher similarity involves what seem to be task-irrelevant criteria. The findings also indicate the presence of sex differences in the definition of the student role.

Studies investigating the relationship between teacher behavior and student behavior have indicated an association between the two, although they suggest that student behavior is more independent of the acts of the teacher on the high school level than on the elementary level. While a few of these studies also find that teacher behavior affects the level of student academic performance, most have focused only upon interaction patterns, ignoring the relation of the patterns to performance.

A number of issues pertaining to this body of research need to be discussed. The findings showing that congruence in student-teacher values, attitudes, and role expectations is related to academic performance raise the question of the causal direction of such relationships. The degree of congruency could be either a determinant or a result of the level of academic performance—or there might be a feedback relationship between the two. With feedback, a moderate degree of congruency might result in a fairly

high level of performance as indexed by the teacher's grades, and this, in turn, might serve to increase the student's identification with the teacher's values and attitudes, thus leading to an even higher subsequent level of academic performance. This question requires further work addressed to the assessment of time sequence in the operation of these variables. Furthermore, if student-teacher congruence is a causal factor determining grades, differential student awareness of teacher definitions of the student role may be a result of differences in social sensitivity. If so, the research in social perception would become relevant to the study of academic performance.

Another issue arising from this research concerns the suggestion of a relation between congruence and performance regardless of the content of the values and expectations used for computing congruence. However, what cannot be ascertained from the research is the degree of correlation between task-relevant and task-irrelevant congruence. It may be that when congruence occurs on task-relevant values, it also occurs on irrelevant values as a result of student identification with the teacher (a "halo" effect). But in the hypothetical case where congruence occurs only on task-irrelevant values, there may be no relation to academic performance. Further work is needed to assess this possibility.

Several other questions are raised but not answered by the research. For example, we know little about the conditions under which students' definitions of their roles converge or diverge from teacher definitions. What are the implications of a divergence between parental and teacher definitions of the student role for the manner in which the student defines his role? The question of the relative importance of the student's different reference groups in determining his value patterns is central here. The problem of the effects on academic performance of a situation where each reference group (that is, the peer group, teachers, the family) holds a different attitude toward school behavior is an especially interesting one; it is amenable to research of the type conducted by Newcomb in the Bennington study.[60] These kinds of questions deserve further investigation.

FAMILY RELATIONSHIPS

Research on the relationship between family factors and academic performance falls into two categories. First, there are studies that focus on certain demographic characteristics of the family. Illustrative is research investigating the number of siblings and birth order in relation to school performance.

Second are studies concerned with the relation of various characteristics of family interaction to a student's school performance. In these studies, family interaction is not usually observed firsthand. Rather, inferences about the quality of interaction are made on the basis of information concerning attitudes of family members.

Sibling Structure of the Family. Bernstein states that family size is inversely related to academic performance; that is, the larger the number of siblings, the lower the level of school achievement.[61] Two facts may help to explain this relationship: first, Nisbet has pointed out that family size is inversely related to intelligence;[62] second, family size is inversely related to socioeconomic status. Presumably, then, large families are significant for educational performance because they are likely to be of lower SES and lower intelligence as compared with smaller families. Of course, this fits in with findings cited earlier showing that

students of lower SES exhibit lower achievement and lower intelligence than students of higher SES. However, Hunt cites evidence showing that the correlation between family size and intelligence holds within all occupational levels except at the very top (where it is possible to afford outside help in the care of children).[63] Thus, Hunt's discussion suggests that family size is independently (of SES) related to both intelligence and academic performance. In this connection, Bernstein and Nisbet suggest an alternative explanation; namely, that the association between family size and intelligence is due to the negative effects of large families on verbal development.[64]

Weitz and Wilkinson found that the academic performance of only children was significantly lower than that of a control group matched for scholastic aptitude.[65] This finding seems to conflict with Nisbet's report of an inverse correlation between family size and aptitude.[66] While the discrepancy cannot be resolved on the basis of evidence, it may be that only-child status is in some way qualitatively different from any situation in which there are two or more siblings. For example, the fact that the only child does not have the experience of a social relationship with sibs may interfere with the acquisition of social skills. This, in turn, might cause difficulties in social adjustment to school, and these might be reflected in lower academic performance. In short, it may be that the negative relationship between family size and achievement holds only for families of two or more children and that only-child status is a unique situation.

In a somewhat different kind of study, Schoonover assessed the effects on academic performance of birth order, sex of sibling, and age interval of siblings.[67] The only factor found to be related to performance was sex of sibling. Sibs of both sexes who had brothers exhibited higher performance on an achievement test than sibs who had sisters.

Brim found that cross-sex siblings have more traits of the opposite sex than do same-sex siblings.[68] This finding was even more pronounced for the younger cross-sex sibling. For example, a younger male sib with an older sister exhibits more feminine traits than a younger male sib with an older brother. Although this study was not concerned with the prediction of academic performance, the findings would seem to bear directly on this question. Thus, some studies have found that overachieving males tend to be higher on so-called femininity scales than underachieving males. Within this context, Brim's findings could be used to derive the prediction that male sibs with older sisters will exhibit higher academic achievement than male sibs with older brothers. It should be noted, however, that this hypothesis seems to conflict with the findings of Schoonover. Only additional research can clarify this issue.

Family interaction Patterns. Strodtbeck has conducted research on the characteristics of family interaction, and one of his purposes was to relate these to the academic achievement of high school boys.[69] He found that characteristics of interaction such as the power distribution in the family and the degree of decision-making consensus were associated with certain personality characteristics which, in turn, were predictive of academic performance. In particular, the degree of decision-making consensus was related to the son's level of achievement motivation. Furthermore, the greater the degree of power the mother and the son have relative to the father, the higher will be the son's score on a test of achievement values. This latter finding is interpreted as an indication that the more power one has, the more likely he is to believe that the world can be rationally mastered, and the belief in one's ability to have some mastery over the world is presumably a prerequisite for believing in the value of achievement. While this study did not attempt to relate directly characteristics

of family interaction to level of academic performance, the fact that such interaction characteristics are associated with achievement-related personality traits suggests that the interaction patterns themselves might be directly predictive of academic achievement.

Several other studies deal with the relationship between characteristics of family behavior and academic performance, although unlike the Strodtbeck research, they do not directly observe family interaction. Thus, one study of college males found that higher achievers had happier, more secure relations with the father.[70] This study did not control for ability, however.

In a study dealing with preparatory school boys of high intelligence who differed widely in academic performance, Kimball discovered that boys whose performance was quite low, unlike the higher achievers, had poor relations with their fathers; that is, the relationship had little warmth and the son feared the father.[71] In another study on the high school level, Tibbetts compared boys varying widely in academic performance level but matched for aptitude.[72] He found that the higher achievers and their parents were more satisfied with family relations, that the boys had greater motivation to please their parents, and that they more often described their parents as thoughtful, understanding, and interested in them.

On the elementary school level, Drews and Teahan studied groups of students who were comparable on aptitude but not on academic performance.[73] They found that the mothers of the higher-achieving students tended to be dominating as well as ignoring. The degree of maternal possessiveness was unrelated to high and low performance levels.

Fliegler found that four home patterns predominate in the case of the gifted, low-achieving child: (1) a neutral or uninterested view of education by the parents; (2) overanxious, oversolicitous, easy-going, or inconsistent parental behavior; (3) lukewarm, indifferent parents; (4) lack of a cooperative spirit in the family.[74] He stated that these patterns lead to distrust of people, a negative attitude toward the learning situation, and a lowered level of aspiration.

Summary and Evaluation. While the findings are not consistent, it seems clear that family life is an important factor in school achievement. The general picture that seems to emerge is that the student who does well in school comes from a family which has a relatively small number of children, in which the parents exhibit warmth and interest, where the child has a relatively high degree of power in decision-making, and where the family is able to arrive with relative ease at consensus regarding important values and decisions.

Although these studies indicate the importance of the family in relation to academic achievement, they are designed so differently that it is difficult to determine just how comparable they are. Some of them base their conclusions about family life on data gathered from the mother; others concentrate only on the father; and still others are concerned with both parents. Thus, some generalizations about the effects of the "family" are in reality generalizations about only very circumscribed aspects of it. Furthermore, no systematic attention has been paid to sex differences or to the extent to which findings at one educational level hold for other levels.

Not even touched upon in these studies are questions we have raised earlier concerning the effects on academic performance of differential identification with various reference groups. An example is the question of what effects the student's differential identification with family and peer groups has in the case where the values of each regarding academic achievement conflict. The answers to such questions await further research.

Summary of the Studies

This paper has reviewed studies concerned with the effects of social factors on academic performance. One type of study emphasizes the effects of ecological and demographic variables. The findings indicate that there are positive relations between socioeconomic status and academic performance at all levels except the upper, where the relationships become inverse. The central significance of SES lies in the fact that it summarizes a variety of other factors that are related to academic performance. Sex, religion, geographic region, and urbanism are also related to academic performance. Once again, these variables summarize a variety of underlying characteristics that serve to explain the observed relationships.

Within the sociological tradition of research which emphasizes role relationships in the educational context, investigations of the student-to-student relationship have shown that sociometric measures of acceptability bear some relation to academic performance, although the causal status of the variable is not clear. Work on the influence of informal peer-group norms upon scholarly attainment is a promising area for study.

Research on the student-teacher relationship suggests two generalizations. First, the more the student's attitudes and values coincide with those of the teacher, the higher the student's academic performance will be. Second, characteristics of teacher behavior may affect the performance level of the student.

Studies dealing with the effects of family relationships upon student performance suggest that several characteristics of family life are relevant. The successful student is likely to come from a family where the parents show warmth and interest, where the child has a relatively strong voice in decision-making, and where the family tends to agree regarding the issues it defines as important.

Notes

[1] Of course it is also possible that in many cases given types of value systems may predispose persons to gravitate into given kinds of life situations.

[2] Francis J. Crowley, "The Goals of Male High School Seniors," *Personnel and Guidance Journal*, 37 (1959), pp. 488–92; W. H. Friedhoff, "Relationships Among Various Measures of Socioeconomic Status, Social Class Identification, Intelligence, and School Achievement," *Dissertation Abstracts*, 15 (1955), p. 2098; Lotus M. Knief and James B. Stroud, "Intercorrelations Among Various Intelligence, Achievement, and Social Class Scores," *Journal of Educational Psychology*, 50 (1959), pp. 117–20; John B. Miner, *Intelligence in the United States: A Survey with Conclusions for Manpower Utilization in Education and Employment* (New York: Springer Publishing Co., 1957); James V. Mitchell, Jr., "A Comparison of the Factorial Structure of Cognitive Functions for a High and Low Status Group," *Journal of Educational Psychology*, 47 (1956), pp. 397–414; Victor H. Noll, "Relation of Scores on Davis-Eells Games to Socioeconomic Status, Intelligence Test Results, and School Achievement," *Educational and Psychological Measurement*, 20 (1960), pp. 119–29; Samuel R. Pinneau and Harold E. Jones, "Development of Mental Abilities," *Review of Educational Research*, 28 (1958), pp. 392–400.

[3] Friedhoff, *op. cit.*

[4] Knief and Stroud, *op. cit.*

[5] Bernard C. Rosen, "The Achievement Syndrome: A Psychocultural Dimension of Social Stratification," *American Sociological Review*, 21 (1956), pp. 203–11.

[6] *Ibid.*

[7] *Ibid.*

[8] Fred L. Strodtbeck, "Family Interaction,

Values and Achievement," in *Talent and Society*, ed. David C. McClelland et al. (Princeton: Van Nostrand, 1958), pp. 135–94.

[9] Louis Schneider and Sverre Lysgaard, "The Deferred Gratification Pattern: A Preliminary Study." *American Sociological Review*, 18 (1953), pp. 142–49.

[10] Orville G. Brim, Jr., and Raymond Forer, "A Note on the Relation of Values and Social Structure to Life Planning," *Sociometry*, 19 (1956), pp. 54–60.

[11] Crowley, *op. cit.;* Herbert H. Hyman, "The Value Systems of Different Classes: A Social Psychological Contribution to the Analysis of Stratification," in *Class, Status and Power: A Reader in Social Stratification*, ed. Bendix, Reinhard, and Lipset (New York: Free Press, 1953), pp. 426–42; William Sewell, Archie O. Haller, and Murray A. Straus, "Social Status and Educational and Occupational Aspiration," *American Sociological Review*, 22 (1957), pp. 67–73; Alan B. Wilson, "Residential Segregation of Social Classes and Aspirations of High School Boys," *American Sociological Review*, 24 (1959), pp. 836–45.

[12] Clyde W. Bresee, "Affective Factors Associated with Academic Underachievement in High-School Studies," *Dissertation Abstracts*, 17 (1957), pp. 90–91; John K. Coster, "Some Characteristics of High School Pupils from Three Income Groups," *Journal of Educational Psychology*, 50 (1959), pp. 55–62; Friedhoff, *op. cit.;* Harold G. J. Gerritz, "The Relationship of Certain Personal and Socioeconomic Data to the Success of Resident Freshmen Enrolled in the College of Science, Literature and the Arts at the University of Minnesota," *Dissertation Abstracts*, 16 (1956), p. 2366; Richard A. Gibboney, "Socioeconomic Status and Achievement in Social Studies." *Elementary School Journal*, 59 (1959), pp. 340–46; Knief and Stroud, *op. cit.;* A. James McKnight, "The Relation of Certain Home Factors to College Achievement," *Dissertation Abstracts*, 19 (1958), pp. 870–71; John P. McQuary, "Some Relationships Between Non-Intellectual Characteristics and Academic Achievement," *Journal of Educational Psychology*, 44 (1953), pp. 215–28; Kate H. Mueller and John H. Mueller, "Class Structure and Academic and Social

Success," *Educational and Psychological Measurement*, 13 (1953), pp. 486–96; Noll, *op. cit.;* Irving Ratchick, "Achievement and Capacity: A Comparative Study of Pupils with Low Achievement and High Intelligence Quotients with Pupils of High Achievement and High Intelligence Quotients in a Selected New York City High School," *Dissertation Abstracts*, 13 (1953), pp. 1049–50; Rosen, *op. cit.*, Robert M. W. Travers, "Significant Research on the Prediction of Academic Success," in *The Measurement of Student Adjustment and Achievement*, ed. W. T. Donahue, C. H. Coombs, and R. M. W. Travers (Ann Arbor: University of Michigan Press, 1949).

[13] E. M. Boyce, "A Comparative Study of Overachieving and Underachieving College Students on Factors Other Than Scholastic Aptitude," *Dissertation Abstracts*, 16 (1956), pp. 2088–89; Junius A. Davis, "Differential College Achievement of Public vs. Private School Graduates," *Journal of Counseling Psychology*, 3 (1956), pp. 72–73; Junius A. Davis and Norman Frederiksen, "Public and Private School Graduates in College," *Journal of Teacher Education*, 6 (1955), pp. 18–22; Charles C. McArthur, "Personalities of Public and Private School Boys," *Harvard Educational Review*, 24 (1954), pp. 256–62; Charles C. McArthur, "Subculture and Personality During the College Years," *Journal of Educational Sociology*, 33 (1960), pp. 260–68; Audrey M. Shuey, "Academic Success of Public and Private School Students in Randolph Macon Women's College: I. The Freshman Year," *Journal of Educational Research*, 49 (1956), pp. 481–92.

[14] Davis, *op. cit.;* Davis and Frederiksen, *op. cit.;* McArthur, "Personalities of Public and Private School Boys . . . ," *op. cit;* McArthur, "Subculture and Personality . . . ," *op. cit.*

[15] Davis, *op. cit.;* Davis and Frederiksen, *op. cit.*

[16] McArthur, "Personalities of Public and Private School Boys . . . ," *op. cit.*

[17] *Ibid.;* McArthur, "Subculture and Personality . . . ," *op. cit.*

[18] Helen H. Davidson and Gerhard Lang, "Children's Perceptions of Their Teachers' Feelings Toward Them Related to Self-Perception, School Achievement and Be-havior," *Journal of Experimental Education*, 29 (1960), pp. 107–18.

[19] Gerritz, *op. cit.;* Donald P. Hoyt, "Size of High School and College Grades," *Personnel and Guidance Journal*, 37, (1959), pp. 569–73; Mildred C. Hughes, "Sex Differences in Reading Achievement in the Elementary Grades," *Supplementary Educational Monographs*, no. 77 (1953), pp. 102–6; Robert A. Jackson, "Prediction of the Academic Success of College Freshmen," *Journal of Educational Psychology*, 46 (1955), pp. 296–301; Arwood S. Northby, "Sex Differences in High-School Scholarship," *School and Society*, 86 (1958), pp. 63–64; Merville C. Shaw and John T. McCuen, "The Onset of Academic Underachievement in Bright Children," *Journal of Educational Psychology*, 51 (1960), pp. 103–8.

[20] Hughes, *op. cit.*

[21] Shaw and McCuen, *op. cit.*

[22] This method of defining underachievement does not meet the criteria discussed in Chapter 2 of *The Prediction of Academic Performance*. It would be more accurate simply to state that within a sample of students comparable as to ability, there are significant differences in level of academic performance.

[23] Talcott Parsons, "Certain Primary Sources and Patterns of Aggression in the Social Structure of the Western World," in *A Study of Interpersonal Relations*, ed. Patrick Mullahy (New York: Hermitage House, 1949), pp. 284–87.

[24] If, as we have stated earlier, the academic performance of females is more predictable than that of males when intellective factors are used as the predictors, then it follows that over- and underachievement should be more frequent for the males.

[25] Strodtbeck, *op. cit.*

[26] Gerritz, *op. cit.*

[27] Peter H. Rossi, "Social Factors in Academic Achievement: A Brief Review," in *Education, Economy, and Society*, ed. A. H. Halsey, Jean Floud, and C. A. Anderson (New York: Free Press, 1961), pp. 269–72.

[28] Merville C. Shaw and Donald J. Brown, "Scholastic Underachievement of Bright College Students," *Personnel and Guidance Journal*, 36 (1957), pp. 195–99; Norman F. Washburne, "Socioeconomic Status, Urbanism and Academic Performance in College," *Journal of Educational Research*, 53 (1959), pp. 130–37.

[29] William B. Sanders, R. Travis Osborne, and Joel E. Green, "Intelligence and Academic Performance of College Students of Urban, Rural, and Mixed Backgrounds," *Journal of Educational Research*, 49 (1955), pp. 185–93.

[30] Lowell Carter, "The Effect of Early School Entrance on the Scholastic Achievement of Elementary School Children in the Austin Public Schools," *Journal of Educational Research*, 50 (1956), pp. 91–103.

[31] Edward Oscar Stephany, "Academic Achievement in Grades Five Through Nine," *Dissertation Abstracts*, 16 (1956), p. 1846.

[32] Vera V. Miller, "Academic Achievement and Social Adjustment of Children Young for Their Grade Placement," *Elementary School Journal*, 57 (1957), pp. 257–63.

[33] Hoyt, *op. cit.*

[34] Esther R. Altman, "The Effect of Rank in Class and Size of High School on the Academic Achievement of Central Michigan College Seniors, Class of 1957," *Journal of Educational Research*, 52 (1959), pp. 307–09.

[35] Dean C. Andrew, "Relationship Between Academic Load and Scholastic Success of Deficient Students," *Personnel and Guidance Journal*, 34 (1956), pp. 268–70; Peter Timothy Hountras, "The Relationship Between Student Load and Achievement," *Journal of Educational Research*, 51 (1958), pp. 355–60; Reed M. Merrill, and Hal W. Osborn, "Academic Overload and Scholastic Success," *Personnel and Guidance Journal*, 37 (1959), pp. 509–10; Gene L. Schwilk, "Academic Achievement of Freshmen High School Students in Relationship to Class Load and Scholastic Aptitude," *Personnel and Guidance Journal*, 37 (1959), pp. 455–56; Shaw and Brown, *op. cit.*

[36] Edward E. Johnson, "Student Ratings of Popularity and Scholastic Ability of Their Peers and Actual Scholastic Performance of Those Peers," *Journal of Social Psychology*, 47 (1958), pp. 127–32.

[37] Robert G. Zumwinkle, "Factors Associated with the Compatability of Roommates: A Test of the Birds of a Feather Hypothesis," *Dissertation Abstracts*, 14 (1954), p. 563.

[38] R. W. Edminston, and Betty Jane Rhoades, "Predicting Achievement," *Journal of Educational Research*, 52 (1959), pp. 177–80.

[39] F. R. Ryan, and James S. Davie, "Social Acceptance, Academic Achievement, and Aptitude Among High School Students," *Journal of Educational Research*, 52 (1958), 101–6.

[40] Evan R. Keisler, "Peer Group Rating of High School Pupils with High and Low School Marks," *Journal of Experimental Education*, 23 (1955), pp. 375–78.

[41] James S. Coleman, "Academic Achievement and the Structure of Competition," *Harvard Educational Review*, 29 (1959), pp. 330–51; James S. Coleman, *The Adolescent Society* (New York: Free Press, 1961).

[42] George C. Homans, *The Human Group* (New York: Harcourt, Brace, 1950).

[43] M. Buswell, "Relationship Between the Social Structure of the Classroom and the Academic Success of the Pupils," *Journal of Experimental Education*, 22 (1953), pp. 37–52; Lloyd R. Grann et al., "The Relationship Between Academic Achievement of Pupils and the Social Structure of the Classroom," *Rural Sociology*, 21 (1956), pp. 179–80.

[44] Lorene Quay, "Academic Achievement Attitudes in Group Perception in Sixth Graders," *Dissertation Abstracts*, 19 (1959), pp. 3042–43.

[45] Anita Yourglich, "Study on Correlations Between College Teachers' and Students' Concepts of 'Ideal-Student' and 'Ideal-Teacher,' " *Journal of Educational Research*, 49 (1955), pp. 59–64.

[46] Eldon G. Kelly, "A Study of Consistent Discrepancies Between Instructor Grades and Term-End Examination Grades," *Journal of Educational Psychology*, 49 (1958), pp. 328–34.

[47] Haron J. Battle, "Relation Between Personal Values and Scholastic Achievement," *Journal of Experimental Education*, 26 (1957), pp. 27–41.

[48] Robert S. Carter, "Non-Intellectual Variables Involved in Teachers' Marks," *Journal of Educational Research*, 47 (1953), pp. 81–95.

[49] Laurence Siegel et al., "Expressed Standards of Behavior of High School Students, Teachers, and Parents," *Personnel and Guidance Journal*, 34 (1956), pp. 261–67.

[50] Howard Moss, "Standards of Conduct for Students, Teachers, and Parents," *Journal of Counseling Psychology*, 2 (1955), pp. 39–42.

[51] Jacob W. Getzels, and Philip W. Jackson, "Family Environment and Cog-

nitive Style: A Study of the Sources of Highly Intelligent and of Highly Creative Adolescents," *American Sociological Review*, 26 (1961), pp. 351–59; a more detailed report of this study is available in a volume by the same authors, *Creativity and Intelligence: Explorations with Gifted Students* (New York: John Wiley, 1962). In a review of this volume, Cronbach points out that these two groups may not be very different in true IQ, and this may account for the fact that they are similar in achievement (in *The American Journal of Sociology*, 68 [1962], pp. 278–79).

[52] Leslie F. Malpass, "Some Relationships Between Students' Perceptions of School and Their Achievement," *Journal of Educational Psychology*, 44 (1953), pp. 475–82.

[53] Davidson and Lang, *op. cit.*

[54] It should be noted that intelligence was not controlled in this study. Thus, perceived favorableness might be simply an indirect index of ability.

[55] Robert L. Baker, and Roy P. Doyle, "Teacher Knowledge of Pupil Data and Marking Practices at the Elementary School Level," *Personnel and Guidance Journal*, 37 (1959), pp. 644–47.

[56] David G. Ryans, "Some Relationships Between Pupil Behavior and Certain Teacher Characteristics," *Journal of Educational Psychology*, 52 (1961), pp. 82–90; David G. Ryans, *Characteristics of Teachers: Their Description, Comparison, and Appraisal* (Washington, D.C.: American Council on Education, 1960).

[57] Howard M. Rosenfeld, and Alvin Zander, "The Influence of Teachers on Aspirations of Students," *Journal of Educational Psychology*, 52 (1961), pp. 1–11.

[58] Clifford M. Christensen, "Relationships Between Pupil Achievement, Pupil Affect-Need, Teacher Warmth, and Teacher Permissiveness," *Journal of Educational Psychology*, 51 (1960), pp. 169–74.

[59] Lorene A. Stringer, "Academic Progress as an Index of Mental Health," *The Journal of Social Issues*, 15 (1959), pp. 16–29.

[60] Theodore M. Newcomb, *Personality and Social Change* (New York: Dryden Press, 1943).

[61] B. Bernstein, "Some Sociological Determinants of Perception; An Enquiry into Sub-Cultural Differences," *British Journal of Sociology*, 9 (1958), pp. 159–74.

[62] J. Nisbet, "Family Environment and Intelligence," in Halsey, Floud, and Anderson, *op. cit.*, pp. 273–87.

[63] Joseph McVicker Hunt, *Intelligence and Experience* (New York: The Ronald Press, 1961).

[64] B. Bernstein, "Social Class and Linguistic Development: A Theory of Social Learning," in Halsey, Floud, and Anderson, *op. cit.*, pp. 288–314.

[65] Henry J. Weitz, and H. Jean Wilkinson, "The Relationship Between Certain Non-intellective Factors and Academic Success in College," *Journal of Counseling Psychology*, 4 (1957), pp. 54–60.

[66] Nisbet, *op. cit.*

[67] Sarah M. Schoonover, "The Relationship of Intelligence and Achievement to Birth Order, Sex of Sibling, and Age Interval," *Journal of Educational Psychology*, 50 (1959), pp. 143–46.

[68] Orville G. Brim, Jr., "Family Structure and Sex Role Learning by Children: A Further Analysis of Helen Koch's Data," *Sociometry*, 21 (1958), pp. 1–15.

[69] Strodtbeck, *op. cit.*

[70] John V. Gilmore, "A New Venture in the Testing of Motivation," *College Board Review*, 15 (1951), pp. 221–26.

[71] Barbara Kimball, "Case Studies in Educational Failure During Adolescence," *American Journal of Orthopsychiatry*, 23 (1953), pp. 406–15.

[72] John R. Tibbetts, "The Role of Parent-Child Relationships in the Achievement of High School Pupils: A Study of the Family Relationships Associated with Underachievement and High Achievement of High School Pupils," *Dissertation Abstracts*, 15 (1955), p. 232.

[73] Elizabeth Drews, and John E. Teahan, "Parental Attitudes and Academic Achievement," *Journal of Clinical Psychology*, 13 (1957), pp. 328–32.

[74] Louis A. Fliegler, "Understanding the Underachieving Gifted Child," *Psychological Reports*, 3 (1957), pp. 533–36.

THE MAJOR portion of the physical area of most schools is broken up into a series of classrooms, and it is here that most students are presumed to do most of their "learning." While the classroom is a comparatively small social world, it has a certain degree of complexity. The sociologist can focus upon the teacher-student relationship or upon the organization and atmosphere of the class as a whole, including patterns of student-student relationships, and within certain general structural limitations there can be considerable variety in the way the class is organized and the way materials are presented. This section will review some possible variations and their implications for student performance.

First a few comments on problems of research design. Ideally the way to evaluate some classroom arrangement or teaching technique is to introduce the "new" or "experimental" method into one or more classes and then to compare the results with those obtained in one or more matched control classes in which the same material is presented in the traditional way (and, if possible, in some *alternative new* ways, to control for a possible Hawthorne effect). There are, however, numerous difficulties in operationalizing this ideal experiment.

Just setting up the experimental and control groups is problematic, because it is so hard to "control" the behavior and personalities of the instructors involved. "It is well known that almost any course works well in the classroom if it is taught by its inventors or by a few of their highly trained converts ... To get a valid test of feasibility, you must turn over the program to teachers who are a fair sample of the people who would be teaching it if it were adopted on the scale for which it was intended" (Moise, 1964, p. 175). But can a teacher who has always run her classes along authoritarian lines, e.g., give a fair test to a teaching device involving much informal interaction among students and with no

Classroom Effects upon Student Performance

Sarane S. Boocock

Reprinted from Sociology of Education, *39 (1966)*, pp. 4–18, by permission of the author and publisher, The American Sociological Association.

predetermined "correct" solutions to problems—even assuming such a teacher was willing to participate in the experiment? How can the researcher be sure that two or more teachers supposedly using the same teaching method are in fact presenting the materials and themselves in the same way? These kinds of questions indicate possible pitfalls in the interpretation of research findings.

The researcher must also consider the possibility of bias if students are assigned to experimental groups any way except randomly. For example, it is difficult to evaluate much of the early research on "progressive" education, since the children attending such classes were probably a self-selected group differing from the general population of children in background, motivation, abilities and other respects.

Then there is what McKeachie terms the "criterion problem" (McKeachie, 1962, p. 319), which amounts to saying that one must be precise in defining just what a student is supposed to learn from any particular teaching experience, that the control group be given the opportunity to "learn" the same content, and that tests be based upon this content. (For a more detailed discussion of experimental design in educational research, cf. Campbell and Stanley, 1963).

The Teacher

In view of the almost universal importance attached to the role of the teacher, it is surprising how little can be said about the kind of teacher and teaching that produce the best learning results. Research has been done on the type of person who goes into teaching as compared to other occupations, on the social background and status of teachers, and on the teacher's position in the school system (relationships with the principal, other teachers, etc.) and in the community. But very little seems to be known about the relationships between what teachers do in the classroom and the subsequent behavior of their students.

A great deal of effort was expended during the 1940's and early 1950's in devising scales to measure "teacher effectiveness," a number of which are described in a review by Medley and Mitzel (1963). All were developed in essentially the same way. Starting with a set of dimensions believed to be related to effectiveness, an observer visited a number of classrooms for short intervals of time, coding the teachers' behavior with respect to these dimensions. Teachers then were designated as "good" or "poor" depending upon their classification on the dimensions.

While the content of the scales varied greatly, they share in common an almost total lack of relationship to any measure of student achievement or gain. Aside from the ridiculous categories used in many of the scales (e.g., "good" teachers are more likely to smile and gesture but less likely to snap their fingers or stamp their feet than poor teachers), Medley and Mitzel feel that they are based upon a fallacy "which says it is possible to judge a teacher's skill by watching him teach," that an intelligent observer "can recognize good teaching when he sees it" (Medley and Mitzel, 1963, p. 257). Given the working definition of learning as a change of some specified sort, and given the uniformly disappointing results of teacher rating scales so far, perhaps a more practical approach to the teacher evaluation problem would be: (1) to designate exactly what learning or change is to be investigated; (2) compare groups of teachers whose students have changed in the desired direction with teachers whose students have manifested less of the desired change for differences in the methods used or characteristics of the teacher (overlooking for the moment the possibility that the changes may be the result of factors other than teacher behavior).

A few clues about the kind of teacher or teaching that are especially conducive to certain kinds of learning can be pulled from scattered studies. There does seem to be evidence that the teacher's training is relevant. In a study of science classes in 56 Minnesota high schools, Anderson (1950) found that the rate of individual student improvement (measured by comparisons of test scores at the beginning and end of the course, adjusted for student's I.Q.) was positively and significantly related to the teacher having done his undergraduate work at some institution other than a teachers' college and having taken a relatively high number of science courses during his college training. In other words, teacher competence does seem to contribute to pupil competence.

Two studies have investigated the relationship between the teacher's classroom behavior as a reflection of his basic personality type and student productivity. Cogan (1958) studied five junior high schools in two different communities, asking students to describe their teachers' behavior. The student responses were classified in terms of degree of teacher's control and organization of the subject matter ("conjunctive" behavior) and degree of warmth and encouragement ("inclusive" behavior). Both variables were found to be significantly related to the child's performance of required work and frequency of self-initiated (non-assigned) projects. A study by Heil, Powell, and Feifer (1960) identified three teacher and four pupil personality types and then compared various teacher-pupil combinations in terms of student achievement. The "well-integrated, self-controlling" teacher type was found to be most effective with all types of students. "Weakly-integrated, fearful" teachers were relatively ineffective with all types of students except "strivers." The "turbulent" type of teacher (a defensively intellectual type, parallel to the personality type found by Anne Roe to be associated with scientific interests) was effective with students classified as "conformers" or "strivers," but not with "opposers" or "waverers," who apparently needed the type of teacher equipped with greater interpersonal skills.

There is some evidence that student performance is improved when the teacher-student relationship is strengthened by providing teachers with information on their students' abilities, home environments, and emotional problems and encouraging them to use this information in planning their class work. In a study by Ojemann and Wilkinson (1939), a sample of ninth graders were individually matched on age, I.Q., achievement and home background and then randomly assigned to experimental and control classes. In the experimental classes only, teachers were given comprehensive data on their students and participated in small group sessions at which pupil problems and possible solutions were discussed. The researchers' conclusion was that the experimental classes made significantly greater academic gains as well as manifesting more positive attitudes toward school and fewer behavior problems. Several studies designed to replicate the basic postulates of the Ojemann-Wilkinson study produced sim-

ilar results. (These same studies also found no relationships between pupil gains and sex of the teacher, a factor often postulated as affecting student response.)

Some observers, noting that many of the schools—especially on the college level—notable for high levels of student achievement are characterized by a small student teacher ratio and relatively frequent, informal relationships between students and teachers, have postulated that it is these close teacher-student relationships which produce high achievement. Newcomb (1962) disagrees with this information, citing findings from an experimental study conducted at Antioch College, in which sections of each of eight different courses were taught with three different levels of student-teacher contact (continuous surveillance, sporadic contact, and almost independent study) and the outcomes (examination results, attitudinal questionnaire responses, amount of extracurricular reading) compared. No significant differences were found, and Newcomb concluded that contact itself is not enough to produce interest and achievement. (Another possibility is that Antioch students may be so homogeneously motivated that a differential reaction to different "treatments" could not be observed. This kind of contextual effect is considered in the next section.) What seems to happen is that high rates of contact tend to occur in a "cluster" of factors characteristic of "good" teachers and quality schools.

There have been a number of studies in which students have been asked to describe their image of a good teacher and/or to rate their own teachers (cf. Riley, Ryan and Lifshitz, 1950). For the most part, these studies do not add much to an understanding of teacher effectiveness, because there seem to be no efforts to relate students' evaluations with their academic performance. That is, there is no evidence that students learn more from the teachers they choose the most on these popularity polls. As a later discussion of value estimates will suggest, whether the popular teacher is also the one who gets the best results in terms of student achievement may well depend upon the extent to which such achievement is valued by different groups of students and by the student body as a whole. One can, e.g., think of schools where the most popular teacher is the "easy" one.

Some of the research of Hovland and his associates on the image of the "communicator" suggests how communication skills may affect learning, especially of materials with value implications. In one of the Yale studies, college students were given a variety of readings expressing opinions on various public issues, and it was found they responded more favorably to opinions perceived as emanating from a "credible" source (e.g., an acknowledged expert in the field, as opposed to a "popular" journalist), although judgment of an opinion as accurate or fair did not always lead to a change in the respondent's own opinions (Hovland et al., 1953, Chapter 2). In this respect, teachers start out with an advantage, for teachers tend to be considered by children—and usually by their parents and the community at large—to be "experts" in learning in general and the particular subject matter that they teach. Perhaps one of the reasons children learn as much as they do as quickly as they do is that in most classroom situations, it is assumed that the teacher knows what he is talking about. The credibility concept may also explain why so few teachers are really effective in shaping students' views on politics, morality, and such—they are simply not perceived as "experts" in these areas. It would be interesting to do some research

relating the degree to which teachers are seen as expert in certain areas and the quality of student learning in these areas.

Thus there are empirical clues but no real theory about what constitutes productive teacher-student relationships. A few writers feel it is time to develop models and laws of effective teacher behavior. Wallen and Travers (1963) suggest working toward a set of laws of teacher behavior with the following general form:

$$T = f(R_g, R_i)$$

where T is the behavior of the teacher, seen as a function of the goals to be achieved (R_g) and the present behavior of the student (R_i). But what actual variables are to be included in the equations is far from clear. All that does seem clear at this point is that there does not seem to be any one type of teacher or teacher-student relationship that is "best" for all kinds of learning and all kinds of students.

The Classroom as a Whole

The present view concerning classroom behavior is that, while the teacher is an important participant, and there are certain things about teachers' personalities and patterns of behavior which will remain constant no matter what particular students they work with, class performance is a function of a constellation of factors, only some of which reside in the teacher (and some of which, in fact, affect the teacher's performance). The classroom is viewed as a social system characterized by a complex set of interpersonal relations and having a "personality" of its own. (For a more detailed statement of this point of view, cf. Withall and Lewis, 1963, who term this a move away from a "single-criterion" formulation of behavior.)

I have divided this discussion into two general categories: studies focusing upon classroom *structuring*, which includes such things as role assignment and organization as well as physical arrangements; and studies focusing upon the general atmosphere or "climate" of the classroom. My impression is that the studies in this section are on a rather higher level of sociological sophistication that the research on the teacher reported in the previous section.

A very basic question—and one which has received much attention in the small groups literature—is whether more, or more effective, learning occurs when students work *individually* (though usually within the group setting of the classroom) or when two or more work *together as a group* on some learning task. (Structurally, this is the kind of distinction described by Lorge et al., 1958, as *non*-interacting face-to-face vs. interacting face-to-face groups.) The notion that the individual produces *different* results when working in a group situation than when working individually seems to have been generally accepted at least since Allport's experimental work in the 1920's, and interest developed early in comparing group and individual performances in terms of some measures of "goodness" or "efficiency."

Lorge et al.'s review of a number of these studies points to two questions that must be resolved:

1. *What* about the group or the individual should be compared? E.g., should one use the average group score with the average individual scores, or the *best* scores at each level, or some kind of summated or aggregated measure?

2. What effect does the *type* of problem have upon the comparison. Lorge mentioned tasks of memorization, judgment, and problem-solving, and also pointed out that each type of task could be of varying length, abstractness, complexity, or difficulty.

A pioneer in this area was Shaw, who experimented with the multi-stage type of problem, requiring correct solution of each stage in order to reach the final correct answer. Shaw found relatively more correct final answers in the group than in the individual situations, and concluded that the value of the group lay in its tendency to reject extreme answers of individual members and to catch errors in reasoning at relatively early stages of the entire process (Shaw, 1932).

Thorndike (1938) carried on this general line of experiment, introducing the variable of complexity and type of problem-solving task. He felt that groups would be more efficient on certain kinds of tasks than on others, and he did find a group superiority on problems with a relatively greater range of possible answers, up to a certain point. E.g., when the task reached the level of complexity of crossword puzzles, it was found that the group did relatively better at solving than creating puzzles, suggesting that tasks with almost infinite and unstructured alternatives may offer too many obstacles in the way of group organization.

The quality of group and individual products is examined in an early study by Allport (1920) dealing with college students' responses to sets of stimulus words. Allport concludes that *more* ideas are produced in the group situation, that the group acts as a kind of stimulus activating the flow of thought, but that "among the ideas so produced, those of superior quality ... are of relatively greater frequency in the solitary than in the group work. Ideas of a lower logical value are relatively more numerous in the group work ... The more intense logical thinking of solitude gives way in the group to extensity of treatment" (Allport, 1920, p. 34).

Perlmutter (1955), experimenting with a memorization task, introduces the possibility of increasing productivity of individuals over time by putting them successively in group and individual situations.

It is beyond the scope of this paper to go into all the details of the small groups literature dealing with this problem (even working through Lorge's synthesis of the more important studies is an arduous task). And the only answer that one can give to the original question of the relative efficiency of the group vs. the individual is: it depends upon the nature and complexity of the task and the composition of the group.

Although the *size* of the classroom group is felt to affect students' achievement or lack of achievement, research on the size factor is rather inconclusive. The most suggestive findings are in the small groups literature, though these studies are usually designed for groups smaller than the typical classroom. Taylor and Faust's (1955) study of problem solving in small groups of different sizes indicated that while adding members to a group does tend to cut down the total amount of time needed to reach a solution, a group of say four cannot really be said to be "faster," in terms of "unit-efficiency," unless it solves a problem at least twice as fast as a group of two—and this was not the case with the groups tested by Taylor and Faust. In other words, there may be a kind of law of diminishing returns in simply increasing the size of a group. Bales' research with groups of different sizes points to increasing role differentiation with increasing size. This manifests itself in an increasingly clear cut distinction between leader(s) and followers, with the former taking over a proportionately larger share of the interaction and the latter directing a greater share of their actions to the leaders (Bales and Borgatta, 1955).

Research in the field of education does not establish the superiority of either large or small classes (cf. Watson, 1963, for some studies on the high school level; McKeachie, 1962, for studies on the

college level). McKeachie suggests that this apparent lack of relationship may be due to two effects working in opposite directions. On the one hand, increasing size increases the resources of the group (e.g., total pool of information available, different approaches to a problem, opportunities for providing feedback from one member to another). On the other hand, the possibility of getting the maximum contribution from all members decreases.

Another possibility is that size is related to *other* factors which affect the classroom situation. For example, if one compares classes in a well-to-do suburb with those in the central city, the latter will probably be greater in size but lower in academic achievement—i.e., an indirect relationship between size and performance. But if one compares urban and rural schools, the latter will probably have *smaller* classes and lower achievement—i.e., a direct relationship between size and performance. In other words, size may well be a causal factor, but it can only be understood when considered simultaneously with other factors.

Given a class of a particular size, it may be organized in a number of different ways, and indeed it seems that much of the past decade's "revolution in teaching" has consisted of manipulating the patterns of student groupings in the classroom. This manipulating may be of two general types. One type structures the class on the basis of the *teaching method* (thus the organization of the room and relationships between student and teacher and between students are clearly different for a lecture, a general class discussion, small team buzz sessions, and individual projects or programmed instruction). The other type structures the class on the basis of certain *characteristics of the students* (thus class groups may or may not be differentiated on the basis of students' abilities, achievement, or interests in certain subjects).

There have been literally thousands of

papers and dissertations comparing one teaching method, or one version of one method, with another. As Wallen and Travers see it, the results tend to be consistent in one respect—"the slight differences found usually favor whatever is designated as the 'experimental' method" (Wallen and Travers, 1963, p. 481). That the relative effectiveness of different methods for specified objectives is simply not known is evidenced by the establishment by the U.S. Office of Education of a research institute at the University of Wisconsin with the five-year assignment of "examining reports dealing with teaching methods and ways to make learning easier for students of all ages" (New York Times, January 13, 1965). Several researchers have made more modest efforts to draw some conclusions about method, and I shall mention a few:

—re: the lecture vs. discussion methods. The lecture is characterized by a high degree of passivity and a low degree of interstudent communication relative to discussions. The lecture seems to be the most effective method for pure transmission of information; the discussion is more conducive to critical examination of ideas, changes in attitudes, and retaining of information and ideas (McKeachie, 1962, pp. 320–27; Bloom, 1963, 425–26);

—re: various methods of lecturing. Research in communications and diffusion suggests that it is important to connect the lecture topic to things that are meaningful and important to the "audience," to present value-oriented material in such a way that it does not seem too dissonant with the students' own beliefs, to draw enough but not too much conclusion for the students, and to make some appeal to their emotions as well as to their intellects (Hovland et al., 1953);

—re: automated teaching devices. The general finding is that TV, films, and other methods in which the student is lectured at or interacts with some kind of non-human device do not seem to do any *worse* than most teachers. This does not seem particularly exciting unless one considers our present teacher shortages and increasing school enrollments, and the possibility of producing such materials inexpensively (McKeachie, 1962, pp. 342–51; Lumsdaine, 1963, 583–682);

—giving students a greater degree of responsibility and autonomy vis-à-vis school "authorities" may produce a high level of achievement and intellectual interest in some students. The extreme of student autonomy is exemplified by Summerhill, based upon the principle that if all adult controls are removed, children will direct their energies to working at the things that truly interest them and to setting up their own organization rather than to resisting adult efforts to coerce them into learning and behaving in certain ways. A less extreme and highly successful use of student responsibility is the Penn State Pyramid Plan, in which much class work is carried on in small groups of six freshmen, six sophomores, two juniors who are assistant leaders, and a senior group leader who has been trained by a faculty member. From data collected from "pyramid" and control classes in psychology, it was concluded students in the former tested higher on "knowledge of the field of psychology, scientific thinking, use of the library for scholarly reading, intellectual orientation, and resourcefulness in problem solving," and more of this group continued as psychology majors (McKeachie, 1962, p. 333).

Before turning from the problem of teaching methods, some comment on tests or examinations seems pertinent, because examinations themselves may be perceived as teaching techniques and because they seem to affect what and how students learn independently of the other techniques a teacher uses. Research evidence indicates that not only do examinations have a built-in motivating mechanism (in that they are so closely tied to the academic reward structure) but that the *type* of exam—or more precisely the *anticipation* of certain types of exam—can shape motivation by promoting certain study patterns and discouraging others. Bloom (1963) reviews three empirical studies in which the amount of memorization, re-reading of assignments, and efforts to remember facts vs. efforts to apply ideas were related to the nature of the examination the student expected. In all cases, students preparing for objective tests (true-false, multiple choice, sentence completion) focused upon small details and the exact wording of textbook materials, with a relatively high amount of memorizing; while students preparing for essay tests were more likely to try to organize material to obtain a general picture, and were also more likely to formulate personal opinions about it. The studies do not say anything about actual test results, not does there seem to be any research on the types of students who respond differently to different types of examinations or to the stimulus of testing generally.

In recent years there has been a good deal of interest in patterns of classroom organization, and currently fashionable is the notion of "homogeneous group" (probably at least partly as a result of our growing sophistication in measuring children's abilities and interests). An example of homogeneous grouping carried to its logical extreme on the whole-school level is the ungraded school, in which a student works on each subject with other students similar to him in achievement in that subject but not necessarily similar to him in chronological age. On a given day, he may meet with several different groups—and may do some individual work, with some kind of programmed learning materials—at several different locations in the school.

The present reports on "grouping" tend to be descriptive rather than experimental (partly a function of the relative newness of the topic), with little specification of the learning objectives for which particular groupings are designed. The only conclusion that seems justified at this point is that no one type of class organization is clearly better than other types, at least not for all kinds of learning (for a brief description of some of these reports, cf. McKeachie, 1962, pp. 337–38; Russell and Fea, 1963, 908–14).

Another area of sociological investigation which suggests structural variables related to classroom achievement is sociometry. The relationship between an individual student's sociometric status and his academic achievement will be discussed in a later section on peer group influences, but the findings that seem relevant here have to do with the sociometric structure of the class as a group.[1]

The typical postulate of sociometry enthusiasts is somewhat as follows (cf. Gronlund, 1959, Chapter 7);

(a)	(b)	(c)
"good" sociometric structure (includes high rate of interpersonal contact within group; no sharp cleavages; no isolates; good leaders) $\longrightarrow$	Satisfying intragroup group relations $\longrightarrow$	1) high individual motivation and achievement; 2) high level of group performance

Gronlund and others do not specify exactly what the "good sociometric structure" is, but one assumes that it has the characteristics listed under (a) above, since these are the kinds of things that tend to be discussed in connection with sociograms and matrices.

The trouble with this formulation is that any empirical evidence that can be brought to bear on it—here I shall draw upon findings from the field of industrial sociology on the factors contributing to worker productivity—indicate that it is not true. More specifically, the studies of factory work groups suggest that while factor (a) does usually lead to factor (b), factor (c) does not necessarily follow. In the Hawthorne studies, the girls in the Relay Assembly Room set a high productivity norm, the men in the Bank Wiring Room a low one. Both groups had the characteristics of "good" sociometric structure. Apparently cohesive groups do provide satisfying environments in which to work, but they do not guarantee a high level of achievement. Seashore concludes that it is dangerous to assume that a cohesive group will be a productive one because "cohesive groups are effective in maintaining group standards, but may set either high or low standards of productivity. Since cohesive groups feel less threatened by management than less cohesive groups, it may be difficult to change their standards" (Seashore, 1954). Applied to the classroom, the implication is that a sociometrically integrated class will assure a high level of academic productivity *if* this group sets a standard of high productivity. Otherwise the good group relations are of no value—and may work against the goals of the school if the group is unified in its non-acceptance of achievement values.

The work of Leavitt and his followers suggest that the amount and accuracy of class group work may depend in part upon the spatial relations in the class as they affect *communication*. Experimenting with different physical arrangements of

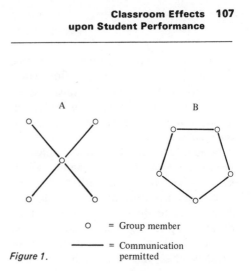

A   B

o = Group member

———— = Communication permitted

Figure 1.

five-man groups (see accompanying figures), Leavitt found that on the *group* level, groups arranged to afford a high degree of centrality (e.g., Figure 1A) tended to organize quickly and to solve "discovery" types of problems with relatively few errors, although the total amount of group activity and over-all group satisfaction were not necessarily high. Leavitt attributed this to the position of the leader, which served as a kind of central office for receiving, organizing and dispatching messages. When centrality was more evenly distributed (e.g., Figure 1B), there was more activity and over-all satisfaction, but lower productivity.

On the *individual* level, both productivity and satisfaction tended to be directly related to centrality of position— the more central one's position in the communication network the more one contributed to the group task and the more satisfaction one felt.

The effect of spatial arrangement upon communication and participation was also explored in Strodtbeck's studies of twelve-man jury sessions (Strodtbeck and Hook, 1961), in which it was found that members' positions around a large table affected who communicated with whom and who assumed group leadership.

Thus it would seem that the teacher

could control classroom output to some degree simply by manipulating communication opportunities, quite apart from individual differences in leadership capacity and other personality factors of the students.

Besides structural characteristics, a group such as a class has certain qualities *as a group* which can perhaps best be described as atmosphere or climate. These have to do with the general tone of the group setting. The original interest in this kind of variable grew out of findings that the most popular, best adjusted children tended to be the best classroom achievers, which led to speculation that a classroom atmosphere conducive to good group adjustment would lead to a high level of class achievement. The rest of this section will explore whether this kind of deduction of a group level phenomenon from an individual level finding is justified.

Undoubtedly the most famous and influential experiments on group atmosphere are the studies begun in the late 1930's by Lewin, Lippitt and associates, in which democratic, authoritarian, and laissez-faire climates were artificially created in children's groups. The discussions of these experiments usually emphasize the higher levels of satisfaction and "group-mindedness" and the lower levels of aggression and hostility in the democratic groups (Lewin, Lippitt, and White, 1939; White and Lippitt, 1962). Less often reported is the finding that the quantity of work produced (in these experiments soap carving, model making and other craft activities) was greater in the autocratic setting, although activity in this setting seems to require the presence of the leader—when the autocratic type of leader left the room, e.g., output tended to drop off. It is also an interesting, and little reported, finding that productivity in the laissez-faire setting, in which there was little formal structure and members were free to do as they pleased, tended to go *up* in the absence of the leader. The authors attributed this to an observed tendency for one of the boys to assume the leadership role when the adult leader was not present. Thus students may be happier and feel more positive toward the teacher and other members of the group in a setting in which the adult acts simply as one of the group and in which decisions are made via group discussion, but they may produce more when the leader or teacher tells them what to do and how to do it. On the other hand, certain learning tasks may be handled effectively by giving students very little direction, forcing them to organize the situation themselves.

Rather similar implications can be drawn from Deutsch's work on the effects of artificially created climates characterized as cooperative or competitive (Deutsch, 1949). Students in an introductory psychology course at M.I.T. were divided into two kinds of groups, each given an assignment involving mental puzzles and discussion and reports on some human relations case studies. In the cooperative groups, evaluation and grading was done by *group*, each member of a given group receiving the same grade and all members of the best group being excused from a term paper. In the competitive groups, individual members of a given group were ranked on their individual contributions, grading was on a curve *within* groups, and the highest ranking individual in each group was excused from the paper. As in the Lewin studies, the cooperative groups showed consistently higher coordination of effort, attentiveness and friendliness toward each other, and a more favorable evaluation of the group and its products. And as in the Lewin studies, there was no evidence of superior output—in this case learning of the content of the course. There was also no greater interest or involvement in the course subject matter.

The nature of the effects of competition

vs. cooperation are further explored and a kind of contextual effect suggested by Blau's study of public employment agency groups (Blau, 1954). Here the researcher did not create group atmospheres but compared work units characterized by cooperative work norms (emphasis upon a "professional" code, with a norm of service to clients rather than simply processing a large number of cases) with those in which members competed against each other for high productivity records, even to the extent of using "illegal" tactics such as hiding case records from each other. Blau found that while the cooperative groups were more productive *as groups* (mean number of cases processed and placements made), the highest levels of *individual* productivity were found in competitive groups.

Studies in the field of industrial sociology reinforce the lack of relationship between group morale and productivity. Reviewing some of his own and other researchers' studies of the electrical industry, Kahn (1956) finds that some show direct, some inverse, and some no relationship, and he concludes that group atmosphere measures are less powerful predictors than measures of individual goals and interests. His formulation is that a worker will have a high rate of production when he perceives high productivity as leading to or having some direct connection with his own individual interests, providing there are no serious barriers. Translated into educational terms, this would say that a student "produces" academically when he sees that it is in his own interest to do so (e.g., when getting good grades is highly rewarded by his peers, or when he is committed to getting into college or some vocational field that requires a good school record), provided that there are no obstacles that seem impassable (e.g., having low ability, or parents with low income).

Recent experimental studies testing the Lewinian thesis indicate that not only is there not likely to be more measurable output in democratic or student-centered classes, but that many students feel dissatisfied or anxious in this kind of setting. From an analysis of thirty-four such studies, Stern (1963) found that of the eighteen in which student reaction was measured in some way, nine were predominantly favorable, four unfavorable, and five had mixed reactions. Only two of the studies showed greater gains in cognitive knowledge of the subject matter in the democratic classes, as compared to five in which the cognitive gain was significantly less; in the rest of the studies there was no significant difference between the two types of classes (Stern, 1963, p. 427, Table 2). Some additional research based on the California F Scale indicated that the type of student with high authoritarian needs is especially uncomfortable in the student-centered class (Stern, 1962, pp. 692–97).

In conclusion, classroom atmosphere —at least as presently measured—does not seem to be related to student performance in any consistent fashion. One possibility is that the concept and components of atmosphere, like those of "teacher efficiency," have not yet been adequately formulated. Another possibility is that this dimension may be related to performance, but in a more complex way than current studies suggest —e.g., it may be related in certain contexts and not others, or as one of a cluster of factors which have not yet been specified.

Note

[1] This individual vs. group-level distinction is not always maintained in the research studies. E.g., Buswell, 1953, claims to be testing the null hypothesis that "there is no relationship between the social structure of a classroom and the achievement in some of the basic elementary school subjects of the members of the class," but her research

design pulls individual students from several different classes in eight different schools and compares all the high status individuals (from all schools) with all the low status individuals.

References

Allport, Floyd H. "The Influence of the Group upon Association and Thought." *Journal of Experimental Psychology*, 3 (1920), 159–82.

Anderson, K. E. "A Frontal Attack on the Basic Problem in Evaluation: The Achievement of the Objectives of Instruction in Specific Areas." *Journal of Experimental Education*, 18 (1950), 163–74.

Bales, R. F. and E. F. Borgatta. "Size of Group as a Factor in the Interaction Profile." In *Small Groups*, P. Hare, E. F. Borgatta, and R. F. Bales. New York: Knopf, 1955, 396–413.

Blau, Peter. "Cooperation and Competition in a Bureaucracy." *American Journal of Sociology*, 60 (1954).

Bloom, Benjamin S. "Testing Cognitive Ability and Achievement." In *Handbook of Research on Teaching*, ed. N. L. Gage. Chicago: Rand McNally, 1963, 379–97.

Buswell, M. M. "The Relationship between the Social Structure of the Classroom and the Academic Success of the Pupils." *Journal of Experimental Education*, 22 (1954), 37–52.

Campbell, Donald T. and Julian C. Stanley. "Experimental and Quasi-Experimental Designs for Research on Teaching." In *Handbook of Research on Teaching*, ed. N. L. Gage. Chicago: Rand McNally, 1963, 171–246.

Cogan, M. L. "The Behavior of Teachers and the Productive Behavior of Their Pupils." *Journal of Experimental Education*, 27 (1958), 89–105 and 107–24.

Deutsch, Morton. "The Effects of Cooperation and Competition upon Group Process." *Human Relations*, 2 (1949), 129–52 and 199–231.

Gronlund, Norman E. *Sociometry in the Classroom*. New York: Harper, 1959.

Hoil, L. M., M. Powell, and I. Feifer. *Characteristics of Teacher Behavior and Competency Related to the Achievement of Different Kinds of Children in Several Elementary Grades*. New York: Office of Testing and Research, Brooklyn College, 1960 (mimeographed).

Hovland, C. I., I. L. Janis, and H. H. Kelley. *Communication and Persuasion*. New Haven: Yale University Press, 1953.

Kahn, Robert L. "The Prediction of Productivity." *Journal of Social Issues*, 12 (1956), 41–49.

Leavitt, Harold J. "Some Effects of Certain Communication Patterns on Group Performance." *Journal of Abnormal and Social Psychology*, 46 (1951), 38–50.

Lewin, K., R. Lipitt, and R. K. White. "Patterns of Aggressive Behavior in Experimentally Created 'Social Climates.'" *Journal of Social Psychology*, 10 (1939), 271–99.

Lorge, I., D. Fox, J. Davitz, and M. Brehner. "A Survey of Studies Contrasting the Quality of Group Performance and Individual Performance." *Psycho Bulletin*, 55 (1958), 337–72.

Lumsdaine, A. A. "Instruments and Media of Instruction." In *Handbook of Research on Teaching*, ed. N. L. Gage. Chicago: Rand McNally, 1963, 583–682.

McKeachie, W. J. "Procedures and Techniques of Teaching: A Survey of Experimental Studies." In *The American College*, ed. N. Sanford. New York: Wiley, 1962, 312–64.

———. "Research on Teaching at the College and University Level." In *Handbook of Research on Teaching*, ed. N. L. Gage. Chicago: Rand McNally, 1963, 1118–72.

Medley, Donald and Harold E. Mitzel. "Measuring Classroom Behavior by Systematic Observation." In *Handbook of Research on Teaching*, ed. N. L. Gage. Chicago: Rand McNally, 1963, 247–328.

Moise, Edwin. "The New Mathematics Program." In *Revolution in Teaching*, ed. A. de Grazia and D. A. Sohn. New York: Bantam Books, 1964, 171–87.

Neil, A. S. *Summerhill*. New York: Hart, 1961.

Newcomb, Theodore M. "Student Peer-Group Influence." In *The American College*, ed. N. Sanford. New York: Wiley, 1962, 469–88.

Ojemann, R. H. and F. R. Wilkinson. "The Effect on Pupil Growth of an Increase in Teachers' Understanding of Pupil Behavior." *Journal of Experimental Education*, 8 (1939), 143–47.

Perlmutter, H. V. and G. de Montmollin. "Group Learnings of Nonsense Syllables." *Journal of Experimental Psychology*, 44 (1952), 360–68.

Riley, J. W., B. F. Ryan and M. Lifshitz. *The Student Looks at His Teacher*. New Brunswick: Rutgers University Press, 1950.

Russell, D. H. and H. R. Fea. "Research on Teaching Reading." In *Handbook of Research on Teaching*, ed. N. L. Gage. Chicago: Rand McNally, 1963, 865–928.

Seashore, S. E. *Group Cohesiveness in the Industrial Group*. University of Michigan Survey Research Center, Pub. No. 14, 1954.

Shaw, M. E. "A Comparison of Individuals and Small Groups in the Rational Solution of Complex Problems." *American Journal of Psychology*, 54 (1932) 491–504.

Stern, George C. "Environments for Learning." In *The American College*, ed. N. Sanford. New York: Wiley, 1962, 690–730.

Strodtbeck, F. and S. Hook. "The Social Dimensions of a Twelve-Man Jury Table." *Sociometry*, 24 (1961), 397–415.

Taylor, D. W. and W. L. Faust. "Twenty Questions: Efficiency in Problem Solving as a Function of Size of Group." In *Small Groups*, ed. P. Hare, E. F. Borgatta, and R. F. Bales. New York: Knopf, 1955, 206–20.

Thorndike, R. L. "On What Type of Task Will a Group Do Well?" *Journal of Abnormal and Social Psychology*, 33 (1938), 409–13.

Wallen, Norman and Robert Travers. "Analysis and Investigation of Teaching Methods." In *Handbook of Research on Teaching*, ed. N. L. Gage. Chicago: Rand McNally, 1963, 448–505.

Watson, F. G. "Research on Teaching Science." In *Handbook of Research on Teaching*, ed. N. L. Gage. Chicago: Rand McNally, 1963, 1031–59.

White, Ralph and Ronald Lippitt. "Leader Behavior and Member Reaction in Three 'Social Climates.'" In *Group Dynamics*, ed. D. Cartwright and A. Zander. Evanston, Ill.: Row, Peterson, 1962, 527–53.

Withall, John and W. W. Lewis. "Social Interaction in the Classroom." In *Handbook of Research on Teaching*, ed. N. L. Gage. Chicago: Rand McNally, 1963, 683–714.

Educational Climates of High Schools: Their Effects and Sources

Edward L. McDill, Leo C. Rigsby, and Edmund D. Meyers, Jr.

This work was supported by the Office of Education, U.S. Department of Health, Education, and Welfare, Contract OE-3-10-080, and The Center for the Study of Social Organization of Schools and the Learning Process, Johns Hopkins University. The authors are indebted to James Fennessey for helpful suggestions on an earlier version of the paper. However, the authors are solely responsible for any shortcomings of the paper in its present form.

Reprinted from the American Journal of Sociology, 74 *(1969), pp. 567–68, by permission of the authors and the publisher, The University of Chicago Press.*

The Problem

IN A RECENT article, Benjamin Bloom[1] has contended that there are few schools in the United States which actually constitute consistent and powerful educational environments. Research evidence by social scientists on the impact of differing contexts, climates, or environments of both high schools and colleges supports such a position. The findings from a number of studies[2] in this area in the last two decades indicate that those school environments in which intellectualism and academic achievement are positively valued and stressed by teachers and students have a positive but only modest impact on the cognitive development of students. Moreover, in the high school studies there has been a tendency to infer the normative climate of schools from the "dominant social class character" of the student body (i.e., the average socioeconomic composition). In other words, there is a conspicuous lack of direct measures for the characteristics of the school environment and their influence on the academic achievement, values, and aspirations of students. As Bloom[3] has noted, steps should be taken to assess school environment more directly in order that policy decisions which will promote the desired academic growth in students may be made.

This paper reports the results of a large-scale study relevant to this concern. More specifically, it focuses on three interrelated problems: (1) the identification of a number of dimensions of educational and social climates of high schools; (2) the assessment of the contextual effects of these environmental dimensions on the academic performance and college plans of students;[4] (3) the investigation of sources of climate effects on the achievement and college plans of students by controlling formal organizational properties of the school and community level variables.

After presenting the results relevant to the above three problems, a discussion will be presented of possible ways of modifying the influence of those factors which seem to be the sources of the effects of school climate and which thereby strengthen the impact of the school environment on the academic growth of students.

Method[5]

Twenty public, coeducational high schools selected in a three-stage, nonrandom manner from seven geographical areas and eight states comprise the sample.[6] This design resulted in a sample of institutions which exhibit marked heterogeneity with respect to demographic, socioeconomic, and community characteristics, and also considerable variation in academic achievement (as measured by one of the standardized achievement tests used in Project Talent) and in rates of college attendance.

Data were collected in 1964 and 1965 from students, teachers, and principals of the twenty schools, using the following instruments.

1. Self-administered questionnaires to 20,345 students in which the subjects were treated as both respondents and observer-informants about the school environment.

2. A self-administered questionnaire completed by 1,029 faculty members in the twenty institutions. In completing the questionnaire, the teacher, just like the student, was acting as both respondent and observer-informant.

3. Principal's questionnaire. Each of the twenty principals completed a questionnaire, providing data on a number of social, demographic, and academic characteristics of the school.

4. Two academic tests from Project Talent administered to the student bodies of the twenty schools. There were (a) Aptitude for Abstract Reasoning (AR), a fifteen-item, multiple-choice test designed to measure ability to determine the relationship among patterns of diagrams. Scores of the AR test provide one indication of a student's intellectual potential which is relatively independent of curriculum content, since formal instruction is not generally provided on this specific reasoning task at any grade level.[7] (b) Achievement in Mathematics (MATH), a twenty-four-item multiple-choice test constructed to provide an indicator of achievement through the ninth-grade level (other than arithmetic computation and reasoning).[8]

The response rates of subjects to each of the instruments were high. Consequently, bias due to non-response cannot have an appreciable effect on the validity of the findings presented below.[9]

Measures of School Climate. The measures of the academic and social

climate of the schools were obtained using a modified version of Selvin and Hagstrom's procedure[10] for classifying formal groups in terms of a large number of variables so that contextual effects on the variation in behavior of members can be assessed. In the present research, thirty-nine aggregative characteristics[11] of the schools based on data from both student and teacher questionnaires were factor analyzed using the principal component solution, and then orgthogonally rotated to simple structure using the varimax method.

Using the eigenvalue criterion, six interpretable factors were extracted, which summarize with a relatively high degree of precision (82 per cent of the total variance) the information contained in the thirty-nine variables. Estimates of factor scores were computed for the schools on each factor, and these estimates were then used to rank the schools for the contextual analysis.

The measures of these various components are considered one of the most important accomplishments of the study since they represent comprehensive, stable, and *direct* indicators of the normative influence of school environment. A number of earlier studies in this area have inferred the level of school climate from indirect indicators such as the average socioeconomic composition of the student body or of the neighborhood in which the school is located—indicators whose overall adequacy has recently been questioned.[12]

Limitations of space do not permit a detailed description of the dimensions of school environment. However, this information is readily available to interested readers.[13] The six dimensions were interpreted and labeled using those variables which have statistically significant loadings ($.05 > p$) on the corresponding rotated factors:

Factor I—academic emulation

Factor II—student perception of intellectualism-estheticism

Factor III—cohesive and egalitarian estheticism

Factor IV—scientism

Factor V—humanistic excellence

Factor VI—academically oriented student status system

Measures of Individual Level Variables.
The AR test is employed as the measure of mental aptitude. Measures of sex, grade in school, and family socioeconomic status (SES) were obtained from single items in the student questionnaires. The measure of family SES is provided by information on father's education.

Students' academic orientations or values are measured by a scale derived from six items contained in the student questionnaire, each tapping a different component within the broad realm of intellectualism-achievement; for example, "learning as much as possible," the importance of "good grades," the degree of satisfaction received from "working hard on studies," and the degree of admiration the subject has for "bright students." The responses to each item were dichotomized, and each respondent was assigned a score based on the number he answered in the positive direction. The reliability estimate of .59 obtained from the KR-20 formula indicates that the scale has an acceptable level of internal consistency.

The measure of one of the two dependent attributes, students' plans regarding college attendance, is inferred from a single item in the student questionnaire. Students' scores on the twenty-four-item MATH test serve as the measure of academic achievement.

The Statistical Technique and Categorization of Variables. To minimize the problem of obtaining spurious climate effects, which is a matter of special concern in contextual analysis, a statistical procedure for use with attribute data was employed using as many categories as possible on the individual level attributes.[15] In this multiple-regression technique, the "effect parameter" for each explanatory attribute may be viewed as closely analogous to an unstandardized regression coefficient. In particular, when the dependent variable is dichotomous (as here), this parameter can be operationally interpreted as follows: It gives the change in probability of being "high" on the dependent attribute, given that the person changes from one level to the next higher level on the independent attribute under consideration, but that his level on all other attributes stays unchanged.

Results

EFFECTS OF SCHOOL CLIMATE AND PERSONAL CHARACTERISTICS ON MATH ACHIEVEMENT AND COLLEGE PLANS

As noted above, contextual analysis requires that the effects of the environment on the dependent attributes be demonstrated while relevant personnel attributes are controlled, since any purported effects of the group level attributes could be attributable to systematic uncontrolled differences in the individual characteristics among the different groups. This is the primary task of this section of the analysis. A second and related task is to assess the relative effects of each of the individual characteristics.

Each row in Table 1 gives the estimated effect parameters for a model in which one of the climate dimensions and three individual level attributes are used as explanatory variables in an attempt to account for variation in MATH achievement. Table 2 gives corresponding results using college plans as the dependent attribute.[16] Thus, in each row of Tables

1 and 2 the same three individual level characteristics are being statistically controlled.

The results for the two dependent attributes will be discussed separately. The most important finding in Table 1 is that, when three relevant individual level attributes are held constant, each of the six climate dimensions has a significant positive effect on MATH achievement. These effects are in the direction which would be expected, given the content of the factors. The effects of dimension I are the strongest of the six dimensions, which is probably attributable to its being the most comprehensive and reliable measure of school environment. In fact, its effect is almost as strong as that of father's education and indicates that the more emphasis on academic performance, competitiveness, and intellectualism by both faculty and students, the more likely students are to achieve "high." The effect of the second dimension indicates that the more the school atmosphere encourages an intrinsic value of knowledge and the more teachers are emotion-

Table 1—Independent Effects of Each of Six Climate Dimensions of Schools and of Three Personal Attributes on MATH Achievement

Climate Dimensions	Weighted Effects of Climate Dimensions	Weighted Effects of Father's Education	Weighted Effects of Student's Academic Values	Weighted Effects of Student's Ability
I. Academic emulation	.110	.119	.137	.299
II. Intellectualism-estheticism	.072	.130	.136	.305
III. Cohesive and egalitarian estheticism	.048	.132	.135	.307
IV. Scientism	.033	.138	.136	.309
V. Humanistic excellence	.042	.133	.136	.308
VI. Academically oriented status system	.046	.134	.136	.308

NOTE: All effect estimates are standardized to dichotomous form and are significant at the .01 level.

Table 2—Independent Effects of Each of Six Climate Dimensions of Schools and of Three Personal Attributes on College Plans

Climate Dimensions	Weighted Effects of Climate Dimensions	Weighted Effects of Father's Education	Weighted Effects of Student's Academic Values	Weighted Effects of Student's Ability
I. Academic emulation	.112	.200	.190	.151
II. Intellectualism-estheticism	.071	.212	.188	.156
III. Cohesive and egalitarian estheticism	.031	.219	.190	.159
IV. Scientism	.002 *	.225	.190	.160
V. Humanistic excellence	.025	.219	.190	.159
VI. Academically oriented status system	.046	.216	.188	.157

NOTE: All effect estimates are standardized to dichotomous form. Unless otherwise noted, effect estimates are significant at the .01 level.
* Not significant at the .05 level.

ally supportive of students, the more likely students are to achieve on the MATH test. Each of the four remaining climate components has less than half the explanatory power for academic performance than does the first. The effect of the third dimension indicates that the greater the degree of social cohesion, democratic values, and intellectual standards for recognition among students, the higher the achievement level of individual students. The small effect parameter for Factor IV indicates a tendency for those schools exerting a strong press toward scientism to have a higher proportion of their students with high MATH achievement than those institutions which do not encourage excellence in this broad substantive area. Likewise, the effects of the fifth construct reveal that the greater the value placed on the humanities by teachers and students and the greater their emphasis on achievement in general, and on an intrinsic value of knowledge, the greater the proportion of students with achievement in a specific substantive area. Finally, the small positive effects of Factor VI suggest that the more the student social system of the school rewards intellectualism and achievement, the greater the tendency for students to achieve. This result is consistent with the widely accepted hypothesis among social scientists that adolescent subcultures of high schools have an impact on the values, aspirations, and achievement of individual students.[17]

Each of the three individual attributes in Table 1 has a sizable effect on achievement in the expected direction, with ability having by far the greatest magnitude. The high degree of association between ability and performance is consistent with the findings of numerous studies which document the considerable predictive power of intellective factors for performance.[18]

The substantial effect of father's education is certainly not unexpected, since family SES is the social background factor which has been most consistently demonstrated to be related to academic performance.

The third personal attribute in the table, students' academic values, also has an appreciable independent influence on their achievement level. This attribute may be viewed properly as an indicator of students' commitment to learning and achievement, and its effect suggests the importance of such a personal value system to the academic development of youth who are in constant demand as the educational and scientific entrepreneurs of modern society.

The results of Table 2 reveal that, in general, the effects of the climate dimensions on college plans are not appreciably different from those on achievement. The single exception is for Factor IV, scientism, which has a small positive effect on MATH but no effect on college plans. One possible explanation for this lack of effect is that the items used in the faculty and student "presses" for scientism, which are the variables with the highest loadings on Factor IV, are inadequate measures of the degree of scientific emphasis in the schools.[19] However, this does not appear to be a completely satisfactory explanation, since Factor IV has a small positive effect on MATH, as shown in Table 1. This result suggests an alternative explanation: The degree of scientific ferment in the high school, although related to MATH performance, is not directly related to college plans. In other words, for the kind of scientific enthusiasm that may prevail in a high school, achievement in mathematics is useful, but college plans are irrelevant. It is not science as a career, but science in the here and now that is being tapped. Two pieces of evidence to support this interpretation are offered. First, the evidence in the study shows that the great majority of students with college plans do not mention "understanding science" as a primary purpose in attending college. In fact, out of a diversified list of ten purposes it ranks next to lowest in importance. Second, only 12 per cent of the students with college intentions indicated they planned to major in science in college.

Turning to the independent effects of the three personal attributes on college plans as shown in Table 2, it can be seen that each has a considerable effect on students' intentions, with father's education having more impact than any of the other attributes. Especially noteworthy is the point that, on the average, father's education has an effect parameter approximately .05 larger than that for student ability. Michael,[20] in his analysis of a nationally representative sample of seniors in 500 public high schools reports similar results; that is, students' socio-economic background exerted a slightly greater influence on their college plans than did ability. Both of these findings seem consistent with the conclusion reached by Sibley[21] twenty-five years ago that the intelligence of the student was more important than family SES in determining whether he would finish high school, but the opposite was true regarding the likelihood of attending college. The fact that the effect parameters for father's education and for students' academic values are larger for college plans than for MATH can be best explained in terms of the qualitative difference between the two dependent

attributes. College plans and aspirations belong to a class of social-psychological phenomena which are highly susceptible to the constraints of significant others in the immediate interpersonal-environment (e.g., parental pressures, of which father's education is an indicator) and to personal motivation and values (as measured by the respondent's academic values). Although the pressures of significant others and personal motivation can enhance students' achievement, such effects are limited simply because there is an upper bound to the ability of the student. Stated differently, it is a truism that the student cannot achieve higher on a standardized test than his ability level permits.

Before turning to a discussion of the sources of school climate effects on achievement and college plans of students, it is important to return to a critical problem in all contextual analyses: the adequacy of the controls for the individual attributes of the respondents. With respect to the dependent attributes under consideration here, there could be concern with the adequacy of father's education as a measure of family background. Consequently, two additional measures of family SES (father's occupation and mother's education) are introduced into the analysis.[22] Table 3 presents the effects of the most important measure of school climate, Factor I, on the two dependent attributes with father's educa-

Table 3—Independent Effects of One Climate Dimension and Five Individual Level Attributes on MATH Achievement and College Plans

Dependent Attribute	Weighted Effects of Factor I	Weighted Effects of Father's Education	Weighted Effects of Mother's Education	Weighted Effects of Father's Occupation	Weighted Effects of Student's Academic Values	Weighted Effects of Student's Ability
MATH achievement	.097	.050	.062	.061	.139	.290
College plans	.091	.081	.114	.084	.179	.139

NOTE: All effect estimates are standardized to dichotomous form and are significant at the .01 level.

tion, mother's education, father's occupation, student's academic values, and ability simultaneously controlled. Thus, the first row of Table 3 is comparable to the first row of Table 1, and the second row of Table 3 is comparable to the first row of Table 2. Holding constant the two additional measures of family background reduces only a negligible amount the effects of the climate dimension on the two dependent attributes. This finding offers further support for the climate effects reported in Tables 1 and 2. In fact, the only noteworthy impact made by the simultaneous introduction of mother's education and father's occupation on the results of Tables 1 and 2 is to reduce by more than 50 per cent the independent effects of father's education on both MATH achievement and college plans. These reductions in the effect parameters reflect the high correlations among father's education, mother's education, and father's occupation.

SOURCES OF CLIMATE EFFECTS ON
THE DEPENDENT ATTRIBUTES

A number of educational researchers and practitioners have asserted that characteristics of the community environment—primarily socioeconomic and "cultural" resources—are important determinants of academic "output." Community factors such as amount of financial support for education and presence of intellectual facilities such as libraries and museums have been viewed as outside-school sources of variation in student achievement and educational aspirations. However, as noted by Boocock, the evidence that such factors have important educational consequences is far from conclusive.[23] Given the lack of consistency of findings in this area, it is especially important to assess the importance of those community characteristics

for which measures are available in the present study.

A second set of factors which will be introduced as potential sources of climate effects are formal organizational properties of the school. These are school characteristics which, for the most part, were included in the original Project Talent survey—characteristics which reflect a few of the many curriculum innovations and organizational approaches being explored in the last two decades. The single most comprehensive piece of research dealing with the relationship of curriculum and school facilities measures to student achievement is the U.S. Office of Education's survey, *Equality of Educational Opportunity*,[24] often referred to as the Coleman report. Among the numerous important findings produced in the highly provocative and controversial work,[25] one is especially relevant to the present discussion: Most of the variation between students' performance on a standardized test of verbal achievement was not explained by school characteristics and resources, such as per-pupil expenditures, number of books in the library, and student-teacher ratio. That is, despite the great diversity of school facilities, curricula, and resources, the variation in achievement among pupils in the same school was roughly four times as large as the variation among schools.[26] However, in a review article, Bowles and Levin[27] seriously question the validity of these results in the Coleman report on a number of grounds. Data are available in the present research on a number of school resources and curricular variables similar to those which were used in the Coleman report. Thus, it should be possible to present additional evidence on the debate concerning the importance of school facilities and resources on student output.

a) *Factors in the Community as Potential Sources of Climate Effects.* Turning first to community characteristics as potential sources of climate effects, a number of "cultural" facilities can be summarily dismissed because they do not vary across communities. In every school, students had access to a public community library; in fifteen of the twenty, "concerts" were readily available to them, and the same holds true for "community theater" in sixteen of the twenty schools. Although the communities showed sufficient heterogeneity on four other cultural resources to justify consideration as potential sources of school environment effects—museum, art gallery, opera, and professional stage[28]—investigation of these facilities failed to produce any consistent relationships with the climate measures and/or the dependent attributes. Thus we conclude that in the present sample the presence or accessibility of a number of community cultural facilities has no impact on the relationship of the educational climates of schools to students' academic performance and therefore cannot be defended as sources of school environmental effects.[29]

However, one community level factor which does appear to function as a source of climate effects is the extent of involvement and interest by parents in school policies and in their children's academic performance. This variable is labeled "Parental Involvement in the High School" (P.I.H.S.), and consists of a summated binary rating scale constructed from three items in the teacher questionnaire.[30] This attribute is introduced as an indicator of the extent to which norms and values regarding academic excellence in the school are shared by the parents and thus the community or neighborhood served by the school. The underlying proposition is that the more prevalent these norms and values are, the more likely the school is to develop an atmosphere which encourages students to higher achievement and educational aspirations. The data of Table 4 lend support to this proposition. School ranks on P.I.H.S. are significantly

and strongly correlated in a positive direction with their ranks on factor scores for each of the six dimensions of school climate.

In introducing P.I.H.S. into the analysis as a potential climate source variable, the schools were ranked according to their median values and then dichotomized at the median of the distribution.

Table 4—Spearman Rank-Order Correlations between P.I.H.S. and Six Climate Dimensions for Twenty Schools

Climate Dimensions	r's with P.I.H.S.
I. Academic emulation	.79**
II. Intellectualism-estheticism	.62**
III. Cohesive and egalitarian estheticism	.78**
IV. Scientism	.68**
V. Humanistic excellence	.76**
VI. Academically oriented status system	.48*

* Significant at the .05 level.
** Significant at the .01 level.

The effects of P.I.H.S. on MATH and college plans—based on data from a representative, 10 per cent subsample of the students in each school[31]—are .194 $(.01 > p)$ and .193 $(.01 > p)$, respectively. Thus, it meets the first criterion as a source of climate effects. The effects of P.I.H.S. on the two dependent attributes for the entire sample, with ability and father's education controlled, are .099 for MATH $(.01 > p)$ and .111 $(.01 > p)$ for college plans. Stated differently, holding constant these two personal attributes reduces the zero-order effects of P.I.H.S. about 50 per cent; however, its impact on each dependent attribute is still significant and substantively meaningful, demonstrating that it meets the second criterion as a climate source variable.

Tables 5 and 6 offer further evidence

Table 5—Independent Effects of Climate Dimensions, P.I.H.S., Ability, and Father's Education on MATH Achievement

Climate Dimensions	Weighted Effects of Climate Dimensions	Weighted Effects of P.I.H.S.	Weighted Effects of Student's Ability	Weighted Effects of Father's Education
I. Academic emulation	*	*	*	*
II. Intellectualism-estheticism	−.006†	.103	.320	.132
III. Cohesive and egalitarian estheticism	.016†	.092	.319	.131
IV. Scientism	.022‡	.093	.320	.130
V. Humanistic excellence	.007†	.095	.319	.132
VI. Academically oriented status system	.000†	.098	.319	.134

NOTE: Results are based on total sample of students, not the 10 per cent subsample. All effect parameters are significant at the .01 level unless otherwise noted.
* The relationship between P.I.H.S. and climate dimension I is sufficiently pronounced that there are no schools *low* on P.I.H.S. and *high* on academic emulation. Consequently, the effects of P.I.H.S. on MATH with academic emulation, ability, and father's education simultaneously controlled cannot be computed. Conversely, the effects of academic emulation on MATH with P.I.H.S., ability, and father's education simultaneously controlled cannot be calculated. (As shown in Table 4, the rank correlation between median school scale scores on P.I.H.S. and factor scores on academic emulation is .79.)
† Not significant at the .05 level.
‡ Significant at the .05 level.

Table 6—Independent Effects of Climate Dimensions, P.I.H.S., Ability, and Father's Education on College Plans

Climate Dimensions	Weighted Effects of Climate Dimensions	Weighted Effects of P.I.H.S.	Weighted Effects of Student's Ability	Weighted Effects of Father's Education
I. Academic emulation	*	*	*	*
II. Intellectualism-estheticism	−.018†	.143	.175	.216
III. Cohesive and egalitarian estheticism	−.011†	.115	.173	.219
IV. Scientism	−.009†	.107	.176	.215
V. Humanistic excellence	−.021‡	.119	.174	.219
VI. Academically oriented status system	−.012†	.110	.174	.217

NOTE: Results are based on total sample of students, not the 10 per cent subsample. All effect parameters are significant at the .01 level unless otherwise noted.
* The relationship between P.I.H.S. and climate dimension I is sufficiently pronounced that there are no schools *low* on P.I.H.S. and *high* on academic emulation. Consequently, the effects of P.I.H.S. on college plans with academic emulation, ability, and father's education simultaneously controlled cannot be computed. Conversely, the effects of academic emulation on college plans with P.I.H.S., ability, and father's education simultaneously controlled cannot be calculated. (As shown in Table 4, the rank correlation between median school scale scores on P.I.H.S. and factor scores on academic emulation is .79.)
† Not significant at the .05 level.
‡ Significant at the .05 level.

that P.I.H.S. is functioning as a source of the climate effects on both dependent attributes. First, the effects of the climate dimensions on both dependent attributes, with ability and father's education controlled, tend to disappear when P.I.H.S. is introduced as an additional control. In fact, none of the climate effects in either of the two tables is statistically significant at the .01 level. On the other hand, the significant effects of P.I.H.S. on MATH and college plans persist with the climate dimensions controlled.[32]

A discussion of the substantive importance of P.I.H.S. as a source variable will be postponed until a number of other potential sources have been considered. However, it should be noted here that these results are consistent with those of a recent large-scale study by Gross et al.[33] on a number of correlates of the "academic productivity" of urban elementary schools. One of the variables most positively correlated with the criterion was the faculty's assessment of the extent of parental interest in the academic performance of their children.

b) Resources and Organizational Properties of Schools As Sources of School Climates. As noted above, one of the most controversial findings of the Coleman report is that economic resources of schools explained only a very small proportion of variance in the verbal achievement of children. Bowles and Levin are highly critical of this finding, arguing that the measurement of variables and the statistical techniques used are "biased in a direction that would dampen the importance of school characteristics."[34] For example, they contend that the measure of per-pupil expenditure used is biased in that it was averaged for an entire school district and therefore did not reflect the variation among schools within a system. They also indicate that their further analysis of data in the Coleman report leads to the implication that another measure of economic resources of schools—teachers' salaries—is

positively related to student achievement. Fortunately, rigorous measures of these two variables are available for each of the twenty schools in the present investigation—average per-pupil expenditure and annual starting salaries for teachers. These data permit the consideration of these two variables as climate sources, which can provide further evidence on this important controversy. It should be emphasized that the twenty schools show a great deal of variation on these two characteristics; per-pupil expenditure ranges from $365 to $1,000 per year, and starting salaries for teachers vary $1,000. Consequently, any failure of these two measures of capital investment to account for variation in climate effects could not be explained in terms of restricted range.

The zero-order effects of these two characteristics on the two dependent attributes for the representative subsample of students are:

Effect of per-pupil expenditure on MATH = $-.008$

Effect of teachers' salaries on MATH = $.008$

Effect of per-pupil expenditure on college plans = $.054$

Effect of teachers' salaries on college plans = $.016$

Both input resources can be eliminated as sources of climate effects since neither is significantly related to the two dependent attributes. Thus, Bowles and Levin's criticisms of the Coleman report notwithstanding, the results for the twenty schools in this sample certainly do *not* contradict Coleman's conclusion that the variance in achievement which is accounted for by a school facilities measure (which included per-pupil expenditure) is of little consequence.[35]

Ten different formal organizational properties of the schools were also examined as possible sources of climate effects. Three facilities measures were dismissed immediately because the schools do not show sufficient variation on them. These were: (1) use of teaching machines as instruction devices;[36] (2) volumes in school library;[37] (3) percentage of students on half-day sessions (i.e., double shifts).[38]

Table 7 lists seven curricular and facilities characteristics on which the schools were sufficiently heterogeneous to permit their consideration as climate sources. Each of these characteristics is based on a single-item indicator in the principal's questionnaire. The zero-order effect parameters for each of these characteristics on both dependent attributes for the 10 per cent sample are also given. (Whenever there is sufficient variation across schools on these characteristics, their effects are based on quartile ranks standardized to dichotomous form.)

Three of the characteristics (average size of math and science classes, average size of classes in non-science courses, and homogeneous grouping of students by ability) are not related at the .05 level to either dependent attribute. (The effects of class size in non-science areas are not in the "expected" direction.) The failure of the two measures of class size to have appreciable predictive power on MATH achievement is highly consistent with Project Talent results,[39] which used average math achievement scores for *schools* as the unit of analysis, and those of the Coleman report,[40] which used verbal achievement scores of *students* as the unit. Bowles and Levin[41] are highly critical of Coleman's conclusion on this point because they feel the measure of pupil-teacher ratio he used, which was obtained by dividing school enrollment by number of teachers, is an inadequate measure of class size, given the fact that unpublished data in the Coleman report *suggest* great heterogeneity in teaching loads within schools. Nevertheless, the results of the Coleman report, Project Talent, and the present investigation are consistent with the general conclusion of numerous studies at both the high school and college levels to the effect that class size shows no clear relationship to learning.[42] Furthermore, at the elemen-

Table 7—Zero-Order Effects of Seven Curricular and Facilities Characteristics of Schools on MATH Achievement and College Plans

INDEPENDENT ATTRIBUTES	DEPENDENT ATTRIBUTES	
	MATH Achievement	College Plans
Size of math and science classes*	−.058†	−.002†
Size of classes in non-science courses*	.023†	.032†
Accelerated curriculum for superior students‡	.065§	.065§
Opportunity to obtain advanced placement and/or credit in college‡	.105	.114
Homogeneous grouping of students by ability‡	−.032†	−.041†
Acceleration policy for graduation‡	.142	.149
Percentage of teachers with more than bachelor's degree*	.076	.124

NOTE: Results are based on a representative 10 per cent subsample of the students in each school ($N = 2,053$). All effect estimates are significant at the .01 level unless otherwise noted.
* Effect estimates for these attributes are unweighted and obtained from school quartile standardized to dichotomous form.
† Not significant at the .05 level.
‡ Effect estimates for these attributes are unweighted and obtained from dichotomies, not school quartiles.
§ Significant at the .05 level.

tary level the evaluation of the More Effective Schools Program in New York City for disadvantaged students (with one of its most distinguishing characteristics being small classes) has failed to show greater academic growth for these students than for the students in the control schools where there were substantially larger student-teacher ratios and larger average class sizes.[43]

The non-significant effects of homogeneous ability grouping are also in the direction opposite to that predicted by the rationale typically offered by educators who advocate this mode of classroom organization: Teachers can achieve better academic results when teaching a group of students who are relatively similar in learning ability. The measure of ability grouping in this study is admittedly weak because it is based on a single-item indicator which classified the schools into two crude categories—those which group for "many" or "all" courses and those which utilized it for only a "few" or "no" courses. However, the results using this measure are consistent with the findings of the most rigorous

and comprehensive study of ability grouping ever undertaken. This is the experimental investigation of elementary school children in New York City recently completed by Goldberg, Passow, and Justman, which produced the following generalization:

The general conclusion which must be drawn from the findings of this study and from other experimental grouping studies is that, in predominantly middle-class schools, narrowing the ability range in the classroom on the basis of some measure of general academic aptitude will, by itself, in the absence of carefully planned adaptations of content and method, produce little positive change in the academic achievement of pupils at any ability level.[44]

The four remaining characteristics in Table 7 have significant effects in the expected direction on both dependent attributes, and Table 8 presents the effects of these four on the dependent attributes for the total sample of students

Table 8—Summary Effects of Four Dichotomized Curricular and Facilities Characteristics of Schools on MATH Achievement and College Plans with Father's Education and Scholastic Ability Simultaneously Controlled

Independent Attributes	Weighted Effects of Independent Attributes on MATH*	Weighted Effects of Independent Attributes on College Plans†
Accelerated curriculum for superior students	.020	.028
Opportunity to obtain advanced placement and/or credit in college	.043	−.003‡
Acceleration policy for graduation	.032	−.017‡
Percentage of teachers with more than B.A. degree	.046	.083

NOTE: Results are based on total sample of students, not the 10 per cent subsample. All effect parameters are significant at the .01 level unless otherwise noted.

* Father's education and ability have approximately constant effects on MATH with each of the four independent attributes controlled. The effects of father's education vary from .142 to .151 and those of ability from .325 to .327.

† Father's education and ability have approximately constant effects on college plans with each of the four independent attributes controlled. The effects of father's education vary from .237 to .243 and those of ability from .178 to .184.

‡ Not significant at the .05 level.

with ability and family SES both controlled. A comparison of these data with those of Table 7 indicates that, although all four characteristics exert a significant effect on MATH (and the same holds true for two of them with respect to college plans), much of their apparent explanatory power is attributable to family status and ability level of students. Consequently, they have only very limited substantive influence on students' academic behavior.[45] The one exception to this statement is the effect of teachers' educational level on college plans and, to a lesser extent, on students' MATH performance. The level of formal education of teachers may be viewed as one indicator of the academic competence of the staff, a variable which previous research has shown to be related to student performance.[46]

Rather than presenting several tables which show (a) the independent effects of each of the four curricular and facilities measures listed in Table 8 on the two dependent attributes when the climate dimensions, father's education, and ability are simultaneously controlled and (b) the independent effects of each of the climate dimensions on the dependent attributes with each of the four curricular measures, father's education and ability simultaneously controlled, the important results may be summarized as follows:

1. The small, statistically significant effects of accelerated curriculum on college plans disappear when each of the six climate dimensions is held constant. However, the effects of each of the climate dimensions are unaffected by controlling accelerated curriculum.

2. The significant effects of educational level of teachers on college plans are unaffected by controlling each climate dimension. Likewise, the effects of each climate dimension are almost totally independent of the educational level of faculty.

3. The small, significant effects of accelerated curriculum on MATH disappear when each of the climate dimensions is controlled. On the other hand, the effects of the six climate dimensions on MATH are not reduced when accelerated curriculum is held constant.

4. The statistically significant effects of advanced placement in college on MATH scores disappear when climate dimensions II, III, V, and VI are held constant; although they remain statistically significant when dimensions I and IV are controlled, they are reduced by approximately 50 per cent. On the other hand, the effects of each climate dimension on MATH are reduced only a minute amount when the effects of advanced college placement are removed.

5. The small, statistically significant effects of an acceleration policy for graduation on MATH disappear when each of the six climate dimensions is controlled. However, the effects of all the climate dimensions remain almost totally intact when graduation policy is controlled.

6. In general, the effects of average educational level of teachers on MATH remain intact when each climate dimension is held constant. Likewise, the influence of each factor dimension on MATH is not appreciably reduced when teachers' educational level is controlled.

These findings, taken together, strongly suggest that none of these four organizational properties of schools is an important source of variation in climate effects on students' academic behavior, since controlling them has no appreciable influence on the magnitude of the relationships between the six climate dimensions and the dependent attributes. However, controlling the effects of the climate dimensions tends to result in the disappearance of the limited effects of these characteristics on the dependent attributes. The one exception to this generalization is the effect of teachers' educational level on both MATH achievement and college plans.

Perhaps the small effects of curricular and facilities characteristics on achievement and educational plans are a *consequence* of variation in community involvement and interest in academic excellence of the schools. That is, schools located in neighborhoods or communities with a strong *social* commitment to quality education for their children are more likely to institute pedagogical innovations and to attract highly competent teachers than communities lacking such a social investment in the quality of education. Although there are no comprehensive measures of community interest available in the present study to test such a proposition, the scale measuring parental involvement in the high school, P.I.H.S., can serve as an indicator of this phenomenon. To test the proposition adequately would require a protracted longitudinal study of communities and their schools, rather than the cross-sectional approach employed here. However, a necessary condition for the proposition to have validity is that there be positive correlations between these curricular and resource characteristics of the schools and P.I.H.S. Each of the four characteristics (indicated in Table 8) has a significant relationship (.05 > p) with P.I.H.S.:

	Product-Moment Correlation
Accelerated curriculum	.423
Advanced placement	.494
Accelerated graduation	.635
Educational level of teachers	.470

Of course, it is possible that P.I.H.S. is generated by school policy and quality and is, therefore, a consequence of such characteristics rather than a source of them. However, it seems, for example, more plausible to argue that competent teachers (as indicated by level of formal education) are attracted to schools in

communities where the residents (especially the parents) and school officials are socially committed to quality education than the converse.[47] Of course, each of these statements is undoubtedly an oversimplification of the complex causal process involved, with a two-dimensional or "feedback" causal relationship being more accurate.[48]

More evidence to suggest the validity of the argument that the extent of the collective parental and community support is one source of variation in the small influence of various indicators of curriculum and facilities on students' achievement and educational plans is found in Table 9, which is identical to Table 8 except that P.I.H.S. is also held constant. A comparison of the effect parameters in the two tables indicates that holding constant P.I.H.S. (1) "washes out" the small effects of an acceleration policy for graduation on MATH achievement, (2) reduces the small effects of advanced college placement on MATH scores, and (3) reduces the small effects of teachers' education on MATH to a point of little substantive significance even though the parameter remains statistically significant.

In sum, the extent of parental and community interest in the school generally functions as a factor accounting for the small net impact of curriculum and facilities on academic behavior of students.

EDUCATIONAL IMPLICATIONS OF FINDINGS ON SOURCES OF CLIMATE EFFECTS

The results of the preceding section, indicating that the critical factor in explaining the impact of the high school environment on the achievement and educational aspirations of students is the degree of parental and community interest in quality education, would appear to have policy implications. The results seem to support a plea recently made by the U.S. Commissioner of Education:

> In all communities—rural and suburban, but especially inner-city—the principal needs to take the initiative in tailoring his school to the character of the community. He needs to solicit parent participation and to help parents understand what kinds of contributions they can make. The principal ought to be welcoming parents and letting them see how the school is run and explaining to them its policies and programs. He should at the same time be converting the school into a community resource that offers adults a center for community activities, for instruction in practical subjects as well as leisure-time activities.[49]

At present there are innovations under way of the type advocated by the com-

missioner—innovations which need to be carefully evaluated over long periods by educational researchers for their potentially positive benefits. The results of the present investigation suggests that these innovations, if kept free of social tensions, might set in motion the feedback mechanism of "parental involvement–intellectually viable school environment" discussed above.

One such innovation is the "community school," which is designed to serve as a community service center where neighborhood residents may obtain health services, counseling services, legal aid, and employment information. In short, the school is conceived as one of the prime loci of community or neighborhood life.[50]

A concept, related to the community school, is the *proposed* experimental program "Family Opportunities for Reaching Goals through Education (FORGE), currently being designed by the Office of Special Programs, Franklin

Table 9—Summary Effects of Four Dichotomized Curricular and Facilities Characteristics of Schools on MATH Achievement with Father's Education, Scholastic Ability, and P.I.H.S. Simultaneously Controlled

Independent Attributes	Weighted Effects of Independent Attributes on MATH*	Weighted Effects of Independent Attributes on College Plans†
Accelerated curriculum for superior students	‡	‡
Opportunity to obtain advanced placement and/or credit in college	.031	§
Acceleration policy for graduation	.018**	§
Percentage of teachers with more than B.A. degree	.026	.061

NOTE: Results are based on total sample of students, not the 10 per cent subsample. All effect parameters are significant at the .01 level unless otherwise noted.

* The effects of father's education, ability, and P.I.H.S. on MATH are almost invariant with each of the three independent variables controlled in this column. The effects of father's education vary from .128 to .132, those of ability from .316 to .319, and those of P.I.H.S. from .092 to .097.

† The effects of father's education, ability, and P.I.H.S. with the measure of teacher's level of education controlled are .217, .171, and .096, respectively.

‡ The positive relationship between accelerated curriculum and P.I.H.S. is sufficiently pronounced that there are no schools with an accelerated curriculum and *low* on P.I.H.S. Consequently, the effects of the former attribute on MATH and college plans with P.I.H.S., father's education, and ability simultaneously controlled cannot be computed.

§ Effects of these independent attributes on college plans were not computed because there is no significant relationship between them and college plans with ability and father's education simultaneously controlled (see Table 8).

** Not significant at the .05 level.

and Marshall College, Lancaster, Pennsylvania.[51] Under this proposed program, poverty neighborhoods and their accompanying schools would be defined and then used as the basic units of the program. The purpose of the program is to encourage the parents of selected elementary school children to become closely involved in their children's education and their local schools. In addition to long-term advisory and support services, the project staff would guarantee total five-year college expenses for each child accepted by a college upon completion of high school. The primary locus of the program would be the neighborhood under the leadership of a resident director. His chief responsibilities would be to provide long-term advice and counsel to parents regarding resources and limitations of neighborhood schools, to promote student and parental involvement in the schools' policies and programs, and to counsel students individually regarding their educational needs and how they can be met. Hopefully, such a program would create the intellectual and social camaraderie between schools and families which appears to be the hallmark of schools with strong academic climates.

As documented by Bloom in his major work, *Stability and Change in Human Characteristics*,[52] highly consistent home environments have more potent effects on cognitive development than those lacking internal consistency. He generalizes this to the relationship between schools and homes: school and home environments which are mutually reinforcing are likely to achieve greater academic growth of students than those lacking such consistency.[53] It would seem that "community schools" and similar organizational innovations in public institutions could perhaps be one mechanism for obtaining support of parents which in turn could provide data for both parents and school officials to achieve consistency between the two environments.

Conclusions

In their summary of the follow-up study of Project Talent high school seniors in 1963 who were ninth graders in the original survey in 1960 (conducted by Shaycoft[54]) the authors conclude that there is a substantial amount of academic growth by students during the high school years and that the schools are of importance in accounting for varying rates of growth. They state:

In summary, schools do vary in effectiveness, but the specific school characteristics that produce results are somewhat elusive. One reason they are so resistant to identification may be that they are elusive *inherently*, not just in the present context. In other words, one of the crucial differences between an effective school and an ineffective one may be something as vague as the *school's atmosphere* [italics supplied]. A school may provide an atmosphere where the motivation to learn is stimulated or it may provide one that produces students whose goal is to "get by." This sort of information cannot be gathered through a questionnaire survey.[55]

The present authors find themselves in agreement with the first of the two major points in the above quote. The evidence from the present research indicates that the educational and social environment of the school does have a moderate effect on the academic behavior of students. However, they cannot accept the second point that adequate measures of school environment cannot be obtained through survey techniques. At the college level there is a substantial body of research—based to a considerable extent on survey techniques—focusing on the kinds of college environments which are conducive to academic achievement and aspirations. The results on climate effects presented in this paper are consistent with the general tenor of findings from other studies at both the high school and college levels, using both survey techniques and other approaches, such as the interview and both participant and non-participant observation.[56] Of course, none of the studies to date has presented conclusive information on the nature of the academic environment of schools which would form the basis for incontrovertible policy prescriptions to school administrators as how to promote particular types of cognitive development in students. Nevertheless, the results of this and other recent studies offer substantial evidence that there are "overachieving" and "underachieving" schools. They point also to the need for more intensive studies of such deviant institutions. Such resesrch should produce, in the foreseeable future, systematic evidence on "the realities of the teaching-learning process as they actually are and as they might be."[57]

Notes

[1] Benjamin S. Bloom, "Stability and Change in Human Characteristics: Implications for School Reorganization," *Educational Administration Quarterly*, 2 (1966), 35–49.

[2] For a list of references which present extensive reviews of research in this area, see Edward L. McDill, Edmund D. Meyers, Jr., and Leo C. Rigsby, "Institutional Effects on the Academic Behavior of High School Students," *Sociology of Education*, 40 (1967), 181–82.

[3] Bloom, *op. cit.*, p. 47.

[4] In order to demonstrate contextual effects on the behavior of individual students, it is necessary to separate the consequences of school conditions from those of the individual's own characteristics for his behavior. Stated differently, one has to demonstrate an impact of school environment on the dependent variables with individual "input" factors such as scholastic aptitude, family socioeconomic status, and their internalized academic orientations controlled. These three variables are among the most important predictors of academic achievement and educational plans. Furthermore, to isolate a contextual effect requires that a relationship between the group level attribute and a dependent attribute at the individual level be demonstrated while the corresponding characteristic for individuals is controlled. In this study, students' academic orientations or values are used as the individual counterpart of the measure of school environment. For an explication of the logic and methodology underlying contextual analysis, see James S. Coleman, "Relational Analysis: The Study of Social Organization with Survey Methods," *Human Organization*, 17 (1958), 28–36; and Peter H. Blau, "Structural Effects," *American Sociological Review*, 25 (1960), 178–93.

[5] A more extensive presentation of the method is found in Edward L. McDill, Edmund D. Meyers, Jr., and Leo C. Rigsby, "Sources of Educational Climates in High Schools" (final report to the Office of Education, U.S. Department of Health, Education, and Welfare under Contract OE-3-10-080, December, 1966). This document is available from the ERIC Document Reproduction Service (Accession No. ED 010 621).

[6] The schools were chosen with the goal of obtaining considerable variation on (1) various "output" measures, such as college-going and achievement levels; (2) a number of "input" measures, such as I.Q. and socioeconomic composition; and (3) demographic and social factors which were expected to relate to school climates.

[7] John Flanagan et al., "Project Talent, Studies of the American High School" (Monograph No. 2, University of Pittsburgh, 1962), p. 6–5.

[8] More complete descriptions of these two academic tests may be found in John T. Dailey and Marion F. Shaycoft, *Types of Tests in Project Talent* (U.S. Department of Health, Education, and Welfare, Office of Education, Cooperative Research Monograph No. 9), Washington: U.S. Government Printing Office, 1961.

[9] For a systematic treatment of this problem, see McDill et al., "Sources of

Educational Climates in High Schools," pp.
III-17–III-27.

[10] Hanan C. Selvin and Warren O. Hagstrom, "The Empirical Classification of Formal Groups," *American Sociological Review*, 28 (1963), 399–411.

[11] Aggregate characteristics are summarizing measures based on smaller units (in this case, individuals) within formal groups. Twenty-seven of the thirty-nine variables are scales; the remaining twelve are single-item indicators.

[12] William H. Sewell and J. Michael Armer, "Neighborhood Context and College Plans," *American Sociological Review*, 31 (1966), 159–68; and McDill et al., "Institutional Effects. . . ."

[13] McDill et al., "Institutional Effects," p. 187 (Table 2).

[14] Harry H. Harman, *Modern Factor Analysis* (Chicago: University of Chicago Press, 1960), p. 177; and William W. Cooley and Paul R. Lohnes, *Multivariate Procedures for the Behavioral Sciences* (New York: Wiley, 1962), p. 172.

[15] For a discussion of the problem of statistical artifacts in contextual research and suggestions for ways to cope with these problems, see Arnold S. Tannenbaum and Gerald G. Bachman, "Structural versus Individual Effects," *American Journal of Sociology*, 49 (1964), 585–95. The multivariate technique is a modified version of Coleman's stochastic model for the multivariate analysis of attribute data (see James S. Coleman, *Introduction to Mathematical Sociology* [New York: Free Press, 1964], chap. 6). Boyle, by slightly modifying Coleman's technique, has demonstrated that it yields parameters for the effects of dichotomous independent attributes on dichotomous dependent attributes which are mathematically equivalent to unstandardized regression coefficients obtained from multiple regression of dummy variables (see Richard P. Boyle, "Causal Theory and Statistical Measures of Effect: A Convergence," *American Sociological Review*, 31 [1966], 843–51). The model has been formally extended by Coleman to make it applicable to the case of polytomous independent attributes, either ordered or unordered, on dichotomous dependent attributes. The analogy to multiple-regression analysis is approximate for polytomous attributes, however. Nevertheless, Boyle has shown that the procedure yields effect parameters which

are close estimates of the coefficients obtained from multiple-regression analysis of dummy variables which are polytomous.

The following classification scheme was used for the variables. (The primary criterion dictating the classification was to retain a sizable number of cases in each cell of the tables which are used in the multivariate analysis. This procedure results in highly reliable estimates of the effect parameters of each independent attribute on the dependent attributes.) Father's education was divided into four categories, approximating a quartile classification. Raw scores on the AR and MATH tests were standardized (using the C-scale technique) by grade and sex, since there were systematic differences in performance by each sex and grade category. The standardized scores for the AR tests were then collapsed into the four categories, which made the number of cases in each of them as near equal as possible. The distribution of scores on the scale measuring students' achievement orientations was also divided into approximately equal quartiles. The two dependent attributes were dichotomized as follows. Students who indicated that they planned to enrol as full-time in college immediately upon completion of high school were classified as having college plans. All other students were considered as not having firm intentions. For the other attribute, standardized scores on the MATH test were dichotomized as closely as possible to the median. Finally, the contextual measures were dichtomized. This was accomplished by ranking the schools on each contextual dimension and then collapsing them as closely as possible to the median. Obviously, a larger number of categories for all contextual variables would have resulted in more precise measurement of the characteristics. However, use of more refined categories was not feasible because in the analysis presented in a later section the measures of school climate and some of the potential sources of school climate effects are introduced simultaneously. The relationships among these characteristics are sufficiently pronounced that using a larger number of categories would have resulted in empty cells in the tables and produced unreliable effect parameters.

[16] Coleman, *Introduction to Mathematical*

Sociology, pp. 218–19, presents a formula for standardizing effect parameters for polytomous, ordered, independent attributes to make them comparable to measures of effect for dichotomous attributes. However, for such adjusted effect parameters to be identical to those obtained from actual dichotomies, the sample has to be rectangularly distributed over the ordered polytomous categories. In all tables in this paper the effect parameters for polytomous independent attributes are standardized to dichotomous form.

[17] Sarane S. Boocock, "Toward a Sociology of Learning: A Selective Review of Existing Research," *Sociology of Education*, 39 (1966), 27–32 and 41. For the present sample it should be noted that, in nineteen of the twenty schools, both "leadership in activities" and "athletics" ("cheerleader" for girls) are viewed as more important for status among other students than "high grades." Furthermore, in all of the twenty schools, both leadership in activities and athletics are considered more important for prestige than "knowing a great deal about intellectual matters." With such evidence it is obvious that the label "academically oriented status system" is not applicable to any of the twenty schools in absolute terms, but only relative to each other. These results are consistent with those of Coleman in *The Adolescent Society*. In each of the ten high schools he studied, scholastic achievement was less valued by students than other activities such as athletics, popularity, and leadership in activities (see James S. Coleman, *The Adolescent Society* [New York: Free Press, 1961]).

[18] An excellent summary of this research is found in David E. Lavin, *The Prediction of Academic Performance* (New York: Russell Sage, 1965), chap. 4, who notes that the correlation is higher at the high school level than at the college level, which can be explained by the more restricted range of ability of college students. Lavin estimates, based on his survey of the literature, that the average zero-order correlation between ability and *grades* for high school students is .60. In the present research, the zero-order, product-moment correlation between AR scores and MATH scores is .52.

[19] There are only five variables with significant loadings on Factor IV. These variables with their loadings are as follows: student perceptions of faculty press for scientism (.901), student perceptions of student press for scientism (.735), faculty perceptions of faculty press for scientism (.883), faculty perceptions of student press for scientism (.756), and faculty perceptions of faculty press for independence (.628). This latter variable is conceptually consistent with a strong emphasis on scientism since it measures the extent of teachers' encouragement of independent and creative work by students. ("Press" refers to the characteristic emphases or pressures of an environment as perceived by the collectivity of informants who constitute its membership.)

[20] John A. Michael, "High School Climates and Plans for Entering College," *Public Opinion Quarterly*, 25 (1961), 594.

[21] Elbridge Sibley, "Some Demographic Clues to Stratification," *American Sociological Review*, 7 (1942), 330. One could argue that a comparison of college plans of high school students with actual college attendance is tenuous, since an unknown number of students are unrealistic about enrolling in college in their responses to the item in the questionnaire. However, the measure of college plans employed here seems not to be an invalid indicator of college attendance: Only those students with definite plans to enroll immediately after graduation from high school were classified as having plans. Those who gave any of the following responses were categorized as not planning to attend: "no, never"; "yes, but not right after high school"; "yes, as a part-time student right after high school"; and "undecided." A comparison in each school of the percentage of the preceding year's graduates who attended college did not yield any substantial differences when compared with the percentage of seniors in this sample who expressed college plans. In a study of Wisconsin high school students it was shown that more than 90 per cent of the seniors with college plans actually enrolled in college the following year. These results are reported in J. Kenneth Little, *A State-wide Inquiry into Decisions of Youth about Education Beyond High School* (Madison, Wis.: School of Education, 1958), cited in William H. Sewell, "Community of Residence and College Plans," *American Sociological Review*, 29 (1964).

[22] The other potential measure of family

SES available in the data—annual family income—could not be used because more than 38 per cent of the students were unable to provide reliable responses to the questionnaire item dealing with this family attribute.

[23] Boocock, *op. cit.*, p. 38; e.g., Coleman, *The Adolescent Society*, p. 65, found no relationship between per-pupil expenditure and achievement in ten Illinois high schools when ability of students was controlled. He also cites a state-wide study of Connecticut high school students which failed to reveal such a relationship when ability was controlled. Finally, at the college level, he cites (p. 329) results from the classic study by R. H. Knapp and H. B. Goodrich, *Origins of American Scientists* (Chicago: University of Chicago Press, 1952), which revealed that the undergraduate institutions which were most productive of scientists were not the most affluent colleges. One large-scale study which showed sizable relationships between community characteristics and test scores was William G. Mollenkopf and Donald Melville, "A Study of Secondary School Characteristics as Related to Test Scores" (Princeton, N.J., Educational Testing Service, 1956 [mimeographed]). However, as noted by Boocock, *op. cit.*, his findings are questionable, since the response rate from principals was less than 50 per cent.

[24] James S. Coleman et al., *Equality of Educational Opportunity* (Washington: U.S. Government Printing Office, 1966).

[25] Christopher Jencks, "Education: The Racial Gap," *New Republic*, October 1, 1966, pp. 21–26, has made the unqualified statement that the report incorporates the most important piece of educational research conducted in recent years. On the other hand, Bowles and Levin challenge the adequacy of the data, the statistical analyses, and the validity of the interpretation of the findings (see Samuel Bowles and Henry M. Levin, "The Determinants of Scholastic Achievement—an Appraisal of Some Recent Evidence," *Journal of Human Resources*, 3 [1968], pp. 3–24).

[26] Coleman et al., *op. cit.*, chap. 3.

[27] Bowles and Levin, *op. cit.*, pp. 8–12.

[28] All of the data on community resources considered thus far were obtained from items in the principal's questionnaire. These measures of the cultural or intellectual atmosphere of the community are crude in the sense that they are merely indicators of

the presence or absence of such facilities. However, it is reasonable to assume that the quality of these facilities is positively correlated with a number of socioeconomic resources of the school and/or community presented below for which ordinal or interval data are available, and which are shown *not* to be sources of climate effects on the dependent attributes. Thus, there is no reason to believe that data on the quality of these three facilities would produce different results as potential sources of school climate effects.

[29] Implicit in this conclusion is a statistical truism: For a given variable to be a source of the effects of climate dimensions on students' academic behavior, the variable has to be related to both the climate dimensions and the dependent attributes.

[30] The three true-false items comprising the P.I.H.S. scale are: (1) Most parents in this school are apathetic to school policies. (2) Parents of students here seem interested in their children's progress. (3) Parents often ask for appointments with teachers to discuss their children's schoolwork. The KR-20 reliability coefficient of .64 is high for a measure containing such a small number of items. It is noteworthy that Neal Gross et al., in a 1966 study of the correlates of academic productivity of urban elementary school pupils from low socioeconomic backgrounds, used a similar approach in constructing a contextual measure of parental interest in the academic performance of their children (see Neal Gross et al., "Some Sociological Correlates of the 'Academic Productivity' of Urban Elementary Schools with Pupils from Families at Low Socio-economic Status" [paper presented at the American Sociological Association Meetings, Miami Beach, Florida, August, 1966]). That is, the measure was based on an average of *teachers'* perceptions of parents' interest in their children's academic activities. The present authors were unaware of Gross's study when this analysis was undertaken.

[31] In the search for source variables, zero-order effects of such variables on the dependent attributes are based on this 10 per cent subsample in order to minimize computer costs, and the .05 level of significance is chosen as the one beneath which a relationship is discounted. For those potential source

variables which show a significant relationship with the dependent attributes for the 10 per cent sample, the effects of such variables on the dependent attributes are then computed for the total population with ability and father's education simultaneously controlled. That is, no community or school characteristic can qualify as a source of climate effects unless the characteristic has a significant effect on a dependent attribute with the ability of the students and family SES both held constant.

[32] In fact, the positive effects of P.I.H.S. on college plans are slightly increased when climate components II, III, and V are controlled, and its effects on MATH are very slightly enhanced when component II is held constant. Furthermore, in every instance in Table 6 and in one case in Table 5 the effects of the climate dimensions are slightly negative. No substantive significance is attached to the fact that in certain instances the effects of P.I.H.S. in Tables 5 and 6 are slightly larger than those when only ability and father's education are controlled and that in six instances out of ten in Tables 5 and 6 the climate effects acquire negative signs. In a recent scholarly article on multivariate techniques, Robert Gordon explains how the distribution of the predictive values of two independent variables (as measured by regression coefficients) can be "tipped" or altered in favor of one or the other by changes in the correlations among a set of independent variables (see Robert A. Gordon, "Issues in Multiple Regression," *American Journal of Sociology*, 73 [1968], 610–11). The more highly correlated the predictors, the more susceptible they are to being tipped. In fact, as the predictors become very highly correlated, the tipping effect can take the following form: One of the regression coefficients assumes a *negative* value and the other a *higher positive* value even though the predictors and the dependent variable are all positively correlated at the zero-order level. Gordon also carefully documents how erroneous substantive conclusions can be reached from indiscriminate use of multiple regression and partial correlation procedures for explanatory variables which are highly correlated *and* not conceptually distinct. Certainly, in the present investigation P.I.H.S. and the climate con-

structs are both conceptually and operationally distinct.

[33] Gross et al., *op. cit.*

[34] Bowles and Levin, *op. cit.*, p. 8.

[35] Coleman et al., *op. cit.*, p. 312.

[36] None of the schools used teaching machines regularly "in many instances," and only four used them regularly "in a few instances."

[37] The adequacy of this measure of library facilities is open to question because the response alternatives for the question measuring library facilities were not presented in sufficient detail. A broader range of response categories would probably have produced sufficient variation for the characteristic to be considered as a source. However, in the Coleman report, *op. cit.* (n. 25 above), p. 316, which showed large variation in library facilities, it was demonstrated that the number of volumes per student had only small and inconsistent relationships with verbal achievement for both Negroes and whites in different geographical regions. Furthermore, the Project Talent survey (Flanagan et al., *op. cit.*, p. 6–14) produced correlations of only .203 and .253 between number of volumes in the library and performance on comprehensive tests of mathematics achievement and reading achievement. It should be emphasized that these two correlations were based on school means, not on individual student scores. Only under most unusual circumstances can correlations on individuals be as large as those based on schools (Flanagan et al., *op. cit.*, p. 5–1). Usually, in the Project Talent survey the correlations based on school means were substantially larger.

[38] Only one of the twenty schools had half-day sessions.

[39] Flanagan et al., *op. cit.*, p. 6–17.

[40] Coleman et al., *op. cit.*, p. 312.

[41] Bowles and Levin, *op. cit.*, p. 12. In both the Project Talent survey and the present study the measures of class size in science and math and in non-science courses were based on responses to the following type of item: "What size is your *average* instructional class in science and math [non-science courses]?" Thus it is highly likely that measures in both studies are "defective" in the manner described by Bowles and Levin.

[42] Boocock, *op. cit.*, p. 11.

[43] David J. Fox, *Expansion of the More Effective School Program* (New York: Center for Urban Education, September, 1967), p.

121. In this evaluation study, a distinction was made between average class size and pupil-teacher ratio (see p. A-1). The former was defined as number of pupils in school divided by number of organized classes, whereas pupil-teacher ratio was obtained by dividing the number of students in school by the total number of authorized teaching positions. To obtain an indication of the large differences between the experimental and control schools on these two measures, consider the following data for October, 1966, the termination date of the evaluation: The average class size in the control schools was 28.5 and only 20.1 for the More Effective schools. Pupil-teacher ratio in the former was 22.2 and only 12.3 in the latter.

[44] Miriam L. Goldberg, A. Harry Passow, and Joseph Justman, *The Effects of Ability Grouping* (New York: Teachers College Press, 1966), p. 167. This conclusion is also supported at the national level by the results of Coleman et al., *op. cit.*, p. 314, who found that ability grouping at the school level accounted for almost no variance in verbal achievement with family background of students controlled.

[45] These findings are in general accord with those of Coleman et al., *op. cit.*, pp. 312–16. Twelve different characteristics of school facilities (similar to those considered in this section) accounted for only a small amount of variance in individual students' achievement when their family background differences were controlled.

[46] Coleman et al., *op. cit.*, p. 318, found that quality of teachers, as measured by scores on a standardized test measuring verbal skills, had a substantially stronger effect on students' achievement than did physical facilities and curricular measures.

[47] That economic investment on the part of the community (as contrasted to *social* investment) is not important in this sample in recruiting quality teachers is evidenced by the fact that the product-moment correlation at the school level between beginning teacher salaries and percentage of teachers with more than the B.A. degree is $-.11$ $(.50 > p > .30)$.

[48] Stated in different terms and at a more general level, school environment and community support interact: communities or neighborhoods with a strong, collective social investment in quality education tend to generate school environments conducive to high educational aspirations and achievement, and these schools attract families to the community who have a strong commitment to quality education. For examples of two-directional relationships involving research on school environments and academic behavior, see Edward L. McDill and James S. Coleman, "High School Social Status, College Plans, and Interest in Academic Achievement: A Panel Analysis," *American Sociological Review*, 28 (1963), 905–18; and Jerome Kirk, "Cultural Diversity and Character Change at Carnegie Tech" (a report on the Carnegie Tech Campus Study, Carnegie Institute of Technology, Pittsburgh, 1965), p. 40.

[49] Harold Howe II, "Picking Up the Options" (address to the Annual Meeting of the Department of Elementary School Principals, National Education Association, Houston, Texas, April 1, 1968), p. 13.

[50] Baltimore City Public Schools, School-Community Relations Division, Bulletin No. 1 (August, 1967). See also, "Reconnection for Learning: A Community School System for New York City" (report of the Mayor's Advisory Panel on Decentralization of the New York City Schools). New York: The Advisory Panel, 1967.

[51] Project FORGE, Office of Special Programs, Franklin and Marshall College, Lancaster, Pa., 1968 (mimeograph).

[52] Benjamin Bloom, *Stability and Change in Human Characteristics* (New York: Wiley, 1964).

[53] Bloom, "Stability and Change . . ." (see n. 1 above), p. 46.

[54] Marion F. Shaycoft, *Project Talent, The High School Years: Growth in Cognitive Skills* (American Institutes for Research and School of Education, University of Pittsburgh, 1967).

[55] "A National Longitudinal Study of American Youth" (Bulletin 6, Project Talent, American Institutes for Research, Pittsburgh, April, 1967).

[56] See Boocock, *op. cit.*, pp. 24–31, for some of the more important work in this area.

[57] Henry S. Dyer, "School Factors and Equal Educational Opportunity," *Harvard Educational Review*, 38 (1968), 55.

The Concept of Equality of Educational Opportunity

James S. Coleman

This article appeared originally in the Winter 1968 issue of the Harvard Educational Review. It was based on a paper delivered at the Conference on the Equality of Educational Opportunity Report sponsored by the Colloquium Board of the Harvard School of Education, October 21, 1967.

Reprinted from the Harvard Educational Review, 68 (1968), pp. 7–22, by permission of the author and publisher, Copyright © 1968 by President and Fellows of Harvard College.

THE CONCEPT of "equality of education opportunity" as held by members of society has had a varied past. It has changed radically in recent years, and is likely to undergo further change in the future. This lack of stability in the concept leads to several questions. What has it meant in the past, what does it mean now, and what will it mean in the future? Whose obligation is it to provide such equality? Is the concept a fundamentally sound one, or does it have inherent contradictions or conflicts with social organization? But first of all, and above all, what is and has been meant in society by the idea of equality of educational opportunity?

To answer this question, it is necessary to consider how the child's position in society has been conceived in different historical periods. In pre-industrial Europe, the child's horizons were largely limited by his family. His station in life was likely to be the same as his father's. If his father was a serf, he would likely live his own life as a serf; if his father was a shoemaker, he would likely become a shoemaker. But even this immobility was not the crux of the matter; he was a part of the family production enterprise and would likely remain within this enterprise throughout his life. The extended family, as the basic unit of social organization, had complete authority over the child, and complete responsibility for him. This responsibility ordinarily did not end when the child became an adult because he remained a part of the same economic unit and carried on this tradition of responsibility into the next generation. Despite some mobility out of the family, the general pattern was family continuity through a patriarchal kinship system.

There are two elements of critical importance here. First, the family carried responsibility for its members' welfare from cradle to grave. It was a "welfare society," with each extended family serving as a welfare organization for its own members. Thus it was to the family's interest to see that its members became productive. Conversely, a family took relatively small interest in whether someone in *another* family became productive or not—merely because the mobility of productive labor between family economic units was relatively low. If the son of a neighbor was allowed to become a ne'er-do-well, it had little real effect on families other than his own.

The second important element is that the family, as a unit of economic production, provided an appropriate context in which the child could learn the things he needed to know. The craftsman's shop or the farmer's fields were appropriate training grounds for sons, and the household was an appropriate training ground for daughters.

In this kind of society, the concept of equality of educational opportunity had no relevance at all. The child and adult were embedded within the extended family, and the child's education or training was merely whatever seemed necessary to maintain the family's productivity. The fixed stations in life which most families occupied precluded any idea of "opportunity" and, even less, equality of opportunity.

With the industrial revolution, changes occurred in both the family's function as a self-perpetuating economic unit and as a training ground. As economic organizations developed outside the household, children began to be occupationally mobile outside their families. As families lost their economic production activities, they also began to lose their welfare functions, and the poor or ill or incapacitated became more nearly a community responsibility. Thus the training which a child received came to be of interest to all in the community, either as his potential employers or as his potential economic supports if he became dependent. During this stage of development in eighteenth-century England, for instance, communities had laws preventing immigration from another community because of the potential economic burden of immigrants.

Further, as men came to employ their own labor outside the family in the new factories, their families became less useful as economic training grounds for their children. These changes paved the way for public education. Families needed a context within which their children could learn some general skills which would be useful for gaining work outside the family; and men of influence in the community began to be interested in the potential productivity of other men's children.

It was in the early nineteenth century that public education began to appear in Europe and America. Before that time, private education had grown with the expansion of the mercantile class. This class had both the need and resources to have its children educated outside the home, either for professional occupations or for occupations in the developing world of commerce. But the idea of

general educational opportunity for all children arose only in the nineteenth century.

The emergence of public, tax-supported education was not solely a function of the stage of industrial development. It was also a function of the class structure in the society. In the United States, without a strong traditional class structure, universal education in publicly-supported free schools became widespread in the early nineteenth century; in England, the "voluntary schools," run and organized by churches with some instances of state support, were not supplemented by a state-supported system until the Education Act of 1870. Even more, the character of educational opportunity reflected the class structure. In the United States, the public schools quickly became the common school, attended by representatives of all classes; these schools provided a common educational experience for most American children—excluding only those upper-class children in private schools, those poor who went to no schools, and Indians and Southern Negroes who were without schools. In England, however, the class system directly manifested itself through the schools. The state-supported, or "board schools" as they were called, became the schools of the laboring lower classes with a sharply different curriculum from those voluntary schools which served the middle and upper classes. The division was so sharp that two government departments, the Education Department and the Science and Art Department, administered external examinations, the first for the products of the board schools, and the second for the products of the voluntary schools as they progressed into secondary education. It was only the latter curricula and examinations that provided admission to higher education.

What is most striking is the duration of influence of such a dual structure. Even today in England, a century later (and in different forms in most European countries), there exists a dual structure of public secondary education with only one of the branches providing the curriculum for college admission. In England, this branch includes the remaining voluntary schools which, though retaining their individual identities, have become part of the state-supported system.

This comparison of England and the United States shows clearly the impact of the class structure in society upon the concept of educational opportunity in that society. In nineteenth-century England, the idea of *equality* of educational opportunity was hardly considered; the system was designed to provide *differentiated* educational opportunity appropriate to one's station in life. In the United States as well, the absence of educational opportunity for Negroes in the South arose from the caste and feudal structure of the largely rural society. The idea of differentiated educational opportunity, implicit in the Education Act of 1870 in England, seems to derive from dual needs: the needs arising from industrialization for a basic education for the labor force, and the interests of parents in having one's own child receive a good education. The middle classes could meet both these needs by providing a free system for the children of laboring classes, and a tuition system (which soon came to be supplemented by state grants) for their own. The long survival of this differentiated system depended not only on the historical fact that the voluntary schools existed before a public system came into existence but on the fact that it allows both of these needs to be met: the community's collective need for a trained labor force, and the middle-class individual's interest in a better

education for his own child. It served a third need as well: that of maintaining the existing social order—a system of stratification that was a step removed from a feudal system of fixed estates, but designed to prevent a wholesale challenge by the children of the working class to the positions held for children of the middle classes.

The similarity of this system to that which existed in the South to provide differential opportunity to Negroes and whites is striking, just as is the similarity of class structures in the second half of nineteenth-century England to the white-Negro caste structure of the southern United States in the first half of the twentieth century.

In the United States, nearly from the beginning, the concept of educational opportunity had a special meaning which focussed on equality. This meaning included the following elements:

1. Providing a *free* education up to a given level which constituted the principal entry point to the labor force.
2. Providing a *common curriculum* for all children, regardless of background.
3. Partly by design and partly because of low population density, providing that children from diverse backgrounds attend the *same school*.
4. Providing equality within a given *locality*, since local taxes provided the source of support for schools.

This conception of equality of opportunity is still held by many persons; but there are some assumptions in it which are not obvious. First, it implicitly assumes that the existence of free schools eliminates economic sources of inequality of opportunity. Free schools, however, do not mean that the costs of a child's education become reduced to zero for families at all economic levels. When free education was introduced, many families could not afford to allow the child to attend school beyond an early age. His labor was necessary to the family—whether in rural or urban areas. Even after the passage of child labor laws, this remained true on the farm. These economic sources of inequality of opportunity have become small indeed (up through secondary education); but at one time they were a major source of inequality. In some countries they remain so; and certainly for higher education they remain so.

Apart from the economic needs of the family, problems inherent in the social structure raised even more fundamental questions about equality of educational opportunity. Continued school attendance prevented a boy from being trained in his father's trade. Thus, in taking advantage of "equal educational opportunity," the son of a craftsman or small tradesman would lose the opportunity to enter those occupations he would most likely fill. The family inheritance of occupation at all social levels was still strong enough, and the age of entry into the labor force was still early enough, that secondary education interfered with opportunity for working-class children; while it opened up opportunities at higher social levels, it closed them at lower ones.

Since residue of this social structure remains in present American society, the dilemma cannot be totally ignored. The idea of a common educational experience implies that this experience has only the effect of widening the range of opportunity, never the effect of excluding opportunities. But clearly this is never precisely true so long as this experience prevents a child from pursuing certain occupational paths. This question still arises with the differentiated secondary curriculum: an academic program in high school has the effect not only of keeping open the opportunities which arise through continued education, but also of closing off opportunities which a vocational program keeps open.

A second assumption implied by this concept of equality of opportunity is that opportunity lies in *exposure* to a given curriculum. The amount of opportunity is then measured in terms of the level of curriculum to which the child is exposed. The higher the curriculum made available to a given set of children, the greater their opportunity.

The most interesting point about this assumption is the relatively passive role of the school and community, relative to the child's role. The school's obligation is to "provide an opportunity" by being available, within easy geographic access of the child, free of cost (beyond the value of the child's time), and with a curriculum that would not exclude him from higher education. The obligation to "use the opportunity" is on the child or the family, so that his role is defined as the active one: the responsibility for achievement rests with him. Despite the fact that the school's role was the relatively passive one and the child's or family's role the active one, the use of this social service soon came to be no longer a choice of the parent or child, but that of the state. Since compulsory attendance laws appeared in the nineteenth century, the age of required attendance has been periodically moved upward.

This concept of equality of educational opportunity is one that has been implicit in most educational practice throughout most of the period of public education in the nineteenth and twentieth centuries. However, there have been several challenges to it; serious questions have been raised by new conditions in public education. The first of these in the United States was a challenge to assumption two, the common curriculum. This challenge first occurred in the early years of the twentieth century with the expansion of secondary education. Until the report of the committee of the

National Education Association, issued in 1918, the standard curriculum in secondary schools was primarily a classical one appropriate for college entrance. The greater influx of noncollege-bound adolescents into the high school made it necessary that this curriculum be changed into one more appropriate to the new majority. This is not to say that the curriculum changed immediately in the schools, nor that all schools changed equally, but rather that the seven "cardinal principles" of the N.E.A. report became a powerful influence in the movement toward a less academically rigid curriculum. The introduction of the new nonclassical curriculum was seldom if ever couched in terms of a conflict between those for whom high school was college preparation, and those for whom it was terminal education; nevertheless, that was the case. The "inequality" was seen as the use of a curriculum that served a minority and was not designed to fit the needs of the majority; and the shift of curriculum was intended to fit the curriculum to the needs of the new majority in the schools.

In many schools, this shift took the form of *diversifying* the curriculum, rather than supplanting one by another; the college-preparatory curriculum remained though watered down. Thus the kind of equality of opportunity that emerged from the newly-designed secondary school curriculum was radically different from the elementary-school concept that had emerged earlier. The idea inherent in the new secondary school curriculum appears to have been to take as given the diverse occupational paths into which adolescents will go after secondary school, and to say (implicitly) there is greater equality of educational opportunity for a boy who is not going to attend college if he has a specially-designed curriculum than if he must take a curriculum designed for college entrance.

There is only one difficulty with this difinition: it takes as *given* what should be problematic—that a given boy is going into a given post-secondary occupational or educational path. It is one thing to take as given that approximately 70 per cent of an entering high school freshman class will not attend college; but to assign a *particular child* to a curriculum designed for that 70 per cent closes off for that child the opportunity to attend college. Yet to assign all children to a curriculum designed for the 30 per cent who will attend college creates inequality for those who, at the end of high school, fall among the 70 per cent who do not attend college. This is a true dilemma, and one which no educational system has fully solved. It is more general than the college/noncollege dichotomy, for there is a wide variety of different paths that adolescents take on the completion of secondary school. In England, for example, a student planning to attend a university must specialize in the arts or the sciences in the later years of secondary school. Similar specialization occurs in the German gymnasium; and this is wholly within the group planning to attend university. Even greater specialization can be found among noncollege curricula, especially in the vocational, technical, and commercial high schools.

The distinguishing characteristic of this concept of equality of educational opportunity is that it accepts as given the child's expected future. While the concept discussed earlier left the child's future wholly open, this concept of differentiated curricula uses the expected future to match child and curriculum. It should be noted that the first and simpler concept is easier to apply in elementary schools where fundamental tools of reading and arithmetic are being learned by all children; it is only in secondary school that the problem of diverse futures arises.

It should also be noted that the dilemma is directly due to the social structure itself: if there were a virtual absence of social mobility with everyone occupying a fixed estate in life, then such curricula that take the future as given would provide equality of opportunity relative to that structure. It is only because of the high degree of occupational mobility between generations—that is, the greater degree of equality of *occupational* opportunity—that the dilemma arises.

The first stage in the evolution of the concept of equality of educational opportunity was the notion that all children must be exposed to the same curriculum in the same school. A second stage in the evolution of the concept assumed that different children would have different occupational futures and that equality of opportunity required providing different curricula for each type of student. The third and fourth stages in this evolution came as a result of challenges to the basic idea of equality of educational opportunity from opposing directions. The third stage can be seen at least as far back as 1896 when the Supreme Court upheld the southern states' notion of "separate but equal" facilities. This stage ended in 1954 when the Supreme Court ruled that legal separation by race inherently constitutes inequality of opportunity. By adopting the "separate but equal" doctrine, the southern states rejected assumption three of the original concept, the assumption that equality depended on the opportunity to attend the same school. This rejection was, however, consistent with the overall logic of the original concept since attendance at the same school was not an inherent part of that logic. The underlying idea was that opportunity resided in exposure to a curriculum; the community's responsibility was to provide that exposure, the child's to take advantage of it.

It was the pervasiveness of this underlying idea which created the difficulty for the Supreme Court. For it was evident that even when identical facilities and identical teacher salaries existed for racially separate schools, "equality of educational opportunity" in some sense did not exist. This had also long been evident to Englishmen as well, in a different context, for with the simultaneous existence of the "common school" and the "voluntary school," no one was under the illusion that full equality of educational opportunity existed. But the source of this inequality remained an unarticulated feeling. In the decision of the Supreme Court, this unarticulated feeling began to take more precise form. The essence of it was that the *effects* of such separate schools were, or were likely to be, different. Thus a concept of equality of opportunity which focused on *effects* of schooling began to take form. The actual decision of the Court was in fact a confusion of two unrelated premises: this new concept, which looked at results of schooling, and the legal premise that the use of race as a basis for school assignment violates fundamental freedoms. But what is important for the evolution of the concept of equality of opportunity is that a new and different assumption was introduced, the assumption that equality of opportunity depends in some fashion upon effects of schooling. I believe the decision would have been more soundly based had it not depended on the effects of schooling, but only on the violation of freedom; but by introducing the question of effects of schooling, the Court brought into the open the implicit goals of equality of educational opportunity— that is, goals having to do with the *results* of school—to which the original concept was somewhat awkwardly directed.

That these goals were in fact behind the concept can be verified by a simple mental experiment. Suppose the early schools had operated for only one hour a week and had been attended by children of all social classes. This would have met the explicit assumptions of the early concept of equality of opportunity since the school is free, with a common curriculum, and attended by all children in the locality. But it obviously would not have been accepted, even at that time, as providing equality of opportunity, because its effects would have been so minimal. The additional educational resources provided by middle- and upper-class families, whether in the home, by tutoring, or in private supplementary schools, would have created severe inequalities in results.

Thus the dependence of the concept upon results or effects of schooling, which had remained hidden until 1954, came partially into the open with the Supreme Court decision. Yet this was not the end, for it created more problems than it solved. It might allow one to assess gross inequalities, such as that created by dual school systems in the South, or by a system like that in the mental experiment I just described. But it allows nothing beyond that. Even more confounding, because the decision did not use effects of schooling as a criterion of inequality but only as justification for a criterion of racial integration, integration itself emerged as the basis for still a new concept of equality of educational opportunity. Thus the idea of effects of schooling as an element in the concept was introduced but immediately overshadowed by another, the criterion of racial integration.

The next stage in the evolution of this concept was, in my judgment, the Office of Education Survey of Equality of Educational Opportunity. This survey was carried out under a mandate in the Civil Rights Act of 1964 to the Commissioner of Education to assess the "lack of equality of educational opportunity" among racial and other groups in the United States. The evolution of this concept, and the conceptual disarray which this evolution had created, made the very definition of the task exceedingly difficult. The original concept could be examined by determining the degree to which all children in a locality had access to the same schools and the same curriculum, free of charge. The existence of diverse secondary curricula appropriate to different futures could be assessed relatively easily. But the very assignment of a child to a specific curriculum implies acceptance of the concept of equality which takes futures as given. And the introduction of the new interpretations, equality as measured by results of schooling and equality defined by racial integration, confounded the issue even further.

As a consequence, in planning the survey it was obvious that no single concept of equality of educational opportunity existed and that the survey must give information relevant to a variety of concepts. The basis on which this was done can be seen by reproducing a portion of an internal memorandum that determined the design of the survey:

> The point of second importance in design [second to the point of discovering the intent of Congress, which was taken to be that the survey was not for the purpose of locating willful discrimination, but to determine educational inequality without regard to intention of those in authority] follows from the first and concerns the definition of inequality. One type of inequality may be defined in terms of differences of the community's imput to the school, such as per-pupil expenditure, school plants, libraries, quality of teachers, and other similar quantities.
>
> A second type of inequality may be defined in terms of the racial composition of the school, following the Supreme Court's decision that segregated schooling is inherently unequal. By the former definition, the question of inequality through segregation is excluded, while by the latter, there is inequality of education

within a school system so long as the schools within the system have different racial composition.

A third type of inequality would include various intangible characteristics of the school as well as the factors directly traceable to the community inputs to the school. These intangibles are such things as teacher morale, teachers' expectations of students, level of interest of the student body in learning, or others. Any of these factors may affect the impact of the school upon a given student within it. Yet such a definition gives no suggestion of where to stop, or just how relevant these factors might be for school quality.

Consequently, a fourth type of inequality may be defined in terms of consequences of the school for individuals with equal backgrounds and abilities. In this definition, equality of educational opportunity is equality of results, given the same individual input. With such a definition, inequality might come about from differences in the school inputs and/or racial composition and/or from more intangible things as described above.

Such a definition would require that two steps be taken in the determination of inequality. First, it is necessary to determine the effect of these various factors upon educational results (conceiving of results quite broadly, including not only achievement but attitudes toward learning, self-image, and perhaps other variables). This provides various measures of the school's quality in terms of its effect upon its students. Second, it is necessary to take these measures of quality, once determined, and determine the differential exposure of Negroes (or other groups) and whites to schools of high and low quality.

A fifth type of inequality may be defined in terms of consequences of the school for individuals of unequal backgrounds and abilities. In this definition, equality of educational opportunity is equality of results given *different* individual inputs. The most striking examples of inequality here would be children from households in which a language other than English, such as Spanish or Navaho, is spoken. Other examples would be low-achieving children from homes in which there is a poverty of verbal expression or an absence of experiences which lead to conceptual facility.

Such a definition taken in the extreme would imply that educational equality is reached only when the results of schooling (achievement and attitudes) are the same for racial and religious minorities as for the dominant group.

The basis for the design of the survey is indicated by another segment of this memorandum:

Thus, the study will focus its principal effort on the fourth definition, but will also provide information relevant to all five possible definitions. This insures the pluralism which is obviously necessary with respect to a definition of inequality. The major justification for this focus is that the results of this approach can best be translated into policy which will improve education's effects. The results of the first two approaches (tangible inputs to the school, and segregation) can certainly be translated into policy, but there is no good evidence that these policies will improve education's effects; and while policies to implement the fifth would certainly improve education's effects, it seems hardly possible that the study could provide information that would direct such policies.

Altogether, it has become evident that it is not our role to define what constitutes equality for policy-making purposes. Such a definition will be an outcome of the interplay of a variety of interests, and will certainly differ from time to time as these interests differ. It should be our role to cast light on the state of inequality defined in the variety of ways which appear reasonable at this time.

The survey, then, was conceived as a pluralistic instrument, given the variety of concepts of equality of opportunity in education. Yet I suggest that despite the avowed intention of not adjudicating between these different ideas, the survey has brought a new stage in the evolution of the concept. For the definitions of equality which the survey was designed to serve split sharply into two groups.

The first three definitions concerned input resources: first, those brought to the school by the actions of the school administration (facilities, curriculum, teachers); second, those brought to the school by the other students, in the educational backgrounds which their presence contributed to the school; and third, the intangible characteristics such as "morale" that result from the inter-action of all these factors. The fourth and fifth definitions were concerned with the effects of schooling. Thus the five definitions were divided into three concerned with inputs to school and two concerned with effects of schooling. When the Report emerged, it did not give five different measures of equality, one for each of these definitions; but it did focus sharply on this dichotomy, giving in Chapter Two information on inequalities of input relevant to definitions one and two, and in Chapter Three information on inequalities of results relevant to definitions four and five, and also in Chapter Three information on the relation of input to results again relevant to definitions four and five.

Although not central to our discussion here, it is interesting to note that this examination of the relation of school inputs to effects on achievement showed that those input characteristics of schools that are most alike for Negroes and whites have least effect on their achievement. The magnitudes of differences between schools attended by Negroes and those attended by whites were as follows: least, facilities and curriculum; next, teacher quality; and greatest, educational backgrounds of fellow students. The order of importance of these inputs on the achievement of Negro students is precisely the same: facilities and curriculum least, teacher quality next, and backgrounds of fellow students, most.

By making the dichotomy between inputs and results explicit, and by focusing attention not only on inputs but on results, the Report brought into the open what had been underlying all the concepts of equality of educational opportunity but had remained largely hidden: that the concept implied *effective* equality of opportunity, that is, equality in those elements that are effective for learning. The reason this had remained half-hidden, obscured by definitions that involve inputs is, I suspect, because educational research has been until recently unprepared to demonstrate what elements are effective. The controversy that has surrounded the Report indicates that measurement of effects is still subject to sharp disagreement; but the crucial point is that *effects* of inputs have come to constitute the basis for assessment of school quality (and thus equality of opportunity) in place of using certain inputs by definition as measures of quality (e.g., small classes are better than large, higher-paid teachers are better than lower-paid ones, by definition).

It would be fortunate indeed if the matter could be left to rest there—if merely by using effects of school rather than inputs as the basis for the concept, the problem were solved. But that is not the case at all. The conflict between definitions four and five given above shows this. The conflict can be illustrated by resorting again to the mental experiment discussed earlier—providing a standard education of one hour per week, under identical conditions, for all children. By definition four, controlling all background differences of the children, results for Negroes and whites would be equal, and thus by this definition equality of opportunity would exist. But because such minimal schooling would have minimal effect, those children from educationally strong families would enjoy educational opportunity far surpassing that of others. And because such educationally strong backgrounds are found more often among whites than among

Negroes, there would be very large over-all Negro-white achievement differences —and thus inequality of opportunity by definition five.

It is clear from this hypothetical experiment that the problem of what constitutes equality of opportunity is not solved. The problem will become even clearer by showing graphs with some of the results of the Office of Education Survey. The highest line in Figure 1 shows the achievement in verbal skills by whites in the urban Northeast at grades 1, 3, 6, 9, and 12. The second line shows the achievement at each of these grades by whites in the rural Southeast. The third shows the achievement of Negroes in the urban Northeast. The fourth shows the achievement of Negroes in the rural Southeast.

When compared to the whites in the urban Northeast, each of the other three

groups shows a different pattern. The comparison with whites in the rural South shows the two groups beginning near the same point in the first grade, and diverging over the years of school. The comparison with Negroes in the urban Northeast shows the two groups beginning farther apart at the first grade and remaining about the same distance apart. The comparison with Negroes in the rural South shows the two groups beginning far apart and moving much father apart over the years of school.

Which of these, if any, shows equality of educational opportunity between regional and racial groups? Which shows greatest inequality of opportunity? I think the second question is easier to answer than the first. The last comparison

Figure 1. Patterns of achievement in verbal skills at various grade levels by race and region.

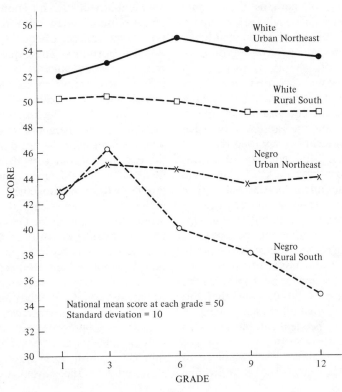

showing both initial difference and the greatest increase in difference over grades 1 through 12 appears to be the best candidate for the greatest inequality. The first comparison, with whites in the rural South, also seems to show inequality of opportunity, because of the increasing difference over the twelve years. But what about the second comparison, with an approximately constant difference between Negroes and whites in the urban Northeast? Is this equality of opportunity? I suggest not. It means, in effect, only that the period of school has left the average Negro at about the same level of achievement relative to whites as he began—in this case, achieving higher than about 15 per cent of the whites, lower than about 85 per cent of the whites. It may well be that in the absence of school those lines of achievement would have diverged due to differences in home environments; or perhaps they would have remained an equal distance apart, as they are in this graph (though at lower levels of achievement for both groups, in the absence of school). If it were the former, we could say that school, by keeping the lines parallel, has been a force toward the equalization of opportunity. But in the absence of such knowledge, we cannot say even that.

What would full equality of educational opportunity look like in such graphs? One might persuasively argue that it should show a convergence, so that even though two population groups begin school with different levels of skills on the average, the average of the group that begins lower moves up to coincide with that of the group that begins higher. Parenthetically, I should note that this does *not* imply that all students' achievement comes to be identical, but only that the *averages* for two population groups that begin at different levels come to be identical. The diversity of individual scores could be as great as, or greater than, the diversity at grade 1.

Yet there are serious questions about this definition of equality of opportunity. It implies that over the period of school there are no other influences, such as the family environment, which affect achievement over the twelve years of school, even though these influences may differ greatly for the two population groups. Concretely, it implies that white family environments, predominantly middle class, and Negro family environments, predominantly lower class, will produce no effects on achievement that would keep these averages apart. Such an assumption seems highly unrealistic, especially in view of the general importance of family background for achievement.

However, if such possibilities are acknowledged, then how far can they go before there is inequality of educational opportunity? Constant difference over school? Increasing differences? The unanswerability of such questions begins to give a sense of a new stage in the evolution of the concept of equality of educational opportunity. These questions concern the *relative intensity* of two sets of influences: those which are alike for the two groups, principally in school, and those which are different, principally in the home or neighborhood. If the school's influences are not only alike for the two groups, but very strong relative to the divergent influences, then the two groups will move together. If school influences are very weak, then the two groups will move apart. Or more generally, the relative intensity of the convergent school influences and the divergent out-of-school influences determines the effectiveness of the educational system in providing equality of educational opportunity. In this perspective, complete equality of opportunity can be reached only if all the divergent out-of-school influences vanish, a condition that would arise only in the advent of boarding schools; given the existing divergent influences, equality of opportunity can only be approached and never fully reached. The concept becomes one of degree of proximity to equality of opportunity. This proximity is determined, then, not merely by the *equality* of educational inputs, but by the *intensity* of the school's influences relative to the external divergent influences. That is, equality of output is not so much determined by equality of the resource inputs, but by the power of these resources in bringing about achievement.

Here, then, is where the concept of equality of educational opportunity presently stands. We have observed an evolution which might have been anticipated a century and a half ago when the first such concepts arose, yet one which is very different from the concept as it first developed. This difference is sharpened if we examine a further implication of the current concept as I have described it. In describing the original concept, I indicated that the role of the community and the educational institution was relatively passive; they were expected to provide a set of free public resources. The

responsibility for profitable use of those resources lay with the child and his family. But the evolution of the concept has reversed these roles. The implication of the most recent concept, as I have described it, is that the responsibility to create achievement lies with the educational institution, not the child. The difference in achievement at grade 12 between the average Negro and the average white is, in effect, the degree of inequality of opportunity, and the reduction of that inequality is a responsibility of the school. This shift in responsibility follows logically from the change in the concept of equality of educational opportunity from school resource inputs to effects of schooling. When that change occurred, as it has in the past few years, the school's responsibility shifted from increasing and distributing equally *its* "quality" to increasing the quality of its *students'* achievements. This is a notable shift, and one which should have strong consequences for the practice of education in future years.

Part II
Auxiliary Readings

Jules Henry, "Attitude Organization in the Elementary School Classroom," *American Journal of Orthopsychiatry*, 27 (1957), pp. 117–33.

The process of bringing the attitudes of children into congruence with adults' views of the social world is viewed as an important aspect of socialization. The author states that this process often involves manipulation of the child's emotions by the teacher. This is illustrated by showing how in different classrooms children's apparently innate tendencies toward peer rivalries and "carping criticism" of one another are rewarded by the teacher, thereby encouraging individualistic competition. Children in these classrooms showed marked anxiety and a high degree of docility in the face of teacher demands. Henry suggests that docility results from attempts to reduce anxiety by "giving the teacher what she wants" in order to receive emotional rewards. He concludes that teachers are often unaware of the consequences of their actions, and seek certain responses from pupils as a result of their own unconscious needs for order, love, etc.

Alex Inkeles, "A Note on Social Structure and the Socialization of Competence," *Harvard Educational Review*, 36 (1966), pp. 265–83.

The author contends that research on socialization has overemphasized primary role-learning while ignoring the socially important end-product of competence. A simple personality model is presented; and the effects of socialization for competence on aptitudes, skills, information, motives and needs, and cognitive modes are discussed. The emphasis of the discussion is the greater access of the more privileged elements of modern society to high capacity role models. In contrast, less privileged groups may be socialized to lack of competence through inadequate socialization mechanisms. This latter process may reenforce discrimination and prejudice even when legal equality is enforced.

Jan J. Loubser, "The Contribution of Schools to Moral Development: A Working Paper in the Theory of Action," *Interchange: A Journal of Educational Studies*, 1 (1970), pp. 99–118.

Using a Parsonian frame of reference, an ideal moral action system is developed. This framework is applied to the schools, and the author concludes that the structure of the educational system is detrimental to the development of moral autonomy and decision-making abilities.

O. K. Moore and A. R. Anderson, "Some Principles for the Design of Clarifying Educational Environment." In *Handbook of Socialization Theory and Research*, edited by David Goslin, Ch. 10. Chicago: Rand McNally, 1969.

The authors develop the theory that socialization in primitive societies consisted primarily of developing techniques to ensure that citizens learned and respected societal models which explained man's relationship to nature, chance, other men, and the normative aspects of group living. In a technological society, where education is a continuous process, these unchanging models are an insufficient basis for education. They suggest that there is a need to change the educational environment in order to produce a more problem-solving orientation. Principles for clarifying the environment would include:

increasing the number of perspectives which the child may take to include assessing, initiating, and reciprocating as well as accepting; allowing the child to develop his own problems in an autotelic environment; making the environment more responsive to the learners' activities (feedback) to allow self-understanding as a learner; and stressing production rather than passive participation.

Talcott Parsons, "The School Class as a Social System," *Harvard Educational Review*, 29 (1959), pp. 297–318.

The author attempts to define the social structure of the classroom and to relate it to the larger structure of society. The school system is seen as differentiated from other agencies for child socialization by its universalistic treatment of students and its achievement orientation. Within the school environment, the teacher's role is to select and reward performances which are valued by society. Peer group solidarity, which crosscuts the achievement axis, functions to keep the differential reward system from producing internal strains in the system. Selection on the elementary level is based on a combination of cognitive and moral achievement; while on the secondary level different types of roles are recognized. Thus, the secondary school is viewed as a bridge between the achievement order of the school and that of adult society. The school is seen as the major institution by which society may funnel its future manpower into appropriate positions.

David E. Wilder, Nathalie Friedman, Robert Hill, and Eva Sandis, *Actual and Perceived Consensus on Educational Goals between School and Community*, ch. 6. New York: Bureau of Applied Social Research, 1968 (USOE Grant No. OE-5-10-238).

The authors study the effects of age, sex and social background on family and school socialization and on school performance. Within the family interaction between mother and child becomes less frequent and more affectively neutral as the child grows older. In the classroom the frequency of both praise and punishment decline markedly with age. For both sexes grades tend to drop with age, although girls consistently receive higher grades. The authors suggest that academic achievement of the child is an important factor in family integration.

III

The School as a Formal Organization

Introduction

MODERN educational systems are comprised of highly complex, formal organizations. There are several reasons for the complexity of the school's structure, chief among them being the magnitude and age-gradedness of the student population, pressures for standardization of the product of education (so that the readiness of a group for advancement to higher levels, and ultimately for certification, can be judged), and the accountability of schools to the constituencies of parents, legislators, and employers. But schools are a special breed of formal organization. While they share many properties with such apparently remote cousins as business firms, government agencies, and industrial units, these properties are mainly of a *bureaucratic* nature: rational goal-setting, a hierarchy of offices, a division of labor with specially trained incumbents, a proliferation of rules, elaborate record-keeping systems, and so forth. Quite obviously, schools are something more than bureaucracies.

Within the broad class of complex organizations which pursue formally prescribed goals, there is a subclass of agencies which is devoted to the *processing* of some object. Schools belong in this subclass—but so do production departments of industrial firms. We therefore need to take a further step and distinguish between the processing of *things* and of *people*. This latter distinction is especially important, for the processing of human beings is quite a different matter from the processing of things. Humans can talk back, they can remain impervious to influence, they can defy reliable prediction of the outcomes of processing, they can evoke responses in their "processors" which are irrelevant and even detrimental to the task at hand, and they have identities outside of the organization. Further, people have a way of banding together to solve common status problems. These features of human processing systems affect the rational, bureaucratic structure of schools (see Part IV, The School As an Informal System). Also, human processing agencies require a certain kind of staff, one which has special qualifications for providing a personal service that is both highly problematic and highly valued by society. Consequenty, the teaching and administrative staff of schools share certain attributes with occupations known as professions (see Part V, Teaching As an Occupation, for an extended discussion of this point). In short, then, schools are not only complex organizations, but they are *professional* agencies.

There is still another distinction to be made among complex organizations which process people: prisons and mental hospitals seek to re-form persons, while schools seek to form them; or, in sociological terminology, schools are engaged in socialization whereas prisons and mental hospitals are engaged in resocialization.

In sum, it is not sufficient to view schools simply as bureaucracies, nor simply as agencies which process human beings; they must be seen as *bureaucratic, professional, socializing* agencies. This means that while schools share specific attributes with other kinds of organization, they combine these attributes into a special form. The restraints, requirements, and opportunities which are posed by the combination of these organizational properties pervade the entire setting and the relations of that setting with its environment, and must therefore be thoroughly comprehended by sociological observers of schools.

The first selection by Stanton Wheeler spells out certain generic features of schools as processing agencies. Although the differentiation of the setting is introduced as one dimension in Wheeler's taxonomy, major emphasis is placed on the *collective* status of recruits and the *serial* order of entry into the system. Wheeler observes that certain consequences of these formal patterns for handling recruits might be detrimental to the goals of socialization, e.g., the formation of a defensive subculture among recruits owing to their collective status. What this analysis suggests, then, are inherent tensions between the way in which recruits are organized and the goals of the system.

The bureaucratic features of schools also impinge on socialization, as suggested by Ronald G. Corwin in the next selection. While Wheeler focuses on the way in which recruits are handled in a complex setting, Corwin emphasizes the complexity of the setting itself. Thus, Corwin attempts to catalogue "elementary properties [which] could form the basis of a universal typology of organizations." These properties are identified by noting certain problems that must be solved by all organizations: coordination, allocation, balancing of autonomy and control, recruitment, direction-finding, and boundary maintenance. While his analysis might have proceeded without any special concern for socializing agencies, he has chosen to exemplify his ideas by reference to schools; and in so doing affords numerous examples of how the solution of organizational problems might affect socialization and the role-performances of the staff. Obviously, a taxonomy which is to prove useful for understanding schools as formal organizations will need to draw upon the perspectives of both Wheeler and Corwin. These selections, therefore, should be read as complementary analyses. Together they furnish a number of starting points for a more elaborate classification of the properties of schools as organizations.

The four selections which follow show how the properties of schools as organizations impinge on each of the three major status-groups in the school: administrators, teachers, and students. Charles E. Bidwell reviews research on the history, orientations, role strains, and leadership styles of *administrators*. Gerald Moeller examines the effect of bureaucratization on *teachers'* sense of power. Philip Jackson shows how the "crowd" (the "collective status of recruits" in Wheeler's terminology) affects socialization in the classroom; and Aaron V. Cicourel and John I. Kitsuse focus on the selection-allocation system.

A common theme in these selections is the *impact* of existing arrangements on the behavior and attitudes of participants. Thus, with reference to administrators, Bidwell comments, "The more rationalized the school-system structure, presumably the narrower the opportunity for variability of performance. At the same time, highly bureaucratized systems may undergo conflicts arising from norms of autonomy among the professional staff." Moeller concludes, however, that teachers in highly bureaucratic schools have a greater sense of *power*. The relationship between professional norms and bureaucratic principles might therefore be more complicated than is generally assumed. With respect to the impact of the organization on students in classrooms, Jackson points out that "the denial of desire is the ultimate outcome of many of the delays occurring in the classroom. The raised hand is sometimes ignored, the question to the teacher is sometimes brushed aside, the permission that is sought is sometimes refused." And finally, Cicourel and Kitsuse view "the differentiation of students as a consequence of the administrative organization and decisions of personnel in the high school."

Schools are also related to a number of other formal organizations. Some of these organizations are integral to the educational system, i.e., colleges and universities, and state and federal educational agencies; while other agencies are "ancillary" to this formal structure, i.e., textbook publishers and accreditation associations. These latter structures exert a great deal of influence on educational decisions at the local level. In fact, they account in large part for the national standardization of curriculum and instructional practices in spite of nominal local control. Thus, in the following selection, Sloan R. Wayland adduces evidence for a national system of education owing partly to a variety of ancillary structures. In short, the control structure of education cannot be understood if we restrict our attention to the internal bureaucratic organization or to the structure of local community control. Account must also be taken of the school's complex relationships with a host of other agencies.

Despite the importance of organizational effects, it seems safe to say that the participants commonly view educational structures as *givens*. As Cicourel and Kitsuse remark, "An interesting feature of our study is that references to inadequacies, defects, or failures of the 'system' by organizational personnel were virtually absent." Within the culture of professional education, inattention to organizational effects is due to a tradition of psychological perspectives on teaching and learning. The writings in Part III should provide an antidote to that viewpoint.

ONE WAY to identify the important qualities of a particular class of phenomena is to examine the implicit classification systems within which the class can be meaningfully located. This procedure can help sharpen the boundaries between related concepts, thus clarifying the structure of one particular class under consideration. Typically the class under study can be located meaningfully in more than one typology or classification system. This seems especially true of the class being considered here: namely, organizations designed to socialize people. A principal reason is that the defining properties of such organizations are likely to have different degrees of relevance depending on whether the agent or the recruit is the focal point for analysis, no matter how much the system of relations between the two is stressed as the common element. Thus it is useful to locate the organizations that process people in two different typologies. The first is more relevant to the processing agency; the second, to those who are ostensibly being socialized.

A Typology of Processing Systems

Organizations that process people are part of a broader typology of systems within which things are processed. The characteristics common to all members of the typology include some more or less clearly defined point of entry for the thing that is to be produced, some notion of movement through a series of stages or steps, and finally some point of exit from the system. In all cases, the product that leaves the system is expected to be different from that of entry. It may be different because a new organization has been put on parts that entered as separate pieces, as in the assembly line production of an automobile. Or it may be different because something new has been added to an already formed product, as when a

The Structure of Formally Organized Socialization Settings: Some Problems of Classification

Stanton Wheeler

Reprinted from "The Structure of Formally Organized Socialization Settings," in Socialization After Childhood by Orville G. Brim, Jr., and Stanton Wheeler (New York: John Wiley & Sons, Inc., 1966), pp. 55–69. Copyright © 1966 by John Wiley & Sons, Inc.; used by permission of the publisher.

bald tire is recapped or when a person attains new knowledge or skills. The important point is that work is done on whatever entered in the hope that its state will be changed when it leaves.

One dimension crucial for understanding such processing systems is the degree of differentiation of the processing agency. At one pole are systems where a single task is performed by an individual. At the other pole are highly differentiated systems, where many specialized tasks are allocated to different individuals or groups. The distinction between degrees of differentiation includes related indicators of complexity such as the sheer size of the organization, the number of separate steps or stages in the process, and the degree to which other elements of bureaucratic structure are present, but it will suffice here to treat all these as elements of differentiation.

Another dimension is the character of what is processed, an important attribute being whether it is a social or a nonsocial object. The primary distinction is between people and things, though this is a distinction too crude for certain instances. For example, a hospital processes people, but usually at the level of the physical anatomy and hence would be classed here as working on a nonsocial object. Where the primary purpose is to change the knowledge, beliefs, attitudes, or skills of those who pass through the system, the work is focused on a social object. The distinction between a nonsocial and a social object, as applied to persons, is roughly similar to that between the biological organism and the personality (12).

A simple typology of processing systems, resulting from cross-classifying the

in the movement from physical to social objects is that people can talk back. Unlike the inanimate object, the person on a production line can respond to his environment and often significantly alter it. He may agree to go along with the program, or he may fight it. His own goals may be at variance with those of the socializing agent. Therefore the whole set of "human relations skills" may have to be brought into play by the agent to accomplish the task at hand. Furthermore, the person is likely to have ties outside the immediate processing system that may exert further pressure on the socializing agents in the system. The influence of youthful peer groups on parents' socialization efforts with their children is a familiar example.

Table I—A Typology of Processing Systems

		Degree of Differentiation of Processing Agency	
		RELATIVELY UNDIFFERENTIATED	RELATIVELY DIFFERENTIATED
	NONSOCIAL OBJECT	Type I Individual craftsman	Type II Mass-production factory
Type of Product			
	SOCIAL OBJECT	Type III Teacher-pupil Mother-child Doctor-patient	Type IV School, prison, mental hospital, trade training center

two dimensions of degree of differentiation and type of product, yields the fourfold pattern indicated in Table 1. Type I is illustrated by the individual craftsman or the family production system. The mass production factory is the best concrete illustration of Type II. Type III is exemplified by any dyadic socialization pair: teacher-pupil, mother-child, doctor-patient. When the complex bureaucracy of Type II is joined by the processing of people, as in Type III, the result is Type IV, the socializing organization: the school, prison, mental hospital, or trade-training center.

Perhaps the most important difference

It is when both these movements—from a relatively undifferentiated system toward a highly differentiated one, and from a nonsocial product to a social one—are joined to form an organization that processes people, that the specific qualities relevant to the study of such settings emerge most clearly. Unlike the simple, often dyadic socialization process, new demands are introduced by the broader organizational form. Now it is not simply one person who can talk back. There emerges a chance for those being socialized together in the mass production process to communicate with each other and establish a social force in the organization not found in the typical manufacturing concern. In addition to whatever problems of communication and social control the organization faces from its lower echelon staff, it is confronted with similar problems from the very units being processed. As a consequence those in the lower echelons of the official system face problems found only at higher levels in the typical factory. The lower operatives in industry are spared the problems of role conflict faced by their superiors, the foremen. But in organizations that process people these conflicts are generated throughout the system, for all employees are in the middle. This heightens problems of communication and role conflict.

The typical dyadic model of socialization in relatively undifferentiated systems may be carried over into the more complex organizational form. In fact, it usually is, as when tutor and pupil are transformed into teacher and student, or therapist and client in a psychiatrist's office become therapist and patient in a hospital. But three new problems are also generated that may significantly alter the relationship between the members of the dyad. First, even though the dyadic relation may remain, it now takes place in a complex organization, and new problems of scheduling and coordination arise. Whereas in the simpler state the agent may have had to handle a number of problems seemingly remote from his primary function, the organization may provide new differentiated units that relieve him of these responsibilities. Bookkeeping departments, attendance offices, and appointment secretaries are examples of forms that remove responsibilities the agent may have carried in less differentiated systems. Theoretically, these may free him for concentration on the socialization task, but there are other forms of control required by the mass production system that may offset these benefits. His work must now be coordinated in time and space with that of

others, and there are features of the setting that must hold for all members despite individual differences in wants, desires, and tastes. Economy may dictate, for example, the quantity ordering of materials such as books, calculators, or other necessary equipment, thus reducing individual autonomy. All these differences are similar in kind to those brought about by the movement toward formal organizations in processing physical objects. They stem from the effort to accomplish just what was done in the simpler and less differentiated system, but to do it more efficiently.

The second problem emerges with the realization that recruits may be influenced in fundamentally new ways by utilizing the organization itself as a mechanism of change. Now it is no longer simply a question of doing more efficiently what was previously done, but of gaining new leverage and a greater range of effects than was possible in the simpler systems. Perhaps the clearest instance has been in therapeutic settings, where the use of group therapy, first justified as a simple expedient to cope with large numbers, came to be seen as having new potentials for effecting personality change. Later, when concern emerged about "the other twenty-three hours," the total organization was viewed as a major factor in rehabilitation (10). This trend leads directly to a search for organizational variables that may produce differences in outcomes for recruits.

Third, these changes raise new potentialities and new problems for the recruits. Although they may perhaps receive more specialized and differentiated training, now both they and the organization face problems of integrating the diverse programs and assuring that the proper balance and fusion results from the influence of separate parts.

Although we are concerned with only one kind of processing system in this work, it is relevant to ask about the conditions under which the various types occur and their consequences for the broader systems in which they are embedded. It seems obvious, for example, that it was not until most of the material problems of survival were solved, and men freed from physical labor by development of an industrial technology, that energies began to be turned in great amounts to the development of occupations and professions for the processing of people. There are still large differences in the extent to which such processing is organized in large bureaucracies. Comparison of the size and other indicators of scale of schools, mental hospitals, and prisons in different societies might suggest some of the conditions leading to differing rates of bureaucratization of the socializing organizations.

A Typology of Interpersonal Settings

When a person moves into a new interpersonal setting, a major problem he faces is understanding the setting and coming to terms with its demands. He must develop a workable "definition of the situation" to guide his action. In addition to whatever definition he derives from his background, much of his orientation can be expected to come from what he learns about the setting itself. The socializing agents will have their version of this process, but since he is a recruit and they are not, his position will be different.

A primary feature of the setting that may aid the recruit in developing a meaningful definition of it is the extent to which others in the setting are or have been in his position and can aid his adaptation. An aspect of this is simply whether he is facing the new setting alone or in the company of others. This can be called simply the *individual* or *collective* status of recruits. As Becker (2) and others have clearly noted, much adult socialization is organized so that a large number of persons are introduced to the new setting simultaneously—a group or class is the target of socialization. Under these circumstances adaptation is likely to proceed much differently from the case where one person enters alone, since the recruits can arrive at a collective solution to the problems they face.

A second and related aspect is whether the recruit has been preceded by others who have been through the same process and who can teach him about the setting. This might be called a *serial* pattern of socialization, to distinguish it from *disjunctive* patterns wherein the recruits are not following in the footsteps of predecessors.

The definition of these two aspects is arbitrary. For example, the number of recruits entering simultaneously may be more important than the simple dichotomy of individual versus collective entry, although studies of individual conformity in the face of social pressure suggest that the presence of just one more like-minded person may radically alter responses (1). The meaning of entering a setting together is also not precise. Individuals may enter the setting at different times, but at intervals small enough that they are thought of as a unit and are "processed" together.

There is similar arbitrariness in the distinction between disjunctive and serial patterns of socialization. For example, even if there are no persons in the setting who have preceded the recruit in his specific position, persons in similar organizations may have done so, and he may attempt to learn from them.

Combining these two characteristics— the individual or collective status of recruits, and the serial or disjunctive character of the setting—results in a fourfold typology arranging socialization settings by the extent to which others therein can help the recruit arrive at a workable definition of his situation (Table 2). The prototype for the individual-disjunctive pattern (Type I) is the oldest child in a family or the first occupant of a newly created job. The collective-disjunctive pattern (Type II) is illustrated by a summer training institute or a group of scholars visiting a particular country in a certain year. Type III, the

second case he can turn only to the latter. The first case seems generally more conservative from the point of view of the organization, since earlier occupants of the position may accumulate, test, and subsequently discard many possible solutions, and since its members can speak to the new recruit with whatever authority seniority and experience offer. It is anticipated that he may look to them for guidance in problem solving, leading to a patterned transmission of the

Table 2—A Typology of Interpersonal Settings

Social Context of Entering Members

		INDIVIDUAL	COLLECTIVE
		Type I	Type II
	DISJUNCTIVE	Oldest child in family; first occupant of newly created job	Summer training institute; group of visiting scholars in foreign country
Social Composition of Other Members		Type III	Type IV
	SERIAL	New occupant of a job previously occupied by another person	Schools; universities; professional training centers (approximated by prisons and mental hospitals)

individual-serial pattern, is frequent in occupational recruitment: the individual is the only one occupying his position, but others have filled it before him and have moved on to other positions in the organization. Finally, the collective-serial pattern typifies large-scale organizations such as schools, universities, and professional training centers and is approximated by prisons and mental hospitals.

To explore the conditions and consequences of each of the four types more thoroughly, consider the two cases in which each influence works separately. In the first, the individual can turn to persons still in the setting who formerly occupied his position, but not to others who are experiencing it with him. In the

organization's culture to new members.

In the second case, labeled the collective-disjunctive type, these influences are missing, but the individual is not thrown solely on his own resources. Since he faces the problems along with others, they may work out a collective solution. The recruits who accompany him can still use past experience, but it is likely to be less relevant, coming as it does from their own backgrounds. The emergent collective solution or style of response is likely to be less stable and predictable than in the individual-serial pattern. The pressures to find a joint solution will probably be unusually great, since there can be no reliance on the stability provided by "older, wiser heads."

The serial pattern, precisely because of its stability, risks stagnation and is likely to be undesirable from the point of view of agents when things are going badly. There is the likelihood that the former recruits will train the new ones using the defeating pattern. Should morale be low, older members introduce the newer ones into the low-morale system. Should lower-level persons be disrupting the program, they are likely to attempt to indoctrinate the new recruits with their viewpoint. Thus, when organizational staff try to get it out of its current rut or to develop novel solutions to problems, they are likely to move toward the disjunctive pattern precisely because of the potent socializing effects of the serial pattern.

An illustration of this process is provided by an innovation in prison and correctional programs. When California's Chino prison was constructed as a model institution demonstrating the best modern penal philosophy, its founders refused to hire any correctional staff who had worked in prisons before, and they took great care in selecting new inmates for the program, with the aim of making a break with the older correctional philosophy. The common-sense observation is that the first class "sets the tone" for future recruits.

The distinction between a serial and a disjunctive pattern may be applied both to the socializing agents and to the recruits or clients, as well as to the higher and lower echelons of the organization in question. Only when a new organization is getting under way, or when there has been a general "house cleaning," will all or most of the participants be in the disjunctive pattern. Frequently, all or most recruits will be in the serial pattern: college students follow others, as do college faculty members. But often a pattern is serial from the point of view

of the socializing agents, yet disjunctive from the point of view of the recruit. This is true wherever there is a position to be filled by only one person, whose predecessor leaves before the new appointment is made. Under these conditions, the socializing agents will have some performance norms to apply to the person, deriving from judgments of his predecessors. Since the recruit was not there when the other person was, he lacks this knowledge. Some of the problems this situation creates are suggested in studies of *succession* in organizations (9).

Occasionally this process is reversed, and the persons ostensibly being socialized build up a knowledge from long-term experience that is likely to be greater than that of those who are to socialize them. This seems true in some prisons and mental hospitals, where staff turnover may equal or in some instances exceed inmate turnover. It is not surprising in such circumstances that the organizations are sometimes literally run by the inmates. This is one of the characteristics that distinguish prisons and mental hospitals from most educational settings, where the possibility of a recruit becoming a "lifer" is more remote.[1]

The collective patterns, as Becker has noted, may provide the recruit with support, should he care to resist the efforts of the socializing agents to change his beliefs, attitudes, or behavior. Where initial commitment is low, as it is among recruits to correctional settings, the collective nature of the process contains the seeds of counterrevolution or at least of a socializing process opposed to that of the staff. Prison is perhaps the most familiar example of how a collective pattern may function to protect recruits from symbolic and actual "pains of imprisonment" (15). It appears to get force both from its serial character, with older inmates providing informal socialization for the newer recruits, and also from its collective nature, with inmates typically being processed in cohorts, as determined by similarity in dates of arrival.

Collective patterns may make a more positive contribution under certain circumstances. If initial commitment to the organization and its recruits is high, the peer group may be harnessed as an aid in socialization, thus intensifying the effects of the formal socialization program. Shil's observations (14) on primary groups in the army and the common feeling in graduate schools that students may learn from each other as much as or more than they do from the faculty are instances of this intensifying effect.

It may be that the collective settings yield quite successful or quite unsuccessful socialization outcomes, depending on the initial commitment and the degree of organization among recruits. This is presumably the reason why personnel in organizations like prisons stress that their recruits should establish individual adaptations, go it alone, mind their own affairs, and have little to do with other inmates, while the agents in colleges and universities encourage student interaction as a meaningful and important part of socialization.

Initial commitment is of course only one of the characteristics that will help determine whether recruits accept or reject the official aims of the organization. The manner in which the staff members work with the recruits and the immediate pressures of the situation, as well as the recruits' initial commitments, will influence the collective response. In some medical schools, for example, despite high initial commitment, the recruits may organize in ways the staff does not approve (3, 4). Consecutive administrators in any type of socialization setting may encourage individual adaptations for fear that the organized recruits may move in unacceptable directions.

Since isolated, individual adaptation seems to go against the usual tendency of persons to desire knowledge about their new setting and companionship while in it, we might expect this pattern to be chosen only under rather special circumstances. Those modes of socialization or resocialization that we think of as most extreme and that have as their goal not a mere change in the skill level or the attitude of the person being socialized but rather a thorough reconstruction of his personality typically involve an individual and disjunctive pattern. A prime example is psychoanalysis. In some cases other recruits may be present but are used to destroy prior patterns rather than to sustain them, to build mutual mistrust rather than action in concert. Examples are brainwashing and thought-reform programs. Indeed, in a recent analysis of radical individual change, McHugh argues that such destructive conditions are necessary before new patterns can be established (11).

The conditions for use of an individual disjunctive pattern are not restricted to radical resocialization. Organizations are likely to create a new position when novel and creative programs are desired. The person entering such a position may be left free to define his role as he sees fit, becoming, in effect, his own socializing agent. And of course these conditions are likely to be personally attractive to those who wish autonomy and the freedom to follow their own paths.

It should be clear that the typology refers to the possibility, rather than the actuality, of interpersonal contacts. Those entering a collective-serial pattern may spend most of their time with persons who have been in the setting longer, or they may spend it with those who entered with them. The conditions and consequences of adopting one or another pattern are not often studied. Wallace's (16) recent study of socialization in colleges shows the potent effect of the serial pattern, even when other alternatives are available. And of course some individuals may remain effectively alone in any setting if they fail to establish ties to other members.

Interesting questions can be raised about the relative frequency of occurrence of the four types. It seems clear that they are not found in equal numbers. Collective-disjunctive patterns, for example, occur fairly rarely. Most collective settings have been programed to have a serial character as well. With industrialization and related institutional processes, the need for mass socialization has led to an increase in the serial-collective patterns relative to others.

Relation to Other Typologies and Concepts

These two typologies present different ways of locating formally organized socialization settings, one calling attention to the general features of processing systems, the other to the possible interpersonal contexts found when the objects processed are human beings. In each case there is one type (Type IV) that tends to be filled by the same concrete social settings. It is the dimensions of variation within those settings that are under consideration. It should be remembered, however, that the distinctions are analytic and that some of the concrete illustrations merge with the other defined types. Prisons and mental hospitals, for example, have all the serial processing qualities noted for schools. Their collective character is a little different, however, since they are continually receiving and releasing recruits, while dates of reception and exit are much more routinized for schools.

Socialization types can, of course, be classified and reclassified in an infinite variety of ways, and much heated verbal argument may ensue about the most appropriate dimensions and labels to be attached to them. The typologies which have been presented earlier must be justified by their ability to clarify the distinctive characteristics of organizations that process people and by suggesting relevant studies that will help inform a comparative analysis of interpersonal situations. It is suggested, for example, that organizations that process people will differ in important ways from those that process things, that within the people-producing variety important differences turn on the complexity of the processing system, and that from the point of view of recruits a critical feature is the extent to which they are accompanied or preceded by others similarly situated.

Different features could have been chosen as bases of classification: whether the recruits are voluntary participants, whether the settings approximate a total institution or community, or any of the variety of dimensions along which social settings can vary. These alternatives were neglected in part because they are already familiar, in part because the dimensions used here help illumine features that are often neglected because they are so obvious. But it may be useful to identify briefly the points of overlap with other typologies and concepts.

Etzioni's classification (7), for example, is based on the nature of the authority and compliance system in the organization and is not sensitive to differences in the type of product. The "lower-level participants" in Etzioni's scheme are sometimes employees of the organization (workers on an assembly line), sometimes persons being processed by the organization (students, patients, inmates). The distinction between these two categories of participant is crucial for the present discussion.

Most socializing organizations would appear in Blau's and Scott's typology as service organizations, that is, organizations in which the prime beneficiary is the client in direct contact with the organization (6). But some socializing organizations might be found in Blau's and Scott's category of commonweal organizations, since the organizations were established to benefit the public. Many organizations that service clients would not appear as socializing organizations. More generally, organizations that merely provide a service (such as shops, dental clinics, or legal aid bureaus) and have no long-range plans for systematic changes in their clients would not qualify as socializing. A recent paper by Bidwell and Vreeland (10) draws distinctions somewhat similar to those introduced in this work and by Blau and Scott.

Parson's classification, based upon the primary function the organization serves for the broader social system, would unite many of the socializing institutions with religious and other organizations on the grounds that both serve the function of pattern maintenance—the provision for cultural continuity across generations. Some others, such as mental hospitals and correctional agencies, would be classified with courts and other structures that serve integrative functions (13).

Lastly, the concept of the socializing organization is closely linked to that of the total institution, as described in the definitive work by Erving Goffman (8). Many of the ideas expressed later owe a debt to Goffman's treatment. His distinctive emphasis is on the encapsulation of the individual by the establishment; the chief defining property is that the organization is set up as a 24-hour living establishment for its inmates. That some total organizations attempt to change their recruits whereas others do not is of only peripheral interest in Goffman's scheme. It becomes a central interest here. But whether or not the system is "total"

in Goffman's sense is not a defining property of the socializing organization.

The two conceptualizations share the binary quality noted so clearly in Goffman's analysis; the distinction between keepers and kept is paralleled by that between socializing agent and recruit. But beyond that, the prime emphasis is the study of socialization is on the problematic relation between what is being taught and what is being learned.

Developmental Socialization and Resocialization

The focus of the remainder of this study will be on sources of variation within the class of organizations that process people. Instead of using a typological framework, the major variables will be simply introduced and discussed serially. However, the common-sense division between schools, colleges, and universities on the one hand, and mental hospitals and prisons on the other, is important enough for special attention.

Schools and universities are familiar examples of what might be called *developmental* socialization systems, where the formal purpose is the training, education, or more generally the further socialization of the individuals passing through. These are the organizations we recognize as legitimate for persons to move through, though not everyone is expected to do so. Contrasting to the developmental socialization systems are what we might call *resocialization* systems, where the formal purpose is to make up for or correct some deficiency in earlier socialization.[2] These are largely the organizations designed to resocialize the deviant, in contrast to those designed for the further socialization of conventional persons.

This simple distinction is so pervasive that it becomes useful for discussing variations in the structure of socialization patterns, especially since the two types are likely to fall at different ends of any dimension along which the patterns vary. Both types are clearly distinguished from those where the primary purpose is merely to hold or detain individuals, with no formally stated mission to bring about personal change. This distinction, like the others mentioned above, is analytic. A specific prison or mental hospital may appear more developmental, and some schools may take on the character of prisons. This is entirely consistent with the argument drawn here, since the intent is to locate dimensions that apply across the range of concrete instances. It is to be expected that the most benign therapeutic community in an open prison might be less prison-like than, say, a prep school organized along military lines. Indeed, when we locate these organizations by their positions on some theoretically meaningful continua there may be good reason for challenging the official labels by which they are known.

Notes

[1] It is interesting to note, however, the concern of university graduate departments about "perpetual" graduate students, the imposition of regulations aimed at forcing such students to obtain an advanced degree within a fixed interval of time or else leave the department, and the role of such students in some of the recent collective demonstrations on university campuses.

[2] A paper prepared for the Social Science Research Council Conference by Yonina Talmon makes useful further distinctions among types of resocialization that this paper passes by.

References

1. Asch, Solomon. "Effects of Group Pressure upon the Modification and Distortion of Judgment." In *Groups, Leadership and Men*, edited by H. Geutz Kow. Pittsburgh: The Carnegie Press, 1951.
2. Becker, Howard S. "Personal Change in Adult Life." *Sociometry*, 27 (1964), pp. 40–53.
3. Becker, Howard S., and Geer, Blanche. "Fate of Idealism in Medical School." *American Sociological Review*, 23 (1958), pp. 50–56.
4. Becker, Howard S., and Geer, Blanche. "Student Culture in Medical School." *Harvard Educational Review*, 28 (1958), pp. 70–80.
5. Bidwell, Charles E., and Vreeland, Rebecca S. "College Education and Moral Orientations: An Organizational Approach." Presented at the annual meeting of the American Sociological Association, August 30, 1962.
6. Blau, Peter, and Scott, W. Richard. *Formal Organizations*. San Francisco: Chandler Publishing Company, 1962.
7. Etzioni, Amitai. *A Comparative Analysis of Complex Organizations*. New York: Free Press, 1961.
8. Goffman, Erving. "On the Characteristics of Total Institutions." *Asylums*, pp. 1–124. Garden City, N.Y.: Doubleday, Anchor Books, 1961.
9. Gouldner, Alvin. *Patterns of Industrial Bureaucracy*, New York: Free Press, 1954.
10. Jones, Maxwell. *The Therapeutic Community*, New York: Basic Books, 1953.
11. McHugh, Peter. Paper delivered at the American Sociological Association meetings, 1964.
12. Parsons, Talcott. "An Approach to Psychological Theory in Terms of the Theory of Action." In *Psychology: A Study of a Science*, Vol. 3, edited by Sigmund Koch. New York: McGraw-Hill, 1959.
13. Parsons, Talcott, "Suggestions for a Sociological Approach to the Theory of Organizations, I, II." *Administrative Science Quarterly*, 1 (1956), pp. 63–85 and 225–39.

14. Shils, Edward. "Primary Groups in the Modern Army." In *Continuities in Social Research: Studies in the Scope and Method of the Modern Soldier*, edited by Robert K. Merton and Paul F. Lazarsfeld. New York: Free Press, 1953.

15. Sykes, Gresham M. *The Society of Captives*. Princeton: Princeton University Press, 1958.

16. Wallace, Walter L. "Institutional and Life-Cycle Socialization of College Freshmen." *American Journal of Sociology*, 70 (1964), pp. 303–18.

The School as an Organization

Ronald G. Corwin

Abridged from Ronald G. Corwin, "Education and the Sociology of Complex Organizations," in On Education: Sociological Perspectives, edited by Donald A. Hansen and Joel E. Gerstl (New York: John Wiley & Sons, 1967), pp. 156–223. Copyright 1967 by John Wiley & Sons, Inc. Used by permission of John Wiley & Sons, Inc., and the author. Since this is a highly abridged version of the original article, the reader with a special interest in the topic should refer to the original.

REGRETTABLY, the study of complex educational organizations is a relatively neglected topic, for sociologists, like educators, have been so impressed by the teaching function itself—the characteristics of teachers and students, the teaching methods, and face-to-face interaction in classrooms—and they have been so concerned with the values that schools teach, that only rarely have they shown genuine interest in the theoretical issues connected with the organization of educational systems.

Nevertheless, evidence has begun to accumulate. This discussion will weld available evidence with conjecture in an attempt to isolate a few selected structural properties which promise to be of more general relevance for describing many types of organizations in addition to schools. These "elementary properties," as they will be called, can be identified through the way organizations function; or, more specifically, their dysfunctional reverberations may be the key. For, like the pressure applied by physical scientists to metals in order to determine their structural properties and hence their tensile strength, organiza-

tional problems produce tensions which, in exposing weaknesses in organizational structure, illuminate the essential properties that always are in operation, though less apparent under normal conditions.

The first problems to be treated—coordination and allocation—originate from the internal principles of organization, the complex system of authority and division of labor. Principles of organization not only prevent conflicts, they often are responsible for them. The tendency for divisions of an organization to become self-sufficient (functionally autonomous) and the corresponding tendency for its parts to change at different rates (structural lag) are prime problems of internal coordination.

Organizations are even less in command of the outside pressures, and for that reason most of their problems concern ways of accommodating to and resisting social forces that eventually impinge upon them. The *recruiting process* represents one mechanism linking them to fluctuations in the environment.

Internal conflicts and inconsistencies, and the precarious balance between organizations and their environments, diminish their ability to control their own *direction*, which is a problem deserving separate treatment. Official goals tend to be replaced by other objectives and unofficial commitments. The comprehensive scope of most public schools has increased their resiliency, but in comparison to more specialized ones, comprehensive schools cannot hope to achieve all their goals with equal effectiveness.

The importance of the intruding environment explains the enormous energy that organizations devote to defining and defending their *boundaries*. Although recruiting practices afford a long-run defense against outsiders (by keeping certain types of people out), more direct strategies are available. The crucial problem of boundary maintenance is how to enlist the aid of outsiders without succumbing to their influence. The capacity to do this depends in part upon the financing procedures employed and the control structure. This problem will be considered at the end of this section.

Coordination Problems

Coordination is the act of unifying the responsibilities of lower echelons. Coordination problems increase with organizational complexity, which in turn is a function of the number of subparts and the degree of consistency among them. It should be noted that school administrators derive power from a complex administrative system. For, in the first place, complexity increases the available alternatives; a wide range of alternatives increases the ability of administrators to bargain for the loyalty of members and to win outside support. Band, chorus, football, and dramatics all contribute to a school's community support, and the availability of these activities increases the likelihood that most students will find something of interest in school. Second, the more complex an organization becomes, the more control it can develop over its noninternal functions and the less dependent it must be on outside assistance. Because they have their own research, testing, and public relations departments, the largest school systems in the country can be impervious to outsiders who may approach them to do research or testing. Similarly, the full-time public relations officers found in the more complex systems protect the organization by serving as permanent watchdogs screening information that might otherwise leak to the public as well as concentrating on favorable publicity.

Yet despite these advantages, a major share of the problems of school systems can be attributed to their complexity. Problems develop because work flow has not been well planned and priorities not assigned to scarce resources; grade levels are improperly arranged so that the work of students does not accumulate progressively; football teams compete with the band for use of the practice field; overlapping basketball and drama schedules create problems in scheduling the use of the auditorium. To counteract this divisiveness, administrative systems are established to coordinate the separate functions. The difficulties likely to be encountered, and the consequent size of the administrative system, increase with complexity. Complexity, in turn, is a function of several characteristics: (1) the division of labor, (2) specialization of personnel, (3) hierarchy of authority, and (4) standardization, or the system of established rules and regulations governing work. Each characteristics will be described briefly.[1]

DIVISION OF LABOR

The way work is divided and allocated determines the number of divisions at each level of the organization. The number of separate education programs in the educational "track" system (e.g., vocational, college prep, and general programs) and the number of separate academic departments and special administrative units are indices of the extent of division of labor in schools.

The division of labor probably tends to increase with organizational size. However, larger organizations do not necessarily have more varied *kinds* of parts than small ones. In this regard, Barker and his colleagues (1962), exploring the relationship between size of high schools and the opportunity of students to participate in extracurricular activities, found that large schools which have 25 times as many students as small ones have only five times as many "behavior settings" and 1.5 times as many varieties of setting (although the schools were not as large as many metropolitan schools, and community size was not controlled). In other words, although small schools have fewer replications of some of their parts, they do have similar parts. The proportion of participants was three to twenty times as great in smaller schools as in larger ones, while the kinds of activities in which students engaged was twice as great in larger schools. (Schools differing in enrollment by 100 percent permitted only 17 percent [median] difference in variety of instruction.) Proportionately more behavior settings were devoted to operation (administration) in larger than in smaller schools. The authors conclude that when better facilities are purchased at the expense of large size, the facilities are likely to be discounted by lower participation rates of students, and hence, that it may be easier to bring specialized and varied behavior settings to small schools than to raise the level of individual participation in large ones.

The distinction between distinctively different parts and those which are merely replicated may prove to be important for estimating administrative complexity and for evaluating the learning experiences that schools provide. For, as this study suggests, the amount of sheer replication can alter learning opportunities.

SPECIALIZATION OF PERSONNEL

Whereas the division of labor is a property of organization, the kind of specialization being referred to here is a personal characteristic: the level of training required of employees. An index of specialization of teaching personnel might include the formal training of a school's faculty and the proportion teaching courses in which they majored in college. It is possible for an extensive

division of labor to be implemented by relatively unspecialized personnel; assembly lines, for example, require very low degrees of specialization, whereas highly specialized personnel, such as lawyers, can function outside of complex organizations.

STANDARDIZATION

To the overlays of structure already mentioned must be added the system of standards embodied in rules and standard procedures. Seeking order and consistency among subordinate units and overall predictability, the administration spins a web of rules and regulations and establishes standards. An index of standardization might include measures of compliance with standard lesson plans and curriculum guides, and the uniformity of tests and textbooks in use in the system.

Standardization produces a number of latent, often ignored side effects. For example, although teachers frequently complain about the constraints of rules and regulations, standardization can increase their power if they are in otherwise insecure positions subject to the caprice and arbitrary judgments of administrators. The way rules compensate for power unexpectedly became apparent in Moeller's study of teachers' sense of power in twenty school systems rated by eight judges on the bases of specified bureaucratic characteristics. (Midwest Administration Center, 1962) The original hypothesis was that bureaucracy is responsible for teachers' feelings that they are powerless to affect teaching policy (as measured by a scale developed for the purpose), but it was not confirmed. On the contrary, teachers in bureaucratic systems sensed more power than those in less bureaucraticized systems, where particularism and lack of policy were more typical.

Perhaps only in an orderly, understandable, and predictable organization can individuals expect to have influence. If a subordinate knows the prescribed course of action, the lines of communication, and the policy on a particular issue, he is at least protected from the caprice of the administration, and rules actually may permit him to make demands which he could not make in the absence of policy. . . .

However, the same uniformities that support *teachers* can jeopardize the nterests of some of their *students*. In their quest for a fully coordinated system, administrators and teachers have attempted to apply uniform methods and curricula to diverse types of students, even when they have not been uniformly relevant. Moreover, the uniform status system which has evolved from the use of homogeneous evaluation critera throughout the system has lowered the effectiveness of teachers with some types of children. Teachers are rewarded for complying with standards applicable to middle-class-oriented schools, even when assigned to situations where these standards cannot be achieved with normal efficiency. Faced with the same evaluation criteria applied to teachers in middle-class schools, slum school teachers are compelled to impose system-wide standards on slum school children for whom they are less relevant. Teachers who modify the curriculum to fit the interests of lower-class children or those who do not require their children to "keep up" with the system-wide rate of progress are likely to be treated as failures. . . .

. . . The fact that valid principles of coordination, so convenient for the organization, can be detrimental to the education of lower-class children again illustrates how organizational principles affect the learning process.

STRUCTURAL LAGS

Social changes create serious handicaps for coordination. Because organizations have only incomplete control over their subparts, some parts will adapt to changes differently than others; hence, organizations can adapt to change only imperfectly. A social change tends to divide the membership into separate coalitions, some of whom welcome it, while others, who owe their positions to the existing system, resist it. Consequently, most complex organizations experience some degree of *structural lag*, that is, an inconsistency throughout the organization due to the fact that the subparts change at different rates. As a result, the organization has difficulty performing its new functions. . . .

Allocation of Power and Authority

The division of labor and standardization represent "horizontal" systems of control, the results of allocating responsibility among peers. Complex organizations also have a vertical division of responsibility, the hierarchy of authority (or the chain of command). The official authority system is an organization's moral spine. Before work can be coordinated and before outside changes and pressures can be accommodated, at least the blueprint of an authority system must be established.

HIERARCHY OF AUTHORITY

The prominence of administration (i.e., activity devoted simply to maintaining the day-to-day operation of the organization) can be expressed as a ratio of the number of administrators in the system to the number of teachers. In one study, it was found that administrators increased disproportionately with the size of the school system (Terrien and Mills, 1955). This tendency may be explained, in part, by the fact that school systems consist of a number of schools at different locations, each requiring separate administrative staffs (Anderson and Warkow, 1961); it also may reflect a particular stage of growth of public schools in this country. A related dimension is the time lapse that occurs before a request by a teacher is acted upon by the administration; the time required increases with the amount of consultation that administrators must do among one another.

Perhaps the most important fact about the hierarchy is the way authority and power are *distributed*. This distribution can be measured along several dimensions (Tannenbaum, 1961). First, the total number of levels of authority can be counted. For example, the authority structure of a system having only a principal and a superintendent differs from one with department heads responsible to a series of assistant principals, curriculum coordinators, and assistant superintendents. Second, the amount of control exercised at *each level* relative to the other levels determines the "slope" of the structure. For example, in one school department heads exercise more control than either teachers below them or the principal above them; while in another, both teachers and the principal exercise equivalent influence in excess of that of department heads. Finally, the *total amount* of control can vary between systems. Two organizations with similar distributions of authority can differ because in one there is more power at every level than at comparable levels of the other. Tannenbaum (1961) reports that the effectiveness of local Leagues of Women Voters studied was related to the distribution of control within each league; in the more effective locals, control was distributed in a more "democratic," less centralized way. It would be instructive to examine the

quality of schools from the same standpoint.

Although they represent an organization's moral system, authority structures are challenged by the tendency of subordinate groups to develop more power than authorized. The problem assumes three forms, which will be discussed: (a) functional divisions having officially equivalent status develop differing amounts of power; (b) subordinates develop informal power structures among themselves, irrespective of their formal status; and (c) subordinates as a group become professionalized, claiming the technical competence that enables them to challenge official authority.

FUNCTIONAL AUTONOMY

The hierarchy of authority produces "social distance" between strata, and thereby reduces the interaction between levels of the hierarchy, hence limiting the opportunity for conflict between supervisors and their subordinates. To a lesser extent, divisions of labor and rules, such as the separation of classrooms and scheduled time periods for particular activities, help to reduce ambiguities which are sometimes a source of conflict in organizations.

However, the two major principles on which cooperation in large-scale organizations is based—hierarchy and division of labor—are responsible for tensions as well. For segments of organizations which perform different functions tend to compete, and become semi-autonomous. Katz postulates that forms of autonomy in school systems develop systematically from patterns of specialization and interaction, including affiliations of members with outsiders (Katz, 1964). Thus, rivalries arise between teachers of academic subjects and athletics and between teachers of "fundamental" and "practical" fields. In many communities athletic programs achieve a degree of autonomy because of their independent income from public attendance and from support of adult-sponsored booster clubs. Katz contends that a group of teachers can accomplish its functions more effectively if it has developed a degree of autonomy from the rest of the system. Similarly, "the school requires a degree of autonomy from local pressures if it is to accomplish its cosmopolitanizing tasks, such as weaning the child from his specific family context."

The fact that teachers are less subject to direct community pressures than school administrators, who work directly with the school board, perhaps puts teachers under less direct pressure than administrators to bargain away the interests of their students. However, it is administrators who often have the primary responsibility for developing and enforcing professional standards.

INFORMAL POWER STRUCTURES

In addition to being segmentalized by official lines of authority and divisions of labor, the organization is further differentiated by informal power structures, or, in other words, cliques of influential teachers and their followers. These leaders derive unauthorized power from their positions and their contacts and use that power in turn to increase the autonomy of their positions. The importance of contacts and the unauthorized influence[2] that subordinates sometimes are able to derive from their positions both are illustrated at one school where a teacher developed an informal arrangement with the secretary to call ahead and warn of the principal's unannounced classroom visits. She also had persuaded the secretary to reschedule her classes for a more desirable time, without the principal's knowledge. . . .

PROFESSIONALIZATION

As school systems become larger and more influential, as pressures for more efficient decision making increase, and as the gap between pedagogical theory and public understanding grows, the staffs and administrators of public schools seem intent on demanding more discretion to exercise their professional viewpoints. . . .

Several crucial differences separate the ideal-type professional from nonprofessional employees. The nonprofessional employee (even though he may be an individualist) is unlikely to distinguish closely between his work responsibilities and his obligation to obey supervisors. He may object to uses of authority that infringe on his personal rights as a citizen (such as no-smoking rules), but he is willing to accept supervision over his job. A good employee is obedient; he has been hired to "do what he is told." Therefore, when he does disobey, he must be ready to sabotage his work and the organization's clients; employees sometimes do disobey with that intent (as in the case of "slow downs" in factories).

The professional employee, on the other hand, denies the principle that his work always must be supervised by administrators and controlled by laymen. Because of his training, pressures from his colleagues, and his dedication to clients, the professionally oriented person considers himself competent enough to control his own work. Hence, he sometimes must be disobedient toward his supervisors precisely in order to improve his work proficiency and to maintain standards of client welfare—especially if there are practices that jeopardize the best interests of students. . . .

Some of the major struggles now going on in educational organizations involve the efforts of teachers to obtain more responsibility for certain types of decisions. In most schools, at least some teachers are attempting to increase their control over the classroom. Sharma's study suggests the norms which are developing. He found sharp differences between what teachers desired and current practice with regard to participation in decision making by groups of teachers. In thirty-two of the thirty-five activities, the percentage of teachers desiring participation in decisions was significantly *higher* than the percentage reporting participation by such groups. They especially wanted responsibility for activities concerning instruction, and they wanted more autonomy for the individual schools in which they teach; the role of citizens in the community, they believed, should be limited to participation in policy making in areas other than professional matters (Midwest Administration Center, 1955).

The struggle of teachers to govern their work necessarily involves militancy, as Solomon has suggested. The more bureaucratized the school, the more resistance they are likely to encounter. Hence, it can be expected that conflict will increase simultaneously with bureaucratization and with professionalization. Comparing seven public schools of varying size, the writer found a positive rank order correlation between the professional climate of the schools (as reflected in the faculty's endorsement of professional norms) and the number of reported conflicts in the school between teachers and administrators and the proportion of teachers in the school reporting that contacts with the principal or his assistants involved disputes. Other evidence collected from interviews also supported the contention that professionalism is associated with conflict between teachers and the administration (Corwin, 1965b). If this evidence is indicative, teachers seem to be exercising more than the traditional amount of leadership in education. . . .

To summarize, it is difficult for an organization to maintain its integrity in the face of internal, semi-autonomous coalitions, each with its own interests and goals. Outside social changes are equally upsetting. This last observation directs attention to the problem of the organization's relation to its environment. The remaining functions of organizations are centrally concerned with regulating and maintaining that relationship.

Recruitment Problems

Balances between coordination and incoordination and between accommodation to change and structural lag can be altered in at least two ways by the recruiting process. First, the type of leaders recruited can influence the rate of change and the stability. Second, certain procedures for recruiting rank-and-file members can protect organizations against their own recalcitrance to change.

TURNOVER OF LEADERSHIP

Carlson's (1962) discussion of school superintendents who come from "inside" and from "outside" the system reveals the instrumental role that turnover plays in promoting or retarding organizational adaptation and lag.[3] The insider, attached to a specific place, his home system, puts place of employment above his career as a superintendent. By contrast, the outsider is career bound and willing to leave the system for a job elsewhere. From his observations of four school systems, Carlson concluded that school boards appoint outsiders when they are dissatisfied with the present administration and want creativity; insiders are appointed when boards are satisfied with the *status quo*. In an analysis of thirty-six successions no insider reported that the school board was unhappy with the way the schools were being administered at the time he was appointed. . . .

The relative influence of successive leaders is likely to depend upon the system's complexity. In more complex organizations, subunits are likely to gain more autonomy, which not only puts subordinates in a better position to resist changes proposed by the chief executive but also creates incentives for them to propose their own innovations (Wilson, 1966). In complex organizations, therefore, rates of turnover among subordinates may produce as much ferment and change as turnover at higher levels.

In any event, a practice seemingly so remote from the classroom as the replacement of superintendents can have a vital effect on the kind of education that people eventually obtain.

PROCEDURES FOR RECRUITING
MEMBERSHIP

The recruitment of rank-and-file members can be as important for an organization's character as the replacement of administrators. The more stringent the recruiting standards, the more control an organization can exercise over its members' values, a fact documented in a study of four sororities and six fraternities at the University of Colorado (Scott, 1965). These organizations were so effective in selecting their members that each new generation reaffirmed the dominant organizational values (e.g., social skills, group loyalty, tolerance of cheating and dependency) more strongly than the senior members. The new members, rather than the older ones, were responsible for maintaining the value system. This perhaps represents a unique case where recruiting procedures were so effective, and the period of membership so short, that a socialization process that had the effect of undermining the value system could be tolerated.

The ability to select new members represents one form of protection to an organization. At the other extreme, even an organization unable to fully regulate its goals by controlling the actual selection of its members, has some assurance of at least survival when membership is compulsory for certain persons. This organization, certainly, is in a less precarious position than one which can neither select its members nor compel them to join. In the public schools, as suggested in the following excerpt by Carlson, the compulsory attendance of students is an especially significant feature which permits schools to operate and flourish with less than perfect efficiency or effectiveness.

If we put the variables of selectivity on the part of the organization and on the part of the client together, we get the possibility of four types of service organization-client relationships as seen in Table 1.

Most of the service organizations we know in the United States are probably Type I organizations: organizations which, either by formal or informal means, select the clients they wish to deal with and are participated in by clients on a voluntary basis. The private university is a good example. Hospitals and doctors' offices also are of this type. In addition, many of the public welfare service units belong to

Table 1—Selectivity in Client-Organization Relationship in Service Organizations

		CLIENT CONTROL OVER OWN PARTICIPATION IN ORGANIZATION	
		Yes	No
ORGANIZATIONAL CONTROL	Yes	Type I	Type III
OVER ADMISSION	No	Type II	Type IV

this type. They apply stringent criteria in the selection of clients, and the potential client is not compelled to accept the service.

Type II service organizations do not select their clients, and participation in the organization is nonmandatory. The state university whose charter specifies that it accept (but not continue to serve) all high-school graduates who are at least 17 years old and who wish to enrol fits this type, for it is not mandatory for high-school graduates to attend college. In addition, most junior colleges and adult-education units fit within this type.

Service organizations of Type III are seemingly very rare or nonexistent. This type of organization selects clients and is one in which clients are compelled to participate. An organization which has such a relationship with its members (not clients) is the citizen army, but it is not a service organization. When laws specify that individuals having certain characteristics must embrace a given service, it seems that the service is always provided by an organization that has no control over admission of clients.

There are a number of service organizations of Type IV, such as public schools, state mental hospitals, reform schools, and prisons. The clients of these organizations receive the service on a mandatory basis, and prisons, public schools, and state mental hospitals cannot exercise choice in the matter of clients. . . .

. . . Though all service organizations, by general definition, establish a social relationship with their clients and thus face a motivation problem, the typology makes it clear that an equal necessity to motivate clients is not placed on all service organizations. It may perhaps be unnecessary to remark that the problem of inducing clients to participate would seem to be most pronounced in Types III and IV, because these organizations are most likely to be in contact with some clients who have no real desire for their services. This factor undoubtedly has many organizational ramifications. To mention only a few, it would seem to bear upon the attitudes which staff members and clients hold toward each other, personality

make-up of staff, prestige of the work, and deployment of organizational resources.

Further, it seems appropriate to call Type IV organizations "domesticated." By this is simply meant that they are not compelled to attend to all of the ordinary and usual needs of an organization. By definition, for example, they do not compete with other organizations for clients; in fact, a steady flow of clients is assured. There is no struggle for survival for this type of organization. Like the domesticated animal, these organizations are fed and cared for. Existence is guaranteed. Though this type organization does compete in a restricted area for funds, funds are not closely tied to quality of performance. These organizations are domesticated in the sense that they are protected by the society they serve. Society feels some apprehension about domesticated organizations. It sees the support of these organizations as necessary to the maintenance of the social system and creates laws over and above those applying to organized action in general to care for domesticated organizations.

Type I organizations, on the other hand, can be called "wild"; they do struggle for survival. Their existence is not guaranteed, and they do cease to exist. Support for them is closely tied to quality of performance, and a steady flow of clients is not assured. Wild organizations are not protected at vulnerable points as are domesticated organizations. . . .

. . . Of particular relevance to this discussion is that the research has pointed out the tremendous importance and the occurrence of adaptation by wild organisms to their changing environment.

This suggests the proposition that domesticated organizations, because of their protected state, are slower to change and adapt than are wild organizations. (Carlson, 1964, pp. 265–67.)

The typology is a simplification, of course, and is subject to several reservations. The parents of public school students do have something to say about where their children will attend school, as they can move, pay tuition to another district, or attend private schools. Schools likewise can gerrymander district lines, expel certain students, and send others to special agencies. Moreover, schools do compete for favored students, as well as faculty; do struggle to perpetuate a favorable reputation. The distinctions are based on official characteristics which do not recognize the informal influence that some administrators in Type IV organizations can have in securing favored clients. In fact, the distinction between wild and domestic seems analogous to the difference between industrial and governmental organizations.

Nevertheless, the scheme is provocative. It can be speculated that bureaucratic regulations will be prominent in Types II and IV, where the organization does not control admission, as a means of controlling members who do not share similar values and who are not involved with the organization's objectives. Type I organizations, by screening out undesirable clients, perhaps tend to have higher social status and more influence than comparable Type IV organizations; the relatively high status of some private schools attests this, although the existence of less influential, low status private colleges also suggests the presence of other factors.

Domesticated organizations, having little opportunity to regulate values, then make structural adjustments to relieve some of the tensions produced by the heterogeneous membership:

> ... Type IV organizations have goals to which they are committed and their achievement is hampered by the presence of the unselected clients, and ... in the course of day-to-day operations there emerge within these organizations adaptive mechanisms which tend to minimize the disruptive factors presented by the unselected clients.
>
> The first adaptive response of domesticated organizations to the environmental condition of unselected clients is *segregation*. Segregation takes several forms. "Dumping ground" is a term well known to educators; it signifies that some part of the school program constitutes a place

where students are assigned or "dumped" for part of their program, for various reasons, to serve out their remaining school days. Students do not get dumped into the academic areas of the program but, most frequently, into the vocational areas. This practice gives clues as to the type of student the school system is most anxious to serve. ...

Frequently a more extreme form of segregation takes place. In California, in some school systems, there are continuation schools for those students who have proved to be too disruptive for the regular high schools. And New York City has its "600" schools. In a sense, they are the dumping grounds' dumping ground. ...

Segregation in domesticated organizations frequently may lead to or is accompanied by goal displacement. Goal displacement is a process whereby the original or overriding goal is abandoned (completely or partially) and another goal substituted. (Carlson, 1964, pp. 268–69.)

Recruiting practices, then, can protect an ineffective organization. Partly because they are guaranteed students and a minimum level of support, schools can endure for long periods of time without improvement. This "kept" status provides security, but permits them to avoid change. Thus, schools continue to stress ancient languages, English literature, and the history and values of the local region in a nation increasingly caught up in a world society, the demands of which logically dictate more modern languages, European and Asian literature, and world history. For similar reasons, until recently, schools have avoided making adjustments necessary to appeal to the one in three high school students who drops out.

At the same time, this protection has permitted educational organizations to subtly transform their objectives, compromising their official goals, for with a guaranteed clientele, it is less essential to be completely effective in fulfilling any given objective. This fact complicates the already difficult problem of setting and maintaining direction in organizations. Attention now will turn directly to this problem.

Policy Problems (*Direction*)

In the process of regulating their precarious relationships to changing environments, in contending with partially autonomous subunits, and in adjusting their structural lags, organizations eventually can lose sight of their objectives, some of which become modified as a result.

GOAL DISPLACEMENT

Social change produces a dilemma, with respect to organizational objectives, which eventually must be faced: if organizations do not adapt their objectives to changing circumstances, they are likely to be judged ineffective; yet, in adapting their objectives, they violate prior commitments.[4] Many organizations do violate old commitments and replace them with new ones. This goal displacement and replacement occurs because they are unwilling or unable to resist new demands made upon them.[5]

An organization's direction is the result of compromises between its acknowledged objectives and the actual circumstances it confronts. It follows that cultural trends and shifts can have enormous influence on those objectives. Largely because they depend so on other social institutions for moral support and direction, the objectives of schools have been sensitive to social changes. In fact, until recently at least, their mode of organization has perhaps changed less than their major objectives, which have readily adjusted through the years to such

diverse purposes as training theologians, scholars, businessmen, technicians, immigrants, and factory workers. Laymen perhaps have had more interest in controlling the objectives of schools than in how schools are run, while educators have had more vested interest in their internal positions than in resisting new demands; indeed, they have strengthened their positions precisely by accommodating those demands. The existing structure of schools therefore has provided a convenient means for indoctrinating each generation with whatever value system is current. . . .

. . . What role, then, *does* rational planning play in the determination of an organization's direction? Do its leaders actually "direct" it toward official goals? Are leaders actually in "command" of their organizations? Different answers to these questions are responsible for two opposing models of organization, identified by Gouldner as the rational model and the natural system model (Gouldner, 1959).

In the rational model, strongly apparent in Weber's work, organizations are assumed to be goal-directed entities. Organizational goals determine the desired course of action and dominate the thinking of leaders, whose decisions are calculated to achieve those goals. Their rationality is, in turn, a function of the number of alternative courses of action considered and the amount of planning done.

In the natural systems model apparent in Michel's writing, on the other hand, direction is more dependent on commitments and constraints than on official goals and planning. A commitment is an obligation initiated by an organization; a constraint, one imposed by outside groups.[6] Schools sometimes commit themselves to unintended courses of action in the process of bargaining. Residents of the small town described by Vidich and Bensman (1960) at one time agreed to permit farmers in the surrounding region to control the school board in exchange for the rural area's support of a consolidated school to be built within the city limits. Over time, the consolidated school maintained a strong vocational agricultural program and other evidences of rural influence, long after rural domination had become useless to high school graduates.

Clark's (1959a) study of an adult education program examines the constraints responsible for that program's precarious development. Being marginal to the school system and facing a school board which favored the public schools in allocating funds, the program's administrators were forced to rely for monies on "enrollment economy" principles—i.e., as many students as possible were recruited to reduce the average cost per student. The program, consequently, became simplified and slanted toward crafts and hobbies in order to achieve popularity. The predominance of crafts and hobbies in adult education, then, evolved from constraints in the competitive enrollment economy rather than from rational planning toward some desirable outcome.

Clark (1960) also has documented a transformation in the official objectives of a junior college designed to provide technical training for high school graduates. Although vocational training officially was the school's primary purpose, the fact that the college was legally required to admit any resident who applied subjected it to the preferences of students, most of whom chose the college curriculum over the vocational program. In order to protect their reputations as college teachers, the faculty began to fail an inappropriately large proportion of students, diverting the college even further from its vocational goals.

To emphasize the prominence of commitments and constraints is not to deny the influence of official goals. Organizations do have goals which are integral to them and separate from the personal goals of their members. They can be considered as the *common* expectations applicable to all roles of the organization. As mutual and overlapping expectations, they apply to all members of the organition, and hence, they are part of the organization's structure. But the point is that organizational goals are only one source of commitment among many possible sources. Furthermore, different groups, even though sharing similar expectations, frequently attach different priorities to them. For example, teachers of both academic subjects and extracurricular activities can accept extracurricular goals while assigning them a different degree of importance. When consensus on the priority of goals throughout the organization is low, other types of commitments and constraints are more likely to predominate.

An integration of the two models, if accomplished, would provide a more coherent concept of organization. They can be compared on essentially three points: (1) the degree of consensus on stated objectives, (2) rational planning for the organization as a whole, and (3) the power of each segment of the organization to achieve its commitments. Rationality can be considered as the *limited case* where there is (a) complete consistency of stated objectives (as indicated by the degree of consensus on their relative importance), where (b) each cental office and subunit within the organization has effective power and knowledge to achieve its commitments, and where there is (c) extensive organization-wide planning, involving consideration of several alternatives over a period of time. However, the natural concept represents the more general case. Complete consensus on objectives is unusual, and with less than full consensus the amount of effective planning that can be done is *inversely* related to the power of the subparts. Even with extensive planning toward several alternatives by a central office, over an extended period of time, an organization cannot achieve rationality if subunits are free to pursue their separate objectives autonomously. Realistically, in most large urban school systems, which are not especially noted for high consensus on objectives, some parts develop autonomy, making the limited case of rationality improbable.

Therefore, focusing on power relationships between subparts (i.e., the locus of decision making) promises to be a more fruitful approach to the study of educational organizations than analyzing the logic behind administrative decisions, a procedure more often preferred by educators.

EFFECTIVENESS

The alternatives available to an organization, and its capacities for adapting to change, are determined by the number of its commitments. Most schools in the nation traditionally have been comprehensive schools, or multifunction organizations, which typically offer a wide variety of programs and activities to heterogeneous student bodies. But because their objectives and other commitments are large in number, comprehensive schools are unlikely to have the capacity to fulfill all of them effectively. The fact that their activities are unequally rewarded by their communities encourages them to concentrate on some commitments more than others. For example, having winning teams or getting students into colleges are visible achievements which, regardless of the logical priority of some other educational objectives, some middle-class communities reward disproportionately. Hence, although they may be committed to a large

number of goals, comprehensive schools in fact tend to informally specialize in a few to the neglect of others.

Some of the disadvantages of comprehensiveness can be overcome through systemwide specialization, i.e., by officially assigning each school in a system limited and distinctive commitments. Specialized schools are able to employ special personnel and resources without fear of being criticized for favoritism or for being "unbalanced." Duplication of services among schools in a system is reduced and the competence and incentive of each to fulfill limited commitments is correspondingly increased.

Some people oppose specialized schools on the grounds that they result in unequal educational opportunities; however, if specialization does increase a school's effectiveness, and if students are allowed to transfer freely between schools as their abilities and interests change, the charge is without much foundation. A more compelling argument is that diversified schools are more adaptable than specialized ones to changing social pressures and times. If public schools had not supported a broad range of objectives during the first part of this century, they would have had more difficulty assuming responsibility for new demands constantly being made of them, for more adult education and extracurricular programs, for example. Recognizing the restrictions that specialization imposes on the capacity for change, Clark says, "An image is a constraint, and the stronger the image, the stronger the constraint. . . . The college that strikes boldly for a highly distinctive character and a unique image is also making connections with the outside world that are not easily revoked. . . . When the times change, image and ingrained character resist change in the college. . . . Alumni and other outsiders remain identified with the old institution, and the old channels of referral and self-recruitment persist. To have a history of distinction is to accumulate resistance to change" (Clark, 1959b, pp. 165–66).

In a society characterized by both specialization and rapid changes, the question is whether a school can be more effective by limiting itself to a specialized objective or by diversifying its commitments in preparation for social change.

Boundary Definition and Maintenance Problems

The degree to which objectives are compromised by outside pressures depends on the organization's ability to defend its boundaries. Boundary definition—the demarcation of jurisdictional limits and the identification of members and the maintenance of boundaries are necessary processes, because organizations depend on outsiders and must solicit their support without at the same time permitting them to interfere detrimentally with internal operations: The price paid by an organization for outside support is determined by its willingness and ability to defend its boundaries. Though legally under local lay control and traditionally subject to a community-school ideology favoring "democratic" participation of parents in school affairs, in fact a school is subject to the same fundamental principle as other organizations—outside control over the organization interrupts its direction, interferes with its coordination and undermines its authority system.

Becker's (1952) study of school teachers describes their efforts to maintain authority in the face of challenges by outsiders. Fearing that parents will exercise their right to complain about school practices, teachers rely upon one another and upon the administration to reinforce their authority. Teachers are not supposed to question one another's teaching, especially in public, and they "stick together" informally. Most important, the principal is expected to support the

teacher, to "back him up" against the weight of parents and students. His patronage is expected even when he personally disapproves a teacher's actions, so long as the teacher acted in good faith.

Although the concept, boundary, is implicit in discussions of school-community relations, the term has been used inconsistently in the literature. The geographical boundaries of public school districts identify one source of membership, but they do not establish the full limits of membership in the system. For example, are school board members outsiders? Are students? Is the P.T.A.? Is the American Legion exceeding its jurisdiction when it succeeds in determining textbook policy?

Boundaries are delineated by the jurisdictions of responsibility of members as opposed to nonmembers. They are based on two distinctions: (a) between insiders and outsiders, and (b) between cooperation and interference. Boundary problems develop when nonmembers interfere with activities that lie clearly within the organization's jurisdiction. But they also arise because distinctions concerning both membership and jurisdiction frequently are ambiguous, these ambiguities often producing challenges to membership rights and jurisdictional disputes.

Two basic types of conflict, then, can develop. First, where membership rights are not at issue, members may compete with nonmembers for jurisdiction over certain activities, e.g., parents compete with teachers for control over selection of textbooks. Second, where jurisdiction is not an issue (i.e., where a decision is clearly the school's prerogative), conflict still may arise over who is authorized to represent the organization; e.g., can the P.T.A.'s public statements on school policy concerning vocational training ethically bind a school administration to that policy? These ambiguities are compounded when a particular party, such as an accrediting association, has a clear but limited jurisdiction within the organization over certain matters, but in all other respects is considered to be a nonmember without authority. Boundary disputes involve all facets. Some of these problems can be clarified by distinguishing between primary and secondary boundaries.

PRIMARY BOUNDARIES

Primary boundaries are fixed by official membership lists. They will be treated here categorically; that is, one is either a member or a nonmember as defined by certain possessions and rites of passage, such as swearing an oath, paying taxes, being on the payroll, signing an employment contract, or being listed on the membership roll. Schools utilize one of the most clear-cut of possible membership criteria, place of residence. However, even distinct school district lines are inadequate for placing some students, such as the many Puerto Rican children who "sleep around" among various relatives living in different parts of a city. . . .

SECONDARY BOUNDARIES

Primary boundaries categorically separate members from nonmembers. However, in practice this elementary dichotomy does not take fully into account the more tenuous relations that many groups develop with schools. For example, are P.T.A. members, the school board, the state department of education, accrediting associations, and even students completely either nonmembers or members? The problem of classifying marginal groups has been handled by modifying

definitions of social positions so that they will fit *a priori* conceptions of boundaries. For example, for some purposes part-time night school students are not considered to be "students," because they do not have complete membership in the school (not because their rights and obligations differ greatly from full-time students). The alternative is to consider them to be students who simply are further removed from the organization's boundaries than those attending full-time. The extent of membership needs to be determined independently from the definitions of positions.

What seems to be needed is an explicit set of criteria for extending boundary profiles beyond simple dichotomies between members and nonmembers without modifying the usual definitions. Some of these criteria are suggested in the commonsense notions of *containment* and *permeability*. Containment refers to how well an organization controls its official members. It includes (1) the *cohesiveness* of relationships among official members, and (2) the *pervasiveness* of control over official members. Permeability refers to how far groups not on the school's official membership list can penetrate into the organization's affairs. This concept includes both (3) the *extensiveness* of their participation, and consequently, (4) the degree of *external influence* they exercise.[7] These properties establish *secondary boundaries*—i.e., those, in addition to official membership, which identify the degree of membership and establish jurisdictions of control. They represent an organization's vulnerability to the influence of nonmembers and its ability to influence its own members. Each concept will be briefly described below.

The *cohesiveness* of an organization refers to the rate of both person-oriented and task-oriented interaction among members, as reflected in the number of mutual friendships among faculty and/or among students, and in the proportion of the student body regularly participating in extracurricular activities. The proto-type of a cohesive school has (a) a fluid clique structure that includes most members and (b) extensive participation in group activities.

Pervasiveness refers to the scope of the activities of members which are controlled.[8] While all schools control the learning process, some, more than others, also regulate dress, language, and personal conduct. A school with well-established norms (rules or traditions) regulating numerous nonacademic spheres of teachers' and/or students' lives represents a pervasive system, while one which confines its regulations to academic or task-related activities is less pervasive. Principals are sometimes able to increase their control by recruiting tractable teachers (often less well-trained women) who are not likely to support the more militant members of the faculty in their efforts to resist the administration's normative controls.

The ability of organizations to defend their internal structure increases with pervasiveness. Regardless of dissent that may exist internally among members, a pervasive school can present a unanimous front, helpful in warding off criticism of outside groups; it is in a position to convey an impression of consensus on its actions (e.g., the children are too young to read Faulkner); and it can maintain enough control over its members to conceal some of its practices from public attention.

Extensiveness refers to the number of nonmember groups participating in the system. Some schools make extensive use of citizens' committees and serve the total community by making facilities, time, and staff available for nonschool-related activities (e.g., the boy scouts), while other schools have much less contact with outside groups and organizations. In an extensive school, then, rates of interaction between school members and outside groups are unusually high.

By *external influence* is meant the ability of a school to control other organizations relative to their control over it. Some schools are able to exert considerable influence over parents, local governments, and voluntary associations in the community, while perhaps more typically, other schools are dominated by these groups. An influential school, then, is able to control outside groups.

Profiles of secondary boundary characteristics can be used to classify nonmembers. For example, the national agency that accredits teacher education institutions (NCATE) would score low on extensiveness but high on influence in teachers colleges because it sets minimum standards and procedures. Thus, in this important sense, NCATE should be included within the secondary boundaries of schools of education.[9]

It should be noted that cohesiveness has been distinguished from extensiveness, and pervasiveness from influence, by whether or not members are interacting with nonmembers. For this discussion primary membership has been identified from official standards, which are independent of the secondary characteristics. However, it should be recognized that in conventional usage, the term "member" implicitly seems to presume certain secondary characteristics—i.e., high rates of interaction with other officials, relatively large numbers of their activities regulated by the administration, and more influence within the organization than most other persons. The conventional usage confuses the fact of official membership with a presumed degree of influence and participation. These two facets of the problem are being distinguished in the present discussion in order to portray boundaries as matters of degree. It seems desirable to visualize boundaries as a configuration of variables rather than as a mere dichotomy.

STRATEGIES OF BOUNDARY MAINTENANCE

The boundaries of schools are partially protected by the financial independence of districts and by other legal provisions, such as those guaranteeing separation of church and state. But the capacity of an organization to defend its boundaries also depends more specifically upon its power to control strategic boundary positions relating to outside groups. One investigator (Kerr, 1964) has enumerated several ways by which officials can control school boards, which perhaps represent the most crucial boundary positions in schools. The fact that in most states board members do not run for office on issues or represent specific constituents to whom they are accountable makes them vulnerable to the administration. Also, the fact that the public usually is split by class and ethnic interests reduces the influence of public sentiment, which might otherwise provide boards with more leverage against administrators. (Although here Kerr does not adequately recognize that cleavages and indifference in communities puts small cliques of citizens in a better position to gain disproportionate influence over school board members). Also, board members are dependent upon administrators both for technical information and for advice about policy. Since internal issues are the special preserve of administrators, board members are likely to feel uninformed about their responsibilities and about the technicalities of administration and teaching. In external issues with wider public appeal board members rely on administrators to define the issues and propose the alternatives, and because their own reputations depend on the success of the administration, they are unlikely to sabotage it in the absence of widespread public dissatisfaction. The visibility of outcomes of school board decisions and the risk of mistakes encourage members to conceal their actions from the public and to patronize the administration.

Vulnerable school boards, then, conspire with administrators against the public. Secrecy is a favorite strategy. Schools routinely withhold information from the public. Gross (1956) reported that all school board meetings were open to the public in only one-seventh of New England school districts, and 10 percent of the superintendents in the study reported that *none* of them were open. Three-fourths of the superintendents thought that newspaper editors should honor requests to withhold unfavorable information about the school from news stories. These and similar practices help to prevent public recognition of situations that might provoke outside interference and criticism.

As another defense, schools may try to confine threatening contacts with outsiders to situations they control. For example, before the local taxpayers' association calls upon him to justify his school bond request, a superintendent may call a public meeting of his own. In one case a principal reportedly succeeded in having some meddlesome women, P.T.A. officers, replaced by men who had less free time than the women to devote to school affairs (Queen, 1965). Principals are universally expected to defend teachers' control over their classrooms in the face of parents' criticisms; whatever punishment the administration may impose upon a deviant teacher secretly, parents will not be permitted to believe they had anything to do with it. The complexity of many large systems also reduces parental influence by channeling complaining parents through an unfamiliar chain of command which extends from the classroom through a hierarchy of administrators, each of whom can disclaim responsibility for settling the problem. These "buck passing" procedures protect individuals in the system from time-consuming and awesome responsibilities which few busy administrators are willing to undertake, and at the same time they discourage outsiders.

Where interaction cannot be regulated by these bureaucratic devices, schools can use several informal strategies: implicit coercion, reciprocity, infiltration, and absorption. As an example of the first, some administrators have successfully coerced their districts into passing bond levies by threatening to close schools or to curtail the athletic program. They also can draw upon outside authorities for support, and superintendents are not above reminding their communities of the preferences of accrediting agencies if it will enhance the chances of a pet program.

School teachers also have cultivated a little-recognized, but effective coercive means of throttling potential parental intervention. Teachers' grading practices and the special recognition and privilege they give or withhold can influence a child's immediate social status among his peers and, ultimately, his later career and the social status of his family. Consequently, some parents live in mortal fear (whether well founded or not) that if they complain too much or too actively oppose school policies, teachers will covertly "take it out on the child," with more homework, more harassment, fewer honorary distinctions and appointments, or lower grades. This implicit threat undoubtedly keeps many parents away from teachers' classrooms. Although perhaps the threat is more imagined than real, since many schools seem to be as willing to bargain with troublemakers by devoting special attention, and perhaps favorable treatment, to their children in order to forestall criticism.

Reciprocity is a principle of bargaining whereby a favor performed by one party indebts another to return it. One's power depends upon obtaining a favorable balance of indebtedness, so that others owe him more than he owes any one of them (Blau, 1964). Using this principle a superintendent might "buy" the support of an influential construction company by arranging for it to secure school building contracts, or of a school board member by helping him to enter politics; the latter case eventually could provide a school with direct access to the community power structure.

A school may bargain away its authority over some activities in order to gain control of others. For example, it may defer to groups who seek to remove specific books from the library shelves in order to appease them with regard to more extensive controls over the school's library. Thus, it concedes a specific demand in exchange for its right to maintain general control over the books. In similar ways, schools sometimes implicitly bargain with specific groups for financial support, for example by teaching a distorted version of the Civil War in order to avoid alienating influential taxpayers.

As still another strategy, school administrators *infiltrate* influential community organizations where they sometimes develop enough influence to use these organizations' resources to support their school's projects. On the other hand, schools also have *absorbed* some activities in order to increase their scope of control. Sponsorship of dances, booster clubs, PTA's, the athletic program, vocational education, and advanced placement programs have helped to pacify outside pressures and at the same time to control these facets of student life and parental concern to a greater extent than would be the case if these activities were not school-sponsored. In the process, schools have extended their own boundaries. The absorption of some activities can also help to divert outsiders' sttention from the school's intrinsic functions to its extrinsic ones. A booster club may interfere with the athletic program, but at the same time it is not concerned with the more critical aspects of curriculum planning and development.

Co-optation is a specific form of absorption in which an organization admits outsiders into its leadership circles in order to control them. In one community, a school which had been criticized by local businessmen for its commercial ventures successfully used the PTA as a front for the same activities while deriving the profits through that organization for its own use. One example of how a school co-opted parents is illustrated in Vidich and Bensman's (1960) study of a small town where a principal gained behind-the-scenes control of the PTA and curtailed the influence of parents while increasing his own. The PTA became a "front" organization and a pressure group for his proposals. By working informally through committees, his ideas were presented to the school board as those of the parent body. Then, the principal could not be blamed either for proposals that were defeated or for those of a controversial nature, while at the same time the PTA provided a sense of legitimacy and community support for his proposals. . . .

DETERMINANTS OF BOUNDARIES

The influence of outsiders depends upon the procedures used to legally control and finance an organization. When both control and support are located in the same group, a school will be more vulnerable than when it has a degree of financial independence from its board of control. . . .

During the course of this chapter, several structural properties have been identified, properties which are of potential significance for explaining how educational organizations function. To the extent that these properties are relevant to *most* complex organizations, in combination they can form the nucleus of a more extensive typology which eventually can become relevant to organizations of diverse purposes. In this sense, they can be considered *elementary properties*.

Carlson's typology, based on the organizations' and the clients' respective control over participation, can serve as a point of departure for building a more elaborate typology from elementary properties. His analysis, however, needs to be elaborated to include variations in levels of professionalization and the organization's relation to the dominant institutions. Sources of control and finance also need to be incorporated within it. To illustrate, at one extreme, where both control and finance are the responsibility of one outside group, the organization is easily accessible to outsiders; the autonomy of its members is at a minimum. As another alternative, control can be distributed among laymen as well as among professional and administrative personnel, with financing controlled by a single outside group, such as is sometimes the case in single-industry communities having only one major source of tax revenue; in this case, coalitions between the financial source and other lay groups and administrators are likely to compromise the otherwise relatively favorable position of professionals stemming from the fact that outside control is distributed rather than concentrated. Third, control can be concentrated in the hands of a dominant group (a school board or a faculty) with financing distributed over a broad base. In this case the controlling group is likely to have a great deal of autonomy, even though some financial supporters may be reluctant to support the program. Finally, both control and financing can be distributed among a number of independent groups and power blocs, as is typical of the more esteemed privately endowed colleges and some of the largest public school systems; group autonomy and conflict will characterize such a system. It seems likely that these configurations of control and financing, in turn, are associated with the functional autonomy of subparts within the system and with profiles of power distributions within the hierarchy.

Secondary boundary profiles also can be incorporated as another dimension of the typology. An organization "high" on all four secondary boundary characteristics—cohesiveness, pervasiveness, extensiveness, and influence—would be a powerful one. However, perhaps the typical school is cohesive, pervasive, and extensive without being influential; it seems unlikely, on the other hand, that a school could have influence without being pervasive. Among pervasive schools, it might be useful to distinguish the cohesive from the less cohesive, for perhaps they have different types of control structures. Similarly, among more extensive schools, those with high influence can be distinguished from those with low influence; each would have very different implications for the meaning of local control.

Structures of control and boundary profiles are probably associated with internal organizational characteristics. For example, the status of professional employees may differ in publicly and in privately controlled organizations; and for a given level of professional expertise and bureaucratic complexity, the authority of outsiders will differ in each class of organization. The way public and

private organizations are controlled also may influence their social prestige and upset the status security of their subunits. In some, the social prestige of subunits is comparable to their autonomy, while in others these statuses are inconsistent, either because a department has more internal autonomy than its outside prestige warrants, or the reverse.

Adding still another layer of concepts to the typology, the complexity of structure can be compared with the level of professional expertise of subordinates (and their supply relative to the demand for their services). The more complex the organization, the more authority administrators will have and the less control laymen can exert. The more professional expertise that subordinates demonstrate, on the other hand, the greater their authority will be relative to that of both administrators and laymen. It is expected that organizational conflict will increase as both professional expertise and organizational complexity increase; that in organizations of similar complexity, conflict will increase with professional expertise. Conversely, in organizations of similar levels of professional expertise, conflict will increase as bureaucratic complexity increases. Professional authority will be modified as well by differing *configurations* of complexity (e.g., combinations of high centralization and standardization compared to low centralization and high standardization). The extent of conflict with laymen is likely to be higher in public organizations because of strong community resistance to professional control.

ELEMENTARY PROPERTIES AND CHANGE

Organizational profiles contrived from combinations of these elementary properties will be of assistance with several key problems, especially the problem of organizational change. Whether or not outside influence can be resisted depends upon the pattern of elementary properties within the organization. For example, if an organization can select its members, it can keep out unwanted influences. But even if it cannot, a well-organized membership can resist outside pressures with the aid of certain tactics; the proportion of members active in professional organizations and unions should therefore be of significance. But while they are in a position to resist changes being advocated by laymen, professional groups are prone to accept and disseminate changes advocated by their colleagues. So it is difficult to anticipate the total *volume* of change.

The ratio of local to nonlocal control also will alter the rate and direction of change. With federal assistance and provocation many schools have changed their math and science programs and teaching techniques extensively during the past few years. In fact, a school which is impervious to local influences may be among the first to succumb to national ones. Educators in public and private schools undoubtedly differ in their willingness and capacity to defend their boundaries effectively from local and national thrusts. With the aid of stringent controls over admitting new members and independent sources of income, well-endowed private schools are in a more favorable position to resist local assaults, and the strategies of defense that are useful to them are not necessarily the most effective for public organizations of equal wealth.

The significance that source of support can have for organizational change was alluded to in Carlson's analysis. Dwelling on the fact that schools are protected and need not attend to all of the ordinary needs of an organization, he asserts that "domesticated" organizations adapt to change more slowly than wild ones. On the other hand, Callahan's thesis appears to be almost the opposite—that public schools are so domesticated and responsive to the dominant social trends that, far from lagging behind, they have been oversensitive to the wishes of reigning groups as each has successively gained national influence. Whenever the *dominant* figures happen to advocate updating the curriculum or other modern trends, the anomoly is complete.

However, the anomoly is more apparent than real. The two writers are not talking about the differences in *rates* of change, actually, but about different sources of pressure toward change. The difference between "domesticated" and "nondomesticated" organizations is not their sensitivity to change as such, but the different sources of pressure to change to which each is subject. Carlson sees few pressures for change originating from the *internal* organization itself. But the very feature which makes a school domesticated—guaranteed clientele and other resources—makes it susceptible to *outside* forces. Domesticated organizations, therefore, quickly adapt to pressures from the outside to modify their *objectives*, while jealously guarding existing *internal procedures* which outsiders have not attempted to control. What from one point of view permits domesticated organizations to withstand required internal changes, from another point of view makes them susceptible to outside pressures for changes.

Summary

To recapitulate, the following is a list of the elementary properties of organizations that were isolated and illustrated in this discussion, properties which, it is proposed, could form the basis of a universal typology of organizations:

A. *Characteristics of the coordination system.*

Number of subparts

Discrepancy between objectives and structure (structural lag)

Level of professional expertise of subordinates and their supply relative to demand

Proportion of activity and personnel devoted to maintaining the system (administration)

Degree of standardization throughout the system (emphasis on rules and common procedures)

B. *Characteristics of the power and authority systems.*

Number of levels of authority

Power distribution profiles

Functional autonomy of subparts

Dependency on a central office and on other organizations in the system

Consistency in levels of autonomy, authority, and prestige

Number of informal power cliques

Drive toward professionalization among subordinates

C. *Characteristics of the recruiting process.*

Selectivity in admitting new members

Members' control over their own participation

Rates of turnover for locals and cosmopolitans

D. *Direction.*

Number of commitments

Consensus on commitments (consistency)

Abstractness of commitments

Discrepancy between commitments and external constraints (goal displacement)

E. *Characteristics of the boundary system.*

Source of legal control—private (religious or secular), public

Sources of finance—local, state, and federal support

Penetration of nonmembers into the organization—extensiveness and influence

Organization's control over official members—cohesiveness and pervasiveness

Systematic comparisons of these properties with one another should gradually produce an empirically based, valid system for classifying organizations. For preliminary analyses, each of the preceding characteristics can be dichotomized into either "high" vs. "low" or "yes" vs. "no" categories. A school's character, then, would be defined by a profile based on the ratio of "high" or "yes" responses to the "lows" or "no's." Once schools have been differentiated among themselves by use of such profiles, hopefully the typology can be extended to noneducational systems. Within the guidelines of such a typology sociological studies of educational organizations can benefit from the growing theory and research on a wide variety of organizations. And this field, in turn, can contribute more systematically to the development of a theory of complex organizations.

Notes

[1] These characteristics, however, are not necessarily directly associated with one another; some complex organizations may be relatively unspecialized and highly centralized, whereas in others the reverse is true.

[2] It is useful to distinguish between a degree of power which permits complete *control* and relatively minor *influence* (Kahn and Boulding, 1964).

[3] Carlson's studies of recruitment parallel the industrial studies of Gouldner (1954) and Guest (1962), and are related to McGee's study of institutional inbreeding in universities (1960).

[4] *Structural* lag occurs when organizations fail to adapt their *procedures* to new com-

mitments produced by changing conditions. This discussion, on the other hand, will focus on the relationship between an organization's *commitments* and external social changes; goal displacement is the process by which an organization substitutes outmoded commitments for new ones.

[5] The degree of goal displacement can be measured by the difference between the priority of public expectations acknowledged by schools and the priority actually given by schools to each expectation in distributing their resources.

[6] A commitment requires evidence that the organization has little alternative but to fulfill its obligations. For example, a contract to pay teachers is a legal commitment; doubling the size of the athletic department and reducing the size of the language department are nonlegal commitments which also reduce alternatives and perpetuate a certain line of action. But, a stated goal does not become a commitment until some type of obligation has been incurred.

[7] However, such evidence does not warrant the conclusion that schools of homogeneously lower-class composition are necessarily more detrimental to students than mixed schools (Havighurst, 1963). In the first place, there is probably a selective factor; children of lower-class families living in predominantly middle-class neighborhoods are likely to have initially higher educational aspirations. More important, the evidence may be a simple reflection of a self-fulfilling prophecy due to schools' neglect of problems in lower-class schools (relative to middle-class schools). Random samples of existing lower-class schools do not provide a fair test of what *could* be done for lower-class schools if special programs, such as the "Higher Horizons" program in New York City, were provided. With educational programs distinctively *designed* for lower-class students, it is possible that homogeneously lower-class schools would be more effective for the "undermotivated" lower-class students than are mixed schools.

[8] A high degree of cohesiveness and pervasiveness in combination define what Goffman (1961) refers to as a "total institution." Schools tend to become total institutions when they apply moral criteria for hiring teachers, and when they regulate students' conduct on the way to and from school.

[9] Operationally, a boundary might be identified as that point at which the attempts of a group to influence the practices of an organization bring successful resistance from members. If a textbook advocated by the American Legion encounters less resistance than one introduced by the principal, then the American Legion is not totally an "outside" group.

References

Anderson, Theodore R., and Warkow, Seymour (1961). "Organizational Size and Functional Complexity." *American Sociological Review*, 26: 23–27.

Barker, Roger G. et al. (1962). *Big School— Small School: Studies of the Effects of High School Size Upon the Behavior and Expectations of Students*. Midwest Psychological Field Station, University of Kansas.

Becker, Howard S. (1952). "Social-Class Variations in the Teacher-Pupil Relationship." *Journal of Educational Sociology*, 25: 451–63.

Blau, Peter M. (1964). *Exchange and Power in Social Life*. New York: Wiley.

Carlson, Richard O. (1964). "Environmental Constraints and Organizational Consequences: The Public School and Its Clients." In *Behavioral Science and Edutional Administration Yearbook, Part II*, edited by Daniel E. Griffiths, Ch. 12. National Society for the Study of Education.

Carlson, Richard O. (1962). *Executive Succession and Organizational Change: Place-Bound and Career-Bound Superintendents of Schools*. Midwest Administration Center, University of Chicago.

Clark, Burton R. (1960). *The Open Door College: A Case Study*. New York: McGraw-Hill.

Clark, Burton R. (1959a). *Adult Education in Transition*. Berkeley: University of California Press.

Clark, Burton R. (1959b). "College Image and Student Selection." In *Selection and Educational Differentiation*. Center for the Study of Higher Education, University of California.

Corwin, Ronald G. (1965b). "Militant Professionalism, Initiative and Compliance in Public Education." *Sociology of Education*, 38: 310–31.

Etzioni, Amitai (1961). *A Comparative Analysis of Complex Organizations.* New York: Free Press.

Goffman, Erving (1961). "The Characteristics of Total Institutions." In *Complex Organizations: A Sociological Reader*, edited by A. Etzioni. New York: Holt, Rinehart, and Winston.

Goss, Mary E. (1961). "Influence and Authority Among Physicians in an Out-Patient Clinic." *American Sociological Review*, 26: 39–50.

Gouldner, Alvin W. (1959). "Organizational Analysis." In *Sociology Today*, edited by Robert K. Merton et al. New York: Basic Books.

Gouldner, Alvin W. (1954). *Patterns of Industrial Bureaucracy.* New York: Free Press.

Gross, Neal (1956). *The Schools and the Press.* New England School Development Association.

Guest, Robert H. (1962). "Managerial Succession in Complex Organizations." *American Journal of Sociology*, 68: 47–56.

Havighurst, Robert (1963). "Urban Development and the Educational System." In *Education in Depressed Areas*, edited by A. Harry Passow. New York: Bureau of Publications, Teachers College, Columbia University.

Kahn, Robert, and Elise Boulding, eds. (1964). *Power and Conflict in Organizations.* New York: Basic Books.

Katz, Fred E. (1964). "The School as a Complex Organization." *Harvard Educational Review*, 34: 428–55.

Kerr, Norman D. (1964). "The School Board as an Agency of Legitimation." *Sociology of Education*, 38: 34–59.

McGee, Reece (1960), "The Function of Institutional Inbreeding," *American Journal of Sociology*, 65: 483–88.

Midwest Administration Center (1962). "Bureaucracy and Teachers' Sense of Power." *Administrator's Notebook*, 11.

Midwest Administration Center (1955), "Who Should Make What Decisions?" *Administrator's Notebook*, 3.

Queen, Bernard (1965). "Boundary Maintenance and the Public Schools." Unpublished research paper.

Scott, William A. (1965). *Values and Organizations.* Skokie, Ill.: Rand McNally.

Tannenbaum, Arnold S. (1961). "Control and Effectiveness in a Voluntary Organization," *American Journal of Sociology*, 67: 33–46.

Terrien, F. C., and D. C. Mills (1955). "The Effect of Changing Size Upon the Internal Structure of an Organization." *American Sociological Review*, 20: 11–13.

Vidich, Arthur, and Joseph Bensman (1960). *Small Town in Mass Society.* Garden City, N.Y.: Doubleday.

Wilson, James Q. (1966). "Innovation in Organization: Notes Toward a Theory." In *Approaches to Organizational Design*, edited by James D. Thompson, Pittsburgh: University of Pittsburgh Press.

The Study of School Administration

Charles E. Bidwell

Reprinted from "The School As a Formal Organization,"
in Handbook of Organizations, *edited by James G.
March (Chicago: Rand McNally & Co., 1965),
pp. 994–1003, by permission of the publisher.
Copyright © 1968 by Rand McNally & Company.*

ACCOUNTS OF THE emergence in the United States of the principalship (Pierce, 1935) and of the superintendency (Gilland, 1935; Reller, 1935) fortunately are available. According to these writers, both administrative offices emerged around the mid-nineteenth century, first in city school systems, with the growth of student populations and with resulting increased school-system size and complexity of instructional procedures. These forces led to the development of graded schools and to a need for some curricular and instructional uniformity—and hence for routinization and coordination. Therefore, at the level of the school unit, full curricular and instructional discretion no longer could reside, as it had to that time, with individual teachers or department heads, or at the system level directly with lay boards of education. The response to these developments at the school-system level was the establishment of the office of superintendent, as executive of the board, to which was delegated at first only responsibility for the academic administration of schools. Fiscal and school-plant administration were retained by the school boards.

Thus, the practice was fixed of recruiting the superintendent from the teaching ranks, as an especially skilled educator. It was not until nearly the turn of the twentieth century, as day-to-day fiscal and plant management grew too complex for direct board participation—with the very rapid growth at that time of student populations and school-system size—that the superintendent became the board's executive in all aspects of school operation, while the board took on a more fiduciary role.

As for the principalship, it was first a set of clerical duties carried by one of the teaching staff, but after 1850, as curricular complexity grew beyond the scope of the superintendency, authority for curricular and instructional supervision was vested in the principal, who, like the superintendent, continued to be recruited from the teaching cadre.

Three aspects of these developments are especially important. First, until the administrative offices were established, the only specifically trained personnel responsible for instructional matters were teachers located within the school units of a system. Thus, the offices of superintendent and principal were added to previously existing school and classroom units. In view of this fact, one wonders about the extent to which the establishment of the administrative offices actually increased the structural looseness of school systems by insulating schools and classroom teachers, whose status in the school organization already was established, from direct board intervention.

Second, the development of the superintendency is also the history of a slow, reluctant, and recent relinquishment by boards of education of direct managerial functions. It seems likely that the division of functions between boards and superintendents is still somewhat ambiguous ideologically, if not legally, especially in smaller school districts which more recently still have followed the lead of the city systems.

Third, the practice of recruiting superintendents and principals from the ranks of teachers was firmly established. Whatever the scope of their official tasks, they must first be specialists in elementary or secondary education. Indeed, not until the 1920s was there the rapid growth, in schools of education, of professional training in educational administration and the insistence by school boards that such training be completed by candidates for superintendencies (see Callahan, 1962, pp. 188–204). Such requirements for principals are becoming more evident, but are by no means widespread.

Given these characteristics of the administrative and control arrangements in school systems, one should expect certain specific consequences for the functioning of these systems. In common with all organizations which are controlled by a lay board and staffed by specially trained personnel, school systems undoubtedly are marked by board-administrator conflicts over matters of policy, as administrative decisions in fact set policies which formally are the province of the board. But given the traditional perquisites of school boards, one should expect these conflicts to be especially severe and widespread in school systems and, more important, to center not only on questions of policy but also on the allocation of responsibility for day-to-day management, including areas of professional competence in curriculum and instruction. Since these conflicts are matters of ideology, rather than of legal definition, it becomes especially important in studying school systems to inquire into factors, such as school-board composition and external political responsiveness, likely to affect board attitudes and behavior along the fiduciary-managerial dimension.

Factors affecting the orientation of the superintendent are equally important, as they affect integration or strain both between superintendent and board and between superintendent and lower administrative and operating echelons.

Given the typical patterns of training for and recruitment to the superintendency, there are three possible directions in which a superintendent may orient himself in the performance of his office: toward the board as its subordinate executive; toward his former teacher-colleagues; or toward his professional peers, as a specialist in school administration. Given the legal status of the superintendent vis-à-vis the board and the relative autonomy of school units, each of these orientations, according to the board's view of its functions and the attitudes and actions of the subordinate staff, should produce distinctive patterns of strain and conflict between the levels of the school hierarchy.

To understand how such tensions may occur and what consequences flow from them, one also must know how the school principals define their functions—whether by emphasizing colleague ties to their teaching staffs or responsibilities to their superordinates. The principal is in the "middleman" position, so that it is important to investigate how the strains inherent in this position are resolved and factors which may affect the modes of resolution. Finally, it seems clear enough that one also should investigate the strength and content of collegial integration among the teaching staff and phenomena in the recruitment and work setting of teachers which presumably determine the form this integration may take.

There is no intent here to discount structural factors. It has been noted that the organizational arrangements of schools appear to be unusual in the degree of autonomy characterizing the operations of school and classroom units. It was suggested that this characteristic of school-system structure, as well as the possibilities for ambiguity in the relations of boards and superintendents, heighten the significance for school-system operation of variability in the performance of staff and board rules arising from variations in the attitudes and orientations of their incumbents. Indeed, two case studies of school systems, one in a Canadian suburb (Seeley, Sim, and Loosley, 1956, pp. 224–76), the other in a small American city (Bidwell, 1957) have reported that the attitudes of school principals, as they affect their administration of individual school units, may redefine and redirect the policies and influence of the superintendent. Consequently, the criteria and procedures for recruiting both staff and board members, as they affect these attitudes and orientations, also assume significance. The task of this chapter must be to discern systematic patterns among these variables.

But one cannot assume that the looseness of school-system structures is fairly uniform across systems. Thus, he must also attend to variations in the bureaucratization of structural arrangements. The more rationalized the school-system structure, presumably the narrower the opportunity for such variability of performance as has just been discussed. At the same time, highly bureaucratized systems may undergo conflicts arising from norms of autonomy among the professional staff.

Briefly, then, this discussion assumes that the functioning of school systems can be understood only as an outcome of complex interactions between structural arrangements (degree of bureaucratization), the attitudes and orientations of staff (degree of professionalization) and board members (fiduciary or managerial), and recruitment to organizational roles.

As is so often true of research into schools, systematic investigations of these phenomena have yet to be undertaken. But there are several existing studies on which to draw for partial evidence.

Evidence concerning the most significant aspect of relations among school officers and boards, their actual patterns of interaction, is presently lacking. With regard to school-board–superintendent relations, for example, there is nothing concerning the frequency or nature of observed conflicts or strategies employed to resolve them, such as attempts by superintendents or board members to mobilize power resources within the school system or in its environment. But there are several studies comparing attitudes of school staff and board members about modes of school-system administration.

Gross, Mason, and McEachern (1958) reported data bearing on consensus among and between Massachusetts school superintendents and their boards of education. Their study was intended primarily as an empirical contribution to the extension and refinement of role theory. While it did indeed succeed in this attempt, its interest here is less in its theoretical contribution than in the substantive findings about school systems. The main dependent variable was the degree of consensus within and among school boards and superintendents concerning the division of policy-making and executive responsibility between the board and superintendent. The effects of a variety of organizational and personal variables presumed to influence degrees of consensus were examined.

Gross and his collaborators limited their study to public school systems in Massachusetts, working with data from 105 superintendents and nearly all of their 517 board members (from a school-system sample stratified by region, type of system, type of community, and level of school expenditure). The data concerning the attitudes and behaviors of the superintendent, and a considerable amount of similar data about the board members as well, were gathered from the superintendent respondents in eight-hour sessions involving both focussed interviews and the administration of a set of forced-choice questionnaires. These questionnaires included indicators of a range of variables relevant to the two roles of board member and superintendent and their interactions. The board members also were interviewed within a more limited frame.

The study design imposed several limitations on the data, the most serious of which was the absence of certain critical items of information which might have been gathered directly from the board members themselves. (For an extended critique of this study see Naegle, 1960). Nonetheless, the work of Gross, Mason, and McEachern constitutes the only systematic study of large numbers of superintendents and their boards and provides a substantial quantity of important data.

Gross, Mason, and McEachern studied the patterning of consensus among school-board members and among superintendents (called intraposition consensus, measured by the variance of responses within groups) and the patterning of consensus between boards and superintendents (called interposition consensus, measured by the squared difference of the superintendent's responses and the mean response of his board). To turn first to intraposition consensus, comparing all superintendent and all board-member respondents, there was, as one might expect, greater agreement among superintendents than among board members.

Gross and his colleagues attributed this finding to the effects of professional training on the superintendents, although other factors may also have entered, e.g., socialization on the job, greater involvement with school affairs, and colleague interaction. Nonetheless, it seems likely that school superintendents do tend to have something of a common occupa-

tional subculture, approximating a professional ideology, while the views of board members may vary more widely according to situational and personal attributes. In the content of items endorsed by the superintendent respondents in this study, with strong supporting evidence from responses of both superintendents and professors of school administration in another study (Bowman, 1963), is clear indication that this ideology centers on expert autonomy for the superintendent and a fiduciary role for the board.

Early in this chapter, it was argued that coordinative problems in school systems should encourage the rationalization of procedures. Although there is no firm evidence for effects of system size, as noted, one might expect larger systems, since they include large numbers of subunits, and large, and perhaps more diverse, student bodies, to encounter greater difficulties of coordination than small systems, and thus to be more highly rationalized. Gross and his associates investigated the effects of school-system size on attitudes presumed to be consistent with rational operation: willingness to delegate responsibility, support of the professional staff and unwillingness to tolerate bypassing administrative echelons. The larger the system, the more likely was the superintendent to display the first two, but not the third, of these attitudes. For board members, as system size increased, the second and third of these attitudes were more prevalent. While the interpretation here is highly tentative, these findings suggest that, as the exigencies of coordination increase, board and superintendent attitudes tend to shift toward favorability to rational procedures, but with the board retaining to a considerable extent the managerial orientation. The superintendents uniformly de-emphasized heirarchic rigidity. This is consistent with problems of authority and control in school systems, arising from staff professionalization, to which the discussion turns shortly.

Gross, Mason, and McEachern also examined intraposition consensus within each school board in their sample. They found that these boards tended to agree among themselves the more homogeneous their composition (along the dimension of political liberalism-conservatism; religion; level of education; motivation for seeking board membership—civic service, political ambition, special-interest representation). They also found that to the extent that board members were well educated and motivated by civic service, their attitudes tended to converge on the professional ideology.

To turn to interposition consensus, boards similar in motives and education were especially likely to endorse "professional" points of view and to agree on such matters with the superintendent. This "professionalization" of their expectations may have been a specific example of a more general attitudinal set, since boards which were more "progressive" in their general educational views also had higher consensus with their superintendents.

Interestingly enough, the characteristics tending to produce high consensus among boards did not, when shared with the superintendent, directly affect interposition consensus, e.g., common religious membership or common political liberalism or conservatism. Thus, the relations of board and superintendent tended to be cast specifically in terms of their definitions of their organizational roles, with status characteristics operating only indirectly through effects on the orientation of the board.

The size of the board and of the school system (with which board size was directly related) was highly related to intraposition school-board consensus and to interposition consensus. Indeed, the effects of religious and educational homogeneity on consensus did not persist when board size was controlled for, although the effects of political attitudes and motivation for board membership remained. Moreover, a negative relation of community urbanization and consensus observed in the data was an artifact of the effects of board size. Gross and his colleagues interpreted this effect of system size as a function of the greater difficulty of achieving consensus within the larger boards which big systems contained.

Bowman's (1963) study suggests that system size may also affect patterns of recruitment to boards and superintendencies and thus influence consensus patterns. He was concerned with factors affecting the views of superintendents and principals concerning the participation of the superintendent in decision-making. He used a sample of school systems of varying size in Illinois, querying the superintendent and each member of his board through a mail questionnaire. Bowman's study replicated certain of the Gross, Mason, and McEachern findings. He noted that both the superintendents and the board members in systems of large size tended to view the superintendent as the chief decision-maker, especially in matters requiring judgments based on technical expertise in education. They also tended to view the board's responsibility as fiduciary. Both superintendents and board members in smaller systems tended to reduce the scope of the superintendent's actions, viewing him primarily as an agent for carrying out decisions made by the board. In addition, however, better-trained superintendents and board members of relatively high levels of education and occupational rank also tended toward the fiduciary view of the board and assigned wide latitude to the superintendent. Superintendents with less training and boards with lower educational and occupational status characteristics tended to endorse the opposite point of view. Finally, as one might expect, the better-trained superintendents and the board members of higher educational status were found in the larger systems.

Unfortunately, Bowman did not cross-tabulate system size and superintendent and board-member status characteristics, lacking adequate numbers of cases. Nonetheless, one probable interpretation of his findings is that school size alone does not fully account for the variance in superintendent and school-board points of view, and that large systems recruit both school executives and board members whose personal attributes predispose them to the professional ideology.

These studies, while they tell a good deal about factors affecting school-board attitudes and consensus, especially the conditions surrounding the recruitment of board members, cast relatively little light on determinants of the superintendent's orientation. A study by Carlson (1961; 1962) extends the understanding of these phenomena. Carlson's work complements the Gross, Mason, and McEachern study by again underlining the importance of recruitment processes. The major contribution of Carlson's study is the delineation of systematic relations among the recruitment criteria used by school boards in hiring superintendents, the career patterns and attitudes of superintendents, the conditions under which they work, and their performance in office.

Carlson used data from the detailed observation of the activities of four school superintendents, interviews with twenty others, and secondary analyses of sample surveys of superintendents. He distinguished two career lines characteristic of these administrators: place-bound and career-bound. The place-bound superintendent was drawn from the lower administrative echelons of the system in which he served, while the career-bound man came from outside, usually from the superintendency of another school system. Carlson found that school boards used different criteria in recruiting superintendents of each type. The place-bound administrator usually followed a superintendent who had been an innovator or in other ways had disturbed the equilibrium of the school system. The board was seeking a man who could consolidate gains made under the previous school executive and stabilize the structure and activities of the system. Career-bound superintendents were sought by boards for one of several reasons connected with improving the school system, e.g., enhancing the system's reputation by means of the new superintendent's professional status, or introducing new policies or procedures.

Carlson further reported that the attitudes and characteristics of the two types of superintendents differed systematically. Place-bound men wished to advance their careers without running the risks of incurring the cost of intersystem mobility or of entering a new situation. They were not highly oriented to career mobility. They did not seek their jobs, but waited to be asked by the board to take the position in their own school systems. On the other hand, career-bound men tended to equate intersystem and career mobility, were mobility-oriented, and sought new jobs actively according to their own career needs. Place-bound superintendents were little known among fellow administrators; career-bound men were well known to their fellows.

There is an obvious parallel between these career types and the cosmopolitan-local typology (see Gouldner, 1957–1958), and although Carlson lacked data on the point, he argued that career-bound men probably were oriented to their professional peers and to the professional ideology of school administration, place-bound men to the existing policies of the schools and the values of the local community.

Indeed, Carlson discovered that the differing conditions under which these types of superintendent were recruited set conditions of work likely to reinforce such attitudes. Career-bound superintendents were in a strong bargaining position vis-à-vis the board. Their alternative job possibilities were fairly numerous, and the board usually sought them for the distinctive skills or qualities which they possessed. The bargaining power of the place-bound administrators was weaker. They lacked access to other superintendencies and were entirely dependent on the board for career advancement. These differences were indicated by their salaries—considerably lower for the place-bound than for the career-bound.

Thus, the career-bound superintendents were given broad personal mandates by their boards; they were expected to produce certain results but were given wide latitude to use their own methods. Moreover, for their new subordinates they were unknown quantities, which gave them the initiative in setting the terms of their relationships. Place-bound superintendents lacked this mandate from their boards, who were likely to specify procedures as well as goals. At the same time, they were already known to their subordinates and obligated to them on the basis of earlier interaction. Career-bound superintendents, at least initially, were relatively free to establish new policies and activities consonant with their own occupational ideologies. The place-bound were not free in this way, necessarily responsive to both the managerial ideas of the board and the prefer-

ences and demands of the school staff. If these were in conflict, the place-bound man was implicated in these conflicts from the outset. One wonders under what circumstances these superintendents may have responded chiefly to the board or to their subordinates.

These differences were reflected in certain of the behaviors in office of the two kinds of superintendents, Carlson found. Early in their job tenure, the career-bound made new rules for system operation and rapidly added new members to their personal staffs. The place-bound emphasized established rules and their support of them, making few changes in the central staff. Carlson concluded that these behavioral differences indicated attempts by the career-bound men to establish their own formulations of policy and to alter central staff loyalties accordingly, attempts by place-bound superintendents to legitimize their right to office on the basis of accepted policy and practice.

Carlson's findings are in part supported, but refined and extended, by a study of Seeman's (1958), using a sample of fifty superintendents from school systems of varied types and sizes. Seeman separately measured the observed job-mobility patterns and the attitudes toward mobility of his subjects, dimensions collapsed by Carlson in his typology. He also secured descriptions of the administrative behavior of these men from the men themselves, their school boards, and their teaching staffs. Administrative behavior was found to be an interaction effect of mobility and mobility attitudes. Maintenance of the *status quo* was characteristic of the less mobile and nonmobility-oriented (Carlson's place-bound), also of the highly mobile and mobility-oriented (perhaps those of the career-bound type who emphasized status advancement more than intrinsic contributions through innovation or school-system leadership). This finding suggests that a more complex typology in Carlson's study might have resulted in more precise findings.

Despite Carlson's finding that the career-bound men established new rules, Seeman found that the highly mobile superintendents stressed considerate relations with subordinates more than the initiation of new structures or procedures. The findings of the two studies are not entirely incompatible, since they may indicate that superintendents from outside the system rely less on official position than on collegial interaction to legitimize, in the eyes of teachers, changes they wish to make. Indeed, as will be seen, this interpretation is consistent with certain findings concerning authority relations in schools. It is also consistent with Carlson's findings that teachers reported more initiation of structure by those superintendents who were both mobile and mobility-oriented than they themselves were willing to admit. In any case, Seeman's study, like Carlson's, underlines the importance of career factors and recruitment practices in influencing performance in the superintendency.

These studies of school-board–superintendent relations raise important questions about the interrelations of the recruitment, attitudes, and behavior of superintendents and school boards. To the extent that recruitment patterns affect the orientations of board members and superintendents, the conditions of recruitment to these roles will be important determiners of consensus or conflict between these levels of the school system. In this way they may color the formation of school-system policies and administrative practices. The way in which the superintendent is recruited apparently influences not only his attitudes, but the scope of his effective jurisdiction to form policies and direct the actions of subordinates.

These factors lead to the consideration of how the recruitment and attitudes of boards and the recruitment and attitudes of superintendents are linked. Some evidence was noted that larger systems tend to recruit board members and superintendents oriented to professional norms governing functional allocations and performance in office, which may well account for the high incidence of interposition consensus reported by Gross, Mason, and McEachern for these systems. It seems likely that professionally oriented boards more frequently will hire career-bound superintendents, and this may account in part for board-superintendent consensus in the larger systems. Structural variables undoubtedly are of equal importance, yet they have received scant attention. It may be that the larger systems, because of their urban settings and greater insulation from local politics, more often recruit board members disposed toward a fiduciary conception of the board's functions. If larger systems tend to be more bureaucratic than smaller ones, regularization of procedure and clear definition of office may both insulate the superintendent from the board and specify clearly the relevance of his specialized competence to his official jurisdiction.

There is, however, no firm empirical evidence of the linkage of size and bureaucratization in school systems. Terrien and Mills (1955) reported such a relationship, but their indicator of bureaucratization—size of the administrative cadre—is of questionable validity. Certainly factors other than size, for example, complexity of function, influence bureaucratization.

New studies are needed which systematically investigate the interaction of variables subsumed under organizational recruitment, structural context, and board and superintendent attitude and action. Such studies should attend to those situations in which boards and superintendents differ in their attitudes toward the responsibilities of their positions, since such situations may not only characterize significant numbers of school systems, but also reveal important sources of strain and conflict inherent in school-system structures. These studies, moreover, should move beyond attitudes to give greater attention to performance in office.

It was also argued that to understand the relations of superintendents and their subordinates requires investigation of the attitudes and degree of collegial integration which exist at lower echelons of the system. There are apparently no published studies of relationships between superintendent and principal, or between principal and teachers, despite the central importance of middle-level administrative echelons in the functioning of school systems. In addition, there are, it seems, no enquiries into the articulation of school units and system-level administrative structures, despite the questions raised by the structural looseness of school systems.

There are, however, a few studies which extend findings on interposition consensus to include the lower levels of the school-system staff.

Halpin (1956) was interested in the expectations held by both board members and the immediately subordinate staff for the administrative behavior of the superintendent and in their perceptions of his performance in office. The samples he used were 50 Ohio public school superintendents, the 237 members of their school boards, and the 350 members of their staffs. Unfortunately, Halpin did not define his staff sample except as the administrative echelon immediately below the superintendency. The value of his study is diminished by his failure to differentiate the responses of incumbents of various staff offices. Since, however, most of the school systems included in the study appear to have been rather small, one can assume reasonably that the staff sample consisted mainly of principals and teachers, that is, of lower-echelon professionals. Halpin's findings are discussed here on this assumption. His data were gathered by administering the Leader Behavior Description Questionnaire (LBDQ). This instrument, developed by Hemphill and Coons (1950), consists of two scales derived by factor analysis, Initiating Structure in Interaction (IS) and Consideration (C). IS leader behavior refers to goal setting, the specification of means, and the establishment of organizational structures for goal attainment. C behavior refers to the granting of personal autonomy to subordinates, the expression of warmth and friendliness to subordinates, and the particularization of their relationships.

Halpin asked his respondents to answer the LBDQ in two ways: according to their perceptions of the superintendent's actual behavior (Real) and their expectations of how he should behave (Ideal). With regard to his data on expectations, Halpin found only moderate variations from school system to school system in the response patterns of either board or staff members. Their expectations stressed both Initiating Structure and Consideration, which Halpin interpreted as evidence for a general norm, a norm which, from the point of view of this chapter, seems to define behavior adapted to the administration of a professionally trained staff.

But within this limit, there were system-to-system differences in staff expectations, that varied in emphasis on Initiating Structure but not Consideration. Board members' expectations were more uniform, but compared with staff personnel, they consistently stressed Initiating Structure more strongly in their expectations, while from system to system they varied in the extent of their agreement concerning Consideration. For these staff members, Consideration formed the core of expectations for the superintendent, while for board members, Initiating Structure was the central theme. Perhaps for both the staff and the school-board samples situational factors produced fluctuations in the alternative domain of expectations.

The superintendents' conceptions of their organizational role, i.e., their responses to the Ideal form of the LBDQ, approximated more closely the expectations of staff than those of board members. While board members tended to emphasize Initiating Structure in their expectations, superintendents centered their role conceptions on Consideration, although they exceeded even the staff sample in this emphasis.

Halpin discovered that perceptions of actual role behavior (Real) were quite different from the pattern of expectations. While staffs and school boards tended to agree among themselves in describing the superintendent's performance, they did not agree with each other. Staff members perceived the superintendent as low on Consideration; board members rated him high on this variable. Thus, the perceptions of the two samples were ordered in a reverse fashion to their expectations. The superintendents saw themselves as acting neither with as much Consideration as did the board, nor with as little Consideration as did the staff. With respect to Initiating Structure, staff and superintendent perceptions tended to agree. But on this variable board members overrated the superintendent compared with both his self-perceptions and perceptions of him by his staff.

Halpin thought that this finding resulted from the superintendents' "playing up" to their boards. This may have been so, but his findings can be interpreted in another way. If professional norms in education stress autonomy and independent technical judgment, then it may be that superintendents must exercise not only rational-legal but also collegial authority vis-à-vis their professional staffs. They would then blend in some way behaviors appropriate to hierarchical position—Initiating Structure—and to the role of *primus inter pares*—Consideration—in their administrative action.

At the same time, the superintendent is primarily an executive and organization officer vis-à-vis his board. Although he may participate with them in policy-making, he does so as an expert subordinate rather than as a peer, and his primary task in the eyes of the board is to carry out their policy decisions. In other words, his interaction with them is primarily concerned with devising and setting in motion organizational structures. Moreover, the greater part of his interactions with subordinates is not directly visible to the board, so that they may be aware of the structuring outcomes of his actions, but less so of the form or content which these actions take.

This interpretation orders Halpin's findings in an interesting way. The expectations of staff and school-board members, despite common elements, reveal certain essential variations in their normative orientations, which differentially legitimize and thus differentially limit the administrative actions of the superintendent. These variations can be viewed as, in part, an outcome of the different tasks of board members and professionals and of variations in their backgrounds and types of training. Given this interpretation, disagreements in perceptions of the superintendent indicate how his performance must vary in relation to his superordinate board and subordinate professional staff (ignoring possible effects of normative orientations upon interpersonal perceptions).

Halpin's sample was limited, and one wonders to what extent the present interpretation of his data can be generalized. Certainly, this interpretation is consistent with other characteristics of school systems. In addition, studies at the University of Chicago (Bidwell, 1957; Guba and Bidwell, 1957), although with equally limited samples, found that teacher expectations for superintendent behavior, centered on dimensions similar to Initiating Structure and Consideration, were patterned in ways similar to those noted by Halpin, and reported that teachers' job satisfaction varied with the extent to which these expectations were met.

References

Bidwell, C. E. "Some Effects of Administrative Behavior: A Study in Role Theory." *Administrative Science Quarterly*, 2 (1957), pp. 163–81.

Bowman, T. R. "Participation of Superintendents in School Board Decision-Making." *Administrator's Notebook*, 11 (1963), pp. 1–4.

Callahan, R. E. *Education and the Cult of Efficiency*. Chicago: University of Chicago Press, 1962.

Carlson, R. O. "Succession and Performance among School Superintendents." *Administrative Science Quarterly*, 6 (1961), pp. 210–27.

Carlson, R. O. *Executive Succession and Organizational Change*. Chicago: University of Chicago, Midwest Administration Center, 1962.

Gilland, T. M. *The Origin and Development of the Power and Duties of the City-School Superintendent*. Chicago: University of Chicago Press, 1935.

Gouldner, A. W. "Cosmopolitans and Locals: Toward an Analysis of Latent Social Roles, I and II." *Administrative Science Quarterly*, 2 (1957–58), pp. 281–306, 444–80.

Gross, N.; Mason, W. S.; and McEachern, A. W. *Explorations in Role Analysis: Studies of the School Superintendency Role*. New York: Wiley, 1958.

Guba, E. G., and Bidwell, C. E. "Administrative Relationships: Teacher Effectiveness, Teacher Satisfaction, and Administrative Behavior, a Study of the School as a Social Institution." *Studies in Educational Administration*, No. 6. Chicago: University of Chicago, Midwest Administration Center, 1957.

Halpin, A. W. *The Leadership Behavior of School Superintendents*. Columbus: Ohio State University Press, 1956.

Hemphill, J. K., and Coons, A. E. *Leader Behavior Description*. Columbus: Ohio State University Press, 1950.

Naegle, K. D. "Superintendency versus Superintendents: A Critical Essay," *Harvard Educational Review*, 30 (1960), pp. 372–93.

Pierce, P. R. *The Origin and Development of the Public School Principalship*. Chicago: University of Chicago Press, 1935.

Reller, T. L. *The Development of the City Superintendency of Schools in the United States*, Philadelphia: Author, 1935.

Seeley, J. R.; Sim, R. A.; and Loosley, Elizabeth W. *Crestwood Heights: A Study of the Culture of Suburban Life*. New York: Basic Books, 1956.

Seeman, M. "Social Mobility and Administrative Behavior." *American Sociological Review*, 23 (1958), pp. 633–42.

Terrien, F. W., and Mills, D. L. "The Effect of Changing Size upon the Internal Structure of Organizations." *American Sociological Review*, 20 (1955), pp. 11–13.

OVER THE SPAN of our nation's history, teaching has ranked low among the occupations available to young people. The typical eighteenth-century teacher who paid for his passage to this country by being indentured to the highest bidder and the contemporary teacher who views greater prestige as the panacea for his professional ills express a common dissatisfaction with their respective positions in the social order.

Poorly paid, insecure in their jobs, and surrounded by petty restrictions, teachers, nonetheless, are regarded by the public with apparent respect and, perhaps, affection. Underlying this, however, is pity for women who failed to find husbands and for men who avoided "real" life by retiring to the classroom. Parents and other citizens in the community have discovered the political inability of teachers to change unfavorable school policies and tax rates. There seems little question that in matters that really count the popularly ascribed role of the teacher, more often than not, is one of impotence to shape his social environment.

It is a matter of conjecture whether teachers agree with this stereotype of themselves. However, it would seem that many of them have, indeed, learned that their authority hangs by a slender thread in encounters with the community of parents. Exhorted to be "professional" and, therefore, self-directed and autonomous in judgment, teachers may feel themselves surrounded by restrictions imposed by the policy structure of their school systems and by their superiors' idiosyncracies of leadership. The dangers in this situation are apparent. If teachers think they are unable to make an impact upon their occupational environment, they may divert their energy from teaching pupils to other activities, avocational or vocational, which are more meaningful to them.

Many factors may induce such a state. The results of a growing body of research have shown that an individual's perception of where he belongs relative to the

Bureaucracy and Teachers' Sense of Power

Gerald H. Moeller

Reprinted from The School Review, 72 (1964), pp. 137–57, by permission of the author and the publisher, The University of Chicago Press.

community power structure is multiply determined.[1] For example, Campbell, Gurin, and Miller, in a study of voter behavior during the 1952 Presidential election, found both sex and socio-economic factors associated with feelings of political efficacy.[2] Men had a higher sense of political efficacy than women; and persons with higher incomes, more extensive educational training, and higher social status felt greater power with respect to public affairs than their less advantaged counterparts. The extent to which a person feels capable of affecting the course of events, whether within the local community or the society at large, may well be a highly generalized attitude. Shipton and Belisle, after showing a close relationship between feelings of local inefficacy among school patrons and their inclination to agree with stereotyped criticisms concerning the schools, suggested that powerlessness reflected "some generalized feelings of futility and dissatisfaction which are projected upon either local government or public education in general."[3] Similarly, Douvan proposed that the feeling of political efficacy is intimately related to a fundamental attribute of personality, the psychological energy which a person has at his disposal.[4]

Since attitudes are learned, it follows that persons who learned that there is a high probability of changing conditions through persistent action will have a different attitude toward existing social conditions than persons who learned that social conditions are impervious to change. It is proposed that teachers who were reared in middle- and upper-class families learned, in a generalized manner, that they could effect changes, while those from lower-class homes learned the futility of such activity. If these attitudes persist into adult life, as Child has indicated,[5] then teachers may initially come to their jobs with different expectations regarding their power in any social system.

Ultimately, whatever orientations or expectations a teacher may have toward power in the abstract will converge with the effects of the school organization and social system, since the organizational structure of the school system both determines and is determined by the social ethos of its members. Accordingly, the focus in this study was directed at organizational complexity and its human antecedents which have been treated by sociologists as a problem of "bureaucracy."

The concept of bureaucracy provided a means for identifying a number of interrelated organizational dimensions which might be found in school systems in company with various effects upon teachers. Such effects, presumably, included sense of power, or, conversely, powerlessness, a concept which, too, has been the subject of recent interest and research among sociologists and social psychologists.

In this study the central issue was the teacher's sense of power with respect to the school system at large—his sense of ability or inability to influence the organizational forces which so importantly shape his destiny. It was not the teacher's feelings about himself and his position with respect to the classroom, nor to the profession, nor to the larger society in which he lives which engaged this investigation. Rather, it was the teacher's sense of power vis-à-vis his school system, as the system varied with regard to its bureaucratization, toward which the study was directed.

Finally, meshed within the organizational structure of the school system are certain situational and social factors which serve to enhance or reduce the teacher's feelings of power. Specifically, cues provided by positions of power he has held in the system (i.e., committee chairmanships and other *ad hoc* decision-making positions), particularistic obligations incurred with administrators,[6] the style of leadership exercised by the chief administrator, and the professional associations and other sources of corporate power upon which he depends, may indicate to the teacher the extent of his potential influence on policy decisions affecting the school system.

While organizational structure may affect individuals in a number of different ways, the issue in this study was restricted to the teacher's sense of powerlessness to influence school system policy.[7] Presumably, school systems in the process of becoming larger and more complex adopt more and more of the elements of bureaucracy. Teachers in such systems are confronted with increased regulations, structuring of the curriculum, and other bureaucratic devices for coordination and control. The major hypothesis, then, was that bureaucracy in school system organization induces in teachers a sense of powerlessness to affect school system policy. Positively stated, it was predicted that the general level of sense of power in a school system varies inversely to the degree of bureaucratization in that system. Secondary hypotheses held that intraschool-system variations in sense of power are induced by factors lying within the individual teacher and his immediate social environment.

To test the hypotheses, twenty school systems employing from 37 to 700 full-time teachers were selected from the St. Louis metropolitan area.[8] Superintendents of these systems were visited by members of the research staff for authorization to contact teachers who were selected from faculty lists by the use of a table of random numbers. Twenty elementary and twenty secondary teachers were chosen, whenever possible, from each school district to receive questionnaires. By additional contacts with non-responding teachers, the research staff brought the final return to 88 per cent of the total, or 692 responses. In order to estimate the bias represented by the non-returns, comparisons were made of the sense-of-power scores of teachers who returned the questionnaire soon after the initial mailing and those who required additional contacts. These differences were found to be insignificant, suggesting that the 12 per cent who did not respond might not differ significantly either.

Since the bureaucratic model had been selected as the means for investigating the influence of organizational structure upon the teacher's sense of power, it was necessary either to find a suitable measure of bureaucratization or to construct one. After an unsuccessful search of the literature such a measure was constructed, using the characteristics of bureaucracy as described by Blau.[9] In an absolute sense, it must be pointed out, American public school systems are highly bureaucratized organizations, governed by a complex body of law and characterized by an elaborate division of labor and a formal structure of administrative authority. Teachers and other employees are certified for their jobs on criteria of technical competence and typically are promoted on the basis of seniority. In some school systems, teachers are protected in their employ-

ment by tenure. Consequently, distinctions drawn among school systems necessarily must be within a relatively narrow range on a continuum of bureaucratization.

Using an eight-item forced-choice instrument, a group of persons with first-hand knowledge of the school systems in the study made judgments which provided the data for ordering the twenty school systems on a bureaucracy scale. The method of scaling the data followed in general the procedures outlined by Riley, Riley, and Toby for construction of an object scale, that is, data from individuals combined to represent collective responses.[10] Each of the twenty school systems was rated by three, four, or five judges. If a majority of judges chose the "bureaucratic" alternative on a given item, a plus was entered for the school; if less than a majority chose the "bureaucratic" alternative, a minus was entered. In this way a single set of ratings over the eight items was obtained for each school system based upon the majority response of the system's judges. This provided the primary data upon which the scale analysis was performed.

Following scale analysis a pattern descriptive of the most to the least bureaucratic school systems emerged (Table 1). On this bureaucracy continuum school systems could be scaled from type 0 to type 8. A school system to which none of the items applied was scored 0 (least bureaucratic), while a school system to which all items applied was scored 8 and was considered "most bureaucratic." In order for a system to be considered most bureaucratic, or scale type 8, all characteristics had to be positive. While the coefficient of reproducibility was found to be .93, the limited number of objects used in scale analysis indicated the need for further evaluation of the data.[11] The question of interrater reliability was most evident. Following the analysis of variance design reported by Ebel when several raters are used. interrater reliability was computed to be .47.[12] In this design it is impossible to take out the between-rater variance which must go into the error term; this is one reason for the low interrater correlation.

These questions indicated the advisability of further analysis. Accordingly, a parallel scale analysis of the data was amount of bureaucracy in any school they rated. Indeed, the subject scale of bureacucracy (for judges) indicated systematic differences between judges in their inclinations to choose the bureaucracy alternative in rating school systems.

To test this possibility, cross-tabulations of subject and object scores were made to determine correlation. The correlation as estimated by the coefficient of contingency was virtually zero. Hence, school scores appear to be independent of the characteristics of the judges by this test.

In sum, the purpose in undertaking these scale analyses of the bureaucracy ratings was to avoid the uninspected assumptions which would have been involved in an arbitrary, although simple, pursued in an attempt to describe the amount of bureaucracy each judge saw in the school systems. In this case, it was the subjects, the judges, who were scored, and not the objects of their judgments, the school systems. The purpose in obtaining scores for subjects as well as for objects (for judges as well as for school systems) was to determine whether or not the bureaucracy score achieved by a school system was an artifact of the kind of judges who happened to rate that system. Conceivably, a school system could achieve a high bureaucracy score by having as its judges persons who were inclined to see a large construction of a bureaucracy index. Only a study conducted on a far larger sample of ratings could verify the unidimensionality which this measure was presumed to possess.

The teacher's sense of power, or the feeling that he can influence the policy direction of the school system, constituted the major issue and dependent variable of the study. Sense of power was conceived of as a continuum upon which teachers may be ordered; at one extreme are those who feel unlimited in the degree to which they can affect school system policy, and, at the other end are those who feel totally powerless to influence its direction in any way. Powerlessness was used as Seeman has defined it, "the expectancy or probability held by the individual that his own behavior cannot determine the occurrence of the outcomes, or reinforcements, he seeks."[13]

Since an extensive search of the literature revealed no measure of sense

Table 1—Scale Items Describing Most to Least Bureaucratic School Systems

Item*	Scale Type
Uniform course of study	8
Communication through established channels	7
Uniform hiring and dismissing procedures	6
Secure tenure for non-teaching personnel	5
Explicit statement of school policies	4
Clearly delimited area of responsibility	3
Specified lines of authority	2
Standard salary policies for new teachers	1

*Systems characterized by none of the above were scaled 0.

of power adaptable to teachers in the social context of the school, it was necessary to construct such a measure. To this end, a set of Likert-type questionnaire items was prepared, tested on a scaling sample of one hundred teachers, and subjected to scale analysis. Six items, whose marginal distributions were well distributed over a range between 0.2 and 0.8, whose cutting points were separated from one another, and whose error counts were low, were selected for the final measure. These six items constituting the sense-of-power scale are listed in Table 2 by order of difficulty, from highest to least high in sense of power:

Later, using the responses of the teachers in the main study, scale analysis was again conducted to determine whether unidimensionality could be cross-validated on a different population. The six items again scaled in the same order as before with a coefficient of reproducibility of .93 when chance reproducibility was found to be .85.

In addition to the sense-of-power scale the teacher questionnaire included indexes of differences among the systems in teachers' exposure to powerlessness-producing effects and in the selection of powerlessness-prone teachers. Specifically included were factors related to particularism in administrator-teacher relations; positions of authority held in the system; repressive authority exercised by the superintendent; teachers' social origins; accessibility of teachers to corporate groups; and sex, length of service, and teaching level.

A measure of the particularism in the teacher-administrator relationship was constructed to determine whether school officials interacted with teachers impersonally or in a highly personal manner conducive to the formation of reciprocal obligations in the framework of their official roles. It was considered that, while universalism might conceivably be considered a goal in some school systems, its attainment was virtually impossible. Hence, all interpersonal interaction between teachers and administrators was on a continuum of particularism bounded by absolute impartiality of treatment or universalism at one pole and extreme partiality at the other. In the measure of particularism, visiting relationships between administrators and teachers were assigned highest weight (3), other teachers who used first names with administrators were assigned a medium weight (2), while all others were assigned a low weight (1).

Table 2—Sense-of-Power Scale

Item	Response	Scale Type
In the school system where I work, a teacher like myself:		
Considers that he has little to say over what teachers will work with him on his job	Disagree	6
Usually can find ways to get system-wide policies changed if he feels strongly enough about them	Agree	5
Feels he does not know what is going on in the upper levels of administration	Disagree	4
Feels he has little to say about important system-wide policies relating to teaching	Disagree	3
Never has a chance to work on school committees which make important decisions for the school system	Disagree	2
Believes he has some control over what textbooks will be used in the classrooms	Agree	1
(Reserved for respondents who indicated the powerless response to each of the above)		0

A measure of the positions of authority teachers had held in their school systems was formed by including all teachers who had been chairmen of committees in the high category and all others in the low category. It was found that committee chairmanship constituted almost the only position full-time classroom teachers held in the power hierarchy of the school. Marginal comments on returned questionnaires indicated that other jobs were viewed as menial extra chores which, if anything, served to emphasize, rather than reduce, the teacher's sense of powerlessness.

Other measures similarly used as control and explanatory variables were an index of repressive authority perceived by teachers to exist in their relations with the superintendent; a measure or corporate power in which teachers were asked, if possible, to name a teachers' organization capable of changing unpopular administrative decisions; and measures of teachers' socioeconomic origins, sex, length of service, and teaching level.

Results

The major hypothesis was denied. Contrary to the hypothesis, teachers in bureaucratic school systems were significantly higher in sense of power than were those in less fully bureaucratized systems ($F = 19.18$, $p < .01$). When teachers were grouped by school system, the more bureaucratic organizations were higher in teacher sense of power than were the less bureaucratic organizations (Spearman rank correlation coefficient $[r_s] = .40, p < .05$). The question confronting us at this point was whether the logic underlying the hypothesis was at fault or whether disproportionate weighting of specific power-inducing or

power-reducing elements in the population had led to this result, masking the effect of organization upon teachers' sense of power. Accordingly, proportions of teachers in the various subgroups noted in Table 3 were examined and held constant when disproportionate in subsequent analyses of bureaucracy and sense of power. Those subgroups considered disproportionate were length of service, social class origins, particularism, repressive authority, and corporate groups. Sex, teaching level, and positions of authority did not differ by more than 1 per cent between high and low bureaucratic systems and were, on this basis, considered proportionate.

The summarized results of the analyses of bureaucracy and sense of power, holding constant disproportionate subgroups, may be seen in Table 4. What is, perhaps, most striking about these findings is the pervasiveness of the bureaucratic variable in its effect upon teachers. Only in one instance, the group of fourteen teachers who chose the welfare committee as a corporate source of power, did teachers in the low bureaucratic systems exceed their high bureaucratic colleagues in sense of power. The low number of teachers involved (total twenty-six) indicates that this is not a dominant factor in the hypothesized relationship.

At this juncture the research strategy pointed toward further examination of the factors other than organization to which sense of power is sensitive.

PARTICULARISM IN THE
ADMINISTRATOR-TEACHER RELATIONSHIP

Particularistic ties between teachers and administrators were more prevalent in low bureaucratic systems than in the high bureaucratic ones. As shown in Table 3, 43 per cent of the high-service teachers reported visiting relationships or high particularism in the low bureaucratic systems compared to 27 per cent

Table 3—Characteristics of the Teacher Population

TEACHER CHARACTERISTICS	HIGH BUREAUCRATIC SYSTEMS		LOW BUREAUCRATIC SYSTEMS	
	Per Cent	N	Per Cent	N
	All Teachers			
Length of service: *				
0–3 years	33	109	44	139
4 + years	67	221	56	178
Total	100	330	100	317
Social class origins: *				
Professional	19	62	10	32
Managerial	26	84	19	58
Clerical	9	28	10	31
Labor	26	85	33	103
Farm	20	69	28	89
Total	100	328	100	313
Elementary:				
Male	4	13	5	16
Female	41	134	40	129
Secondary:				
Male	29	93	30	90
Female	26	81	25	75
Total	100	321	100	310
	High-service Teachers Only (4+ Years)			
Positions of authority:				
High	47	104	48	85
Low	53	116	52	92
Total	100	220	100	177
Particularism: *				
High	27	60	43	77
Low	73	160	57	101
Total	100	220	100	178
Repressive authority: *				
High	30	58	34	53
Medium	47	93	51	79
Low	23	45	15	24
Total	100	196	100	156
Corporate groups: *				
Union	14	30	6	10
Welfare committee	6	12	8	14
Local organization	65	141	54	92
No organization	15	33	32	55
Total	100	216	100	171

*Factors considered disproportionately distributed and hence subjected to further analysis as intervening variables in the relationship of bureaucracy and sense of power.

of the teachers in the high bureaucratic systems. Yet, teachers in the high bureaucratic systems with personal ties with administrators were significantly higher in sense of power than those lacking such ties ($\chi^2 = 6.79$, $p < .01$). Apparently, particularism held no significance for sense of power among the high-service teachers in the low bureaucratic systems ($\chi^2 = .50$), or among low-service teachers in high bureaucratic systems ($\chi^2 = .38$), or in low bureaucratic systems ($\chi^2 = .04$).

Particularistic connections between teachers and administrators in bureaucratic systems were infrequent. It seems reasonable that, if only a few teachers have access to the administrator in an informal, social way, those teachers who do have access will have a higher sense of power than those without such ties.

On the other hand, in the low bureaucratic systems, particularistic ties were relatively easy to acquire and may have become commonplace; for example, any teacher wishing to do so could establish visiting relationships with the administrator. The openness of this avenue in the low bureaucratic systems may have made particularism appear ineffective in enhancing any one teacher's sense of power.

POSITIONS OF AUTHORITY HELD BY
TEACHERS IN THE SCHOOL SYSTEM

The proportions of teachers with high service reporting positions of authority

Table 4—Sense-of-Power Means For Variables Disproportionately Distributed in High and Low Bureaucratic School Systems

TEACHER CHARACTERISTICS	HIGH BUREAUCRATIC SYSTEMS		LOW BUREAUCRATIC SYSTEMS		COMPARISONS
	Means	N	Means	N	
Length of service:					
0–3 years	3.06	109	2.46	139	Hi vs. Lo Bur, $F = 26.93$†;
4 + years	3.19	221	2.55	178	Hi vs. Lo Serv, $F = 3.29$†
Social class origins:					
Professional	3.29	62	2.81	32	Hi vs. Lo Bur, $F = 20.51$†;
Managerial	3.15	84	2.41	58	between origins, $F = 2.40$*
Clerical	3.32	28	2.25	31	
Labor	2.75	85	2.21	103	
Farm	3.23	69	2.83	89	
Particularism:					
High	3.73	60	2.64	77	Hi vs. Lo Bur, $F = 3.80$;
Low	3.01	160	2.50	101	Hi vs. Lo Part, $F = 61.45$†
Repressive authority:					
High	2.29	58	1.53	53	Hi vs. Lo Bur, $F = 12.60$†;
Medium	3.33	93	2.81	79	repressive authority,
Low	3.98	45	3.33	24	$F = 20.70$†
Corporate groups:					
Union	3.63	30	2.60	10	Hi vs. Lo Bur, $F = .31$;
Welfare committee	4.33	12	4.71	14	organizations vs. no
Local association	4.56	141	3.39	92	organizations, $F = 12.54$†; between organizations, $F = 9.75$†
No organization	3.09	33	2.78	55	

*Significant at less than 0.05 level.   †Significant at less than 0.01 level.

in high and low bureaucratic systems were remarkably similar, as noted in Table 3. However, when such positions and sense of power were compared, a significant relationship was found among the teachers in the high bureaucratic systems ($\chi^2 = 4.56$, $p < .05$) but not among the teachers in the low bureaucratic systems ($\chi^2 = .23$). Again, as in the results of comparisons of particularism and sense of power, teachers in the low bureaucratic systems did not see positions of authority as a route to power.

ADMINISTRATOR'S REPUTATION FOR REPRESSIVE AUTHORITY

The extent to which teachers in high or low bureaucratic systems saw their superintendent as exercising restrictive and oppressive authority over the faculty depressed their sense of power accordingly ($F = 20.70$, $p < .01$, as shown in Table 4).

One element of bureaucratic administration is the reliance upon reason or rationality to achieve organizational objectives. Hence, it had been anticipated that in the high bureaucratic systems where rationality was the administrative mode, few teachers would report repressive authority in relations with the administration. But, as noted in Table 3, this was not borne out in the findings which showed larger numbers of teachers reporting repressive authority in the high bureaucratic than in the low bureaucratic systems. Apparently, rationality in bureaucratic organization does not preclude the use of restrictive and coercive measures. As Gouldner has noted, bureaucracies may be punishment-centered, using compulsion and sanctions, or bureaucracies may be representative and use human relations techniques, feedback, and education to attain compliance with organizational objectives.[14] Or it may be that teachers with strong aspirations to autonomy may see *all* administrative direction or struc-

ture as repressive authority, incompatible with their professional roles.

CORPORATE GROUP MEMBERSHIP

Teachers with organizational ties, as noted in Table 4, were found to possess significantly higher sense of power than teachers without such corporate instruments of power. And teachers in the bureaucracies felt that such organizations were more readily available to them than did their colleagues in the less bureaucratized systems (Table 3). Again the pervasive effect of bureaucracy was in evidence. With one exception (the welfare committee) members of organizational groups in the bureaucracies had a higher sense of power than did their counterparts in the low bureaucratic systems. In the high bureaucratic systems 65 per cent of the teachers saw the local teachers organization as the most potent source of power available to them compared to 54 per cent in the low bureaucratic systems. Unions appeared to sustain sense of power in 14 per cent of the high bureaucratic teachers and in 6 per cent of the low bureaucratic teachers. The welfare committee, which usually consisted of a group of teachers chosen by popular vote, was the choice of 6 per cent of the high bureaucratic teachers and 8 per cent of the low bureaucratic group. Interestingly, the latter group had the highest sense of power scores when the data were classified by groups. The analyses of teacher groups again pointed up both the variability of teachers in their orientations to power and the strength of the bureaucratic variable in determining a system-wide level of sense of power.

SOCIAL-CLASS ORIGINS OF TEACHERS

The home background of teachers in their formative years appeared to be a factor in sense of power. When all teachers, irrespective of school system, were grouped by social origins, sense of power ranked, from high to low, as follows: professional, farm, business-managerial, clerical-white collar, and labor (between origins $F = 2.40, p < .05$, in Table 4). The high sense of power of teachers reared on farms brings into question the use of economic indicators in measurement of power. The knowledge that their environment is controllable may, indeed, characterize groups other than the upper strata of society. In each grouping, however, the teachers from the bureaucracies indicated higher sense of power than did similar teachers in the low bureaucratic systems ($F = 20.51, p < .01$ in Table 4).

SEX AND TEACHING LEVEL

Male teachers felt themselves more powerful than did female teachers ($F = 10.30, p < .01$, data not shown) and elementary teachers, as a group, more powerful than secondary ($F - 12.63, p < .01$, not shown). With one exception, however, the differences between groups were relatively small. This group, the male elementary teachers, was smallest in size (29 men to 263 women in the elementary grades) and had the highest sense of power.

LENGTH OF SERVICE

As noted in Table 3, teacher turnover was less evident in the bureaucracies with 67 per cent of the teachers having 4 or more years of service than in the low bureaucratic systems with 56 per cent of the teachers in this category. This stability of employment was accompanied by higher sense of power (relative to the low bureaucratic systems) at all points in

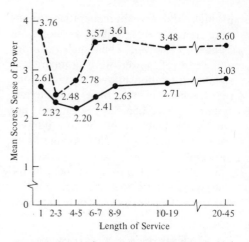

Figure 1. Sense of power among teachers in high bureaucratic systems (dotted line) and among teachers in low bureaucratic systems (solid line).

the teachers' careers ($F = 26.93, p < .01$, in Table 4 and, graphically, in Figure 1). Particularly striking in Figure 1 is the shape of the curves in high and low bureaucratic systems when teachers' careers were viewed longitudinally. First-year teachers had a high sense of power which dropped and then rose again in the second- to fifth-year group to a point where it remained rather constant for the more senior teachers in the sample. Since these data are cross-sectional, selective fears may have operated, first, to eliminate those with high sense of power and, later, those with low sense of power. In any event, the pattern similarity between high and low bureaucratic systems suggests that length of service relates to sense of power in a manner unrelated to bureaucracy.

As further noted in Figure 1, first-year teachers in the contrasting organizations differed strikingly in sense of power. A t-test showed that this difference was significant at less than the 0.05 level. These data, however, were obtained after the first-year respondents had been teaching for 5 months, and the data might have looked different had they been collected earlier in the year. But, the total evidence suggests no organizational effects on sense of power unique to bureaucratized or non-bureaucratized systems.

The foregoing results are summarized in Figure 2, which shows those variables augmenting or reducing a teacher's sense of power in the school systems studied.

Sense of Power and Policy

Sense of power to influence the policy direction of the school system was found to be high in the bureaucratic systems when teachers as individuals, when school system means, and when all other sub-groups of teachers were compared. In contrast, sense of power was consistently low among teachers in the low bureaucratic school systems.

It is the position taken here that the firm policy of the more heavily bureaucratized school systems enhanced rather than reduced a teacher's sense of power. As functionaries of organized school systems, teachers are in no sense "free" agents but are subject to many restrictions imposed by law, local customs, limited finances, and, perhaps, by their their own indecision. The issue, there-

fore, is not one of policy direction of the administration versus professional autonomy of teachers, as is so often proposed in current debate; rather, the issue appears to be policy direction versus capricious, infirm, and poorly conceived decisions made by the administration in response to each new challenge generated within or outside of the school system.

It seems apparent in the low bureaucracy schools that nearly everyone—teachers, parents, and the general public —has access to the administrative policymakers on a friendship basis—or realizes that he can go to the superintendent if he chooses. This, in effect, tends to devalue this avenue, for if everyone has access, then all should benefit equally. Since particularism pervades the entire teaching staff of a low bureaucratic system, relatively few are disenfranchised and the possibility for invidious comparisons of power is greatly reduced. Without the stabilizing benefit of a comprehensive and uniform written set of rules for the school system, many decisions arise for which adequate policy is unavailable.

Figure 2. Summary of major findings: variables augmenting (solid line) or reducing (dotted line) a teacher's sense of power.

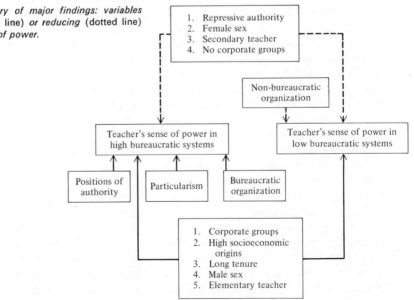

This, it would seem, leads teachers in the low bureaucratic systems to be uncertain as to such decisions and the element of unpredictability inherent in the system tends to abrogate their sense of power. In short, only in an orderly, understandable, and predictable organization can any individual expect to influence the direction the organization will take. This factor seems crucial in the low sense of power of the low bureaucratic teachers and leads to the postulation of predictability as a major organizational element differentiating the high and low bureaucratic systems. Teachers who know that most events will follow a prescribed course and will be dealt with in a predictable and rational manner are in a much better position to influence these events than are teachers who never know what action the administration will take. In such an ambiguous situation, teachers must view each new situation with foreboding, not knowing which cues are dependable guides for action.

In systems characterized by firm policy, we may postulate that teachers' knowledge of that policy is, in itself, a form of power. When policy is applicable to all, then any individual who knows the rules by which the system is governed is able to predict how any particular situation will be handled. This factor enables the teachers in the bureaucratic school systems, by the expedient of learning the rules; to anticipate how the administration will act in most problems confronting it. More importantly, knowledge of policy enables teachers to know the most effective course of action to take in order to influence the policy-maker. Accordingly, in the bureaucratic school systems, firm policy enables teachers to predict accurately, providing an effective basis for action and thereby enhancing sense of power. With the advantage of a firm policy structure, teachers in the bureau-

cracies, as a group, have a higher general sense of power than teachers in the low bureaucratic systems.

A Reassessment of Bureaucracy and Sense of Power

From the findings reported in this study have emerged a number of postulates regarding bureaucracy in the public school setting. Certainly bureaucracy, as a rational and, hence, predictable form of organization, does not induce in teachers feelings of powerlessness or alienation from the system. The greater predictability seems to stem from the published policy of these systems which assures teachers of specific avenues of communication up the line to the decision-making centers of the administration. Then, too, the rationality of the bureaucracies pressed toward effectiveness of operation and efficiency in employment of personnel, insuring teachers the best possible working conditions within the limits of available resources.

By definition the low bureaucratic school systems are less complex organizations with fewer and less explicit written policies. Without specified rules to guide them, administrators of these systems must rely on unanticipated decisions or on traditional community norms—either of which are subject to misunderstanding and, hence, are less predictable than a well-defined policy structure would be.

When the focus is shifted from the school system organization to the individual teacher, the dimension of comparative evaluation becomes relevant. Each member of a social system learns his role in that system and, in so doing, assesses his power in relation to others. This knowledge of relative position in the power hierarchy enables teachers with greater service, of higher social-class origins, and the males in elementary schools to score high on sense of power whether they were employed in high or low bureaucratic systems.

In short, sense of power appears to be influenced by many diverse variables lying within the teacher himself, in his past, in his social groups, in his relations with his superiors, and in the organizational structure of the school in which he is employed. The general level of sense of power seems to be limited by the organizational variable. Bureaucracy provides the teacher with an understandable and predictable ethos in which to pursue his profession. This predictability, far from reducing sense of power, sets a higher level of sense of power than is found in the less bureaucratized school organizations. To the general level of sense of power set by the organization of the school system the teacher brings his own personal characteristics which differentiate him from his colleagues and enable him to make comparisons of his power in relation to that held by others. Thus, the school system sets the general level of sense of power and the teacher varies from this level by his own personal orientation toward power.

Notes

[1] Wayne E. Thompson and John E. Horton, "Political Alienation as a Force in Political Action," *Social Forces*, 38 (1960), pp. 190–95. This article succinctly summarizes and presents results emerging from research in this area.

[2] Angus Campbell, Gerald Gurin, and Warren E. Miller, *The Voter Decides* (Evanston, Ill.: Row, Peterson, 1954), p. 187.

[3] James M. Shipton and Eugene L. Belisle, "Who Criticizes the Public Schools?" *Phi Delta Kappan*, 37 (1956), pp. 303–7.

[4] Elizabeth Douvan, "The Sense of Effectiveness and Response to Public Affairs," *Journal of Social Psychology*, 47 (1958), pp. 111–26.

[5] Irvin L. Child, "Socialization," in *Handbook of Social Psychology*, ed. Gardner Lindzey. (Reading, Mass.: Addison-Wesley, 1954), p. 681.

[6] An interpersonal relationship is said, in Parsons' terms, to be particularistic when each participant evaluates the relationship in terms of his own and the other individual's personal relations. On the other hand, a relationship is universalistic when each individual evaluates the other as an instance of a general class of persons, irrespective of personal elements. A more complete discussion may be found in Talcott Parsons and Edward A. Shils, *Toward a General Theory of Action* (Cambridge: Harvard University Press, 1952), p. 81.

[7] Gerald H. Moeller, "The Relationship between Bureaucracy in School System Organization and Teachers' Sense of Power" (unpublished Ed.D. dissertation, Washington University, 1962). This study was part of a larger project performed pursuant to SAE Contract 9009, project No. 929, with the United States Office of Education, "Teacher Perception of Administrator Behavior," W. W. Charters, Jr., Principal Investigator.

[8] The school systems participating in the study are located in St. Louis and Jefferson Counties in Missouri and in Madison and St. Clair Counties in Illinois.

[9] Peter M. Blau, *Bureaucracy in Modern Society* (New York: Random House, 1956), pp. 28–33.

[10] Matilda W. Riley, J. W. Riley, Jr., and J. Toby, *Sociological Studies in Scale Analysis* (New Brunswick, N.J.: Rutgers University Press, 1954), ch. 5.

[11] The coefficient of reproducibility is the quantity of one minus the number of errors divided by the number of item responses.

[12] R. L. Ebel, "Estimation of the Reliability of Ratings," *Psychometrika*. 16 (1951), pp. 407–24.

[13] Melvin Seeman, "On the Meaning of Alienation," *American Sociological Review*, 24 (1959), p. 784.

[14] Alvin W. Gouldner, "Organizational Analysis," in *Sociology Today*, ed. Robert K. Merton and Leonard S. Cottrell, Jr. (New York: Basic Books, 1959), p. 403.

Organizational Constraints in the Classroom

Philip Jackson

From Chapter 1, "The Daily Grind," from Life in Classrooms by Philip W. Jackson, pp. 11–19. Copyright © 1968 by Holt, Rinehard and Winston, Inc. Reprinted by permission of Holt, Rinehart and Winston, Inc.

ANYONE WHO HAS ever taught knows that the classroom is a busy place, even though it may not always appear so to the casual visitor. Indeed, recent data have proved surprising even to experienced teachers. For example, we have found in one study of elementary classrooms that the teacher engages in as many as 1000 interpersonal interchanges each day.[1] An attempt to catalogue the interchanges among students or the physical movement of class members would doubtlessly add to the general impression that most classrooms, though seemingly placid when glimpsed through the window in the hall door, are more like the proverbial beehive of activity. One way of understanding the meaning of this activity for those who experience it is by focusing on the teacher as he goes about channeling the social traffic of the classroom.

First, consider the rapidity of the teacher's actions. What keeps him hopping from Jane to Billy to Sam, and back again, in the space of a few seconds? Clearly much of this activity is done in the interest of instruction. Teaching commonly involves talking and the teacher acts as a gatekeeper who manages the flow of the classroom dialogue. When a student wishes to say something during a discussion it is usually the teacher's job to recognize his wish and to invite his comment. When more than one person wishes to enter the discussion or answer a question at the same time (a most common event) it is the teacher who decides who will speak and in what order. Or we might turn the observation around and say that the teacher determines who will *not* speak, for when a group of students have signalled the desire to enter the dialogue, several of them may be planning to say the same thing. Therefore, if Johnny is called on first, Billy, who also had his hand raised, may now find himself without anything to say. This fact partially explains the urgency with which the desire to speak is signalled to the teacher.

Another time-consuming task for the teacher, at least in the elementary school, is that of serving as supply sergeant. Classroom space and material resources are limited and the teacher must allocate these resources judiciously. Only one student at a time can borrow the big scissors, or look through the microscope, or drink from the drinking fountain, or use the pencil sharpener. And broken pencil points and parched throats obviously do not develop one at a time or in an orderly fashion. Therefore, the number of students desiring to use various classroom resources at any given moment is often greater than the number that can use them. This explains the lines of students that form in front of the pencil sharpener, the drinking fountain, the microscope, and the washroom door.

Closely related to the job of doling out material resources is that of granting special privileges to deserving students. In elementary classrooms it is usually the teacher who assigns coveted duties, such as serving on the safety patrol, or running the movie projector, or clapping the erasers, or handing out supplies. In most classrooms volunteers are plentiful, thus the jobs are often rotated among the students. (A list of current job-holders is a familiar item on elementary school bulletin boards.) Although the delegation of these duties may not take up much of the teacher's time, it does help to give structure to the activities of the room and to fashion the quality of the total experience for many of the participants.

A fourth responsibility of the teacher and one that calls our attention to another important aspect of classroom life, is that of serving as an official timekeeper. It is he who sees to it that things begin and end on time, more or less. He determines the proper moment for switching from discussion to workbooks, or from spelling to arithmetic. He decides whether a student has spent too long in the washroom, or whether those who take the bus may be dismissed. In many schools he is assisted in this job by elaborate systems of bells and buzzers. But even when the school day is mechanically punctuated by clangs and hums, the teacher is not entirely relieved of his responsibility for watching the clock. The implications of the teacher clock-watching behavior for determining what life in school is like are indeed profound. This behavior reminds us, above all, that school is a place where things often happen not because students want them to, but because it is time for them to occur.

All of the teacher's actions described so far are bound together by a common theme. They are all responsive, in one way or another, to the crowded condition of the classroom. If the teacher dealt with one student at a time (as does happen in tutorial settings) most of the tasks that have been mentioned would be unnecessary. It is, in part, the press of numbers and of time that keeps the teacher so busy. But our ultimate concern, it must be remembered, is with the student and the quality of *his* life in the classroom. Therefore, the frenetic activity of the teacher as he goes about calling

on students, handing out supplies, granting privileges, and turning activities on and off, is of interest, within the present context, only insofar as that behavior tells us something about what school is like for those who are at the receiving end of the teacher's action.

The things the teacher does as he works within the physical, temporal, and social limits of the classroom have a constraining effect upon the events that might occur there if individual impulse were allowed free reign. If everyone who so desired tried to speak at once, or struggled for possession of the big scissors, or offered a helping hand in threading the movie projector, classroom life would be much more hectic than it commonly is. If students were allowed to stick with a subject until they grew tired of it on their own, our present curriculum would have to be modified drastically. Obviously, some kinds of controls are necessary if the school's goals are to be reached and social chaos averted. The question of whether the teacher should or should not serve as a combination traffic cop, judge, supply sergeant, and time-keeper is somewhat irrelevant to the present discussion, but the fact that such functions must be performed, even if the responsibility for performing them falls upon individual students, is far from irrelevant. For a world in which traffic signs, whistles, and other regulatory devices abound is quite different from one in which these features are absent.

One of the inevitable outcomes of traffic management is the experiencing of delay. In crowded situations where people are forced to take turns in using limited resources, some must stand by until others have finished. When people are required to move as a group toward a goal, the speed of the group is, necessarily, the speed of its slowest member.

Almost inevitably, therefore, in such situations some group members are waiting for the others to catch up. Moreover, whenever the future is thought to be more attractive than the present—a common perception among school children—slow movement can sometimes seem like no movement at all.

All of these different kinds of delay are commonplace in the classrooms. Indeed, when we begin to examine the details of classroom life carefully, it is surprising to see how much of the students' time is spent in waiting. The most obvious examples are to be found in the practice of lining up that has already been mentioned. In most elementary schools students stand in line several times a day. The entire class typically lines up during recess, lunch, and dismissal, and then there are the smaller lines that form sporadically in front of drinking fountains, pencil sharpeners, and the like. Furthermore, it is not uncommon for teachers to hold these lines motionless until talking has ceased and some semblance of uniformity and order has been achieved.

Nor does the waiting end when the line has disappeared. Even when students are sitting in their seats they are often in the same position, psychologically, as if they were members of a line. It is not uncommon, for example, for teachers to move down rows asking questions or calling for recitations or examining seatwork. Under these conditions students interact with the teacher in a fixed order with the consequence of each student waiting until his turn arrives, speaking his piece, and then waiting for the teacher to get to him again in the next round. Even in rooms where teachers do not operate "by the numbers," as it were, the idea of taking turns during discussion and recitation periods is still present. After a student has made a

contribution in a more informally run class the teacher is less likely to call on him again, at least for a brief period of time. Conversely, a student who has said nothing all period is more likely to have his raised hand recognized than is a student who has participated several times in the lesson. Unusual variations from this procedure would be considered unfair by students and teachers alike. Thus, even during so-called free discussion invisible lines are formed.

In rooms where students have considerable freedom to move about on their own during seatwork and study periods, the teacher himself often becomes the center of little groups of waiting students. One of the most typical social arrangements in such settings is that in which the teacher is chatting with one student or examining his work while two or three others stand by, books and papers in hand, waiting to have the teacher evaluate their work, give them further direction, answer their questions, or in some other fashion enable them to move along. At such moments it is not unusual for one or two of the seated students also to have their hands raised, propped at the elbow, waiting patiently for the teacher to get around to them.

A familiar arrangement in the lower grades is for the teacher to work with a part of the class, usually a reading group, while the remainder engage in seatwork. Not uncommonly the students working by themselves finish their assignments before the teacher is finished with the group with which he is working. Under such circumstances it is not uncommon for the teacher to admonish the students to "find something to do" until it is time for a new activity to begin. These students may obey the teacher and thus appear to be busy, but their busyness is analogous to that of patients who read the old magazines in the doctor's waiting room.

A final example of the kinds of delay to be observed in the classroom involves the situation in which the group is given a problem to solve or an exercise to complete and some students complete the work long before others. At such times the teacher may be heard to ask, "How many need more time?" or to command, "Raise your hand when you have finished." This type of delay may only last a few seconds, but it occurs very frequently in some classrooms. Further, it is a kind of delay that is not experienced equally by all students, as are some of the others that have been mentioned, but tends, instead, to be encountered most frequently by students who are brighter, or faster, or more involved in their work.

Thus, in several different ways students in elementary classrooms are required to wait their turn and to delay their actions. No one knows for certain how much of the average student's time is spent in neutral, as it were, but for many students in many classrooms it must be a memorable portion. Furthermore, delay is only one of the consequences of living in a crowd and perhaps not even the most important one from the standpoint of constraining the individual. Waiting is not so bad, and may even be beneficial, when the things we are waiting for come to pass. But waiting, as we all know, can sometimes be in vain.

The denial of desire is the ultimate outcome of many of the delays occurring in the classroom. The raised hand is sometimes ignored, the question to the teacher is sometimes brushed aside, the permission that is sought is sometimes refused. No doubt things often have to be this way. Not everyone who wants to speak can be heard, not all of the student's queries can be answered to his satisfaction, not all of their requests can be granted. Also, it is probably true that most of these denials are psychologically trivial when considered individually. But when considered cumulatively their significance increases. And regardless of whether or not they are justified, they make it clear that part of learning how to

live in school involves learning how to give up desire as well as how to wait for its fulfillment.

Interruptions of many sorts create a third feature of classroom life that results, at least in part, from the crowded social conditions. During group sessions irrelevant comments, misbehavior, and outside visitors bearing messages often disrupt the continuity of the lesson. When the teacher is working individually with a student—a common arrangement in elementary classrooms—petty interruptions, usually in the form of other students coming to the teacher for advice, are the rule rather than the exception. Thus, the bubble of reality created during the teaching session is punctured by countless trivial incidents and the teacher must spend time patching up the holes. Students are expected to ignore these distractions or at least to turn quickly back to their studies after their attention has been momentarily drawn elsewhere.

Typically, things happen on time in school and this fact creates interruptions of another sort. Adherence to a time schedule requires that activities often begin before interest is aroused and terminate before interest disappears. Thus students are required to put away their arithmetic book and take out their spellers even though they want to continue with arithmetic and ignore spelling. In the classroom, work is often stopped before it is finished. Questions are often left dangling when the bell rings.

Quite possibly, of course, there is no alternative to this unnatural state of affairs. If teachers were always to wait until students were finished with one activity before they began another, the school day would become interminable. There seems to be no other way, therefore, but to stop and start things by the clock, even though this means constantly interrupting the natural flow of interest and desire for at least some students.

Another aspect of school life, related to the general phenomena of distractions and interruptions, is the recurring demand that the student ignore those who are around him. In elementary classrooms students are frequently assigned seatwork on which they are expected to focus their individual energies. During these seatwork periods talking and other forms of communication between students are discouraged, if not openly forbidden. The general admonition in such situations is to do your own work and leave others alone.

In a sense, then, students must try to behave as if they were in solitude, when in point of fact they are not. They must keep their eyes on their paper when human faces beckon. Indeed, in the early grades it is not uncommon to find students facing each other around a table while at the same time being required not to communicate with each other. These young people, if they are to become successful students, must learn how to be alone in a crowd.

Adults encounter conditions of social solitude so often that they are likely to overlook its special significance in the elementary classroom. We have learned to mind our own business in factories and offices, to remain silent in libraries, and to keep our thoughts to ourselves while riding public conveyances. But there are two major differences between classrooms and most of these other settings. First, except for the first few days of school, a classroom is not an *ad hoc* gathering of strangers. It is a group whose members have come to know each other quite well, to the point of friendship in many cases. Second, attendance in the room is not voluntary, as it is in many other social situations. Students are there whether they want to

be or not and the work on which they are expected to concentrate also is often not of their own choosing. Thus, the pull to communicate with others is likely somewhat stronger in the classroom than in other crowded situations.

Here then are four unpublicized features of school life: delay, denial, interruption, and social distraction. Each is produced, in part, by the crowded conditions of the classroom. When twenty or thirty people must live and work together within a limited space for five or six hours a day most of the things that have been discussed are inevitable. Therefore, to decry the existence of these conditions is probably futile, yet their pervasiveness and frequency make them too important to be ignored. One alternative is to study the ways in which teachers and students cope with these facts of life and to seek to discover how that coping might leave its mark on their reactions to the world in general.

First, we must recognize that the severity of the conditions being described is to some extent a function of social tradition, institutional policy, and situational wealth and poverty. In some schools daily schedules are treated casually and in others they are rigidly adhered to. In some classrooms a rule of no talking is in force almost all of the time, while a steady murmur is tolerated in others. In some classrooms there are forty or more students, in others, at the same grade level, there are twenty or less. Some teachers are slow to recognize an upraised hand, others respond almost immediately. Some rooms are equipped with several pairs of big scissors, others have only one.

Despite these differences, however, it is doutbful that there is any classroom in which the phenomena we have been discussing are uncommon. Space, abundant resources, and a liberal attitude toward rules and regulations may reduce the pressure of the crowd somewhat but it certainly does not eliminate it entirely.

Indeed, most of the observations on which the present analysis is based were made in so-called advantaged schools whose teachers were proud of their "progressive" educational views.

Second, as we begin to focus on the ways of coping with these institutional demands, it should be recognized at once that adaptive strategies are idiosyncratic to individual students. We cannot predict, in other words, how any particular student will react to the constraints imposed on him in the classroom. We can only identify major adaptive styles that might be used to characterize large numbers of students.

The quintessence of virtue in most institutions is contained in the single word: *patience*. Lacking that quality, life could be miserable for those who must spend their time in our prisons, our factories, our corporation offices, and our schools. In all of these settings the participants must "learn to labour and to wait." They must also, to some extent, learn to suffer in silence. They are expected to bear with equanimity, in other words, the continued delay, denial, and interruption of their personal wishes and desires.

But patience is more of a moral attribute than an adaptive strategy. It is what a person is asked to "be" rather than what he is asked to "do." Moreover, when we consider how a person *becomes* patient—that is, the behaviors he must engage in in order to earn the title—it becomes apparent that patience is more clearly determined by what a person does *not* do than by what he does. A patient man is one who does not act in a particular way, even though he desires to. He is a man who can endure the temptation to cry out or to complain even though the temptation is strong. Thus patience has to do principally with the control of impulse or its abandonment.

Returning to the situation in our schools, we can see that if students are to face the demands of classroom life with equanimity they must learn to be patient. This means that they must be able to disengage, at least temporarily, their feelings from their actions. It also means, of course, that they must be able to re-engage feelings and actions when conditions are appropriate. In other words, students must wait patiently for their turn to come, but when it does they must still be capable of zestful participation. They must accept the fact of not being called on during a group discussion, but they must continue to volunteer.

Thus, the personal quality commonly described as patience—an essential quality when responding to the demands of the classroom—represents a balance, and sometimes a precarious one, between two opposed tendencies. On the one hand is the impulse to act on desire, to blurt out the answer, to push to the front of the line, or to express anger when interrupted. On the other hand, is the impulse to give up the desire itself, to stop participating in the discussion, to go without a drink when the line is long, or to abandon an interrupted activity.

Whether or not a particular student acquires the desirable balance between impulsive action and apathetic withdrawal depends in part, as has been suggested, on personality qualities that lie outside the scope of the present discussion. In most classrooms powerful social sanctions are in operation to force the student to maintain an attitude of patience. If he impulsively steps out of line his classmates are likely to complain about his being selfish or "pushy." If he shifts over into a state of overt withdrawal, his teacher is apt to call him back to active participation.

But the fact that teachers and peers help to keep a student's behavior in line does not mean that the demands themselves can be ignored. Regardless of his relative success in coping with it, or the forces, personal or otherwise, that might aid in that coping, the elementary school student is situated in a densely populated social world. As curriculum experts and educational technologists try to experiment with new course content and new instructional devices, the crowds in the classroom may be troublesome. But there they are. Part of becoming a student involves learning how to live with that fact.

Note

[1] Philip W. Jackson, "Teacher-Pupil Communication in the Elementary Classroom: An Observational Study," Paper read at the American Educational Research Association meeting, Chicago, February, 1965.

Among the variety of theoretical and research problems in occupations that interest sociologists is that concerned with the processes by which a population becomes distributed within the occupational structure of the society. Any society must develop techniques for selecting and training its members to fill occupational positions. In modern industrial societies, these techniques have become increasingly specialized and organized within educational institutions.

With the increase in occupational specialization, college training has become the major criterion for stratifying occupations of high and low occupational skill, income, and social prestige. The strategic importance of college training for the occupational distribution of the population has in turn increased the significance of the high school in the structure and process of social stratification, because admission of high school graduates to colleges is often contingent upon their performance in secondary schools.[1] Thus, in their studies of how populations are occupationally differentiated and distributed, sociologists have directed their investigations to the processes of socialization in general, and more particularly to the temporal points within these processes at which the range of occupational aspirations becomes narrowed and focused, choices are made between alternatives, and preparatory activities are begun.

Approaches to the Problem

The standard approach to the study of students who are and are not admitted to college begins with examination of the characteristics of college-qualified graduates to determine how they differ from those of nonqualified students. The findings of investigations oriented by this approach suggest that the more "obvious" explanations, such as that the college-qualified students have higher

The School as a Mechanism of Social Differentiation

Aaron V. Cicourel and John I. Kitsuse

From The Educational Decision-Makers *by Aaron V. Cicourel and John I. Kitsuse, pp. 3–20. Copyright © 1963 by The Bobbs-Merrill Company, Inc. Reprinted by permission of the publishers.*

I.Q. scores, higher grade records, greater financial support from their parents, etc., than their non-college-qualified peers, are inadequate to account for students who are qualified but do not get to college. For example, a recent volume[2] reports a finding by Stouffer that many students with high I.Q. scores did not go to college. He reports also that of the high I.Q. students who did not go to college, many had consistently good academic records during their high school careers.

In view of such findings, social scientists have increasingly directed their attention to "non-intellective" determinants of educational, occupational, and general life aspirations. Among students whose tested capabilities and course grades are high, the determinants of college-going aspirations and actual college enrollment have been sought in cultural, social, and motivational factors. Performance and achievement are conceived to be products of ability and motivation when talent is above a minimum level considered necessary for success in college. Thus, Turner,[3] using a sample of male college students, has investigated the motivational significance of the standards of reference groups used by future-oriented students to evaluate the relative success of their own performance. Strodtbeck[4] has also emphasized the social and cultural motivational sources of academic achievement in his study of Jewish and Italian high school students. His findings suggest the motivational significance of group differences in family interaction, particularly power relations in the socialization process and value orientations toward achievement. Similarly, Parsons,[5] Kahl,[6] and others have underlined the importance of social class membership as a major determinant of the occupational aspirations and achievement of youth. They have emphasized class-related differentials in the socialization of children and the consequences of such differences for the attitudes of youth toward academic achievement, occupational aspirations, and plans for college education.

Hollingshead's study of adolescence in Elmtown[7] presents a somewhat different perspective on the relation between social class and the social as well as academic status of students within the school system. His concern with the organization of adolescent activities among the youth in Elmtown directed him to investigate the influences of social class membership upon clique formation and the effects of such cliques upon the treatment and evaluation of students by administrative and teaching personnel within the school. Since the publication of Hollingshead's book, peer groups and related peer cultures and their influences upon the organization of adolescent attitudes, activities, and achievement have been subjects of sociological investigation, both theoretical and empirical.[8] In his recent study, Coleman[9] specifically examined these influences by investigating the normative effects of peer group climates upon the relative valuation of peer achievement in academic, athletic,

and social activities among the student populations of ten high schools varying in size and organization.

In the following pages we present an alternative formulation that conceives of the differentiation of students as a consequence of the administrative organization and decisions of personnel in the high school. We shall contend that the distribution of students in such categories as college-qualified and non-college-qualified is to a large extent characteristic of the administrative organization of the high school and therefore can be explained in terms of that organization. We shall be concerned primarily with the relation between the administrative organization of the high school and the ways in which the students are processed through it. More specifically, we wish to investigate how the routine decisions of the guidance and counseling personnel within the high school are related to the college/non-college decisions and, by implication, to the occupational choices made by students.

Our more general concern with the allocation of personnel within the occupational structure of the larger society is similar to that of Parsons. We view as problematic, however, his assumption that the "virtually ascribed" college-going expectation among the middle- and upper-class segments of the population *accounts for* the higher rate of students from those social classes who do in fact go to college.[10] Although he identifies the school and prior academic achievement as the institutional setting within which the college-going expectation is expressed, he does not systematically consider how the formal organization of the school affects the realization of those expectations. In stressing the class-ascribed character of the college aspiration, he assumes that the organizational processing of the aspiration is routine and non-problematic. We wish to question this assumption in our study.

Although heightened competition for

college facilities has stimulated the growth and development of colleges throughout the nation, it has also given impetus to a policy of restricted enrollment for "quality" education and raised the entrance requirements among the "better" colleges to which students of the middle and upper social classes aspire. In view of the changing ratios of supply and demand in college facilities, it should also be noted that the theoretically significant distribution of high school seniors is not the gross college/non-college dichotomy, but the distribution of students according to their admission into colleges, ranging from those having the highest applicant/enrollment ratio and admission requirements to those accepting any high school graduate. Class-ascribed college-going expectations might be considered an adequate explanation of the gross college/non-college distribution, but it cannot explain how students are distributed among hierarchically ranked (prestige) colleges. An explanation of such a distribution requires an investigation of the ways in which admission to various colleges is subject to specifically *organizational* contingencies.

Assuming that parents have college aspirations, to whatever quality of college, for their children, and assuming that their children have internalized those aspirations, whether or not such students do in fact become eligible for college entrance depends upon: (1) the communication by parents and/or the student to the school of the student's intention to prepare for college admission; (2) the enrollment of the student in high school courses that will qualify him for college— i.e., courses that will meet college entrance requirements; (3) the satisfactory completion of such courses;[11] and (4), in some instances, the recommendation of high school authorities in support of the student's college applications, particularly in the case of applications to the "better" colleges. Organiza-

tional decisions and actions that affect those preconditions may occur at any point in the student's transition through the school system and may be quite independent of either his or his parents' aspirations.[12]

In stressing the significance of such organizational contingencies for the explanation of college/non-college or "good"/"better"/"best" college distributions of the student population, we do not deny that the formal organization of the high school progressively implements the college and occupational goals of the majority of students. Such student goals, however, are processed and actualized through a system subject to the contingencies of organizational processes. Indeed, it is precisely the routine aspects of the organizational processing activity that are of interest and are revealed by the variety of "problems" that attend the movement of a cohort of students through the high school system.

The Conceptual Framework

In his classic study of suicide,[13] Emile Durkheim underlined the central importance of rates of social phenomena for sociological theory and research. The sociological problem of rates may be stated simply as follows: How are the patterned variations in the rates of certain social phenomena to be accounted for as characteristics, not of individuals, but of the social and cultural organization of the groups, communities, and societies with which they are regularly associated? For example, how is it that rates of juvenile delinquency are higher among Negroes than whites, working-class than middle-class, urban than rural adolescents?

The rates taken to be the "facts to be explained" by sociologists are generally constructed by using statistics compiled and assembled by persons other than sociologists for purposes other than that of scientific research. In establishing the existence of differences in the rates of juvenile delinquency among various segments of the population, for example, the sociologist frequently depends upon statistics made available by law-enforcement and other agencies of control. Sociologists generally recognize and acknowledge that such statistics contain errors of under- and over-enumeration that result from the variation between and within agencies of the definitions of categories used in compiling the statistics, the biases of agencies in identifying and processing cases, misclassification of those cases that are identified, etc. The statistics are, nevertheless, used by the sociologist as bases for constructing rates on the justification that, as a practical matter, they are the best available data. A major consequence of such use of agency statistics is that the sociologist, after acknowledging the questionable bases of the rates, assumes the rates as given and proceeds to correlate those rates to various social characteristics— e.g., age, sex, race, family background— of *individuals* who are represented in the rates. This procedure, however, obscures the fact that the variations in the rates that the sociologist seeks to explain are inextricably related to the organizational activities of the agencies that produced the statistics and thus the rates.

In formulating our research, therefore, we proposed to address specifically the problem of investigating the processes by which persons come to be defined, classified, and recorded in the categories of the agency's statistics.[14] If the rates of college-going students, underachievers, "academic problems," etc., are to be viewed sociologically as characteristics of the high school as a complex organization, then the explanation for such rates

must be sought in the patterned activities of that organization and not in the behavior of students *per se*. The theoretical significance of student *behavior* for variations in the rates is dependent upon how the personnel of the high school interpret, type, and process that behavior. Thus, the problem was formulated as follows: If the rates of various student types are conceived to be products of the socially organized activities of the personnel, then the question is "How do these activities result in making a student a statistic in a given category?" Or stated in a more general form: "How are the equivalence classes of given social categories produced?" So stated, our problem was to investigate the day-to-day activities of high school personnel and the conceptions, definitions, and criteria they employed to identify, classify, and record "cases" in the categories of the school's statistics.

The orientation that guided our research application of the problem of rates was drawn from the work of Alfred Schutz[15]—who takes the position that the perspectives of the actors (i.e., the organizational personnel) whose actions produce the ongoing social organization are of central importance for any investigation of how organizations come to define, record, and treat persons as instances of certain social categories. Throughout his work, Schutz underlines the theoretical and methodological principle that the social sciences must deal with social behavior in terms of the *commonsense interpretations of social reality* currently in use by members of the group, organization, or society under investigation. In stressing this principle, Schutz insists that the concepts of the social sciences must be "constructs of the second degree." He states:

The observational field of the social scientist . . . has a specific meaning and relevance structure for the human beings living, acting and thinking therein. By a series of common-sense constructs they have pre-selected and pre-interpreted this world which they experience as the reality of their daily lives. It is these thought objects of theirs which determine their behavior by motivating it. The thought objects constructed by the social scientist, in order to grasp this social reality, have to be founded upon the thought objects constructed by the common-sense thinking of men, living their daily lives within their social world. Thus, the constructs of the second degree, namely constructs of the constructs made by the actors on the social scene, whose behavior the social scientist has to observe and to explain in accordance with the procedural rules of his science.[16]

This theoretical orientation to the study of social organization may be applied to the present problem of explaining the variations in rates of college-going and other student types. Such rates, constructed by the sociologist from the various statistics of the high school, may be conceived as products of the socially organized activities of its personnel. Attention must therefore be directed to those definitions applied and procedures followed by the personnel whereby students are differentiated, labeled, and processed as "college material," "academic problems," "troublemakers," etc. The use of such definitions and their effects upon the interpretations of student behavior by the organizational personnel become the primary source of data for understanding how students come to be classified and distributed among the various categories of the high school's statistics. Schutz states the theoretical importance of these definitions as follows:

The typifying medium *par excellence* by which socially derived knowledge is transmitted is the vocabulary and syntax of every-day language generalization referring to the relevance system prevailing in the linguistic in-group which found the named thing significant enough to provide a separate term for it. The *pre-scientific* vernacular can be interpreted as a treasure house of readymade pre-constituted types

and characteristics, all socially derived and carrying along an open horizon of unexplored content.[17]

Thus, the first research task in our investigation of the rate-producing process was to explore the "vocabulary and syntax" of the language employed by the school personnel to identify the variety of student types recognized as significant in the day-to-day activities of the high school. Such types are the common-sense constructs by which the personnel interpret student behavior and classify them into organizationally provided categories.

The second task was to examine the consequences of these identification and classification processes for the direction and development of any given student's career within the high school. Our use of the term career follows Hughes' suggestive statement that a study of careers "may be expected to reveal the nature and 'working constitution' of a society."[18] As applied to our research, the day-to-day organizational activities of identifying and classifying student types may be conceived to produce a range of careers that lead to different outcomes for students processed through the system. Some careers may qualify students for entrance to accredited colleges and universities and lead to professional occupations. Others may lead to terminal junior college certificates and into the lower ranks of white collar positions, and still others to immediate entrance into the labor market. The concept of career provides us with a method of describing and charting the sequence of the organizational decisions made and actions taken toward students in their movement through the high school system.

In a current study of patient selection in a psychiatric out-patient clinic, Garfinkel and Brickman deal explicitly with the social processes by which a population is differentiated within a social organization. Their study is concerned with "the socially organized and socially controlled ways in which patients and clinic personnel make decisions that decide a patient's transfer from one clinic status to a succeeding one. We wish to study whether and how these ways account for the features of patient load and flow."[19] The design of their study provides us a method of investigating the processes by which different outcomes are produced in an organizational setting. The present formulation follows the framework of their study.

An Overview of the Substantive Issues

In the following chapters we shall direct our attention to how the high school as a socially organized system of activities differentiates talented from average and low-ability ·students and college-going from non-college-going students, and how such activities may affect the future occupational careers of the student population. We shall not undertake the task of investigating a wide range of phenomena pertaining to student attitudes, values, and behaviors that presumably differentiate the college-going from non-college-going populations. Our interest in these pheneomena will be guided by their organizational relevance. That is, the theory of social organization followed here will be applied to decide which of the phenomena are pre-selected and pre-interpreted as significant by the personnel of the high school.

In our study we wish to examine the thesis advanced in earlier studies that social class and organizational sponsorship, as opposed to capability, are critical

for the manner in which students are processed through the school system. Since our student sample is drawn from an upper-income community, the students should, consistent with Parsons' hypothesis, be predominantly college-oriented. We seek also to show, however, that the notion of class-ascribed aspirations from which Parsons' hypothesis is derived must be articulated with a conception of organizational processes if we are to understand how effectively those aspirations are implemented for the majority of such students. We hope to shed light on how parental and student knowledge and activity regarding the college-going program influence the organizational processes of the high school.

The theory of social organization that orients our study leads us to conceive of a college-qualified high school senior as the product of the organizational actions of school personnel who record the college/non-college declaration of freshmen students, classify them into ability groups, assign them to types of course programs, review and evaluate their performance, and define, interpret, and counsel them on their problems. We may ask, then: are students with college-going expectations automatically assigned to courses that will qualify them for college entrance at the end of their high school careers? Or, is such assignment subject throughout their high school years to specific organizational contingencies?

The "problems" that are attributed to students by school personnel should not be those which are widely, but generally, discussed as the so-called "adolescent problem." The lables of "underachiever" and "overachiever" and the variety of social and psychological interpretations that are made of them—e.g., "emotionally disturbed," "social isolate," "anti-social"—should be generated by the organizational activities of the school personnel. Our research formulation directs our attention to organizational factors for an explanation of how such students present problems for the high school.

We contend that the organizational production of various student problems is related to the bureaucratization of the counseling system and the professionalization of its personnel. Thus, the organization of the counseling system and the activities of its personnel have been a central focus of our study. Our interviews with counselors were designed to reveal that the clinical orientation of their professional training leads to the fusion of academic problems with personal problems of students. We suggest that among full-time counselors, and particularly among school social workers, the clinical interpretation of academic problems has become a means of explaining deviant cases of students who have capability but who fail to perform at their expected level.

Our study is indirectly tied to the larger question of whether and how the high school in American society operates to provide equal access to higher educational facilities to those of equal capability. The theoretical orientation we follow suggests that one of the major consequences of the current search for academic talent in the high school should be a limitation of access to future occupational opportunities by organizational decisions and actions that occur as early as the students' last year in junior high school. The activities of counseling personnel are of major importance in such organizational decisions and actions and therefore deserve close examination.

Organizational Processes and High School Careers

In the organization of contemporary adolescent life, the high school is the major if not the single formal organizational structure in which the adolescent's achievement in his progress toward adult-

hood is systematically assessed and recorded. Excluded as he is from equal participation in the social, economic, and political activities of the larger society, the adolescent's school activities provide the major formally organized avenue of achievement that links his present status to his projected adult career. The school, therefore, occupies a strategic position in the organization and control of the adolescent status transition. It serves as a sort of clearing house for other community agencies that come into contact with the adolescent. Thus, the school is the agency to which the police, civic organizations, and welfare agencies, as well as parents, go with their reports, if not complaints, concerning the actual or suspected "problems" of students. The often incomplete records of such communications are filed in the student's cumulative folder. The folder constitutes an official biography reflecting the state of his career at any particular time. As any teacher or counselor would acknowledge, however, a student's career within the school system may also be documented by an unofficial biography that not only supplements the officially recorded information but frequently provides the critically significant interpretation of it. The information, therefore, that is *not* included in the official biography should be an important determinant of the manner in which students are organizationally defined and processed.

Compulsory education, which in most states prescribes school attendance until the age of sixteen, insures the passage of each generation of youth through the school system and an organizational record of their careers within it. The authority and responsibility that are legally delegated to the school are assumed as mandates to "educate the young" in the broad sense of that phrase.

Accordingly, the school as an agency of socialization has undertaken the task of developing responsible citizenship and "well-rounded" personalities as well as scholarship among its students. Participation and performance in the school-sponsored and organized extracurricular activities have come to be viewed by school personnel as an important index of the personal, emotional, and social "adjustment" of students.

The recent emphasis on the identification and development of talent in the high school has sharpened the focus of organizational efforts to raise the academic achievement of students. In their implementation of these efforts, the high schools are in many ways thrust into a nation-wide competition for rank and prestige. The criterion of evaluation is productivity, and the gross measure of a school's productivity is the proportion of its seniors who are admitted to colleges. With the increase in production of college-qualified seniors, however, quality as well as quantity has become the standard for judging the excellence of high school programs. The competition for national rank and reputation has been given increasing publicity in recent years, and high schools have sought to maximize their productivity by the application of "scientific" techniques to identify academically talented students and of bureaucratic methods to develop systematically the talent identified.

The Bureaucratization of the Search for Talent

The development and application of techniques to identify potentially talented students early in the educational process is one reflection of the increasing specialization of occupational structure in industrial societies. The period of formal educational instruction required to develop potential academic talent into the technical competence required of specialists has extended beyond undergraduate college training to graduate, and in some instances, to postgraduate work. Thus, the investment required in terms of educational facilities and resources has stimulated efforts to increase the efficiency of methods of identifying and recruiting the talented into occupations of critical importance to the society. The current search for academic talent in the high school is the most striking and publicized manifestation of this trend.

A major consequence of the policy of identifying talented students at an early stage in the educational process is that the high school tends to control the students' access to higher educational facilities and, in turn, their life chances. The practice of so-called "ability grouping" is an important structural feature of this control. The assignment of students to ability groups is primarily based on the interpretation of counselors and teaching personnel of the students' performance on aptitude tests. Since students classified as "low ability" in one or another section of the aptitude tests are not permitted to enroll in courses required for college entrance, ability grouping is significantly related to the distribution of educational opportunities among the student population. We wish to investigate the criteria employed by the school personnel to interpret test results as well as other, less objective measures of student performance in the processing of students through the system.

Our preliminary field investigations indicated that the counseling process provided for periodic reviews of student performance as the major method by which student problems were identified for investigation by counselors. The routinization of this counseling activity suggests that the academic as well as personal, emotional, and social "adjust-ment" of all students will be subjected to examination for evidence of difficulties. As specialists in the identification, inter-pretation, and treatment of student problems, counselors would occupy a strategic position in the network of communications concerning the general demeanor, conduct, association, activi-ties, and performance of students both in and out of classrooms, Schools with highly bureaucratized counseling systems, therefore, may be expected to identify more students with problems.

Preliminary field work also revealed that students with discrepancies between their tested ability and achievement are particularly subject to counselor atten-tion. Failure to achieve at the expected level alerts the counselor to investigate the "problem" for indications of "diffi-culties." An underachiever, for example, may reveal in a conference with the counselor that he simply failed to submit his homework in a course ("lacks motivation") or that his mother always expects him to do better than his brother ("sibling rivalry") or that he doesn't need any counseling ("reaction against depen-dency needs"). On the other hand, although students are expected to achieve up to their ability, evidence that a student has to work harder than he should for his grades may be considered prejudicial to his over-all development.

The interpretation of such "problems" in psychological and clinical terms has important consequences for the degree to which the policies and methods of the school system remain open to evalu-ation of their effectiveness and to proposals for modifications. Our coun-selor interview schedule was constructed to focus investigation on the variety of academic problems that come to their attention. We sought to explore the extent to which some counselors seek explanations by use of a clinical vocabu-lary that would lead them to interpret those problems in terms of the student's "motivation," "family situation," "peer adjustment," etc.

The presence of social workers in the school we studied prompted us to ask if the failure of the student to respond to psychologically oriented treatment would tend to lead counselors and social workers to look for "deeper problems." We reasoned that, if the student is summoned by the counselor and en-couraged to discuss his "difficulty," he may in the face of such solicitous treat-ment provide information to confirm the clinical interpretation of his "prob-lem." Thus, the organizational efforts to "help" the student may redefine the initial basis of the student's "problem" —i.e., the discrepancy between his capa-bility and classroom performance. One consequence of such an orientation of "help" would be to deflect school administrators from examining the orga-nization and methods of the school system, including the activities of coun-selors, as sources of academic prob-lems.

Another consequence of this orienta-tion would be the creation of a population of students organizationally differentiated as clinical cases in need of therapeutic treatment. Such a differentiation would presuppose some criteria of normal or healthy adjustment that counselors would presumably apply to identify and inter-pret problems. We asked, therefore, if there were consensus among school counselors and social workers concerning such criteria. If so, what are the empirical bases for their classifications? We sought also to determine whether and how such interpretations are communicated to the student and to his parents and teachers. When the student is defined as "emotion-ally disturbed," "anxious," or some similar term by counseling personnel, do the student, his parents, and his teachers accept the clinical labels, or do they propose alternative explanations of the academic problem?

Whether or not they accept the clinical labels, or indeed, even though they may be unaware that imputations concerning the student's "adjustment" have been made, his career within the school system and in later life may be significantly affected by the counselor's judgment. For the counselor's activities involve him in many aspects of the student's life. In addition to the personal counseling discussed above, his duties include vocational guidance, advising students on the programming of courses, certifying them as qualified to participate in extracurricular activities, writing letters of recommendation in support of college and job applications. Thus, we were interested to know when and how the counselor decides that a student with academic problems needs special guidance concerning the college to which he should apply, the occupational careers for which he is most suited, the extracurricular activities in which he should be allowed to participate. To what extent are decisions affected by the counselor's characterization of such students as "insecure," "emotionally unstable," or "aggressive and authoritarian?"

The introduction of clinical terminology and interpretations into the school system is one reflection of the increasing concern in American society for the maintenance of health, particularly mental health. This concern is manifested in virtually all aspects of daily life by such notions as the "emotional maturity" necessary for marriage and parenthood, the "alienative" tendencies of modern life, and the deteriorative effects of the "psychological isolation" of the aged. With the diffusion of such terminology into the vocabulary of everyday life, the individual's status as a "good risk" creditor, employee, scholar, or club member is dependent upon the maintenance of an unmarred reputation as a socially and mentally "well-adjusted" person.

In the context of this increasing stress upon good social and mental adjustment, our study examines the counselor's position of authority and power as a validating agent for the student's future occupational opportunities and careers. Many colleges and employers routinely request unofficial as well as official information in the form of recommendations from school personnel. In many schools such requests presumably would go to counselors as the personnel most intimately informed about the student's high school career. We are interested in knowing what information the counselor recalls about the student and how he recalls it, how these recollections inform his interpretation of the official records, and how the recommendation is phrased. In view of the trend toward the progressive coordination of records and information between the school and other agencies within the society, the student's school career, what is recorded about it, and the counselor's interpretation of it are of more than incidental significance for the processes of social mobility and stratification.

Notes

[1] Junior colleges, which have recently increased at a phenomenal rate, particularly in California, provide an alternate route to college admission for students whose high school records disqualify them at the time of graduation for applications for college entrance. The applications for transfer of junior college students, however, are differentially evaluated to their disadvantage, according to a study by Burton R. Clark. (*The Open Door College: A Case Study.* [New York: McGraw-Hill, 1960]). See also Leland L. Medsker, *The Junior College: Progress and Prospect* (New York: McGraw-Hill, 1960).

[2] David C. McClelland et al., *Talent and*

Society (New York: Van Nostrand, 1958). The paper by Samuel A. Stouffer, "Social Mobility of Boys in the Boston Metropolitan Area," delivered at the SSRC Conference on "Non-intellective Determinants of Achievement," Princeton, New Jersey, 1953, is cited on page 16.

[3] Ralph H. Turner, "Reference Groups of Future-Oriented Men," *Social Forces*, 34 (1955), pp. 130–36.

[4] Fred L. Strodtbeck, "Family Interaction, Values and Achievement," in *Talent and Society*, ed. David C. McClelland et al. (New York: Van Nostrand, 1958), pp. 135–91.

[5] Talcott Parsons, "General Theory in Sociology," in *Sociology Today*, ed. R. K. Merton et al. (New York: Basic Books, 1958), pp. 3–88.

[6] Joseph A. Kahl, "Educational and Occupational Aspirations of 'Common Man' Boys," *Harvard Educational Review*, 23 (1953), pp. 186–203.

[7] August B. Hollingshead, *Elmtown's Youth* (New York: Wiley, 1949).

[8] See David Riesman et al., *The Lonely Crowd* (New Haven: Yale University Press, 1949), esp. ch. 3; Carolyn Tryon, "The Adolescent Peer Group," *43rd Yearbook* of the National Society for the Study of Education (Chicago: University of Chicago Press, 1944), Part I, "Adolescence"; James S. Coleman, *The Adolescent Society* (New York: Free Press, 1961); Talcott Parsons, "Age and Sex in the Social Structure of the United States," *American Sociological Review*, 7 (1942), pp. 604–16; C. W. Gordon, *The Social System of the High School.* (New York: Free Press, 1957); Frederick Elkin and William A. Westley, "The Myth of Adolescent Culture," *American Sociological Review*, 20 (1955), pp. 680–84.

[9] Coleman, *op. cit.;* also "The Adolescent Sub-Culture and Academic Achievement," *American Journal of Sociology*, 65 (1960), pp. 337–47.

[10] Parsons, *op. cit.*, p. 27.

[11] "Satisfactory" in this context means that the student earned grades that were adequate for admission to the college of his choice.

[12] The consequences of such organizational activity may be unknown to the student or his parents until he seeks admission to a college, or indeed, they may never become known to him. The articulation of parental and/or student aspirations with the organizational processes that differentiate and channel students through the school system cannot, therefore, be assumed, for it requires a flow of information to, from, and within the family and school organizations.

[13] Emile Durkheim, *Suicide* (New York: Free Press, 1951), pp. 41–53; 297–325.

[14] This view of rates is taken from the work of Harold Garfinkel and can be found in his "Common Sense Knowledge of Social Structures," paper read at the Fourth World Congress of Sociology, Milan, Italy, September, 1959.

[15] The following represent a selection from Schutz's writings: "On Multiple Realities," *Philosophy and Phenomenological Research*, 5 (1945), pp. 533–75; "The Problem of Rationality in the Social World," *Economica*, 10 (1943), pp. 130–49; "Common-Sense and Scientific Interpretation of Human Action," *Philosophy and Phenomenological Research*, 14 (1953), pp. 1–37; "Concept and Theory Formation in the Social Sciences," *The Journal of Philosophy*, 51 (1954), pp. 257–73. Harold Garfinkel's paper, "The Rational Properties of Scientific and Common Sense Activities," *Behavioral Science*, 5 (1960), pp. 72–83, contains a detailed discussion of the present use of the notion of common-sense interpretations of social reality.

[16] Schutz, *op. cit.*, "Concept and Theory Formation . . . ," pp. 266–67.

[17] Schutz, *op. cit.*, "Common-Sense and Scientific Interpretations . . . ," p. 10. Italics added.

[18] Everett C. Hughes, "Institutional Office and the Person," *American Journal of Sociology*, 43 (1937), pp. 404–13. For another related conception of career, see Erving Goffman, "The Moral Career of the Mental Patient," *Psychiatry*, 22 (1959), pp. 123–42.

[19] Harold Garfinkel and Harry Brickman, "A Study of the Composition of the Clinic Patient Population of the Outpatient Department of the UCLA Neuropsychiatric Institute," unpublished manuscript, n.d., p. 16.

Interrelationship Between School Districts

Sloan R. Wayland

Reprinted from "Structural Features of American Education As Basic Factors in Innovation," in Innovation in Education, edited by Matthew B. Miles, (New York: Teachers College Press, 1964), pp. 587–605, by permission of the author and publisher.
In the remaining portion of Professor Wayland's article the effects of the formal organization of local schools are discussed.

ONE OF THE dominant elements in the formal organization of the American school system is the independence and autonomy of the local educational system. Under the Constitution, the provision for education is a state function; the states in turn have delegated the responsibility for the operation of schools to local school districts. The consequence is that education is administered through some 37,025 local districts. These districts hire and fire their administrators and teachers, establish their curricula, and handle the finances for the schools. Lateral relationships between districts are not usually provided for in the organizational structure of a state system, as they are between schools within a single district. Sometimes, collaboration for specialized functions may be officially established between districts on a regional basis. In some instances, local districts collaborate with other districts under state regulations in the provision of secondary or other special schools. In general, however, there is no authority in a line position between the local school district and the state. Local control of schools is a well-established feature of the American ideology.

We are faced at this point with a paradox. The 37,025 school districts are ostensibly locally controlled; this is socially valued as a grass-roots system which will permit the local area to have the kind of educational system it wants. Yet the differences among these districts are relatively small, as will be seen below. *The formal organization of the schools, and their curricula, do not vary markedly throughout the country.* Since this similarity is not the function of an over-all formal organization, and cannot be assumed to be a matter of chance, other types of structures must exist which have brought it about.

The assumption underlying this section of the paper is that *we have, in fact, developed a national educational system, with the consequence that serious innovation at the local level is extremely difficult to introduce and to maintain.* The fact that this national system is not provided for in the formal organization (i.e., that there is no central ministry of education charged with the responsibility for running a national system) does not mean that a national system does not exist. Assuming that such a system does exist, our task becomes that of identifying the types of structures which make it function.

No effort will be made here to demonstrate in detail the common character of the school system throughout the country. Several aspects will be considered, however, and others will be analyzed in the process of looking at the types of existing structures.

Evidence for a National System

In countries with a legally established national educational system, the courses of study which are to be offered at each level are specified, the instructional materials are provided for all, and an

230

evaluation system, including inspectors and external examinations, is provided. As noted above, none of these exist in the United States as publicly controlled activities. State departments of education do issue curriculum guides, and these serve as a framework within which local curriculum decisions are made. *However, no one knows in any detail what is taught in the American schools.* Since we do not have direct data, it is necessary to rely on indirect evidence. The four items listed and discussed below constitute such evidence, and at the same time are factors which partially account for the common curriculum.

1. *National recruitment of teachers.* Although each state has its own system of certification of teachers, the training process for teachers makes it relatively easy for teachers to move from one state to another. Teachers trained in Arkansas are regularly recruited by suburban schools around Chicago. California school systems send representatives to the East Coast to recruit teachers. Active negotiations are under way to prevent the loss of pension rights when teachers move from one state to 'another. If differences exist between these systems as they affect teachers, they are apparently of minor importance. These minor differences are a function both of the similarity in educational systems and the ease with which the college graduate can learn to do what he is assigned to do.

2. *Successful movement of students from school to school.* The extensive mobility of the American population results in frequent tests of the degree to which the instruction in one school system meshes with that of another. Research on the problems associated with such movement has been limited, but the few studies at hand indicate that students do not suffer from such mobility, unless they move many times in a short period.

3. *National market for instructional materials.* Although teachers are urged to prepare their own instructional materials, textbooks and similar instructional materials serve as the central feature of most courses. The textbook industry functions on a national basis. In order to take advantage of large-scale production, extensive adoption of texts is a desirable goal for any one publisher. And in view of the sequential or cumulative character of many segments of the curriculum, series of texts are issued for different levels, with the exception that a particular school system will buy an entire series. Many publishing companies publish such series, in a variety of different subject areas.

Texts are prepared by educators, and the textbook editors and their consultants are frequently people who have had some association with the school system. Authors of texts frequently test out their materials in their own classrooms, or gain the cooperation of others in trying them out before they are published. However, most of the structures involved in the preparation and distribution of texts are ancillary, and not part of the formal structure. The linkages referred to above, and others such as feedback from teachers to salesmen, serve as mechanisms to insure that the formal and the ancillary structures mesh with each other. (This pattern operates in the Roman Catholic parochial school system as well as in the public educational system. Private publishing companies specializing in production of textbooks for such schools are not part of the formal structure of the church.)

In summary, textbooks are a central feature in setting the framework of what students are taught, and they are distributed on a national basis. Although it is not contended that textbooks by different companies are the same, their differences in most areas of instruction are not marked. Furthermore, school systems do not like to change textbooks as long as the existing inventory is usable. Three- to five-year use of such materials seems to be common, and retention for much longer periods is not unusual.

4. *National examination systems.* Over a period of years, several different testing and examination systems have been developed which operate on a national basis. The factors giving rise to these testing and examination systems vary. The National Merit Scholarship system has the manifest function of providing opportunity for college study for qualified students, regardless of their financial resources. The tests developed and administered through the College Entrance Examination Board have been devised to provide colleges with standardized information about applicants, supplementing data from local school systems, which may be difficult to interpret. The various achievement tests, such as the Iowa or Stanford tests, make it possible for local school systems to measure their achievement against a norm established on a national basis.

The fact that such tests and examinations could have been developed and administered on a national basis—and the fact that the results are taken as a basis for action—indicates the extent to which a basically common system has developed. In a sense, these ancillary structures have an effect which is in the direction planned for (through the use of inspectors and external examinations) in countries with formal national educational systems.

Variations in content and quality of school programs are frequently *not* sources of pride, but of concern. Dr. Conant has followed the logic of many educational leaders in urging the building of large educational systems, to facilitate the introduction of courses which cannot be provided economically in small schools. State and federal aid is urged as a means of insuring that inadequate education is not due to lack of resources. The argument is usually made in terms of the extent to which school systems deviate from a norm; inability of a deprived area to establish its unique program is not usually mentioned.

Structures Supporting a National System

To the extent that a relatively common educational program exists, it is necessary to look for explanations outside of the formal structure. The various ancillary structures which exist are numerous and of quite different orders, and only brief and general examination of their operation can be made here.

In the first place, the structures which have been cited as indicators of the common character of the program are also contributory structures. For example, the movement of teachers and administrators from place to place is a mechanism for diffusion of educational practices. Similarly, the parents who move around the country serve as a diffusion mechanism. The textbook industry, through its publications and the actions of its salesmen, makes available to local school systems curriculum patterns which are in existence in other school districts. The results obtained through the administration of national tests and examinations serve as a guide for modifications of the curriculum—modifications designed to insure more favorable results on subsequent administration of the same tests.

Another major set of structures is composed of *national organizations* of persons involved in various ways in the educational system. State and national organizations for teachers (at all levels and for all specialties) and for administrators, school board members, parents, textbook publishers, and teacher training personnel serve as communication devices and also as status-giving and rewarding systems. Through formal papers, informal discussions, publications, and policy-making actions, models for appropriate actions are made available on a national basis. Although most of the personnel involved are parts of the formal structure, these organizations are ancillary structures, and provide systemic linkages which the formal organization does not. A special case in this general category is the Council of Chief State School Officers, an organization which has no legal status but which is a very significant mechanism in a society without any formal structural provisions for handling interstate problems.

Teacher training institutions usually have no direct formal relationships with the schools. A significant proportion of teachers is trained in private institutions which take state requirements into account as they choose. Only about 120 of 1,300 institutions engaged in teacher preparation are teachers colleges. Graduate schools of education, whether public or private, tend to function as nonlocal institutions, as noted earlier. Leadership personnel in teacher training programs are likely to have strong professional ties outside the local area. Too strong a commitment to local ties may hinder advancement within the profession, and the rewards for strong professional ties are high.

Accreditation associations represent another ancillary structure which brings local school systems and teacher training institutions within a common framework. Although these are extralegal associations, they can exercise sanctions which cannot be ignored by educational systems. For example, college admissions officers usually discount units offered by students graduating from nonaccredited high schools. Recently, the threat of loss of accreditation status at the University of Mississippi has apparently been of more serious concern to state and university officials than legal sanctions had been. Although accreditation associations may try to reject the concept of a single pattern for the institutions which they serve, they do have an evaluative function and also communicate a system of values. Since the members of accreditation teams are also on the staffs of accredited institutions, they serve as additional linkages between formal systems.

In addition to the types of structures which have been identified above, another type exists which is not as closely tied to the educational structure. This is the *ad hoc* group—either an independent group, or an agency of an organization with a program which may involve education. For example, national organizations interested in safety, alcoholism, conservation, patriotism, and mental retardation attempt to focus attention on their areas of concern by gaining inclusion of materials in the curricula of schools throughout the country. Once such programs are adopted, the organizations resist efforts to eliminate or reduce the attention given to their interest.

Groups in special positions in the educational system, or operating as ancillary structures, may serve to reinforce the national character of the system. For example, an influential figure such as Dr. James Conant, with support of a respectable foundation like the Carnegie Foundation and using national media, has been able to set a pattern which mediates between somewhat different emphases. In a similar way, new programs in physics (and other disciplines) have been developed by ancillary structures; through linkages with the formal structures at many points, such programs have been established throughout the country.

Since ancillary structures are not a part of the formal organization of the school, they are not easily subject to public control. However, changes in the formal system will be felt in these ancillary structures, and such changes may or may not be in the self-interest of such structures. To the extent that a proposed change is not in their interest, resistance to it may be anticipated.

Implications for Innovation

In this section, attention has been directed to the set of structures which serve to develop and maintain a national educational system. These structures are primarily ancillary, since the formal organizational structures are limited and weak. At a number of points, the functions of ancillary structures in the United States have been shown to be parallel to those of elements in the formal organizational structure of nations with centralized educational systems.

However, the central point of this analysis is not the demonstration of the existence of a national educational system, but the identification of features of the American system which influence innovation. If in fact local school districts functioned as autonomous units with no significant linkages outside the local area, the problems of innovation would be limited to the type discussed under formal organization of local schools, below. But as the Arkansas–Ford Foundation experience shows, even the states, which are legally autonomous educationally, are in fact so linked with other states through ancillary structures that real limits on innovation exist.

It is particularly instructive to compare the relative success of the Ford Foundation, with all its resources, and that of the special education movement, working as an essentially lay movement. Although the content of the interests of these two ancillary structures is of some relevance to the comparison, the special education movement has apparently operated with substantially greater appreciation for the structure of the American educational system. Its leaders have not been deceived by the ideology of local autonomy of schools or by the assumption that well-trained teachers will solve all educational problems. No judgment is being made here as to the merits of the innovations which have been proposed; nor is it assumed that the leadership of the special education movement ever made explicit their understanding of the structure of American education. It *is* assumed that their actions were sufficiently in conformity with the demands of the structure to lead to success.

James G. Anderson. *Bureaucracy in Education*. Baltimore: Johns Hopkins Press, 1968.

The author posits a basic tension between the rational system of the school based on competence and expertise, on the one hand, and the control mechanisms of the social system, on the other. Several types of control patterns, including supervision, impersonal mechanisms, and professional standards, are presented and discussed in terms of functional and dysfunctional aspects. The level of rules within the school is related to size of department, academic discipline of department, percentage of females in the department, socioeconomic level of the students, and the professional training of the teachers. The author concludes that effective, professionalized teaching is incompatible with the proliferation of rigid means of control over the school population.

Robert G. Barker and Paul V. Gump. *Big School, Small School*. Stanford; Stanford University Press, 1964.

This is an extensive study of the effects of school size on students' participation in school activities, satisfactions and participation in community activities. The study is noteworthy for its derivation of clearcut hypotheses from a theoretical framework based on prior research on groups and organizations, which research is reviewed in an early chapter. In light of the consistently beneficial effects of small size, the authors suggest that "it may be easier to bring specialized and varied behavior settings to small schools than to raise the level of individual participation in large schools."

Charles E. Bidwell. "The School as a Formal Organization." In *Handbook of Organizations*, edited by James G. March. Chicago: Rand McNally, 1967.

In this review of the literature, the author begins by describing four main charac-

Part III
Auxiliary Readings

teristics which differentiate the school from other organizations. The work of Willard Waller is discussed at length as an example of one of the few comprehensive treatments of the school. Areas of research which are covered include the school as a small society, student social structure and relations between teachers and students, classroom structure and educational outcomes, and the school as a bureaucracy.

Neal Gross and Robert Herriott. *Staff Leadership in Public Schools: A Sociological Inquiry*. New York: Wiley, 1964.

The purpose of this book is to study the efforts of the elementary school principal to fulfill his obligation to improve the quality of his staff and of his school. Executive Professional Leadership (an index of the principal's behavior as reported by teachers) was found to be highly related to teacher morale, teacher performance, and student performance. High EPL scores are related to low formal preparation, lack of experience in the position, and youth of the principal; they are unrelated to previous teaching and administrative experience. Individual attributes, such as interpersonal skills and intellectual ability, are also related to effectiveness.

Fred Katz. "The School as a Complex Social Organization." *Harvard Educational Review*, 34 (1964), pp. 428-55.

Challenging the Weberian concept of rational bureaucratic structures, the author argues that the diversity of roles and functions within the organization, and affiliations outside the organization, produce constant strains toward autonomy on the part of various groups in the organization. These "autonomy patterns" provide a conceptual link between the previously disconnected theories about formal and informal organization, according to the author. A typology of autonomy structures is developed and applied to the school.

David Rogers. *110 Livingston Street*, pp. 267–305. New York: Random House, 1968.

The history of attempts to institute racial integration in the New York City schools is used to illustrate "bureaucratic pathologies" in urban education. Overcentralization and overspecialization, bureaucratization of recruitment and promotion, compulsive rule following, and informally decentralized authority not accountable to any source are discussed as major causes of ineffective administration.

IV

The School as an Informal System

Introduction

OF ALL the areas of sociological interest in education, perhaps the least well understood is the school viewed as an informal social system or, more accurately, as a collection of subcultures in interaction producing a relatively self-contained society. To be sure, this society is influenced by the backgrounds of participants, the occupational characteristics of teachers and administrators, the formal features of the school as a rational organization, and the school's relations with its environment. But because the relationships that emerge within the school take on a life of their own —creating a consensus that bridges background differences among peers, shaping occupational values and role-performances, modifying the formal structure, and affecting the community's commitment to the school—they deserve to be treated as a separate topic.

Indeed, one of the greatest potential contributions of the sociology of education resides in a full account of the effects of the school's emergent social system on the attainment of educational goals. And yet, it is safe to say that our knowledge of the informal structure of the school is woefully inadequate. One reason for this state of affairs might be the reluctance of academic social scientists to become identified with the day-to-day activities and interests of professional educators. Also, by virtue of the fact that social scientists have spent the majority of their pre-adult years within schools, the school is regarded as familiar territory. Many academic observers, therefore, feel qualified to assert their expertise without any special study of the phenomenon. As a consequence, careful sociological analyses of the school's informal system are few and far between.

The seriousness of the problem can be gauged from the fact that the most thoroughgoing analysis of the internal life of schools was written forty years ago by Willard Waller; and that the intervening years have failed

to produce any major research effort devoted to the substantiation, refinement, or extension of Waller's ideas. We begin our section on the school as
an informal system, therefore, with two excerpts from the work of this
seminal sociologist. The first excerpt elaborates the notion of the "separate
culture" of the school, and the second focuses on teacher–student relationships in the classroom.

In Waller's view, the school is a congeries of subcultures with a high
potential for conflict. The strains between students and teachers are
especially interesting because they bear directly on the process of socialization. As the adults of the school go about imposing their expectations on
students, the latter form defensive alliances, which in turn generate a defensive subculture among teachers. Consequently, two conflict groups stand
face-to-face in an uneasy equilibrium of power. This confrontation takes
place within two distinct settings: inside and outside the classroom. A
careful reading of Waller reveals different modes for the resolution of the
conflicts associated with each of the two settings: (1) outside the classroom
—through the emergence of student extracurricular "activities," which
drain off tensions and provide for the management of student commitment;
and (2) in the classroom—through the development of informal relationships between teachers and students. Waller therefore directs attention to
what might be called the *dual* social system of the school, and also to the
importance of informal mechanisms of social control in the classroom as
well as in the larger school setting. In particular, his analysis of the techniques of classroom control, classified "approximately in the order of
their utilization of the institutional and the arbitrary, and inversely to
their dependence upon personal influence," reveals the teacher's shift
from a reliance on formal prerogatives to affective relationships. Thus,
Waller is not content just to establish the *existence* of the distinctive culture
of the school, but he goes on to spell out the functional significance of that
culture for social control and socialization.

The next selection carries Waller's analysis a step farther. Gertrude
McPherson notes that the elementary teacher not only uses techniques
of control which depart from arbitrary commands based on a presumption
of authority, but that she eventually becomes "identified" with her class.
This process of identification not only provides the teacher with a leverage
for control, but may also afford a dependable source of approval for
individuals whose role performances are not directly observable by peers,
administrators, or parents. Thus, the teacher is able to enjoy esteem and
even love inside the classroom, and also to gain recognition from the
world outside the classroom for her success in the management of
children. But McPherson also mentions several dysfunctions of classroom
identification: the rewarding of conservatism and the penalizing of
enthusiastic new teachers, the weakening of the solidarity of the teacher
group, and the exposure of the teacher to possible manipulation by
students. We are therefore alerted to the possibility that the emergent
culture of the classroom may interfere with the formal goals of socialization and with professional interaction among colleagues.

A threat to the achievement of formal goals stemming from the student subculture can also be discerned in the activities that take place *outside* the classroom, which brings us to the larger setting of the school noted by Waller. James S. Coleman, the author of the next selection, studied the status systems of the adolescent communities in ten high schools. And here we see that the status aspirations of high school students are often at variance with the professional academic goals of education. Thus, students who are regarded as belonging to the "leading crowd" more often desire recognition as athletes, thereby setting up standards for the dispensing of social rewards within the status system of adolescents. Moreover, Coleman shows that the status system of adolescents may restrain the academic effort of students. In short, the student system undermines the official reward system, which is engaged in the allocation of grades for academic work. These findings should be examined in the light of Waller's contention that student "activities" may be employed to direct commitment to the school's official goals. Apparently, owing to the solidarity of the student society, social control which is gained through the promotion of "activities" is required at the expense of reduced commitment to academic goals—a possibility which Waller himself recognizes. But this conclusion does not entirely vitiate the value of extracurricular activities for social control, as Coleman points out, and he proposes the creation of inter-scholastic, academic competitions in which the outstanding student might "bring glory to his school" and thereby elicit the commitment of more students to academic goals.

Teachers also belong to a peer culture that holds up certain standards, punishes deviation from those standards, provides an adult buffer to the world of the child, diffuses information, softens the impact of administrative dictates, and affords an opportunity for the expansion of the teacher's personality in a number of directions apart from classroom roles. Further, just as the adolescent subculture develops its own criteria of recognition, there are probably determinants other than expertise operating in professional influence among teachers. Since we have been unable to locate definitive research on these issues, however, we must regretfully omit a selection in this domain. (See the Auxiliary Readings for research on selected aspects of this general area.)

The selections discussed so far have tended to emphasize the solidarity of the relationships that emerge from the day-to-day interaction of participants. It is equally important to realize that the participants are also exposed to *conflicting* expectations. This issue brings us back to Waller's discussion of the school as a setting for potential and often manifest conflict. For example, the teacher might be subjected to demands from students which are incompatible with the expectations of peers. And students might be subjected to cross-pressures stemming from teachers and from other students. Moreover, even *within* one's subculture, there are often expectations originating with one set of peers which collide with those originating with another set. Both sorts of normative conflict arise from the occupancy of a single position. But there is a third type of conflict which arises from occupancy of multiple position, e.g., teacher and mother, student and child, administrator and husband, and so on. The first two types of conflict are sometimes called "role conflict" and the third "status conflict"; or, in Neal Gross' terminology in the next selection to be considered, "intra-role" and "inter-role" conflict, respectively.

In their study of conflicting expectations, Gross, McEachern, and Mason draw our attention to a status group in the school hitherto ignored in this section: administrators. Because they function as mediators between school and community, and between groups within the school, superintendents are exposed to a wide array of expectations, many of which are incompatible. By noting the *legitimacy* with which an expectation is perceived, the *sanctions* at the disposal of the role-partner for nonconformity, and the subject's *predisposition* to give greater weight to either sanctions or legitimacy, Gross et al. are able to predict the ways in which school superintendents resolve incompatible expectations for their office.

TEACHERS HAVE always known that it was necessary for the students of strange customs to cross the seas to find material. Folklore and myth, tradition, taboo, magic rites, ceremonials of all sorts, collective representations, *participation mystique*, all abound in the front yard of every school, and occasionally they creep upstairs and are incorporated into the more formal portions of school life.

There are, in the school, complex rituals of personal relationships, a set of folkways, mores, and irrational sanctions, a moral code based upon them. There are games, which are sublimated wars, teams, and an elaborate set of ceremonies concerning them. There are traditions, and traditionalists waging their world-old battle against innovators. There are laws, and there is the problem of enforcing them. There is *Sittlichkeit*. There are specialized societies with a rigid structure and a limited membership. There are no reproductive groups, but there are customs regulating the relations of the sexes. All these things make up a world that is different from the world of adults. It is this separate culture of the young, having its locus in the school, which we propose to study. To work out all the details of this culture would be a task long and difficult, and, for our purpose, not altogether necessary. We shall be content to mark out the main lines of the cultural background of school life.

In part the discussion of the school in cultural terms has been anticipated in a preceding section. We have advanced the notion that the school is a center of cultural diffusion; we have shown that the school serves as a point from which the cultural standards of the larger group are mediated to the local community. The organization of higher and lower schools for the purpose of cultural diffusion may be thought of as analogous to the organization of wholesale and retail merchandising for the distribution of material goods. The goods, here

The Separate Culture of the School

Willard Waller

Reprinted from The Sociology of Teaching (*New York: John Wiley & Sons, Inc·, Science Editions, 1965*), pp. 103–119, by permission of the publisher.

certain cultural traits, are sent out from centers in job lots, to be distributed by retailers by their own methods at their own price. There is a certain amount of central control of education, as there is central control of the merchandising of certain material objects. We have noted also that the school is engaged in the transmission of a vast body of culture which is passed on from the old to the young. The school must pass on skills and it must implant attitudes; most of these are not new in the community. At any time and in any community the major portion of the work of the school is that of imposing these preexistent community standards upon children.

Certain cultural conflicts are at the center of the life of the school. These conflicts are of two sorts. The first and most obvious is that which arises from the peculiar function of the school in the process of cultural diffusion. A conflict arises between teachers and students because teachers represent the culture of the wider group and students are impregnated with the culture of the local community. Where the differences concern matters of religion or of fundamental morality, the struggle which then ensues may become quite sharp and may seriously affect the relation of the school to the community. A second and more universal conflict between students

241

and teachers arises from the fact that teachers are adult and students are not, so that teachers are the bearers of the culture of the society of adults, and try to impose that culture upon students, whereas students represent the indigenous culture of the group of children.

The special culture of the young grows up in the play world of childhood. It is worth while to note that it arises in the interstices of the adult social world. Thrasher's *The Gang* is a study of the conflict between the established social order and the interstitial group which has sprung up and grown strong in the sections of society where the adult order does not hold. But this is by no means a complete explanation of the behavior norms of childhood groups. Another fact of importance is that the child does not experience the world in the same manner as does the adult. The child perceives the world differently from the adult in part because he sees it in smaller and simpler configurations. The adult sees social situations as falling into certain highly complex configurations; the child, with a simpler mental organization, does not see these, but breaks up his sensory data into different wholes. The sensory patterns of childhood, then, arise in part from imperfectly experienced adult situations. What the child appropriates from the cultural patterns around him must always be something which it is within his power to comprehend. This is usually one of the simpler and more elementary forms of adult behavior, as the criminal behavior followed out by the gang, or it is a split-off part of a more complex whole common in the culture of adults. . . .

Age is not the only factor that separates people who nominally drink of the same cultural stream from actual community of culture. Mental ability, education, subtle differences of interests and of

personality may likewise sort people into cultural pigeonholes. So completely is the individual immersed in the culture of his own age and social level that he often has difficulty in realizing that any other kind of culture exists. He is separated by invisible walls from those about him who follow different gods. Persons living in different segments of our culture, as determined by age and life situation, may find difficulty in communicating with each other or in understanding each other at all. The old cannot understand the young, the prudent cannot understand the heedless, the married can have little sympathy for the unmarried, parents can never commune with non-parents; each person in the world is surrounded by many with whom he must communicate by smoke signals and by only a few with whom he can converse. But the greatest chasm is that which separates young persons and old. . . .[1]

Though an enlightened pedagogy may ameliorate the conflict of adults and children, it can never remove it altogether. In the most humane school some tension appears between teacher and students, resulting, apparently, from the role which the situation imposes upon the teacher in relation to his students. There are two items of the teacher's duty which make it especially likely that he will have to bring some pressure to bear upon students: he must see to it that there is no retrogression from the complexity of the social world worked out for students of a certain age level,[2] and he must strive gradually to increase that complexity as the child grows in age and approximates adult understanding and experience. Activities may reduce conflict, but not destroy it.

Children have something which can be regarded as a culture of their own. Its most important loci are the unsupervised play group and the school. The unsupervised group presents this culture in a much purer form than does the school, for the childish culture of the school is partly produced by adults, is sifted and selected by adults, and is always subject to a certain amount of control by teachers. The culture of the school is a curious mélange of the work of young artisans making culture for themselves and old artisans making culture for the young; it is also mingled with such bits of the greater culture as children have been able to appropriate. In turning to more concrete materials, we may note certain aspects of tradition in the school. It will illustrate well this mingling of cultures if we divide the tradition which clusters about the school into three classes: tradition which comes entirely, or almost entirely, from the outside; tradition which is in part from outside the school and in part indigenous; and tradition which is almost entirely indigenous. It is roughly true that tradition of the first class exists in the community at large, that of the second class among teachers, and that of the third class among students.

Tradition of the first class, that which for the particular school comes altogether from the outside, is a manifestation of a culture complex diffused throughout the whole of West European culture. The historic school has of course had a part in the formation of this complex, but any particular school is largely the creation of it. Tradition of this sort governs the very existence of schools, for, without such a culture complex, schools would not exist at all. This traditional culture complex governs also the general nature of the life in the schools. It determines that the old shall teach the young, and not that the young shall ever teach the old, which would be at least equally justifiable in a world that changes so rapidly that an education twenty years old is out of date. Tradition governs what is taught and it holds a firm control upon the manner in which it is taught. Tradition determines who shall teach; we have already discussed some of the traditional requirements for teaching.

It is this same sort of tradition also which largely determines how students and teachers shall think of each other.

The best example of a mingled tradition in part absorbed from the general culture of the group and in part produced in the particular institution is the tradition of teachers. In so far as this tradition of teachers is derived from outside a particular school, it is drawn by teachers from the general culture, and from association with members of the teaching profession everywhere. In so far as it is a purely local product, it is produced by the teachers in the institution and is passed on from one teacher to another. We may mention some cardinal points of the teacher tradition as it is usually encountered, making due allowance for local variations. There is a teacher morality, and this morality regulates minutely the teacher's relations with his students and with other teachers; it affects his relations with other teachers especially where the standing of those teachers with students might be affected. There is a character ideal of the teacher; nearly every group which lives long in one stereotyped relation with other groups produces its character ideal, and this ideal for teachers is clearly observable. When teachers say of a colleague, "He's a school teacher," they mean that he conforms to this local character ideal. (It usually implies that the individual puts academic above other considerations, is conscientious in his duties, and exacting in the demands he makes upon himself and others.) There is a taboo on seeking popularity among students, and this taboo operates with dreadful force if it is thought that popularity seeking is complicated by disloyalty to the teacher group. There is a traditional attitude toward students; this attitude requires that a certain distance be kept between teachers and students. The desire to be fair is very likely not the strongest motive that teachers have for keeping students at a distance, but it is certainly one of the consequences of the policy, and it has in its own right the compelling value of an article of faith. None may violate the code of equality with impunity. Teachers have likewise a certain traditional attitude toward each other. The most obvious manifestation of this traditional attitude is the ceremoniousness of teachers toward each other and toward the administration of the school. It seems clear that this is the ceremoniousness of a fighting group which does not care to endanger its prestige with underlings by allowing any informality to arise within itself. Another interesting observation that has often been made about particular groups of teachers is that they discriminate markedly between veterans and new men. This distinction is in the folkways. Occasionally there is a more or less definite ceremony of initiation, more rarely, actual hazing.

The indigenous tradition of the school is found in its purest form among students. This tradition, when it has been originated on the spot, is passed on, largely by word of mouth, from one student to another. Some of the indigenous tradition has been originated by the faculty, and then imposed upon the students; once it has been accepted by students, however, it may be passed on by student groups, Some of the traditional observances which students follow are not home-grown; there is a great literature of school life, and students occasionally appear who are obviously playing the parts of storybook heroes. Besides, there exists in the culture of any community a set of traditional attitudes toward school and school life, varying from one social class to another, and from family to family; these attitudes influence profoundly the attitudes which

students have toward school life. Nevertheless the tradition of students is very largely indigenous within the particular school. Although this sort of tradition varies much in detail from one school to another, we may mention certain characteristics of the fundamental patterns.

Like teacher morality, student morality is the morality of a fighting group, but differences appear in that the student group is subordinate, and its morality is relevant to that situation. Social distance between student and teacher seems as definitely a part of the student code as of the teacher code. The student must not like the teacher too much, for that is naiveté. There is the well-known schoolboy code, the rule that students must never give information to teachers which may lead to the punishment of another student. Certain folkways grow up in every group of school children, as the folkway of riding to grade school on a bicycle or of not riding to high school on a bicycle, and these folkways have a great influence over the behavior of all members of the group. These groups of children are arranged in stairsteps. Membership in the older group implies repudiation of the folkways of the younger group. No one more foolish than the high-school boy on a bicycle, or the college boy wearing a high-school letter! Interlocking groups look forward only, each group aping its elders and despising its juniors. In modern schools, there is a whole complex of traditions pertaining to activities; it seems that all activities are meritorious, that they are in some way connected with the dignity and honor of the school, that some activities are more meritorious than others. . . .

The cultural anthropologists have taught us to analyze the actions of human beings living in a certain culture into culture patterns. Those partially formalized structures of behavior known as "activities" will serve as excellent examples of culture patterns existing in the school. Among the "activities" to be found in most public schools may be mentioned athletics, work on the school paper, oratory and debating, glee club work, Hi-Y work, dramatics, participation in social clubs, departmental clubs, literary societies, fraternities, etc. Each of these activities may be thought of as representing a more or less ritualized form of behavior carried out by the individual as a member of a group and, often, a representative of the larger group. There is a set form for these activities. There is merit in these activities, and that merit seems to rest ultimately upon the notion that group welfare and group prestige are involved in them; the honor of the high school is damaged if the team loses. ("Our team is our fame-protector, On boys, for we expect a touchdown from you—" is unpoetic, but explicit on this point.) But there is intrinsic, irrational merit in them, too, as in the trading of the Trobriand Islanders. There is distinction in these activities for individuals. That distinction rests in part upon the prominence which participation in them gives the individual in the eyes of the school at large, and in part upon the recognition which the adult group accords them. The variety of activities is almost endless, for each of the activities mentioned above has many subdivisions; these subdivisions are sometimes arranged in something of a hierarchy as in athletics, where the greatest distinction attaches to football, a little less to basketball, less yet to baseball and track. These activities are commonly justified on the grounds that they actually prepare for life, since they present actual life situations; their justification for the faculty is in their value as a means of control over restless students. It is noteworthy that a competitive spirit prevails in nearly all activities. Not all activities are really competitive, but the struggle for places may make them so, and the desirability of having some place in some

school activity makes the competition for places keen. One "makes" the school orchestra or glee club quite as truly as one makes the football team.

These culture patterns of activities are partly artificial and faculty-determined, and partly spontaneous. In so far as they have been evolved by the faculty, they have been intended as means of control, as outlets for adolescent energies or substitutes for tabooed activities. They represent also the faculty's attempt to make school life interesting and to extend the influence of the school. Any activity, however, which is to affect the life of students at all deeply, any activity, then, which aspires to a greater influence than is exerted by the Latin Club or the Cercle Français, must have a spontaneous basis, and must appeal to students by presenting to them behavior patterns of considerable intrinsic interest. Each activity usually has some sort of faculty connection, and the status of the faculty adviser is thought to rise or fall with the prosperity or unprosperity of the activity which he promotes. Activities, then, increase in importance and gain recognition from the faculty through the efforts of interested faculty members, as well as through their own intrinsic appeal to students. (A change is taking place in our teacher idiom. The young teacher now refers to himself not as the teacher of a certain subject, but as the coach of a certain activity.)

Of all activities athletics is the chief and the most satisfactory. It is the most flourishing and the most revered culture pattern. It has been elaborated in more detail than any other culture pattern. Competitive athletics has many forms. At the head of the list stands football, still regarded as the most diagnostic test of the athletic prowess of any school. Then come basketball, baseball, track, lightweight football, lightweight basketball, girls' basketball, girls' track, etc. Each of these activities has importance because the particular school and its rivals are immersed in a culture stream of which competitive athletics is an important part. Each school has its traditional rivals, and a greater psychic weighting is attached to the games with traditional rivals than to those with other schools. Schools are arranged in a hierarchy, and may therefore win moral victories while actually suffering defeats. Pennsylvania wins, but Swarthmore triumphs. . . .

The author would be inclined to account for the favorable influence of athletics upon school life in terms of changes effected in group alignments and the individual attitudes that go with them. It is perhaps as a means of unifying the entire group that athletics seems most useful from the sociological point of view. There is a tendency for the school population to split up into its hostile segments of teachers and students and to be fragmented by cliques among both groups. The division of students into groups prevents a collective morale from arising and thereby complicates administration; the split between students and teachers is even more serious, for these two groups tend to become definite conflict groups, and conflict group tensions are the very antithesis of discipline. This condition athletics alleviates. Athletic games furnish a dramatic spectacle of the struggle of picked men against the common enemy, and this is a powerful factor in building up a group spirit which includes students of all kinds and degrees and unifies the teachers and the taught. In adult life we find the analogue of athletics in war; patriotism runs high when the country is attacked. Likewise we find the most certain value of punishment to be the unification of the group which punishes.[3] Athletic sports use exactly the same

mechanism in a controlled way for the attainment of a more limited end.

By furnishing all the members of the school population with an enemy outside the group, and by giving them an opportunity to observe and participate in the struggle against that enemy, athletics may prevent a conflict group tension from arising between students and teachers. The organization of the student body for the support of athletics, though it is certainly not without its ultimate disadvantages, may bring with it certain benefits for those who are interested in the immediate problems of administration. It is a powerful machine which is organized to whip all students into line for the support of athletic teams, and adroit school administrators learn to use it for the dissemination of other attitudes favorable to the faculty and the faculty policy.

In yet another way an enlightened use of athletics may simplify the problem of police work in the school. The group of athletes may be made to furnish a very useful extension of the faculty-controlled social order. Athletes have obtained favorable status by following out one faculty-determined culture pattern; they may be induced to adopt for themselves and to popularize other patterns of a similar nature. Athletes, too, in nearly any group of youngsters, are the natural leaders, and they are leaders who can be controlled and manipulated through the medium of athletics. Those who are fortunate enough to be on the squad of a major sport occupy a favored social position; they are at or near the center of their little universe; they belong to the small but important group of men who are doing things. They have much to lose by misconduct, and it is usually not difficult to make them see it. They have, too, by virtue of their favored position, the inevitable conservatism of the privileged classes, and they can be brought to take a stand for the established order. In addition, the athletes stand in a very close and personal relationship to at least one faculty member, the coach, who has, if he is an intelligent man or a disciplinarian, an opportunity to exert a great influence upon the members of the team. The coach has prestige, he has favors to give, and he is in intimate rapport with his players. Ordinarily he uses his opportunities well. As the system usually works out, the members of the major teams form a nucleus of natural leaders among the student body, and their influence is more or less conservative and more or less on the side of what the faculty would call decent school citizenship. The necessarily close correspondence between athletic prowess and so-called clean living is another factor which effects the influence of athletes upon non-athletes. We have here stated a theory of the ideal use of athletics in school control, but it is the part of common sense to concede at once that it does not always work out so. An anti-social coach, or a coach who allows his players to believe themselves to be indispensable, so that they wrest control of athletics from his hands, can vitiate the whole system. When the system does go wrong, athletes and athletics become an insufferable nuisance to teachers. A teacher who had had numerous unpleasant experiences with athletes summed up the situation in her school by saying, "I learned that whenever I ran into some particularly difficult problem of discipline I could look for a boy wearing the school letter."

There are other activities. Their effects upon the school group, and upon the personalities of the individuals who participate in them, differ widely. . . .

. . . The growth of school activities in recent years, and not the development of new theories of education, would seem to have been chiefly instrumental in making school interesting for the student, and undoubtedly helps to account for the recent success of the public schools

in holding their students through the years of high school. There is added the fact that most of the activities carried on in the schools would probably exist in one form or another whether the faculty fostered them or not. If the faculty is able to foster and control them, there is at least a greater likelihood that they will subserve ends acceptable to the faculty than there would be if activities were quite spontaneous. Activities are indeed so thoroughly a part of the school system at the present time that school administrators have grown superstitious about them. They have learned to expect trouble when there is a lag in the activities. In the private boarding schools, a relative lull in activities occurs somewhere in midwinter, usually just after the onset of wintry weather has put a stop to widespread participation in athletics. The experience of these schools seems to show that serious cases of discipline and general discontent with school life are more likely to be encountered in this period than in any other.

Unquestionably, activities contribute much to make the schools livable and are more effective than any other feature of the school in the molding of personality. But we should not allow these facts to blind us to the truth that they often tend to interfere with other important features of school life. Every activity has its faculty sponsor, who in addition to his teaching is charged with the promotion of that particular activity. His prestige among the faculty and students, and often his salary as well, are largely determined by the success of that activity; it is no wonder, then, that activities accumulate and make increasing demands upon the school time and the attention of students. It would, of course, be perfectly possible to educate through activities alone, and the present writer would be the last to argue against such a system if one could be devised, but we must not forget that education through activities as at present organized is at best scattering and sporadic, and needs systematic supplementation through the basic training in facts and skills which it is the formal purpose of the schools to give. And it would not be possible to take even so tolerant an attitude toward activities whose chief motivation is a business one, as seems to be the case with college football.

Notes

[1] The fact that the world of the child is organized into configurations of a different kind from the configurations composing the base of the adult's universe seems to constitute, by the way, the best justification we have for lying to children. The greatest argument for the teaching of falsehood seems to be that different orders of truth exist for different mental levels. Children should therefore be taught the kind of truth they are able to understand. There is truth in this argument in that children are likely to break up into simpler configurations the complicated configuration which results for the adult mind in the weighing of virtue against vice, and they are likely to get a final result which is, for the adult, distorted and beside the point. No one who has seen the demoralization produced in some not overly intelligent youths by contact with cynical but well-balanced and earnest adults can fail to see that there is some argument for the simple virtues, even if they are based upon falsehoods. But one wonders whether demoralization is not even more likely to result from building up in the child's mind a structure of beliefs which he is likely to take sometime for complete lies because they are partly false. That such demoralization often occurs will be apparent to all who have ever been in a position to witness the changes wrought in the moral fiber of students when they enter the greater world or make the transition from secondary schools to universities. Nor should we fail to remark in this connection that the policy of lying to children presupposes that one should be intelligent enough and dexterous enough to deceive them completely. This is often not the case at all, for shrewd children, judging their elders by their behavior rather than by their words, are frequently able to cut through the adults' rationalizations to the amoral core of their behavior. Since children, even the shrewdest of them, do not make allowance for rationalizations as rationalizations, as phenomena beyond the conscious control of the individual, they judge their elders more harshly, sometimes, than they deserve. They think their elders both knaves and fools when those elders are in fact too high-minded to admit their selfishness to themselves. Perhaps, when all the alternatives are considered, we shall do better to stick to the simple virtues ourselves, and to speak truth, while taking such precautions as we may against unwarranted generalizations from facts which run contrary to the accepted views of ethics. The virtue that we shall so engender will be a tough-minded virtue. It may be less comprehensive than some would desire, but it will not be brittle.

[2] A strong tendency toward such retrogression in the direction of simpler and easier structures seems to exist, especially in the intermediate stages. This retrogression appears as "silliness." Much conflict between teachers and students arises from the desire of the teacher to eliminate "silliness".

[3] Mead, G. H., "The Psychology of Punitive Justice," *American Journal of Sociology*, 23 (1918), pp. 577–602.

THE TEACHER–PUPIL relationship is a form of institutionalized dominance and subordination. Teacher and pupil confront each other in the school with an original conflict of desires, and however much that conflict may be reduced in amount, or however much it may be hidden, it still remains. The teacher represents the adult group, ever the enemy of the spontaneous life of groups of children. The teacher represents the formal curriculum, and his interest is in imposing that curriculum upon the children in the form of tasks; pupils are much more interested in life in their own world than in the desiccated bits of adult life which teachers have to offer. The teacher represents the established social order in the school, and his interest is in maintaining that order, whereas pupils have only a negative interest in that feudal superstructure. Teacher and pupil confront each other with attitudes from which the underlying hostility can never be altogether removed. Pupils are the material in which teachers are supposed to produce results. Pupils are human beings striving to realize themselves in their own spontaneous manner, striving to produce their own results in their own way. Each of these hostile parties stands in the way of the other; in so far as the aims of either are realized, it is at the sacrifice of the aims of the other.

Authority is on the side of the teacher. The teacher nearly always wins. In fact, he must win, or he cannot remain a teacher. Children, after all, are usually docile, and they certainly are defenceless against the machinery with which the adult world is able to enforce its decisions; the result of the battle is foreordained. Conflict between teachers and students therefore passes to the second level. All the externals of conflict and of authority having been settled, the matter chiefly at issue is the meaning of those externals. Whatever the rules that the teacher lays down, the tendency of

Teaching as Institutionalized Leadership

Willard Waller

Reprinted from The Sociology of Teaching (*New York: John Wiley & Sons, Inc., Science Editions, 1965*), pp. 195–209, by permission of the publisher.

the pupils is to empty them of meaning. By mechanization of conformity, by "laughing off" the teacher or hating him out of all existence as a person, by taking refuge in self-initiated activities that are always just beyond the teacher's reach, students attempt to neutralize teacher control. The teacher, however, is striving to read meaning into the rules and regulations, to make standards really standards, to force students really to conform. This is a battle which is not unequal. The power of the teacher to pass rules is not limited, but his power to enforce rules is, and so is his power to control attitudes toward rules.

Rules may be emasculated by attrition through setting up exceptions which at first seem harmless to the established order but when translated into precedent are found to destroy some parts of it altogether. One value of experience in teaching is that it gives the teacher an understanding of precedents. A trivial favor to Johnny Jones becomes a ruinous social principle when it is made a precedent. Or students defeat a rule by taking refuge in some activity just beyond its reach; what the rule secures, then, is not conformity but a different kind of non-conformity. Both teachers and pupils know well what hinges on these struggles over rules and evasions of rules. Johnny

249

goes to the blackboard but he shuffles his feet; he is made to walk briskly but he walks too brisky; he is forced to walk correctly but there is a sullen expression on his face. Many teachers learn to cut through the rules to deal with the mental fact of rebellion; this is a negation of institutionalized leadership and requires a personality strong enough to stand without institutional props.

Most important in making conformity to external rules harmless are habitual adjustments to the inconveniences which teachers can impose upon students. A certain boy is in rebellion against the school authorities; he violates many rules and he devises new offences which are not covered by rules. Penalties do not stop him from breaking rules, for he is used to penalties, used to "walking the bull ring" or staying in after hours, and toughened to beatings. New penalties, likewise, do not stop him long, for he soon becomes accustomed to them as thoroughly as to the old. Likewise, it does little good to devise rules to cover a wider range of contingencies, for the new laws, the new risks, and the new penalties are soon a part of life. A social machine, however finely worked out, can never make a human being go its way rather than his own, and no one can ever be controlled entirely from without.

Dominance and subordination in the schools are usually discussed as "discipline." On the objective side, discipline is a social arrangement whereby one person is able consistently to exert control over the actions of others. Subjectively, discipline is the morale obtaining under institutionalized leadership. It is observable in the social interaction of the persons concerned, and it rests upon psychic arrangements in the minds of those persons. "Discipline" is often used as a value term to denote something regarded as constructive and healthful for the student or something of which the teacher approves. . . .

Discipline is partly personal influence and partly the social standing of an office. It is the resultant from the filtering of the teacher's personality through the porous framework of the institution. The larger the pores in the framework, the more personalities come into contact through it, and the more profound and permanent are the effects of social interaction. The more evident the social pattern in the schools, the less are personalities involved.

Discipline is a phenomenon of group life. It depends upon a collective opinion which superiors cause inferiors to form of superiors and of the tasks imposed by superiors. Essentially it depends upon prestige, which is largely a fiction, upon the ability of leaders to capture and hold attention (and by shifting objectives, to maintain the tonus of the relationship), upon formality setting the stage for social interaction, upon social distance which keeps primary group attitudes from eating away at formal relations, upon the reenforcement of respect for superiors by the respect of superiors for each other and upon the reenforcement of the inferior's respect for the superior by the respect which other inferiors pay him. (The maintenance of discipline may depend also, in the long run, upon the establishment of channels for the hostility of subordinates to superiors.) Discipline shows itself, in the group, as a one-way suggestibility.

The techniques used by teachers to maintain this mixed rapport, discipline, may be classified, approximately in the order of their utilization of the institutional and the arbitrary, and inversely to their dependence upon personal influence, as follows: (1) command, (2) punishment, (3) management or the manipulation of personal and group relationships, (4) temper, and (5) appeal.

(1) Institutionalized dominance and subordination appears in its purest form

in the command.[1] A command is a suggestion directed by the superior at the subordinate relating to the behavior of the subordinate. As a suggestion mechanism, it depends for its effectiveness upon the general conditions of suggestibility, upon the inherent suggestibility of the subordinate, upon the one-way rapport between superior and inferior, and upon the personal prestige of the individual from whom the command emanates. The command as such is most effective when most formalized, that is, when given without any personal implications. The presumption is present that the superior is willing to back up the command with all the (unknown) resources of his personality and of the organization of which both the superordinated and the subordinated one are a part. Army officers are accustomed to speak of a voice of command, which is strong and virile, but flat and entirely unemotional, takes obedience for granted, and is formalized as far as possible. On this latter point, note the military custom of mechanizing as many commands as possible. "Attention" means but one thing, and there is but one way of calling for attention. Likewise all commands relating to military maneuvers are completely formalized. There is a tendency for even these bare words to be reduced to their essential parts; thus "Attention" becomes "Tenshun" with an accenting and a drawing out of the first syllable and a sliding over of the last, and "March" becomes symbolized by "Ho."

It seems clear that the reason for a command should never be explained. Although it may be desirable on other grounds to explain it, it should be recognized that the explanation, by introducing an element of doubt concerning the command, or by the suggestion that it might not be obeyed, or by the mere weakening of the stimulus word by bringing it into connection with others, detracts from the force of the command. Certainly a command should

never be coupled with a statement of grievance, for that will revive hostility and sometimes induce disrespect for the person weak enough to allow grievances to arise when he is presumed to be in control of the situation; this is an error common among mothers and weak teachers. Likewise a command that is couched in the language of the whine or the complaint operates powerfully to bring about its own frustration, for it calls into being a whole system of disgust reactions which militate against obedience. A plea is often used to back up a command, but it seems certain that where this technique enables a person to obtain control it is the plea that does the work and not the command. A threat is commonly attached to a command, and the threat sometimes operates to give force to a command by attaching a fear sanction to it, but the threat detracts from the efficacy of the command as a pure command by presenting the alternative of disobedience, and by calling out the hostile attitudes implicit in the situation of dominant and dominated persons. It is likewise unfortunate to give a command in the form of a question, such as, "Will you shut up?" The giving of a command implies authority, real or theoretical, formal or personal. A command without authority becomes a mere exhortation, which is usually quite meaningless. In actual human relationships an attenuation of authority occurs by its being spread over a field so wide that it cannot hold. Thus a great theoretical but unenforceable authority is congruous with the issuance of exhortations, while the person of more limited authority can give commands.

(2) The sanction enforcing the command is formal punishment. Punishment is a measured pain or inconvenience imposed according to rule by the rep-

resentative of authority upon those subject to that authority. Punishment is impersonal, unemotional, and proportioned to the offence rather than to the offender, every care being taken, in the pure case, to separate the offender and the offence, and to keep apart the punishment and the person inflicting the punishment. Punishment is usually justified according to a hedonistic theory of discipline. To every infraction of the rules must be attached a penalty just severe enough to make it unattractive. Students will be good because it will pay them to be good. Without embarking upon a theoretical refutation of hedonism, we may remark that punishment often fails to accomplish its purpose, even when the pains connected with it are multiplied far beyond any possible pleasure connected with a violation of the rules, because the causes from which offences come are more deep-seated than the remedies superimposed, so that the only effect of punishment is to enhance mental conflict, or to produce a more complex mental organization. It is not possible by punishment to produce very much effect upon a deep-lying personal hostility, except to increase it, or to deal with an irrational, unconscious attitude of rebellion.

A real value of punishment is that it serves to define the situation. It puts the student in the way of distinguishing clearly the permitted and the not-permitted, the right and the wrong within the complex social situation of the school. If consistently and unvaryingly applied, it tends to set up certain rules as essential limitations to action within the situation, and the student comes in time, unless motivated otherwise to rebellion, to accept those basic limitations and to adapt his behavior to them. A further value of punishment as it takes place in the actual social situation of the school

room is that it removes the offender from the group. When the dominance of the teacher is threatened by some act of a student, it is imperative that action of some sort be taken in order to prevent others from copying the behavior and reenforcing each other in their derelictions. It is the use of formal punishment to put an abrupt end to the process of interaction which might ultimately lead to concerted rebellion by removing from the group the one from whom offence first comes. It may be that the individual is punished by some form of banishment, such as sending from the room, sending to the principal's office, suspension, or expulsion; in this case the isolation from the group is physical. If the offender remains physically in the group, the fact that he is under the ban, that he has an ordeal to face, or that he has lost standing through humiliation serves to isolate him from the group phychically and to lessen his influence upon other students. The effect of the punishment on the person isolated is another matter. . . .

Punishment is probably used more often for personal reasons than for reasons inherent in the formal relation; offences, likewise, often arise from the clash of personalities rather than from the formal structure. The usual thing is for the machinery of punishment to be made the means of carrying on the teacher's part of a conflict in which teacher and student become involved but which neither understands. It should be noted that punishment used for personal ends ceases to be punishment and becomes a feud or a struggle for status, an aspect of social life in the school which we have noted elsewhere.

Some further generalizations may be made concerning the use of punishment in the schools. The first of these is that there is in the school very little punishment as strictly defined. It is very difficult to keep punishment impersonal, under conditions of physical intimacy and constant association such as those in which teacher and student are thrown together, and therefore it is hard to keep punishment punishment. When the personal element enters into punishment, an intense hostility is aroused on both sides. The system of punishment is apparently at its best when the entire group, the teacher as well as the student, is regarded as subordinated to a principle; in this case the teacher is not the source and spring of punishment, but the channel through which it comes. If the principle is consistently but not fanatically adhered to, it may help to remove the personal element from punishment almost entirely. The difficulty is in finding a principle. We should note, furthermore, that punishment is bearable in proportion to the social distance of the person inflicting it from the person upon whom it is imposed; hence the advantage for the teacher of belonging frankly to the adult group and the teaching group. . . .

(3) A means of control that is important for many teachers we may refer to in the absence of a better name as management. Under this heading we should include all means of getting the teacher's definition of the situation accepted and the teacher's wishes carried out without a direct clash of wills between teacher and student. One of the most important devices to be included under this head is that of indirect suggestion, which many teachers have learned to use most effectively. Indirect suggestions are such suggestions as are carried in stories, fables, anecdotes, and general expressions of attitude toward actual or potential behavior. We should also include under the heading of management the principle of precipitating conflict at the time most advantageous to the teacher, at a time when the opponent, though definitely in the conflict, is unready or in some other way at a disadvantage. The policy most often followed by teachers is that of attempting to precipitate conflict before the student is emotionally ready; this is

the policy, to use the slang phrase of teachers, of "getting the jump on them." Many sagacious teachers have also learned to apply this principle with reverse emphasis, to postpone dealing with an angry or rebellious student until his emotions have had an opportunity to cool. Both these empirical principles are apparently based upon a sound psychology; the emotions are of value in a struggle, they have a temporal quality, they cannot be called immediately into play, and they cannot last forever.

Under the heading of management, too, should be included all manipulation of the student in his social relations. Isolation is a powerful weapon. The teacher may ignore a student, or he may state or infer that this person does not really belong to the group, or he may, by curtailment of privileges, actually deprive him, for a time, of his opportunities for association with other youngsters. This is a long lever that makes dreadfully for conformity. The limitations upon it are the limitations of the teacher's ability to manipulate the pupil group and the undesirable effects upon the personality of the student if this technique is used recklessly and successfully. The teacher, again, may attempt to manipulate group alignments so that the ukase of the teacher appears to be backed up by the authority of the student group; a subtle example of this is the use of the first person plural in giving reprimands or rebukes, as, "We don't like that, John," or "You are disturbing us," or "Can't you see we are busy?" Ridicule is sometimes used as a means of depriving the individual of status before punishing him. The effectiveness of these devices depends upon the effectiveness of the teacher's personality. If the teacher is thoroughly in control, the members of his class may feel flattered at being admitted into partnership with him, and will be carried on by this feeling to form their attitudes after this; but if he is not already in command of the situation, the whole procedure becomes absurd. Likewise, the teacher may attempt to manipulate home and community relationships with reference to himself and his students in such a way as to increase his own prestige. Thus he may cultivate acquaintance with parents, and may, in his dealings with children, refer to talks he has had with parents and attitudes expressed by them in those conversations. A classic device is that of holding the parent's ideals before the child. The teacher says, "Now, John, I know your mother would not want you to do that," or, "John, I know your parents want you to do well in school and grow up to be one of the outstanding men in the community." This device is mostly ineffective. If the relationship of parent to child is meaningful, and the meaning is of a positive nature, the child may resent having his parents dragged in by the heels by someone who has less weight or a different kind of meaning altogether. If the attitude toward the parent is mixed with a considerable rebellion, as it often is, the teacher-pupil relationship will be unduly complicated by the release within it of affects belonging elsewhere in the scheme of life.

There are other devices for playing upon the group alignment of children. Catching the child in one group, teachers attempt to obtain his assent to some general principle that carries over into the school group. If subtly done, this technique may be effective. When it is subtle enough to be effective, it proceeds no further than indirect suggestion, or at most to verbalization of things already in the child's mind. In the unsubtle extreme, it amounts to seizing a favorable opportunity to preach a sermon without receiving backtalk, or to mere posing in the presence of parents. The compartmentalization of the child's mind whereby one set of attitudes comes to expression at one time and another at another time —so that the child is hard and then soft— this too may be played upon. But such suggestions as are offered to a child when he is in a melting mood must be very indirect, else he will build up his defences and be soft no more in the presence of that particular person. Teachers are sometimes able, by long and serious talks, "heart-to-heart" talks, to induce this softened mood in their students and then to preach them a sermon. But if this is done, the teacher must not speak from the teaching role, for that will destroy any favorable effect, but as one human being to another. He must also be prepared to accept a resumption of the old relationship when the mellow mood has passed, with reserves restored and no further reference to the incident of communication and no effect traceable except perhaps a slight modification of the general attitude.

(4) Teachers also control by displays of temper. The display of temper is marked by diminution of social distance, by sloughing of social inhibitions and reserves, menacing behavior, and obvious, weakly controlled, or uncontrolled emotion. Control by temper is far down on the scale of social distance and high on that of actual human influence. Passion has become too much for social forms. The ritual has broken down and human personalities have come into contact without the intermission of buffers. It is implicit in the school situation that hates should sometimes run so high that they break through all barriers, and it has also become a part of the code. It is unwritten law that the only emotion a teacher can display is anger, that all else is softness. It should be noted that the technique of control by anger is often mingled with punishment, or confused with it. Strictly speaking, anger destroys punishment as

punishment, but the machinery of punishment may be used as a part of the technique of control by anger, and it is probably so employed more often than it is administered without passion.

A person who teaches usually acquires a temper worthy of remark, or, if he is already blessed with such a characteristic, he learns how to use it more effectively. The manner in which this personality change ensues will be elaborated elsewhere, but we may note it briefly here. The strain of a situation created by the behavior of students mounts, in the absence of a technique for neutralizing it, until it becomes intolerable. An outbreak of temper ensues. Perhaps the teacher himself is surprised at the violence of his emotion. (Most new teachers report at least one such experience.) The teacher gains his point. He finds the school room thereafter easier to live in, his students respectful and perhaps even affectionate.[2] He cultivates a rapid-fire, intense temper. He expresses his grievances as they arise without reserve. Or the teacher does not gain his point, in this case he becomes frantic and meets the situation with redoubled emotion and with increased energy, perhaps attaining ultimate success. Quickness in organizing anger, enough violence of emotion to carry one through the crisis and to inhibit all disposition to temporize, ability to maintain an angry attitude until the last vestige of rebellion has been crushed, all appear to be requisites of the schoolteacher temper. The formation of a technique for expressing anger is important also in that the expression of the teacher's anger enables him to deal with the situation calmly afterwards and to minimize the holding of grudges. . . .

(5) The technique of appeal is most often used for dealing with minor infractions of the rules, or, in a more important case, for effecting a change in the general attitude of the student. The appeal is an attempt to manipulate the child by calling into play, usually through verbal reference, some basic attitude or strong trend in his personality which it is thought will be effective in bringing him to conform to the teacher's wishes. An appeal may be direct or indirect, public or private, positive or negative in its nature. A direct appeal is what it purports to be and amounts to an exhortation with special reference to some supposed attitude of the child. An indirect appeal may imply this reference or it may be couched negatively, in the form of a challenge or a shaming reference.

Some of the supposedly dominant attitudes of children to which appeal is made are the parents' ideals, fair play, honesty, chivalry, or self-esteem. A favorite appeal is that to the ideals which the parents, especially the mother, are supposed to entertain concerning the child. "Don't do anything you would be ashamed to have your mother see you do." "I know what your mother would think of that," says the teacher, and the boy is then supposed to be ashamed of himself. Likewise an attempt is made to assimilate the school to the home: "I know you would not act like that in your own home. Why should you do it here?" There are reasons enough why he should, but the child does not know them! The sense of fair play is also called upon to enforce a certain amount of law and order in the school room, sometimes effectively. "Henry," asks the teacher, "do you really think it's fair to treat a smaller boy that way?" If Henry does not think it fair, he may conform to the teacher's wishes. An appeal is likewise made to honesty, usually in the form of praise for certain honest actions, and it is often successful. The self-esteem of the child is of course played upon in all these instances. Sometimes the appeal to self-esteem is even more direct. "I'd be ashamed, a great big boy like you, Leo, to make silly faces like a six year old."

Or, "I'm surprised at you. I always thought you were such a gentleman." Women teachers commonly appeal to the sense of chivalry of the male students. In the unsubtle cases, the appeal takes about this form: "Well, just go on, now. I can't do anything with you. I'm just a poor weak woman." Women who know how to capitalize their sex more subtly may be able to do so with a considerable degree of success. Usually such appeals are quite hopeless, as is, for instance, the double-barreled one which assimilates the woman teacher to the mother: "All that I ask is that you show the same respect to me you'd show to your mother. Your mother's a woman, too, and she would understand."

Appeals which are most effective are those which are most delicately made. A frank appeal for help which a teacher makes because he cannot otherwise go on will usually, also, get a favorable response. More than once it has happened that a class which took no prizes for orderliness while the teacher was well and hearty became very cooperative when she sprained her ankle. The challenge, in the hands of a vigorous personality, can accomplish remarkable results. It is sometimes very strong. "You lazy boob, all you do is warm a seat. Do you think you'll ever learn anything? You're the biggest fool in school." When the teacher is vigorous enough to lay down his challenges in such a way that they cannot be avoided, he can often secure very effective control through that technique. It is a technique, however, which induces failure at least as often as success, and the wise teacher will use it soberly and sparingly.

Factors which limit the effectiveness of the technique of appeal are the social distance and antagonism between teacher and student and the lack of a suitable technique on the part of the teacher for discovering the dominant complexes of the student and adapting his procedure so that a real connection between them and the intended appeal can be made. Social distance obstructs appeal because it makes it difficult for the teacher to speak to the child as one human being to another. Antagonism between teacher and student tends to neutralize the effect of an appeal that really hits the mark; after one or more appeals the preexisting antagonism may cause the student to increase the social distance between himself and the teacher. Chiefly important in making the technique of appeal difficult is the utter lack of ability of most teachers in practical character diagnosis; the importance of this is obvious, because one must know what to appeal to before he can attempt to make an appeal; an appeal that goes wrong does more harm than good. Teachers sometimes attempt direct appeals in a very foolish manner and one that disregards wholly the existing attitudes of a child. Teachers commonly do not realize how necessary is a favorable rapport for any such suggestions as those we have been discussing; nor do they understand the technique of getting hold of a person a little at a time, of gradually building up a favorable feeling tone before attempting to make the relationship carry a heavy weight of suggestion. So little do teachers realize what emotional factors are involved in the appeals that they are trying to make that they sometimes do not hesitate to make their most intimate and touching appeals in the presence of a large group.

These are by no means all the techniques used by teachers in the attempt to maintain this mixed rapport which we call discipline. Probably all teachers use all these techniques and more, but with different emphasis and in different degrees. . . .

[1] N.B. Commands are often given in the non-institutionalized relations, but these are not formal commands. They proceed from whole personalities, and are directed at whole personalities; it is precisely this which is forbidden in institutional relations.

[2] It seems paradoxical that affection should be won in this way, and yet there is much evidence that it often happens so. The explanation seems to be that the teacher has established leadership, and that students are grateful for the opportunity to be dependent. We must not forget that institutional leadership, for all the conflict that is in it, is real leadership.

The Teacher and the Class: An Investigation of the Process and Functions of Identification

Gertrude McPherson

THE ROLE-SET[1] of the public school teacher has as its core the relationship between teacher and pupil: the role-expectations of the teacher for the pupil and her response to and handling of the expectations she perceives directed at her about this relationship from her other role-partners-parents, administrators and the pupils themselves. In the course of my investigation of teacher role-set[2]—its dimensions, strains, and modes of articulation—in one particular school, I discovered that a significant aspect was the relationship of the teacher to her class as a group, and that it was not sufficient just to study her relationship to individual pupils. It is this aspect on which this paper focuses. How does the relationship change from social distance to identification and what functions does this growing identification serve for the teacher in articulating her role-set?

It is important to mention briefly the methods of investigation that I used in the study since they provide clues both to the limitations and to the significance of my conclusions. I taught as an inter-mediate (fifth and sixth grade) teacher in a small rural New England school for ten years, during which time I conducted the study, intensively for one year, more casually for the other nine. My role as participant observer was concealed; the other teachers saw me as a colleague and did not know that I was also acting as sociological observer. My data were collected through observation of myself and of the other teachers and were recorded as fully as possible from memory at the end of each school day. My placement with a group of children in a particular grade for the greater part of each day naturally limited what I could see, how much I could observe. My own orientations and values as an intermediate teacher no doubt also limited both my understanding of the orientations and expectations of my role-partners and my understanding of the orientations of teachers in other positions in the school structure (symbolized by the location of intermediate teachers upstairs, primary teachers downstairs). These limitations were compensated for by my complete and intimate involvement in the school, the fact that I was fully accepted as a colleague, and that, therefore, what I experienced myself and observed in other teachers was the role-set from inside, as it is experienced, not as it looks to the outsider.

One of the norms accepted by all the teachers in the Adams Schools was that of loyalty to the teacher group and to teacher solidarity against the pressures from others, whether parents, principal, or pupils. One pupil cannot significantly weaken this united front, but a class as a group does have a significant influence on this solidarity. The relationship between a teacher and her class is complex and involved and not all of the power in the relationship devolves to the teacher alone.[3]

The kindergarten teacher has the hardest job in the school. The children, unfamiliar with what is expected of them, must be molded from an unorganized mass into some kind of group which can be taught.[4] Mrs. Garten, the kindergarten teacher, remarked that most of her time was spent familiarizing the children with the necessity for routine and regularity in order to prepare them to be instructed in first grade. "That's why we need kindergarten—to save the first grade teacher all that stuff." At Adams the group constituted in kindergarten remains, almost unchanged, throughout the elementary years. Working and playing together one hundred and eighty days each year they develop a sense of group identity, share common standards of action and value and consistent patterns of behavior and expectation. They think of themselves as a group and are so considered by the teachers.[5]

Even those classes divided in fifth grade for the departmental program develop over the year distinct group characteristics, partly through the ways in which each teacher treats them as a separate entity. When Mrs. Crane reprimanded her homeroom class for the misbehavior of a few, someone objected: "But only a few of us were bad." She answered: "But that is all that is needed to get this class a bad reputation in the building." The teacher talks to her class as to an individual and praises it or blames it as she does the individual pupil.

Over time the group moves towards a central tendency. The teachers label one class as "good" (hard-working and eager) and another as "bad" (lazy, disobedient). One eager enthusiastic pupil may be the spark needed to ignite the others and his class becomes known as that "eager fifth grade." A wide gap between the top and the bottom students in a class or a predominance of average pupils may produce a group the teachers label as "dull." Two or three troublemakers with strong leadership qualities and a sense of mischief may turn a group into that "difficult sixth grade."[6]

A group labeled as good or exciting attempts to keep its label, to push its members towards the accolade, "the nicest class I ever had," A group labeled as bad is pushed by its label towards further "bad" behavior. Labels are hard to outgrow. A class considered to be the noisiest, laziest, worst-behaved on the upper floor referred to itself this way. Years later its reputation as that "difficult" class preceded it through high school.

So, except for the kindergarten teacher, every teacher must deal with what is already a group with its own standards, patterns of behavior, its own expectations of school and teacher, the complex product of earlier experiences in school and constant classroom association over time. And each teacher must make this group her own and define the "teacher dominant situation" by incorporating its standards to hers, its expectations to hers. The experienced teacher knows what she must do quickly in the first few weeks of the school year. The new teacher, with less idea of what she wants and less knowledge of how to get it, operates with less conviction and less sureness, but she too establishes some modus vivendi with her class during that difficult month of September.[7] No teacher accepts the class definitions completely. She always has some personal standards she wishes to incorporate, if only to show that she is in charge. To the frequent pupil objection: "But that's not the way Mrs. Smith did it," she responds: "But you are in the fourth grade now. We do it this way"; or "When . . . in the fifth grade you can [do] a book report in a new way"; or "Fourth graders don't need afternoon recess. They are too grown up."

Most Adams teachers are grateful for the number of ways they do not feel compelled to change. The standard classroom procedures can be taken for granted. Since the standards and traditional rules accepted as sacrosanct by the pupils become quite rigid over the years, it is to the advantage of the teacher to accept what has gone before as right. The conservatism of the pupils is encouraged by and encourages the conservatism of the teacher. To break pupil habits, particularly those of a whole class, requires time and effort and every teacher must decide how important it is to her to change. Any change takes time and energy she might be using in other aspects of her teaching.

As the teacher molds her class and is molded by it, she begins to identify herself with it.[8] Because of the status and power differences between her and her pupils this identification never becomes complete, but the relationship moves from the impersonal to the personal, and social distance between teacher and pupils is notably reduced.[9] The teacher begins to experience certain sentiments that resemble those attached to property—exclusive control, jealousy of interference, pride in possession and display. There are distinct similarities to the type of relationship, as described by George Homans, characteristic of the Tikopian father and son, sea captain and seamen, officer and soldiers.[10] The original separation of interests, the class as *they*, as the outgroup, begins to fade away and the purely formal impersonal rights and obligations become imbued with affect and even internalized. The teacher, spending six hours a day almost exclusively with her class, begins to see the world through the eyes of the class, its interests as her interests, even as she continues to be separate from the pupils because of her authority and the requirement that she must teach, judge, and control them.[11]

The process of identification reveals the shifting by Adams teachers between idealistic and realistic role-expectations.[12] Each September the teachers hold what seem to an outside observer to be utopian and unrealistic expectations for their classes. These expectations cannot survive the daily routine and are progressively scaled down during the school year to more realistic but still normative expectations by June. Yet, in the context, the original ideal expectations may seem "realistic" to a teacher, who brings each fall to her new unshaped September class recollections of her matured and departed June class. No matter how willing she may have been in June to get rid of a class, by September it has taken on an aura of virtue—infinitely more attractive, more intelligent and docile than the new, awkward, confused group which she must mold. I have heard every Adams teacher say at some time in September: "This is the worst class I have ever had." But no teacher seems to remember having said it before, and the perennial process of reduction of expectations occurs each year without any particular self-awareness of it among the teachers.

September is a grueling month as the teacher learns to know the children, to discover their clique relationships, to determine which child can be trusted, which should not be given responsibility, who should sit near whom. She is careful not to respond too quickly to those pupils eager to attach themselves to her, since often these are the marginal members, those least likely to help her establish her control over the class.[13] Finally, she copes with what seems to be total ignorance and the insistence by the children that "we never had *that* before."

During September the teacher speaks of "them" and is never heard to refer to "my class" or "my homeroom." When towards the end of the month she speaks of "my class," it is usually to compare it unfavorably with other classes she has had. During this period she indirectly criticizes previous teachers who are responsible for this confused mass of ignorance. Thus she can remain competent, unhappily saddled with a badly prepared class. Sometimes a teacher even asks the teacher she is indirectly criticizing for support and sympathy in her difficult situation.

For a few more weeks she holds the class at a distance, preserving her own status by denying that its work, its behavior, and its test results have anything to do with her. She claims neither credit nor blame for the class. But then a subtle change begins to occur, more rapidly if she has an intelligent, well-behaved, and likable group of children, but eventually even with a slow and difficult group.

Mrs. Gregory, the fourth grade teacher, said in September: "If you think the group you have now is bad, wait until you get this crowd. I will never train them," and in October: "This is the worst fourth grade I have ever had. They can't reason." But even then she was beginning to impose her rigid standards of order on the group and beginning to judge their work in itself rather than in relation to her dimming recollection of her previous class. By November she remarked: "I guess my class knew I didn't feel well. They made no trouble and I didn't have to raise my voice once."

After December Mrs. Gregory never expressed criticism of her class as a whole. She boasted about "my class" and rejected any criticisms other teachers might direct at the group. And she demanded for her class all the advantages of every other class. Although angered when a child asked for a Christmas party (he was "uppity"), she decided to have one since "I couldn't have them left out."

Hers is a typical transformation. Even the highly critical second grade teacher, who spoke disapprovingly (in September) of the noise her class made as done by *them*, was saying in May: "Did you hear *us* today? We didn't mean to disturb you upstairs, but we were having a wonderful time learning a new dance."

The introduction of a departmental system in the intermediate grades at Adams disturbed and complicated but did not destroy each teacher's identification with her homeroom class. It was hard for the teacher to make the transition from the parent-teacher role, in which she was responsible for the total school life of her class, to a subject-teacher role, in which she was responsible only for teaching one subject to four different groups of pupils. To some degree each homeroom teacher made her identification with her homeroom class and competed for its rights against the other three teachers. This meant that to some degree she rejected the other three groups of children, a rejection which led to internal ambivalence since she also had to teach all three of the other groups. One of the four teachers carried the process of identification so far that she interfered with the work of other teachers with her homeroom class. This led to rather intense ingroup tension among the teachers. As Erving Goffman has noted, too great identification by one teacher with her class may convince the other teachers that "the impression they are trying to maintain of what constitutes appropriate work is threatened."[14]

When a teacher identifies with her self-contained classroom and no other teacher comes into much contact with the pupils, interclass comparison is difficult and competition is limited. However, in the early stages of a departmental program, competition may become cutthroat as the differences among the classes are exposed to all the teachers. As the intermediate teachers at Adams become more and more identified with their subject areas, it seems clear that they will identify less and less with the homeroom class and resemble the high school teachers more than they do the primary teachers. During the years under study, identification with the class was the common pattern. The process occurred year after year and provided some important functions for a teacher in articulating her role-set.

First, identification tends to encourage respect for tradition, to reward conservatism, and to penalize the new enthusiastic teacher. For a teacher to undo established habits of writing book reports, to unteach faulty knowledge about space, to encourage individualized reading programs, often produces resistance and confusion in the class. Often it is far easier to carry on the old ways. For the older teacher this seems self-evident since she usually shares with the lower grade teachers standards relating to classroom management—order of procedure, type of paper to be used, bathroom regulations—as well as those relating to methods of teaching and standards of academic performance. For the newer teacher who, because of different background and training, may consider the weight of tradition an obstruction to her own ideas about education, the urge to change is greater. But, unfortunately, she is also less able to keep order, to set up the teacher-dominant situation. So the newer teacher too begins to settle for the "tried and true." As Willard Waller once noted: "Enthusiasm does not comport well with dignity."[15] It is a rare teacher who persists and succeeds in redefining the traditional order, since the experienced teacher who might have the skill to do this is usually too accustomed to the traditional ways to consider overthrowing them.

A second function of this identification with the class is that the solidarity of the teacher group tends to be weakened, sometimes providing one teacher with an ally in her competition with or jealousy of another teacher. We have seen that this became a problem at Adams with the introduction of departmentalization. It also occurred, however, even among teachers who, teaching different grades with a lot of individual insulation and autonomy, still used the class to jockey and dispute with other teachers. The continual territorial disputes on the playground illustrate the teacher's concern for her class's rights and her hostility to other teachers who might threaten these rights. Mr. Hanson, the principal, had to appoint a neutral teacher's committee to divide the playground into rigid zones in order to mitigate the conflict between the second and the fourth grade teachers. A dispute between the fourth and the sixth grade teachers as to who had the right to the baseball field at noontime led finally to a name-calling contest, avidly enjoyed by all the pupils in both classes.

A third function of identification seems a response to the isolation of the teacher from her peers during the school day and the desire she has for approval and love. The importance of this third function is greatest in the primary grades where there is some internal definition of the teacher's role as that of mother substitute. In upper grades the teacher more often fluctuates between seeking love and retreating from it for the sake of her dignity and acceptance of the standards of universalism and affective neutrality.[16]

A fourth function of identification is that it provides the teacher with a symbol, a way of representing her role to the outside world. Since much of her role is played out within the schoolroom, it is only her class's proclaimed achievements and perceivable department that represent to others her success or failure. At times, the teacher might prefer to reject the picture of herself provided by her class, but at other times, this picture provides her with the only measurable tokens of her success, at least her success in her expectations for producing docility and order.

Criticism of her class by others becomes criticism of her. She may know that her class needs to be reprimanded: "If they are bad, please feel free to punish them," but she resents it if any other teacher actually does this. Any interference, however graciously accepted, is soon followed by an unpleasant remark about the interfering teacher. And the interfering teacher is usually very careful to apologize for her interference: "I know it was your class and it wasn't my business, but since I was right there I spoke to them."

Like the traditional patriarchal father, the teacher holds discipline as her exclusive prerogative and resents all aspersions on her class. None of them could have chalked the obscene writing in the lavatory or broken the window. If the accusation is proved, however, the teacher's righteous anger with her class outstrips that of any outsider.

With the class as her symbol, each teacher attempts to procure benefits for it and resents seeming slights against her class as slights against herself. So she is alert not to get cheated out of any available supplies for "my class," protesting angrily that "she took the books that were obviously meant for third grade."

Through this symbolization the teacher may even begin to resemble her class.[17] Associating continually with a group of children and only occasionally with her peers, identifying her interests more and more with these children and standing with them against the world, she may begin to think and act as her pupils do. A first grade teacher regales her colleagues with first graders' jokes and expects them to be as delighted with these jokes as she obviously is. The fourth grade teacher fought for her pupils' playground space with all the vehemence of one of her fourth graders

defending his rights. A teacher who had taught in third grade for twenty years was never able to adjust her ways to a fifth grade class, where her "third grade" mannerisms (such as always referring to herself in the third person) led to delighted mimickry by her more sophisticated pupils.

Finally, identification may have the function for the teacher of augmenting the power and authority she has in teaching and molding her class. Manipulation through love and approval may provide the teacher in the unstable classroom situation with the leverage she needs for control, beyond that provided by her formally constituted status. As has been noted in various studies,[18] this may become a two-edged sword; the teacher may be able to manipulate pupil conformity, but at the same time she leaves the way open for pupil and class manipulation of her and of her expectations. This last function is put forth tentatively. My own data are not sufficient to do more than suggest it as having possible significance. I frequently found myself manipulated by my class. Whether other teachers were more impervious to this than I it is hard for me, from my own vantage point and isolation, to say.

It is not possible to push much further with the process and functions of identification on the basis of this one study. That it is an important aspect of the teacher's role-set is clear to me, and other kinds of studies might provide interesting and significant extensions of our understanding. In order to probe this subject further we need to search out innovative methods that can be used in studying the insides of the role-set, methods that would have the advantages derivable from participant observation and the case study, but that would be more widely generalizable and that could be used by investigators who do not have the time, inclination, or opportunity to immerse themselves within the role in order to study it.

Notes

[1] ". . . that complement of role relationships which persons have by virtue of occupying a particular social status." Robert K. Merton, *Social Theory and Social Structure* (New York: Free Press, 1963), p. 423.

[2] Gertrude H. McPherson, "The Role-Set of the Elementary School Teacher: A Case Study" (New York: Columbia University, 1966).

[3] Willard Waller, *The Sociology of Teaching* (New York: Wiley, 1965), ch. 18, "The Definition of the Situation."

[4] See Harry L. Gracey, "Learning the Student Role: Kindergarten As Academic Boot Camp," In *Readings in Introductory Sociology* ed. Dennis H. Wrong and Harry Gracey (New York: Macmillan, 1967), pp. 288–99.

[5] Redl and Wattenberg note the development of a distinctive personality in each school class. The group creates the conditions and then the individual members respond. Fritz Redl and William Wzttenberg, *Mental Hygiene in Teaching* (New York: Harcourt, Brace, 1951), p. 213.

[6] Waller, *op. cit.*, p. 162. "A class, as a crowd, develops a definite personality. . . . A sort of specialized and cumulative leadership grows up through the years of classroom association."

[7] *Ibid.*, p. 297.

[8] The term *identification* is used in a limited sense here; not as identification with a reference group, either comparative or normative, which involves seeking to approximate the behavior and values of the individual or group to which one aspires to belong (Merton, *op. cit.*, pp. 356–58). Nor is it used in the sense employed by some psychologists and sociologists, as assimilation of feelings, emotional absorption, living in and through others. See, for example, Gardner Murphy, Lois Murphy, and Theodore M. Newcomb, *Experimental Social Psychology* (New York: Harper, 1937), pp. 188–89, 208, 210; or Talcott Parsons and Edward Shils, ed., *Towards A General Theory of Action* (Cambridge: Harvard University Press, 1951), p. 308.

[9] George Homans, *The Human Group* (New York: Harcourt, Brace, 1950), pp. 244–47.

[10] *Ibid.*

[11] In this context, see the discussion and citation of research on the conflict endemic in the teacher role between the pressures for universalistic standards and affective neutrality and the pressures to be nurturant and particularistic, in Charles E. Bidwell, "The School As a Formal Organization," in *Handbook of Organizations* ed. James G. March (Chicago: Rand McNally, 1965), pp. 930–92.

[12] This is not the same as the distinction noted by Neal Gross, Ward Mason, and Alexander McEachern, *Explorations in Role Analysis: Studies of the School Superintendency Role* (New York: Wiley, 1958), pp. 58, 59, between role-expectations (normative) and role-anticipations (behavioral). Realistic role-expectations are normative, but they represent a scaling down of idealistic role-expectations in the face of behavioral deviation.

[13] Ferenc Merei, "Group Leadership and Institutionalization," *Human Relations*, 2 (1949), pp. 33–34.

[14] Erving Goffman, *The Presentation of Self in Everyday Life* (New York: Doubleday, Anchor Books, 1959), p. 201.

[15] Waller, *op. cit.*, p. 390.

[16] *Ibid.*, p. 252.

[17] *Ibid.*, p. 59. "If the teacher is to control understandingly it must be by the sacrifice of some of his own adulthood."

[18] Peter Blau and W. Richard Scott, *Formal Organizations* (San Francisco: Chandler, 1962) p. 142. See also Charles Bidwell, *op. cit.*, pp. 978–84, 990, for summary of studies dealing with this process.

INDUSTRIAL SOCIETY has spawned a peculiar phenomenon, most evident in America but emerging also in other Western societies: adolescent subcultures, with values and activities quite distinct from those of the adult society—subcultures whose members have most of their important associations within and few with adult society. Industrialization, and the rapidity of change itself, has taken out of the hands of the parent the task of training his child, made the parent's skills obsolescent, and put him out of touch with the times—unable to understand, much less inculcate, the standards of a social order which has changed since he was young.

By extending the period of training necessary for a child and by encompassing nearly the whole population, industrial society has made of high school a social system of adolescents. It includes, in the United States, almost all adolescents and more and more of the activities of the adolescent himself. A typical example is provided by an excerpt from a high-school newspaper in an upper-middle-class suburban school:

SOPHOMORE DANCING FEATURES CHA CHA

Sophomores, this is your chance to learn how to dance! The first day of sophomore dancing is Nov. 14 and it will begin at 8:30 A.M. in the Boys' Gym. . . .

No one is required to take dancing but it is highly recommended for both boys and girls. . . .

If you don't attend at this time except in case of absence from school, you may not attend at any other time. Absence excuses should be shown to Miss —— or Mr. —— .

In effect, then, what our society has done is to set apart, in an institution of their own, adolescents for whom home is little more than a dormitory and whose world is made up of activities peculiar to their fellows. They have been given as well many of the instruments which can

The Adolescent Subculture and Academic Achievement

James S. Coleman

The research discussed in this paper was carried out under a grant from the United States Office of Education; a full report is contained in "Social Climates and Social Structures in High Schools," a report to the Office of Education. The paper was presented at the Fourth World Congress of Sociology, Milan, Italy, September, 1959.

Reprinted from the American Journal of Sociology, 65 (1960), pp. 337–47, by permission of the author and the publisher, The University of Chicago Press.

make them a functioning community: cars, freedom in dating, continual contact with the opposite sex, money, and entertainment, like popular music and movies, designed especially for them. The international spread of "rock-and-roll" and of so-called American patterns of adolescent behavior is a consequence, I would suggest, of these economic changes which have set adolescents off in a world of their own.

Yet the fact that such a subsystem has sprung up in society has not been systematically recognized in the organization of secondary education. The theory and practice of education remains focused on *individuals*; teachers exhort individuals to concentrate their energies in scholarly directions, while the community of adolescents diverts these energies into other channels. The premise of the present research is that, if educational goals are to be realized in modern society, a fundamentally different approach to secondary education is necessary. Adults are in control of the institutions they have established for secondary education; traditionally, these institutions have been used to mold children as individuals toward ends which adults dictate. The fundamental change which must occur is to shift the focus: to mold social communities as communities, so that the norms of the communities themselves reinforce educational goals rather than inhibit them, as is at present the case.

The research being reported is an attempt to examine the status systems of the adolescent communities in ten high schools and to see the effects of these status systems upon the individuals within them. The ten high schools are all in the Midwest. They include five schools in small towns (labeled *0–4* in the figures which follow), one in a working-class suburb (*6*), one in a well-to-do suburb (*9*), and three schools in cities of varying sizes (*5, 7,* and *8*). All but No. *5,* a Catholic boys' school, are coeducational, and all but it are public schools.

The intention was to study schools which had quite different status systems, but the similarities were far more striking than the differences. In a questionnaire all boys were asked: "How would you most like to be remembered in school: as an athletic star, a brilliant student, or most popular? The results of the responses for each school are shown in Figure 1,[1] where the left corner of the triangle represents 100 per cent saying "star athlete"; the top corner represents 100 per cent saying "brilliant student"; and the right corner represents 100 per cent saying "most popular." Each school is representedly a point whose location relative to the three corners shows the proportion giving each response.

The schools are remarkably grouped somewhat off-center, showing a greater tendency to star "star athlete" than either of the other choices. From each school's point is a broken arrow connecting the school as a whole with its members who were named by their fellows as being "members of the leading crowd." In almost every case, the leading crowd tends in the direction of the athlete—in all cases *away* from the ideal of the brilliant student. Again, for the leading crowds as well as for the students as a whole, the uniformity is remarkably great; not so great in the absolute positions of the leading crowds but in the direction they deviate from the student bodies.

This trend toward the ideal of the athletic star on the part of the leading crowds is due in part to the fact that the leading crowds include a great number of

Figure 1. Positions of schools and leading crowds in boys' relative choice of brilliant student, athletic star, and most popular.

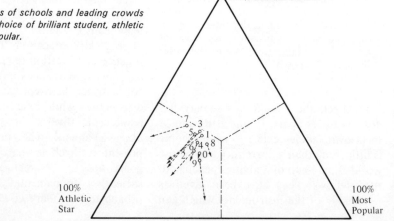

athletes. Boys were asked in a question-naire to name the best athlete in their grade, the best student, and the boy most popular with girls. In every school, without exception, the boys named as best athletes were named more often—on the average over twice as often—as members of the leading crowd than were those named as best students. Similarly, the boy most popular with girls was named as belonging to the leading crowd more often than the best student, though in all schools but the well-to-do suburb and the smallest rural town (schools 9 and 0 on Figure 1) less often than the best athlete.

These and other data indicate the importance of athletic achievement as an avenue for gaining status in the schools. Indeed, in the predominantly middle-class schools, it is by far the most effective achievement for gaining a working-class boy entrée into the leading crowd.

Similarly, each girl was asked how she would like to be remembered: as a brilliant student, a leader in extra-curricular activities, or most popular. The various schools are located on Figure 2, together with arrows connecting them to their leading crowd. The girls tend slightly less, on the average, than the boys to want to be remembered as brilliant students. Although the alternatives are different, and thus cannot be

directly compared, a great deal of other evidence indicates that the girls—although better students in every school—do not want to be considered "brilliant students." They have good reason not to, for the girl in each grade in each of the schools who was most often named as best student has fewer friends and is less often in the leading crowd than is the boy most often named as best student.

There is, however, diversity among the schools in the attractiveness of the images of "activities leader" and "popular girl" (Figure 2). In five (9, 0, 3, 8, and 1), the leader in activities is more often chosen as an ideal than is the popular girl; in four (7, 6, 2, and 4) the most popular girl is the more attractive of the two. These differences correspond somewhat to class background differences among the schools: 2, 4, 6, and 7, where the activities leader is least attractive, have the highest proportion of students with working-class backgrounds. School 9 is by far the most upper-middle-class one and by far the most activities-oriented.

The differences among the schools correspond as well to differences among the leading crowds: in schools 2, 4, and 6, where the girls as a whole are most oriented to being popular, the leading

Figure 2. Positions of schools and leading crowds in girls' relative choice of brilliant student, activities leader, and most popular.

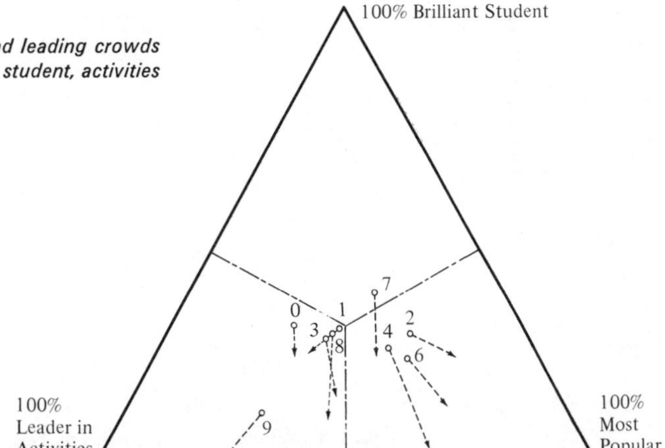

crowds are even more so; in the school where the girls are most oriented to the ideal of the activities leader, No. 9, the leading crowd goes even further in that direction.[2] In other words, it is as if a pull is exerted by the leading crowd, bringing the rest of the students toward one or the other of the polar extremes. In all cases, the leading crowd pulls away from the brilliant-student ideal.

Although these schools vary far less than one might wish when examining the effects of status systems, there are

differences. All students were asked in a questionnaire: "What does it take to get into the leading crowd?" On the basis of the answers, the relative importance of various activities can be determined. Consider only a single activity, academic achievement. Its importance for status among the adolescents in each school can be measured simply by the proportion of responses which specify "good grades," or "brains" as adolescents often put it, as a means of entrée into the leading crowd. In all the schools, academic achievement was of less importance than other matters, such as being an athletic star among the boys, being a

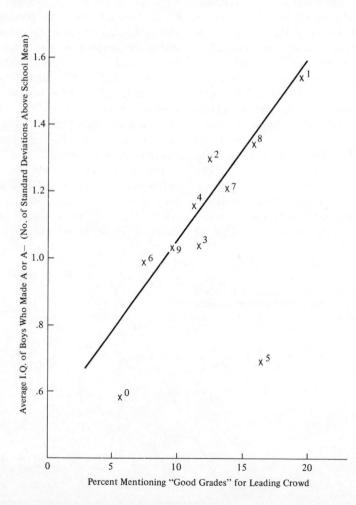

Figure 3. I.Q.'s of high achieving boys by importance of good grades among other boys.

cheerleader or being good-looking among the girls, or other attributes. Other measures which were obtained of the importance of academic achievement in the adolescent status system correlate highly with this one.[3]

If, then, it is true that the status system of adolescents *does* affect educational goals, those schools which differ in the importance of academic achievement in the adolescent status system should differ in numerous other ways which are directly related to educational goals. Only one of those, which illustrates well the differing pressures upon students in the various schools, will be reported here.

In every social context certain activities are highly rewarded, while others are not. Those activities which are rewarded are the activities for which there is strong competition—activities in which everyone with some ability will compete.—In such activities the persons who achieve most should be those with most potential ability. In contrast, in unrewarded activities, those who have most ability may not be motivated to compete; consequently, the persons who achieve most will be persons of lesser ability. Thus in a high

Figure 4. I.Q.'s of high achieving girls by importance of good grades among other girls.

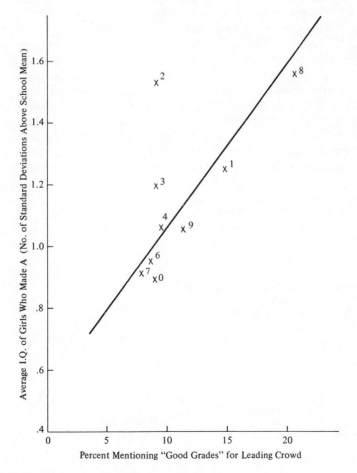

Percent Mentioning "Good Grades" for Leading Crowd

school where basketball is important, nearly every boy who might be a good basketball player will go out for the sport, and, as a result, basketball stars are likely to be the boys with the most ability. If in the same school volleyball does not bring the same status, few boys will go out for it, and those who end up as members of the team will not be the boys with most potential ability.

Similarly, with academic achievement: in a school where such achievement brings few social rewards, those who "go out" for scholarly achievement will be few. The high performers, those who receive good grades, will not be the boys whose ability is greatest but a more mediocre few. Thus the "intellectuals" of such a society, those defined by themselves and others as the best students, will not in fact be those with most intellectual ability. The latter, knowing where the social rewards lie, will be off cultivating other fields which bring social rewards.

To examine the effect of varying social pressures in the schools, academic achievement, as measured by grades in school, was related to I.Q. Since the I.Q. tests differ from school to school, and since each school had its own mean I.Q.

and its own variation around it, the ability of high performers (boys who made A or A—average)[4] was measured by the number of standard deviations of their average I.Q.'s above the mean. In this way, it is possible to see where the high performers' ability lay, relative to the distribution of abilities in their school.[5]

The variations were great: in a small-town school, No. *1*, the boys who made an A or A—average had I.Q.'s 1.53 standard deviations above the school average; in another small-town school, No. *0*, their I.Q.'s were only about a third this distance above the mean, .59. Given this variation, the question can be asked: Do these variations in ability of the high performers correspond to variations in the social rewards for, or constraints against, being a good student?

Figure 3 shows the relation for the boys between the social rewards for academic excellence (i.e., the frequency with which "good grades" was mentioned as a means for getting into the leading crowd) and the ability of the high performers, measured by the number of standard deviations their average I.Q.'s exceed that of the rest of the boys in the school. The relation is extremely strong. Only one school, a parochial boys' school in the city's slums, deviates. This is a school in which many boys had their most

Figure 5. Positions of schools and leading crowds in boys' relative choice of brilliant student, athletic star, and most popular (two private schools [10, 11] included).

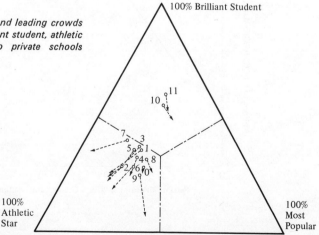

important associations outside the school rather than in it, so that its student body constituted far less of a social system, less able to dispense social rewards and punishments, than was true of the other schools.

Similarly, Figure 4 shows for the girls the I.Q.'s of the high performers.[6] Unfortunately, most of the schools are closely bunched in the degree to which good grades are important among the girls, so that there is too little variation among them to examine this effect as fully as would be desirable. School 2 is the one school whose girls deviate from the general relationship.

The effect of these values systems on the freedom for academic ability to express itself in high achievement is evident among the girls as it is among the boys. This is not merely due to the school facilities, social composition of the school, or other variables: the two schools highest in the importance of scholastic achievement for both boys and girls are *1* and *8*, the first a small-town school of 350 students and the second a city school of 2,000 students. In both there are fewer students with white-collar backgrounds than in schools *9* or *3*, which are somewhere in the middle as to value placed on academic achievement, but are more white-collar than in schools *7* or *4*, which are also somewhere in the middle. The highest expenditure per student was $695 per year in school *9*, and the lowest was little more than half that, in school *4*. These schools are close together on the graphs of Figures 3 and 4.

It should be mentioned in passing that an extensive unpublished study throughout Connecticut, using standard tests of achievement and ability, yielded consistent results. The study found no correlation between per pupil expenditure in a school and the achievement of its students relative to their ability. The effects shown in Figures 3 and 4 suggest why: that students with ability are led to achieve only when there are social rewards, primarily from their peers, for doing so—and these social rewards seem little correlated with per pupil expenditure.

So much for the effects as shown by the variation among schools. As mentioned earlier, the variation among schools was not nearly so striking in this research as the fact that, in all of them, academic achievement did not count for as much as other activities. In every school the boy named as best athlete and the boy named as most popular with girls was far more often mentioned as a member of the leading crowd, and as

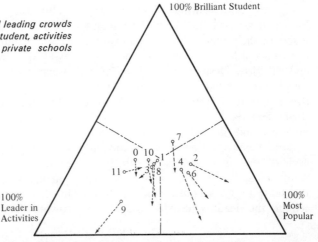

Figure 6. Positions of schools and leading crowds in girls' relative choice of brilliant student, activities leader, and most popular (two private schools [10, 11] included).

someone to "be like," than was the boy named as the best student. And the girl named as best dressed, and the one named as most popular with boys, as in every school far more often mentioned as being in the leading crowd and as someone "to be like," than was the girl named as the best student.

The relative unimportance of academic achievement, together with the effect shown earlier, suggests that these adolescent subcultures are generally deterrents to academic achievement. In other words, in these societies of adolescents those who come to be seen as the "intellectuals" and who come to think so of themselves are not really those of highest intelligence but are only the ones who are willing to work hard at a relatively unrewarded activity.

The implications for American society as a whole are clear. Because high schools allow the adolescent subcultures to divert energies into athletics, social activities, and the like, they recruit into adult intellectual activities people with a rather mediocre level of ability. In fact, the high school seems to do more than allow these subcultures to discourage academic achievement; it aids them in doing so. To indicate how it does and to indicate how it might do differently is another story, to be examined below.

Figures 1 and 2, which show the way boys and girls would like to be remembered in their high school, demonstrate a curious difference between the boys and the girls. Despite great variation in social background, in size of school (from 180 to 2,000), in size of town (from less than a thousand to over a million), and in style of life of their parents, the proportion of boys choosing each of the three images by which he wants to be remembered is very nearly the same in all schools. And in every school the leading crowd "pulls" in

similar directions: at least partly toward the ideal of the star athlete. Yet the ideals of the girls in these schools are far more dispersed, and the leading crowds "pull" in varying directions, far less uniformly than among the boys. Why such a diversity in the same schools?

The question can best be answered by indirection. In two schools apart from those in the research, the questionnaire was administered primarily to answer a puzzling question: Why was academic achievement of so little importance among the adolescents in school 9? Their parents were professionals and business executives, about 80 per cent were going to college (over twice as high a proportion as in any of the other schools), and yet academic excellence counted for little among them. In the two additional schools parental background was largely held constant, for they were private, coeducational day schools whose students had upper-middle-class backgrounds quite similar to those of school 9. One (No. 10) was in the city; the other (No. 11), in a suburban setting almost identical to that of No. 9. Although the two schools were added to the study to answer the question about school 9, they will be used to help answer the puzzle set earlier: that of the clustering of schools for the boys and their greater spread for the girls. When we look at the responses of adolescents in these two schools to the question as to how they would like to be remembered, the picture becomes even more puzzling (Figures 5 and 6). For the boys, they are extremely far from the cluster of the other schools; for the girls, they are intermingled with the other schools. Thus, though it was for the boys that the other schools clustered so closely, these two deviate sharply from the cluster; and for the girls, where the schools already varied, these two are not distinguishable. Furthermore, the leading crowds of boys in these schools do not pull the ideal toward the star-athlete ideal as do those in almost all the other schools. To be sure, they pull away from the idea of the brilliant student, but the pull is primarily toward a social image, the most popular. Among the girls, the leading crowds pull in different directions and are nearly indistinguishable from the other schools.

The answer to both puzzles, that is, first, the great cluster of the boys and now, in these two additional schools, the greater deviation, seems to lie in one fact: the boys' interscholastic athletics. The nine public schools are all engaged in interscholastic leagues which themselves are knit together in state tournaments. The other school of the first ten, the Catholic school, is in a parochial league, where games are just as hotly contested as in the public leagues and is also knit together with them in tournaments.

Schools *10* and *11* are athletically in a world apart from this. Although boys in both schools may go in for sports, and both schools have interscholastic games, the opponents are scattered private schools, constituting a league in name only. They take no part in state or city tournaments and have almost no publicity.

There is nothing for the girls comparable to the boys' interscholastic athletics. There are school activities of one sort or another, in which most girls take part, but no interscholastic games involving them. Their absence and the lack of leagues which knit all schools together in systematic competition means that the status system can "wander" freely, depending on local conditions in the school. In athletics, however, a school, and the community surrounding it, cannot hold its head up if it continues to lose games. It *must* devote roughly the same attention to athletics as do the schools surrounding it, for athletic games are the only games in which it engages other schools and, by representation, other communities.

These games are almost the only means a school has of generating internal cohesion and identification, for they constitute the only activity in which the school participates *as* a school. (This is well indicated by the fact that a number of students in school *10*, the private school which engages in no interscholastic games, has been concerned by a "lack of school spirit.") It is as a consequence of this that the athlete gains so much status: he is doing something for the school and the community, not only for himself, in leading his team to victory, for it is a school victory.

The outstanding student, in contrast, has little or no way to bring glory to his school. His victories are always purely personal, often at the expense of his classmates, who are forced to work harder to keep up with him. It is no wonder that his accomplishments gain little reward and are often met by ridiculing remarks, such as "curve-raiser" or "grind," terms of disapprobation which have no analogues in athletics.

These results are particularly intriguing, for they suggest ways in which rather straightforward social theory could be used in organizing the activities of high schools in such a way that their adolescent subcultures would encourage, rather than discourage, the channeling of energies into directions of learning. One might speculate on the possible effects of city-wide or state-wide "scholastic fairs" composed of academic games and tournaments between schools and school exhibits to be judged. It could be that the mere institution of such games would, just as do the state basketball tournaments in the midwestern United States, have a profound effect upon the educational climate in the participating schools. In fact, by an extension of this analysis, one would predict that an international fair of this sort, a "Scholastic Olympics," would generate interscholastic games and tournaments within the participating countries.

Notes

[1] I am grateful to James A. Davis and Jacob Feldman, of the University of Chicago, for suggesting such graphs for presenting responses to trichotomous items in a population.

[2] This result could logically be a statistical artifact because the leaders were included among students as a whole and thus would boost the result in the direction they tend. However, it is not a statistical artifact, for the leading crowds are a small part of the total student body. When they are taken out for computing the position of the rest of the girls in each school, schools 2, 4, 6, and 7 are still the most popularity-oriented, and school 9 the most activities-oriented.

[3] Parenthetically, it might be noted that these measures correlate on imperfectly with the proportion of boys or girls who want to be remembered as brilliant students. These responses depend on the relative attractiveness of other ideals, which varies from school to school, and upon other factors unrelated to the status system.

[4] In each school but 3 and 8, those making A and A— constituted from 6 to 8 per cent of the student body. In order to provide a correct test of the hypothesis, it is necessary to have the same fraction of the student body in each case (since I.Q.'s of this group are being measured in terms of number of standard deviations above the student body). To adjust these groups, enough 6's were added (each being assigned the average I.Q. of the total group of 6's) to bring the proportion up to 6 per cent (from 3 per cent in school 3, from 4 per cent in school 8).

[5] The I.Q. tests used in the different schools were: (0) California Mental Maturity (taken seventh, eighth, or ninth grade); (1) California Mental Maturity (taken eighth grade); (2) SRA Primary Mental abilities (taken tenth grade); (3) California Mental Maturity (taken ninth grade; seniors took SRA PMA, which was tabulated as a percentile, and they have been omitted from analysis reported above); (4) Otis (ninth and tenth grades; taken eighth grade); Kuhlman Finch (eleventh and twelfth grades, taken eighth grade); (5) Otis (taken ninth grade); (6) California Mental Maturity (taken eighth grade); (7) California Mental Maturity (taken eighth grade); (8) Otis (taken ninth or tenth grade); and (9) Otis (taken eighth grade).

[6] For the girls, only girls with a straight-A average were included. Since girls get better grades than boys, this device is necessary in order to make the sizes of the "high-performer" group roughly comparable for boys and for girls. Schools differed somewhat in the proportion of A's, constituting about 6 per cent of the students in the small schools, only about 3 per cent in schools 6 and 7, 1 per cent in 8, and 2 per cent in 9. In 8 and 9, enough girls were added and assigned the average grade of the 7 (A—) group to bring the proportion to 3 per cent, comparable with the other large schools. The difference, however, between the large and small schools was left.

IN CERTAIN situations an individual may find himself exposed to conflicting expectations: some people expect him to behave in one way, others in another, and these expectations are incompatible. How will individuals behave when faced with such conflicts? This is the problem with which our paper is concerned. Later we shall offer a theory of role-conflict resolution and present a test of its usefulness. Before doing this it is necessary to try, first, to clarify the meaning of role conflict and introduce definitions of the concepts we shall employ; second, to present the methods we used in a study of role conflicts of school superintendents; and third, to describe their behavior when they perceived their exposure to conflicting expectations.

Concepts

An examination of the literature concerned with "role conflict" reveals that this term has been given different meanings by different social scientists. Some have used it to denote incompatible expectation situations to which an actor is exposed, whether he is aware of the conflict or not. Other social scientists use "role conflict" to mean situations in which the actor *perceives* incompatible expectations. A foreman's subordinates and his boss may hold quite opposite expectations for his behavior but he may or may not be aware of this discrepancy. Some formulations of role conflict specify that the actor must be exposed to conflicting expectations that derive from the fact that he occupies two or more positions simultaneously. For example, a young man may occupy simultaneously the positions of son and a member of a fraternity, and his father and his fraternity brothers may hold contradictory expectations for his "drinking behavior." Other formulations include in role conflict those contradictory expectations that derive from an

Role Conflict and Its Resolution

Neal Gross,
Alexander W. McEachern,
and Ward S. Mason

The article represents a condensed and simplified version of the analysis of role conflict which may be found in Neal Gross, Ward S. Mason, and Alexander McEachern, Explorations in Role Analysis: Studies of the School Superintendency Role (*New York: Wiley, 1957*). *For a more detailed treatment of the problems considered in this paper and a critical appraisal of the theory presented, the reader is referred to chs. 15, 16, and 17 of* Explorations.

From Readings in Social Psychology, 3rd edition, *edited by E. E. Maccoby T. M. Newcomb and E. L. Hartley pp. 447–59. Copyright 1947, 1952,* © *1958 by Holt Rinehart and Winston, Inc. Reprinted by permission of Holt, Rinehart and Winston, Inc.*

actor's occupancy of a single position. A professor may be expected to behave in one way by his students, in another way by his dean.

Some writers limit role conflict to situations in which an actor is exposed to conflicting *legitimate* expectations or "obligations" whereas others do not make this restriction.

In view of these differences it is necessary to specify the way we defined and limited our problem. First, our interest was in role conflicts which were *perceived* by the individuals subject to them. Second, we were concerned with incompatible expectations resulting from an actor's occupancy of single as well as of multiple positions; *intra-role* as well as *inter-role* conflicts were within the focus of inquiry. Third, the analysis was not restricted to incompatible expectations which were perceived as legitimate.

Attention was directed to situations involving both legitimate and illegitimate incompatible expectations.

Limiting the problem in this way the following definitions of basic concepts were used. A *role congruency* is a situation in which an actor as the incumbent of one or more positions perceives that the same or highly similar expectations are held for him. A school superintendent who perceived that his teachers, principals, students, and school board all expected him to handle a discipline problem in the same way would be confronted with a role congruency.

There are situations, however, in which an actor perceives that he is exposed to expectations which are incompatible. A school superintendent may think teachers and parents hold conflicting expectations for his behavior in dealing with a truant child. Any situation in which the incumbent of a position perceives that he is confronted with incompatible expectations will be called a *role conflict*.

The person for whom an expectation is held may consider it to be *legitimate* or *illegitimate*. A legitimate expectation is one which the incumbent of a position feels others have a right to hold. An illegitimate expectation is one which he does not feel others have a right to hold. An expectation which is felt to be legitimate will be called a *perceived obligation*. One which is felt to be illegitimate will be called a *perceived pressure*.

A *sanction* is either a reward or a punishment, conditional on how an individual behaves. For our analysis we will not be concerned with negative sanctions, nor will we be concerned with *actual* sanctions, but rather with an individual's *perceptions* of the sanctions others may apply to him. Whether or not the perceived and actual sanctions are the same in any given situation is an

empirical problem which will not be relevant to these analyses.

Methodology

One hundred and five school superintendents were included in the study. They represented a 48 percent stratified random sample of all school superintendents in Massachusetts in 1952–1953. The data to be reported were obtained from each of these superintendents in the course of an eight-hour interview conducted in the staff research offices.

After considerable experimentation with various methods of isolating the role conflicts to which superintendents were exposed, the following procedure was developed. Four situations were presented to the superintendent, each involving problems with which all superintendents must deal and which, on the basis of the pretests, were judged likely to arouse incompatible expectations. They concerned (1) the hiring and promotion of teachers, (2) the superintendent's allocation of his after-office hours, (3) salary increases for teachers, and (4) the priority the superintendent gives financial or educational needs in drawing up the school budget. For each situation we offered three alternative expectations that incumbents of relevant counterpositions might hold. For example, in the situation which is concerned with teachers' salaries these three expectations were described:

A. Expect me to recommend the highest possible salary increases for teachers so that their incomes are commensurate with their professional responsibilities.

B. Expect me to recommend the lowest possible salary increases for teachers.

C. Have no expectations one way or another.

Eighteen potentially relevant groups or individuals were then listed, and each of the superintendents was asked to indicate which of the three statements most nearly represented what each of the groups or individuals expected the superintendent to do in the situation. If he said that one or more individuals held expectation A and one or more held expectation B, then he was reporting incompatible expectations from incumbents of positions counter to his own.

In addition, the superintendents were asked whether or not they felt that the expectations they said others held were "legitimate." Furthermore, if incompatible expectations were perceived by the superintendent, the interviewer probed with open-end questions to discover how much anxiety was thus created, how the conflict was resolved, and what sanctions the superintendent thought would result from selecting one or the other of the incompatible alternatives.

An example of a city superintendent's responses to the role conflict instrument

Table 1—A Sample Questionnaire

Three Attitudes of Various Groups and Individuals Which One Superintendent Perceived in His Community

	A	B	C		A	B	C
1. Politicians		×		11. Service clubs	×	×	
2. Church or religious groups		×		12. Fraternal organizations			×
3. Farm organizations			×	13. Veterans organizations			×
4. Business or commercial organizations			×	14. Individual school-committee members	×	×	
5. Labor unions	×			15. Town finance committee		×	
6. Parents (PTA)	×	×		16. My wife, family	×		
7. Teachers	×			17. Chamber of commerce			×
8. Personal friends	×	×		18. The press		×	
9. Taxpayers' association		×		19. Other			
10. Individuals influential for economic reasons		×					

DIRECTIONS: For each group or individual listed above please check the box which most nearly represents what they think you should do about this:

A. Expect me to recommend the *highest* salary increases possible for teachers so that their incomes are commensurate with their professional responsibilities.

B. Expect me to recommend the *lowest* possible salary increases for teachers.

C. Have no expectations one way or another.

illustrates the exact method of securing the data for this analysis. Table 1 summarizes the responses of this superintendent to the question of which groups or individuals held which expectations for him with respect to salary increases for teachers.

It is clear that he perceived incompatible expectations. He perceived that labor unions, the Parent-Teacher Association (PTA) and parent groups, some teachers, some of his personal friends, some service clubs, some of the school-board members, and his family expect him to recommend the highest possible salary increases. A number of other groups and individuals hold the contrary expectation; these are politicians, religious groups, some parents, some personal friends, taxpayers' association, economic influentials, service clubs, some school-board members, the town finance committee and the press.

In four cases some members of a given category held one expectation, according to the superintendent, while others in the same category held the contrary expectation. School-board members, parents, personal friends, and service clubs were all described by the superintendent in this way.

The Incidence and Resolution of Role Conflict

In view of space limitations it is necessary to limit consideration of the incidence and resolution of role conflict to only one of the four situations studied. The teacher-salary issue will be used. An examination of this potential area of role conflict will serve as a background to the theory of role-conflict resolution and yield part of the data with which one test of it can be made.

That the teacher-salary issue is a fertile source of role conflict is clear from the fact that 88 percent of the superintendents perceived that they were exposed to conflicting expectations in this area. Table 2 reports the proportions of superintendents who perceived that incumbents of each of the listed counterpositions held: (1) the expectation that he recommend the highest salary increases possible; (2) the expectation that he recommend the lowest salary increases possible; (3) mixed expectations (that is, some held the A and others the B expectation); (4) no expectations regarding this issue.

Whereas 99 percent of the superintendents perceived that their teachers expected them to recommend the highest salary increases possible, 75 per cent of those with taxpayers' associations in their communities reported that these associations held the opposite expectation (column 2). Similarly a majority of the superintendents said that their town finance committee or city council and local politicians expected them to minimize salary increases for teachers. In addition to reporting that their teachers expected them to recommend the highest possible salary increases, a majority of the superintendents reported that labor organizations, parents and the PTA, personal friends, individual school-board members, and their wives held the same expectation. Relatively few superintendents, however, are confronted with the "mixed" expectation from members of the same group or category, school-board members obtaining the highest percentage (14 percent in column 3) and town finance-committee members the next highest (12 percent in column 3).

From these data it is possible to conclude not only that superintendents are frequently confronted with role conflicts with respect to their teacher salary recommendations, but also that these conflicts may stem from different groups and individuals or from groups and individuals of the same kind. For the 88 percent of the superintendents who perceived that they were exposed to incompatible expectations, there is clearly a problem which must be resolved. How do superintendents act when they perceive that some groups or individuals expect them to behave in a contradictory manner?

When a superintendent had indicated that he was exposed to incompatible expectations, he was asked how he resolved the dilemma implied by this condition. Of the 92 superintendents (88 percent) who were exposed to role conflict in this situation (13 were not), seven gave insufficient information to permit coding their behavior, 54 conformed to the expectation of recommending the highest possible salary increases (64 percent of the 85 who told us what they did), eight recommended the lowest possible

increases (9 percent of 85), and 23 (27 percent of 85) adopted some kind of strategy which did not require them to make an unequivocal choice between the two incompatible alternatives. Before we turn to an effort to predict which people will resolve the conflict in which way, let us examine briefly the different resolution techniques of those 23 superintendents who did not make a definite choice but developed a procedure whereby they could to some degree satisfy (18 or 21 percent) or ignore (5 or 6 percent) both demands.

One of the five superintendents who ignored both demands was not yet on

Table 2—Percentage of Superintendents Who Perceived Particular Expectations from Specified Groups and Individuals with Respect to Their Salary Recommendations

Group or individual	A High salary expectation (percent)	B. Low salary expectation (percent)	C. Mixed expectation (percent)	D. No. expectation (percent)	N*
1. Politicians	14	51	6	29	105
2. Church or religious groups	34	6	3	57	104
3. Farm organizations	12	17	2	69	62
4. Business or commercial organizations	15	34	4	47	105
5. Labor unions	63	2	2	33	53
6. Parents (PTA)	78	1	9	12	105
7. Teachers	99	0	1	0	105
8. Personal friends	57	1	5	37	105
9. Taxpayers' association	9	77	4	11	61
10. Individuals influential for economic reasons	11	45	7	37	105
11. Service clubs	35	7	7	50	87
12. Fraternal organizations	19	3	3	74	93
13. Veterans' organizations	27	5	4	64	104
14. Individual school- committee members	70	14	14	2	105
15. Town finance committee or city council	18	60	11	10	103
16. My wife, family	71	0	0	29	103
17. Chamber of commerce	20	27	7	47	65
18. The Press	28	25	2	45	88

*When N is less than 105 it is usually because the group or individual did not exist in a number of communities; the "no answers" when the group or individual did exist are also excluded.

tenure and perceived that his school board members, the town finance committee, the taxpayers' association, and individuals who were economically influential all expected him to recommend the lowest possible salary increases, whereas his teachers held the contrary expectation. He described his situation in this way:

I put it all in the hands of the school committee. It's a hot potato so I let the school committee handle it. The teachers feel I should represent them; the school committee feels I should represent them: I'd hang myself by getting involved. But I go along with the school committee recommendation one hundred percent, whatever they decide.

Four of the 18 superintendents who compromised assumed the position of negotiator when confronted with this dilemma. They apparently worked on the assumption that, although the expectations they face conflict, it is their duty to negotiate "a settlement" that will be most satisfactory to everyone. One superintendent perceived that his teachers, the school board, and the PTA expected him to recommend high salary increases to hold and attract competent personnel, while the town finance committee and taxpayers' association expected him to recommend the lowest increases, because they felt that the town was approaching a financial crisis. This superintendent says: "I use the salesman's technique. I tell the town, 'You don't want cheap teachers if you want a good school system.' I tell the teachers they have to be reasonable, that there has to be a compromise . . . if I completely agreed with the teachers, I'd be out of a job."

Three of the superintendents who compromised rejected both sets of expectations and substituted a new criterion in making their recommendations. They took the position that since they could not fully conform to both sets of expectations they try to develop a defensible rationale for their recommendations which is independent of the incompatible expectations of others. One of the superintendents recommended that the salary increases be contingent on a cost of living index. The others recommended an increase that would keep their school system in a competitive position with those of comparable size and wealth. One superintendent said he tried ". . . to do what's fair in light of what other communities are doing. I don't want my teachers to be at a disadvantage, but neither do I want our system to be a leader in the salaries we pay."

Ten of the 18 superintendents who compromised resolved the salary dilemma by trying to modify the conflicting expectations of one group so that they more nearly approximated the expectations of other groups. This technique differs from that of the superintendents who tried to adopt the position of negotiator, in that no attempt was made by these ten to modify both sets of expectations, and additionally, once one group's expectation had been modified, the superintendents gave their clear support to it. One superintendent told his teachers that if they gave him ". . . a reasonable request, I'll fight for it. If it's unreasonable, I won't. Then I tell them what I think is reasonable according to the town's ability to pay. . . . It's the realistic way to support the profession."

The remaining superintendent who compromised combined several of the previously described strategies. His primary objective was to obtain the maximum salary increases possible. According to his assessment, however, the way to do this was a little at a time. This superintendent said that he worked on this principle: "He who fights and runs away, lives to fight another day." He went on to say that ". . . it's a give and take matter. If your goal isn't damned you haven't lost. I have friends operating for better salaries for teachers who are on the town finance committee. This is the effective way to get results over time, if done consistently. You have to make compromises, and get part of what you want one year, and part the next. You can't move too fast. The idea is to make steady progress."

The above excerpts from interviews have illustrated strategies of compromise or avoidance. We saw earlier that while some superintendents compromised, others made a clear choice between the two kinds of behavior expected of them. What determines the choice an individual will make in resolving role conflict?

The Theory

The starting point for this theory of role-conflict resolution is the actor's definition of the situation. We assume that actors will have perceptions of whether or not the expectations to which they are exposed are legitimate. Furthermore, we assume that they will have perceptions of the sanctions to which they would be exposed if they did not conform to each of the expectations. In addition, we assume that individuals may be differentiated into three types according to whether they are primarily oriented toward legitimacy or sanctions in making decisions.

The first type characterizes the person who, when faced with a role conflict, gives most weight to the legitimacy of expectations. His definition of the situations places stress on *the right* of others to hold their expectations and de-emphasizes the sanctions he thinks will be applied to him for nonconformity to them. We shall say such a person has a *moral* orientation to expectations. He will be predisposed to behave in a role-conflict situation in such a way that he can fulfill legitimate expectations and reject illegitimate ones. If one of the incompatible expectations is viewed as

legitimate and the other is not, he will be predisposed to conform to the legitimate expectation, regardless of what sanctions are involved. If both are legitimate he will adopt a compromise behavior in order to conform, at least in part, to both of them. If both are perceived as illegitimate, he will be predisposed to conform to neither of them and will adopt in consequence some type of avoidance behavior. In short, for an individual with a moral orientation to expectations we will ignore his perceptions of the probable sanctions in making predictions about his behavior. From his definition of the legitimacy of the expectations we can make predictions about his behavior, and in Table 3 these predictions are specified.

The second type of orientation to expectations may be called *expedient*. An individual who has this orientation is one who gives priority to the sanctions others will bring to bear if he does not conform to their expectations. Such a person, we will assume, will act so as to minimize the negative sanctions involved in the role-conflict situation. He will try to provide the best defense for himself in view of the relative severity of the sanctions he feels others will apply to him for nonconformity to their expectations. Whether others have a right to hold certain expectations is irrelevant or of secondary importance to him. When he perceives strong sanctions for nonconformity to one expectation and weaker sanctions for nonconformity to the other, he will conform to the expectation which would result in the stronger sanctions for nonconformity. If he perceives that equally strong sanctions result from both, he will compromise in order to minimize sanctions. If he perceives no sanctions for nonconformity to either of the expectations, then the sanctions dimension will be of no value as a predictor of his behavior. Under this condition the other factor in the model, the

Table 3—Predicted and Actual Behaviors of Moralists in 16 Types of Role Conflict

	Types of role conflict				Predicted Behavior*	Number of Moral Superintendents Exposed to Each Type of Conflict	Frequency of Actual Behavior	Proportion of Correct Predictions
	SUPERINTENDENT'S PERCEPTION OF:							
	EXPECTATION A		EXPECTATION B					
	Is it legitimate?	Sanctions for nonconformity	Is it legitimate?	Sanctions for nonconformity?				
1.	Yes	Yes	Yes	Yes	c	2	c = 2	2/2
2.	Yes	No	Yes	Yes	c	1	c = 1	1/1
3.	Yes	Yes	Yes	No	c	0	—	—
4.	Yes	No	Yes	No	c	0	—	—
5.	Yes	Yes	No	Yes	a	4	a = 3; c = 1	3/4
6.	Yes	No	No	Yes	a	4	a = 4	4/4
7.	Yes	Yes	No	No	a	7	a = 7	7/7
8.	Yes	No	No	No	a	1	a = 1	1/1
9.	No	Yes	Yes	Yes	b	0	—	—
10.	No	No	Yes	Yes	b	0	—	—
11.	No	Yes	Yes	No	b	0	—	—
12.	No	No	Yes	No	b	0	—	—
13.	No	Yes	No	Yes	d	0	—	—
14.	No	No	No	Yes	d	0	—	—
15.	No.	Yes	No	No	d	0	—	—
16.	No	No	No	No	d	0	—	—
					Total:	19		18/19 (.95)

*The abbreviations used in this column are as follows: a = conformity to expectation A, b = conformity to expectation B, c = compromise, and d = avoidance.

legitimacy dimension, would be the only basis for predicting his behavior. In Table 4 the predictions for expedients are specified.

A third type of orientation to expectations will be called *moral-expedient*. A person who has this orientation does not give primacy to either the legitimacy or sanctions dimensions but takes both relatively equally into account and behaves in accordance with the perceived "net balance." For some role-conflict situations the decisions of an individual with a moral-expedient orientation are relatively simple since both the legitimacy and sanctions elements lead him to the same behavior. If, for example, expectation A is perceived as legitimate and expectation B illegitimate and if he perceives greater sanctions for nonconformity to expectation A than for nonconformity to B, he will conform to expectation A. In general, if the legitimacy dimension leads him to the same behavior indicated by the sanctions dimension, no problem exists for him. Either criterion leads him to the same behavior.

By comparing Tables 3 and 4 and observing which types of role conflict lead moralists and expedients to the same behavior we can easily isolate all the non-problematic situations for the moral-expedients.

What is required as a basis for predicting his behavior in the remaining types of role conflict? A person with a moral-expedient orientation is one who takes both the legitimacy and sanctions dimensions into account and is predisposed to adopt a behavior that emerges from a balancing of these two dimensions. Thus, if expectations A and B are both viewed as legitimate but he perceives greater negative sanctions for nonconformity to A than to B, he will conform to expectation A. Weighing the two dimensions would result in clear-cut resolutions of the role conflict in types 2, 3, 5, 9, 14, and 15 of Table 5. In each of these instances on the basis of the sanctions and legitimacy dimensions there are two predis-

positions to one of the behaviors and only one to the other.

How would a moral-expedient behave when the sanctions and legitimacy dimensions lead him to conform to opposite expectations, as in types 6 and 11? In type 6, the legitimacy dimension would require conformity to expectation A, but the sanctions dimension would lead to conformity to expectation B. Since the actor is a moral-expedient he will try to do both or compromise because this seems to be the best balancing of the two dimensions when they lead to opposite behaviors; he is predisposed to do A on the basis of legitimacy and B on the basis of sanctions, and is, therefore, predisposed to both A and B, or to a compromise of the two.

We are left with one additional type in Table 5, type 13. In this case neither of the expectations is viewed as legitimate but nonconformity to both is perceived as leading to strong negative sanctions. The legitimacy dimension leads him to an avoidance behavior and the sanctions dimension suggests a compromise. It seems clear that he will not conform to expectation A or to B. To minimize sanctions he would compromise or try to conform to both A and B, and to emphasize legitimacy he would avoid or fail to conform to both A and B. It is clear that an avoidance reaction does not conform at all to either A or B; but it seems equally clear that a compromise fails to conform in part to both A and B and, therefore, is partially an avoidance. Consequently, the most probable resolution of situations of this kind by moral-expedients would be a compromise, which in part avoids and in part conforms to both expectations.

In Table 5 the predictions made on the basis of legitimacy and sanctions for "moral-expedients" are specified. Tables 3, 4, and 5 together describe all of the predictions made on the basis of the theory.

Table 4—Predicted and Actual Behaviors of Expedients in 16 Types of Role Conflict

Types of role conflict

	SUPERINTENDENT'S PERCEPTION OF: EXPECTATION A		EXPECTATION B		Predicted Behavior*	Number of Expedient Superintendents Exposed to Each Type of Conflict	Frequency of Actual Behavior	Proportion of Correct Predictions
	Is it legitimate?	Sanctions for nonconformity	Is it legitimate?	Sanctions for nonconformity?				
1.	Yes	Yes	Yes	Yes	c	3	c=1; d=2	1/3
2.	Yes	No	Yes	Yes	b	2	b=2	2/2
3.	Yes	Yes	Yes	No	a	2	a=2	2/2
4.	Yes	No	Yes	No	c	0	—	—
5.	Yes	Yes	No	Yes	c	3	c=3	3/3
6.	Yes	No	No	Yes	b	4	b=4	4/4
7.	Yes	Yes	No	No	a	7	a=7	7/7
8.	Yes	No	No	No	a	0	—	—
9.	No	Yes	Yes	Yes	c	0	—	—
10.	No	No	Yes	Yes	b	0	—	—
11.	No	Yes	Yes	No	a	0	—	—
12.	No	No	Yes	No	a	0	—	—
13.	No	Yes	No	Yes	c	1	c=1	1/1
14.	No	No	No	Yes	b	0	—	—
15.	No	Yes	No	No	a	1	a=1	1/1
16.	No	No	No	No	d	0	—	—
					Total	23		21/23(.91)

*The abbreviations used in this column are as follows: a = conformity to expectation A, b = conformity to expectation B, c = compromise, and d = avoidance.

If the superintendent's responses to the salary instrument revealed that contradictory expectations were held for his behavior, we designated the situation as a role conflict. On the basis of his answers to the interview questions, each of the superintendents was then coded on (1) his perception of the legitimacy or illegitimacy of the expectations, (2) the perceived sanctions for noncompliance with each expectation, and (3) how he resolved the role conflict.

The remaining element of the theory that requires consideration is the superintendent's orientation to expectations, that is, whether he was a moralist, expedient or moral-expedient. The superintendent's responses to another and completely independent instrument provided the data used for this categorization. Each item in this instrument refers to expectations that could be applied to a superintendent. For the 37 items in this instrument, he was asked: "As a school superintendent, what obligation do you feel that you have to do or not to do the following things?" The response categories were: absolutely must; preferably should; may or may not; preferably should not; absolutely must not.

We reasoned that a person who would typically react to expectations in terms of "it depends" is one who possesses an *expedient* orientation to expectations. In operational terms he would respond to the expectation items with the "preferably should," "preferably should not," or "may or may not" response categories.

On the other hand, a person whose typical response is not a contingent one but is in terms of "absolutely must" or "absolutely must not" carry out expectations is one who is primarily oriented toward their rectitude. He does not think in terms of factors in the situation that would lessen his obligations. Such a person would be predisposed "to honor" legitimate expectations regardless of the sanctions involved in the situation. Such a person would be a moralist.

One who shows no "typical" response to expectations but vacillates between the conditional and mandatory categories in his reactions to expectations would possess the characteristic required for the moral-expedient orientation. This lack of consistency in orientation to expectations suggests that he is the type of person who would tend to take *both* the sanctions and legitimacy dimensions into account in reacting to perceived expectations.

This line of reasoning led to the following procedure. Each superintendent was given a score of 1 for each item in this instrument for which he gave a mandatory response (absolutely must, or absolutely must not). This provided a range of scores from 1 through 30 for the 37 items in the instrument. The estimated reliability of these scores is .884. These scores were then split into the following three categories: 1–9, 10–18, and 19–30. On the reasoning outlined above those superintendents who fell into the low mandatoriness group (1–9) were defined as expedients, those who fell into the high mandatoriness group (19–30) were considered moralists, and those who fell in the middle category (10–18) were categorized as moral-expedients.

A Test of the Theory

If we accept each of these operational indexes as adequately representing the variables and conditions described by the theory of role conflict resolution, we can use our data to perform an exploratory test of the theory. We have 48 possible "types" of situations. That is, the moralists, expedients, and moral-expedients can each be subdivided into four groups according to their judgments about the legitimacy of the expectations directed toward them (i.e., both expec-

Table 5—Predicted and Actual Behaviors of Moral-expedients in 16 Types of Role Conflict

	Types of role conflict				Predicted Behavior*	Number of Moral Expedient Superintendents Exposed to Each Type of Conflict	Frequency of Actual Behavior	Proportion of Correct Predictions
	SUPERINTENDENT'S PERCEPTION OF:							
	EXPECTATION A		EXPECTATION B					
	Is it legitimate?	Sanctions for nonconformity	Is it legitimate?	Sanctions for nonconformity?				
1.	Yes	Yes	Yes	Yes	c	6	c=5; d=1	5/6
2.	Yes	No	Yes	Yes	b	2	b=2	2/2
3.	Yes	Yes	Yes	No	a	6	a=6	6/6
4.	Yes	No	Yes	No	c	1	c=0; d=1	0/1
5.	Yes	Yes	No	Yes	a	4	a=3; c=1	3/4
6.	Yes	No	No	Yes	c	3	c=2; d=1	2/3
7.	Yes	Yes	No	No	a	20	a=19; c=1	19/20
8.	Yes	No	No	No	a	1	a=1	1/1
9.	No	Yes	Yes	Yes	b	0	—	—
10.	No	No	Yes	Yes	b	0	—	—
11.	No	Yes	Yes	No	c	0	—	—
12.	No	No	Yes	No	b	0	—	—
13.	No	Yes	No	Yes	c	0	—	—
14.	No	No	No	Yes	b	0	—	—
15.	No	Yes	No	No	a	0	—	—
16.	No	No	No	No	d	0	—	—
					Total:	43		38/43 (.88)

*The abbreviations used in this column are as follows: a = conformity to expectation A, b = conformity to expectation B, c = compromise, and d = avoidance.

tations legitimate; both illegitimate; A legitimate and B illegitimate, and A illegitimate and B legitimate). Each of the resulting 12 groups can be further subdivided into four categories according to whether the subject believed sanctions would be forthcoming for nonconformity to A, B, both, or neither.

By comparing the behavior predicted on the basis of the theory for each of these 48 types with the actual behavior of the superintendents who fell within these categories, we may say whether or not the theory has led in each case to the correct prediction.

As can be seen in Tables 3, 4, and 5 for 77 (91 percent) of the 85 role-conflict cases the theory led to the correct prediction. In order to test the theory it is necessary to ask whether the proportion of correct predictions obtained could have occurred by chance. To answer this question, the numbers of correct and of incorrect predictions were compared with the numbers expected on the basis of chance. Statistical details are presented elsewhere.[1] The theory led to significantly more correct predictions than would be expected by chance (at the .01 level). We are consequently led to the conclusion that the findings provide significant support for the theory in the teacher-salary role-conflict situation.

A review of the predictions made for moralists, moral-expedients, and expedients will reveal that for many of the types of role conflict the theory leads to exactly the same prediction no matter what the orientation of the individual involved. It is particularly interesting, therefore, to ask how well the theory does in the "difficult" cases. How well will the theory do in predicting the behavior in only those cases of role conflict where it makes a difference (according to the theory) what the orientation of the individual is? It would be inappropriate to apply a significance test to only those cases, but it is nevertheless revealing of the power of the theory to consider them separately.

Let us consider those cases for moralists and those for expedients in which the theory makes a prediction which differs from the one made in the case of the moral-expedient orientation. In types 2, 6, 11, 13, 14, and 15 of the moralist orientation and types 5, 6, 9, and 11 of the expedient orientation the theory leads to a prediction which differs from the one to which it leads for the moral-expedients. There were 12 school superintendents with either a moralist or expedient orientation who experienced role conflicts of these types. For how many of these did the theory lead to the correct prediction? For how many would the correct prediction have been made by assuming that their resolution of role conflict would be the same as that of moral-expedients? The answer is that in all 12 cases (as may be verified by reviewing the appropriate types of conflict in Tables 3 and 4) the theory led to the correct prediction, and in none of these cases would the correct prediction have been made on the basis of the assumption that these moral or expedient individuals resolved their conflicts in the same way as do moral-expedients.

In this paper we have not been able to consider a number of questions that the critical reader would ask about the theory. How does this theory differ from others? What accounts for the errors in the predictions? Have we ignored certain variables which affect the resolution of certain types of role-conflict situations? We have tried to consider these problems elsewhere.[2]

Notes

[1] See Neal Gross, Ward S. Mason, and Alexander McEachern, *Explorations in Role Analysis: Studies of the School Superintendency Role* (New York: Wiley, 1957).

[2] *Ibid.*

Part IV
Auxiliary Readings

Howard Becker. "The Teacher in the Authority System of the Public School." *Journal of Educational Sociology*, 27 (1953), pp. 128–41.

The teacher is portrayed as an individual who must attempt to maintain her sphere of legitimate authority in the face of threats from outside sources. The main source of challenge is parents, and the teacher depends on organizational resources such as the principal and on the seclusion of the classroom to maintain her authority. Teachers develop means of handling potential intrusions on their sphere of authority.

H. Otto Dalke. *Values in Culture and Classroom.* New York: Harper, 1958.

The theme of this work is that the values and norms of our culture are reflected in both the structure and content of the educational system. The relationships between cultural norms and the school are traced through the formal and informal organization of the school, the teaching profession, and school-community relations.

John C. Glidewell, Mildred B. Kantor, Louis M. Smith, and Lorene A. Stringer. "Socialization and Social Structure in the Classroom." In *Review of Child Development Research*, edited by Lois Wladis Hoffman and Martin L. Hoffman, vol. 2, pp. 221–56. New York: Russell Sage Foundation, 1966.

A comprehensive review of research on the social structure of the classroom is provided by the authors. The development, stability, and awareness of peer relationships are discussed by reference to numerous studies. The effects of a diffuse or centralized structure, of teacher power and background characteristics, and of personal and social attributes of pupils on social relations and mental health are covered.

C. Wayne Gordon. *The Social System of the High School.* New York: Free Press, 1957.

The major hypothesis of this book is that the social behavior of high school students is related to the positions which they occupy in the social structure of the school. It was found that the students' participation in the area of extra-curricular activities was most important in determining their status, while achievement in the formal, academic realm was least important. The network of inter-personal relations (measured by sociometric data) and the students' ascriptive characteristics were of moderate importance. Since the teachers' criteria for judging student performance conflicts with the rewards of the students' society, teachers are often subjected to role strain. Teachers often resolve their role conflict by succumbing to the perspectives of informal groups of teachers and students and abandoning strictly achievement-oriented criteria for judgments of students' work.

Ellen Greenberger and Annemette Sørensen. "Interpersonal Choices Among a Junior High School Faculty." *Sociology of Education*, 44 (1971), pp. 198–216.

This report uses concepts from Blau to generate and test predictions about how individuals make choices to consult, respect, or like their colleagues. Choices were analyzed according to individual attributes and choice criterion. Sex is a significant determinant of whom teachers choose for advice about a classroom problem. Other determinants of choice are departmental affiliation, age, and organizational status. Teachers do not necessarily confer with peers whom they regard as outstanding teachers, but more often seek advice from those with whom they share certain attributes or who have higher organizational status.

Robert Rosenthal and Lenore Jacobson. *Pygmalion in the Classroom.* New York: Holt Rinehart and Winston, 1968.

The authors seek to test the hypothesis of the self-fulfilling prophecy in the classroom by informing teachers that a randomly selected sample of their students "showed a high potential for academic development." The IQ gains of these students are analyzed according to school track, minority group status, age, and sex.

Richard A. Schmuck. "Some Relations of Peer-liking Patterns in the Classroom to Pupil Attitudes and Achievement." *The School Review*, 71 (1966), pp. 337–59.

It is proposed that peer group conditions may substantially affect the pupil's self-concept and thereby his academic performance. High group affect in the classroom is associated with a less centralized sociometric structure; and pupils who are highly involved in the classroom have a more positive sense of self as the group structure moves from centralized to diffused. Highly involved pupils who are either actual or self-perceived outcasts utilize their abilities less, have a lower self-image, and dislike school more than their more popular peers.

Donald I. Warren. "Variations on the Theme of Primary Groups: Forms of Social Control within School Staffs." *Sociology of Education*, 43, 3, 1970; pp. 288–310.

Four mechanisms of social control are analyzed in relationship to a typology of school staffs which in several respects resemble primary groups. Mechanisms of selective recruitment and selective expulsion are used extensively by staffs whose members internalize and share values. The mechanism of socialization is important in a school staff with a heterogeneous membership when the members interact informally away from the work setting. Isolation is employed to punish deviants in a staff whose members interact frequently in the course of their work. Data from eighteen elementary schools in a large urban center are used to test hypotheses.

V

Teaching as an Occupation

Introduction

TO THE layman, an occupation is defined solely in terms of what its practitioners *do*. The doctor heals, the carpenter builds, the teacher teaches, and so on. But there are large, *socially patterned* differences among occupations which must be taken into account if we wish to understand their role in society and how their distinctive features affect *what* its practitioners do and *how* they do it.

In differentiating among occupations, it is useful to distinguish three major classes of sociological attributes: (1) the *social background* of practitioners, that is, the statuses (past or present) which the practitioners occupy apart from their occupational role; (2) the *social system* of the occupation itself (occupational socialization, role orientations, peer relationships, etc.); and (3) the *work setting* in which the occupation is typically pursued. The attributes in each of these categories influence those in each of the other categories. In short, social background, the social system of the occupation, and the work setting are interdependent domains, and a full understanding of their interdependencies is necessary to a complete sociological portrait of a field of work. In our discussion of the selections which follow, the content of each domain and their interconnections will become clearer.

W. W. Charters' survey of the social background of teaching furnishes a wealth of information about teachers' nonoccupational statuses. Thus, we learn that the modal category of teachers is composed of married, middle-aged females with a college education. Because of local recruitment practices, the racial and religious characteristics of teachers and their communities of origin seem fairly representative of American society as a whole. The social class origins of teachers are less clear-cut, since most studies of this topic have been highly localized (and also because many of the studies are out of date). What *is* apparent is wide variation in social class origins among different regions and communities. Further, there is evidence of background variation by field of teaching and level of assignment within the school. (Selectivity of teachers according to certain of these background factors has been shaped by historical trends in education, as pointed out by Dan Lortie in the selection that follows.)

Insofar as certain values, beliefs, and resources are associated with the background statuses mentioned above, the identification of these statuses and their possible effects on occupational performance are matters of great importance. Indeed, in addition to reporting the backgrounds of teachers, Charters reviews the evidence for an impact of *social class* on behaviors and values manifested in the classroom. But a second and equally important reason for understanding the external statuses of practitioners is their possible effect on the *social system* of the occupation —which brings us to the second major domain of sociological interest. The fact that teachers are predominantly female, for example, accounts partly for the inability of the occupation to develop the features that typify full-fledged professions. As Lortie notes, "To date the only occupations which have clearly achieved professional recognition have been male occupations. We have yet to see whether any occupation predominantly feminine in composition can or will achieve clear title to the honorific designation 'profession'. "

Lortie poses four "issues" for analysis of the social system of teaching which go beyond the impact of external statuses: how the individual relates to the market; the nature of knowledge and skill possessed by members of the occupation; the relation established to the polity; and the extent to which those performing similar activities influence the careers of members of the occupation. With respect to each of these issues, Lortie argues that elementary teaching diverges from the established professions in its "mode of resolution." Consequently, in Lortie's view, teachers have not developed a subculture which is capable of buttressing its claims to full professional status against the administrative authority of the school. This latter observation directs our attention to the third domain of occupational characteristics, namely, the *work setting*. But before considering the ways in which the organizational context influences occupational values and roles, it is important to examine another aspect of the social system of teaching: commitment to teaching as a long-term career.

Pursuing a line of analysis similar to Lortie's, Blanche Geer shows how commitment is undermined by the typical features of teaching as an occupational system. Specifically, Geer notes that the social system of reaching prevents the accumulation of "valuables" which might serve to sustain commitment to a teaching career when confronted with alternative activities, such as marriage or another job. Finally, Geer offers certain tenative proposals for changes in the occupational structure which might increase the commitment of teachers.

A third area of sociological interest focuses on the structure of the *work setting* and its effects on values and role performance. The selection by Henry J. Meyer et al. approaches the subject from a comparative perspective. Finding differences between the values held by social workers and by teachers, the authors hypothesize that it is the organizational context which accounts for these differences. Since the two occupations occupy the same social class position, the external status of social class is ruled out as an explanatory factor. Also, since both occupations may be characterized as "semi-professions," value differences cannot be attributed to the weak development of a professional subculture among teachers. But the authors are still confronted with the possibility that pre-service socialization might account for the observed differences, and therefore they attempt to show that the structural context of teaching has a decisive influence.

As mentioned earlier, the sociological character of an occupation cannot be satisfactorily comprehended without taking note of the interrelationships among the three major domains of occupational variables. The importance of this dictum is clearly demonstrated in the conflict between the professional value of *autonomy* held by many teachers (a feature of the occupation's social system) and the *bureaucratic* organization of schools (a feature of the work setting). The literature on formal organizations is rife with references to the conflict between professional and bureaucratic principles for organizing work. In particular, the professional values of autonomy and collegial control are presumably opposed to the bureaucratic principles of standardization and hierarchical authority. Since teaching is an incomplete profession, as discussed by Lortie and Geer, this conflict has not eventuated in widespread revolt against bureaucratic (and also lay) controls. But many teachers today *do* hold strong professional values, and for these individuals the conflict between professional and bureaucratic principles may lead to protest and even to rebellion. That professionalism provokes a militant stance vis-à-vis bureaucratic authorities in local school systems is suggested by research on the topic (see Ronald G. Corwin's article in Auxiliary Readings). On a larger scale, this conflict may have contributed to the growth of militant organizations of teachers in the past decade. Thus, it would be a mistake to assume that the present clamor for more power is restricted to traditional areas of unionization, i.e., bread and butter issues and security.

The specific policy domains in which the leaders of teachers' organizations in five cities desire more power are discussed by Alan Rosenthal in our final selection. The greater militancy of the unions as compared with the more traditional associations is clearly revealed by Rosenthal's data. Further, with regard to the core professional domain of "curriculum and instruction," it is noteworthy that the great majority of the union leaders in almost all of the locals desire greater power; and in about half of the locals the leaders want *at least* as much voice in the formulation of curricular and instructional policy as enjoyed by the local board or administration. While there is much variation among the teachers' organizations in the amount of power desired across the different policy domains, it is by now abundantly clear that a new militancy has arisen among the teachers of America and that much of this militancy reflects a desire for greater control over the educational process itself.

The selections included here are more illustrative than conclusive with regard to the three major domains of sociological interest in occupations. A full-scale portrait of teaching as an occupation awaits further research and theoretical formulation.

A WEALTH OF information is available to describe the American teacher in terms of his nónoccupational statuses, especially the more readily ascertainable statuses of age, sex, marital status, educational attainment, and the like. The U.S. Office of Education, the Research Division of the National Education Association, and the U.S. Bureau of the Census regularly publish population statistics for the teaching occupation. Data also have been assembled through the years in survey studies of the "social composition" or the "social and economic status" of teaching. Some of these surveys were specifically directed to the problem which concerns us here. Thus, the earliest studies of social composition were predicted on the belief that knowledge of the social origins and characteristics of teachers would illuminate teaching "efficiency" in the classroom; the same rationale underlies some surveys today. Many surveys of teacher characteristics and conditions, however, were motivated by other interests, especially the desire for information regarding teacher supply and demand. Discovery of the societal sources of teacher supply and of the social and economic circumstances in which teachers work is presumed to suggest ways in which more and better teachers may be attracted to and retained in the profession. Whatever the purpose of the surveys, the fund of data is large and, in some cases, highly dependable.

Social Composition and Social Class Background of Teachers

W. W. Charters, Jr.

Reprinted from "The Social Background of Teaching," in Handbook of Research on Teaching, edited by N. L. Gage (Chicago: Rand McNally, 1963), pp. 718–22 and 730–41, by permission of the American Educational Research Association.

Population Characteristics of Teachers

AGE, SEX, AND MARITAL STATUS

The modal American teacher, in the late 1950's, was a married woman between the ages of 46 and 55 years, representing approximately 19 per cent of the total occupational group (National Education Association, 1957). Teaching clearly draws heavily from the female population. Currently, slightly less than three-quarters of the teachers are women, a figure which has varied substantially during the past 100 years. Most teachers, both male and female, are married or previously married (the "old-maid school teacher" now represents only about 11 per cent of the teaching force), but the married woman in teaching is a recent phenomenon. In 1931, married women constituted less than one-fifth of the total teaching group. Today, male teachers are predominantly young, female teachers are middle-aged.

COMMUNITY ORIGINS

There is a persistent belief that teachers are drawn heavily from small towns and rural communities. L. A. and E. F. Cook (1950, pp. 438–39) argued strongly in this vein, citing data from Greenhoe's (1941) national survey just before World War II. Greenhoe reported that about one-half of the responding teachers had been born in areas with populations of 2,500 or less and had spent most of their life in such places. More recently, McGuire and White (1957) found that nearly three-quarters of the Texas teachers they studied had been born in communities of less than 20,000. Tabulations from a national sample of teaching population in 1957 (National Education Association, 1957) showed that 32 per cent of the teachers came from farm homes. An agrarian or small town background certainly is strongly represented in the present teaching group, but this group, with a median age of around 40 years, also represents an earlier generation when urbanization of our society was considerably less marked. Whether teacher recruits today are being drawn disproportionately from "provincial" backgrounds is an unanswered question. An inadequately controlled study of a group of Detroit teachers (Wattenberg, 1957b) suggests a changing pattern: Where 20 per cent of the teachers over 40 came from farm families, only 2 per cent of the younger teachers had a farm origin.

EDUCATIONAL ATTAINMENT

Whatever may be the American teacher's provincial origins, he has, with relatively few exceptions, been exposed to the liberalizing experience of four years of college education. In 1957, over three-quarters of all teachers held at least a bachelor's degree, and one-quarter of them a master's degree. Six out of every seven beginning teachers in the fall of 1954 were college graduates (National Education Association, 1956). The college graduate in teaching, like the married woman teacher, is a phenomenon of the last 20 or 30 years. In 1931 only one-third of the public school teachers had four years of college education (Evenden, Gamble, and Blue, 1933).

NATIVITY, RACE, AND RELIGION

Dependable national statistics regarding the nativity, the race, and the religious affiliation of public school teachers are less abundant, but it is probably safe to say that the overwhelming majority of American teachers are native-born, white, and Protestant. The 1950 census, for example, reported that Negro and other nonwhite races constituted less than 7 per cent of the teaching population (U.S. Department of Commerce, 1952).

Social Class Origin and Mobility

In the last 20 years, a growing interest in the relationship between social stratification and education, stimulated by the community research of W. Lloyd Warner and his colleagues, has resulted in a number of studies of the social class origins of teachers. "The overwhelming proportion of teachers in the grammar schools and high schools are middle-class, often lower-middle-class," Warner concluded in one of his commentaries on the subject (Warner, 1953, p. 176). He estimated that 94 per cent of American teachers were members of the middle class. This figure was based upon three intensive community studies—Yankee City in the East, Old City in the Deep South, and Hometown (Elmtown) in the Midwest. The detailed social class distributions of teachers in the three communities are shown in Table 1. Warner, Havighurst, and Loeb noted, with respect to the *differences* in social class distributions displayed in Table 1:

In the East and the South, where class lines have been established longer, the teachers are usually in the upper-middle class, and many of them have risen from lower-middle class families. In the Middle West and the West, the teachers are usually lower-middle class, and many of them have risen from lower-class families (Warner, Havighurst, and Loeb, 1944, p. 101).

Because conclusions based on these data have been so widely cited, they are worth considering more fully. First, it is apparent that Warner's data refer to the social class position *attained* by teachers, not their social class *origins*. With this in mind, a subsequent passage in the Warner, Havighurst, and Loeb volume raises the question of how the social class position of teachers was established:

The social position of teachers is indefinite. Their social participation is often limited to their own professional group. . . . The unmarried Hometown female teachers live together in groups of two to five, either boarding or renting apartments. Where social participation is used as the test of social status [as Warner does], the teachers are difficult to locate in the social structure, because they participate so little in the social life of the community (Warner, Havighurst, and Loeb, 1944, p. 103).

World War II, we question the wisdom of resting conclusions on such limited and dated studies.

Finally, the *particular* figure Warner offers for the proportion of middle-class teachers might well be questioned. While other research bears out the concentration of teachers in the middle class, the conclusion that nearly 19 out of 20 are so located may be misleading. Data on the occupation of teachers' fathers go back as early as 1911, and a number of surveys have been conducted subsequently.[1] In the early studies, the majority of teachers were found to come from families of farmers, an occupational group which falls largely outside the social stratification schemes of Warner and other students. Thus, Coffman (1911) reported that at the time of his study 52 per cent of the nation's teachers derived from farm families.

Table 1—Social Class Distribution of Teachers (White Teachers Only)

Class	Hometown (%)	Yankee City (%)	Old City (%)
Upper upper	0	2	2.5
Lower upper	0	1	2.5
Upper middle	26	76	72.5
Lower middle	72	21	20.0
Upper lower	2	0	2.5
Lower lower	0	0	0.0

SOURCE: Warner, Havighurst, and Loeb (1944, p. 101).

Second, Warner's conclusions are generalizations from three communities, none of them metropolitan. Only Yankee City, a town of 17,000 inhabitants, approximates a modern, industrialized city; Old City (13,000) and Hometown (6,000) are small, agrarian communities relatively untouched, at the time of the studies, by the sweep of urbanization and suburbanization in our society. In light of massive changes in the composition of the teaching population since

A substantial percentage of teachers with labor backgrounds is shown in many of the studies. Of Coffman's teachers, 26 per cent had fathers whom he classified as "artisans" and "laborers," and 22 per cent had fathers who were professionals, businessmen, and public officials (p. 74). Thirty years later, Greenhoe's (1941) national survey of teachers showed 18 per cent whose fathers were day-laborers. Of 198 Detroit teachers taking in-service training in mid-1950, 29 per cent had fathers in unskilled or semiskilled labor occupations, a proportion especially pronounced among the younger teachers in the group (Wattenberg, 1957b). While occupational classification is not strictly comparable to Warner's scheme for social class placement, Warner's distinction between the middle and lower social classes corresponds, by and large, to a distinction between the white-collar and blue-collar or manual worker. A study of Texas teachers offered data more closely comparable to the Warner classification: of 100 elementary and secondary school teachers sampled from in-service training programs, 18 per cent had their origins in lower-class families (exclusively the upper-lowers), 79 per cent in middle-class families (predominantly the lower-middles), and 3 per cent in upper-class families (McGuire and White, 1957).

Thus, to conclude that teaching is virtually monopolized by persons of middle-class origin is probably to overstate the case. It may hold in some locales, but available research suggests that there may be variation from one type of community or school system to another, and a number of the surveys of teacher origin going back to the early 1900's show that a small but significant proportion of teachers came from the working class. It would be no exaggeration to conclude that the teaching occupation draws heavily from the middle ranges of the American social class structure: the lowest and highest classes are under-represented in the profession.

As to the social class *mobility* of teachers, Warner frequently cites the generalization that teaching is an avenue for moving upward in the class structure and that large numbers of teachers are, indeed, upward mobile. The generalization is based principally on case studies of teachers which, of course, provide no evidence regarding the prevalence or frequency of upward mobility. But the one study directly examining teacher mobility does support the generalization; McGuire and White (1957) compared the social class positions attained by teachers and other school personnel (counselors and administrators) in Texas with the social class position of their parents and found that slightly over one-half of the sample of 150 had moved upward.

Summary and a Qualification

We have sought to describe the American teacher in terms of the societal statuses he occupies in addition to his occupational status. We find that American teachers may be characterized as predominantly college-educated, native-born, Protestant, white, middle-aged, married females of middle-class and possibly rural or small-town origin. The modal description is based upon the occupational group as it is currently constituted and does not necessarily represent the kinds of people now being recruited into teaching.

Such a characterization of the teaching population in America, however, is overdrawn. Not only does it discount variations from the norm, a danger inherent in any modal description, but in this case it hides the *systematic nature* of such variations. In particular, the detailed statistics often show remarkable differences in social composition between rural and urban school districts, between elementary and secondary schools (and, within the secondary school, among teaching fields), between Negro and white schools (where segregated), and among states or regions of the nation. When these dimensions are cross-classified with one another (yielding, for example, rural, white, elementary schools of New England or urban, white, elementary schools of the South), the differences in the social characteristics of teachers are of such magnitude as to suggest that the various "teaching situations" represent discrete occupational categories with social compositions shaped by distinct arrays of forces.[2]

In the school year of 1930–1931 (for which unusually comprehensive statistics are available), the median age of elementary school teachers in the open country schools of Connecticut was 23 years; in similar California schools it was 32 years, a nine-year difference (Evenden, Gamble, and Blue, 1933). Elementary school teachers in the large city schools of these two states were substantially older— 29 years old in Connecticut and 36 in California. Senior high school teachers (unspecified by community size) were older still—32 and 37 years, respectively. The same data showed even more dramatic variations in sex distribution. For example, the percentage of male teachers in elementary schools ranged from 2 per cent in New Hampshire, Connecticut, and Maine to a high of 41 per cent in Indiana.

Within the secondary school, differences among teaching fields may be equally impressive. Some fields, such as home economics and vocational agriculture, are clearly sex-typed, others less obviously so. Wattenberg (1957b) reported that his Detroit teachers with laboring class backgrounds principally supplied the fields of physical education, industrial education, home economics, and social studies, although his data do not make a strong case. Research on personal atributes of high school teachers, such as interest patterns, personality characteristics, values, and so on, supports the observation of differences among teaching fields (Lieberman, 1956, pp. 219–20; Ryans, 1960, pp. 322–27).

Besides variations among teaching situations, major changes in social composition have occurred over the years, possibly at different rates in different teaching situations. Within recent years, teaching has undergone a transformation

so great as to render obsolete many popular conceptions of the occupation. We have already alluded to a few of these. While the data are scanty, it is reasonably clear that the social forces shaping occupational composition have never been constant for any extended period in our history. The sex distribution is a case in point. The teacher in the colonial period and through the first half of the nineteenth century typically was a male, though this fact depended, as Elsbree (1939) carefully pointed out, upon region of the country and type of school. From the latter part of the nineteenth century until 1920, the proportion of males declined steadily to 14 per cent; since then it has climbed, with setbacks during war periods, to the present figure of 26 per cent.

Variations of these kinds should be viewed as evidence of phenomena to be understood, not hidden by modal descriptions. Fortunately, data on certain teacher characteristics are abundant in the files and reports of the Office of Education, the Research Division of the National Education Association, and the Bureau of the Census. Many national and local surveys reporting the "general status" of teachers are scattered through the professional literature, some of them dating back to 1905. Betts, Frazier, and Gamble (1933) provided an exhaustive bibliography of such studies covering the first two decades of this century. Conceivably, the very act of summarizing data on changes over the years in teacher characteristics in the various teaching situations would illuminate the nature of forces operating on the social composition of the teaching occupation. In turn, the variations in social composition offer an opportunity to examine and test the effects of these forces on the teaching-learning process. . . .

Value Orientations:
The Case of Social Class

Sociologists and anthropologists associated with Warner's theory of social stratification regard the social class strata as the most important set of subcultures in American society. In this view, the social class structure consists of a series of loosely formed groups larger than the friendship circle but smaller than the entire community and ordered on a scalar dimension of prestige.[3] Personal interaction tends to be limited between members of the different classes but relatively intense within class strata, a circumstance which favors the emergence of unique culture patterns and value systems within each class. A child born to a family within a particular stratum is acculturated by means of unique patterns of child training and then comes to internalize the appropriate value orientations. Nevertheless, personal movement from one stratum to the next is not uncommon in American society. Indeed, exponents of this theory of social class consider the aspiration to enhance one's social standing (or to maintain a favorable standing) as an extremely important human motivation. Movement from one stratum to another is never easy, and in some cases, for example, when the host stratum excludes those without a proper family lineage or those without white skin color, it is impossible. To be mobile, a person must acquire the value orientations, attitude, language habits, manners, and other cultural trappings appropriate to the host stratum, and this frequently requires him to renounce the values and way of life of the stratum from which he moves, running the risk, consequently, of alienating himself from his family and earlier friends.

In the view of the theorists, the school assumes a highly significant function in the stratification system of twentieth-century America (Warner, Havighurst, and Loeb, 1944). On the one hand, the school is one of the few remaining avenues of upward mobility from the lower to the middle classes or, within the middle class, from its lower to its higher reaches. Formal educational training is a *sine qua non* of membership in higher social strata. Not only is educational attainment itself a criterion for membership but it is a prerequisite for more "respectable" occupational or professional opportunities and higher or more secure incomes. Moreover, the theorists propose that the public school is a middle-class institution in the sense that it embodies the middle-class culture and thereby serves the upward mobile child of the lower class as a secondary acculturating agency, a place where he can assimilate the values, customs, morals, and manners essential to acceptance in the higher strata.

On the other hand, the school preserves the stability of the stratification system by limiting upward mobility to those youth who are willing and able to play within the rules of the game or, more specifically, to acquire the value orientations and motivations appropriate to middle-class membership. The public school serves as a sifting and sorting mechanism which differentiates between those who go to college and those who do not. Among those who do not go on to college, the school makes differential allocations to the various levels of occupational opportunity in the community; among the college-bound, to the various types of advanced training. As one analyst recently suggested (Parsons, 1959), the sorting process begins as early as the elementary school.

Our purpose is not to assess the adequacy of the social class theory nor to review the research which serves as its underpinning. Our discussion is offered as background for the task of examining the research pertinent to the impact of the teacher's social class position upon the teaching-learning process in the classroom. In undertaking such an examination, we will identify and elaborate on the main links in the chain of reasoning which connects the teacher's social class origins to his classroom performance. Given the fact that teachers derive principally from the middle class, one can draw certain conclusions concerning how the degree of success pupils will experience in the classroom and school will depend on the pupils' own social class position. But these conclusions can be drawn from the given fact only if three basic assumptions, or tenets, also hold. These tenets relate to (1) social class differences in values, (2) teachers' internalization of middle-class values, and (3) the manifestation of middle-class values in the classroom interaction process.

SOCIAL CLASS DIFFERENCES IN VALUES

The first basic tenet is that persons raised in middle-class families (or upper-class families) will hold values in their adulthood differing in certain critical respects from those held by persons raised in lower-class families. Two implications of this statement demand elaboration and some qualification. The statement reflects the strong emphasis social class theorists place on childhood as the formative period of adult character. While theorists of the Warner school do not disregard the influence on the adult's behavior of his contemporary social class position or of his social class aspirations and mobility, they are inclined to stress the enduring attributes of personality acquired during the early acculturation period. Hence the significance of their research on class differences in child training practices. The statement also posits major differences in value orientations and cultural patterns among the social strata of American society. This assumption has been

abundantly supported by empirical research over the years, especially regarding differences between the middle and lower classes. Such demonstrated differences, however, do not preclude the existence of a dominant or core value system in American society, more or less internally consistent, more or less integrative of the variant values and ideologies in the several social strata and other subcultures.

At the risk of oversimplifying the research findings, we will outline some of the more important differences in ideology and value orientation between the middle class (representing most closely what Warner and others call the "common man" or lower middle class) and the lower (or working) class.[4] Orientation of the middle class is toward sacrifice of immediate gratifications to attain future rewards, together with long-term planning to tie future goals to instrumental acts of the present; orientation of the lower class is toward immediate impulse gratification and "getting by" in the present rather than "getting ahead." This difference in orientation is related to several other divergences, including the valuation of expressions of "raw" emotions. In the middle class, strong taboos are associated with the direct expression of aggressive or sexual impulses; such impulses are neither controlled nor denied in the lower class but, rather, are rewarded when prowess is displayed. In the middle class, money, property, and material goods are things to be accumulated and cared for; in the lower class, they are regarded as things to be used. Personal "ownership" is a concept less applicable to goods in the lower class; in the middle class, the distinction between "your" possessions and "mine" is taught early and reinforced by sanctions.

Schooling, study, and academic achievement, in the middle class, are viewed as instrumental to the attainment of occupational aspirations and "success"; in the lower class, they are either irrelevant or only vaguely instrumental, representing primarily a delay in entering the labor market and in establishing one's status as a non-dependent adult. The person who is "too educated" is a misfit in the lower-class community. In the middle class, respect for a person depends on the extent of his conformity to standards of propriety, including proper forms for eating, address, greetings, exchange of gifts, expression of sympathy, offering of apology, language usage, and standards associated with tidiness of person, apparel, and possessions. In the lower class, respect is accorded on the basis of attributes of the person, such as being a "good fellow" or a "good-hearted woman," unmediated by conformity to many formal conventions. In the middle class, value is associated with the nuclear, but not the extended, `family, with participation in formal organizations, and with allegiance to and respect for institutionalized authority. In the lower class, the extended family is the proper base of one's associations, and institutionalized authority of the law and courts, of the school, and of formal community organizations is feared or treated opportunistically, not respected.

The preceding sketch, as well as the evidence on which it is based, describes modal value orientations of the middle and lower classes in the aggregate. Even when the social strata are broken down into five or six divisions, or when classification is made on the basis of self-identification rather than objective placement, characterizations of the various classes represent modal tendencies distilled, in effect, from comparisons of statistical averages. Inspection of the original data reveals sizable departures from the modal tendencies within each stratum, due in part to the crudity of measurement. Such intrastratum variability is probably due in larger part, however, to differences among stratum members in their exposure to a wide gamut of value-forming experiences other than social class. This point becomes relevant as we examine the second tenet of the social class reasoning.

SOCIAL CLASS VALUES OF TEACHERS

The second basic tenet is that teachers are drawn from the middle stratum of the American class structure and, therefore, hold middle-class value orientations. Evidence for the first part of this tenet has been reviewed earlier. It is almost certainly true that a majority of the families of persons currently teaching are from the middle class. The second part of the tenet, however, does not necessarily follow from the first part. Does teaching select those middle-class members who hold the value orientations of the middle class? Is the teacher a member of the middle class who is fully imbued with the notions of sacrifice of present desires and denial of emotional expression, fraught with taboos regarding sex and aggression, conventional and proper, convinced of the instrumental worth of education? According to the popular stereotype, the answer would be yes, but the answer must be sought in facts. Other possibilities are open. In any event, empirical investigation relating to the latter half of the second tenet is meager.

Few studies of class-related attitudes or values have been conducted so as to permit either (1) comparison of teachers with the general population from which they are drawn or (2) comparison among teachers of different social class memberships. The most relevant is Sims's (1951) study of several hundred public school teachers attending a summer session at the University of Alabama. Sims asked these teachers the six questions Centers (1949) had asked a nationwide sample five years earlier to assess positions on a "conservatism-radicalism" dimension of politico-economic attitudes. The questions were of the following kind: Do you agree or disagree that America is truly a land of opportunity and that people get pretty much what's coming to them in this country? In strikes and disputes between working people and employers, do you usually side with the workers, or with the employers? (Sims, 1951, p. 332).

Centers had found a substantial positive relationship between degree of conservatism, as derived from responses to these questions, and social class membership, when measured either by self-placement or by objective placement. The distribution of attitude scores for the Alabama teachers showed them to be more conservative, on the average, than any of Centers' occupational categories except businessmen; they were more conservative in scores than the white-collar workers whom they would most closely approximate in social-class position.

Sims's study is far from definitive in regard to the issue of social class selectivity. One would anticipate higher conservatism scores from a Deep South sample, whether or not composed of teachers, than from a cross-sectional sample of the nation. Moreover, the Alabama summer session teachers almost certainly were largely composed of non-urban persons, a factor which Centers showed was associated with conservatism. Nevertheless, to the author's knowledge, Sims's study remains the most direct attempt to test the second tenet of the social class theory.

A test of the proposition that middle-class teachers internalize the value orientations of their social class might be sought in research, such as Wickman's (1928), on the kinds of pupil behavior teachers regard as serious problems. If

teachers' standards of conduct were found to correspond to the values associated uniquely with the middle class, the hypothesis would be supported, assuming, of course, that the teachers studied were principally of middle-class origin. Among the 12 problems most frequently cited as serious by 511 elementary school teachers in Wickman's (1928) study, three related to sex taboos (heterosexual activity, masturbation, obscene notes and pictures), two related to disrespect for property (stealing, destroying school materials), two related to disrespect for authority (impertinence and defiance, disobedience), and one related to unbridled aggression (cruelty and bullying). Two of the remaining might also be regarded as class-typed standards—truancy, unreliability, and irresponsibility—but the last two might better be considered as related to core values of American society—untruthfulness and cheating.

As evidence for the second tenet, however, Wickman's data are highly equivocal. There is no assurance that social class differences would be shown *on these particular items.* Furthermore, certain variations appear in Wickman's data where no variations in social class of teachers would be expected, and no variations appear where differences in social class might be expected. In Wickman's study (1928, pp. 246–47), 35 teachers in three villages in Minnesota and New York State (probably not varying substantially from the urban teachers in social class position) regarded selfishness, smoking, and profanity as among the most serious behavioral problems, matters of considerably less concern to the teachers of New York City, Cleveland, and Newark. These differences may be more closely associated with the puritanical code of the rural areas than with social class mores. In his data from experienced teachers enrolled in college classes, Wickman observed that the departure of their ratings from the public school sample in some instances could be attributed to the course instruction and its emphases (pp. 105, 108–9). This would suggest that teachers' norms with respect to pupils are affected by professional training. Finally, Wickman obtained ratings from 10 male teachers in a private academy near Cleveland; these teachers, conceivably of a higher social class than the remainder of the public school sample, nevertheless rated pretty much the same problems as the most serious (pp. 106–7).

Several replications of the Wickman study in the 1940's and 1950's supported the contention that influences other than social class membership affect standards of judgment regarding undesirable pupil behavior (Mitchell, 1943; Schrupp and Gjerde, 1953; Stouffer, 1952). While the same kinds of behavior problems that appeared in 1926 (when Wickman's data were collected) still appeared in the top ranks of seriousness—such as heterosexual activity, stealing, cruelty, obscenity, and lying—certain subtle shifts in ranking were observed. Mitchell (1943), for example, reported that such nonaggressive behaviors as sullenness, unhappiness, and resentfulness increased in rank between 1926 and 1940. Where the correlation between teacher rankings and the rankings by mental hygiene experts had been—.08 in the Wickman study, Mitchell's teachers and mental hygienists in 1940 agreed to the extent of a .70 correlation. Mitchell, however, gave his mental hygiene experts different instructions from those Wickman had given, and the two studies were hence not strictly comparable.

Schrupp and Gjerde (1953) exactly replicated the Wickman study and found a correlation of .56 between the rankings of teachers and of mental hygienists in 1951. These authors showed that it was the teachers and not the experts who had changed their rankings in the intervening 25 years. Stouffer's (1952) study provided very similar evidence.

It is reasonable to attribute the shifts in teachers' judgments of behavior problems to changes which occurred in professional education in this period and even to the Wickman study itself. The Wickman research appeared just at the time the mental hygiene point of view was gaining a foothold in teacher-training curricula, and the conclusion widely drawn from Wickman's data, rightly or wrongly, that teachers do not appreciate the significance of withdrawal and autism as symptoms of personality disturbance in children, became a point of departure for mental hygiene courses and textbooks. There is no doubt that the generations of teachers trained after 1930 have been sensitized during their training to problems of personal and social adjustment far more than were earlier generations of teachers.

The simple fact is that no definite conclusion can be drawn from existing data regarding the extent to which teachers internalize the value orientations unique to their social class position. One might anticipate considerable variation among teachers here, but the empirical tests have not been made.

MANIFESTATION OF VALUES IN TEACHING

The third basic tenet, completing the connection between the teacher's social class position and the teaching-learning process, is embedded in the following statement: "Since the teachers' judgments of the children and of standards of performance are inevitably based on their own personal standards, buttressed by those set up by the school as an institution, the lower-class child is at a disadvantage when competing with children from the middle classes" (Warner, 1953, p. 177).

The key phrase here is that teachers' judgments of pupils are "inevitably based on their own personal standards," meaning, in the context of the paragraph, on their own *social class* standards. Thus, the tenet states that teachers guide their classroom behavior according to the general cultural values of the social stratum in which they were raised. This is a critical assumption, for it could very well be that, even though a teacher had thoroughly internalized the value orientations of his social class, his performance in the role of teacher is governed by frames of reference and value orientations other than those of his social class, such as those provided by his specialized occupational training, by the core values of society, or by requirements of the social organization of the learning process. Dahlke (1958) poses the latter alternative forcefully:

> A current interpretation of the public school is that it merely reflects and upholds middle-class values. The norms apparently support this idea, but continuity of school and middle-class norms is incidental. Many of the norms and even value emphases occur not because of middle-class influence but because the school is a group. Emphasis on work, punctuality, getting the job done, control of aggression, avoidance of conflict, and being relatively quiet are necessary conditions if any group is to persist (Dahlke, 1958, p. 253).

Nevertheless, the assumption that the performance of teachers in the classroom is governed by their middle-class values is central to the line of argument. Davis and Dollard (1940, ch. 13) used this reasoning in the most thoroughly detailed analysis of the operation of social class standards in the teaching-learning process available to us. In accord with the learning theory developing in the Yale Institute of Human Relations at the time (Miller and Dollard, 1941), Davis and Dollard proposed that behavioral responses of human beings are reinforced

when accompanied by reward, especially the social rewards of privilege and approval, or when they reduce anxiety produced by the threat of punishment or of social disapproval. To understand the classroom situation, it is necessary to consider the teacher's distribution of social rewards and punishments and to examine the behavioral responses of pupils with which they are associated. Davis and Dollard argued that, initially at least, the teacher distributes rewards on the basis of the child's social class membership, not on the basis of his classroom performance.

> [Children of middle- or upper-class membership] begin to receive favors and status privileges . . . as soon as they enter school. They must work, as their parents and teachers demand, but they are also immediately rewarded. Their anxiety is thus reduced, and they are reinforced in repeating those actions which have pleased the teacher. Before long, the person of the teacher, her smile or praise, become sub-goal responses in themselves. The average lower-class child, however, who on status grounds is systematically punished by his teacher, becomes a sullen, hostile child. Anger, overt or repressed, is a barrier to effective learning. . . .
> He sees the upper-class and upper-middle-class children being accorded preference, not only in classroom recitations but also in school entertainments and in intimate friendship relations with the teacher. He finds that he is not granted these privileges; instead, he is stigmatized by teachers and their favored students on grounds of the "ignorance" of his parents, the dialect which he speaks, the appearance of his clothes, and, very likely, the darkness of his skin. It does not take him long to discover that something is wrong and that the teacher's "pets" of high status are the only ones who can make the prestige goal responses. If there is no reward for learning, in terms of privilege and anxiety-reduction, there is no motive for work (Davis and Dollard, 1940, pp. 281–85).

The lower-class child is "systematically punished" for what he *is* and not for what he *does*. It is thereby impossible for him to learn which behavioral responses are instrumental in obtaining reward or in avoiding punishment. The case of the child of higher social class position is different. Initially, he is favored for what he is, but he is also "reinforced in repeating those *actions* which have pleased the teacher." This means that the teacher differentially rewards the behavioral responses of the middle-class child but not those of the lower-class child. This phase of the Davis and Dollard argument is rather awkward, for it leaves unexplained why in the one case reward and punishment remain attached to the class membership of the child and in the other case they are transferred to the behavioral responses of the child. But whether it is the child's social position as such or whether it is the propriety (by middle-class standards) of his behavior which inclines the teacher's actions, the fact remains, Davis and Dollard would argue, that lower-class children monopolize the punishments, higher-class children the rewards.

Reward and punishment, according to the underlying learning theory (Miller and Dollard, 1941), have very different consequences for the pupil. In brief, the middle- and upper-class child learns how to succeed in school while the lower-class child learns how to escape punishment in school. There are, of course, many ways of escaping punishment besides becoming a success. And, as the quoted passage intimates, punishment induces anger and aggressive impulses which not only interfere with cognitive learning but also, when overtly expressed, are likely to bring further punishment. A "circular reinforcement" process is instituted in the interaction between teacher and pupil which over time stabilizes the teacher's

inclinations to favor the higher-class child and to discriminate against the lower-class child. The social reinforcement which a favored child receives from his teacher has consequences for the child and also for the teacher. In the first place, the acts of the teacher in praising the pupil and granting him dominant relationships to his fellow students diminishes the pupil's anxiety and thus reinforces him in learning his lessons and in maintaining good "deportment." At the same time, the student's successful learning reinforces the teacher in continuing her acts of preference toward him. The teacher is herself a member of the class system. She is rewarded by the behavior of the good student, first, because his habits are evidence that she is a proficient teacher, and, second, because through the child she is able to gain the approval of his upper middle-class or upper-class parents (Davis and Dollard, 1940, pp. 281–82). The upshot of the analysis by Davis and Dollard is that the social class value orientations of the teacher enter the teaching-learning process in two ways: by governing the teacher's distribution of reward and punishment, and by determining what kinds of pupil behavior will be rewarding to the teacher.

A markedly different form of analysis was offered by Brookover (1953) in which he centered his concern less on how the teacher's values govern his classroom behavior than on what the teacher's values and social class position represent to the pupil.[5] In so doing, he proposed four ideal types of teacher which he called "upper-class," "established middle-class," "striving middle-class," and "unranked" teachers. These teacher types vary not only in the behavior patterns and beliefs they manifest but in such attributes as their sense of security in the stratification system, their capacity to appreciate, understand, and communicate with pupils of various social class levels, and their ability to provide the skills and incentive for upward mobility. Depending upon the social class position of the pupils involved, each type of teacher differs both in the kind of behavioral model he provides the pupil and in the likelihood that he will serve as a model at all. The pupil's identification with a given type of teacher is a major determiner of the pupil's own orientation to the social class structure. While Brookover advanced a number of specific hypotheses on these themes, none of them have been tested to date.

CLASSROOM STUDIES OF MANIFEST SOCIAL CLASS VALUES

What of the research evidence for the assumption that teachers govern their classroom behavior in accordance with the cultural orientations of their social class? Direct evidence on the issue is scanty, entailing, as it must, classroom observations of teacher-pupil interaction; we will shortly review the one study which bears precisely on the issue. Some circumstantial evidence is available in teachers' reports about their pupils and, as in studies of the Wickman type cited above, about the behavior of pupils which distresses them. We will first look at a few studies of teacher reports on pupils and pupil behavior, beginning with Becker's sociologically oriented investigation.

During interviews with 60 teachers in the Chicago public schools about the problems of teaching, Becker (1952b) found them spontaneously making evaluations in terms of the social class of the pupils they taught. (Becker presented no evidence regarding the incidence of these evaluations.) Problems with pupils centered in three areas, each varying in severity and kind with the pupils' social class. The first area was the problem of performing the task of teaching successfully. As Becker said, "The teacher considers that she has done her job adequately when she has brought about

an observable change in the children's skills and knowledge which she can attribute to her own efforts . . ." (p. 453). In this respect, pupils in the "better neighborhoods"—i.e., of the upper middle class—furnished the teacher with the greatest reward, and those of the "slum" schools—i.e., the lower lower class—offered the least reward. "Ambivalent feelings are aroused by children of the middle group. While motivated to work hard in school they lack the proper out-of-school training . . ." (p. 455). The second area related to problems of discipline. "Slum" children were considered the most difficult to control, but those of the "better" neighborhoods were also hard to handle in some respects by virtue of their disinclination to submit to the authority of the teacher. The middle group was regarded as the least difficult to discipline.

Neither of the preceding two problem areas, however, directly implicates teachers' middle-class values. Indeed, they suggest that the occupational role of teacher induces standards of evaluation quite apart from the general cultural standards of the social stratum. The third area, on the other hand, directly involves social class standards—the problem of the moral acceptability of the students. Becker offers a variety of instances in which teachers were concerned with pupil transgressions against deeply felt moral standards, especially those of "health and cleanliness, sex and aggression, ambition, and work, and the relations of age groups" (p. 461). The most severe instances involved children of the "slum" schools, but again children of the "better" neighborhoods often violated teachers' standards regarding smoking, drinking, and respect for their elders. "Children of the middle group present no problem at this level, being universally described as clean, well dressed, moderate in their behavior, and hard working" (p. 461).

Kaplan (1952) summarized annoying forms of pupil behavior as those which either violated the teachers' personal standards or challenged the teachers' authority in the classroom. He had asked elementary school teachers to write freely on "What problems or situations disturb or annoy you in your work and life as a teacher?" About one-half of the responses of teachers related to pupil behavior; others related to problems of school organization, professional status, and out-of-school obligations and pressures. From these free responses he prepared a 100-item check list and administered it to 250 experienced elementary school teachers in an Oregon summer school. Those pupil behaviors which two-thirds or more of the dealers agreed were "very disturbing" or "greatly annoying" referred to such matters contravening the teachers' sense of morality as stealing, lying, cheating, aggression, and destruction of property—items reminiscent of the Wickman list. Teachers also agreed on the annoying character of such matters as inattentiveness, indifference to school work, reluctance to work except under compulsion, nonconformity, and refusal to follow regulations, which Kaplan regarded as challenges to the teachers' roles as "leaders, disciplinarians, and instructors." A similar theme is found in Clark's (1951) report, but his conclusion—that teachers are more annoyed by behavior disruptive of classroom decorum than by behavior personally threatening to them—is not warranted by his data.

Teachers' ratings of the personal or social adjustment of particular pupils have been found to correlate with the social class position of the pupils in a number of studies. Objective measures of adjustment, however, often indicate that lower-class pupils are indeed less well adjusted. Hence, it is more parsimonious to attribute the correlation to veridical estimations by the teacher rather than to a "social class bias" on their part. A recent study (Glidewell, Gildea, Domke, and Kantor, 1959) demonstrated that teachers tend to see a lower incidence of adjustment problems among middle-class pupils than among either upper- or lower-class pupils, but the data they obtained simultaneously from parents led them to reject the "social class bias" explanation.

Thus, the ratings and reports of teachers about pupil behavior are not substantial evidence regarding the operation of social class values within the teaching-learning situation. More convincing would be investigations of the flow of classroom interaction, especially in terms of the privileges, favors, and attention accorded by the teacher to his pupils.

The study by Hoehn (1954) is the only systematic test made along this line to determine the extent of teachers' "unconscious discrimination against lower-class children."[6] Using a modification of the Anderson-Brewer schedule of dominative-integrative teacher behavior, he recorded the frequency and kinds of teacher contact with children high and low in social class position in 19 third-grade classrooms in central Illinois. The teachers were all middle class, Hoehn reports, but were heterogeneous with respect to age, experience, and marital status. He found no relationship between the frequency of teacher contacts, regardless of kind, and social class position of the child; children of low social class position were just as likely to receive the teacher's "attention" as those of high social class position. With respect to the *kind* of contact involved, however, some differentiations were noted. The proportion of "domination with conflict" contacts was greater for low social class children than for high social class children. The proportion of "integration with evidence of working together" contacts was greater for high than for low social class children, and the ratio of integrative to dominative contacts favored the higher class children.

Hoehn introduced a note of caution in interpreting these results: He had studied the relationship between teacher contact and the achievement level of the pupils, measured by the Progressive Achievement Test. He reported that the low achievers received a greater share of the teacher contacts but also a greater proportion of the "less favorable" kinds of contact (dominative and conflictful) than the high achievers. The question was raised by Hoehn as to whether the teachers' discrimination against the lower-class children is not simply a reflection of their discrimination against low achievers, since the two are highly correlated. If we take the Davis and Dollard analysis seriously, though, we would expect to find a relationship between teacher discrimination by social class and discrimination by pupil achievement. Discrimination by social class leads to differential learning success which, in turn, stabilizes the teacher's social class discriminations (Davis and Dollard, 1940).

A more important qualification is found in Hoehn's remark that the absolute magnitude of the differences in teacher behavior toward low- and high class pupils was small. (His presentation of data does not show the amount of difference; it only shows the number of the 19 classrooms in which differentiation occurred in *some* degree and the direction of such discrimination.) Hoehn was considerably more impressed by the variation *among teachers* in the extent of their discriminatory behavior. On the basis of his inspection of the data, he noted that some teachers did not discriminate consistently between either group of pupils, other teachers con-

sistently favored the high social class children, and in one of the classrooms the teacher consistently favored the low social class pupils with the greater proportion of integrative and the smaller proportion of conflict contacts. Recall that all of these teachers, nominally at least, were members of the middle class.

Hoehn's study ties in with a long line of research on the implications of teacher-pupil interaction for promoting a healthy learning environment for pupils. Some of these studies, like Hoehn's, find teachers directing their promotive acts principally at high achieving pupils and their disruptive acts at the low achievers. Recording interaction in four New York State classrooms by means of a Teacher Approval-Disapproval Scale, DeGroat and Thompson (1949) found that children who received many approval responses but few disapproval responses from the teacher were significantly higher in intelligence test scores and in achievement than were those who received few approval but many disapproval teacher responses.

Subsequently, Meyer and Thompson (1956) recorded a sex discrimination in teachers' interactions with pupils in three sixth-grade classrooms: boys received a substantially greater proportion of the (female) teachers' disapproval responses than girls. No strong sex difference appeared in the approval responses. The authors interpreted the sex discrimination in terms of an interplay between the middle-class values of teachers and the societal definition of the male and female roles, especially as it regards assertive behavior. Boys are expected to be more aggressive, they argue, and in fact they are more aggressive in the classroom than girls. But this aggressive behavior of boys is unacceptable to teachers on the grounds of their middle-class standards, and the teachers consequently direct more disapproval toward the boys. The authors fail to explain, however, why teachers do not share in the societal expectations of differences in the male and female roles.

The key assumption of Warner and his followers—that teachers' middle-class standards inevitably determine their class-room responses—stands virtually un-tested at the present time. Persuasive as the illustrative anecdotes of writers may be, provocative as the indirect evidence may be, one central question remains unanswered: Do teachers with value orientations of the lower or the upper class behave differently in the classroom than those professing middle-class values? Affirmative evidence respecting relationships between teachers' social class and their distributions of reward and punishment, or respecting the value premises underlying their classroom actions and communication, would be compelling. To generalize, we submit that the greatest fruit will be borne by research which pits the assumption that middle-class values determine teacher behavior against one or more competing assumptions concerning the source of teachers' classroom standards. Such research would require specification of distinct points of discontinuity or conflict between middle-class values and pro-fessional values, or between middle-class orientations and orientations of the "core culture" of American society, or between middle-class standards and standards imposed by the requirements of social order in the classroom. Where conflict or discontinuity can be specified, obser-vation in the classroom can be directed toward assessing the relative potency of the opposing forces acting on the teacher. Research can be set the task of delineat-ing the conditions which predict which

force will ultimately govern the teacher's performance in the teaching-learning situation. If, on the other hand, it is found impossible to specify points of discontinuity, serious doubt would be cast upon the conceptual stature of the social class argument.

SOCIAL CLASS DIFFERENCES IN
PUPIL "SUCCESS"

The final link in the chain of reasoning concerning the teacher's position in the social class structure remains to be stated explicitly, although we have alluded to it throughout our discussion. Recall our three basic assumptions: (1) that persons raised in middle-class families hold values in their adulthood differing from those held by persons raised in lower-class families, (2) that teachers are drawn from the middle stratum of the American social class system and thereby hold those values characterizing the middle class, and (3) that teachers guide their classroom behavior according to the values of their social stratum. Given these three basic tenets, it is proper to conclude that pupils of the lower classes will experience frustration and failure and pupils of the higher classes will ex-perience gratification and success in their educational experiences. The evidence supporting this conclusion is over-whelming.

To categorize youth according to the social class position of their parents is to order them on the extent of their partici-pation and degree of "success" in the American educational system. This has been so consistently confirmed by re-search that it now can be regarded as an empirical law.[7] It appears to hold, regardless of whether the social class categorization is based upon the ex-haustive procedures used in Elmtown (Hollingshead, 1949) or upon more casual indicators of socioeconomic status such as occupation or income level. It seems to hold in any educational institution, public or private, where there is some diversity in social class, including universities, colleges, and teacher-training institutions as well as elementary and secondary schools. Social class position predicts grades, achievement and intelligence test scores, retentions at grade level, course failures, truancy, suspensions from school, high school drop-outs, plans for college attendance, and total amount of formal schooling. It predicts academic honors and awards in the public school, elective school offices, extent of participation in extra-curricular activities and in social affairs sponsored by the school, to say nothing of a variety of indicators of "success" in the informal structure of the student society. Where differences in prestige value exist in high school clubs and activities, in high school curricula, or in types of advanced training institutions, the social class composition of the membership will vary accordingly.

The predictions noted above are far from perfect. Inasmuch as social class position rarely accounts for more than half the variance of school "success," the law holds only for differences in group *averages*, not for differences in individual success. The relationship in some instances may be curvilinear rather than linear, but the data rarely have been assembled to test this possibility. Finally, there are a few cases in the literature in which the expected relationships have failed to emerge. Nevertheless, positive findings appear with striking regularity.

The weight of evidence supporting the conclusion of the chain of argument does not, however, necessarily justify the assumptions from which the conclusion is drawn. To infer that it does is to commit the logical fallacy of affirming the consequent. Conditions other than the teacher's position in the social class structure may account equally well for the relationship between the pupil's social class position and his degree of success in the educational system. The com-

plexity of the situation was well recognized by Warner and his associates. In discussing the correspondence between social class and high school dropouts, Warner drew this conclusion:

> We believe this is a two-way relationship. On the one hand, the class culture of the child provides him with certain beliefs and values about the high school and what it has to offer. On the other [hand], the institutional values of the school, represented by the Board of Education, the professional administrators and teachers, as well as the students, develop differential attitudes toward persons in different positions in the social structure which act as attractive or repellent agents to keep the adolescent in, or to force him out of, school (Warner et al., 1949, p. 206).

During the 1950's, research efforts moved strongly in the direction of explaining school success in terms of the motivational structure and cultural experiences provided by the pupil's family rather than in terms of the "bias" of the educational institution. Representative studies include those of Davie (1953), Douvan and Adelson (1958), Drews and Teahan (1957), Girard and Bastide (1955), Hieronymus (1951), Hyman (1953), Kahl (1953), and Toby (1957).

Conclusion: The Consequences of Occupational Selectivity

It is obvious that teachers are drawn selectively from various statuses in the American social structure. At the same time, assumptions have been made regarding what this selectivity means for the teaching-learning process; some of these assumptions have been naïve and some sophisticated. In either case, research which tests the veridicality of the assumptions is meager, and what findings there are suggest that the assumptions are gross oversimplifications of the processes involved. We submit that the absence of positive findings regarding the relationship between societal statuses and performance in the teaching-learning situation is attributable in large part to the fact that programs of research and theoretical development have not concentrated on this problem as such. The research we have had to draw upon has more often emerged as a by-product of other research movements, such as those aimed at specifying the qualities of the "good teacher," the conditions under which more and better teachers may be induced to enter the teaching occupation, the mental hygiene implications of the classroom behavior of teachers, or the relation of social stratification to societal stability and change. Conceptualizations developed for these other purposes may be highly provocative for the problem of the relationship between occupational selectivity and the teaching-learning process, yet they are not necessarily adequate for the task. Indeed, they are almost bound to be partial accounts of the relationship. If and when the relationship in question is itself taken as a problem for investigation, theoretical models will almost certainly arise which will be capable of accounting for the complexities of the interdependence between the teacher's statuses in society and his conduct in the classroom. Such theoretical models, however, will also have to come to terms with other environmental forces acting on the teacher. . . .

Notes

[1] Most studies on occupational background have surveyed teachers-in-training, not teachers on the job. Generalizing from such data to the teaching population at large is hazardous. Aside from the fact that substantially less than 100 per cent of these students enter teaching, a fact which introduces the possibility of unknown bias, several studies have demonstrated important differences among types of college in background characteristics of their students. Teacher-trainees in the small teachers colleges, for example, are more likely to come from agricultural and laboring families than teacher-trainees in liberal arts colleges or the larger universities (Evenden, Gamble, and Blue, 1933; Kiely, 1931; McGuire and White, 1957).

[2] Mobility of teachers from one teaching situation to another does not contradict the presumption of "discrete occupational categories." The movement of teachers from rural to urban schools or from elementary to secondary schools is probably no longer the important avenue of vertical mobility it once was. But, to the extent that such mobility does exist, it is in itself a selective process which shapes the social characteristics of teachers in schools on all levels of the mobility ladder.

[3] The Warner theory of social stratification departs in a number of important respects from classical Marxian theory and other sociological theories. Since educators are inclined to regard it as *the* theory of social class, the author recommends to them the excellent, authoritative review of contemporary social class theories by Mayer (1953) which places the Warner theory in perspective.

[4] It is impossible in the space available here to cite the supporting evidence regarding social class differences in culture patterns, and the literature *summarizing* the evidence is, perhaps, more voluminous than the research itself. In the following sketch we have drawn heavily upon the systematic schematization of value orientations presented by C. Kluckhohn and Kluckhohn (1947). The reader wishing to pursue the evidence should consult a standard textbook on sociology or social stratification.

[5] Getzels (1957) has approached the matter of value learning in much the same way as Brookover, emphasizing the process of the pupil's *identification* with the teacher.

[6] Hoehn cited a dissertation by Clifton (1944) in which observations of the dominative-integrative behavior of teachers in second-grade classrooms were reported. The classrooms were located in three different

socio-economic areas. According to Hoehn, Clifton found little difference between the classrooms in the nature of teacher contacts with pupils, but there were somewhat fewer conflict contacts and somewhat more integrative contacts in the schools of the highest socioeconomic area.

[7] We cannot undertake to document each of the following statements separately. The reader is referred to the bibliographies of Dixon (1953) and Gordon (1957b), to the various community studies in the social class tradition, especially Hollingshead on Elmtown (1949), and Warner, Havighurst, and Loeb's (1944) monograph on education, to the comprehensive selection of readings in Stanley, Smith, Benne, and Anderson (1956, Part 2), and to the competent summaries of Brookover (1955b, ch. 5) and Havighurst and Neugarten (1957, chs. 10, 11).

References

Becker, H. S. "Social-class Variations in the Teacher-Pupil Relationship." *Journal of Educational Sociology*, 25 (1952), pp. 451–65.

Betts, G. L.; Frazier, B. W.; and Gamble, G. C. *Selected Bibliography on the Education of Teachers*. Washington, D.C.: U.S. Department of the Interior, Office of Education, Bull. 1933, No. 10, Vol. 1.

Brookover, W. B. "Teachers and the Stratification of American Society." *Harvard Educational Review*, 23 (1953), pp. 257–67.

Brookover, W. B. *A Sociology of Education*. New York: American Book Co., 1955.

Centers, R. *The Psychology of Social Classes*. Princeton: Princeton University Press, 1949.

Clark, E. F. "Teacher Reactions toward Objectionable Pupil Behavior." *Elementary School Journal*, 51 (1951), pp. 446–49.

Clifton, D. E. "Dominative and Socially Integrative Behavior of Twenty-five Second Grade Teachers." Unpublished doctoral dissertation, University of Illinois, 1944.

Coffman, L. D. "The Social Composition of the Teaching Population." *Teachers Coll. Contr. Educ.*, 1911, No. 41.

Cook, L. A., and Cook, Elaine F. *A Sociological Approach to Education* (2nd ed.). New York: McGraw-Hill, 1950.

Dahlke, H. O. *Values in Culture and Classroom*. New York: Harper, 1958.

Davie, J. S. "Social Class Factors and School Attendance." *Harvard Educational Review*, 23 (1953), pp. 175–85.

Davis, A., and Dollard, J. *Children of Bondage*. Washington, D.C.: American Council on Education, 1940.

DeGroat, A. F., and Thompson, G. G. "A Study of the Distribution of Teacher Approval and Disapproval among Sixth-grade Pupils." *Journal of Experimental Education*, 18 (1949), pp. 57–75.

Dixon, N. R. "Social Class and Education: An Annotated Bibliography." *Harvard Educational Review*, 23 (1953), pp. 330–38.

Douvan, Elizabeth, and Adelson, J. "The Psycho-dynamics of Social Mobility in Adolescent Boys." *Journal of Abnormal Social Psychology*, 56 (1958), pp. 31–44.

Drews, Elizabeth M., and Teahan, J. E. "Parental Attitudes and Academic Achievement." *Journal of Clinical Psychology*, 13 (1957), pp. 328–32.

Elsbree, W. S. *The American Teacher*. New York: American Book Co., 1939.

Evenden, E. S.; Gamble, G. C.; and Blue, H. G. *Teacher Personnel in the United States*. Washington, D.C.: U.S. Department of the Interior, Office of Education, Bull. 1933, No. 10, Vol. 2.

Getzels, J. W. "Changing Values Challenge the Schools." *School Review*, 65 (1957), pp. 92–102.

Girard, A., and Bastide, H. "Orientation et Selection Scolaires: Une Enquete sur les Enfants a la Sortie de l'Escole Primaire," *Population*, 10 (1955), pp. 605–26.

Glidewell, J. C.; Gildea, Margaret C. L.; Domke, H. R.; and Kantor, Mildred B. "Behavior Symptoms in Children and Adjustment in Public School." *Human Organization*, 18 (1959), pp. 123–30.

Gordon, C. W. "The Sociology of Education." In *Review of Sociology: Analysis of a Decade*, ed. J. B. Gittler, pp. 500–519. New York: Wiley, 1957.

Greenhoe, Florence. *Community Contacts and Participation of Teachers*. Washington, D.C.: American Council on Public Affairs, 1941.

Havighurst, R. J., and Neugarten, Bernice L. *Society and Education*. Boston: Allyn & Bacon, 1957.

Hieronymus, A. N. "Study of Social Class Motivation: Relationship Between Anxiety for Education and Certain Socioeconomic and Intellectual Variables," *Journal of Educational Psychology*, 42 (1951), pp. 193–205.

Hoehn, A. J. "A Study of Social Status Differentiation in the Classroom Behavior of Nineteen Third Grade Teachers." *Journal of Social Psychology*, 39 (1954), pp. 269–92.

Hollingshead, A. B. *Elmtown's Youth*. New York: Wiley, 1949.

Hyman, H. H. "The Value Systems of Different Classes: A Social Psychological Contribution to the Analysis of Stratification." In *Class, Status, and Power*, ed. R. Bendix and S. M. Lipset, pp. 426–42. New York: Free Press, 1953.

Kahl, J. A. "Educational and Occupational Aspirations of 'Common Man' Boys." *Harvard Educational Review*, 23 (1953), pp. 186–203.

Kaplan, L. The Annoyances of Elementary School Teachers." *Journal of Educational Research*, 45 (1952), pp. 649–65.

Kiely, Margaret. "Comparison of Students of Teachers Colleges and Students of Liberal Arts Colleges." *Teachers Coll. Contr. Educ.*, 1931, No. 440.

Kluckhohn, C., and Kluckhohn, Florence R. "American Culture: Generalized Orientations and Class Patterns." In *Conflicts of Power in Modern Culture*, eds. L. Bryson, L. Finkelstein, and R. M. MacIver, pp. 106–28. New York: Harper, 1947.

Lieberman, M. *Education as a Profession*. Englewood Cliffs, N.J.: Prentice-Hall, 1956.

Mayer, K. "The Theory of Social Classes." *Harvard Educational Review*, 23 (1953), pp. 149–67.

McGuire, C., and White, G. D. "Social Origins of Teachers—in Texas." In *The Teacher's Role in American Society*, ed. L. J. Stiles, pp. 23–41. New York: Harper, 1957.

Meyer, W. J., and Thompson, G. G. "Sex Difference in the Distribution of Teacher Approval and Disapproval Among Sixth-Grade Children." *Journal of Educational Psychology*, 47 (1956), pp. 385–96.

Miller, N. E., and Dollard, J. C. *Social Learning and Imitation*. New Haven: Yale University Press, 1941.

Mitchell, J. C. "A Study of Teachers' and Mental Hygienists' Rating of Certain Behavior Problems of Children." *Journal of Educational Research*, 36 (1943), pp. 292–307.

National Education Association, Research Division. "First-year Teachers in 1954–55." *NEA Research Bulletin*, 34 (1956).

National Education Association, Research Division. "The Status of the American Public School Teacher." *NEA Research Bulletin*, 35 (1957).

Parsons, T. "The School Class as a Social System: Some of Its Functions in American Society." *Harvard Educational Review*, 29 (1959), pp. 297–318.

Ryans, D. G. *Characteristics of Teachers*. Washington, D.C.: American Council on Education, 1960.

Schrupp, M. H., and Gjerde, C. M. "Teacher Growth in Attitudes Toward Behavior Problems of Children." *Journal of Educational Psychology*, 44 (1953), pp. 203–14.

Sims, V. M. "The Social-class Affiliations of a Group of Public School Teachers." *School Review*, 59 (1951), pp. 331–38.

Stanley, W. O.; Smith, B. O.; Benne, K. D.; and Anderson, A. W., eds. *Social Foundations of Education*. New York: Dryden, 1956.

Stouffer, G. A. W., Jr. "Behavior Problems of Children as Viewed by Teachers and Mental Hygienists." *Mental Hygiene, New York*, 36 (1952), pp. 271–85.

Toby, J. "Orientation to Education as a Factor in the School Maladjustment of Lower-class Children." *Social Forces*, 35 (1957), pp. 259–66.

U.S. Department of Commerce, Bureau of the Census. *Census of Population: 1950*, Vol. 1, *Number of Inhabitants*. Washington, D.C.: U.S. Government Printing Office, 1952.

Warner, W. L. *American Life: Dream and Reality*. Chicago: University of Chicago Press, 1953.

Warner, W. L.; Havighurst, R. J.; and Loeb, M. B. *Who Shall Be Educated?* New York: Harper, 1944.

Warner, W. L.; Meeker, Marsha; and Eells, K. *Social Class in America*. Chicago: Science Research Associates, 1949.

Wattenberg, W. "Social Origins of Teachers—A Northern Industrial City." In *The Teacher's Role in American Society*, ed. L. J. Stiles, pp. 13–22. New York: Harper, 1957.

Wickman, E. K. *Children's Behavior and Teachers' Attitudes*. New York: Commonwealth Fund, 1928.

PUBLIC SCHOOL circles are rife with talk of professionalism. Those familiar with the resistance administrators encounter from technical personnel in hospitals, universities, and business might surmise that the gap between the stated and the actual in school organization stems from the professionalization of teachers.[1] That interpretation, however, assumes that processes of professionalization among teachers are sufficiently institutionalized to constrain the actions of boards and administrators. How accurate is that assumption? What part do collegial ties among teachers play in "softening" hierarchical authority? In looking for answers to these questions, we shall examine several facets of professionalization among elementary teachers. Specifically, the examination includes a brief review of the history and current status of the occupational group, a comparison of the teacher's role with a model of professionalized work, and inquiry into teacher socialization and the technical subculture of the occupation.

The Partial Professionalization of Elementary Teaching

Dan Lortie

Reprinted with permission of The Macmillan Company from The Semi-Professions and Their Organization, edited by Amitai Etzioni, pp. 15–30. Copyright © 1969 by The Free Press, A Division of The Macmillan Company.

A Brief History of Teacher Professionalization

Stinchcombe argues that conditions associated with an organization's founding have lasting effects on its subsequent development.[2] Ambiguities in the position of the elementary teacher today are rooted in the organizational history of schools; control by laymen, lack of clarity in colleague group boundaries, limited prestige and money income, and feminization of the occupation have taken place over a protracted period of time.

Bailyn writes that the contribution of the Colonial Era was to initiate the concept of school as a necessary instrument for socializing colonial children into a novel way of life.[3] Englishmen in Tudor times relied primarily on family

and apprenticeship to conduct their young from infancy to adulthood. Migration to the New World meant rearing children in a setting where older forms of socialization, inappropriate to the new environment, lost their effectiveness and reliability. Education became a designed and conscious affair undertaken to replace the old. The advent of the school created financial problems, and the solution of these problems eventuated in local and public control. "Dependent for support upon annual and even less regular gifts," states Bailyn, "education at all levels during the early formative years came within the direct control, not of those responsible for instruction, but of those who had created and maintained the institutions."[4] Lower schools, unlike the colleges, failed to develop alternative sources of support; today elementary and secondary education are financed and controlled by the local citizenry. The persistence of such "layman control" has had significant consequences for the shape of the teaching occupation.[5]

Teaching was not regularized during the Colonial Period; no special arrangements existed to regulate entry, and the necessary credentials were limited to sufficient literacy to teach reading, writing, and elementary arithmetic.[6] Those who taught did so for limited periods of time, for most of them were on the way to something else—ministerial students preparing for a pulpit, indentured servants accumulating the price of their bond. Incomes and prestige were low. Teaching was ranked in terms of the age of the students, with those teaching the early grades receiving the lowest monetary and deference rewards. The men who taught (most teachers were male) were expected to show themselves proper and religious in conduct, and, as part of their regular duties, were expected to help out around the church by doing menial chores. Then, as today, these men needed extra income and often took on extra employment. Colonial Americans thought of teaching as a rather easy task —they did not think of it as taxing the full strength of a man.

State school systems as we know them today began to emerge between the Revolution and the Civil War. Those whose names are featured in histories of education (Mann, Bernard, Wiley) asserted the urgency of a free and public system of common schooling;[7] they managed to build the first such system in history. Yet few major changes occurred in the role of the teacher; during the Jacksonian years, public school teaching, like much else, was absorbed into the spoils system. As salaries were small and communities were loath to raise them, women entered the work and, in line with practices of the time, accepted incomes lower than those paid to men. Elementary teaching became work for girls with little formal schooling—most had finished elementary school and a year or two of grammar school. Normal schools (imported from Prussia) began before the Civil War, but it was several decades before a majority of teachers

received the year-or-two's training they offered to elementary school graduates. The Civil War emptied the schools of men; veterans, finding numerous other opportunities in the expanding economy, rarely returned to the classroom.

The role of the elementary teacher took firmer shape in the years following the Civil War; by 1917, the principalship and the superintendency were institutionalized.[8] Elementary schools expanded to cope with millions of children whose parents had immigrated from Europe, and the demands for teachers rose. "Tappan's Law," which stipulated that a teacher should have completed the level immediately above that which she aspired to teach, emerged as the guide to school officials; elementary teachers came to be women with high school education.

The superintendent emerged as the key school administrator around the turn of the century. Callahan documents how superintendents were swept up in the enthusiasm for "Scientific Management" which marked the first two decades of this century.[9] This view of school management conceptualized the teacher much as industrial workers were seen by their managers; the teacher was to execute, under minute prescription and intimate supervision, the plans developed by experts in the central office. The teacher associations which had survived fused into the National Education Association and its complex array of state and local affiliates. The domination of associational life by men in administrative positions was flagrant, and in 1920 a reorganization, the result of a teacher revolt, gave somewhat greater influence to classroom teachers.[10] It is important to note, however, that the main body of teachers who continued with the NEA did *not* insist on separating out their role in professional development. The formation of the American Federation of Teachers was in opposition to administrators, but it failed to attract more than a minority of teachers. The

National Education Association formed and sustained internal units which differentiated by role, such as the Classroom Teacher's Department and the American Association of School Administrators. But to this day, those participating within the NEA complex have averred the importance of a "unified profession" composed of teachers, administrators, guidance personnel, and others who perform "professional" functions in the school.

The years from 1918 to today have not, generally speaking, seen many structural changes in the role of the elementary school teacher. Tenure arrangements, begun just before World War I, spread during the twenties and thirties; the equalization of elementary and secondary salaries occurred in that period. Entry standards rose to require college attendance, and certification machinery was constructed; the National Education Association grew enormously (from 8,500 members in 1918 to almost one million today) and added numerous functions and functionaries to its central headquarters. Managerial ideologies shifted from "scientific management" to "democratic administration" to the analytic and social scientific orientation emerging at present.[11] The current ideology of administration appears somewhat uncertain and tentative; we are in a period marked by greater concern with means than with ends, with pedagogical efficiency within prevailing forms than with new conceptions of school purpose.[12]

The current situation reflects the centuries during which teachers were defined solely as employees. It is interesting that teachers have not challenged their formal subordination; unlike most who claim professional status, teachers have not contested the right of persons outside the occupation to govern their technical affairs. Although teacher associations have sought to influence legislation at all levels of government, they have generally accepted the structural order within which they work. The American Federation of Teachers, presumably the most aggressive of teacher organizations, has worked to define relations between teachers and superordinates as relations between employees and employers. Concentrating on "welfare" issues of money and working conditions, it has not launched any serious attacks on the right of citizen boards to control instructional affairs. Whatever the ideology of professionalism among teachers may be, it does not currently constitute a direct challenge to public, lay control over school affairs.

Elementary teaching has been "regularized" in the sense that pathways *into* the occupation have been institutionalized. It is not clear, however, what constitutes leaving the occupation. Are elementary principles members of the "profession"? Whereas most fields claiming professional status manifest great concern with the clarification of membership qualifications, the exact boundaries of colleague-group membership remain unclear within public school teaching. The definition put forth by the largest occupational association, the National Education Association, is extremely broad. NEA policy calls for a "unified profession" encompassing teachers, principals, superintendents, counselors, and —optimistically—college professors. Yet the same association, ironically, includes subgroups which act in ways divergent from the policy of the group as a whole. The American Association of School Administrators recently revised its rules to make it more difficult for teachers and principals to gain entry. Although teacher unions stress solidarity among classroom teachers, they have not sought to capitalize on such solidarity as the basis for professionalization. If elementary teaching be a profession, it is a profession with ambiguous membership.

Professional status carries connotations of high prestige.[13] The prestige of elementary teachers, as distinguished from high school teachers, is not known, but the general standing of public school teachers can be inferred from the National Opinion Research Center's studies of occupational ranking. The survey conducted in 1947 accords "public school teacher" a rank of 35/90 and a position below such occupations as medicine, college teaching, the clergy, dentistry, law, and engineering, and above journalists, welfare workers, and the skilled trades of electrician, machinist, and carpenter.[14] No significant differences in overall rankings or the specific position of teaching occurred in the replication done in 1963.[15] It is useful, however, to examine the prestige of teaching in light of the sexual division of labor in our society. Although teaching ranks thirty-fifth on the NORC list in general, it is first among those occupations largely populated by women.[16] Within the range of occupations "open" to women (open in the sense that participation is clearly more than token), the prestige of teaching is very high. Teaching is socially desirable for American women, but for men it occupies a rank well below the topmost levels of work achievement.

Occupations can be arrayed in terms of the ratio between those granted admission and those seeking entry. Some occupations regularly turn away large numbers of would-be members, while others, like teaching, fall into the category of fields of chronic "shortage." The percentage of college seniors choosing teaching has risen steadily of late, but expansion of teaching staffs, coupled with high turnover, has resulted in demand exceeding supply.[17] A situation of shortage undermines attempts to raise entry standards; the certification machinery already developed has been violated

by thousands of teachers working with "temporary" certificates. The unfavorable competitive position of elementary teaching has prevented leaders from employing strategies of prestige enhancement based upon more rigorous or restricted entry. The social characteristics of teachers have added little to its overall standing, for as the National Education Association reports,

teachers constitute, in social origin, a fairly representative cross section of the American people, except that the families of the managerial and professional groups appear to be over-represented by teachers and that unskilled and service workers appear to be under-represented.[18]

Although teaching salaries have risen steadily (particularly since 1947) they are marked by a "low ceiling" and are generally low in comparison with the average annual earnings of male college graduates.[19] Most men who teach in public schools find it necessary to supplement their salaries by additional employment.[20] The level of teaching salaries is not sufficiently high to maintain men and their families at a living standard associated with "professional" styles of life in our society.

. . . As far as elementary teaching is concerned, it is clearly congruent with feminine socialization, work styles, and familial roles. Compared to other realistic alternatives for women, teaching offers attractive prestige and money. The decentralized nature of school organization means local hiring in almost every community; teaching is thus accessible to women who are relatively immobile members of the work force.[21] The absence of interpersonal rivalry for monetary rewards fits the socialization experiences Caplow attributed to American women.[22] The work schedule of teachers facilitates the participation of women with school-age children—their work hours coincide with those during which their children are outside the home.

The slow-changing technology of teaching permits teachers to be away for protracted periods (as during the early years of child-rearing) and to return without excessive loss of skill. An obvious but important correlative fact should also be mentioned: in our society, as in most, the care of small children is culturally defined as women's work.

It is easy to forget the recency of large-scale participation by women in the general labor market. To date the only occupations which have clearly achieved professional recognition have been male occupations. We have yet to see whether any occupation predominantly feminine in composition can or will achieve clear title to the honorific designation "profession."

Elementary Teaching and the Established Professions

Although sociologists have not achieved consensus on a single set of criteria for the identification of professions, there is general agreement that a few fields clearly belong within the category. Examples are medicine, law, and architecture. But such fields are fee-for-service professions where the practitioner renders service to an aggregate of clients. The problem is to find organizational characteristics peculiar to professions which can, with equal facility, be applied to salaried occupations. Direct and concrete applications of fee-for-service categories create confusion. (Who is the client of the elementary teacher: students? parents? taxpayers? the school system?) We can, however, locate certain issues which must be resolved in all occupations, and, noting the peculiar resolution employed in clearly established professions, test individual fields in terms of the proximity of their resolutions to professional ones. We use four such issues here:

1. How the individual relates to the market.
2. The nature of knowledge and skill possessed by members of the occupation.
3. The relation established to the polity.
4. The extent to which those performing similar activities influence the careers of members of the occupation.

The established practitioner in a well-established profession occupies a favored position in the market.[23] He can assert himself vis-à-vis a single client without serious economic risk, for the multiplicity of his clientele and their lack of organization reduces his economic dependence upon any single individual. This economic independence provides him with a basis for professional autonomy; he can choose to act in ways congruent with professional norms when the latter collide with the wishes of a client. He can withstand pressures which he considers contrary to his professional principles or interests.

Elementary teachers receive their income from "one big client." But is it not true that tenure arrangements serve to balance the exchange and give the teacher an autonomy similar to that enjoyed by the professional practitioner? There are differences between the functions served by multiple clienteles and tenure; tenure protects the individual in his position only within a given school district. It is difficult for elementary teachers to build a reputation which transcends their local area; teaching, even superb teaching, throws a short shadow. Since mechanisms for broadcasting one's competence are limited, the teacher cannot be entirely unconcerned with her employer's goodwill. Since employment elsewhere can be threatened by negative recommendations, the teacher is wise to avoid actions which would antagonize her "one big client."

The knowledge and skill possessed by those practicing established professions are recognized both as vital to individual and social welfare and as esoteric in nature. The layman experiences here his vulnerable status—he knows he needs the professional's service and lacks the professional's knowledge and skill. The critical point is that of evaluation by relevant publics; whatever the actual state of professional knowledge in scientific terms, the relevant publics (clients, political agencies, and the like) *believe* that knowledge to be both essential and restricted to members of the professional group. The possession of esoteric knowledge over a period of time strengthens those within the profession vis-à-vis the public in *general* terms. There are indications that protracted occupancy of professional status permits an occupation to play an important role in defining the very nature of the service it will provide. Thus, lawyers have influenced the meaning and substance of justice, and, in some respects, doctors have defined the essential characteristics of health and illness.

"No one ever died of a split infinitive" is a quip which throws the less-than-vital nature of teaching knowledge into relief. Nor can elementary teachers point to an arcane body of substantive or technical knowledge to assert professional status vis-à-vis the school board or the public-at-large. That which is taught in elementary school is presumed to be known by almost all adults, and teachers have not been able to convince many critics— and more importantly, legislatures—that "methods courses" constitute a truly distinct and impressive body of knowledge.[24] The subjects teachers themselves believe useful in teaching (e.g., child psychology) are primarily the property of others. Lacking the clear autonomy

which leads to the assurance that professional knowledge will provide the basis of action, teachers have not developed codified and systematic bodies of professional knowledge; lacking that knowledge, their stance vis-à-vis laymen is, in turn, weakened.

The state can ill-afford to ignore well-established professions and the claims of persons to their powers, for, since the service is presumed to be vital, the charlatan can threaten the welfare of citizens. Complex licensure arrangements develop which are mainly delegated by political authorities to members of the profession who implement them. Such delegation is not, however, a formal abrogation of powers: there is the implied threat to reclaim the government of affairs by political officials should the profession lose their confidence.

The situation in licensing elementary teachers is somewhat quixotic. A complex and elaborate procedure exists which, as Conant indicates, is by-passed by thousands of teachers.[25] Lieberman points out that educational licensing boards are *not* controlled by members of the teaching profession.[26] Further confusion is evident when we observe that some high-status schools, such as private preparatory schools, employ teachers without regard to such certification specifics where they can do so.

Those outside a well-established profession, acknowledging their ignorance of its special knowledge, are inclined to delegate much of its governance to members of the professions. It makes sense to conceptualize this process as one of exchange by means of which the profession can retain its self-governing perquisites as long as it retains the trust of political authorities. Professions possess and use complex formal machinery for the discipline of errant members who threaten that exchange. But what is less widely realized is that in important sectors of the professions, senior colleagues hold enormous and sustained power over the careers of those aspiring to full recognition.[27] Informal referral systems in medicine and partnership probation periods in law and architecture enable senior practitioners to undertake protracted testing of the technical competence and normative integrity of aspirants.

The ambiguity of colleague group boundaries makes it difficult for an observer to decide whether teachers are subjected to collegial scrutiny in their career progression. The tenure promotion, for example, is assessed by administrative superiors (the principal and superintendent normally recommend candidates to the board) but not by fellow teachers. It is a curious fact, unexplained by Sharma, that teachers in his national sample did not wish to participate in personnel decisions about other teachers.[28]

This review of four issues reveals as much dissimilarity as similarity to professional modes of resolution. We encounter serious ambiguities on each count; the role of the elementary teacher differs significantly from that found in situations where professional status is uncontested.

The Incomplete Subculture

The controls one finds in well-established professions are more than external mechanisms for rewarding the faithful and punishing the deviants. Members of a profession are supposed to internalize the standards of their profession—they talk of "professional conscience." But the inculcation of such standards requires an elaborate subculture buttressed by complex machinery for its transmission to neophytes.[29] Witness, for example, the protracted socialization we find in medicine with its pre-medical curriculum, its four years of specialized schooling, its complex internship and residency arrangements. Established professions take few chances with newcomers—the neophyte is subjected to years of scrutiny and indoctrination by professors and members of the profession.

Elementary teaching represents, at best, a faint replica of such inculcation of technical and moral practices. Although inquiry into teacher socialization is still very limited, it is possible to note some important ways in which teaching, as a subculture, differs from what is associated with a high degree of professionalization.

Entrants to most professions are, as materials for professional socialization, largely unformed. Few students entering law or medicine or architecture are intimately familiar with the working round of practitioners or feel qualified to make judgments about professional performances. Teaching, on the other hand, is well known to entrants, and they have already formed opinions about what constitutes an effective teaching performance. Teachers interviewed by the author were able to describe their outstanding public school teachers in considerable detail, and some volunteered the information that they currently employ techniques learned as young students.[30] Those seeking to socialize their students into a particular conception of teaching must overcome such pre-existing attitudes and values. It is noteworthy that the same teachers who found it easy to describe their former teachers had difficulty in describing colleagues of outstanding competence; their replies frequently contained the phrase "we never see each other at work." These data suggest that the flow of influence from generation to generation encounters less influence from colleagues than we associate with professional fields and may, in fact, account for the conservatism ascribed to school people by Waller and Durkheim.[31]

We have noted that the public school network, as a series of linked organizations, can eliminate those who, as students or beginning teachers, fail to show the appropriate characteristics and attitudes. To test for *general* acceptability, however, is not the same process as indoctrinating beginners with a set of clear, precise, and usable specifications for the performance of the occupation's tasks. The role of college preparation for teaching is not well understood at the present time, but it appears that its potency, in confronting students with extended prior exposure to teaching, is limited. Teachers themselves tend to discount the contribution of pre-service courses in influencing their current work habits and choices.[32] Some studies point to a shift in teacher attitudes as they move from professional training courses to actual classroom confrontation.[33] One study indicates that actual experience in teaching tends to "wash out" earlier differences associated with attendance at different types of undergraduate colleges.[34] There is no evidence that pre-service experiences provide those exposed to them with a significant body of directives for teaching or affect their work values in lasting fashion.

There is indication that work socialization occurs primarily during the beginner's actual confrontation with responsibility in performing occupational tasks.[35] Elementary teachers acquire their substantive knowledge through sixteen years of studentship, but what of the core interpersonal skills involved in their craft? Learning to control a class of thirty students, determining appropriate levels of vocabulary and effective sequences of presentation, realizing variations in individual potentials for learning —these are complex accomplishments requiring immersion in actual teaching. Elementary teachers usually undergo a period of practice teaching before assignment to a regular class and one study shows that the tutelage of the supervising teacher has an important influence.[36] But it is significant to observe that the first year of actual teaching experience—the point of full involvement in accountable teaching responsibility— is generally not accompanied by regular or intensive contact with senior colleagues. The beginning elementary teacher is, of course, "visited" by the principal and probably a central office supervisor, but the fraction of working time which is supervised is very small. (Twelve visits of two hours' duration each would be high and would consist of less than 3 per cent of the teacher's first year, estimated at thirty-eight weeks of thirty hours each.) Where obvious trouble arises with a beginning teacher, special attention will be paid; otherwise, she may be left almost entirely to her own resources in mastering her new role. Other teachers have little time available, for they too are caught in the time and space economy of elementary schools which permits them little time away from students. The system of supervising beginning teachers is compatible with the exercise of gross control and of centering on trouble points; it does *not* suggest a precise instrument of work socialization through which the organization or professional colleagues engage in on-the-spot assistance to the newcomer. Elementary teachers learn their core skills in isolation from other adults.

Occupational cultures, no less than other types, grow through protracted interaction and communication among members of the group. Teaching, as an activity involving contact with students, is carried on by individuals whose contacts with one another are essentially at the periphery of the central transactions. Such conditions are neither likely to produce a culture marked by rich, specific, and detailed technical terms and procedures nor calculated to develop norms which operationalize values. We can see this in the state of practical knowledge about teaching, for, in addition to the private nature of this activity, there are no regular mechanisms for overcoming its evanescent qualities. Teaching techniques are developed and used by thousands of individuals in restricted contact with one another; there are no general expectations that individual teachers should record their experiences in such a way that it becomes the general property of the professional group. No provisions are made in the daily schedule of the teacher for such activity. Yet we note that physicians since Galen (with important historical gaps) have identified and described syndromes and have tested and recorded alternative therapies and their effects. Law, through its elaborate, refined procedures for recording the deliberations and decisions of courts, represents the distillation of generations of practitioner effort. The successes and failures of architects are recorded in stone, wood, and steel. Experience in these professions has a cumulative quality; what teachers learn is largely lost. It is not possible for the professor of education to gain ready access to decades of "cases" for critical review and scientific testing; nor is it easy for the beginning teacher to get the feeling that she begins where predecessors left off.

The absence of a refined technical culture is evident in the talk of elementary school teachers. Analysis of long, somewhat "open" interviews with teachers reveals little by way of a special rhetoric to delineate the essence of their daily grappling with interpersonal and learning problems. The language one finds, as might be expected from the foregoing paragraph, is the language of persons of their general educational and class background.[37] Where trade jargon is used, it is frequently characterized by various meanings among different speakers (e.g. "growth" is advanced perform-

ance on achievement tests for one, the overcoming of shyness for another). Isolation and evanescence seem to have had the expected effects.

The general status of teaching, the teacher's role and the condition and transmission arrangements of its subculture point to truncated rather than fully realized professionalization. The ideology of professionalism among elementary teachers has yet to result in the structural characteristics or collegial assertiveness found in clearly established professions. It appears that considerable militancy and knowledge-building must occur if teachers are to acquire the work arrangements and technical apparatus associated with high-prestige professions.

In view of the truncated nature of professionalization among elementary teachers, it seems highly unlikely that collegial ties play a major part in reducing the potency of hierarchical authority. It may be, of course, that board members and administrators occasionally restrain their assertions of authority in deference to the attributed expertise of teachers. But professional ways of organizing work have yet to be institutionalized in the public schools. The absence of such institutionalization suggests skepticism rather than credulity on the count of teacher professionalization, and this skepticism should, in the writer's opinion, extend to ruling out *a priori* formulations which grant professional controls a major part in containing administrative authority. The autonomy possessed by elementary teachers is not the collectively shared right of recognized professionals.

Notes

[1] Howard M. Vollmer and D. A. Mills, *Professionalization* (Englewood Cliffs, N.J.: Prentice-Hall, 1966) esp. sec. 8; and Amitai

Etzioni, *Modern Organizations* (Englewood Cliffs, N.J.: Prentice-Hall, 1964), ch. 8.

[2] Arthur L. Stinchcombe, "Social Structure and Organizations," in *Handbook of Organizations*, ed. James G. March (Chicago: Rand McNally, 1965), p. 153.

[3] Bernard Bailyn, *Education in the Forming of American Society* (Chapel Hill: University of North Carolina Press, 1960), p. 21.

[4] *Ibid.*, p. 44.

[5] See Myron Lieberman, *Education as a Profession* (Englewood Cliffs, N.J.: Prentice-Hall, 1956).

[6] R. Freeman Butts and Lawrence A. Cremin, *A History of Education in American Culture* (New York: Holt, 1953).

[7] *Ibid.*, p. 256.

[8] Paul Revere Pierce, *The Origin and Development of the Public School Principalship* (Chicago: University of Chicago, 1935). T. L. Reller, *The Development of the City Superintendency of Schools in the United States* (Philadelphia: Author, 1935).

[9] Raymond E. Callahan, *Education and the Cult of Efficiency* (Chicago: University of Chicago, 1962), chs. 2, 3.

[10] L. Cremin, *The Transformation of the School: Progressivism in American Education, 1876–1957* (New York: Knopf, 1961).

[11] Raymond E. Callahan and H. Warren Button, "Historical Changes in the Role of the Man in the Organization: 1865–1950," in *National Society for the Study of Education Yearbook*, ed. Daniel Griffiths (Chicago: NSSE, 1964), pp. 73–92.

[12] See paper by Dan C. Lortie in *Challenge and Change in American Education*, ed. Seymour Harris (Berkeley: McCutchan, 1965), pp. 149–56.

[13] Howard S. Becker, "The Nature of a Profession," in *Education for the Professions*, National Society for the Study of Education Yearbook, ed. Nelson B. Henry (Chicago: NSSE, 1962), 61, pt. 2, 31 (whole section from pp. 27–46).

[14] National Opinion Research Center, "Jobs and Occupations: A Popular Evaluation," in *Class, Status, and Power*, ed. R. Bendix and S. M. Lipset (New York: Free Press, 1953), pp. 411–26.

[15] Robert Hodge, Paul M. Siegel, and Peter Rossi, "Occupational Prestige in the United States, 1925–63," *American Journal of Sociology*, 70 (1964), pp. 286–302.

[16] NORC, *op. cit.*

[17] National Education Association, Research Division, "Teacher Supply and Demand in Public Schools, 1965," *Research Report 1965–R10* (June, 1965).

[18] National Education Association, Research Division, "The American Public School Teachers, 1960–61," in *Research Monograph 1963–M2*, p. 15.

[19] Charles S. Benson, *The Economics of Public Education* (Boston: Houghton Mifflin, 1961), pp. 403–4.

[20] NEA, *Research Monograph 1963–M2*, p. 21.

[21] Benson, *op. cit.*, p. 417.

[22] Theodore Caplow, *The Sociology of Work* (Minneapolis: University of Minnesota Press, 1954), p. 243.

[23] Dan C. Lortie, *The Striving Young Lawyer*, p. 182.

[24] The legislatures of California and New York have recently augmented the discipline-based study required of all elementary teachers.

[25] James B. Conant, *The Education of American Teachers* (New York: McGraw-Hill, 1963), Appendix G (pp. 242–46).

[26] Lieberman, *op. cit.*, pp. 91–97.

[27] Oswald Hall, "Stages of a Medical Career," *American Journal of Sociology*, 53 (1948), pp. 327–36; Dan C. Lortie, "Laymen to Lawmen: Law School, Careers and Socialization," *Harvard Educational Review*, 29 (1959), pp. 352–69.

[28] Chiranji La. Sharma, "Practices in Decision-Making as Related to Satisfaction in Teaching," unpublished Ph.D. dissertation (Department of Education, University of Chicago, 1955).

[29] Everett C. Hughes, *Men and Their Work* (New York: Free Press, 1958), ch. 9.

[30] The interviews referred to were part of the Boston Area Study.

[31] Emile Durkheim, *Education and Sociology* (New York: Free Press, 1956); Willard Waller, *The Sociology of Teaching* (New York: John Wiley & Sons, Inc., Science Editions, 1965).

[32] Teachers dismiss most of their courses as "too theoretical." It seems that they are referring less to an inappropriate level of generalization than to overly idealistic depictions of what it is possible to attain in classrooms.

[33] J. W. Getzels and P. W. Jackson, "The Teacher's Personality and Characteristics," in N. L. Gage (ed.), *Handbook of Research*

on *Teaching* (Chicago: Rand McNally and Co., 1963), p. 574.

[34] Egon G. Guba, Philip W. Jackson, and Charles E. Bidwell, "Occupational Choice and the Teaching Career," *Educational Research Bulletin*, 38 (1959), pp. 1–12.

[35] Lortie, "Laymen to Lawmen."

[36] Laurence Iannoccone and H. Warren Button, *Functions of Student Teaching; Attitude Formation and Initiation on Elementary School Teaching*, Cooperative Research Project No. 1026 (St. Louis: Graduate Institute of Education, Washington University, 1964).

[37] Emil Haller, in the course of research on teacher socialization, sampled conversation from the author's tape-recorded interviews with elementary teachers and compared it with the Thorndike-Lorge Word List, a listing of the frequency with which English words are used. He found that 89.6 per cent of the words used in the interviews coincided with the 2,200 most commonly used words on the list. Words with prefixes and suffixes were not included; Haller estimated that such words would account for half the remaining words. Such heavy use of common vocabulary in discussion of their work does not support the beliefs that teachers possess and employ an extensive technical rhetoric. See Emil J. Haller, "Technical Socialization: Pupil Influences on Teachers' Speech" (Unpublished Ph.D. dissertation, Department of Education, University of Chicago, 1966).

Occupational Commitment and the Teaching Profession

Blanche Geer

Much of my thinking for this paper has been stimulated by the work of Everett C. Hughes. I am indebted to Howard S. Becker for critical readings and constructive advice.

Reprinted from The School Review, 74 (1966), 31–47, by permission of the author and publisher, The University of Chicago Press.

OCCUPATIONAL commitment is one of the chief values in our society. It is a mark of adulthood among us to settle down to a consistent line of activity, a career in a chosen field. With few exceptions, we have structured our organizations in such a way that they operate best with a low turnover of workers, and it is the mark of a good administrator to keep them at their jobs. Similarly, the occupation which people leave does not seem to us a good one; we value most those occupations which people choose early and work at into old age. Particularly in occupations aspiring to be professions or in doubt of their status, there may be great concern about commitment because it is considered a mark of the real profession.

Teaching is a profession, or would-be profession, presently so concerned about commitment that its concern has stimulated research on the extent and sources of the problem. Studies have found that 26 per cent of the graduates in education do not immediately enter teaching[1] and that 60 per cent of the recruits do not stay in teaching for five years.[2] Another study, widely cited to demonstrate lack

of commitment, found that half of a sample of beginning teachers expected to leave teaching within five years.[3]

Discussions of this last study usually fail to note that only about 20 per cent expect to leave teaching permanently for other occupations or family duties. While only 29 per cent of the men and 16 per cent of the women plan to teach until retirement, an additional 51 per cent of the men and 9 per cent of the women expect to stay in the schools in some capacity, and 58 per cent of the women hope to reenter teaching when family duties permit. Thus the problem is not one of permanent loss to the schools; teachers can be said to lack commitment only insofar as women do not want to teach continuously, and men want advancement beyond the classroom.[4] Nevertheless, in the eyes of administrators who need people in their classrooms and to those who want teachers to be more like other professionals (or what they conceive these to be), teachers are insufficiently committed. They do not want to make teaching an uninterrupted, lifelong career.

Research on the sources of the problem has taken two forms. Surveys have found high turnover in secondary schools and among women.[5] Following the lead of industrial sociology, other investigators have found teachers dissatisfied with their pay and working conditions.[6] But as yet no one has approached commitment in broad sociological terms. The basic questions as to the nature of commitment as a process have not been related to those aspects of occupational structure which may facilitate commitment or impede it. In this paper I shall attempt to outline the possibilities of such an approach.

In a ground-breaking paper, Becker suggests that commitment to any consistent line of activity occurs when an individual, confronted with an opportunity to depart from it, discovers that in the course of past activity he has, wittingly or not, accumulated valuables of a kind that would be lost to him if he makes a change.[7] We can apply this conception of commitment (as Becker does briefly in illustrating his thesis) to commitment to an occupation. In doing so, we shall be concerned not so much with commitment as an individual process, as with certain occupational and organizational structures which appear likely to facilitate the accumulation of valuables resulting in commitment. Since there is evidence that the well-established professions produce high levels of commitment,[8] we shall in most instances compare the kinds of valuables generated by certain aspects of the structure of medical practice, college teaching, and research, as well as some of the arts, to the valuables characteristic of school-teaching.

Training

One aspect of occupational structure is the familiar division into apprentice, journeyman, and master paralleled in the professions by student, beginner or intern, and full-fledged practitioner. We may suppose that commitment may occur in any of the three stages of a career. Since it minimizes waste for both occupation and trainee, commitment during training has obvious advantages.

In some occupations, the trainee acquires sufficient valuables to make it quite likely that he will feel himself committed before his training has been completed. Medicine is a good example. Our data on medical students suggest that the high position of medicine in the external structure or hierarchy of occupation allows the student to regard medicine as the best of the professions. He feels that in doing so he has the support of society, his community, friends, relatives, and parents. Having once announced publicly that he wishes to enter medicine by applying to medical

school and actually beginning the term, he cannot face the thought of what people would think of him if he did not graduate and eventually begin practice. For him, there is no other occupation equal in status and desirability.[9] He has staked his pride and self-esteem—valuables he must lose if he discontinues medical training.

Not infrequently, an internal occupational structure characterized by long, expensive, and arduous training occurs in occupations with high rank in the external hierarchy of occupations. Medical school and the obligatory internship take five years; a residency in order to specialize, several years more. In addition, the would-be physician has often taken a heavy load of science courses in college and even in high school in order to speed his progress. In effect, he has invested twelve or more years of his life (sacrificing other interests) and a tremendous amount of effort and money in his medical training.

Perhaps the most compelling form of valuable that an occupation or profession can provide is specificity of knowledge and skill. What the medical student learns can only be used in one occupation, and there is a strong professional society legally capable of excluding those without the one training, license, and degree. Medicine has another advantage over many less catholic occupations in that one medical degree prepares for all medical careers. The single label "physician" describes a large number of styles of work and living.

Since his patients are not likely to be very sick, the specialist in dermatology works a nine-to-five office day; general practitioners and obstetricians work longer and more irregular hours. According to whether he chooses a specialty in demand only in large cities or a type of practice needed in small communities, the physician can choose his style of life.[10] Main Street, the Alaskan wilds, and Park Avenue are all possibilities for him, although in the case of the last he will have had to choose his medical school carefully. Careers in administration, teaching, and research are other possibilities. Paradoxically, the high specificity of medical training to the physician's work, under the present strong organization of the profession, provides the student with a variety of choices of career. His specialized knowledge and skills are forbidden to others; they constitute valuables difficult to abandon.

In contrast, the student preparing himself to be a schoolteacher associates himself with an occupation far from the top of the prestige ladder. There are many kinds of work he can take up without losing self-esteem, occupations popularly considered to make equal or superior contributions to society. As he continues his courses, he does not accumulate the kind of knowledge or skill which would make it a great social waste if he did not spend his life in the classroom. Thus, the pressure of cultural expectations will be relatively light for him.

His training requires no greater investment of time and money than any other college major. He is as free (and this is quite free insofar as we can judge by our present study of undergraduates) to develop interests outside of the field of education, as his classwork is less difficult and time-consuming than that of many majors.[11] It usually includes no more than two years of specifically professional training which has not required unusual preparation in high school. Since a B.S. in education is as acceptable a ticket as a B.A., the graduate is not limited to schoolteaching in his choice of occupation. Nor does he have knowledge and skills belonging only to

him. Under present conditions of shortage, his professional associations are not strong enough to protect him from the encroachments of the partially trained. Perhaps most tellingly, his training fits him only for one kind of work in the school system—classroom teaching. He can seldom hope for advancement without experience in the classroom, followed by more education. He will enter schools which, despite their variety, nationally impose quite similar hours and tasks. He can choose between city and country and find work in many regions, but the styles of life open to him are probably much more limited than those open to other professions. Although there are individual exceptions, it is probable that most education students graduate without having completed, and in many cases scarcely having begun, the accumulation of valuables likely to commit them to a lifelong teaching career.

In fact, it might be better to think of the education major as a valuable associated with commitment to some career other than teaching. At the state university we studied, students having difficulty making their grades in liberal arts often took education courses because they were easier. In this sense, courses in education are a form of academic insurance.

They may also provide occupational insurance. Students primarily interested in athletics and the fine arts take education in order to have an alternative career to fall back on if they do not succeed in their first choice.

For the very many women students whose major occupational commitment is marriage, an education major is insurance in still another sense. A young woman will hesitate to major in a field which may lead to a job that is too interesting or well paying to leave without sacrifice. She wants training in a field that provides equally good job opportunities wherever her husband goes, and the schools are an ideal solution. Many women, including brilliant students, switch to an education major when they become engaged, because they can be certain of helping their husbands financially. In later life, they anticipate teaching in case of a husband's illness, a divorce, or other misfortune.

It is probably true that not entering an occupation for which one has trained involves some loss of face. Particularly if one has done well at school, peers and superiors will express opposition, but the woman who gives up teaching to look after her husband and children fulfils, rather than violates, cultural expectations.

Work-Related Commitment

Opportunities to acquire and retain valuables are often closely related to one's work. They may derive from the particular nature of the work itself, from the structure of the occupation, or from the structure of the employing organization and the devices it uses to hold its employees. In comparison with other professions, business, and industry, teaching offers few opportunities for work-related commitment. A brief examination of some of the processes of commitment in other occupations may clarify the point.

KNOWLEDGE AND SKILLS

If, for the moment, we consider knowledge apart from skills, it should be clear that some occupations are so structured that the people in them have opportunities to advance the fund of knowledge in their field. The work of some scientists, scholars, and engineers fits this pattern; their understandings are cumulative, often rare or unique. While it occasionally happens that a man at the peak of his abilities finds he has run through his field and begins a new career, or sees a way to apply his knowledge to

another field (as some physicists have done), most men in creative occupations find their accumulated learning so valuable, such an irreplaceable yet expanding basis for further work, that a change to another occupation, even one which seems quite similar to outsiders, is unthinkable.

There are, of course, other kinds of knowledge which we often call (for lack of better terms) "know how," skill, or experience. To work at any job, trade, or profession is to acquire a body of experience unique to it. One learns the culture of an occupational group, the "ropes"—which rules must be followed, which can or must be broken, the quirks of people and things that ease everyday performance. Most of this knowledge is so localized, so peculiar to the immediate situation, that it is not in itself useful in other occupations. It is useful only insofar as the individual has been made aware of his need for similar understanding in any occupation, and has had practice in acquiring it. Nevertheless, such knowledge is a valuable that many workers are unwilling to lose by changing occupations. Especially as they grow older, they cannot face the prospect of starting again in an unfamiliar environment.

Unlike that of the scholar-scientist or creative artist, the schoolteacher's job is to spread other people's butter.[12] He is a conveyor and transmitter, but not a creator of knowledge. The commitment resulting from the cumulative acquisition of this form of valuable is seldom possible in a life regulated by the school bell.

Teaching skills and experience are another matter. Over the years, they may become so specific to one locality, type of school, or child, that they constitute a constraining valuable, one likely not only to keep him teaching but teaching in the same classroom. As Becker has pointed out, the teacher in the slum school may become expert at maintaining discipline and getting slow learners to pass. In time he is fitted to teach only in the school where this sort of child is in the majority.[13] It is probably one of the few instances in which the teacher approaches commitment through his own achievement.[14]

CLIENTELE

In professional partnerships and solo practice, and many service occupations and small businesses, the practitioner, owner, or manager recruits his clientele. He spends time and money (if he has a business) acquiring clients, and throughout his career must devote himself to pleasing them.

Since clients voluntarily seek him out, he knows that his dealings with one individual may affect his chances of getting and retaining others. A growing clientele is his tangible reward, a proof of good work. It is a reciprocal but lopsided relationship. To the practitioner or businessman, his clients are a major investment; he must have them to make his living and to do his work. They demand continuing effort, since they not only require the services he can supply but are at liberty to go elsewhere for them. Furthermore, the kinds of clients a man has determine his status in his community and affect his daily work. Janitors, as Gold notes,[15] do not recruit their clients; they must accept what tenants come their way. Yet the janitor tries to hold on to a building with the "right" kind of tenant. The wrong kind can lower his prestige among his peers and make his life miserable with unreasonable demands. It is not surprising, therefore, that holding a clientele preoccupies the practitioner-manager.

Once secured, a good clientele makes possible a sense of continuing responsibility, pride, and satisfaction not otherwise obtainable. In time, a poor one may be improved. Such a concrete, yet tantalizing, valuable is not easily abandoned.

As an employee, the schoolteacher's relationship to his clients—his pupils and their parents—is mediated by the school administration. The teacher-client relationship is involuntary on both sides. With rare exceptions, pupils do not choose their teachers, nor teachers their pupils.[16] The teacher receives those assigned him and loses them after a year or so, no matter how close and rewarding the relationship or how much responsibility he feels for them. In fact, his proof of a successful relationship, his reward for doing his job well, is to pass his clients on to others and start afresh with new ones.

Unsatisfactory as it may frequently be in one's daily work to have a captive clientele which one cannot expand by his own efforts, the teacher is further handicapped by the fact that, unlike the practitioner or proprietor, he must divide the rewards of success with his colleagues and the school. No pupil is uniquely his own, no matter how much he may have inspired him. Many feel little need of the teacher and less dependence.

Devoted as they often are to children, many teachers do not recognize the force of still another professional handicap—the low status of their clients. Nevertheless, children and adolescents (despite many cries of alarm to the contrary) are a powerless group in society, and the fact that schoolteachers serve minors rather than adults means that they are deprived of opportunities available to other service occupations to establish useful and prestigious relationships during their daily work.

As the chief focus of their work, pupils must provide teachers with most of their rewards; they are important valuables, but so ephemeral that they seldom constrain occupational choice. If pupils keep teachers in teaching, they must do it in the most abstract and faceless sense, devoid of the continuing responsibilities to individuals of other client relationships.

PUBLIC AND AUDIENCE

Professional athletes and performing and creative artists undergo training and refine their skills throughout their careers in a continuing effort to please a public. With the help of managers, agents, or directors, the performer-artist engages in what is essentially a recruiting process to attract and maintain public interest over the years. Limited at first to one locality, if the performer is to define himself as a success, his public must become nationwide, an expanding group to which he presents himself on tour or to whom others distribute his work. Although the relationship can hardly be called face-to-face as with clients, the performer-artist responds to the approval or disapproval of his public and engages in a reciprocal relationship in which he maintains or improves his standards of work in order to maintain or increase its regard. The kind of public an artist has (loyal, discriminating, or distinguished), as well as its size, measures his success and constitutes his chief career valuable.[17]

Performers also have an audience of colleagues. A much smaller group, it contains professional friends and acquaintances. By turns critical and supportive, colleagues are often as valuable an audience as the general public.

Somewhat incongruously, scholars, scientists, and professionals engaged in research also have an audience. It consists largely of colleagues who follow their publications in professional journals. A man who publishes in the journals of applied fields may even acquire an audience of men of action who seek his

advice as consultant. Over time, the scholar-researcher gathers a network of people who share his interests. The process is one of accretion. To meet someone who has read your work or whose work you have read may be to make a friend; it will certainly broaden and deepen the relationship. Initial interaction is eased by shared ideas and experiences. Making such a friend leads to meeting his colleagues and having him meet yours. As the pattern of interaction enlarges, it both expands and confirms the intellectual concerns and professional understandings of each participant. Office in professional societies may follow, bringing still another increment in interests and colleagues. There is a free flow of professional "gossip"—news of job openings and working conditions about the country. Network members have a national orbit. No longer dependent upon local contacts and employees, they are loyal to peers scattered about the country. In time, the network becomes a valuable that binds a man to a particular branch of his profession.

Shut in by the four walls of his classroom, the schoolteacher has neither a public nor an audience of colleagues which he can increase by the excellence of his work as in the performing and creative arts, or bind into a helpful peer group as in research. He seldom writes for publication, is not asked to consult or display his skills to anyone but his pupils—a small proportion of the children in one school. He may establish a reputation among them which brings him tearful praise at commencement time and more tractable classes, but children are without power in an adult world. They cannot, as colleagues can, expand one's career within or beyond the confines of the local community. He is denied the rewards which, in other occupations, spur people on to new tasks and responsibilities. Instead, he faces always the routines of repetitive work.

Teaching has been and often still is, in spite of the proliferation of public-address systems, a curiously secretive process for one which takes place in a group. Doctor and patient in the hospital are more subject to interruption and observation than a teacher in his classroom. Supervisors may look in, but in most schools visitors of all kinds—parents, fellow teachers, the principal himself—are kept out. The privacy of teaching makes it difficult for others to evaluate the teacher and for him to evaluate himself. Lacking both a public and an audience of colleagues, the teacher lacks valuables which might well commit him to teaching.

PROMOTION

Many industries, business organizations, and government bureaucracies have a differentiated, hierarchal structure. Complexity of function engenders numerous divisions and sections within an organization, each with several kinds of personnel. Within sections and from one section to another there are promotions which bring new titles, higher pay, and more interesting and responsible work as one moves up. Workers define movement up this ladder as a reward for achievement. Once caught by the system, to stand on one rung of the ladder is to reach for the next. Climbed rungs are an investment increasingly difficult to abandon as the climbing process (rather than work itself) becomes, for many workers, a central value. It is, at the same time, a gamble which takes "know how" and experience and can fill dull days with effort and suspense.

The structure of our educational system presents two faces—one to the student passing through it, another to those who teach. For the student, the several units of the structure are serially linked. Good work insures uninterrupted promotion from elementary school through junior to high school, and predisposes the student to continue the sequence in college and often beyond. For the teacher, the segmented character of the school system is paramount. Most schools of education require specialization of their students. Separate programs prepare teachers for elementary- and high-school teaching. With few exceptions, the teacher's career is bound to the segment of the public-school system for which he is trained.

With additional training at night school and over summers, a few teachers leave the classroom to become guidance specialists, supervisors, or administrators. But the number of positions available in a given school, as in any organization with a two- or three-step hierarchy and relatively undifferentiated work, is small in relation to the number of people (in this case, teachers) on the bottom rung of the ladder. In this respect, teaching is a dead-end job without the traditionally compelling valuable—promotion.

In the absence of vertical mobility, horizontal mobility sometimes provides workers with another form of promotion. Becker's studies of Chicago schoolteachers suggest that horizontal mobility may be characteristic of large-city systems.[18] Beginning teachers start where there are the most vacancies—the slum schools—but there is a transfer list. With luck and the passage of time, a teacher may be able to move to a school in a middle-class neighborhood where working conditions are less arduous. Like the promotion ladder provided by industry, accumulated time on a transfer list is not something a worker wants to give up. It is a ticket to something better within the system.

Classroom teachers outrank each other in length of service (often accompanied by pay increases) and may be elevated to the position of department head, but the distinctions are minimal in comparison with those of a larger bureaucracy. Doing well at the job is not usually recognized by promotion, and distinguishing titles are seldom employed. What differences there are in teachers' status in a school are usually related informally to seniority. Just as the youngest cab driver gets the oldest cab and the man with most seniority the newest, the longer a teacher stays at his job, the more likely he is to have the sunniest classroom, the best sections to teach, and fewer nonteaching duties. If such privileges were formalized, they would be inducements to remain in teaching. Since they are usually informal, they are peculiar to one school and one administration. A new principal may disregard seniority as a matter of policy (he has to show the old guard he is boss), or he may break patterns of privilege simply because he does not know who has been there longest.

Administrative policy often provides employees with the chance to acquire committing valuables in the form of retirement plans which build up over the years into large sums. These are more likely to influence teachers nearing retirement age and already settled than uncommitted young ones with opportunities to leave but to whom old age is improbably distant.

Off-the-Job Commitment

Occupations differ in the amount of leisure they offer and the degree of identification with a community they permit. At one extreme, executives of large corporations spend long hours on the job and take work home at night. Their limited leisure reduces involvement with local friends, voluntary associations, politics, sports, and hobbies. If the company shifts them from one plant to another at frequent intervals, they have

even less opportunity or inclination to cement local ties. The executive who sticks to his career under these conditions does so largely for the sake of valuables immediately related to his work.

Schoolteaching is at the opposite extreme. Localized in one area, the school system cannot foster geographical mobility; it is in competition with other school systems for teachers. The schedule offers several vacations and, in comparison with other professionals and many executives, short working hours.[19] The schedule permits teachers to "moonlight." They run summer camps or after-school businesses—often insurance. According to an NEA survey in 1960–61, 73 per cent of the men in teaching had such additional jobs.[20] The man with a family may initially phrase his outside work as a financial necessity because of his low teaching pay; once started, it easily becomes an important or even a central interest which ironically binds him to teaching, since continuous schedules in other occupations would make his moonlight job impossible.

Fewer women moonlight (16 per cent),[21] but much the same mechanism operates for them, if with reversed emphasis. They continue in teaching or return to it after marriage because the family has become used to the extra income. Begun as an insurance occupation, a second best to marriage, teaching becomes a valuable in the marriage; to give it up would be a family loss.

Needless to say, a teacher may pursue interests during his free time which eventually conflict with a commitment to teaching. He can educate himself up and out of the classroom or find that his moonlighting has expanded to full time. Nevertheless, the combination of stable residence and relatively large amounts of leisure may well result in more constraining valuables than any other aspect of teaching. The teacher continues to teach because it has become convenient —a negative form of commitment which may not result in good teaching.

Discussion

Several of the mechanisms of commitment in other occupations which we have discussed suggest changes that might be brought about in the teaching profession if lifelong commitment on the part of more teachers is desired. But as we have seen, commitment is a process so closely fitted to occupational structure that changes in it would necessarily involve structural change in teaching as a profession, which would, in turn, affect the organization of the school system in ways that might prove disruptive to other desirable goals.

In such a situation, the sociologist should be conservative: I offer the following suggestions for change very tentatively, indeed; they may well be too sweeping for serious consideration.

Although medicine may now be passing out of this phase (there are many things to be said against it), one degree and one set of courses for all those who wish to work in the schools (I hesitate to say what it should be called) and less emphasis on training people for elementary and high schools, specialties, and administration is a possibility. An initial year of interning as ordinary teachers, similar to the Master of Arts in Teaching program, might also be salutary.[22]

Perhaps it is too radical to suggest that teachers be given opportunity to express among their peers their accumulated experience of the job—to write, speak, and visit other schools. Currently, everyone except teachers seems to write and speak about them. In this way, they would acquire an audience of colleagues

with all the expansion of professional interests this implies.

In a sense, the increase of teaching by television may be providing a few teachers, at least in part, with the rewards of a public. It is even possible that such differentiation of function among teachers still in the classroom could form the basis of a promotion system within the school which would not destroy the rather uneasy equality teachers now enjoy. At worst, such devices suggest solutions to administrative difficulties in evaluating teachers' work.

Were teaching a year-round job, fewer teachers would back into commitment via moonlighting and other outside interests, perhaps at the profession's cost. Certainly the most sweeping change possible would occur if women ever permit themselves to regard work outside the home as the obligation of both sexes.[23]

The devices usually recommended to increase commitment—higher pay, better working conditions, and an improved professional "public image"—have probably not been successful. These are certainly valuables for the worker, but not necessarily committing valuables, since still better pay, conditions, and prestige can be obtained by leaving teaching for other occupations. Teachers' pay has risen but, as we all know, so has that of other professions, and manipulation of the external structure of occupations (their relative rank) is a task only the higher agency of government can undertake successfully.[24]

Occasionally, however, when change is under way in one part of a social structure, unanticipated possibilities of change in other parts develop. The many current changes in education suggest that changes in the occupational commitment of teachers are also a possibility.

Notes

[1] National Education Association, Research Division, *Teacher Supply and Demand*

in Public Schools, 1964 (Research Report 1964–R9 [Washington, D.C., 1964]), pp. 28–29.

² William Rabinowitz and Kay E. Crawford, "A Study of Teachers' Careers," *School Review*, 58 (1960), pp. 377–99.

³ Ward S. Mason, *The Beginning Teacher: Status and Career Orientations* (U.S. Department of Health, Education, and Welfare, Office of Education, Circular No. 644 [Washington, D.C.: Government Printing Office, 1961]), p. 102.

⁴ *Ibid.*, p. 103, table 73.

⁵ Frank Lindenfeld, *Teacher Turnover in Public Elementary and Secondary Schools 1959–60* (U.S. Department of Health, Education, and Welfare, Office of Education, Circular No. 675 [Washington, D.C.: Government Printing Office, 1963]), p. 10.

⁶ Jack W. McLaughlin and John T. Shea, "California Teachers' Job Dissatisfaction," *California Journal of Educational Research*, 11 (1960), pp. 216–24; Frederick L. Redefer, "The School Board and Teacher Morale," *American School Board Journal*, 145 (1962), pp. 5–7; James Leon Turner, *Morale-Building Techniques in the Secondary Schools of Texas* (Austin: Texas Study of Secondary Education, February, 1960).

⁷ Howard S. Becker, "Notes on the Concept of Commitment," *American Journal of Sociology*, 66 (1960), pp. 32–35. I have used the term "valuable" (p. 39) throughout for "side bet."

⁸ Harold L. Wilensky, "Varieties of Work Experience," in *Man in a World at Work*, ed. Henry Borow (Boston: Houghton Mifflin, 1964), p. 137.

⁹ Howard S. Becker, Blanche Geer, Everett C. Hughes, and Anselm Strauss, *Boys in White: Student Culture in Medical School* (Chicago: University of Chicago Press, 1961), ch. 5.

¹⁰ *Ibid.*, ch. 18.

¹¹ The data were gathered at a large midwestern university by Howard S. Becker, Blanche Geer, and Marsh Ray. The study, supported by a grant from the Carnegie Corporation, is now being written up by Becker and Geer.

¹² Graham Wallas, *Our Social Heritage* (New Haven: Yale University Press, 1921), p. 149.

¹³ Howard S. Becker, "The Career of the Chicago Public School Teacher," *American Journal of Sociology*, 57 (1952), pp. 473–77.

¹⁴ For an insightful discussion of still other skills characteristic of teachers, see J. M. Stephens, "Spontaneous Schooling and Success," *School Review*, 68 (1960), 152–63.

¹⁵ Ray Gold, "Janitors versus Tenants: A Status-Income Dilemma," *American Journal of Sociology*, 57 (1952), pp. 486–93.

¹⁶ For a discussion of the importance of such variables in the relation of client and medical practitioner, see Eliot Freidson, "Client Control and Medical Practice," *American Journal of Sociology*, 65 (1960), pp. 374–82.

¹⁷ For a fascinating description of ballet training that supports this view, see Marilyn Fortescue and Pauline Kolenda, "Ballet Company" (unpublished MS., November, 1964).

¹⁸ Becker, see n. 13 above, pp. 470–77.

¹⁹ Harold L. Wilensky, "The Uneven Distribution of Leisure," *Social Problems*, 9 (1961), pp. 32–56.

²⁰ National Education Association, Research Division, *The American Public-School Teacher, 1960–61* (Research Monograph 1963-M2 [Washington, D.C.: 1963]).

²¹ *Ibid.*

²² For a report on this program, see Francis Keppel, "Masters of Arts in Teaching," in *American Education Today*, eds. Paul Woodring and John Scanlon (New York: McGraw-Hill, 1963).

²³ For an analysis of this problem, see Helen Mayer Hacker, "Women as a Minority Group," *Social Forces*, 30 (1951), pp. 60–69.

²⁴ Wallas, *op. cit.* For a discussion of this problem in England some years ago, see ch. vi.

Introduction

TWO BASIC APPROACHES to studying the effect of occupational milieu on value orientations have been emphasized in sociological literature. One approach, that of "social class" analysis, is the predominant one. Whether derived from á Marxian or a Weberian point of view, or from a less theoretical classification system, a basic assumption of this approach is that occupations may be classified in terms of basic dimensions that reflect the social class system. Persons in a given category of occupations, regardless of the particular occupation, are hypothesized to share common behavior patterns, attitudes, and values with persons in this category but to differ in distinctive ways from persons in other "classes." Those who embark from Marxist assumptions will select as the crucial source of differentiation the relationship of the "class" to the means of production. Weberians argue that it is the "probability of achieving life chances" based on position in the marketplace that is central. A pragmatic researcher might utilize income level to differentiate occupational groupings. Under all of the formulations suggested, occupations such as teaching and social work would tend to fall under a common heading.

A contrasting line of sociological thought takes occupations themselves, rather than social classes, as significant social milieux. Emile Durkheim is a central intellectual progenitor of this point of view. A number of studies of occupational cultures—that of lawyers, doctors, and restaurant employees, to list a few examples—derive from such a sociological tradition.[1] In this paper, we would like to present some evidence regarding the variation of values between and within occupational groups that fall within a single class categorization. We shall show that teachers differ in values from social workers and that the social

Occupational and Class Differences in Social Values: A Comparison of Teachers and Social Workers

Henry J. Meyer,
Eugene Litwak, and
Donald Warren

Revision of a paper presented at the Annual Meeting of the American Sociological Association, Los Angeles, August 1963. Because of an ongoing experiment, we cannot at this time identify by our grateful acknowledgment the school system whose teachers and officials made this research possible. We can acknowledge support from the Russell Sage Foundation Social Work and Social Science grant to The University of Michigan. More recent phases of the research continue under a grant from the U.S. Office of Education. We wish also to acknowledge the assistance of Ronald Feldman in the analysis of data.

Reprinted from Sociology of Education, *41 (1968), pp. 263–81, by permission of the authors and publisher, The American Sociological Association.*

values of teachers are further differentiated by occupational setting.

In considering value differences between social workers and teachers, one of two lines of reasoning could be followed. Where a society has a multiplicity of values which are not always consistent but are equally desired, it may be necessary, in order to preserve these differences, to provide organizational autonomy to such values.[2] Put more specifically, social work as a profession may be viewed as having emerged historically to stress different values as compared to teaching.

A second factor that may produce value differences is the nature of the work setting. In some ways, there are considerable differences between the two professions. This is especially true if one takes the extremes of each profession—for example, the mathematics teacher in a high school and the psychiatric caseworker. Let us consider dimensions of work that separate these extreme cases. First, the teacher deals directly with a group—20, 30, 40 or more—whereas the caseworker usually deals directly with a single individual. Secondly, the teacher works with children or adolescents where there is a clear status difference coupled with an important social mandate to inculcate knowledge and to socialize the "client," and this mandate carries considerable coercive backing for a one-way influence to change. By contrast, the mandate for change is not a clear-cut one for the caseworker, nor are the criteria for satisfactory change uniform. The caseworker frequently deals with an adult client, with no sharp age status differences involved. The relationship has considerably less coercion built into it than teaching; success is based mainly on persuasion. In addition, through the institution of "supervision," the social worker is in constant touch with a fellow professional—the supervisor—and their discussion of the "case" or "patient" takes place within almost a colleague type relationship. In contrast, the teacher has much less formal contact with fellow professionals about any given pupil, and the teacher's immediate supervisor—a principal or assistant principal of the school—has a clearly higher status. This relationship is more likely to be a hierarchical, evaluative one rather than the colleagal one the social worker usually has with a "supervisor."

Teaching and social work also differ in the degree of specialization found within each profession. The teacher of one particular subject often has distinctive knowledge and skills that are not easily transferred to other subjects. A chemistry teacher requires different training from a music teacher or an English teacher. Moreover, the teacher must deal with a broad range of the population of children; the caseworker usually deals with a narrower segment. With compulsory education for all children, the demand for teachers exceeds the demand for caseworkers and the teaching profession cannot afford as stringent a selection procedure or training program as that of professional social work. Finally, teaching and social work, to a large extent, appear to start from different premises and to have different goals. Thus, the social worker is involved in changing personality, inter-personal relations, and conditions of living whereas the teacher tends to be concerned mainly with transmitting a body of information, knowledge, or "culture" that does not necessarily assume that the person or his situation must be changed. In fact, one common viewpoint in teaching is that the individual's capacity to absorb knowledge is a biological phenomenon and that recognizing and adapting to this fixed capacity is a necessary part of the teaching job. This is often an important assumption of the differentiated high school curriculum consisting of college preparation, general education, and vocational training. In this regard, schools follow a pattern that characterized social work at the turn of the century when the assumption was made that mental illness was a biologically based disease not amenable to treatment. Those who were ill were merely placed in an asylum for custody and those less severely afflicted were kept at home without hope of recovery.

From analysis of this sort, we would argue that the social work profession acts as a guardian of humanitarian values and its practitioners tend to operate in a human relations type of bureaucratic structure. It treats personality and social relations as variables capable of change. It has a relatively small professional cadre which permits a high degree of selection and intensive training. Conversely, the teaching profession tends to focus on the transmission of knowledge and cultural values defined in a relatively fixed manner. Teachers generally function within a rationalistic bureaucratic environment where recognition of fixed personality attributes and capacities is stressed.[3] The large population served by teachers results in less restrictive recruitment procedures and consequently a weaker form of occupational socialization.

Granted such points of difference between social work and teaching, how do these factors generate divergent value orientations if such exist? To examine this question, we take a baseline drawn from a study by Meyer and McLeod.[4] From examination of social work literature, they describe ten value dimensions that characterize the social work profession. In this paper we shall employ five of these dimensions to reflect values of professional social workers. Although Meyer and McLeod could not determine what selective factors, if any, operate to produce "social work values" among social workers, they were able to demonstrate that the more professional training social workers have, the more they adhere to the values we use in the present study. Meyer and McLeod also demonstrate that the more obvious selective attributes such as race, religion, and age do not account for the differences in values between the more trained and less trained social workers. This means, aside from selective recruitment or out-movement, that direct socialization into a set of values may occur due to training and associated experiences.

Our effort to demonstrate that the influence of occupational setting operates despite class similarities in occupational groups will be based on three lines of evidence. First, we will show that social work and teaching, which by all definitions of class are occupations falling within the same category, have major differences in value orientation. Second, we will show that the older and more experienced teachers have values that contrast most with those of social workers and with younger and less experienced teachers, suggesting processes of socialization or selective dropout. Third, we will show that when the work setting of teachers approaches that of the social work setting, the values of teachers approach those of social workers. The latter task will be accomplished in two ways: (1) by indicating that where school structures have been altered to approach social work patterns the values of teachers differ accordingly; (2) by showing that teachers in elementary schools (where tasks and job milieu are more like social work than those of secondary schools) have values more like social workers than do high school teachers.

Discussion of Values[5]

Brief descriptions of the five values used in this paper follow:

1. *Individual worth vs. System goals.* A primary social value in our society centers around the idea of worth and dignity of the individual as contrasted with the idea that the goals of the group, the state, or social system are preeminent. Although ideologically both social workers and teachers may be presumed to share an emphasis on individual worth, the characteristic one-to-one relationship between social worker and client might be expected to support this value to a

greater degree than the responsibility of the teacher facing a group of children collectively as a class. Furthermore, social and cultural norms are traditionally stressed in the content of public school education in contrast to the stress in social work (associated with psychoanalytic doctrine) on minimizing psychic tensions of individuals.

2. *Group responsibility vs. Individual responsibility.* Social work has a strong tradition asserting the responsibility of the group—the family, the community, the government—for the welfare of its members in contrast to the position of primary or exclusive individual responsibility. The teacher, not institutionally responsible for social reform on behalf of individual welfare, does not often directly confront this issue but, on the contrary, tends to emphasize individual achievement in assignments and tests. Furthermore, the adult-child status relationship in teaching may heighten the sense of the teacher's own responsibility for the outcome of teaching, in contrast to the necessarily shared responsibility of the social worker with the client in the usual adult-adult relationship. Likewise, the collegial context of professional social work supports the conception of collective rather than individual responsibility whereas the hierachical structure of the school may tend to fix responsibility more on the individual in his fixed status.

3. *Security-satisfaction vs. Struggle-suffering-denial.* Again related to psychoanalytic doctrine, the view that security and the satisfaction of biological and culturally acquired needs underlie the realization of individual potential is strongly represented in the ideology of professional social work. The more puritan belief in the importance of struggle, denial, and punishment as ennobling is rejected. In his practice the social worker usually faces the deprived client exhibiting minimum security; the teacher faces a group of children whose impulses and needs must be disciplined

to permit knowledge to be transmitted to the class by the teacher. There is less reason, therefore, for the teacher to contest the pervasive belief in American society that discipline, control, denial are positive conditions for the creation of "good character."

4. *Innovation-change vs. Traditionalism.* The social reform heritage of social work, built on reactions against Social Darwinism and on belief in the power of legislation, has persisted as a theme within the profession despite later psychological emphasis which diminished its dominance. Continuity and conservation characterize school teaching in its role as preserver and transmitter of culture. Exposed to deviant social groups, social workers are likely to confirm their belief in change; exposed to children, ignorant but not deviant, teachers are likely to stress transmission of existing knowledge and values. The structure of separate and relatively small social agencies as work places contrasts with that of large public school systems where change may be viewed more as disruptive than supportive.

5. *Interdependence vs. Individual autonomy.* The ideology of social work sees, as an existential belief, the dependence of individuals on others, of families on surrounding conditions, of one undesirable social condition on another. The autonomy of the individual is viewed as limited. No such ideology seems particularly relevant to the teaching profession. Both the tasks of the teacher and the work setting would, rather, encourage the sense that the person is himself capable of determining his own destiny.

The foregoing comments on these five values[6] are intended only to suggest their content and its possible relation to more obvious characteristics of social work and teaching. Much more detailed presentation would be required to establish historical evidence of differential ideologies. Even more difficult would be the demonstration that values are direct expressions of the social structural features of the two occupations. For our purposes it is sufficient to indicate that such relationships are plausible, since our objective is to show that there are empirical differences in values between social workers and teachers and to argue that one may seek explanation for such differences in the characteristics of the occupations and their structural settings rather than in their social class location.

Differences in Social Values of Social Workers and Teachers

Meyer and McLeod sampled three groups of social workers: (1) those who were fully trained in their profession (holding a master's degree in social work); (2) those who were in training (in school of social work); and (3) those who had little or no professional training (social workers in public welfare and other public programs).[7] They found that the more fully trained the social worker, the more he or she is likely to adhere to Individual worth rather than

System goals, to Innovation-change rather than Traditionalism, to Group responsibility rather than Individual responsibility, to Security-satisfaction rather than Struggle-suffering-denial, and to Interdependence rather than Individual autonomy.[8] This outcome apparently involves some kind of socialization or selective screening-out of individuals for professional training. However, the differences between trained and untrained social workers persist when background characteristics — including ethnicity, religion, and age, which are related to value positions—are controlled.[9] On the basis of these findings, we will accept as an appropriate indication of "social work values," for purposes of this paper, those values espoused most strongly by the professionally trained social workers in the Meyer-McLeod sample.

To compare the value orientation of teachers to social workers a revised but over-lapping version of the Social Values Test was administered to 721 public school teachers in a large city.[10] Because only some items, common to both versions of the test, were answered by both social workers and teachers, we cannot compare the total value dimension scores for social workers and teachers. We have, however, made item-by-item comparisons for each value dimension, using only common questions. Where the social workers adhere to the value

Table 1—Comparison of Social Workers (N = 293) and Teachers (N = 721) on Identical Items of Social Values Test by Value Dimensions*

VALUE DIMENSION	Number of Identical Items	Number of Items S. Workers Have Higher Proportions Than Teachers	AVERAGE PROPORTION ADHERING TO VALUE	
			S. Ws.	Teachers
Individual worth	6	6	73	54
Group responsibility	8	8	78	50
Security-satisfaction	6	6	81	55
Innovation-change	6	5	62	57
Interdependence	6	6	70	40

NOTE: Because of the nature of our samples, we have used a sign test that makes minimal assumptions. Using this test almost all our comparisons of value differences in Tables 1–9 are significant at the .06 level for the two-tailed test and .03 for the one-tailed test. In the above table, the innovation change differences do not meet this criterion.

*Stated as the value position preferred by professionally trained social workers.

positions of professional social work more than the teachers, we would argue that this is evidence for the hypothesis of systematic occupational differences between the two groups. Where teachers adhere to such values more than social workers, such a difference would not be explainable in the structure of reasoning we have presented. Table 1 indicates that with regard to the items of all value dimensions considered, substantially more social workers adhere to these values than do the teachers.

From Table 1 we can see that social workers are consistently higher than teachers in their responses to common items in each of the five value dimensions.[11] For all of the values combined, there were 32 common items, and, on 31 of these, social workers had a larger proportion than teachers professing the indicated pole of the dimension. Despite the fact that both social work and teaching are usually grouped in the same social class, these findings are evidence that, within a given class, occupational groups may exhibit distinctive value positions.

Recruitment vs. Socialization and Selective Drop-out

The question now arises as to whether the association between teachers and particular values is a consequence of selective recruitment, socialization on the job, or a process of selective withdrawal from the profession. To examine this question, we will first examine the relationship, if any, between experience in the occupation—in this case teaching—and value orientation. If socialization, or selective elimination, is operating, then teachers who have been in the profession longer are more likely to exhibit the values which characterize all members of the occupation than newer teachers. Teachers were divided into two groups—those with ten or fewer years of teaching and those with eleven or more years of teaching. As can be noted in Table 2, those with more teaching experience are less likely than less experienced teachers to adhere to values characteristic of social work.[12] It can be seen that for four of the five value dimensions, the socializing or selective effects are substantially apparent. This is evidence that, aside from any initial selectivity into teaching, there is a subsequent factor differentiating value positions associated with years of service in the profession.[13] Since years of teaching experience and years of age are obviously correlated, it is not surprising to report a consistent decrease with age in proportions of teachers giving high responses on the value dimensions, with the most striking shift occurring between the 20–29 year category and the older age

Table 2—More Experienced Teachers Are Less Likely than Less Experienced to Adhere to Social Work Values

	PERCENT OF TEACHERS SCORING HIGH ON EACH VALUE	
VALUE DIMENSION	0–10 Years Teaching Experience	11 or More Years of Teaching
Individual worth	47	43
Group responsibility	57	39
Security-satisfaction	54	36
Innovation-change	65	42
Interdependence	54	41
$N = 646$	(358)	(288)

categories. Occupational socialization or selection may account for this relationship. If the former, some evidence may be derived from the following analysis of teachers in schools believed to have different work milieux.

Project and Non-project Schools

The sample included teachers in working class schools where a special project was in progress, in working-class non-project schools considered comparable to project schools, and in middle-class schools.[14] The intent of the project— an official effort by the school system— was to introduce significant changes in educational and community programs and to re-orient the school toward educational problems of deprived areas. If the intent was realized and if the milieu for teachers in project schools was thereby modified in a direction more in keeping with social work orientations, the values of project school teachers ought to reflect this difference. If, furthermore, teachers are otherwise similar in background characteristics in the three sets of schools, we will have some support for the hypothesis that work milieu produces a structural effect on social values within the teaching occupation.

At the time when the values test was administered, seven of the 16 schools were project schools. All of these were in the lowest income areas of the city. The project provided a number of structural innovations. For each school, three full-time staff members were added to organize special programs for pupils with reading difficulties, to aid families who were having social-emotional problems, and to develop closer school-community interaction. In addition, funds were provided to keep the schools open in after-school hours and to hire additional personnel to work with children and adults in the neighborhood. Moreover, additional funds were provided to the project schools for extra supplies, for fields trips, and to give additional training to teachers. The overall result of these structural changes was to reduce the teacher-pupil ratio, to increase the per-pupil investment by approximately eight percent, and to stress values that were closer to contemporary social work values. Thus, the assumption of the project was that the learning level of children did not reflect a fixed I.Q., but that motivation and home training could bring about significant alterations. The assumption was that it is necessary for the schools to work alongside the family in a closer manner than had been the case in order

Table 3—Teachers in Project Schools Adhere to Social Work Values More than Teachers in Matching Working Class Schools

PERCENT OF TEACHERS SCORING HIGH ON EACH VALUE

VALUE DIMENSION	Teachers in Middle Class Schools	Teachers in Project Schools	Teachers in Working Class Non-project Schools
Individual worth	49	52	27
Group responsibility	57	67	1
Security-satisfaction	51	61	4
Innovation-change	63	62	6
Interdependence	52	62	11
N = 646	(190)	(311)	(145)

to produce a higher educational attainment among children. Therefore, one would expect schools in the project to have value orientations which were closer to those of social workers than schools not in the project.

In Table 3 it can be seen that teachers in the project schools are much more likely to express values like professional social workers than those in non-project working class schools. Furthermore, the distributions of value responses in project schools are much more like those in the middle class schools than those in the comparable working class non-project schools. Since the project has not changed the pupil populations, factors other than the social class served must apparently be sought to explain these similarities and contrasts.[15]

The contrast between working class non-project schools and middle class schools indicates the strong relationship between social class of area served and values of teachers. Although it is the exception to this relationship of the working class project schools that interests us, we may note a number of possible explanations for the class difference itself. Aside from selective factors differentiating teachers in middle class and working class schools, it is possible that a "drift" of teachers leaning toward social work values takes place toward middle class areas. It is further possible that the character of middle class children and families permits value expressions that are suppressed in working class areas. Perhaps the values of the area served are themselves different and teachers reflect the differences. Finally, conditions associated with social class of the area may permit or require the working milieu that more nearly approaches that of social work, and this may be expressed in value orientations.[16]

This latter explanation is the implication of the difference between project and non-project working class schools. Before this implication is accepted, however, it is necessary to see whether some discernible selective factor, itself associated with social value positions, differentiates the teachers of these two groups of presumably comparable schools.[17]

Tables 4 and 5 show that both race and religion are associated with value responses, white teachers and Catholic teachers being least likely to respond like social workers. Tables 6 and 7 show that value differences between project and non-project working class schools persist when race and religion are controlled.

Although the data are not presented here, project and non-project school teachers in our sample do not differ appreciably on the following variables that might be expected to define a selective bias for project schools: age, sex, self-perceived social class status, graduate credits in education, willingness to

Table 4—Negro Teachers Adhere to Social Work Values More than White Teachers

PERCENT OF TEACHERS SCORING HIGH ON EACH VALUE

VALUE DIMENSION	Negroes	White	No Answer
Individual worth	58	42	45
Group responsibility	65	45	51
Security-satisfaction	64	40	42
Innovation-change	66	51	51
Interdependence	60	43	40
$N = 646*$	(134)	(450)	(47)

*Fifteen teachers are not included who were classified as "other" than Negro or White.

Table 5—Catholic Teachers Are Less Likely than Other Teachers To Adhere to Social Work Values

PERCENT OF TEACHERS SCORING HIGH ON EACH VALUE

VALUE DIMENSION	Jewish	Protestant	Catholic	Other and No Answer
Individual worth	56	46	38	43
Group responsibility	78	48	47	48
Security-satisfaction	78	44	40	41
Innovation-change	66	54	51	53
Interdependence	73	48	36	43
$N = 646$	(41)	(419)	(132)	(54)

go into teaching again if there were a choice, years of teaching experience, and years teaching in present school.

We are led to the tenative conclusion that milieu effects of the project, rather than selective factors, account for the value orientations of teachers in the project schools. This is in keeping with the hypothesis that conditions of occupational experience are critical determinants of social values of teachers.

Elementary and Secondary Schools

Differences between the social milieux of elementary and secondary schools may constitute a further test of the hypothesis that intra-occupational work situations of teachers are associated with variations of social values. In contrast to the high school, the elementary school usually has fewer teachers and pupils,

Table 6—Effects of Project Schools on Social Values Hold for Both Negro and White Teachers

PERCENT OF TEACHERS SCORING HIGH ON EACH VALUE

VALUE DIMENSION	Race of Teacher	Middle Class Schools	Working Class Project Schools	Working Class Non-project Schools
Individual worth	Negro	. .	63	30
	White	49	44	24
Group responsibility	Negro	. .	79	0
	White	55	63	2
Security-satisfaction	Negro	. .	74	10
	White	51	51	2
Innovation-change	Negro	. .	76	0
	White	65	65	7
Interdependence	Negro	. .	73	8
	White	52	55	11
$N = 134$	Negro	(2)	(108)	(24)
$N = 460$	White	(177)	(162)	(121)
$N = 62$	Other and No Answer	(11)	(41)	(10)
$N = 656$		(190)	(311)	(155)

Table 7—Effects of Project Schools on Social Values Holds for Each Religious Group

PERCENT OF TEACHERS SCORING HIGH ON EACH VALUE

VALUE DIMENSION	Middle Class Schools	Working Class Project Schools	Working Class Non-project Schools
		Jews*	
Individual worth	76	44	60
Group responsibility	94	82	0
Security-satisfaction	100	78	0
Innovation-change	78	70	0
Interdependence	89	70	20
N = 41	(19)	(17)	(5)
		Protestants	
Individual worth	48	55	26
Group responsibility	44	71	0
Security-satisfaction	40	65	5
Innovation-change	65	70	7
Interdependence	49	66	11
N = 419	(110)	(215)	(94)
		Catholics	
Individual worth	44	40	28
Group responsibility	70	60	2
Security-satisfaction	56	52	5
Innovation-change	62	72	5
Interdependence	38	58	5
N = 132	(45)	(50)	(37)

*Differences among Jewish respondents are in the right direction but do not meet the statistical criterion of .06.

less differentiated structure of departments and specializations, greater concern with socialization aspects for its younger student body relative to concern with transmission of subject matter. The tendency of elementary schools is toward a human relations rather than a rationalistic social structure. In these respects, the elementary school shares more features of the social agency than secondary schools do. It would, therefore, be expected that the social values of teachers in elementary schools would more nearly resemble those of social workers than would be the case with teachers in junior high and high schools.

This hypothesis is tested by the data in Table 8, where adherence to values characteristic of social work are presented for teachers in working class project and non-project schools and in middle class schools, by educational level of the schools within the school system. Although there are some exceptions, the trend is unmistakable: elementary school teachers are more likely than secondary school teachers to have high scores on the value dimensions.[18]

Contextual Effect of Majority Value Positions in Individual Schools

Our analysis thus far leads us to believe that what we have called the "occupational milieu" of the school affects the value orientations of teachers and pro-

Table 8—Adherence To Social Work Values Is Greater for Teachers in Elementary than in High Schools

		PERCENT OF TEACHERS SCORING HIGH ON EACH VALUE		
		Elementary Schools	Jr. High Schools	High Schools
VALUE DIMENSION	Class Level of Schools			
Individual worth	Wk. class project	58	55	35
	Wk. class non-project	40	28	20
	Middle class	54	48	44
Group responsibility	Wk. class project	84	72	25
	Wk. class non-project	0	3	0
	Middle class	65	67	35
Security satisfaction	Wk. class project	79	62	20
	Wk. class non-project	10	3	1
	Middle class	63	56	29
Innovation-change	Wk. class project	77	82	38
	Wk. class non-project	8	7	7
	Middle class	72	76	45
Interdependence	Wk. class project	73	66	34
	Wk. class non-project	8	17	11
	Middle-class	56	58	38
$N = 311$	Wk. class project	(135)	(112)	(64)
$N = 145$	Wk. class non-project	(40)	(29)	(76)
$N = 190$	Middle class	(81)	(54)	(55)
$N = 646$		(256)	(195)	(195)

duces substantial intra-occupational differences. We have been able to characterize the milieu of schools only generally from our data.[19] We can, however, examine one aspect of the teacher's occupational milieu: the context of value positions held by a majority of teachers in the building. We have already shown that teachers with more years of experience profess values less like social workers than teachers with fewer years of experience (see Table 2). We would, however, expect teachers, regardless of length of experience, to reflect the value positions of the majority of their work associates (where a clear majority obtains).

This contextual effect is examined in Table 9. The 16 schools have been grouped into those where 60 percent or fewer of the teachers are less experienced (have been teaching less than eleven years), those where 60 percent or more

teachers are more experienced (have been teaching eleven years or more), and those schools in which there is no clear majority of less or more experienced teachers. Teachers in these groups of schools have, in turn, been divided into those with less and those with more years of experience similarly defined. Reading across the rows of Table 9 for each value dimension, we find a consistent pattern of greater proportions of teachers, whatever their years of teaching experience, having high scores in the group of schools where the majority of teachers have less experience and hence tend toward value positions of social workers. Reading down the columns for each value dimension, we may note generally that teaching experience has the previously demonstrated effect on value positions, but this effect is least evident in the group of schools where the majority are more experienced.

Put more succinctly, the minority in terms of experience tends to express values along the same lines as the majority in their building. This is not to say that years of experience of the individual teacher makes no difference. If one looks down the columns of Table 9, it can be noted that there is a trend for the experienced teacher in any given school milieu to have lower value scores than the less-experienced teacher. There seem to be simultaneous effects of the group structure of the teaching staff in a given building and teacher's own length of experience in the occupation whether in that building or not.

Our data do not permit us to introduce controls (or trend data) to determine whether this contextual effect results from socialization in the school or selection of teachers tending to hold the values of the majority. We do have indirect evidence (presented in Table 10) that teachers who have taught longer in their present schools are more likely to report

that their "philosophy of education" has changed.[20]

Conclusion

The central theme of this paper has been that divergent work situations may produce differences in social value orientations between groups in occupations sharing the same social class position and, indeed, within a single occupation. Although our data are confined to the two professional occupations of social work and teaching, and therefore cannot claim generalization to other occupations, the evidence presented indicates considerable intra-class variation in the value positions of social workers and teachers. It further indicates considerable intra-occupational variation in values among social workers and among teachers. The

Table 9—Years of Teaching Experience of Majority of Teachers in School Affects Value Positions of Teachers Whether They Have Less or More Individual Teaching Experience

		PERCENT OF TEACHERS SCORING HIGH ON EACH VALUE		
VALUE DIMENSION	Years of Experience of Individual Teachers	Schools Where at Least 60% of Teachers Have Less Than 11 Years of Experience	Schools with No Clear Majority	Schools Where at Least 60% of Teachers Have 11 or More Years of Experience
Individual worth	Less than 11 yrs.	55	46	28
	11 yrs. or more	47	44	41
Group responsibility	Less than 11 yrs.	70	57	25
	11 yrs. or more	66	44	21
Security-satisfaction	Less than 11 yrs.	65	51	16
	11 yrs. or more	55	40	21
Innovation-change	Less than 11 yrs.	77	59	30
	11 yrs. or more	59	48	34
Interdependence	Less than 11 yrs.	61	53	27
	11 yrs. or more	74	37	27
$N = 646$	Less than 11 yrs.	(181)	(113)	(64)
	11 yrs. or more	(70)	(98)	(120)

former we have been able from our data to relate primarily to differences in amount of professional training. The latter we have shown to be related to years of teaching experience, and to the social class level of the school population served. We have additionally shown effects on value positions held by teachers in schools where a special project has sought to modify the milieu so that it is more nearly like that of the social agency. Further, we have shown that the values of teachers in elementary schools more than those in secondary schools approach the positions of social workers and we have argued that elementary school social milieux are closer to those of the social agency. Finally, we have shown that the value positions of the majority of teachers in schools affect the positions of all teachers in the schools, suggesting a contextual effect on values within the occupation.

Throughout the paper we have been sensitive to the explanation—alternative to that of differential socialization—that

persons are selectively recruited or eliminated to produce differential value positions within the occupation. Although our evidence is far from conclusive, we believe that both selection and socialization processes are at work to produce variation within and between occupations falling within the same social class. It seems clear, however, that research on social values and social class, when it is defined by occupational groupings, must consider both selection and socialization effects of the social milieu within which the occupation is performed.

In the absence of data comparing values of social workers and teachers, on the one hand, and persons in occupations of different social classes, on the other hand, we cannot, obviously, claim more than negative evidence to show that occupation *per se* rather than the social class location of the occupation differentiates social values. We have only shown that values differ between and within occupations of a single social class. As in the case of other phenomena —such as parental behavior, participation in primary relations and secondary groups, and neighborhood integration,

Table 10—Teachers Who Have Taught Longer in Their Present Schools Are More Likely To Report that Their "Philosophy of Education" Has Changed Very Much or Somewhat

Percent of Teachers Reporting Indicated Degree
of Change in "Philosophy of Education"

Amount of Change Reported in "Philosophy of Education"	MIDDLE CLASS SCHOOLS		WORKING CLASS PROJECT SCHOOLS		WORKING CLASS NON-PROJECT SCHOOLS	
	Less than 3 Years in School	3 or More Years in School	Less than 3 Years in School	3 or More Years in School	Less than 3 Years in School	3 or More Years in School
Very much or somewhat	64	70	51	64	48	54
A little or hardly at all	31	24	49	34	50	38
No answer	5	6	..	2	2	8
N = 721	(97)	(197)	(59)	(159)	(61)	(148)

to give examples[21]—occupational characteristics may operate independently of
class in their effects on social values.

Occupational and Class Differences   **349**
in Social Values

Our prior speculations suggest at least
two general types of variables that might
be fruitfully explored to discern distinctive occupational effects on social
values. First, we may mention the goals
of the occupation together with the
historically emergent ideology associated
with them. Thus, we have suggested that
schools having as a major task the transmission of current culture might sensitize
teachers to values different from those of
social workers where the concern is more
with individual adjustment. The second
type of variable is the bureaucratic
context in which the occupation is performed. In this study we have suggested
differences in bureaucratic structures of
schools and of social work agencies,
with the former tending to approach
the Weberian, rationalistic model and
the latter tending to approach a human
relations model. More specifically, we
suggest that differences might be related
to the extent to which authority is
hierarchical (as opposed to collegial), to
the degree of affective involvement, to
the extent to which tasks can be defined
a priori and are specialized rather than
diffused. We do not see these structural
factors as exhaustive of occupational
milieux, but they do point to one direction of promising research to link more
closely the study of social class and
occupational effects on social values.

Addendum

Almost two years after this study was
completed, we sought to replicate part
of it within a different study. We investigated 18 elementary schools, including four of our original project schools
but none of the other schools. Included
in an extensive questionnaire to 528
teachers was a modified version of the
social values test, consisting of 40 items

representing ten value dimensions. When
the responses were analyzed, they did not
indicate the differences previously found
between the inner-city project and non-
project schools. The responses of teachers
in the inner-city nonproject schools
tended to move in the direction of the
inner-city project schools. All outer-city
schools and inner-city project schools
tended to have the same response
patterns.

Considering the marked differences we
found in the earlier study, we are uncertain about the meaning of the partial
replication, but we should like to offer
interpretations, in addition to noting
differences in the samples. Between the
first and second studies there may
indeed have been a shift in the value
positions of teachers in this urban school
system, or it is possible that a different
type of teacher has been recruited into
the inner-city schools, or both of these
changes may have occurred. This was a
period of active reevaluation by educators of their teaching methods in the inner
city. It was such a reevaluation that led
to the inner-city school project in the
first place. About the time of the second
study, it became the policy of the school
system to require, in effect, that new
teachers spend at least three years in an
inner-city school, and accompanying
this policy was a deliberate effort to
develop a greater social work orientation
among the teachers. This may well have
encouraged the teachers to respond more
in line with what they felt to be school
system expectations. It is also possible
that the results of the first study had
become known to the teachers and in the
second study they responded accordingly.
We note also that, in its second administration, the values test was part of a
larger questionnaire which might cause
a difference in response. Furthermore,
the shortened version of the values test

used in the second study (using four items rather than eight for each value dimension) might have made it more transparent, allowing teachers to give socially expected responses.

Although we could not replicate this part of our findings, the strength of the findings in the first study encourages us to present them with this reservation noted, and with due caution, so that other researchers might be stimulated to pursue the question further of effects of organizational milieux similar to that of the project schools on social values of teachers.

Notes

[1] The development of the sociology of occupations is perhaps best indexed by the fact that most major professional schools such as medicine, law, social work, nursing, have as a regular part of their staff a sociologist. Illustrative of the kind of empirical work developing in this field are the following: Robert K. Merton, George G. Reader, and Patricia L. Kendall, eds. *The Student Physician* (Cambridge: Harvard University Press, 1957); Leonard Reissman and John H. Rohrer, eds., *Change and Dilemma in the Nursing Profession* (New York: Putnam, 1957); Erwin Smigel, "Recruitment and the Large Law Firm," *American Sociological Review*, 25 (1960), pp. 56–66.

[2] Eugene Litwak and Lydia F. Hylton, "Interorganizational Analysis: A Hypothesis on Coordinating Agencies," *Administrative Science Quarterly*, 6 (1962), pp. 395–99.

[3] For discussion of human relations and rationalistic (Weberian) bureaucratic types, see Eugene Litwak, "Models of Bureaucracy Which Permit Conflict," *American Journal of Sociology*, 67 (1961), pp. 177–82.

[4] H. J. Meyer and D. B. McLeod, *A Study of the Values of Social Workers*, 1961 (mimeographed). A summary of this research, under the same title, is found in E. J. Thomas, ed. *Behavioral Science for*

Social Workers (New York: Free Press, 1967), pp. 401–16.

[5] Social values, as conceived by Meyer and McLeod, include both judgments of "ought," "should," etc. and existential beliefs concerning social relations and collective welfare. The five social values used in this paper are selected from value dimensions inferred from the ideology of the social work and teaching professions and may be thought of as a specification of more general American values but by no means inclusive of all major values of American society.

The values are represented as a range of positions expressed along dimensions inferred from responses agreeing or disagreeing with attitude statements designed to reflect the dimensions and included in a Social Attitudes Questionnaire, called the Social Values Test. This test (when administered to teachers in the present study) consisted of 72 items selected by cluster analysis from a matrix of 100 items responded to by a sample of social workers so as to provide 9 sub-tests of 8 items each. The clusters, although moderately intercorrelated, remained relatively stable in item content for both social worker and teacher samples and could not, by factor analysis, be reasonably reduced to fewer dimensions.

Items are scored on a four-point scale from "strongly agree" to "strongly disagree" and dimension (or value) scores are the unweighted sums of the scores of items in the dimension.

[6] The other four value dimensions, not used here, are designated as follows: Personal liberty vs. Societal control; Relativism-secularism vs. Absolutism-sacredness; Changeable human nature vs. Inherent human nature-fatalism; Diversity-heterogeneity vs. Consensus-homogeneity-conformity.

[7] The 103 professionally trained social workers were members of local chapters of the National Association of Social Workers; 66 percent were women and about one-half were 40 years of age or older. Social workers in training ($N = 92$) were first- and second-year students in the School of Social Work, The University of Michigan; 59 percent were women and 71 percent were under 30 years of age. The 98 untrained social workers were primarily employed in public welfare and other public agency programs in Detroit and Washtenaw County, Michigan; 61 percent were women and about one-half were under

30 years of age. On most background characteristics the three groups were approximately similar, except for educational level and disproportionally more Jews among the professionally trained (23 percent compared to 9 percent of the students and 1 percent of the untrained social workers).

[8] H. J. Meyer and D. B. McLeod, *op. cit.*, Table 7, p. 38.

[9] *Ibid.*, pp. 40–46.

[10] This sample constituted the faculties of 16 schools, 9 of which were elementary schools, 4 junior high, and 3 high schools. Seven of the schools (4 elementary, 2 junior high, and 1 high school) were part of an experimental project intended to improve educational opportunities for children in deprived areas of the city. The remaining 9 schools were selected as comparable working class or contrasting middle class schools. Thus, the schools ranged across social class lines, excluding the very highest income areas. The teachers in these schools cannot be taken as a random sample of all public school teachers in the city although no obvious groups of teachers are unrepresented.

[11] For the other four dimensions, social workers are higher on common items as follows: Personal liberty—4 out of 5 items; Relativism-secularism—4 out of 4 items; Changeable human nature—3 out of 3 items; Diversity-heterogeneity—4 out of 4 items.

[12] In this and in subsequent tables, we will use the value scores based on the 9 items of each scale. The population has been dichotomized at the median and in each sub-group the proportion above the median is designated. Since 75 of the teachers had incomplete tests, the basic population size for value analyses is reduced to 646.

[13] For the other value dimensions the trend is similar, with 2 of the 4 additional value dimensions showing pronounced differences by teacher experience: Relativism—61 percent for less experienced, 40 percent for more experienced; Changeable human nature—62 percent compared to 43 percent, respectively.

[14] By social class of schools, we refer to the socio-economic level of the population and area generally served by the schools.

[15] We could find no evidence that the project schools were selected *because* their teachers held different values from the working class non-project schools chosen as comparable. However, since the choice of project and non-project schools was not random, we cannot conclusively eliminate this possible selective factor. To suggest as we have done that there is a difference in value expression of project and non-project personnel does not say anything about the depth of such a shift. It would be important to know if this represented mere lip service or something more basic.

[16] The findings of recent studies provide a context for such hypotheses but do not directly address them. See Robert E. Herriott and Nancy N. St. John, *Social Class and the Urban School* (New York: Wiley, 1966); Sam Sieber and David Wilder, "Teaching Styles: Parental Preference and Professional Role Definition," *Sociology of Education*, 40 (1967), pp. 302–15.

[17] The project had been under way for two years in two of the project schools and one year in the other five. Stability of teaching staff indicates that there was little deliberate recruiting of teachers during these years for project schools.

[18] We do not present here the data for this relationship with possible selective factors controlled. Compared to elementary schools, high school teachers in our sample have higher proportions of teachers who are men, white, have 33 or more graduate credits in education, over 20 years of teaching experience, and 11 or more years teaching in present school. Where size of the sub-groups permits analysis, the trend of value responses persists despite these differences.

[19] Research in progress, under a grant from the U.S. Office of Education, will permit a more explicit differentiation of the social milieux of different school buildings so that variation of bureaucratic structure and administrative style can be related directly to social values of teachers.

[20] Because we would expect differences between middle-class, working-class project and working-class non-project schools, data on reported change in "philosophy of education" are presented in Table 10 for each of these categories of schools. It is also possible that our findings represent the length of time the respondent has been teaching (i.e., the longer time they have been teaching, the more chance of change occurring.)

[21] The following are some studies which seek to examine occupational effects, independent of class dimensions, of work: Martin Gold and Carol Slater, "Office, Factory, Store—and Family: A Study of Integration Settings," *American Sociological Review*, 23 (1958); Daniel R. Miller and Guy E. Swanson, *The Changing American Parent* (New York: Wiley, 1958); Harold L. Wilensky, "Orderly Careers and Social Participation," *American Sociological Review*, 26 (1961); Phillip Fellin and Eugene Litwak, "Neighborhood Cohesion Under Conditions of Mobility," *American Sociological Review*, 28 (1963).

For some years now conflict between school employees and school managers has been on the rise. Not long ago, for example, the president of the National Education Association (NEA), in an address to public education's foremost establishment, spoke forcefully about the right of teachers to participate in the formulation of public school policy. In laying it on the line to the nation's school administrators, he disclaimed any intention by teachers to seize control but was unequivocal in demanding for his classroom colleagues full partnership in the educational enterprise.[1] Words and action both signify a new militancy which characterizes teachers as they are organized today. Unlike the docile pedagogues of the past, the current armies manning the battlements of elementary and secondary education are in "a state of ferment bordering on rebellion."[2] One spokesman for the militant American Federation of Teachers (AFT), and president of the United Federation of Teachers (UFT) in New York City, has commented on the new movement in the following way:

> Teachers are demanding more and more decision making power. Power is never given to anyone. Power is taken, and it is taken from someone. Teachers, as one of society's powerless groups, are now starting to take power from supervisors and school boards. This is causing and will continue to cause a realignment of power relationships.[3]

This argument, as well as those made by numerous others, maintains in essence that (1) educational power now is held largely by schools boards and administrations, with teachers powerless by comparison, and (2) teachers are now demanding more power, primarily in order to achieve a significant voice in the processes of educational decision-making.*

*[Editor's note: For presentation of data bearing on the first issue, see the original article. The present excerpt deals only with the second issue.]

Pedagogues and Power

Alan Rosenthal

"Pedagogues and Power" by Alan Rosenthal is reprinted from Urban Affairs Quarterly, 2 (1966), pp. 83–85, and 94–102, by permission of the author and the publisher, Sage Publications, Inc.

To explore the bases of these contentions, this paper will examine the views of leaders of teacher organizations in five large cities. These cities, which have seen varying degrees of teacher militancy and conflict, are New York, Boston, Chicago, San Francisco, and Atlanta. Four of the teacher groups whose leadership views have been surveyed are affiliated with AFT: New York's United Federation of Teachers (UFT), the Boston Teachers Union (BTU), the Chicago Teachers Union (CTU), and the San Francisco Federation of Teachers (SFFT). Three others are tied to NEA: the Chicago Education Association (CEA), the San Francisco Classroom Teachers Association (SFCTA), and the Atlanta Teachers Association (ATA).[4] Two have no national affiliation: the Boston Teachers Alliance (BTA) and the Teachers Association of San Francisco (TASF). In late 1965 and early 1966, questionnaires were mailed to members of the executive boards of these nine groups.[5] Completed questionnaires have been received from 185 of the 270 board members (a response rate of 68.5 percent), and these individuals constitute our leadership sample for the present analysis.[6] On the basis of responses to structured items in the survey instrument, we intend to describe and compare leadership perceptions of power and attitudes concerning power with regard to several domains of educational policy-making. Underlying this design was a suspicion that perceptions and attitudes would differ considerably, depending upon whether the relevant policy domain was general or, more specifically, salary, personnel, curriculum and instruction, or the organization of the school system.[7] . . .

A furious competition now rages between NEA and AFT, each of which seeks to represent the nation's teachers in their struggles to gain material benefits and improve their status. One group advocates professional negotiations, the other calls for collective bargaining. However the two may differ, both vigorously encourage affiliates, and particularly those in cities, to increase their influence in the decision-making processes of public education. In view of pressures from these national bodies as well as the escalating effects of local rivalry, we would expect that teacher leaders are dissatisfied with the low-power estates of their own organizations. This is more or less the situation in the five cities under discussion.

An expansion in the power of teacher organizations can come about in a number of ways. If the influence of other participants remains stable while that of teachers grows, the result would be a net gain for teachers. A similar result would ensue if the influence of all core participants expands, but not as greatly as that of teachers. Alternatively, a decrease in the influence of boards, superintendents, and bureaucracies coordinate with maintenance on the parts of teacher groups would lead to a like outcome. The greatest change would probably occur given a diminution of the power of all other participants and a simultaneous enhancement of the power of teacher organizations. In light of these possibi-

lities, we endeavored to discover how teacher leaders feel about a redistribution of power in the various policy-making domains of each city. Our method resembles the one used previously in assessing the distribution of power. By way of prescription, respondents indicated whether they believed that participants, ranging from the mayor to school principals, should have "more," "the same amount," or "less" power than they presently had.[8]

Leaders in the total sample substantially agree on two points only: Their own groups should have more power, and mayors and municipal officials should have less. The belief pervading professional doctrine and cherished by administrators and teachers alike is that education should be kept entirely separate from politics and that school departments should be completely autonomous of other local agencies. It is predictable, then, that leaders of the nine teacher organizations, subscribing to traditional tenets, want public schools in their cities to have less influence in school affairs. Two-thirds of them, in fact, expressed the view that mayors should have less to say about educational policy in general, while only one-third wanted to leave the meager power of municipal officials intact. Similar proportions concurred in advocating the reduction of mayoral influence in the particular policy domains of salary, personnel, curriculum and instruction, and school organization. Nor does it matter in most cases whether the mayor was perceived to have had power in the first place. In Atlanta, where his influence was thought to be minimal, members of the ATA executive board overwhelmingly desired that it be reduced further. Where his influence was apparently greatest, leadership opinion was divided. Boston leaders almost unanimously favored a shift in fiscal authority from the mayor to the school committee. On the other hand, UFT leaders, who in the past had benefited from intervention by City Hall, generally agreed that no change in the mayor's role was necessary.

As we mentioned earlier, the loci of educational power are the central offices of the school departments. Depending upon the type of issue and the particular city, school boards, superintendents, and administrative chiefs share in fashioning educational policies. Should these dominants have more or less to say on various kinds of matters? There is little consistency in the patterns of response revealed by the leadership sample. Certainly no overall desire on the parts of teacher organizations to curb the powers of the powerful emerges from these data. Nor is there a correlation, either positive or negative, between the ways in which leaders would allocate power among dominants and the manner in which they think it is presently distributed. In Atlanta, executive board members are pretty well content with the current allocation. In Boston, leaders of both groups tend to favor a somewhat greater authority for the committee, superintendent, and bureaucracy. The discernible difference here is that the union would prefer the school committee and the independent association would prefer the superintendent to have more of a voice in salary determination. Despite the obvious predominance of Chicago's superintendent, leaders in this city show little disposition to restrict his powers. The AFT affiliate, however, would strengthen the board, while the NEA local would strengthen the bureaucracy. Of the three teacher organizations in San Francisco, two of them, one linked to NEA and the other independent, evidence no dissatisfaction with the present distribution of power at the central office.

Seven teacher groups, therefore, would likely shun a strategy designed to reduce the policy-making prerogatives of either board, superintendent, or administrative bureaucracy. Apparently, they make little

linkage between their own power and that of key participants. The two remaining organizations, however, take a more militant posture, presumably relating their own aspirations to the overwhelming influence of the educational establishment. Leaders of UFT and SFFT prescribe lesser amounts of power for all other core participants. Perhaps because it has not yet achieved comparable status, the San Francisco union takes an even firmer stance than UFT. In all four policy areas, SFFT's executive board splits, with about half the members advocating less, another half the same amount, and scarcely any favoring more power for the board or administration. The prescriptive views of UFT executive board members vary to a somewhat greater extent. Leaders of this entrenched organization seem least unhappy about the superintendency and most discontent with influence exercised by deputy and assistant superintendents at school headquarters.

On one element of prescription, there is naturally a high degree of consensus. Hardly a leadership respondent believes that the power of his own organization should be diminished. Yet the cohesiveness of leaders, in terms of their commitments to pursuing power, does vary from one organization to another. As Table 1 clearly shows, teacher groups differ substantially, ranging from those where leaders are unanimous or nearly unanimous in desiring greater power to those where about half are satisfied with the current status of their organization. If we exclude the two independent groups (BTA and TASF), a consistent organizational pattern emerges. NEA associations and AFT unions diverge sharply in their aspirations for increased influence. Aggregate percentages in Table 1 demonstrate that, with regard to educational policy generally or any single domain, union leaderships are solid, while association leaderships are divided in desiring power for their own groups. Specifically, the four union locals (SFFT, UFT, BTU, and CTU) rank higher from one policy domain to the next than do the three associations (SFCTA, CEA, and ATA). In fact, with the exception of salaries where the rankings of individual organizations shift somewhat, the order is almost the same whatever the policy area being considered. Among the unions, the ones in San Francisco and New York, which are most desirous of curtailing the influence of other participants, appear also to be the most militant regarding the enhancement of organizational power. Union leaderships in Boston and Chicago are less cohesive in this respect. Among the associations, all of which rank lower, those in San Francisco and Chicago are notably more prone to pursue power than is ATA in Atlanta.

Intercity comparisons likewise prove interesting. Generally, leaders in New York, San Francisco, and Boston are more concerned with group power than are their counterparts in Chicago and Atlanta. In the latter cities, as well as in Boston, teacher organizations of whatever affiliation seem most intent on enhancing their influence over salary policy. Fewer leaders in these places care much about group power in the domains of personnel, curriculum, or school organization. In contrast, salary power is less important in New York and San Francisco. This is understandable, since UFT already carries considerable weight here and San Francisco teachers earn salaries which compare quite favorably with those paid in other large cities across the nation.

Teacher organizations understandably want more power. But how much, particularly when compared to that held by educational dominants? This question leads us to examine the roles teacher organizations seek to play in the arenas of educational policy-making. Today especially, professors of school administration and superintendents abstractly

Table 1—The Pursuit of Power: Percentages of Leaders Desiring More Power for Their Own Organizations

| | | POLICY DOMAIN | | | | |
CITY	ORGANI-ZATION*	Policy in General	Salary Policy	School Organi-zation	Personnel Policy	Curriculum and Instruction
New York	UFT	97	77	92	92	92
Boston	BTU	82	93	79	89	82
	BTA	88	100	75	88	88
Chicago	CTU	65	83	67	78	61
	CEA	50	72	39	61	50
San Francisco	SFFT	100	91	88	100	96
	SFCTA	55	59	64	64	68
	TASF	86	86	71	86	86
Atlanta	ATA	45	55	30	45	30
	NEA Locals	50	62	45	57	50
	AFT Locals	89	85	83	90	85

*The number of responses for each organization is reported in note 6.
Total number of NEA leaders = 61; total number of AFT leaders = 109.
The actual number of responses varies slightly by policy domain.

agree that teachers should be involved in deciding matters of import. "Teacher participation" has become a new shibboleth of American education. What it really means, however, is unclear. One aim of the present study is to see how teachers themselves view participation. What do local leaders think their organization's proper role should be? In this inquiry we have posited for each domain five possible levels of participation in the formulation of school policy. Respondents were asked to denote a preference as to whether teacher organizations (1) should have more to say than the board and/or administration; (2) should have a voice equal to that of the board and/or administration; (3) should be consulted and have their advice weighed heavily; (4) should be kept informed, but not necessarily called upon for advice; or (5) should not be involved.[9]

On the basis of the pronouncements of national officials as well as the responses about power cited above, we would hypothesize that union locals aspire to more decisive participation than professional associations or independent groups. Totals for AFT and NEA in Table 2 suggest that this is indeed the case. Depending upon the policy area, from one-half to two-thirds of the union leadership subsample opts for a major or equal voice in decision-making. The proportions of NEA leaders choosing the same roles are much lower, ranging from about one-tenth to one-quarter. In places where several organizations exist, intracity comparisons reveal that in every instance higher percentages of union than of other leaderships desire to participate significantly in the several areas of policy formulation. Naturally, the agreement among leaders on organizational objectives varies from one domain to another. In general, teacher leaders are likelier to desire major participation on salaries and curriculum. Proportionately fewer insist on a comparable level when policy concerns personnel or school organization. Specifically, in Boston and Chicago, salaries and then curriculum evoke greater

Table 2—Participation in Policy-making: Percentages of Leaders Desiring High Participative Roles

		POLICY DOMAIN				
CITY	ORGANI-ZATION*	Policy in General	Salary Policy	School Organi-zation	Personnel Policy	Curriculum and Instruction
New York	UFT	77	82	71	74	66
Boston	BTU	57	52	29	32	46
	BTA	13	38	25	00	25
Chicago	CTU	22	33	22	28	28
	CEA	05	21	00	06	00
San Francisco	SFFT	83	83	75	67	88
	SFCTA	41	32	27	27	33
	TASF	29	14	14	29	57
Atlanta	ATA	10	20	00	10	30
	NEA Locals	20	25	10	15	22
	AFT Locals	64	66	53	54	59

*The number of responses for each organization is reported in note 6.
Total number of NEA leaders = 61; total number of AFT leaders = 109.
The actual number of responses varies slightly by policy domain.

desires for high participation on the part of teacher groups. In San Francisco and Atlanta, the order is reversed.

If the participative roles prescribed by leaders are any indication, we might easily conclude that UFT in New York and SFFT in San Francisco rank as the most militant organizations. This conforms with other evidence previously presented. BTU trails well behind, while either CTU, the most conservative union, or SFCTA, the most militant association, comes next. As far as participation in policy-making is concerned, leaders of CEA in Chicago and ATA in Atlanta seek not a major or equal voice but rather a consultative role for their own groups.

Power, Participation, and Militancy

Many, if not all, discussions of the new militancy stress its behavioral features —aggressive activity, hard conflict, open warfare. An appreciation of the militancy of teacher organizations, we believe, requires that several dimensions be taken into account. From the standpoint of teacher leaders, we have considered three: how power is distributed; how it should be redistributed; and what role teacher organizations should play in educational policy-making. Leadership perceptions of influence may not be entirely accurate, but they do conform closely to the views of other observers of school politics in these five cities. In any event, it is important to realize how leaders feel when comparing their own influence to that of school boards and administrators. Given low self-images, teachers inevitably desire enhancement of their own power holdings. Otherwise, there is no discernible relationship between the distribution of influence on the one hand and leadership advocacy of its redistribution on the

other. While they want more for themselves, most leaders of most organizations are relatively content with the power allegedly possessed by boards, superintendents, and bureaucratic chiefs.

If a common strategy involves gaining increased power (while not depriving others of their present shares), a principal goal is regular participation in the policy-making processes of public education. Conceivably, some groups could desire far greater power than they had and still be satisfied with a passive role in deciding policy. Others could desire somewhat less and yet seek an active role. Our expectations, however, demonstrate a close relationship between the pursuit of power and the desire for a significant voice in the processes of policy-making. Rank order correlations, using Kendall's tau, between power aspirations and policy-participation objectives are all positive: educational policy in general, .81; salary, .62; school organization, .81; personnel, 1.00; curriculum and instruction, .81. With the exception of salaries, the San Francisco Federation of Teachers, the United Federation of Teachers, and the Boston Teachers Union consistently rank highest and, with only one additional exception, the Chicago Education Association and the Atlanta Teachers Association rank lowest on both types of ordinal scale.[10] Thus, where leaderships are solidly committed to increasing group power, their intention is to convert that power into a full partnership in educational policy-making.

Our descriptive survey admittedly has ignored many crucial questions. Whatever their evaluations of influence, their power ambitions, and their objectives, the militancy of teacher organizations hinges also on their willingness to fight. Unless groups are disposed to act forcefully in pursuing their goals, the militant label should not be applied.[11] Combative dispositions do not necessarily lead to actual conflict, however. Nor does open conflict necessarily enable teacher organizations to succeed in attaining their objectives. Thorough understanding of the militancy and achievement of teacher organizations in large cities demands that careful scrutiny be given to at least three broad categories of factors.

First, we must explore further the characteristics of teacher organizations themselves. In profiling leadership attitudes, this study has made a modest beginning. Attention must also be paid to the stage of an organization's development, since groups with small, fervent memberships may operate differently from those with large, passive memberships. Rank-and-file satisfaction with the educational status quo, organizational resources in terms of skills and finances, and competition between or within groups must be considered.

Second, the attitudes and behavior of other core participants presumably affect the way teachers feel, what they do, and just how much they accomplish. Superintendents and boards of education have a choice when responding to teacher demands. Through adamant opposition, benevolence, or plain weakness, they may either encourage or discourage militancy.

Finally, cultural, political, and situational variables must be taken into account. State legislation regulating employer-employee relationships, community folkways, and patterns of political practice all appear important and all vary among cities. Strikes or strike threats may be viable tactics in New York but self-defeating in Boston. Open conflict may be legitimate and productive in Chicago, but personal diplomacy may prove better suited to Atlanta. In one city, a particular issue can be salient and furnish the spark for collective action; in another, no such catalyst might appear.

Only after probing into these uncharted areas will we add substantially to our knowledge of the characteristics, roles, and impact of local teacher organizations. Along the way, we may be able to shed further light in general on the educational politics of large city school systems.

Notes

[1] Richard D. Batchelder, speaking before the 98th annual meeting of the American Association of School Administrators, Atlantic City, N.J., February 15, 1966 (NEA press release).

[2] These words are quoted from Allan M. West, Assistant Executive Secretary for Field Operations and Urban Services, NEA, "What's Bugging Teachers," *Saturday Review*, October 16, 1965, p. 88.

[3] Albert Shanker, "Teacher-Supervisory Relationships: A Symposium," *Changing Education*, 1 (1966), p. 23.

[4] The cooperation of one teacher organization in Atlanta could not be obtained.

[5] Mailings also went to the professional executive secretaries or directors of several nonunion groups, whose views are included here. These people, like the full-time presidents or business managers of unions, have major influence within their own organizations.

[6] By organization, the response was as follows: UFT, 39 of 47 (83%); BTU, 28 of 40 (70%); BTA, 8 of 17 (47%); CTU, 18 of 40 (45%); CEA, 19 of 32 (59%); SFFT, 24 of 33 (73%); SFCTA, 22 of 26 (85%); TASF, 7 of 8 (88%); and ATA, 20 of 27 (74%).

[7] In emphasizing specialization, our treatment of the educational arena is patterned after recent investigations which have shown power to be differentially exercised in a community according to the type of issue being decided. See, for instance, the following: Edward C. Banfield, *Political Influence* (New York: Free Press, 1961); Robert A. Dahl, *Who Governs?* (New Haven: Yale University Press, 1961); Roscoe C. Martin et al., *Decisions in Syracuse* (Bloomington: University of Indiana Press, 1961); and Wallace S. Sayre and Herbert Kaufman, *Governing New York City* (New York: Russell Sage Foundation, 1960).

[8] A "power prescription" index was constructed, with scores of 1, 0 and −1 assigned for each "more," "same amount," and "less"

response. Although scores are not reported in this paper, they provide a basis for part of the ensuing discussion.

[9] Questionnaires included these items for educational policy in general and for each of the four policy domains. For present purposes, we have dichotomized responses, with choices of (1) or (2) signifying "high" participative objectives and (3), (4), or (5) signifying "low" participative objectives.

[10] The reversed rankings of UFT and BTU with regard to salary on the power and participation scales are probably attributable to two factors. First, at the time the questionnaire was sent, BTU had just won a collective bargaining election. It was about to enter into negotiations, the major element of which concerned salaries. Hence, its desire for greater salary power. Second, UFT already has, and is conscious of having, a considerable say on salary matters. Thus, although leaders agree on a high level of participation, they are less inclined to feel the need for even more power to achieve their objective.

[11] In our investigation we have found that teacher organizations ranking high in the pursuit of power and on policy-making participation also are most disposed to engage in combat.

Howard S. Becker. "The Career of the Chicago Public School Teacher." *American Journal of Sociology*, 57 (1952), pp. 470–77.

The author describes several alternative career patterns which are pursued by teachers in the Chicago public school systems. The most common is the movement from a less desirable slum school to a middle-class school. A less frequent career type is exemplified by the teacher who is socialized to the slum environment and who moves up within the informal hierarchy at a particular school. The basic issue for the teacher is viewed as a dilemma between his expectations and changing his environment.

Stephen Cole. "The Unionization of Teachers: Determinants of Rank and File Support." *Sociology of Education*, 41 (1968), pp. 66–86.

Several background characteristics of teachers are shown to be related to support of militant strategies. Democratic political affiliation, affiliation with the Jewish religion, and lower- or working-class social origins are all highly associated with support of teacher strikes. More important, however, is the respondents' prior attitude toward unionism. Men, who experience more relative deprivation than women, are also more supportive of militant tactics aimed at raising the status of the profession. Older teachers are more conservative on this issue. The author concludes that increasing militancy in the teaching profession may be traced to a large extent to changes in the composition of the occupation.

Ronald G. Corwin. "Militant Professionalism, Initiative and Compliance in Public Education." *Sociology of Education*, 38 (1965), pp. 310–31.

This article reports that teachers who are disposed toward exercising initiative in professional matters are prone to endorse

Part V
Auxiliary Readings

professional as contrasted with bureaucratic-employee roles, and are also more often involved in overt conflict with bureaucratic authorities. Further, teachers with a high professional orientation and a low bureaucratic orientation (the "functional bureaucrats") are more conflict-prone than other types of teachers. However, militancy among teachers does not necessarily entail strong professional values. Also, the officers of teachers' organizations are not necessarily more militant, for many have dual allegiances to the profession and to the organization.

Donald E. Edgar and Rodney L. Brod. "Professional Socialization and Teacher Autonomy" (Technical Report No. 12). Stanford: Center for Research and Development in Teaching, 1970.

This study examines two connected problems: how new teachers become socialized into their profession, and how this socialization process affects their attitudes toward professional autonomy. A pre-test–post-test correlational design investigates the effects of both organizational evaluators' attitudes and prevailing school-staff climate on teacher attitudes toward professional autonomy.

Estelle Fuchs. *Teachers Talk*. New York: Doubleday, Anchor Books, 1969.

The beginning teacher undergoes a period of induction and transition during which she learns to think of herself as a teacher and to adapt to the work setting. The impact of the employing school is documented through diaries kept by teachers in inner-city schools during their first year. Emphasis is placed on the discontinuity between expectations and theories learned in teacher training, and the degrading, frightening, and often disillusioning experiences which are met on the job.

W. K. Hoy. "The Influence of Experience on the Beginning Teacher." *The School Review*, 76 (1968), pp. 312–22.

Student control is viewed as a central problem for teachers. Teacher training focuses on an ideal of humanism, but when the real world of teaching is entered, the teacher may become socialized into acceptance of a more custodial and authoritarian orientation toward students. A group of teachers were tested on a Pupil Control Ideology form before practice teaching, after practice teaching, and after their first year of work. Teachers were significantly more custodial after one year of teaching, while a control group which completed teacher training but did not go into teaching did not change.

Myron Lieberman. *Education as a Profession*. Englewood Cliffs, N.J.: Prentice-Hall, 1956.

The author questions whether teaching should be considered a profession. He points out that education lags far behind the full-fledged professions in function and scope, authority, certification, ethics, and professional groupings. He states that differentiation among teaching positions and functions, and a redefinition of the educator's tasks, are prerequisites for acceptance of teaching as a profession.

Ward S. Mason, Robert J. Dressel, and Robert K. Bain. "Sex Role and the Career Orientations of Beginning Teachers." *Harvard Educational Review*, 29 (1959), pp. 270–83.

The authors analyze some of the relationships between sex and occupational roles which appear to account for the high percentage of loss from the occupation. Women show a pattern of leaving the occupation and then returning while men tend to view teaching as a means of occupational advancement into administrative positions or into other fields. The authors conclude that efforts to reduce teacher turnover in the schools should entail differential inducements for each sex.

Alan Rosenthal. "The Strength of Teacher Organizations: Factors Influencing Membership in Two Large Cities." *Sociology of Education*, 39 (1966), pp. 359–86.

Longitudinal aggregate and individual data are used to explore the correlates of membership strength of the teacher unions in New York and Boston. It is reported that men are more likely to join unions than women, that the sex-ratio of schools affects membership strength, and that new teachers are likely to be active. It is pointed out that the context of the communities is very important in explaining the effect of these variables.

School-Community Relations

Introduction

DESPITE increasing federal and state support for public education in the United States and increasing signs of an emerging national system of education (see the selection by Sloan R. Wayland in Part III), schools continue to receive a major portion of their support from local sources, and the norm of local autonomy is jealously guarded. One consequence of our traditionally decentralized system is that a number of administrative decisions, such as which books and equipment to purchase and how much to pay teachers, must be made at the local level. The necessity for raising money and making these decisions at the local level has resulted in the schools' occupying an especially vulnerable political position in our society, such that school policy may sometimes be determined by the votes of the local public whose taxes support the schools. Another consequence of local autonomy is the proliferation of positions for lay members of the community who, as school board members, are entrusted with hiring professional educators to run the schools. Not surprisingly, local autonomy also tends to make the relative limits of the roles of lay members of the community and professional educators somewhat ambiguous and overlapping, and, no doubt, the American educators concern with educating the "whole child" has contributed to this confusion. Hence the relations between schools and the communities in which they are located present an especially fertile research site for sociologists. The selections that follow represent only a portion of the problems that have been studied, but an attempt has been made to provide illustrative examples of the different levels on which school-community relations can be studied.

In the first selection, Sieber and Wilder distinguish four styles of teaching by differentiating the extent to which adult authority is utilized and the amount of emphasis placed on subject matter. The preferences of mothers for the style of teaching they would choose for their children are then contrasted with the self-images of the teachers who teach their children. This analysis reveals that mothers' preferences vary considerably according to the grade level of children and the social context within which the school is located, but a majority of teachers see themselves as discovery-oriented at all levels and in all social settings. Hence, a large majority of mothers in every setting *perceive* the teacher as being the type they prefer. Thus, while there is considerable *actual* disagreement between mothers and the teachers of their children, mothers are unable to observe these differences in the vast majority of cases. Moreover, potential conflict over teaching styles between professional educators and their constituencies of parents is highest in working-class areas of the cities—the areas where contact between parents and the schools has been the lowest, and where the norm of local autonomy has seldom been honored.

The contrast between laymen and professional educators is also a major concern of Norman D. Kerr in his analysis of the behavior of school board members in two suburban school systems. While the board members have been elected to represent the community and to set policy in conjunction with the superintendent whom they technically employ, in reality it is usually the superintendent whose views prevail. This displacement of goals takes place for a number of reasons, but partly because members have no constituency and are unfamilair with school programs and with board activities. As a result, new members are socialized by old members and by the superintendent when they are at an obvious disadvantage. Community pressures operate in such a way that the board tends to become aligned with the superintendent and dependent upon his expert knowledge. Hence the board is converted to a role of legitimizing the professional orientations of the superintendent to the community, rather than representing the community in relation to the schools.

The most volatile subject of school-community relations in recent years has been race, and there is considerable evidence that it will continue to be an explosive issue in the near future. It is especially difficult to collect the type of systematic information needed in order to make sociological generalizations in the midst of heated controversy, but Robert L. Crain and David Street managed to surmount many of these difficulties in their case comparisons of desegregation in eight cities and extended work in Chicago. Perhaps most interesting, in view of the preceding selection by Kerr, is their finding that the boards, rather than the superintendents, made the decisions about school desegregation in most cases since there is no legitimate expertise that the superintendent can bring to bear on these issues. Moreover, they found that there is usually an initial "key response" by the board to desegregation demands that is correlated with the final level of acquiescence, and that the level of acquiescence is highly related to the status composition of the board. That is, if boards consist mainly of high status members of the community, they will tend to make liberal-acquiescent decisions; whereas low status (political) boards tend to resist desegregation demands and to be less autonomous because of internal conflicts.

Crain and Street provide a unique comparison of school-community decision-making processes in large city schools in that they are able to operationalize their key concepts in a manner that permits quantitative analysis. They are careful to point out, however, that organizational features of large city school systems make implementation of desegregation decisions extremely difficult, and that actual desegregation levels are extremely low in most cities.

Desegregation and integration represent only one type of solution to the problem of ensuring that disesteemed minorities are afforded the benefits of formal education. And in light of the increasing proportion of racial and ethnic minorities in the cities, this solution has been seen as a partial one, if not one that is wholly outdated by social trends. A controversial alternative is "community control" of schools, a reform intended to reallocate decision-making power to the black ghettoes of urban America. In appraising this development it is virtually impossible to separate educational goals from political goals, and indeed the advocates of community control view the two sets of goals as mutually reinforcing— to achieve full citizenship, the black community needs to control its own educational destiny; and in order for the black community to acquire this control, white society must accept the larger political goal of self-determination. The equation of political and educational aspirations is a familiar one in the history of American minority groups, although it has been usually confined to the domain of higher education. In the domain of public school education, this equation has fostered controversy among educational experts for two reasons: (1) it implies a retreat from the common school goal of furnishing a universal socialization experience (as contrasted with the parochialization of educational content), and (2) it augments lay authority at the expense of professional autonomy.

The first of these two issues is a direct descendant of the Durkheimian problem of providing *both* universal socialization and specialized education for a particular stratum, referred to earlier in the Introduction to Part I, Classical Perspectives. The second issue arises from the organizational, and hence occupational, separateness of the school from society, which has been touched on at numerous points in earlier selections. In essence, the innovation of community control revives a fundamental conflict in American education. On the one hand, professional control is viewed as a necessary mechanism for secular-universal education; on the other, indigenous control of an educational process that affects the life-chances of a particular stratum is viewed as a defining feature of equalitarian society.

This dilemma is elaborated in the selection by Leonard J. Fein. Following an extremely thoughtful analysis, Fein suggests that the dilemma may be more imagined than real: "the social system has never been as secular in its operation as the norm of universalism implies or as many American liberals generally suppose. . . . the history of the schools can be read as an example of creative tension between the particular and the universal." Precisely how this "creative tension" has been sustained in the past, and what its fate will be under the stress of black militancy, are problems that deserve the most careful analysis, both for the benefit of education and for the advancement of sociological theory.

In the final selection, Eugene Litwak and Henry J. Meyer discuss the problem of linking schools as organizations with families as primary groups in the local environment. Thus the problem identified by Dewey —the problem of discontinuity between the socialization styles of the home and the school—reappears, but this time as an aspect of the problem of integrating different groups within the community. In an earlier selection by Edward L. McDill et al. (see Part II), we found that parental involvement in the schools was strongly related to achievement and aspiration of students; but Litwak and Meyer would question the extent to which this finding can be generalized. First, they distinguish the types of tasks they believe can best be accomplished by bureaucracies and primary groups, and conclude that these are respectively uniform and nonuniform events. Next, they argue that schools cannot afford either a complete "open door" or "closed door" policy in relation to parents, but that they must seek a midpoint where "limiting effects are minimized and complementary contributions of both . . . are maximized." Finally, they differentiate seven mechanisms for communication between schools and families and analyze each according to four common dimensions: initiative, intensity, focused expertise, and scope. Thus Litwak and Meyer move directly from sociological theory and a Weberian image of bureaucracy to an analysis of the problems that face contemporary schools in the urban ghetto and possible strategies for solutions.

ALL ASPECTS OF public education are matters of public interest and concern both by law and by tradition. Public participation in school-related activities, however, has often been shown to vary from one social setting to another. Generally, whether the activity is voting in school elections or membership in the PTA, participation is higher in communities or among individuals with relatively high socioeconomic status.[1] This tendency has been interpreted by some observers as reinforcement for inequalities which already exist in the schools and as a barrier to improved education in working-class settings. In recent years, civil rights leaders and poverty area workers have attempted to provoke higher participation from parents, particularly in urban slum areas; and school protests (such as the ones in New York City during 1966–1967) have been one of the outgrowths of this movement. Some schools, in turn, have gone on record as favoring decentralization of administration and direct public involvement in school matters.[2] These recommendations are directed at the improvement both of education and of school-community relations. However, it is possible that there are differences in the values and expectations of parents and educators which will lead to open conflict as parental involvement in the schools increases, and as parents and educators become more aware of their differences.[3]

One area of potential conflict between parents and educators is that of the appropriate role behavior of teachers. The role behavior of teachers can be regarded as reflecting instrumental processes as distinguished from terminal goals or the eventual outputs desired from education. It seems probable that the purposes of education must be diffuse in order to accommodate the different values and expectations of the different interested groups. Indeed, the ultimate goals of education are often stated in platitudes. As a result, there are seldom

Teaching Styles: Parental Preferences and Professional Role Definitions

Sam D. Sieber and David E. Wilder

This study was made possible by a grant from the U.S.O.E. We are indebted to Professor William S. Goode for his helpful comments on the first draft of this article.

Reprinted from Sociology of Education, 40 (1967), 302–15, by permission of the publisher, The American Sociological Association.

public disputes between parents and teachers over the purposes of education. In contrast, instrumental processes concern the daily behavior of teachers and students. Both parents and teachers may have rather specific ideas about what this should be like, and open disputes may more readily result.[4]

The preferences and images of parents regarding instructional practices has been a subject of considerable debate in the past ten years. Spokesmen on both sides of the "great debate" concerning the most suitable kind of education for the post-Sputnik era have imputed attitudes to the community to support their own preferences. Thus, the critics of progressive education have claimed that parents are dismayed by the poverty of instruction in the basic subjects, while the defense has argued that current instructional approaches reflect the desires of local publics, and that parents are highly concerned about the school's

Table 1—Profiles of Attendance Areas and Numbers of Respondents*

Attendance Area	Median Family Income	% in White-Collar Occupations	Median yrs. of School Completed	% Negro	% Increase in School Pop. (1960–1963)	NUMBER OF INTERVIEWS Mothers	Teachers	Students	Principals
City neighborhoods									
White middle-class (el.)	$10,000	55%	12	>5%		92	13	0	1
White working-class (el.)	$6,000	40%	8	>5%		92	18	0	1
Mixed Negro and white (el.)	$4,500	20%	8	40%		84	9	0	1
Negro (el.)	$4,500	15%	8	90%		66	16	0	1
Cross-section (high school)						138	29	157	1
Suburbs									
Stable middle-class	$15,000	75%	13	>1%	5%	131	22	59	2
Growing middle-class	$10,000	70%	13	>1%	15%	128	31	48	2
Stable working-class	$6,000	30%	9	>1%	1%	111	25	49	3
Growing working-class	$7,000	35%	11	>1%	41%	142	48	45	2
Small towns									
Middle-class (pop. 4,000)	$6,300	50%	12			154	23	45	2
Working-class (pop. 6,000)	$6,200	40%	10			125	30	56	2
Rural community (pop. 2,500)†						127	19	49	2

*All census figures are approximate in order to preserve community anonymity. The 1960 U.S. Census was used.
†Census data not provided.

contribution to the emotional and social development of their children.[5]

In the midst of this controversy, some educators have become worried that teachers themselves have been misled by a vocal minority of prominent critics. They fear that teachers wrongly believe that parents favor more academic pressure on pupils at the expense of other kinds of growth.[6] By examining how parents feel about various styles of teaching, we hope to furnish a partial

discourse of practitioners and parents.

Two especially important aspects of the teaching role are widely discussed in the literature: (1) the extent to which subject matter is emphasized, and (2) the extent to which adult authority is exercised. By dichotomizing and combining these two dimensions, we obtain four distinct styles of teaching:

		EMPHASIS ON SUBJECT MATTER	
		High	Low
RELATIONS BETWEEN TEACHER AND CHILD	*Adult Centered* (authoritarian)	Content-oriented	Control-oriented
	Child-centered (permissive)	Discovery-oriented	Sympathy-oriented

answer to the practical question of what sorts of instruction are preferred by what types of parents. And by juxtaposing self-images of teachers against the expectations of parents, we should be able to see how parents' desires compare with teachers' own role-definitions.

Methods

Styles of teaching can be thought of in many ways—for example, authoritarian versus permissive, pupil-directed versus content-oriented, or businesslike versus unplanned. Several writers have developed lists of teaching styles.[7] But just what teachers actually do is still very much an open question.[8] The main reason for the lack of research evidence on what teachers do in the classroom is the difficulty of measuring classroom behavior. But despite the absence of empirically documented styles, a number of ideal-constructs have been derived from "philosophies" of teaching, from controversies over progressive versus traditional education, and from the everyday

The four styles singled out for study are not exhaustive of the popular conceptions of teaching and are not wholly accurate reflections of behavior patterns, but they do represent some of the most common images that are held of teaching at the elementary and secondary levels.

The four styles of teaching were presented to first, fifth, and tenth grade *teachers*, to the *mothers* of many of these teachers' pupils, to the *pupils* of selected tenth grade English teachers, and to the *principals* of the schools where the teachers were located. (The sample design is discussed below.) The questions that were posed were the following:

Mothers and Students—

Although teachers have to concern themselves with many different things in their jobs, some teachers emphasize certain things more than others. Suppose there were four first (fifth, or tenth) grade teachers in (school) and you could choose the one you wanted to be (M: child's teacher; S: your 10th grade English teacher). Which of these would be your first choice?

Which of these best describes (M: child's teacher; S: name of English teacher)?

Teachers—
Although teachers have to concern themselves with many different things in their jobs, some teachers emphasize certain things more than others. We would like to know which one of the following four types of teachers you think best describes you.
Which of these four types of teachers do you think most of the mothers of the students in your class prefer?
How about your principal? Which type do you think he (she) prefers?

Principals—

(Same basic question as above, but:) Which of these four types of teachers do you prefer having as a teacher in (school)?

The four teaching styles were described as follows:

(Control-oriented)

Teacher #1 is most concerned with maintaining discipline, seeing that students work hard, and teaching them to follow directions.

(Content-oriented)

Teacher #2 feels it's most important that students know their subject matter well, and that he (she) cover the material thoroughly and test their progress regularly.

(Discovery-oriented)

Teacher #3 stresses making the class interesting and encourages students to be creative and to figure things out for themselves.

(Sympathy-oriented)

Teacher #4 thinks it's most important that a teacher be friendly and well liked by students and able to understand and to handle their problems.

School attendance areas were selected in order to maximize the homogeneity of certain social and ecological characteristics. (See Table 1 for profiles of the communities and numbers of respondents.) A city school system provided four elementary attendance areas. Three of these were predominantly working-class areas: one was mostly white, one was mostly Negro, and one was mixed. The fourth elementary attendance area in the city was mainly composed of white middle-class residents. In the same city a high school which received the students from the schools already mentioned was also selected. Outside of the city, four suburbs, two small towns, and one rural community were chosen. The suburbs were selected according to both SES of the residents (middle versus working class) and rate of growth (stable versus growing). The two small towns were selected according to SES and commuting rate.

All the mothers of pupils in the classrooms of two teachers in each school building at each of three grade levels (first, fifth, and tenth) were in the sample. Wherever possible, the two teachers in each grade represented a slow and a fast track, or a non-college and a college track. The tenth grade teachers were teachers of English. All teachers in the elementary schools were also interviewed; all English teachers were interviewed in each high school. All principals and all tenth grade English students were also respondents.[9]

Results

Before looking at the correlates of preferred teaching styles, it needs to be emphasized that the expectations that mothers hold are by no means of minor importance to them. For if mothers do not believe that teachers are meeting their role expectations, they tend to be dissatisfied with the teacher.

As noted above, the mothers were asked to select the style that they preferred and also the style that "best describes" the teacher. By matching the mothers' *preferences* with their *perceptions* of teachers, we are able to designate mothers who desire a teaching style that is at odds with what they believe the teacher is actually doing in the classroom. As a measure of satisfaction with the teacher's performance, we have employed the following question:

Are there any things that you think it is important for (teacher) to be doing differently than he (she) is in order to help (child) get the most out of school?

Table 2 shows that mothers who perceive the teacher as deviating from their expectations much more often desire some modification in the teacher's behavior. Only 15 percent of those who perceive *conformity* desire other behavior, contrasted with 40 percent of those who perceive *deviance*. These figures at once lend credibility to the responses of mothers about preferred teaching styles, and demonstrate the practical value of studying parental preferences.

Perceived deviance with respect to two of the four styles is especially highly related to dissatisfaction. These styles are the two *intellectual* ones: content-orientation and discovery orientation. Almost half of the mothers who see the teacher as failing to conform to these desired styles would welcome a change in the teacher's behavior. As we shall see in a moment, these are also the two patterns of teaching that are most commonly preferred at all three grade levels.

Preferred Teaching Styles at Different Grade Levels

It is generally assumed that elementary and secondary teachers are expected to perform their teaching roles quite differently. As the pupil passes from lower to higher grade levels, he is expected to become more intellectually serious, and especially so if he wishes to enter college. One would therefore predict that parents with children in the higher grades would place greater emphasis on teaching of *content*. Also, one would expect parents of younger children to desire greater support or sympathy from teachers.

Despite these common impressions, our data show only a slight trend in the

Table 2—Mothers' Dissatisfaction with Teachers, According to Mothers' Perception of Teachers' Conformity to Preferred Styles of Teaching

	TEACHING STYLES		DISSATISFACTION (% Mothers Who Say That Teacher Should Be Doing Something Differently)			
	Preferred	Perceived				
Perceived Conformity	Control	Control	16%	(140) *	15%	(680)
	Content	Content	16%	(251)		
	Discovery	Discovery	14%	(228)		
	Sympathy	Sympathy	13%	(61)		
Perceived Deviance	Control	(Not control)	27%	(134)	40%	(614)
	Content	(Not content)	44%	(227)		
	Discovery	(Not discovery)	48%	(181)		
	Sympathy	(Not sympathy)	33%	(72)		

*Numbers in parentheses are the N on which the percentage is based.

direction of parents' placing greatest emphasis on *content*-orientation from lower to higher grade levels, and practically no difference with respect to preferences for the *sympathy*-oriented teacher. As shown in Table 3, 33 percent of the mothers of first graders would choose a teacher who was content-oriented, compared with 38 percent of the mothers of fifth graders, and 43 percent of the mothers of tenth graders. There is a clear trend, but it is much less pronounced than common sense would predict. The sympathy-oriented style was favored by only 11 percent of first grade mothers, 11 percent of fifth grade mothers, and eight percent of tenth grade mothers.

The greatest difference occurs with respect to preferences for the *control*-oriented teacher: 26 percent of the first grade mothers, 22 percent of the fifth grade mothers, and 13 percent of the tenth grade mothers desire this teaching style. Thus, the younger the child, the more likely are their mothers to want a non-intellectual authoritarian style. This would appear to be in direct conflict with the professional educational ideology that stresses the importance of a permissive classroom climate in the early grades.

To sum up thus far, mothers of older children more often desire the two styles of teaching that emphasize *subject matter*, content-orientation and discovery-

orientation. But the overall difference between first and tenth grade mothers is not very pronounced, suggesting that variations in the expectations of parents with children in different grade levels has been overestimated by professional educators.

Perhaps of greater significance is the observation that *within each grade level*, the mothers prefer the *content*-oriented first and the *discovery*-oriented teacher second in order of frequency. Only a small percentage of the mothers opted for the *sympathy*-oriented teacher. In short, it is not true that mothers are only secondarily concerned with the intellectual maturation of their children. Even in the elementary grades, only about a tenth of the mothers prefer a teacher who is primarily oriented to playing a nurturance role with pupils (i.e., the sympathy-oriented teacher). The critics of educational practices who claim that parents are mainly concerned about the intellective aspects of education are by and large correct in their assessment, and especially with reference to the higher grade levels.

Preferred Teaching Styles and Social Position

The sample design permits us to examine the expectations of teachers that prevail in different social contexts. In the following discussion we shall use the features of the community to define the characteristics of respondents. In other

Table 3—Teaching Styles Preferred by Mothers with Children in Different Grade Levels

| TEACHING STYLE | GRADE LEVEL OF CHILD | | |
	1st	5th	10th
Control	26%	22%	13%
Content	33	38	43
Discovery	30	29	36
Sympathy	11	11	8
	100%	100%	100%
N mothers	(453)	(494)	(424)

words, instead of classifying the mothers according to their own socio-economic position and race, we shall classify them according to the socio-economic and racial composition of their community. Further analysis will draw upon both sources of classification simultaneously, but for the purposes of this paper it is sufficient to note variations according to community characteristics alone.[10]

The variation in preferences of mothers by the social class composition of the communities is at least as great as the variation by grade level; and with respect to certain styles of teaching it is much greater. The most consistent difference between working-class and middle-class communities, controlling for grade level of child, relates to the preference of the middle-class for the *discovery*-oriented style. As shown in Table 4, mothers in the middle-class communities much more often prefer this style of teaching. Thus, 23 percent of the working-class residents compared with 38 percent of the middle-class residents with grade school children prefer the discovery-oriented teacher; and the respective figures for mothers of tenth graders are 25 percent and 47 percent.

Evidently, the middle-class emphasis on training for independent effort reasserts itself in the preferences of mothers regarding their children's formal education.[11] One important implication of this finding is that teachers who actually use the "discovery method" will be more successful with middle-class than with working-class children, because of the cultural support for independent effort that middle-class students receive in the home. This is a possibility that has so far been overlooked in the psychological literature on the subject.[12]

Mothers located in working-class communities prefer the *control*-oriented and the *sympathy*-oriented styles of instruction more often than do mothers in middle-class communities. (This is mainly the case among grade school mothers.) As mentioned earlier, these two images refer to non-intellectual mechanisms of socialization. Indeed, the two styles refer to socialization sanctions employed by mothers themselves, namely, disciplining and giving affective support. It appears then that working-class mothers, and especially those with grade school children, are more likely to desire a teacher who is a prototypical parent-surrogate. This tendency to expect teachers to perform in ways that are similar to informal socialization of the young might stem from the working-class tendency to view the world in more simplistic and personal terms.[13] Isolation from the internal workings of formal organizations and from professional role-

Table 4—Teaching Styles Preferred by Mothers with Children in Different Grade Levels, According to SES of Community

TEACHING STYLE	1ST AND 5TH GRADES		10TH GRADES*	
	Working Class	Middle Class	Working Class	Middle Class
Control	30%	17%	12%	8%
Content	32	39	55	40
Discovery	23	38	25	47
Sympathy	15	6	8	5
	100%	100%	100%	100%
N mothers	(495)	(372)	(114)	(129)

*Excludes the city high school because it contains a mixture of social class backgrounds.

playing might limit their understanding of the extent to which teachers are prepared to play a specialized role in dealing with children.

Of the two images more often preferred by working-class mothers of grade school children, it is a preference for the *control*-oriented teacher which more clearly differentiates the two social classes. Seventeen percent of the middle-class mothers of grade school children prefer this teaching style compared with 30 percent of the working-class mothers. At the tenth grade level, however, it is the *content*-oriented style that most clearly distinguishes the working-class from the middle-class (55 percent vs. 40 percent, respectively). These apparent differences between grade levels mask an important underlying similarity. It will be recalled that control- and content-orientation are the two styles which we have designated as *authoritarian*. The proportion of working-class, tenth grade mothers choosing *both* of these styles remains high in comparison with first and fifth grade mothers. Thus, there is simply a shift from one authoritarian stance (control-orientation) to another (content-orientation), although this shift of emphasis crosses the boundary from the non-intellectual, parent-surrogate styles to the intellectual realm of teaching. Stated in relation to the preferences of middle-class mothers, the difference between the two social classes shifts from the question of *whether* subject matter should be emphasized to the question of the appropriate *manner* of emphasis. To sum up, when the working-class mothers choose an intellectual style at the tenth-grade level, they choose "authoritarian intellectualism" (content) rather than "permissive intellectualism" (discovery).

These results are in accord with research that reports a tendency among working-class members to value authoritarian social relationships,[14] and particularly the child-rearing studies that show greater emphasis on parental dominance among working-class mothers.[15]

The social class differences we have observed are not confounded by the different racial compositions of working, and middle-class schools. Table 5 makes this quite clear. In this table we show the styles of teaching preferred by mothers of grade school children who are located in the one city in our sample. (As mentioned earlier, the three working-class grade schools in the city were selected according to their racial composition.) Table 5 shows that the mothers' desires do not differ systematically according to the proportion of Negroes in the school. But what is more significant, all of the major differences previously noted between middle-class and working-class mothers of grade school children *persist* regardless of racial composition. Working-class mothers more often prefer the

Table 5—Teaching Styles Preferred by Mothers of Grade School Children in the City, According to Racial Composition and SES of School Attendance Area

| | WORKING CLASS | | | MIDDLE CLASS |
TEACHING STYLE	White	Mixed	Negro	(Mostly White)
Control	40%	41%	35%	21%
Content	33	25	26	40
Discovery	17	13	22	30
Sympathy	10	21	17	9
	100%	100%	100%	100%
N mothers	(81)	(92)	(65)	(91)

control-oriented and the sympathy-oriented teachers, while middle-class mothers more often prefer the content-oriented and the discovery-oriented teachers.[16]

But we have not yet looked at the teachers themselves. In order to determine the amount of consensus between teachers and mothers on styles of classroom teaching, we need to compare the expectations of mothers with the role-definitions of teachers. This question is especially important if we wish to see whether teachers are more likely to conform to the expectations prevailing in the world of professional education than they are to the expectations flowing from outside the system.

Concensus on Styles of Teaching between Teachers and Parents

We saw earlier that mothers who believe that teachers are *not* teaching the way they would like them to teach are much more often dissatisfied with teachers. Apparently there is much room for dissatisfaction, for when we compare the teaching styles preferred by parents with the teachers' definitions of their role, we find considerable discrepancy. For example, as we see in Table 6, only 30 percent of the grade school mothers desire the *discovery*-oriented style, but 56 percent of the teachers claim that this

is the style that best describes them. And even a larger gap occurs between tenth grade mothers and teachers.

Teachers also diverge widely from parents' expectations in the category of *content*-oriented teaching. Thus, 43 percent of the tenth grade mothers prefer this style, but only 16 percent of the teachers describe themselves in this fashion. In short, mothers most often prefer the content-oriented style, while teachers tend to espouse the discovery-oriented style. This contrast confirms the critics of public education who claim that parents want more attention devoted to the basic content of school subjects while school personnel favor a more permissive intellectual approach stressing "independent discovery."

Regardless of the merits of these two instructional patterns, it is obvious that many parents and teachers have quite different educational philosophies. Specifically, *69 percent of the mothers in our study have a teacher for their child whose role-definition is not in accord with their preferences.* The proportions of mothers with various role-preferences whose teachers describe themselves in various ways are shown in Table 7.

Mothers whose expectations are most often violated (at least with respect to the teacher's definition of her role) are those who favor a *sympathy*-oriented

Table 6—Teaching Styles Preferred by Mothers Compared with Teachers' Own Role-Definitions (by Grade)

	1ST AND 5TH GRADES		10TH GRADE	
TEACHING STYLE	% Mothers Who Prefer Type	% Teachers Who Describe Selves	% Mothers Who Prefer Type	% Teachers Who Describe Selves
Control	24%	20%	13%	10%
Content	35	18	43	16
Discovery	30	56	36	72
Sympathy	11	6	8	2
	100%	100%	100%	100%
N	(947)	(175)	(424)	(104)

Table 7—Teachers' Role-Definitions According to the Expectations of Their Pupils' Mothers

TEACHERS' SELF DESCRIPTIONS	STYLE PREFERRED BY MOTHERS			
	Control	Content	Discovery	Sympathy
Control	27%	24%	17%	21%
Content	16	13	12	17
Discovery	55	59	67	57
Sympathy	2	4	4	5
	100%	100%	100%	100%
N mothers	(278)	(510)	(401)	(136)

style. Only five percent of these mothers have teachers who describe themselves as sympathy-oriented. But only a small proportion of mothers prefer this style. More serious in terms of possible strain between family and school is the large minority of mothers (23 percent of the entire sample) who expect the teacher to be content-oriented but whose teachers describe themselves as discovery-oriented.

The discrepancy between parental and professional role expectations becomes even larger when we compare mothers with principals. Table 8 shows that teachers occupy a position midway between parents and principals with respect to the proportion espousing the discovery-oriented style. This style, which we earlier characterized as "permissive intellectualism," is preferred by 30 percent of the mothers, 62 percent of the teachers, and 90 percent of the principals. In short, the degree of integration into the educational subsystem determines the extent to which the value of "permissive intellectualism" is held.

The differences observed might not be only due to background differences among the three status-groups. The importance of degree of involvement in the educational structure is suggested when we examine the role-expectations of students, who occupy the overlapping status of "client within the organization." Thus, students stand with one foot in the community and the other in the organization. And as shown in Table 9, the teaching styles favored by students reflect their degree of involvement in the educational system.

Whether the emphasis on discovery and deemphasis on content of professional educators reflects a functional requirement of our educational system or merely an educational fad cannot be determined here. But whatever the source, "permissive intellectualism" is clearly a part of the value system of education, as shown by our data, and is differentially espoused according to the degree of involvement in the educational structure.

Table 8—Preferences of Mothers and Principals for Various Styles of Teaching, and Teachers' Own Role-Definitions

Teaching Style Preferred	Mothers	Teachers*	Principals
Control	22%	16%	5%
Content	38	17	5
Discovery	30	62	90
Sympathy	10	5	..
	100%	100%	100%
N	(1334)	(271)	(20)

*Percentages refer to own role-definition.

Table 9—Preference of Tenth Grade Mothers, Students, and Principals for Various Styles of Teaching, and Tenth Grade Teachers' Own Role-Definitions

Teaching Style Preferred	Mothers	Students	Teachers*	Principals
Control	13%	7%	10%	..
Content	43	22	16	14%
Discovery	36	57	72	86
Sympathy	8	14	2	..
	100%	100%	100%	100%
N†	(424)	(418)	(104)	(7)

*Percentages refer to own role-definitions.
†This table contains only 10th grade teachers, mothers of 10th grade students, and principals of high schools, so that results can be compared with the students.

Conclusions

By comparing the preferences of mothers among four typical teaching styles with the self-images of their children's teachers, it was found that mothers prefer a content-oriented style more often than any other, while a majority of teachers see themselves as discovery-oriented. In addition, over two-thirds of the mothers expressed role preferences that were not in accord with the self-descriptions of their child's teacher. A higher proportion of the mothers of 10th graders than mothers of first and fifth graders were found to prefer the two subject matter oriented styles, but somewhat larger differences were found between mothers in communities with different socio-economic composition. Working-class mothers had a higher preference for the two authoritarian styles of teaching, while middle-class mothers tended to share the preference for a discovery-oriented style with teachers. The latter finding was interpreted as suggesting compatibility between the independence training stressed by middle-class parents and the teaching styles advocated by teachers. It is not clear whether the preference of teachers for the discovery-oriented style is a reflection of professional socialization or a functional requirement of the teaching role in American schools. The high consensus on teaching styles among teachers, however, and especially the even higher consensus among principals suggest a pervasive educational ideology.

Evidence that instrumental goals of education are potential sources of conflict was shown by the higher dissatisfaction among mothers whose perceived and preferred teaching styles were dissimilar. This demonstrates the importance of studying what teachers do, and are thought to do, in the classroom, as distinct from the more diffuse purposes of education.

In view of the current agitation for increased parental participation in the schools in working-class areas, the especially high preference for the control-oriented teaching style among the mothers of the elementary school children in such areas might be a potential source of parent-teacher conflict. If increased participation results in increased awareness among mothers of their differences with teachers, then the likelihood of conflict should also increase unless (a) the schools are able to legitimate teacher behavior which is not in accord with parental expectations, for example, by persuading parents in working-class areas of the virtues of discovery-oriented teaching, or (b) teachers change their role definitions in accord with the expectations held by the constituency of parents.

Notes

[1] For a summary statement of the social characteristics of voters and non-voters in school elections see R. F. Carter, *Voters and Their Schools* (Stanford University, California, 1960). For evidence regarding differential participation in P.T.A., see especially P. C. Sexton, *Education and Income* (New York: Viking, 1961), and R. E. Herriott and N. H. St. John, *Social Class and the Urban School* (New York: Wiley, 1966). A doctoral dissertation is being written by Nathalie Schacter Friedman based on data from this study which further elaborates and corroborates these relationships and investigates some of the consequences of differential parental observability and participation in the schools.

[2] Two notable examples are the New York City schools (see the minutes of the Board of Education, December 21, 1966) and the recommendation made to the schools of Washington, D.C. by A. Harry Passow as a result of an extensive and much publicized study. (See A. H. Passow, *A Study of Washington, D.C. Schools.*)

[3] The larger study of which this is part will explore several of the areas of possible conflict in a forthcoming report. Some of the normative differences between teachers and parents have been described by D. Jenkins, "Interpersonal Perception of Teachers, Students, and Parents," NEA, 1951, and John M. Foskett, *The Normative World of the Elementary School Teacher*, (Eugene: University of Oregon, The Center for the Advanced Study of Educational Administration, 1967).

[4] Traditionally, educators have maintained that the purposes or terminal goals of education should be determined by the citizenry, but that professional educators should be left to decide how subject matter will be taught. Citizens have not always shared this definition of the situation judging from the controversies over methods of teaching reading, for example, and the pronouncements of popular critics of American education, including Admiral Rickover and Martin Mayer. The limits of lay authority become especially relevant when parents participate in school activities: and in New York, parents have recently demanded the right to participate in the selection of professional school personnel.

[5] See, for example, Winfield C. Scott, Clyde M. Hill, and Hobert W. Burns, *The Great Debate—Our Schools in Crisis* (Englewood Cliffs, N.J.: Prentice-Hall, 1959).

[6] This study of parents' and teachers' opinions about the roles and goals of education was originally prompted by precisely this concern on the part of officials in one of the State Education Departments.

[7] The most extensive list of dimensions for classifying teacher behavior has been developed by Ryan as part of the Teacher Characteristic Study, *Characteristics of Teachers* (Washington, D.C.: American Council on Education, 1960). More sociologically oriented conceptualizations can be found in Orville Brim, *Sociology and the Field of Education* (Philadelphia: Russell Sage, 1958); W. W. Charters, Jr., "The Social Background of Teaching," in *Handbook of Research on Teaching*, ed. N. L. Gage (Chicago: Rand McNally, 1963), pp. 715–813; and Charles E. Bidwell, "The School As a Formal Organization," in *Handbook of Organizations*, ed. James G. March (Chicago: Rand McNally, 1965). Bidwell's recent restatement of Waller (W. Waller, *The Sociology of Teaching* (New York: Wiley, 1932) in terms of two conflicts faced by teachers, the use or non-use of affect in controlling students, and whether to emphasize nurturance or student achievement, produces four types very similar to those we have used.

[8] Norman E. Wallen and Robert M. W. Travers, "Analysis and Investigation of Teaching Methods," in *Handbook of Research on Teaching*, ed. N. L. Gage (Chicago: Rand McNally, 1963), pp. 448–505.

[9] For a detailed discussion of the sample design, including problems in its development, see David E. Wilder and Nathalie Schacter Friedman, *Project Memorandum #1—"Selecting Ideal-Typical Communities and Gaining Access to Their Schools for Social Research Purposes,"* Columbia University, Bureau of Applied Social Research, October, 1965. Response rates for the various groups were as follows: mothers, 83%; teachers, 99%; principals, 100%; and students, 97%. Interviews with mothers were conducted in the homes by Roper Associates. The interviews lasted 90 minutes on the

average. Teachers and students were interviewed in the schools, and interviews averaged 60 minutes.

[10] For stylistic convenience we shall occasionally refer to mothers residing in the various types of social context as "middle-class" or "working-class" mothers; but it should not be overlooked that we are really speaking of mothers who reside in certain types of communities. As previously mentioned, the communities were selected partly on the basis of internal homogeneity of socio-economic characteristics, and therefore this characterization of mothers is accurate in the vast majority of cases.

[11] For a review of research on "independence training" according to social class of parents, see Urie Bronfenbrenner, "Socialization and Social Class through Time and Space," in *Readings in Social Psychology*, ed. Maccoby, Newcomb, and Hartley, 3rd ed. (New York: Holt, 1958), pp. 400–25.

[12] See, for example, Jerome S. Bruner, "The Act of Discovery," *Harvard Educational Review*, 33 (1963), pp. 124–35.

[13] Seymour M. Lipset, "Democracy and Working-Class Authoritarianism," *American Sociological Review*, 24 (1959), pp. 482–501.

[14] Richard Christie, "Authoritarianism Re-Examined," in *Studies in the Scope and Method of the "Authoritarian Personality,"* ed. Richard Christie and Marie Jahoda (New York: Free Press, 1954), pp. 123–96.

[15] Bronfenbrenner, *op. cit.*

[16] It is clear from comparing Tables 4 and 5 that working-class mothers of grade school children in the city prefer the control-oriented style of teaching over the content-oriented style, while the opposite is true for elementary school mothers in working class settings which are not in the city.

The School Board as an Agency of Legitimation

Norman D. Kerr

Reprinted from Sociology of Education, 38 (1964), pp. 34–59, by permission of the author and publisher, The American Sociological Association. This article may be identified as publication No. A-404 of the Bureau of Applied Social Research, Columbia University.

MEMBERS OF BOARDS of education are supposedly elected to represent the community in the making of local educational policies. Since the allocation of authority in professional matters to laymen in the local community has important implications for educational policy, boards of education have frequently been studied to determine the social backgrounds of the members. The assumption has been that background factors affect decisions on the board. For the most part, however, this assumption has remained untested and one researcher who has reviewed the field has called for a moratorium on purely descriptive studies in favor of explanatory investigations of the decision-making process.[1]

Although only a few studies have sought to relate the social status characteristics of board members to their role performance, it is noteworthy that the findings of these studies have not borne out the assumption that the attitudes or behavior of members are unambiguously related to their social characteristics. Campbell, for example, has concluded from a study of the records of 172 board members in 12 western cities from 1931–

40 that there was "little or no relationship between certain social and economic factors and school board competence."[2] And Caughran reports from a survey of Illinois school board members that measures of socio-economic status were not related to the members' attitudes toward several issues of educational financing.[3]

Perhaps the most systematic study of the influence of social characteristics on members' attitudes is contained in Gross' report on schools in Massachusetts. From this study we learn that the only characteristic which was clearly related to "Educational Progressivism" was the members' amount of education. Income, religion, motivation for seeking election to the board, activity in politics, age, length of residence in the community, number of children, and type of school attended by their children—none of these factors revealed a clear-cut relationship to Gross' scale of progressivism.[4] Further, Gross was unable to find a relationship between either economic or educational homogeneity of school boards and consensus among the members.[5] Nor was homogeneity with respect to income related to their agreement with the superintendent. And while religious and politico-economic homogeneity were related to the members' consensus, neither was related to their agreement with the superintendent on what their roles should be.[6]

These findings imply that the social structure in which local school boards are imbedded in some way screen out or otherwise nullify the usual effects of social backgrounds on attitudes. The purpose of this paper is to explore several facets of the context and internal structure of boards of education which intervene between social background and the performance and attitudes of board members.

More specifically it will be argued that under some conditions, which may not be uncommon, school boards chiefly perform the function of *legitimating* the policies of the school system to the community, rather than *representing* the various segments of the community to the school administration, especially with regard to the educational program. This unintended function of school boards may be viewed as an organizational defense which counteracts the threat to the school system's institutional security inherent in local control by laymen.

Methods and Research Sites

While other studies will be cited for supporting evidence, our conclusions will be drawn mainly from intensive observations and interviews carried out in 1962–63 in two suburban school districts located about 25 miles from a large northern city.*

School districts were selected which were adjacent to each other and located within the same county and township. One of the districts was undergoing rapid expansion due to the influx of former city dwellers, and was almost three times the size of the other in terms of enrollment. The percentage increase in enrollment over the previous year had been 18 per cent. This district also attracted a large proportion of Jewish residents as a consequence of having once been a Jewish resort area. (It was estimated that 55 percent of the high school students were Jewish.)

The smaller system was growing much less rapidly due to its location a few miles farther from the city. The percentage increase in enrollment over the previous year was 5 per cent. The population was predominantly Protestant, with a large Catholic minority. Both districts

* A residency stipend from the Russell Sage Foundation for an investigation of the problems of education in the light of sociological theory and prior research made it possible to carry out the study.

contained a high proportion of commuters, and both contained nuclear villages around which commuters tended to locate their homes.

The terms of office of the two superintendents were fairly typical for the type of succession represented by each of them. The superintendent of the smaller district had held the position for 11 years, and had formerly been the high school principal. The superintendent of the larger district had held the position for 6 years after moving from another suburban district. According to a national study of the succession of school superintendents, the mean time in office of "insiders," or individuals who have moved up within the system, is 10 years; for "outsiders" it is 8 years.[7]

In statistical profile, the two districts were rather typical of large and small suburbs, respectively, as defined by Martin in his analysis of data gathered in a national survey in 1959–60 for his study of *Government and the Suburban School*.[8] Some statistical comparisons with Martin's sample are shown in Table 1, together with additional information about the two districts which was not presented in Martin's monograph. Table 2 sets forth some details of the composition of school boards in the two districts. The differences in religion and political party affiliations reflect the community differences. The differences in average tenure of board members reflect differences in legal terms of office rather than in turnover.

With respect to several community features—size, religion, political preferences, population density, and rate of growth—the smaller district may be regarded as part of a more traditional community. Likewise, the smaller school district exhibited less specialization, fewer formal regulations, and less emphasis on the academic as contrasted

Table 1—Profiles of Two Suburban School Districts Compared with National Data

	Larger District	National Survey	Smaller District	National Survey
Population	29,000 (district)	More than 10,000 (cities)	15,000 (district)	10,000 or less (cities)
Enrollment	7,888	8,900 ($\overline{X}$)	2,911	4,700 ($\overline{X}$)
Teaching staff	309	365 ($\overline{X}$)	158	179 ($\overline{X}$)
Public schools				
Secondary	3	3 ($\overline{X}$)	1	2 ($\overline{X}$)
Elementary	9	10 ($\overline{X}$)	$4\frac{1}{2}$	6 ($\overline{X}$)
Parochial schools				
Jewish	5	*	0	*
Catholic	1	*	4	*
Educational program				
Kindergarten	Yes	72%	Yes	71%
Special education courses	Yes	61%	Yes	45%
Adult education program	Yes	87%	Yes	42%
Summer school	Yes	81%	Yes	42%
College attendance as % of graduating class	70%	*	54%	*

*Not reported in Martin, *op. cit.*

Table 2—The Social Composition of School Boards in Two Suburban Districts

	Larger District	Smaller District
No. of members	9	7
Men	8	6
Women	1	1
Professional	5	2
Businessman	3	4
Housewife	1	1
Jewish	6	0
Catholic	2	0
Protestant	1	7
White	8	7
Negro	1	0
Republican	2	6
Democrat	6	1
DK	1	0
Legal term of office	3 years	5 years
No. of years served on school board:		
All members since centralization ($\overline{X}$)	4.6 years (13 years)	6.7 years (22 years)
Current members ($\overline{X}$)	5.4 years	9 years

with the athletic program. Despite these differences between the two districts, however, my observations of the school boards and their relations with the superintendents showed them to be strikingly similar. Some exceptions will be mentioned later on.

It is not claimed that these two suburban school districts are representative of suburban schools, much less of the totality of American school districts. All that can be claimed is that the two districts are not grossly atypical.[9] In any case, the chief contribution of case studies in social research is the identification of variables that at least must not be overlooked in future inquiries, and the generation of hypotheses which may be tested in other contexts.

Analysis and Interpretations

The main forces shaping school board members' attitudes and performance will be dealt with under the following headings: school board politics, pressures for conformity throughout the process of socialization on the board, and community pressures generated by the school system's impact on the public.

SCHOOL BOARD POLITICS

There were two major features of school board politics in the two districts which seemingly had considerable effect on the role behavior of board members: (1) the relative absence of clear-cut constituencies, and (2) the candidates' lack of familiarity with school board activities and with the educational program.

1. *The absence of constituencies.* If candidates for the school board do not represent visible constituencies which support their candidacy, ensure their election, and watch the behavior of their representatives after election, then the mandate which board members receive permits considerable freedom in adjusting to the expectations of school

administrators and older board members.

That only a minority of school board candidates obtain the backing of particular groups in the community is suggested by one of the findings in Gross' study. Drawing on the replies of a sample of superintendents in Massachusetts, Gross found that only 29 per cent of the school board members represented some group when they sought election. The motive of "gaining political experience" was attributed to 21 per cent of the board members by the superintendents, while the motive of "civic duty" was attributed to 64 per cent.[10]

The notorious paucity of issues in school board elections also testifies to the absence of constituencies. This situation perplexed a candidate in the larger district who was searching earnestly for a platform. During a meeting in which the local Citizens Council for Better Schools was planning a campaign for one of their members, the candidate grew exasperated because no one could supply him with an issue: "I can't just say I'm for better schools—that's what everybody says." The kinds of issues which finally emerged in this campaign, and the doubtful validity of most of them, will be mentioned later on. What was striking about this particular candidate, however, was that even though he had the backing of a citizens' organization, he was at a loss to provide a cogent issue for his campaign.

The only type of organized group with specific objectives which supports candidates with notable frequency is a taxpayers association.* But ordinarily these groups are temporary coalitions with the limited purpose of running an economy-minded candidate. Since the scope of their concern is much narrower than the

* [Editor's note: This assessment was made in 1964, prior to the emergence of black educational politics.]

range of decisions which members of the school board are required to make, it is unlikely that the attention of such a group is sustained throughout the school year. Further, if new trustees are elected several months before the new budget is prepared, a taxpayers group has little with which to concern itself during the interim period. This was the case in both of the districts. Consequently, once the campaigns came to an end, the taxpayers groups dissolved before the boards turned their undivided attention to the budget. In the larger district, the most prominent taxpayers group was actually a civic association in a particular neighborhood which quickly became preoccupied with other issues after the campaign was ended.

But even when a taxpayers group remains intact all year round, the specificity of its goal does not provide a standard according to which their representative can settle the many issues which are brought to his attention while serving on the board. Thus, the influence of a taxpayers group is limited—unless, of course, it manages to reduce expenditures below the level sufficient to maintain a minimally adequate school program. But in many suburban school budgets, there is considerable leeway above this minimal level.

Illustrative of these generalizations was the election of a school board member in the smaller district with the support of a taxpayers association. The association was organized for the first time in behalf of this particular candidate. A local builder, the candidate was expected to trim the budget of "nonessentials" in the school plant and to oversee the construction of a new school building. Soon after the candidate's election, the association ceased to exist. To my knowledge, none of the members of the group attended a board meeting in the following year. And as one of the board trustees remarked in an interview several months later, "Once Mr. Stevens got in, he never said boo about the budget. He saw that you can't reduce the budget."

If we examine the context of local control of education, we find several factors which account for the relative absence of pressure groups other than taxpayers associations. In the first place, because of the emphasis on education as a uniquely governmental function, school board candidates do not publicly identify themselves with political parties.[11] Indeed, nonpartisanship is proudly proclaimed by school boards, sometimes to the detriment of a concerted attack on problems.

A second possible source of constituencies is the social class structure. But the socio-economic homogeneity of school board members, which has been documented in numerous studies, testifies to the absence of clearly formulated issues based on social class differences. (All of the board members in the two districts were either prominent professionals or well-to-do businessmen, with the exception of two housewives who were married to prominent professionals.) The assumption on the part of the electorate that school board candidates should be highly educated, since they will shape the policy of an educational institution, may explain in large part the social class homogeneity of school boards. There is probably also a tendency to match the prestige of school board membership with the prestige of certain occupations, apart from the specific educational function of the school board. The desire of property owners to have representation in setting policy on property taxes is also a factor in some communities. The political apathy of lower status groups is obviously another factor, but one which is not unique to school politics. Whatever the cause, the striking consequence is that the class homogeneity of school boards militates against the emergence of class-based issues.

On the other hand, it is the extreme heterogeneity of parental interests which blocks the emergence of issues concerning the school program. The wide array of interests represented by parents with children at different levels in the school system, located in different buildings, and representing different class and ethnic groups rarely permits a sizable portion of school patrons to organize around any particular grievance concerning their children's education. Many of the grievances which do emerge, moreover, are carried to the teacher or to the building principal, and sometimes to the PTA. Since many of these complaints do not reach the school board, they do not enter into the election campaigns.[12]

Because of the absence of visible constituencies, new board members are highly receptive to the pressures for conformity which stem from the incumbent board members and from school administrators. Gross' study affords suggestive evidence on this point also. Gross found that the motive of "civic duty" for running for the school board was highly related to subsequent conformity with the expectations of the superintendent (.52), while the alternative motives of "representing some group" and "gaining political experience" were found to be negatively related to conformity.[13] Moreover, the motive of "civic duty" was more related to conformity with the superintendent's expectations than several other factors, including board members' level of education, their agreement with the superintendent on role definitions, and their evaluation of him.

Gross explains the relationship between the motive of "civic duty" and conformity to the superintendent's expectations in terms of "the extent to which the (board members) are motivated to

achieve the goals of the system."[14] An alternative explanation seems equally plausible, namely, that the absence of constituencies releases the board members from community constraints, thereby rendering them highly receptive to pressures for conformity. But in order to confirm this point, we need to consider another facet of school board politics: the candidates' familiarity with the goals of the system. For if it is primarily through interaction with incumbent board members and school administrators that new board members learn about professional expectations of the superintendent and about the goals of the system which he represents, then Gross' explanation needs to be reexamined. This brings us to our next topic.

2. *Unfamiliarity with school board activities and with the school program.* The candidates' ignorance about the school program is difficult to document because of the lack of studies which have measured this factor. We know a great deal about the knowledge of the public in general, however, and the evidence points to considerable ignorance and apathy about the local schools.[15] For suggestive evidence of the candidates' ignorance, we shall have to rely on our observations in the two suburban districts.

a. *Unfamiliarity with the school program.* One of the two successful candidates in the smaller district revealed her ignorance of the school program in her first public pronouncement. When asked in a public meeting if there were "any areas in which you feel the school should be doing a better job," she mentioned the vocational training program:

We teach kids to make bookshelves, but not how to make alterations on a house. We haven't set our sights high enough in vocational training.

The clerk of the board pointed out to the candidate that the county ran a separate program for vocational students for one-half of each school day, which prepared them thoroughly in the mechanical arts. He further explained that the school's shop program, which is what the candidate had in mind, was never intended to provide vocational training. In short, the candidate was misinformed about the issue which was most meaningful to her. This was all the more surprising in view of the fact that she had formerly been a teacher in the district, and was currently the president of a "Committee for the Presentation of School Board Candidates."

Another candidate for the board in the same district revealed even greater uncertainty. When asked for her views of the schools' needs in the same public meeting, she replied:

> I'm not an educator. I feel it's a good system, but there's room for improvement. I'm willing to learn about the operations of the school board. I don't have any ideas about changes because I don't know enough about the operations of the system. I would love to serve; I would have to learn. I've been reading about it in the papers is all.

Nor was this candidate, who was not elected, as apathetic about community affairs as her reply suggests. She had one child in the high school, was a member of the Parent-Faculty Association, was the activities director of a local recreations commission, and had served as chairman of a number of community fund drives.

The other two candidates were somewhat better informed about the school program. This was understandable since one was an assistant principal of a city elementary school, and the other had been a board member in the district two years earlier. Neither of these candidates was elected, however.[16]

There is not space here to document in detail the knowledge of the school program possessed by the ten candidates who ran for the board in the larger district (two additional candidates were incumbents seeking re-election.) An indirect measure of their familiarity with the program was attempted by means of a content analysis of the platforms written by all the candidates at the request of the local League of Women Voters and published in the newspapers.

On the basis of this material, all of the new candidates devoted greatest attention to non-educational issues, such as financing new buildings, setting up citizens' advisory groups for the building program, improving school bus transportation, and exploring the possibility of a statewide purchasing system. All but one of the candidates made general statements about the needs of a good educational program, such as "I would try for a real breakthrough in curriculum," or "(we should) utilize a sound philosophy of education to meet the needs of each individual child." But a total of only 15 concrete recommendations was made. And most significant is the fact that 12 of these 15 recommendations were already being implemented in the school system. These included a syllabus for advanced students, special classes for the retarded and for the emotionally disturbed, a low drop-out rate (12 per cent), and guidance for college-going students. Moreover, the candidates failed to mention several innovations which had *not* been incorporated into the program, such as foreign languages in the elementary schools, the ungraded primary school, teaching machines, and educational television. These omissions suggest that the candidates' recommendations for the school program were gleaned randomly from popular articles about education with little reference to the needs of their particular school system. To the voting public, who may have been only a little less informed than the candidates, the irrelevance of the recommendations was not always apparent.

b. *Unfamiliarity with school board activities.* The candidates probably possessed greater knowledge of the school program than of school board activities. They could at least draw upon their children's experiences in the schools, and they could exploit their relationships with teachers, either through PTA meetings or through more personal contacts. But they seldom attended public school board meetings. None of the ten candidates in the larger district attended a single school board meeting during the preceding year, and only one of the four candidates in the smaller district attended a meeting.

Further, many meetings of school boards are executive sessions from which the public is barred. According to a recent survey by the U.S. Office of Education, 68 per cent of suburban school boards hold one or more executive sessions during the year, and 52 per cent of these hold more than six executive sessions.[17] Private meetings are necessary in order to conceal differences of opinion from a public which is greatly affected by school decisions.[18] The following dialogue, which took place during an executive meeting devoted to teachers' salaries in the smaller district, is illustrative (all names are fictitious):

SUPERINTENDENT I'll ask for your approval of this next Tuesday night, unless there's some question now.
MR. DONALDSON This is disagreeing night; next Tuesday (public meeting) is agreeing night.

The other members laughed approvingly. When a similar situation arose in the larger district, the Superintendent stated, "We might have an informal discussion of this now. I don't think you want to have an open session with the press here."

The real work of weighing alternative goals, referring to state laws and local board policies, consulting with the administration, and persuading one another to adopt a course of action is carried out in these closed meetings. Public meetings in the two districts were usually reserved for formal action; but during my period of observation, almost none of the considerations that actually produced the boards' decisions were revealed in public meetings. Consequently, public meetings were typically routine and dull.

Public meetings were also reserved for less important issues. This practice was demonstrated by the following exchange which took place in a private meeting. The superintendent had raised the question of whether the new ceiling in an old building should be 12 or 14 feet high.

MRS. GRAY Do we have to talk about that now?
SUPERINTENDENT Why? Do you have to leave early?
MRS. GRAY No, I just thought that would be a good thing to talk about in a regular meeting.
MR. VINSON It's a good harmless thing to talk about in a regular meeting, isn't it?

Citizens who attended public meetings did so to present a specific complaint or to ask permission to use the school property. (The only exceptions were the members of the Committee for the Presentation of School Board Candidates who sent one or two women to about half of the public meetings in the smaller district.) And it was standard procedure to invite the visitors to address their questions to the board at the beginning of the meeting. After the visitor received a reply he departed, which was understandable in view of the uneventfulness of such meetings.

In sum, owing to the policy of holding executive meetings to deal with "delicate matters," it was impossible for aspiring board members to learn much in advance about the intricate and often exciting business of decision-making which took place on the school boards. Therefore, freshmen board members were very dependent upon the school administration and the incumbent board for information about the goals and means of the system, and they were also unprepared to resist the pressures for conformity which stemmed from the superintendent and from older board members.

SOCIALIZATION AND PRESSURES FOR CONFORMITY

1. *The induction phase.* It is impossible to draw a sharp line between the induction phase and later socialization on the board. We have simply defined this phase as comprising the early contacts of the new board member with school authorities. Our observations suggest that this is a crucial stage in the process of defining the role of new board members.

a. *Induction by the administration.* The superintendent in the larger district invited new board members to an "orientation" in his office before the new members were exposed to the incumbent board. In these orientations the conversation focussed on legal and financial affairs of the school. In one case, however, the new member interrupted the superintendent to mention a recommendation which Conant had made about suburban school programs. Since he could only vaguely recall the idea, he asked the superintendent if a copy of Conant's book were available in the office. The superintendent replied that it was, but that it was more important for

him to explain the legal aspects of board membership. He then continued to pile a great deal of legal and financial material in front of the new board member, advising him to spend the next few weeks studying it. Finally, at the close of the meeting, the superintendent firmly directed the new member to refer all complaints about the school program to his office or to the principal of the school which was involved before attempting to reply to anyone. Nothing more was said about the school program, even though this member had been outstandingly articulate and inquisitive about the educational program during his campaign. As he left the superintendent's office, he only expressed dismay about the mountain of material which he was obliged to master. In the smaller district, measures were taken to indoctrinate only those candidates who appeared to be especially threatening. For example, the candidate of the taxpayers association was inducted by means of guided tours of the school plant. These tours were conducted by the assistant superintendent for buildings and grounds, and lasted several days. In the course of the tours, the new member was impressed by the numerous maintenance and construction problems and by the economies which had been achieved in handling these problems. As a result of common occupational interests and mutual respect for one another's competence, the assistant superintendent and the new board members became close friends. We have already mentioned that this board member never did initiate the economy drive that the school authorities had feared. When I asked the assistant superintendent about the member's influence on school expenditures, he replied:

It hasn't changed. As a matter of fact, it's increased. When you put on a new project, you automatically get an increase, and John saw the need. . . . Our tax rate has gone up each year. . . .

These episodes drawn from the two school districts illustrate the ways in which the administration can influence the role behavior of new board members before they ever sit down with the school board. That one superintendent practiced diversionary tactics while the other used total coöptation was probably due to the different positions of the two superintendents vis-à-vis the board members. The superintendent in the smaller district (total coöptation) had greater security as a result of longer tenure and greater stability of the school system. There was also a slower rate of turnover among the school board members. Lacking these sources of security, the superintendent in the larger district (diversionary tactics) was compelled to confront new board members privately before they became active members, and to redirect their energies into the more harmless areas of school board responsibility.

b. *Induction by incumbent board members.* The board members in the two districts were equally adept at defining role behavior for new members in a way which reduced the new members' threat to the ongoing system. In the first place, new members are seldom unknown quantities to older board members, for the latter follow the campaign very closely. In fact, they discuss the candidates privately among themselves and pick their favorites. This makes them better prepared to deal with the new member. And as the president of the school board in the larger district informed me, "There's usually some fear when a new member comes on the board, but usually we're able to make them see our policies."

There were several means by which the two school boards sought to obtain the conformity of new members. First, the new member was assigned to a freshman status with the clear implication that he was to be a learner rather than a spokesman for an indefinite period of time. Condescension, paternalism,

chiding, and even humiliation were sanctions which kept the new member in his freshman status. The success of these methods depended upon the greater familiarity of older members with technical matters and past board policies. Success also depended upon the greater power of the board president who shared with the superintendent the responsibility for guiding the discussions.[19]

An example of mild humiliation was recorded. In a closed meeting a new member in the larger district was visibly disturbed by the guesswork involved in planning the cost of a new bond referendum. The architect responded by saying, "Something was said about uncertainty. . . . Architects don't add up nuts and bolts; it's a matter of experience." Then an older member added, "Marvin is aghast, but you have to make guesses." Finally, the president raised his voice angrily, "You'll have the complete figures in 48 hours! And that's the man who will get them," he added, pointing to the architect. "Turn around and look at him! Go ahead, turn around!" Whereupon the new member turned sheepishly to the architect, quite visibly shaken by the assault.

The election of a faction rather than a single individual presents the board with an especially difficult problem. And if the newly elected faction joins forces with an incumbent board member who is dissatisfied with the other members, then the problem is intensified. This situation was handled adroitly by the president in the larger district.

When trips were arranged for the purpose of interviewing architects and appraising their buildings, the president sent the members of the faction to different towns. He instructed a friendly board member with the largest girth to sit between the incumbent deviant and the two new members during the board sessions so that they had trouble exchanging signals. He appointed each new member to the chairmanship of different committees, thereby giving them a formal status on the board which was not enjoyed by the incumbent deviant, and also segregating them into different work groups. Meanwhile, the president taunted the old deviant member of the board into demonstrations of irresponsibility. For example, when the deviant said that he was unable to meet with the Salary Committee on Saturday because he had to tend the children while his wife worked, which was well known to the president, the president responded angrily, "All right, Jim, we'll make our decisions without you." Jim resented the attack, and therefore refused to meet with the committee even on weekdays. As the president summed up the story to me: "So that Jerome (a new member) was confronted with the same kind of behavior we've been confronted with for years." Later on, the relationship between the deviant and the two new members was destroyed. The new members began privately expressing their disapproval of him; and eventually, they too split up.

This episode demonstrates how an extreme threat to the stability of the social system can be met with equally extreme measures. Milder sanctions ordinarily sufficed to restrain less serious transgressions.

2. *Later socialization and control.* The indoctrination of new board members did not end with their initial contacts with the administration or with the incumbent board members. There was still a great deal to learn about state laws, financial practices, the school program, and school board policies, written and unwritten. It was also important to discover the best way to influence other members of the board without antagonizing them. Thus, the later period of socialization was prolonged over several months.

Owing to their unfamiliarity with the work of the school boards, the self-confidence of new members was sometimes severely strained. As one of the board members in the smaller district confessed in a meeting with the public for the selection of board candidates:

> It takes almost a year to understand the language. It's like speaking another language—like aid for each child, the language of the administration. There's a period of adjustment that you have to go through, and sometimes you feel like you ought to quit. I know that Mr. Adams, when he first came, wasn't sure if he was at a school board meeting or some other kind of meeting.

Thus, ignorance of school board activities may plague new members for a considerable period of time, thereby prolonging their exposure to pressures for conformity. When the new members began to demonstrate their grasp of board functions and their willingness to conform to the ground rules, the manipulative measures of the president or of the superintendent were relaxed. If a member remained critical of the board or the administration, however, pressure continued.

In the larger district the severest pressures were felt by the incumbent deviant whom we have already mentioned. This individual had broken the district's "gentleman's agreement,"[20] and had persisted in criticizing the school program, the administration, and the board itself. His rejection by the board took a variety of forms: the other members avoided being photographed with him for the press; the PTA, whose coordinating chairman was the board president, invited him to speak only once; the Educational Standards Committee, of which he was a member, was convened by the president only four times in three years; the president rebuked him at a public board meeting for failure to attend the meetings of the salary committee; and, as already described, the president successfully turned the sentiments of the newly elected members against him. The deviant's lonely position at the far end of the school board table symbolized his rejection. Subsequently, he refused to run for re-election, although the local Citizens Council for Better Schools offered support. His feeling was that re-election would be a futile gesture. As he later complained to a reporter in a lengthy interview, "I have been a victim of school censorship."

Occasional deviations of a less extreme nature were handled more gently, but firmly nevertheless. In contrast with the controls exercised during the phase of induction, when the initial ignorance and lack of confidence of the new members rendered them more pliable, the controls that normally operated during the later phase drew their power from the affective relationships which emerged among the members. Meeting as frequently as they did, and sharing common problems and criticisms from the public, the board members tended to develop affective ties. As the relationships became more intimate, the sanctions became more subtle and more personal. The way in which the former candidate for the taxpayers association was restrained is illustrative. As an older member remarked in an interview:

There was quite a lot of concern about that—that he would be a pennypincher. But he's turned out to be a cooperative member of the board. . . . We've gotten *close enough* to where I *laugh him out of some of those things.*

The superintendent in the district was keenly aware that a congenial atmosphere on the board produced greater cohesion, and consequently, from his point of view,

greater malleability. He described a special annual supper for the members as follows:

SUPERINTENDENT This is one of the ways I *weld the school board together*. They get to know one another personally.
INTERVIEWER But aren't there other school board suppers during the year?
SUPERINTENDENT Yes, but this is the only one to which their wives are invited. So they don't talk business, and get to know one another socially.

One of the most striking characteristics of the board's discussions was the relative absence of concern with the educational program. Because this sub-cultural "trait" was so obvious, it is worthwhile examining the way in which new board members were indoctrinated with the attitude that education was the province solely of the school administration.

In order to determine the amount of time that was devoted to various topics during board meetings, a careful record was kept of almost all regular, special, and executive meetings for the entire year. The way in which time was distributed is shown in Table 3. In thirteen meetings of the board in the smaller district, 58 per cent of the time was devoted to financial affairs, while only 10 per cent of the time was devoted to the educational program. In the larger district the respective figures were 45 per cent and 13 per cent. Even if we eliminate the time spent preparing the bond issue referenda, it can be seen in Table 3 that far more attention was devoted to non-educational than to educational matters in both districts.

The omission of the education program for the boards' deliberations was sustained by several mechanisms. Some of these involved manipulation by the administration; others derived from fundamental features of the structure of

Table 3—Amount of Time Devoted to Various Topics by Two Suburban Boards of Education*

	Larger District		Smaller District	
Finances				
Routine (bids, contracts, audits, treasury reports, taxes, budget)	17%		23%	
Bond issue referendum for new buildings and sites (includes planning the campaign)	21	45%	21	58%
Salaries	2		12	
State Aid	5		2	
Physical facilities				
Buildings and grounds maintenance	1		6	
School bus transportation	4	15%	2	12%
Enrollment trends and accommodations	8		1	
Requests for use of school property	2		3	
Personnel				
Appointments; resignations; conference requests; leaves of absence	7	7%	8	10%
Problems in staff relationships	..		2	
Educational program				
Curriculum; student progress	9		9	
Educational research; consultants; in-service program	1	13%	1	10%
District workshops (reports)	3		..	
Requests or questions from public	6		2	
Relationships with local government	2		1	
All other topics (e.g., reading minutes, planning meetings, receiving legal consultation)	13		13	
Total minutes	2,206		1,651	
Total hours	36.8		27.5	
No. of meetings	15		13	

*Includes public and closed meetings on regularly scheduled nights, but excludes workshop sessions (which were chiefly financial and board committee meetings with teachers (which were chiefly concerned with salaries). Totals exceed 100 per cent because some time units were placed in two categories.

the relationship between a professional educator and laymen.

One means by which the administration manipulated the visibility of the educational program involved the school board agenda. In both districts the agenda was prepared by the superintendent, with occasional suggestions from the board members. Items concerning the educational program were conspicuously absent from the agenda. In addition to following the agenda, the superintendents were adept at directing the discussion by means of tactical silence or outright diversion. Once when I remarked to the superintendent in the smaller district that the school board seemed to devote very little time to education, he replied:

They don't know anything about it; but the things they *know* they talk about, like sidewalks, sites, and so forth. I let them go on sometimes because I don't want them to talk about curriculum. This is another thing they don't put in the books.

Another method of diverting attention from the school program was to anticipate the board's interest in a manner which disarmed them. This was achieved mainly by detailed reports on the school program. With rare exceptions, the educational program was discussed in both districts only when the superintendents presented a report, either personally or through one of their administrative assistants.[21] These reports invariably displayed the achievements of the program rather than the unresolved problems. By casting a favorable light, they signified that further attention from the board was superfluous. (One example from the smaller district was a report on the low drop-out rate and how the administration felt it had been achieved. An example from the larger district was a report on curriculum guides which had been written by the staff, printed, and already distributed.)

Sometimes a board member requested a report on some aspect of the school program. It was usual, however, for several weeks to elapse before the report was presented, during which time steps were taken to insure that it would be favorable. (When I asked the superintendent in the larger district what he would do if a board member insisted on a change in the school program, he replied that he would implement the request "only if I could get agreement on a more important matter." Upon further inquiry he admitted that the board had not once caused him to change a decision about the educational program during the six years of his superintendency.)[22]

In addition to these manipulative measures of the administration, there were structural features of the school-board superintendent relationship which facilitated the superintendent's autonomy. Perhaps the most important feature of this relationship was the board's dependence upon the superintendent's performance as an educator. School board members are held accountable by the community for the superintendent's performance because the board members are by definition his superiors, at least in the eyes of the public. And since there is the danger that the superintendent's commitment to effective performance will be undermined if he is forced to abandon his professional goals, it is important for board members to confer on the superintendent a goodly portion of the autonomy which the latter considers his prerogative as a professional.

Gross' study suggests that the willingness of school boards to allocate educational decisions to superintendents is widespread. The highest degree of consensus on different aspects of the division of labor between board members and superintendents concerned the professional educational tasks of the superintendents, such as the selection of new textbooks and the shaping of instructional policy.[23]

What deserves emphasis here, however, is that the school board's attitudes often originate in the socialization process, rather than in a uniform predisposition on the part of candidates regarding the professional prerogatives of the superintendent. There are two pieces of evidence for this proposition. First, as we have already seen, the school board candidates in the two districts paid a fair amount of attention to needed reforms in the educational program during their campaigns, despite their ignorance of the current program. The contrast between this behavior and their performance as board members must be attributed to the socialization process which we have delineated.

Second, it was observed that older board members occasionally warned freshmen members not to invade the domain of educational policy. The following exchange, which took place in a closed meeting in the smaller district is illustrative. The topic was teachers' salaries, and the question arose whether the merit plan (which had been administered chiefly by the superintendent) was sound. Knudsen, the freshman board member, spoke with authority since he was a professor of education and had formerly taught in the school system.

KNUDSEN This all comes down to the fact that we don't have clear-cut criteria for merit.
VINSON I disagree with that very strongly.
ARNOLD That's not something that school boards should get into. That's for the administration.

Arnold, the president, and Vinson were among the three oldest members of the board. A similar warning was issued by an older board member in the larger district when a new member sought to inquire into educational policy.

Thus far we have presented an essentially passive picture of the school boards' role in legitimating the school systems and the administrators. There were also occasions when the board members actively justified the superintendents' decisions to the public. In order to understand how a formally representative body may be converted into an active agency of legitimation, we need the board's relationship with the community.

COMMUNITY PRESSURES

School boards operate in a context of potential crisis owing to the pervasive effect which their decisions have on the community. As a consequence, school boards sometimes undergo (1) alienation from the public, and (2) concealment. This was the case in both suburban districts.

1. *Alienation from the public.* Since the issues which came before the school boards were often quite complex, they were only partially understood by the community. In the two districts, considerable ignorance of financial and legal affairs was demonstrated by the uninformed questions, the unrealistic proposals, and the misguided criticisms which flowed from public assemblies. But the school board members were obliged to note that the public's ignorance did not deter them from drawing conclusions about the school board's competence. The following cases are examples.

A local builder took ten minutes of a board meeting to present a proposal that local residents build the three million dollar high school with their own labors "the old church raising type of idea."

Hundreds of residents claimed vociferously that a two-story school building was cheaper than a one-story building, despite public testimony to the contrary by architects, and evidence from studies made by building experts throughout the nation.

The editor of a local newspaper editorialized for months in opposition to home economics before he discovered that it was required by State law. It was the superintendent who finally told him.

A local builder attacked the school board for securing property at exorbitant prices, and had to be informed in detail about the requirements of terrain for school buildings, and of the real estate practice of marking-up the property which was being considered by the board.

Several residents confessed that they did not know what a bond issue was, although a community-wide campaign had been conducted for a number of weeks, which included daily coverage on the front pages of most local papers.

A woman threatened to go straight to the *board of education* if she could not get satisfaction from the *school board*.

Every one of these criticisms required tactful and exhaustive explanations in public meetings of the board or in public assemblies attended by hundreds of residents. But an explanation at a single meeting seldom sufficed, and so the board repeated the same explanations continually but with mounting impatience. The situation was especially acute in the larger district which was compelled to deal with many recent migrants from the city whose school taxes were increasing yearly. As a leader in the League of Women Voters remarked, "When we come out from the city, we know nothing about taxes and how you pay them. And when they got this terrific knock over the head, it's no wonder they dropped dead." There is also the possibility that many new residents projected their alienation from the centers of urban power into the suburban school scene. Provided with this new access to highly visible local authorities, many expressed old hostilities to political power.[24]

Under these circumstances, it was not surprising that the school board members grew increasingly cynical about the value

of representing the public's wishes. At one time or another, most of the school board members in the larger district expressed their alienation from the community. For example, during a debate in a closed meeting about erecting either one- or two-story buildings, one of the board members revealed a sentiment with which the others tended to concur:

That we should do what the community wants—this goes against my grain as a board member. We should make up our own minds about what makes sense.

Another board member expressed the rationale for this attitude:

This is a community of experts, and no matter *what* we do, they'll find something wrong with it.

It was to be expected that such an attitude would vex the new board members who had recently made commitments to represent the will of the people. At one point during another closed meeting, a freshman objected to an older member's reference to the community's recalcitrance:

STEINBERG Ben, you keep saying "they" as though these are very strange people.
JACOBS They are strange to me. (laughter)
MARTIN The difference is *you* understand the problem and *they don't.*

Martin's explanation was basically sound. The board's alienation from the community developed from the members' greater understanding of the needs of the system, combined with the community's unwillingness to grant them superior knowledge. As a consequence, the board members in the larger district were further released from community restraints and more exposed to the values of the administration. They therefore became preoccupied with the task of explaining and justifying the needs of the system to the community. Since this process was mainly observed in the larger, more rapidly growing district, it seems that a school board's alienation is closely related to the public's lack of understanding.

2. *Concealment from the public.* As Vidich and Bensman have pointed out, the visibility of the consequences of school board decisions generates a need for the board to conceal itself from the public.[25] One way in which this need is met is by maintaining unanimity. In effect, a unanimous vote reduces the visibility of arguments against the decision.

The two suburban school boards were no exception to the rule of unanimity. There had been only one split vote in the past two years in the smaller district, and the board members attributed the only budget defeat they had suffered in the ten years since centralization to this lapse in observing the principle of unanimity. The following statement by the board president in the larger district, urging the members to reach a decision on the school board referendum, reveals the pressures that promote agreement:

I would hate like the dickens for our vote to be hung up like this at that time [i.e., when the public is admitted], because there are people in the community who will take note. That's why I want to reach a consensus *now*.

It should be noted, however, that the superintendents had to be included in any consensus that was reached. The importance of gaining the superintendent's approval in presenting a decision to the community was illustrated in a closed meeting of the board in the larger district. For almost three hours the members debated and polled themselves on the relative advantages of wide and narrow corridors in a new elementary building. All of them preferred wide corridors, but several feared that the public would consider it a waste of money and would therefore defeat the entire building program. The superintendent at this time was particularly apprehensive about public reaction, and firmly stated his position to the members of the board. Finally, one of the board members spoke up:

JOHNSON If the administrators aren't enthusiastic for wide corridors, we can't sell it.

ABRAHAM Yes. We've got to have the enthusiasm, and our administrators don't have it.

SUPERINTENDENT I frankly haven't got enough experience or research to be enthusiastic about it at the moment.

This final statement clinched the debate. Narrow corridors were put into the plans.

A board member in the smaller district expressed the same concern for reaching decisions which coincided with the superintendent's desires:

It's terribly important in public meetings to show complete agreement, especially in supporting the administration.

The superintendent's support seems to be important for two reasons. First, he has to join the board in selling the decision to the public. If the superintendent failed to demonstrate his support for the board's decision, then the members were exposed to suspicion no less than if a board member had dissented. The second reason concerns a factor which we have already mentioned, namely, that the school is judged by the effectiveness with which the superintendent performs his duties. The board must therefore be careful not to force their views upon him lest they undermine his professional motivation. As a consequence, it was largely the decisions of the administration which were legitimated through recurrent expressions of unanimity among board members.[26]

There were also occasions when board members played an even more active role in presenting the views of the administration to the community. The members appeared before PTA meetings and other public gatherings to promote the budget or the bond issue. And there were innumerable opportunities for them to urge support of the school system through more personal contact.

The importance of personal contacts was strikingly demonstrated by the board member in the smaller district who received the support of the taxpayers association. In fact, the career of this board member illustrates several points made earlier. During an interview three years after his first election, and immediately following his re-election he stated:

> A school trustee *has* to support the superintendent. If he didn't, it would be terrible with the staff and the public. You've *got* to back up the superintendent.

When I asked if the board had ever turned down the superintendent's recommendation for a new teacher, he answered: "Never. On what grounds could we? We aren't qualified." Finally, it was plain from the comments of the assistant superintendent who had introduced the board member to the school plant, and of a board member who had served with him for three years, that the former taxpayers' representative had become very useful in legitimating the school system to the most economy-minded sector of the community. As the assistant superintendent noted:

> Maybe we have a person now who can communicate with some people we were missing before. They can ask him questions and get direct answers. Now they feel they have a representative.

And as the school board member pointed out:

> He reaches people on the street who don't have children in the school—old timers, part of the old community whose parents were here.

Summary and Conclusion

We have dealt with a number of factors in the social structure of American education which constrain school boards to legitimate the school system to the local community. Since the process is a complex one, it may be helpful to examine the diagram in Figure 1, which recapitulates the discussion in the form of a flow-chart. The diagram does not pretend to be an elegant theoretical model. Its chief purpose is to summarize the discussion graphically so that future research may be directed to strategic linkages in the network of relationships.

The *Community's demand for representation* (1) has not been discussed at length because it is so obvious a feature of the American school system. While this factor actually provides the impetus for the whole network of processes, we have entered it into our diagram at only one point.

The *community's ignorance about schools* (2) no doubt lies behind the candidates' ignorance, since the latter are more or less typical members of the community with respect to their amount of information. Hence, this influence has been shown as antecedent to the candidates' ignorance. Of course, as already mentioned, the ignorance of the community about the school board's job also promotes the board's alienation from it. Finally, it will be noted that the *professional self-image of the superintendent* (5) is the only major causal factor which

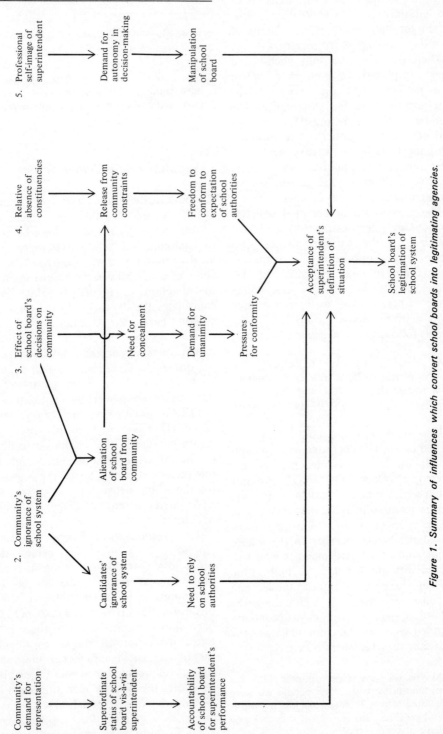

Figure 1. Summary of influences which convert school boards into legitimating agencies.

does not reside in the nature of the local community.

In conclusion, our analysis has sought to identify a number of influences which act upon school board members in such a way as to deflect behavior from formally prescribed goals, and even from the candidates' own goals for the system. Thus, we have argued that under certain conditions the chief contribution of school boards to the continuance of our educational system is their legitimation of the schools' policies, rather than their representation of the community.

Within the framework of a more general theory of organizations, the function of legitimation may be regarded as arising from the organizational prerequisite of attaining security in the environment.[27] Due to the "openness" of American school systems at the *top*—because of school boards—and at the *bottom*—because of the presence of students inside the organization—the system is threatened with loss of professional control. Our attention has therefore focussed upon one set of organizational mechanisms which tends to restore security and maintain this control.

Notes

[1] W. W. Charters, Jr., "Beyond the Survey in School Board Research," *Educational Administration and Supervision*, 41 (1955), pp. 449–52.

[2] Roald F. Campbell, "The Social Implications of School Board Legislation" (unpublished doctoral thesis, Stanford University, 1942); "Are School Boards Reactionary?" *Phi Delta Kappan* (Nov. 1945), p. 27; pp. 82–83, 93.

[3] Roy W. Caughran, "The School Board Member Today," *American School Board Journal*, 133 (Nov. 1956), p. 39; and 133 (Dec. 1956), p. 26.

[4] Neal Gross, *Who Runs Our Schools?* (New York: Wiley, 1958), ch. 11, and pp. 179–181.

[5] Neal Gross, Ward Mason, and

Alexander McEachern, *Explorations in Role Analysis* (New York: Wiley, 1958), pp. 190–91.

[6] *Ibid.*, p. 191.

[7] Richard O. Carlson, "Succession and Performance among School Superintendents," *Administrative Science Quarterly*, 6 (1961), p. 223.

[8] Roscoe C. Martin, *Government and the Suburban School* (Syracuse, N.Y.: Syracuse University Press, 1962), p. 24–25.

[9] One source of atypicality is the large Jewish population in the larger district. It is not unusual, however, for suburbs to develop according to segregative patterns. Cf. William M. Dobriner, *Class in Suburbia* (Englewood Cliffs, N.J.: Prentice-Hall, 1963). A more serious problem in representativeness concerns the enrollment increases in this district. Many suburbs, however, have gone through similar spurts of growth.

[10] Gross, *Who Runs Our Schools?* ch. 7.

[11] Martin, *op. cit.*, pp. 59–60.

[12] It is noteworthy that when a portion of the community rises to protest some aspect of the educational program, the protest is usually facilitated by a nationwide controversy which has been carried to the community by the mass media. The criticisms of current reading instruction over the past several years is illustrative. In the absence of national controversy, the individualized nature of parental complaints forestalls the emergence of community-wide issues concerning curriculum or instruction.

[13] Gross et al., *Explorations in Role Analysis*, p. 239. In measuring these relationships, Gross eliminated from the "civic duty" category any members who were also said to be representing some group or to be seeking political experience. Thus, these categories were made mutually exclusive.

[14] *Ibid.*, pp. 238–39.

[15] Cf. Martin, *op. cit.*, p. 56.

[16] I was unable to assess the information of a fifth candidate who filed at the last moment, and who was elected primarily in opposition to a Jewish candidate from the same village.

[17] Martin, *op. cit.*, p. 44.

[18] We shall return to this point in a later section.

[19] The imposition of a freshman status on the new board members is similar to what

Michels has called a "quarantine" of the new recruits to the leadership cadre of a political party. *Political Parties* (New York: Dover, 1959), p. 170.

²⁰ "Gentlemen's agreements," which are entered into at the time of centralization, seek to insure that there will always be at least one school board member representing each of the pre-centralization districts. Thus, a candidate from one former district must not run against an only candidate from another former district. The agreement has no legal status within the state where the two districts are located.

²¹ Only once was a report presented by an instructor in the smaller district; and this person was actually the administrator of the physical education program and a close friend of the superintendent. Likewise, in the larger district, a group of older high school teachers once presented a report during the year.

²² The superintendents were not the only administrators in the two districts who disapproved of the board's intervention in professional matters which legally came under the board's jurisdiction. For example, a questionnaire survey in the two districts included a question concerning the role that the school board should play in hiring teachers: "To what extent do you think the following persons or groups *should* influence the selection of new teachers?" Eight out of 13 administrators in the larger district and 5 out of 8 in the smaller district replied that the school board should be "not at all" involved in selecting teachers.

²³ Gross et al., *op. cit.*, ch. 8.

²⁴ For an outstanding study of the relationship between feelings of powerlessness and opposition to school bond issues, see John Edwin Horton, "The Angry Voter" (unpublished doctoral thesis, Cornell University, 1960).

²⁵ Arthur J. Vidich and Joseph Bensman, *Small Town in Mass Society* (New York: Doubleday, 1960), pp. 176–78.

²⁶ Roberto Michels has put the issue of unanimity more concisely, if less analytically: "When there is a struggle between the leaders and the masses, the former are always victorious if only they remain united." *op. cit.*, p. 157. Another means of concealment advocated by board members in both districts was the omission of certain statistics from brochures which described the building program. Still another means, of course, was executive or closed sessions. The intense pressures for conformity exerted by the board while socializing new members were probably also dictated by the need to achieve unanimity on specific decisions.

²⁷ Philip Selznick, *TVA and the Grass Roots* (Berkeley and Los Angeles: University of California Press, 1949). Selznick's concept of "formal cooptation" as practiced by the TVA in response to organizational insecurity is, of course, extremely pertinent to our analysis of school boards. In the case of school boards, however, an inherent feature of school systems is converted into a legitimating agency; while in the case of the TVA, the structure of local representation was initiated for purposes of legitimation.

IN MANY WAYS the school desegregation issue is an ideal context in which to examine the general question of how school systems make policy decisions. First, it is an issue of some importance, so that the decision-making process uncovered can be assumed to be a non-trivial one. Second, it is a relatively new issue, so that the system can make decisions without much reference to traditional decision-making rules; this means that the social scientist need not be greatly concerned with the impact of prior historical accidents. Finally, the issue has arisen in nearly every large city with only minor differences among cities in the way in which it has been raised and with such idiosyncratic factors as the taxing power of the system being of minor importance. This means that the setting is almost ideal for comparative analysis.

This paper principally discusses some of the conclusions of a comparative study of integration in eight northern large city school systems carried out by the National Opinion Research Center in 1965.[1] Data were gathered by teams of graduate students who spent ten man-days in each city interviewing school administrators, school board members, civil rights leaders, political leaders, members of the civic elite, and other informants. The cities were selected by a modified random sampling design from the cities having a population between 250,000 and 1,000,000 of which at least 10 per cent was Negro. The findings are supplemented by observations made in the course of research on the social organization of the large city school system carried out principally in the Chicago schools.[2]

The Issue

Very little research has been devoted to the school desegregation issue as a problem in policy-making. Consequently,

School Desegregation and School Decision-making

Robert L. Crain and David Street

"School Desegregation and School Decision-Making" by Robert L. Crain and David Street is reprinted from Urban Affairs Quarterly, 2 (1966), pp. 64–82, by permission of the authors and the publisher, Sage Publications, Inc.

almost everyone, including most social scientists, have been dependent upon the popular media for information about the issue. This has produced a widespread acceptance of some important misconceptions. Perhaps the most common is the view that intense conflict over school desegregation is unavoidable because civil rights leaders want major concessions which the white voters are too prejudiced to give. This statement contains, we believe, three errors: First, our findings indicate that in some circumstances intense conflict is avoidable. In the eight cities studied, three (Newark, Baltimore, and St. Louis) have at least temporarily resolved their conflict with the civil rights movement. In three other cities (Pittsburgh, San Francisco, and Buffalo), the controversy has cooled down and shows promise of being resolved. In the two remaining cities the controversy is still raging. Second, our data indicate that most civil rights leaders will be satisfied (or at least call off their attacks) if they receive even minimal concessions. Third, survey data have indicated relatively little opposition to school desegregation in national samples of white voters.[3]

In short, the school system has some freedom to establish a policy which will prevent conflict. This is not the same as saying that the school system has the power to develop a policy which will actually alter the basic nature of the schools' treatment of Negro students; indeed, we doubt that any big city school system can do this. Thus, it will be necessary to divide our discussion into two sections: first, viewing school desegregation as an issue of symbolic politics, and then looking at the actual outputs of the school system—the extent of school integration and the extent to which educational opportunities can in fact be equalized.

Symbolic Politics: The Demands of the Civil Rights Movement

Traditional civil rights groups have pressed for school integration in all eight cities studied in the NORC research. To these groups the integration issue means two things: (1) the prevention of discrimination in allocating students to schools; and (2) the acceptance on the part of the school system of the principle that integration is desirable. Beyond these rather minimal goals, the civil rights prefer, of course, a maximum amount of actual integration, but most of them view true integration as a nearly unattainable goal.[4] If the school system can be persuaded to make racial integration one of its major goals, the civil rights groups will have achieved an important victory, for this commitment exerts normative pressure on the total community to accept the principle of racial equality and to define the efforts to segregate Negroes as illegitimate. Thus, for the traditional civil rights movements, the written policies and pronouncements of the school system are important regardless

of their impact. (Of course, if the system took no efforts to implement the policy, the civil rights leaders would raise the cry of hypocrisy.) The civil rights groups would probably endorse the definition of integration given by the Pittsburgh Urban League: "We regard a community as integrated when opportunities for the achievement of respect and the distribution of material welfare are not limited by race."

One is tempted to draw parallels between the school desegregation issue and labor-management negotiations. The major difference is that the corporation is required by law to negotiate with a labor union, while the school board is not. The school board is in the position of the corporation of four decades ago, when management had to decide whether it was wise or morally proper to negotiate with labor unions. The Northern school board is not required to recognize the civil rights movement as legitimate, and indeed many whites who appear otherwise unprejudiced do not consider it so. But another problem is that even when the school system decides that negotiation is proper, the question remains of whom to recognize as the true spokesmen for the civil rights movement. For these two reasons, actual back-room negotiations with the civil rights movement are not common. In our eight cities, only two school systems have been able to maintain this sort of communication with the civil rights groups. This means that we will have to analyze the school systems' policy-making as taking place with only limited private face-to-face communications between the "negotiators."

The First Stage of the Desegregation Decision: The School Superintendent As Decision-maker

We shall see that the policy decision on desegregation is made by the school board, not the superintendent. However, in each case the board attempted to avoid making a decision for as long as possible. The typical school board seems to operate in a highly pragmatic, fire-fighting fashion. It has limited time, resources, and information with which to make policies, and the result is that it seems not to have a clear policy perspective but primariy makes *ad hoc* decisions as issues become "hot."[5] In the case of desegregation, none of the eight school boards took action when the issue was first raised, and this placed the burden of decision-making on the superintendent. Of ten superintendents who served in the eight cities during the racial controversy, seven can be said to have acted autonomously without board direction to reject demands made by the civil rights movement, while three urged the board to take a liberal position. This comes as no surprise. It is now fashionable to accuse superintendents as a group of being narrow-minded and arrogant in their dealings with civil rights leaders. As our data indicate, superintendents do not uniformly reject civil rights demands, but enough do to require us to discuss this point.

The statements of school superintendents frequently stress three themes. The first is that the appropriate stance should be "color blindness"—the refusal to pay any attention to race. This sometimes leads to statements that racial census of school children is illegal or at least immoral. Coupled with this concern with color blindness is the stress placed on a narrow definition of the function of the school as "educational" rather than "social." The third theme which recurs (although with somewhat less frequency) is an extreme defensiveness and an intolerance for "lay" criticism. Lay persons are dismissed as unqualified to make recommendations, and their criticisms are frequently answered with flat disagreement or with vague, overly detailed, and off-the-point replies.

Of course, these reactions are common to all organizations which must meet criticism, but the educators go further than most public officials in reacting defensively to political demands. Educational administrators are insistent on defining themselves as professionals and have an entrenched ideology that grants lay control but stresses the importance of the teaching certificate and "educational experience" as the boundary between the expert and the layman. In part, the response to the demands for integration is only another instance of the professionals' tendency—developed through generations of conflict over political interference, progressive education, charges of communism in the schools, and other issues—to perceive any criticism as an "attack upon education."

Further, civil rights demands also strike deeply at one of the most firmly held tenets of the ideology of the large city superintendent: universalism. In the development of the large city schools, insistence on equality of programs for all populations in the city marked a dramatic accomplishment as it gave the schools protection from the pleas for special treatment from various political and ethnic groups. Without this universalism, Northern schools would be more segregated than they are; even after World War I, biracial high schools still discriminated against their Negro students in extracurricular activity participation.[6] Yet, demands by the civil rights movement give the lie to the assumption of universalism, thereby provoking a defensiveness around a highly salient theme and, often, the administrators' counterattack that civil rights demands are themselves a case of special pleading. The defensive response may also be increased by the superintendent's knowledge that even if he were wholly com-

mitted to making integration a prime
value of the schools, many of his personnel are too traditionalistic, too prejudiced,
or too recalcitrant to make the needed
adjustments without great resistance.

Thus, we can understand the superintendents' initial defensive response. But
in most cases, the school board has little
difficulty taking control of the decision
from the superintendent. Why is this?
The answer seems to lie in what areas
the superintendents can make believable
claims to expertise. On many issues—
for example, curriculum construction,
textbook selection, or design of facilities
—the superintendents' judgments generally go unchallenged, not only because
they usually fall into areas of indifference
but also because the superintendents'
accumulation of detailed information,
his technical background, and his appeals
to standard or good practice argue well
for honoring his professional claims. On
such issues, the superintendent in effect
runs the schools. Any criticism in these
areas may cause the superintendent
to accuse the board of interference with
his administrative role.

But it is only in the extreme case of
Benjamin C. Willis in Chicago that a
superintendent has been willing to take
the stand that he must have autonomy
or he will resign over a racial issue.[7] This
is understandable, for there is not truly
marketable expertise on racial integration
anywhere, and there is certainly little
claim possible in this area from within
the education profession. Therefore, the
superintendent, after his initial negative
response, often finds his upstaging by
the board to be the least awkward exit.

In addition, the origins and backgrounds of the large city superintendents
generally do not provide them with a
sensitivity to urban social change and
problems and to the current revolution
of rising racial expectations in the large

cities which would lead these men to
play a leadership role in the absence of
professional claims. Evidence bearing
on this point comes from the biographies
of the eleven big city superintendents
contained in *Who's Who*. Of the ten
whose birth date was given, the mean age
was fifty-seven. Nine of the eleven began
as teachers, and only one finished
graduate school before beginning his
career. Six of the ten American-born
superintendents were from very small
cities or farms, and none of the eleven
attended a first-rank undergraduate
college. Seven of the eleven began their
teaching in small towns, and much of
the administrative experience of all but
four had been outside the large cities.

While many of these men had been
administrators in smaller, suburban,
and often vanguard or experimental
school systems, their experiences in the
large cities have not stimulated their
desire to be experimental. The financial
problems of the large city systems, the
sheer administrative problems of size,
scale, and change, and the often inert
middle-level personnel and principals
(who frequently are political appointees
left over from an earlier era) tend to move
these superintendents toward an emphasis
upon a traditionalistic philosophy of
education that stresses the three R's, the
standard neighborhood school, and
"sound programs." When racial and
other social changes place new demands
on the schools, these superintendents
generally are unable to articulate a
leadership ideology dealing with integration and broadened welfare goals.

The Second Stage of the
Controversy: The School Board
Takes Over

In the typical city studied, the civil
rights movement first approaches the
board cautiously over a period of a year
or two, making statements and testifying

at hearings. In general, the school system does not respond to this; the issue is still below the level of saliency. The integrationists then step up their campaign, and their demands are rejected by the school superintendent at this point. When the movement replies to this with demonstrations or threats of demonstrations, the school board begins to take the issue seriously and responds in a variety of ways. At this point, the second stage of the controversy has begun. The board has taken over racial policy-making. In six of the eight cities it is possible to find a point at which the superintendent's recommendations were ignored or a point when he was instructed to alter his policy. In the other two cases, the system changed superintendents without changing its policy, so that we must assume that the board supplied policy continuity to the system.

The first response made by the school system during this second phase we call the "key response," because it sets the tone for the remainder of the conflict. This key response by the board seems to be made with almost complete autonomy. One might expect the community political and civic elites to exert great influence, but we have only one clear case where this was done successfully. In two cases, the school board seemed to ignore the recommendations of the mayor; in another case, the community's most prominent industrialist was flatly rebuffed. It is not possible to describe all the actions taken by various actors in this short paper, but in general it seems clear that there is less direct influence exerted on the board than one would expect and that attempts to influence the board usually are not very successful.

The most complex question is: To what extent can the civil rights movement control the outcomes of the school desegregation decision by their use of power? The evidence seems to indicate that they have surprisingly little influence.

The civil rights movement can force the school system to deal with the issue, of course; few if any of these systems would have done anything about civil rights if they had not been pressured by the movement. Generally, the movement is successful in part—that is, the system will usually desegregate schools to some limited extent, and all of the eight cities have adopted a policy statement advocating integration. But concessions may be minimal and may come so late and be given so grudgingly as to be nearly meaningless.

Apparently, there is little that the civil rights leadership in a typical city can do to prevent this. Once the key response of the board is taken, the process is "locked in." If the key response is conciliatory, continued low-keyed civil rights activity will extract additional concessions; if the key response is negative, the civil rights movement will retaliate with demonstrations, but this usually leads to an escalation of the conflict and the school board's subsequently becoming more reluctant to negotiate or make additional concessions. The only way in which the movement can control the outcome is by introducing a new authority—for example, the state government may step in to order desegregation, and this is sometimes very effective.

Altogether, the findings mean that the school board usually is nearly autonomous in its policy-making on racial issues. It generally is not effectively influenced by political or civic leadership, by its superintendent, or even by the behavior of the civil rights movement, despite the fact that the decision on race is probably the issue of greatest immediate importance to the largest number of actors.

In order to demonstrate this conclusion, the research staff of the eight-city study ranked the cities on four variables: the level of civil rights activity prior to the key response, the level of civil rights activity after the key response, the degree to which the key response indicated a willingness to acquiesce to the civil rights demands, and the final level of acquiescence of the board to the demands made. Acquiescence is based on the number of demands met and the general public tone taken by the schools with respect to the civil rights movement. Put another way, the research staff attempted to rank the cities according to the degree to which a typical civil rights leader would feel satisfied with the response of the school system. The eight cities varied greatly in their acquiescence. In Pittsburgh, for example, the school board reacted very early to civil rights demands with a transfer plan which integrated two previously all-white schools. When demands for integration reappeared later, the school board committed itself, in a long and candid statement, to integration; adopted some short-range integration programs; and began planning for large scale educational parks as the long run answer to the integration question. In Baltimore, a demand for the elimination of overcrowding in Negro schools led to a summer of negotiation between the civil rights leaders and the school board, resulting in a decision to transport 4000 Negro students and eliminate all double-shift schooling in the system, effective only six months after the issue was first raised. These two school systems are scored at the top of the acquiescence scale. At the opposite extreme, two school boards have refused to meet any of the demands for integration made, despite repeated demonstrations and pressure from other governmental officials. These two systems are located at the bottom of the scale.

Figure 1 diagrams the rank-order correlations between the initial level of civil rights activity, the acquiescence of the key response, the level of civil rights activity following the key response, and the total level of acquiescence of the school system. The correlations indicate that the key response is not dependent upon the level of civil rights activity directed at the board, and also that the key response predicts quite accurately the final amount of acquiescence of the school system. If the rank correlations are accurate, they indicate that the civil rights movement principally responds to the behavior of the school system rather than being a cause of the character of the school system's behavior.

This is only indirect evidence that the boards can be quite autonomous in their decision. We also have some direct evidence of this. In Figure 2, the eight

Figure 1. Rank-order correlations between civil rights activity and acquiescence of school boards to civil rights demands.

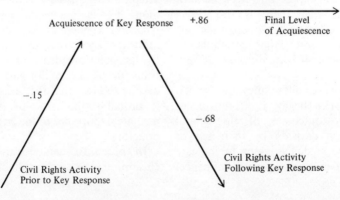

boards have been ranked by a combination of two closely correlated variables: the percentage of the board members having high socioeconomic status (men from large businesses, corporation lawyers, or professionals) as against the percentage who are professional politicians or related in other ways to the political parties in their city. (High-status men are, of course, generally independent of the parties.) This single variable predicts quite well the final level of acquiescence of the school system. Since the variable is clearly independent of the actual decision situation, this seems to be strong evidence.

The autonomy of the nonpolitical board is not so surprising. However, the five boards which are partly or wholly made up of political appointments are also largely autonomous. Two of these boards are elected boards in cities where political power is quite decentralized. In a third city, the mayor's recommendations seem to have been largely ignored. In another, the mayor's appointments have disagreed strongly with each other and have involved the city in a lengthy controversy. In the fifth city, the mayor seems to have maintained control over the school system, and here the board has been persuaded twice to change its position on a racial issue.

It is usually assumed that political leaders wish to maximize their power and, therefore, detachment from school politics may seem surprising; but the mayor who tries to run the schools would be taking a great risk for a very small reward.

Before considering the implications of these findings, we also should consider why it is that the civic board is more acquiescent than the political board. The answer is a simple but empirical one: On our measures, the civil board members are more liberal on racial issues and the political board members are more conservative. This is not a trivial statement, because it is certainly not necessary that there be a high correlation between the

personal attitude of government officials and their public actions. In fact, a similar study of Southern school boards indicates that there is at best a weak correlation between racial attitudes and behavior regarding school desegregation.[8] The presence of this high correlation in the North indicates the extent to which the school desegregation issue is unstructured. In the absence of clear legal guidelines for action, of efficient communication between the contesting parties, and of a coherent educational ideology to draw upon, the school board members are "on their own" in deciding what to do. Board members are very conscious of this; more than one has publicly appealed for a decision by a local or Federal court to clarify the situation. Buffalo, New York, furnishes a striking example of what this kind of clarification by an authority can do. The state commissioner of education, James E. Allen, demanded that the board desegregate the schools, and immediately the board became a cohesive decision-

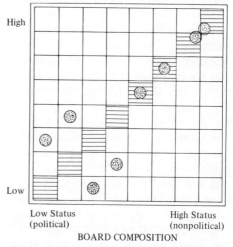

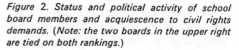

Figure 2. *Status and political activity of school board members and acquiescence to civil rights demands. (Note: the two boards in the upper right are tied on both rankings.)*

making body even though it had been torn by internal conflict for well over a year prior to his intervention.

The lack of structure and clarity in the civil rights arena is, we think, also reflected in the fact that heterogeneous school boards and boards with a history of internal conflict have the greatest difficulty in meeting civil rights demands. Only two of the eight boards have contested elections for membership (five are appointed while another is *de facto* appointed by a slating committee); these two boards were the least acquiescent, probably because of their heterogeneity and the pressures on the boards to make their disagreements public. The board with internal conflict cannot acquiesce to the demands made on it for two reasons: First, it cannot agree on what is being asked of it, and what strategies are available to it; second, it cannot prevent public controversy which polarizes the community and further limits the alternatives available to it.

The great debate over community power structure hinges about the amount of autonomy which governmental officials have and the extent to which the civic elite are able to influence policy. The findings of this research suggest that it is possible for government officials to have great autonomy and at the same time for the civic elite to have great influence. In the case of the schools, the nature of the local civic elite is a principal factor in determining the composition of the school board, and thus the elite indirectly controls policy, even though it makes little or no effort to influence any single decision (and probably could not do so if it tried). The three most acquiescent cities all have high-status school boards, and the civic elite in all three cases plays an important role in locating school board members. These three cities have elites which are highly active across a wide range of local policy issues. In the

other five cities, the elites are weaker, and the result is that school board members are selected either from the ranks of the political parties, or from the leadership of voluntary organizations or in order to represent various ethnic groups.

Even the degree of heterogeneity and internal conflict in the school board has its roots in the structure of the political parties and the nature of the elite. The conflict-ridden boards which resist desegregation appear in cities with weak political parties, for example. Thus, the school board is autonomous in its decision-making procedure, yet the degree of acquiescence of the school system is determined by the overall political structure of the city.

Symbolic Politics and Real Outputs

To this point we have not discussed the real outputs of the school system's racial policy—the actual changes in quality of education or the actual increase in the number of students in integrated schools. It is not difficult for a school system to adopt a racial policy which will partially satisfy civil rights leaders without actually making a large impact on the operation of the schools. (These symbolic victories may have a considerable impact on the attitudes and behavior of individual Negro students, but this is outside the range of the two studies.) Conversely, it is also possible for the school system to have in operation policies which increase school integration without satisfying the civil rights groups. In two cities, Negro students were routinely bussed into white schools, but the school adamantly refused to state that such integration was desirable, and the board in each case was subject to a great deal of attack.

The actual amount of integration is, of course, small. Among the eight cities, the greatest acquiescence, as judged by the research staff, was in Pittsburgh,

Baltimore, and St. Louis. In Pittsburgh, the school system has succeeded in remaining on cordial terms with the civil rights leaders and has committed itself wholeheartedly to integration; but to date, Pittsburgh has done little to increase integration. St. Louis and Baltimore have adopted bussing programs which have successfully relieved overcrowded Negro schools, but less than 5 per cent of the Negro students are directly involved. In the eight cities, the proportion of Negro elementary school children attending schools which are at least 90 percent Negro varies from a low of 30 percent in San Francisco to a high of 86 percent in St. Louis; the median for the eight cities is 68 percent. If the largest cities— Chicago, Detroit, Cleveland, Philadelphia, Washington, and New York City— had been included in the study, the picture would look even bleaker.

The school board may commit itself to a policy of integration but find its efforts to implement this policy restricted by a number of factors outside of its control. The superintendent may undermine the design and implementation of the policy through his role in developing technical details of the plan. Voluntary plans for pupil-transfer may have a minimal effect because of a lack of interest among Negro parents, or may even further segregation by allowing whites to transfer out of integrated schools. (This is another example of universalism; transfer plans explicitly based on the race of pupils involved are quite *avant-garde*.) Or track systems or practices of homogeneous grouping, discriminatory or not, may segregate pupils rigidly within the "integrated" school. And in cities where racial tensions are especially high, such as in Chicago and Cleveland, Negro students attending white schools have been assaulted, and it is often a community prophecy (and in a part a self-fulfilling one) that integrated schools will become all Negro.[9]

More important, the school system cannot control its own personnel. The

heart of successful integration is the classroom teacher, and many big city teachers do not feel comfortable teaching Negro students or handling an integrated class. Further, it is a big city tradition that the integrated school is a "changing" school, where teachers transfer out, morale drops, and high-level programs are phased out as no longer appropriate to the clientele.

The difficulties encountered by the school systems in implementing effective integration go beyond the particular personality problems of the individual actors. They are tied to basic inadequacies in the organizational capacities of the large city school systems for adapting to social change. Briefly, these inadequacies include the following:

1. A bureaucratic rigidity flowing from the statutory and quasi-legal restrictions placed on the school systems by states and accrediting associations. These restrictions limit the scheduling of the school year, prescribe certain courses and curricula, bureaucratic teacher recruitment, etc. This rigidity is related to the great emphasis upon universalism, a stress which in large part is a heritage of many cycles of reform. The result is administration by numbers: an attempt at innovation becomes merely an elaborate formula for assigning X numbers of specialists to Y numbers of schools. Another example is the procedure of allowing teachers to pick whatever schools they want on the basis of seniority, a practice which usually undermines the "difficult" school. And a crucial result is the highly standardized curriculum, which exists despite obvious differences in the needs of different schools.

2. The fact that teachers are basically solo practitioners. Unlike most professions, teaching offers relatively little opportunity for collegial contact which could provide the opportunity not only for respite but for communication of

new practices and the development of new attitudes. In-service training tends to be restricted to short-term workshops which are likely to have a minimal impact on teacher attitudes relevant to racial change. Yet, intensive resocialization procedures are apparently essential because of the conventional perspectives with which persons enter teaching.[10] Further, rewards for the teachers are largely ascriptive, based on seniority and on graduate work which in most schools of education is not oriented to the problems of urban education. As solo practitioners, the teachers frequently are reluctant to have anyone enter their classrooms, including subprofessionals or volunteers who could play a significant role. Principals and middle-level administrators face similar problems of poor lateral and vertical communication except on purely administrative matters.

3. Given these patterns, the large city school systems have very primitive mechanisms of control, which limit them severely in producing change. These systems are overcentralized in the sense that standardized curricula and administration by formula do not provide enough fiscal and administrative autonomy to permit "decentralized" administrators to vary their programs to local needs with any real facility. Yet they are undercentralized in the sense that it is very difficult for decisions made at the top of the organization to alter the traditional operating procedures. This is particularly the case in cities where principals or other personnel have become highly entrenched in their positions; the man who has been principal of the same school for twenty years is not responsive to supervision. Commitment to the status quo is often heightened by in-breeding and by the associations of principals and other personnel which act as mutual protective associations.[11]

4. Also limiting the school system in producing innovations in racial practices and programs for the deprived is their general weakness in research and development. The large systems have numerous special projects for dealing with Negro pupils, and many have generated a sense of success and excitement. But evaluation research is usually poor, and attempts to expand the program to other schools are so haphazardly administered that few survive to become incorporated into standard operating procedure.

Cumulatively, these characteristics of the large city school system imply that more adequate integration of the large city schools will require not only higher levels of leadership in broadening and pursuing educational goals, but also substantial tarnsformations in the organizational format.

Conclusion

It has often been said that in a large and complex organization the leadership does not have control over the operation of the system. These data indicate that there is considerable truth in this. Control over the classroom teacher is limited by the fact that she cannot be supervised directly and by the nature of her contract and the character of her professional organization. Control over individual principals is limited because supervision must be from a distance and by a strict universalism in administration. The board cannot supervise a school superintendent unless he supplies information to them, presents the full range of policy alternatives, and permits the board to believe that it knows something about how to run a school system. Similarly, the men who select the school-board members must defer to them as "experts" once the selection has been made.

On the other hand, we do see a clear line of influence which runs from the top of the system to the bottom. When members of the mayor's staff or members of the civil elite choose school-board members (and in most cities they do choose them), they have in mind an operational image when they say they want a "good man" for the job. It is hardly a surprise that they get the kind of man they want most of the time. These men then control the schools "image" on racial matters and to a limited extent this style can filter down to the classroom. The board selects the superintendent, and some boards have definite criteria in mind; if he does not meet them, he may then be subject to what one board member called a "learning experience." And the superintendent, through his choice of subordinate administrators and his use of policy directives and public relations, can project a "style" into the school system. Granted there is no close isomorphism between this "style" and the actual day-to-day operations of the schools, but at least there is some order in the system.

Notes

[1] This research is reported in Robert L. Crain, Morton Inger, Gerald A. McWorter, and James J. Vanecko, *School Desegregation in the North: Eight Comparative Case Studies of Community Structure and Policy Making* (Chicago: National Opinion Research Center, Report #110A). The research was sponsored by the U.S. Office of Education.

[2] This research was supported by the Russell Sage Foundation. Major findings will be reported in David Street, *The Public Schools and Metropolitan Change*.

[3] For a general review of this and other survey data, see Paul B. Sheatsley, "White Attitudes Toward the Negro," *Daedalus*, 95 (1966), pp. 217–38; and Harriet B. Erskine, "The Polls: Race Relations," *Public Opinion Quarterly*, 26 (1962), pp. 137–48.

[4] It is for this reason that we have chosen to use "desegregation" rather than "integration" in the title of this paper.

[5] Support for this hypothesis is provided by L. L. Cunningham, "Decision-making Behavior of School Boards," *American School Board Journal* (February, 1962).

[6] J. H. Tipton points out that in the late 1940s Negro students were not allowed to use the swimming pool in one high school in Gary, Indiana. See his *Community in Crisis* (New York: Bureau of Publications, Columbia Teachers' College, 1953).

[7] Willis' temporary resignation was apparently triggered by a taxpayer's suit charging that he had arbitrarily changed a voluntary transfer plan designed by the board to further integration. The incident is described in Joseph Pois, *The School Board Crisis* (Chicago: Aldine, 1964), pp. 109–14.

[8] See Robert L. Crain, Morton Inger and Gerald A. McWorter, "School Desegregation in New Orleans: A Comparative Study in the Failure of Social Control" (Chicago: National Opinion Research Center, Report #110B).

[9] Each of these problems is potentially subject to remediation as shown, for example, in St. Louis's ability to bus approximately 2600 Negro students into white schools in 1965–1966. The bussing program seems to have an informal "quota"; none of the integrated schools is over 40 percent Negro. After the initial shock, there has been virtually no opposition in this border city, and bussing of Negro students is now taken for granted.

[10] The tendency for even city-bred teacher trainees to have quite negative orientations toward the challenges of "problem schools" in the inner city is described in Bryan Roberts, "The Effects of College Experience and Social Background on Professional Orientations of Prospective Teachers" (unpublished dissertation, University of Chicago 1964). Findings of an experiment conducted by Bruno Bettelheim in cooperation with the Russell Sage project indicate that teachers' difficulties in dealing with Negro children who present behavior problems flow not principally from racial prejudice but from social class views in which the teacher assumes that the children are unlikely to learn. The Bettelheim work also seems to demonstrate that really intensive in-service training can produce a reduction in these stereotypic views.

[11] For a discussion of the power of this sort of clique, see W. S. Sayre and H. Kaufman, *Governing New York City* (New York: Norton, 1965), pp. 279–80.

Community Schools and Social Theory: The Limits of Universalism

Leonard J. Fein

Reprinted from Community Control of Schools, *edited by Harry M. Levin (New York: Simon & Schuster, Inc., Clarion Books, 1970), pp. 76–98. Copyright 1970 by The Brookings Institution, 1775 Massachusetts Ave., N.W., Washington, D.C. 20036. Reprinted by permission of the author and The Brookings Institution.*

WRITING IN THE late 1950s, Myron Lieberman put quite plainly what was, until recently, the dominant view of liberal critics of the public school system: "The public interest is almost invariably better served by leaving professional questions to the professionals.[1] . . . Local control results in the same kind of intellectual protectionism that characterizes schools in totalitarian countries."[2] At the time that Lieberman was writing, critics of public education were particularly concerned with issues of censorship, growing out of the McCarthy period, and with problems of desegregation, growing out of the 1954 Supreme Court decision.[3] In both cases, it seemed to the critics that the barrier to reform was persistence of local control.

As intellectuals were concerning themselves with structural reforms that would temper the parochializing power of local communities, those communities were becoming increasingly alarmed at the prospect of a decrease in their autonomy. These were the post-Sputnik years, and talk of national standards and federal involvement was widespread. Against such pressures, communities asserted their own historic jurisdiction and were, in the main, successful—largely by virtue of their movement toward the necessary reforms within the prevailing structures.

A good deal has happened in the past decade, and now we find the liberal critics badly split. Many continue to stress the virtues of a secular system, as against the threatened parochialization that neighborhood control suggests; at the same time, large numbers appear to endorse a more elaborate degree of neighborhood control over the schools than was ever seriously contemplated by the traditional exponents of local autonomy.

This shift has been sudden, and it is, to say the least, most curious. Even if important public policy issues were not involved, this shift should elicit our attention as an interesting footnote to intellectual history. Since it does, in fact, embrace pressing matters of public policy, careful attention to the change in perspective is all the more important. Moreover, as we shall see, analysis of the split within the liberal community takes us a long way toward understanding the central issues of the current debate.

It must be evident at the outset that the debate is based, in large measure, on a general disagreement over both the meaning and the legitimacy of community in American society. This problem is at the heart of our present perplexity, and much of what follows here is an effort to thread through its mysteries and clarify its ambiguities. But we must recognize that the concept of community is not the only source of confusion, and, therefore, we shall turn first to a set of related problems that require clarification.

One major theme in the recent literature on the subject couches the demand for community control in terms of historical precedent. It calls for a return to an earlier and more manageable arrangement. "Once upon a time, the people created public schools, and the schools belonged to them."[4] But as the cities have grown, the school system has become a hyperbolic enterprise, too large to be effectively influenced, let alone controlled, by the community. Thus, the schools "have taken on the shape of massive corporate enterprises," and now, at last, "the public is seeking to repossess its schools."[5]

This position does not depend critically on a negative assessment of the present performance of public schools. From a logical standpoint, it could as easily be tied to normative theories of democracy, insisting on more popular participation in school management as an end in itself. But the fact is, of course, that those liberal intellectuals who call for a return are induced to do so largely because they believe that the schools have failed.[6] For this reason, their expression of nostalgia should not be mistaken for the instinctive response to nationalizing trends that is so common to local school people. Furthermore, most of them know that there never was a time in industrial America when schools were definitively controlled by the local community, much less the neighborhood. The tension between professional judgment and community values has been part of the story of public education in the United States at least since educators began to view themselves (and, occasionally, to be viewed by others) as professionals. And, in general, intellectuals have sided with the professionals in the continuing debate, for they have seen community control as essentially repressive rather than liberating.

Hence, talk of return or repossession is misleading. It proposes a return to a time that never was, and to a commitment that intellectuals rarely shared.[7] From what, then, does the current interest derive?

In the epidemiology of American ideological currents, we often find that the experiences of New York City are the infecting bacillus. For better or for worse, what happens in New York is then writ small around the country. In New York City, there have been reports calling for one form of decentralization or another in the public schools in 1933, 1940, 1942, 1949, 1962, 1965, 1967, and again in 1968.[8] Yet decentralization in New York has yet to take place.[9] Since New York is at the same time the largest public school system in the nation and, evidently, the most rigid, the conclusion seems warranted that reform can take place only through radical change in the very structure of the system. In other words, although it might be true that moderate parceling out of the central system's powers would be sufficient to introduce the required flexibility, we must recognize that heavily centralized systems are unlikely to permit any real reduction in their power. It follows that the only alternative is a radical structural transformation, in which the power to allocate power among the participants in the system is taken away from the central agency.

Moreover, and apart from New York, there is a severe crisis in the observed effectiveness of the schools, and a significant frustration with attempted reforms. The crisis in effectiveness is both general and specific. The general, and continuing, crisis is a result of the growing disagreement about what the schools ought to be teaching. Neither in traditional societies, where the task of the schools was the transmission of consensual culture, nor in societies that required large numbers of competent and autonomous mechanics, such as our own until quite recently, were questions regarding the substantive orientation of public education particularly critical. But it has now become evident that no person can become the intellectual master of his environment, for the environment is far too complex, far too technical, to permit universal mastery. It is not even clear that the schools, staffed in the main by people at the periphery of the technical environment, have anything particularly useful to say about it. Nor, finally, have the schools been able to bridge the gaps gracefully between our several competing ideologies of education, some stressing the virtues of personal autonomy, some the importance of ethical guidelines, still others the current requirements of the collectivity for teamwork.

It is not surprising, then, that the schools are in trouble, nor that they tend to cling to external indexes, such as college admission rates, or to tradition as measures of their success.[10] And this general crisis is likely to endure for some time, at least until we have come to terms with the new relationship of man to things, and to other men, implied by the developing technology.

At the same time, a more specific and more urgent crisis affects the public schools. This is the special crisis of their effectiveness with respect to low-income people and, in particular, to black people. There is general agreement that no matter what the schools are supposed to be teaching they are not teaching it very well to the poor and the black. In an era when it was commonly believed that blacks could not learn what others could, the inequity in product was of little public moment. But in our present egalitarian mood, the continuing inequity is a source of very sharp unrest.

Thus a reformist spirit developed, determined, more or less, to redeem the schools. If we take just the last decade or so as our time span, we can readily identify the leading doctrines of the reformers. The first was the professional-technical approach: Our teachers are

not qualified and our classrooms are crowded. Raise salaries, reform teachers' education, build schools, and all will be better, if not well. We then realized that teachers, who were predominantly recruited from the lower-middle class, had special problems and anxieties in communicating with lower-class children. Several solutions were pursued. Teachers' salaries were raised, in order to make them less status-anxious; they were offered courses designed to evoke empathy with their students; the students were told repeatedly that if only they would shape up, middle-class success would be theirs. And most teachers continued in the reliable defense pattern, which was (and is) to believe that their students were not, and would not be, successful, as society defines success.

Since these were either unacceptable or ineffective solutions, reformers turned in new directions. Attention was directed away from professional-technical characteristics and toward the psychological phenomenon of educational deprivation. The most urgent reforms, it was concluded, were enrichment programs for the culturally deprived to compensate for the inadequacy of their home-neighborhood environment. If low-income children suffered because they had less educational resources than their more affluent peers—less space to study, fewer books, a limited vocabulary—the solution was to offer them compensatory programs.

It did not take long to realize that more of the same might not be an adequate remedy. The issue was not simply the lack of specifically educational resources but also victimization by an environment that distorted self-image, made a mockery of hope, and challenged the relevance of the school, even when it had elaborate compensatory programs. Eventually, a more macroscopic sociological stance began to replace the individualized approach of educational psychology, and emphasis shifted to a comprehensive

None of the attempted reforms has revolutionized the condition of education for the poor and the black. The hasty conclusion that each reform was inadequate has led to a renewed search for more effective remedies.[12] In that search, two tendencies predominate. One view considers the chief reason for the failure of the attempted reforms to be the inertia of the school bureaucracies. That is, the reforms themselves are not at issue but our failure to give them sufficient support. According to the second view, it is the reforms that are inadequate because they have missed the point. Even if they had been fully implemented—and those who hold this view agree with the others that they have not been—they would have been insufficient, for, in important ways, they would have exacerbated the very conditions they were designed to relieve.

In particular, we are now witness to a specific rejection of what had been generally regarded, and is still regarded by many, as a most enlightened view of educational deprivation. That view, emphasizing environmental disadvantage, argues that the culture of poverty, passed on from parent to child, is educationally disabling, and that the children who are its victims cannot, therefore, be expected to thrive in school. It simultaneously acknowledges inequities in capacity and relieves the incapacitated of any moral blame.

The theory is enlightened insofar as it does not depend on genetic inferiority; on the contrary, it depends upon a relatively sophisticated social psychology. Unfortunately, however, it can also be used to relieve the schools of any fundamental responsibility for inequitable educational results. The argument based on this theory would reason as follows: "We understand how difficult it is and how unfair, therefore, it is to expect low-income (more commonly, disadvantaged) children to do as well as the more affluent. We can, and we shall, try to repair the inequities. But we are only one agency among many, and unless there is basic change in the culture of poverty itself, there are limits to the likelihood of our success." Schools are used to dealing with individuals. The less we blame the individual for his failings, the more we hold the environment responsible; the more we hold the environment responsible, the less we can expect of the school.

There are, however, more serious problems with the now conventional concept of educational disadvantage. Some of these have to do with the validity of the theory, an issue that has already evoked a substantial literature. But even beyond the question of validity we now discover that its application is problematic. This is so not only because it provides a too convenient excuse for the failure of the schools, but because to an even greater extent it has come to be recognized as an untoward self-fulfilling hypothesis. By holding that the poor cannot be held to the same level of academic performance as the affluent, the theory, by its enlightened, even empathic, lowering of expectation has produced a continuing inadequacy in performance.[13] Hence, though the case of poor performance is now seen as benign, at least so far as the children are concerned (it is now the society at large that is held culpable), it is not necessarily seen as more malleable. Compensation helps, but compensation coupled to reduced expectation reinforces the conviction of both teacher and child that the poor are problem cases.

Out of frustration and impatience with recent approaches at reform, critics have turned in several directions. In the view of some, especially when dealing with New York City, any change is seen as beneficial: ". . . a change—almost any change—would stir the city's schools in useful ways."[14] Here, evidently, the chief problem is seen as systemic rigidity. Others believe that school officials, especially when threatened, cannot—or will not—be relied upon to care enough; thus, "Parents can be trusted to care more than anyone else for the quality of the education their children get."[15] But regardless of the specific remedy proposed, more and more observers agree with the general indictment: ". . . it appears that the present system of organization and functioning of urban public schools is a chief blockage in the mobility of the masses of Negro and other lower-status minority group children."[16]

Thus the search for a villain comes to focus on the organization of the system itself. There is increasing agreement that reorganization of the educational system is, at the very least, a necessary condition (some would also say sufficient) for educational reform. It is important to recognize that, having identified the system as a leading culprit, we are not inevitably led to endorsement of community control, or even of the more innocuous decentralization. Instead, the importance of greater independence, or more expertise, or improved professional standards might have been stressed. It is a mark of the unusual level of dissatisfaction that such avenues have, in the main, been rejected in favor of the more radical call for major institutional reorganization.

We should not conclude, however, that the call, widespread though it is, is consensual. The outward appearance of a concerted effort, focused on increasing community participation and control, is, in fact, the least consensual of recent proposals for educational reform. This is true not only because it is a threatening doctrine to many participants in the system, but because its adherents come to it for diverse reasons and mean by it conflicting things. The earlier alliance of educational reformers has come apart; the appearance of an alliance is a function of the ambiguities of the concepts, the issue to which we now turn.

Those who believe that the schools have been inept in instituting the various reforms of recent years generally blame that ineptitude on conventional bureaucratic resistance to innovation and on a cumbersome bureaucracy. While it is not obvious that decentralization of the bureaucracy is the way to induce innovation, some causal relationship between the two is assumed. Thus, in a recent interview, William Haddad, a member of the New York City Board of Education, argued that "decentralization could aid reform because local election of local school boards could help parents get power that could be 'translated into modernization of the system.' Up to now . . . the New York City system has been plagued by 'heavy bureaucracy that stifles creativeness.' "[17]

In its simplest version, the thrust toward decentralization is based on insights derived from administrative theory. It is a traditional argument with immediate appeal only in large school systems, and it is not necessarily linked to the call for greater community control. It is logically possible, for example, to seek at the same time both greater decentralization and greater insulation from politics—hence continuing insulation from public control.

The movement toward community control, as distinct from decentralization, derives not so much from the general crisis of effectiveness of the schools, but rather from the specific failure of the schools in dealing with the poor, and, more particularly, with black children. Indeed, it is unthinkable that we would now witness so dramatic a turn of interest to community control were it not for the civil rights movement and the crisis in black and white relations in America. Although the crystallization of support grows out of diverse experiences —in some cases the recognition that integration is demographically improbable, in others the conviction that white school boards will never provide the necessary resources to black schools and will be sluggish about integration, and in still others a more direct response to the general doctrine of participatory democracy—it is an aspect of the civil rights struggle rather than of educational reform per se. It draws from a different and much more recent tradition, and it carries with it, therefore, substantially different implications. It is not, for the most part, that the administrative reformers, seeking decentralization, and the political reformers, seeking community control, have converged upon a common stance. The appearance of commonality is, as noted, a function, first, of ambiguity, and second, of an occasional similarity in views between some of the variations on the broader themes.

Thus, among the administrative reformers, there are those who believe that community control is the only tactic that has a chance of achieving the goal of decentralization. And, among black supporters of community control, there is a significant number whose advocacy is less political than educational in origin. Their view, briefly, is that black children have special educational needs, and that preeminent among those is exposure to positive role models and knowledge of their own past. These specific needs have little validity in and of themselves but must be met in order to unblock the impediments to general learning. Variants of this approach stress the inevitable racism of white teachers, or the inequity in the distribution of educational investments by school boards

oriented to white middle-class children.

But the powerful thrust toward community control goes far beyond the simple allegation of ineffectiveness. Together with black reformers interested particularly in educational reform, the advocates of community control view the present system as grossly ineffective, but they go on to insist that ineffectiveness is a necessary corollary of the prevailing educational structure. Community control is no longer seen as merely one way to revitalize a rigid system but as the only way in which the school system can be made legitimate. In the extreme version of this perspective, the present school system, as managed by whites, would be no more acceptable even if the various indexes of performance were suddenly transformed. This is so because the overriding crisis of the schools is one of goals, not performance.[18] . . .

At the beginning of this chapter, it was suggested that many liberals shifted from an enthusiastic espousal of professional control to a more community-oriented position. Further elaboration is now necessary. While some have moved toward positions favoring administrative and educational reforms, which do not emphasize professionalism nearly as much as leading doctrines did a decade ago but which fall short of endorsing community control, others—far fewer— have, indeed, moved to support political reform, or community control per se. But many have not moved at all and are, as noted, deeply troubled by the current thrust of their former allies. Their trouble derives from their recognition that what black militants now seek violates the basis of the liberal tradition in fundamental ways.

The liberal commitment, in education

as in other spheres, is to universalism. We approach liberal salvation as we move from the sacred to the secular, from *Gemeinschaft* to *Gesellschaft*, from folk society to urban society, from tradition through charisma to rational bureaucracy. The liberation of man, which is the aim of secular wisdom, proceeds on diverse fronts: liberation from nature, achieved through science; liberation from bondage, achieved through law; liberation from self, achieved through psychoanalysis; liberation from myth, achieved through education; liberation from the past, achieved through commitment to progress; liberation from the confines of time and space, achieved through intellectual and physical mobility, through the good offices of the mass media. At the very least, scholars have generally seen the process of secularization as inevitable: "Secularization . . . and its concomitant rationalization may be good, or it may be bad, but it is our destiny. . . . To him who cannot manfully bear this destiny . . . the doors of the old churches stand forgivingly open . . . if he will but make 'the sacrifice of the intellect.' "[19]

The descriptive proposition that modern, industrial society requires a transformation of folk culture requires no elaboration. It is a central precept of virtually all the social sciences, and especially of students of modernization as the following two quotations illustrate:

> Relationships among individuals [in small groups] . . . are mainly *ascribed* (fixed by birth or other involuntary membership), *diffuse* (covering a wide and open-ended range of rights and duties), and *particularistic* (based on particular relations to particular persons or statuses, not on generalized, impersonal rules). In modern complex societies, the four basic structures [kinship, territorial community, social stratification,

and ethnic grouping] are interlaced and overlaid by economic and political systems that are organized in considerable part on radically different principles—the principles of achieved, competitive placement rather than ascription by birth, of impersonal universalistic norms, and of highly specific, narrowly defined relations among persons. Also, in our society [the United States], the major religious traditions all stress universalism in the ethical domain.[20]

> . . . The passage from "traditional" to "modern" society . . . involves a complex set of changes in the organization of the society and in man's perspective on his society. There is a movement from identification with primary groups to identification with secondary groups, from social norms in which status is derived from inherited place in the order (ascription) to the function that one performs in society and how well one performs it (achievement). It is a movement toward more complex, highly differentiated and specialized social institutions and social roles. Life becomes less viewed as a whole, less diffuse, within the setting of the village and traditional agriculture. . . . Modern society [similarly] requires a different sort of political order, one serviceable to a much expanded notion of the relevant community, as the scope of social life changes from the order of the village to the order of the nation.[21]

But more than simple description is generally implied in such characterizations of the process of modernization. For liberal intellectuals have cast their own lot with the forces of modernization, and hence with secularism, rationality, and universalism, and against tradition, ritual, and — community. As Robert Nisbet has pointed out, "To regard all evil as a persistence or revival of the past has been a favorite conceit of liberals nourished by the idea of Progress. . . . Present evils could safely be regarded as regrettable evidences of incomplete emancipation from the past—from tribalism, from agrarianism, religion, localism, and the like. In one form or another, the theory of cultural lag has been the secular approach to the problem of evil."[22] Or, "The demands of freedom appeared to be in the direction of the release of large numbers of individuals from the statuses and identities that had been forged in them by the dead hand of the past. A free society would be one in which individuals were morally and socially as well as politically free, free from groups and classes. . . . Freedom would arise from the individual's release from all the inherited personal interdependencies of traditional community, and from his existence in an impersonal, natural, economic order."[23] . . .

Liberal commitment to the secular city is supported by the American myth of the melting pot. The commitment is not total; some instances of the survival of folk culture are still viewed as quaint rather than threatening. Nevertheless, the traditional liberal perspective maintains its utopian commitment to a world of universal brotherhood, a world in which the private community would be obsolete.

Insofar as the educational system promotes the secular ideal, it conforms to the liberal perspective. For this reason the public school has always emphasized liberty and equality over fraternity, except when fraternity has been understood to encompass all mankind. Relying heavily on the storied experience of New York City during the days of its heavy in-migration, liberals have seen the public schools as society's best hope for achieving comprehensive integration.

From this broad perspective, a number of specific theorems derive: The schools should embrace heterogeneous populations; schools are to be ethically neutral, except for their endorsement of the scientific ethic; the curriculum is to be secular, and is to emphasize the shared culture; school personnel should be selected and advanced according to their merits, the best approximation being the civil service laws; children fail for idiosyn-

cratic (individual) reasons, or because of insufficient funds or wisdom, not because they occupy a special stratum in society.

These several beliefs are directly at odds with the theses now propounded by defenders of community schools. In fact, they conform quite closely to the views of the present educational establishment in most cities. The reason for this is that most establishment managers, no matter how conservative in their administrative behavior, are liberals in their social ideology. Moreover, nothing in these views logically requires a commitment to intense centralization of authority. Therefore, the decentralizers, too, can share the social theory, even though they dispute the administrative arrangement. And that is why the difference between school authorities and administrative reformers, however obstinate, is not logically fundamental. . . .

. . . The emergence of community consciousness among blacks flagrantly violates the traditional liberal ethic of universalism. It parochializes society instead of secularizing it; it evokes a mystical bond instead of a rational contract.

Liberal guilt over white failings permits many white liberals to accept the new direction of the black community, at least in part, albeit always with the hope that society will move fast enough to "outgrow" the need for community soon. But liberal commitments to the secular city prevent an even larger number of liberals from any empathy with present directions of the civil rights movement.[24] Hence, we are witness to an increasingly problematic relationship among historic allies.

The linkage of these general issues, here so briefly touched upon, to the question of community control is quite specific, and more basic even than rejection, by liberals, of so explicit an assertion of community—though that is a major aspect. The liberal axiom that society is an aggregate of independent individuals, rather than an organic compact of groups, necessarily points to a policy in which all legitimate authority is vested in the state.[25] Assertion that a sacred entity[26] should be viewed as a legitimate partner to the secular authority threatens not only the institutions of liberal society but its assumptions as well; the movement toward community control is a profound rejection of the core of liberal ideology.

If Negroes were not involved, but some other ethnic community, the battle would be far more intense, for liberals would doubtless recognize the threat and act with vigor to reduce it. It takes only memory, not imagination, to visualize the intensity of liberal rejection of parochial management of the schools, whether the parochialism is expressed by Southerners opposed to integration, Rotarians opposed to the *New Republic*, or Catholics committed to prayer in the schools. Lieberman has expressed the dominant liberal mood of the 1950s: ". . . national survival now requires educational policies and programs which are not subject to local veto. . . . It is becoming increasingly clear that local control cannot in practice be reconciled with the ideals of a democratic society. . . . Local control is a major cause of the dull parochialism and attenuated totalitarianism that characterizes public education in operation."[27] As it is, the reaction of white liberals to black people is so mixed with guilt, with patronization, and with anxiety that the force of liberal opposition to the parochial threat is blunted.

In short, insofar as liberals have countenanced the concept of community at all, they have sought what Scott Greer calls "the community of limited liabi-

lity," a community based on either shared taste, shared neighborhood, or shared specific interest.[28] This is quite different from the diffuse organic community, based as much on mystique as on reason, acting as a primary group to its members and speaking a private tongue.[29] Black people, in increasing numbers, having despaired of their acceptance under the terms of liberal writ, have begun to emphasize the organic community. What debate there is among black militants on this issue is over the question of whether building community is a temporary tactic (the community will be used as a springboard into the secular society) or an end goal (black separatism).

Once the underlying logic of community is understood, we can also move toward an understanding of the position of the political reformers. Their position does not depend, as so many white radicals think, on a romantic belief in the inherent wisdom of "the people." Their insight is not that black parents are more likely to provide effective educational programs for black children than white professionals are but rather that black parents (or their agents) are the legitimate managers of such schools; whites are not and cannot be. The schools, in short, are to be community schools in a sense that differs dramatically from previous usage in American educational history. They are to belong to a community that is defined organically rather than contractually, and their ownership by the community will in turn help to establish the point that the community does exist as a legitimate social entity.

They are political reformers precisely because their insistence on the legitimacy of community is inevitably associated with an equal insistence on the need for a redistribution of power within the society. The issue of power—less relevant, perhaps, to other ethnic groups, which were neither so systematically excluded from power nor so dependent on politics as a source of power—is not a specific aspect of educational theory, nor even simply a way of guaranteeing sufficient attention to black children. It is rather a corollary of a social theory requiring that communities within the whole be made viable. Acceptance of the concept of organic community necessarily points to decentralization; acceptance of the desirability of educational reform does not.

In this view, therefore, the question of whether the schools, if managed by blacks, could do a better job than they are now doing, or even a better job than they might do if various proposed administrative and educational reforms were instituted, becomes meaningless. For the word "better" can only be taken to mean better according to some secular standards, and it is precisely those standards that are now rejected. The purpose of teaching black children African languages is not solely to develop in them the kind of confidence and pride that will then permit them to do better work in the conventional curriculum; it is ideological rather than tactical. The theory is highly specific; there is no intimation that the schools ought to be controlled by their neighborhoods, a view held by some white liberals. Instead, the theory holds that organic communities of interest— which may, coincidentally, be neighborhood based—be considered legitimate. The schools are not, then, ineffective simply because they are badly organized or ignorantly operated but because they lack legitimacy. And they lack legitimacy because they are incapable of taking into account the special requirements of diverse groups. This incapacity is most serious for blacks, for other groups that feel they have special needs can often bend the system to their needs *sotto voce*, without appearing to disturb the secular norms of the system.

In brief, blacks are treated particu-

laristically and ascriptively, but are held to universalist standards of achievement. The administrative and educational reformers seek to change the treatment; the political reformers, despairing of change in the treatment, seek to change the standards. They thereby endorse a theory of social structure that is directly at odds with the prevailing liberal theory. ...

The present tempest in America has led to some shifts in the conventional liberal perspective. In particular, the notion that the nation is best governed by a highly centralized bureaucracy has begun to lose respectability, and it is possible that the commitment to a secular bureaucracy will, similarly, weaken. Some liberals do argue for suspension of the civil service regulations in specific instances, although this deviation from tradition is countered by the continuing commitment to national standards on key policy issues. It is, however, folly to predict a major ideological transformation, since the sources of such transformations remain so mysterious.

There is some logical relationship between the doctrine of participatory democracy and a parochialization of social theory. Obviously, the more power that is provided to people to make their own political rules, the more likely those rules are to be particularistic rather than universal. At this stage in the movement toward participatory democracy, however, it seems no more warranted to predict its eventual victory than to suggest that its limits will be set by its threat to the secular tendencies of the system.

There is, then, one mode of reconciliation left—admittedly a rather academic mode, worth more as solace than as program. It is to accept that the social system has never been as secular in its operation as the norm of universalism implies or as many American liberals generally suppose. The evidence for this view is somewhat speculative, but three different arguments lend it weight.

First, there is the persistence of ethnic identities, not only as a psychological phenomenon but also as reflected in the economy. Different groups have established themselves in different sectors, and their persistence as identifiable groups, in the face of a social ideology that is chilly toward them, suggests that they cannot be dismissed lightly as an aberrant anachronism. As Glazer asserts, "The ethnic group in American society [has become] not a survival from the age of mass immigration but a new social form."[30] Whether this new form is benighted, as the ideology suggests and scholars often assert, or is socially functional, is beside the point; it exists, and belies the inevitability of secularization.

Second, it can be argued that the political system itself has not been as secular as is assumed. Such an argument has genuine validity in the case of black Americans, who have obviously not been encompassed by the doctrine of universalism. The current challenges to American political institutions, and especially to universities, suggests that this argument may be valid in other spheres as well. Those challenges may be interpreted as a rejection of elaborate institutions which profess their neutrality but which, in fact, operate to the advantage of particular groups within the society. Moreover, institutions play favorites independently of the good will of those who manage them, since the rules of the game and institutional inertia conspire to overwhelm modest efforts at reform. What is obvious with respect to Negroes is no less true, if less obvious: the structure of the system, which is to say, of our institutions, and the rules according to which they are managed, preserve a reality of particularism and of ascription, elaborately disguised by a mythology of universalism and achievement-orientation.

Third, despite the prevailing myth that education is a secular institution, the history of the schools can, and should, be read as an example of creative tension between the particular and the universal. The standard compromise has been to create largely parochial structures while emphasizing fundamentally universal content. On the face of it, this seems an implausible development, since conventional sociology informs us that there is necessarily an identity between structure and content. But if the two tendencies are viewed, after Parsons and Shils,[31] as representing a continuing dilemma, it becomes clear how they might have been played off against one another. Unable or unwilling to commit itself wholly to the one choice or the other, society has managed, however improbably, to sustain both together.

The operational implication of this failure to choose, if it is to be continued, is, first, that the best of two worlds may be available, or, at least, the worst of both may be avoided. There is, after all, a cyclicality to these affairs, and the balance, most recently heavily weighted toward the universalist norm, now needs to be adjusted to favor the particularistic. This implies a greater openness to community control as long as certain universalist criteria are maintained.

In other words, the fear of balkanizing the society through endorsement of community schools would be warranted only if many other institutions, and particularly the mass media of communications, were not on the side of nationalizing, hence secularizing, education. If all the secular educational inputs are added together, a school system based on more parochial claims may seem less threatening to the traditional ideology and more a way of preserving some balance between consensus and diversity.

Further, we must emphasize the degree

to which universalist doctrine is fundamentally normative rather than descriptive. Liberals who insist on applying universal norms are unable to make exceptions for black people without undermining their fundamental ideological commitments. They therefore either reject current Negro demands or rise to defend community control of the schools as if it were a helpful doctrine everywhere, a position few of them seriously entertain. The obvious resolution of this problem is to recognize the exceptional position of the black community—exceptional because of history, exceptional because of current needs, and exceptional particularly by virtue of the growing degree of community consciousness. It is difficult, of course, for liberals to accommodate such exceptions, to recognize that what may be good, or appropriate, or legitimate for one group need not be a secular standard for all groups. But such recognition is bound to be less tortured than the continued rejection of the demands, on the one hand, or the fatuous endorsement of the demands as a new and comprehensive norm for the entire educational system, on the other.

Notes

¹ Myron Lieberman, *The Future of Public Education* (Chicago: University of Chicago Press, 1960), p. 60.

² *Ibid.*, p. 38.

³ *Brown* v. *Board of Education of Topeka*, 347 U.S. 483 (1954).

⁴ Mario D. Fantini in his Foreword to Marilyn Gittell, *Participants and Participation: A Study of School Policy in New York City* (New York: Praeger, 1967), p. vii.

⁵ *Ibid.*

⁶ Whether the extraordinary interest in participatory democracy to which we are now witness would have occurred had our institutions not faced a crisis of effectiveness is a moot question. It is, however, reasonable to suppose that the popular (as distinguished from intellectual) enthusiasm for the idea that is now developing, especially in the

Negro community, would have been substantially reduced.

⁷ Indeed, there was a time when communities had more to say about how their children would be educated. This was not so much because schools were subject to more community authority then but rather because extraschool educational inputs were more systematic and more manageable. In pre-urban, preliberal, and, especially, pre-television America, parents could and did feel more confident that the established institutions were effectively transmitting their own values to the young. But tasks once assumed by the family and the church have now passed, by and large, to the mass media, and parents have no control over the stimuli to which their children are exposed. This situation has become so acute that genuine community efforts to retain (or to reassert) control over the schools may be regarded as a last attempt to gain some control over the education of the young—an effort directed at the schools not because they are the traditional transmission belts of community values but because they are the only educative institution that remains, to some degree, vulnerable to direct political pressure.

But this perspective, once again, is not what intellectuals are talking about. For intellectuals, far from lamenting the erosion of parochial influence on the schools, have remained firm in their commitment to secular education, and hence to the increasing nationalization of the curriculum content of the schools.

⁸ Cited by Jason Epstein in "The Politics of School Decentralization," *New York Review of Books*, 10 (June 6, 1968), p. 26.

⁹ At least as of this writing. And it can safely and sadly be predicted that if the situation has since changed, it will have been with greater stress and bitter dispute.

¹⁰ See the works of Edgar Z. Friedenberg for an astonishingly elegant statement of the problem, especially *Coming of Age in America* (New York: Random House, 1965) and *The Vanishing Adolescent* (Boston: Beacon, 1959).

¹¹ See John Seeley's Introduction to Morris Gross, *Learning Readiness in Two Jewish Groups* (New York: Center for Urban Education, 1967), for a brief, useful,

and somewhat different summary of recent educational policy.

[12] Hasty, of course, in the typical American way. We promise too much for each proposed reform, invest too little in it, and then profess disappointment with the results In this regard, see Aaron Wildavsky, "The Empty-head Blues: Black Rebellion and White Reaction," *Public Interest*, No. 11 (Spring, 1968), pp. 3–16.

[13] A point intriguingly demonstrated in recent experiments, discussed in Robert Rosenthal and Lenore Jacobson, *Pygmalion in the Classroom: Teacher Expectation and Pupils' Intellectual Development* (New York: Holt, 1968).

[14] Theodore R. Sizer, "Report Analysis," *Harvard Educational Review*, 38 (New York: (1968), p. 180.

[15] Mayor's Advisory Panel on Decentralization of the New York City Schools, *Reconnection for Learning: A Community School System for New York City* (1967), p. 68.

[16] Kenneth B. Clark, "Alternative Public School Systems," *Harvard Educational Review*, 38 (1968), p. 109.

[17] As reported in *The New York Times*, Sept. 8, 1968, p. 51. Note also that Haddad is speaking of a specific form of decentralization, one in which parents would have some power over local school officials.

[18] *Ibid.*

[19] Max Weber, "Wissenschaft als Beruf" ("Science as a Vocation"), in *Gesammelte Aufsätze zur Wissenschaftslehre*, translated and cited in Howard Becker and Harry Elmer Barnes, *Social Thought from Love to Science* (New York: Dover, 1961), p. 770.

[20] Robin M. Williams, Jr., *Strangers Next Door: Ethnic Relations in American Communities* (Englewood Cliffs, N.J.: Prentice-Hall, 1964), p. 356.

[21] Charles W. Anderson, Fred R. von der Mehden, and Crawford Young, *Issues of Political Development* (Englewood Cliffs, N.J.: Prentice-Hall, 1967), pp. 4–5.

[22] Robert A. Nisbet, *Community and Power* (Oxford University Press, 1962), p. 214.

[23] *Ibid.*, p. 22.

[24] One mark of the historic success of liberals is the persistent acceptance of secularism as utopia by the masses of Afro-Americans.

[25] This point is elaborated by Nisbet, *Community and Power, passim.*

[26] "Sacred," as Becker uses the term, to distinguish nonrational ties from the secular rational. See Howard Becker, *Through Values to Social Interpretation: Essays on Social Contexts, Actions, Types, and Prospects* (Durham, N.C.: Duke University Press, 1950).

[27] Lieberman, *The Future of Public Education*, p. 34.

[28] *The Emerging City*, ch. 4, pp. 107–37.

[29] Recognizing implicitly the legitimacy of a private language, some educators have proposed that black children be taught middle-class English as a second language, rather than as the correct replacement of the natural language.

[30] Glazer and Moynihan, *Beyond the Melting Pot*, p. 16.

[31] Talcott Parsons and Edward A. Shils, eds., *Toward a General Theory of Action* (Cambridge: Harvard University Press, 1954), esp. Parsons and Shils, "Values, Motives, and Systems of Action," pp. 45–275.

SOCIOLOGISTS HAVE generally been more concerned with incompatibilities between bureaucratic organizations and primary groups than they have with their complementarities. Max Weber, emphasizing the efficiency of rational formal organization for industrial society, suggested that industrialization might well be delayed where the family system was very strong.[2] Some students of the family have implied that the transfer of traditional functions from the family to formal organizations casts doubt on the viability of the modern family.[2] Less extreme views of contemporary theorists hold that certain necessary functions, such as early socialization of the child and management of tensions of both adults and children, are best performed in the family and constitute its central contribution.[3] They argue, however, that antithetical principles of bureaucratic and family organization require that the two forms be relatively isolated from each other. Thus they point out that a nuclear family structure with a sex-linked division of labor tends to limit the number of family members who will have to bridge the worlds of family and occupation and minimize the clash between their antithetical atmospheres. A parallel view among some educators can be called the "locked-door" policy. . . .

An alternative viewpoint which seems to be gaining increasing support among educators is what we have called the "open-door policy." In essence, this position holds that maximum education will occur where the families and schools are brought close together, where families are drawn into the schools and schools taken into the community. It is significant that the implicit sociological theory of this position—that maximum goal achievement in contemporary society occurs where bureaucratic organizations and families are intertwined—is rarely expressed in sociological analysis of industrial society. Educators holding this view argue that motivation is central

The School and the Family: Linking Organizations and External Primary Groups

Eugene Litwak and Henry J. Meyer

Condensed from Chapter 19 of The Uses of Sociology, edited by Paul F. Lazarsfeld, William H. Sewell, and Harold L. Wilensky, (New York: Basic Books, Inc., 1967), pp. 522–43. Reprinted by permission of the authors and publisher.

in educating the child, and the best way to motivate him is by relating the teaching situation to his ongoing life experiences, which are always partially unique because [they are] dependent on his particular family situation. Therefore, it is necessary to take learning experiences into the community and to bring the community into the school if one is to achieve maximum motivation in the child. . . .

If one takes seriously such responses of practitioners to the empirical world, modification of the earlier theory of bureaucracy-primary-group relations is necessary. The "open door" viewpoint suggests that the earlier positions do not conform to experience. The primary group is thought to increase effectiveness in achievement of organizational goals and the family to perform more functions than basic socialization and tension management. Among those with practical organizational problems to solve there seems to be as great a tendency to bring primary group and bureaucracy together as there is to keep them apart.

Reconsideration of the Functions of Primary Groups and Bureaucracies

In the face of practitioner experience, it becomes necessary to reopen the theoretical inquiry into the alternative functions of primary groups and bureaucratic organizations. . . .

We would approach the issue by noting those dimensions of organization that define the respective structures. As an ideal type, primary-group structure has been described in terms of the following dimensions: face-to-face contact, diffuse, noninstrumental, and relatively permanent relations.[4] One ideal-type bureaucracy has been described in terms of these dimensions: hierarchy of authority, use of rules to guide behavior, impersonal social relations, a priori definition of duties and privileges, separation of policy and administrative decisions, use of specialists, and the appointment and advancement of personnel on the basis of merit, that is, their competence to accomplish the tasks of the organization.[5] We shall use this simplified formulation of Weber's analysis because it highlights the points at issue. More contemporary theories of bureaucracy are also consistent with the approach developed later in this chapter.

If the dimensions of such a Weberian bureaucracy are examined, its claim for efficiency rests primarily on the fact that the organization is designed to bring the maximum amount of knowledge and experience to bear on any task. Specialization and appointment on the basis of knowledge are the chief means for insuring maximum knowledge and experience. To protect against favoritism or the introduction of personal rather than organizational goals, policy is

separated from administrative decision, duties and privileges are defined in advance, and relations are depersonalized. Finally, in order to insure that specialists and trained experts are coordinated (necessary where there is a large organization), rules are developed for standardized tasks and a hierarchy of authority is used to decide when rules have not been set.

By contrast, the primary group provides no support for the trained expert. Admission to the primary group is not by merit, but by birth or by personal affection, and as such is relatively permanent. The group is not task-limited, but encompasses many interests of its membership (diffused relations). It does not have sufficient size (with face-to-face contact) to develop specialists within its boundaries, but defines roles only generally.

It seems quite clear that the structure of the bureaucratic organization serves to support and encourage the trained expert, whereas the primary group tends to do the opposite. Therefore to answer the question "Under what circumstances are primary groups more effective than formal organizations?" we must seek to answer a prior question, "Under what circumstances are trained experts of little use in achievement of goals?" For it is in exactly the areas where the trained expert is of little use that the primary groups may be more efficient in goal achievement than the bureaucratic organization.

There are at least three classes of tasks for which there is no substantial advantage in using a trained expert. First, and most obvious, are those tasks where the knowledge required is so simple that everyone is expert enough to perform it. Thus, pulling a child out of the path of an automobile requires no special training beyond that which the average person can readily learn. Dressing a child, feeding him, insuring that he is in bed at a certain time, seeing that he is studying rather than at the show, having him up in time for school, seeing that he has eaten, has dressed appropriately for the given weather, and so forth, are all tasks which the average parent can learn to do satisfactorily without special training. Little would be gained by having professional experts do these jobs.

A second class of tasks comprises those that fall at the opposite extreme: problems for which we have very limited knowledge. The advantage in having the advice of an expert is greatly diminished if in fact the state of knowledge is such that his advice is not clearly superior to that of an untrained person. There are many tasks and decisions to which the expert cannot bring sufficiently definitive knowledge to guide action. For example, consider the following: how to carry out parental socialization functions that lead to the internalization of achievement orientation in children, the management of marital relations to ease tensions, the assessment of which of two candidates would make the better president, the decision to encourage nuclear disarmament, and so forth. These are not only incredibly complex problems involving many inadequately specified variables; they also represent problems in which expert opinions may conflict. Under such circumstances the function of the expert would seem to depend more on attribution of legitimacy to his role than on superior knowledge. Therefore, when faced with such problems, persons often seem satisfied to rely on the advice of trusted nonexperts. This is not to deny a function for experts in such areas—a function whose characteristics have been only partially explored[6]—but it is to suggest that experts do not have a clear and obvious utility for this class of tasks.

A third class of tasks which gain little from the use of trained experts consists of those involving essentially idiosyncratic events. Sometimes events are so unique to a given time or a given person that there is no opportunity to train an expert or it would be too expensive to train one. Thus, since earthquakes occur rarely and at unpredictable places, it is economically and socially prohibitive to train experts who specialize in taking care of consequences of earthquakes. Likewise, if an event may happen to a given individual but it is difficult to say when it will happen, it becomes prohibitive to assign experts to that individual. In addition, there are aspects of the role behavior of participants in work, educational, leisure, religious, and all other social activities that are idiosyncratic, socialization into roles is never perfect. Although the more standardized forms of role behavior may benefit from expert assistance, the non-standardized are unlikely to do so. In particular, since they are largely internalized, the motivational aspects of role behavior tend to have more idiosyncratic components and fewer known regularities about which expertness can be developed.

To refer to all three classes of tasks, or behavioral situations, where trained expertise may be of limited advantage (knowledge required too simple, knowledge too limited, or behavior idiosyncratic), we use the term *nonuniform events*. If our theoretical analysis is correct, the availability of the trained expert in the bureaucratic organization gives it no advantage over the primary group in dealing with nonuniform events.

Furthermore, there appear to be actual disadvantages for bureaucracies when faced with nonuniform events. Larger numbers of persons and long chains of communication become impediments in contrast to immediate, face-to-face communication among the smaller number of the primary group. We are not saying that the primary group can act faster or with more flexibility than the formal organization *in general*, but only that it can do so when dealing with nonuniform events. Moreover, there is some evidence that specialists tend to develop commitment to the procedures of their specialties, so that specialization may actually reduce flexibility.[7] As critics of Weber's view of bureaucratic efficiency have pointed out, the use of rules in idiosyncratic situations tends to inhibit the solution of organizational problems or leads to inappropriate decisions since a new rule must be developed for every such situation, or a decision on it must be obtained at higher levels of the hierarchy, or an existing but not applicable rule must be applied.[8] There is also some evidence that internalization of organizational goals that may direct even idiosyncratic behavior toward common ends occurs more readily among persons in reciprocal affective interaction.[9] The emphasis on impersonal relations and organizationally evaluated performance in bureaucratic organizations might well impede such internalization of goals. The possible difficulties we have been discussing are usually noted in analyses of the functions of primary groups, or "informal organization," *within* bureaucracies,[10] but they are equally evident when considering functions of external primary groups for organizational effectiveness with nonuniform events.

In sum, we suggest that nonuniform events present problems for which the expertise that especially characterizes the bureaucratic organization is not useful or is actually disadvantageous and that the characteristics of the primary group might provide a better organizational base for goal achievement under such conditions. This position is put forth as a theoretical conclusion; we do not argue that other factors may not play a part in determining which organizational form will be considered most efficient for some social objective. . . .

If we accept the conclusion that primary groups are more effective in nonuniform areas and formal organizations more effective in uniform areas, can we distinguish in fact between nonuniform and uniform social tasks? We would answer that all social tasks have both uniform and nonuniform aspects. In the first place, insofar as science and technology can be brought to bear, behaviors become predictable and hence subject to treatment as uniform; nonuniformity appears to be reduced, although not eliminated. Second, social interaction and imperfect role socialization inevitably seem to yield some nonuniformity. Finally, technological innovations and demographic factors seem for our society to present continuing sources of unanticipated circumstances. For reasons such as these we argue that most areas of social endeavor must take account of both uniform and nonuniform tasks and therefore will be most effectively carried on when both bureaucratic and primary-group organizational forms are involved. This is not to say that at any time the balance between uniform and nonuniform aspects of a given social task may not change. It is only to say that in principle both aspects will be involved and both must, in the achievement of most social objectives, be considered.

The Policy Paradox

If the foregoing reasoning is used as a guide to a policy to govern a program of school-community relations, such as that of the Great Cities Project, it would seem to lead to contradictory implications:

1. Families and schools must work closely together to achieve educational goals.

2. Families and schools must be kept separated since their basic organizational principles are antithetical.

Nothing in our analysis has challenged the observation that primary groups and formal organizations have antithetical atmospheres. On the contrary, their very difference in form of social relations accounts for the differential efficiency of each when dealing with uniform and non-uniform tasks.

The paradox can be resolved if we accept both statements as simultaneously true: educational objectives will be relatively limited both by keeping schools too far apart from families and by bringing them too close together. The optimal solution is therefore some midpoint where limiting effects are minimized and complementary contributions of both organizational forms are maximized. We have given the name "balance theory of co-ordination" to this theoretical viewpoint. Such a linkage theory of relations between bureaucratic organizations and primary groups is proposed as an alternative to theories which view relations between these forms as conflicting.[11]

Mechanisms of Co-ordination between Bureaucratic Organizations and External Primary Groups: An Empirical Typology

This theoretical analysis has led us to a basis on which a program to alter school-community relations can be formulated. Such a program should seek a complementary balance. Therefore, it must look for linking mechanisms of two types: (1) those that can increase the "social distance" without destroying communication necessary for co-ordination and (2) those that can decrease the "social distance" without the destructive consequences of mutual interference. What procedures might be followed to bring families closer, but not too close, to the schools?

There has been little attention in sociological theory to types of linking mechanisms, but social practitioners have devised many types from the empirical necessities they have faced. The implicit theories underlying such mechanisms are, indeed, in advance of stated theories. From examination of practitioners' writings we have distinguished seven linking mechanisms that seem to account for most of the types in use. No claim can be made that these types are mutually exclusive or exhaustive. A brief description of each of these empirically observed types follows.

1. *Detached-worker approach.* In this procedure professionals from the bureaucratic organization go into the "home" of the primary group and develop an informal relationship with the family they seek to convert to organizational goals. Among practitioners the most successful use of this procedure has probably been the county agent of the agricultural extension services. Its most dramatic use in the urban environment has probably been by social workers who attach themselves to delinquent "street gangs."[12] A version of this approach has been used in the Detroit schools by some school-community agents working more often with families than with gangs.

2. *Opinion-leader approach.* In this approach the organization communicates with the community through the indigenous leaders. The conceptual elaboration of this approach has been most clearly stated in the fields of consumer and political behavior.[13] Earlier, Shaw and McKay used such a procedure as a key element in their delinquency-control programs.[14] In private fund raising this is frequently a prime technique. In Detroit, both school principals and school-community agents often make efforts to reach "key people" in their school districts.

3. *Settlement-house approach* is one where physical facilities and professional personnel are provided in geographical proximity to the potential clientele. The name is borrowed from social work, but we use it here in a more restricted sense. Social agencies occasionally locate their services in "store-front centers." Branch libraries, neighborhood clinics of health departments, local political party offices, and so forth, which bring services directly into the neighborhood, are all making use of a settlement-house approach. Schoolmen sometimes use the term *lighted school* to designate a type of settlement-house program. A lighted school is one kept open after school hours so that adults and children in the community can make use of the physical facilities and special programs set up for their use.[15] This approach is a major part of the experimental programs of school systems in a number of cities, including Detroit.

4. *Auxiliary voluntary association approach.* An auxiliary voluntary association through which the organization communicates with the community may be established. Among schools, the P.T.A. and homeroom mothers' clubs are examples of this approach. Hospital service groups, volunteer fund-raising organizations for charitable agencies, alumni associations of universities, military officers' associations, act in this capacity as well. These are all associations attached to organizations, not independent voluntary associations.

5. *Common-messenger approach* takes advantage of individuals who are members of the bureaucratic organization and the family system at the same time. Because he occupies this dual position, the individual becomes a communication link between the two social systems. The child most obviously acts in this capacity for the school. The breadwinner linking family and occupational structure, as noted by Parsons, is a common messenger. Since all organizations are linked in this fashion to families, it is not surprising that this is a frequent channel of communication. It is surprising, however, that common messengers are not more often deliberately created by organizations. Parents brought into school to perform various services and teacher-aid tasks become available as common messengers.

6. *Mass-media approach* is one where the organization resorts to newspapers, printed notices, mass mailings, and so forth to communicate with families. Of all mechanisms, the problems and theories of mass media have been most thoroughly studied by sociologists, and probably most widely used by practitioners. Some of the basic principles of communication that have emerged from the study of mass media take on new meaning when applied to other linking mechanisms.

7. *Formal-authority approach.* Some organizations have a legal or a strong normative basis for communication and often for enforcement of their purposes. The juvenile court can compel the presence of parents in a court procedure. Schools may use the formal authority of the truant officer to visit the home of a family and demand compliance with compulsory attendance laws. It is the capacity to communicate through this mechanism, rather than coercive power of the organization, that we wish to emphasize here.

These mechanisms have been described in terms of communication *from* the organization *to* the family or the neighborhood. Communications initiated from the primary group toward the bureaucratic organization may use some, but not all, of these mechanisms; other mechanisms may be identified as operative in this direction, but they will not be described here.[16]

Mechanisms of Co-ordination Between Bureaucratic Organizations and External Primary Groups: A Tentative Theoretical Analysis

According to our earlier analysis, a balance at some point between isolation and intimacy would constitute the relation between school and family most likely to optimize educational objectives. Therefore, linking mechanisms must be assessed with reference to their capacities to effect this balance by increasing social distance when school and family are too close, decreasing it when they are too far apart, and maintaining it when they are in balance. Determination that an optimum balance has been achieved is a difficult theoretical and empirical problem that we shall not deal with here.[17] Lack of balance, however, has not been difficult to observe.

For example, some middle-class families with high educational or professional backgrounds in some school districts, often suburban, place such value on academic performance that their children are under constant pressure and exceptional demands are made on their schools. Such parents may even seek to influence what the school does with respect to grading, curriculum, type of academic assignments, and other functions which are presumably the responsibility of competent professional educators to whom the community has delegated the job of education. Oversensitized to the demands of such parents, teachers may make judgments in terms of parental pressures, rather than educationally appropriate standards. Although the children may do very well in school, the quality of their education may suffer by the confusion of family and school criteria. In our terms, family and school are too close for optimum educational goals to be achieved.

The opposite situation is more common, particularly in areas of low-income and transient families where parents may have little educational background. Whatever their verbalized opinions may be, some parents see little advantage in education, are suspicious of the school, fail to see a relation between home conditions and school success, and generally avoid contact with the school. They do not attend P.T.A. meetings and rarely see principal or teacher unless a problem with their child becomes severe enough for them to be sent for. This gap between school and family may be further increased because cultural values may differ from those of the teachers, who may add further distance by inadvertent middle-class bias.[18]

From the viewpoint of balance theory, the problem is to adopt mechanisms to increase distance in the first example and to decrease it in the second.

Sociologists working in the area of communication have particularly been concerned with bridging social distances, since the practical problems of political and consumer influence usually entail hostile or indifferent target groups. Four problems delineated by such students are particularly pertinent to our interests: (1) the problem of selective listening, (2) the problem of selective interpretation, (3) the problem of sufficient feedback when complex messages are communicated, and (4) the problem of scope, that is, extensiveness of numbers reached.[19] Although there are other problems in communication theory not here included, these seem to be especially relevant to school-family communication, and it was with them in mind that we developed the following general criteria for assessing the empirical linking mechanisms:

1. *Organizational initiative.*—Communication studies have pointed out that an unsympathetic audience frequently cannot be reached because it

will not listen to the message in the first place. Parents whose children are seen by the school to be most in need of help are frequently the least likely to come to P.T.A. meetings or to pay attention to school suggestions. In political campaigns it has been noted that people rarely listen to the opposition candidate.[20] In order to overcome this problem of selective listening, the communication procedures or linking mechanisms must permit the organization to take the initiative in reaching families who disagree with organizational goals, rather than leave the initiative to the family. If we examine the various linking procedures we see that they differ in the amount of initiative they permit the organization. Thus the detached-worker approach and the formal-authority approach permit the organization considerable initiative in confronting the family. By contrast, the mass-media and the voluntary-association approaches assume that the family will take the initiative. As a consequence the former are expected to be better procedures for communicating where there is a great social distance and selective listening is likely to muffle communication, whereas the latter should serve well for communicating across narrow social distances where selective listening and family initiative favor communication.

2. *Intensity.*—Even where people can be reached, they may selectively absorb or selectively forget parts of the communication so that it has little effect on their views.[21] Thus the principal might bring a parent into the school under threat of formal authority and force him to listen, but the parent might nevertheless misinterpret the principal's statements or forget those parts of the message with which he disagrees. Katz and Lazarsfeld suggest that where the individual is encased in a primary-group

atmosphere which is hostile to the views of the communicator, it is virtually impossible to produce change.[22] We would argue that in order to reach very distant families—those organized in primary groups and holding views antithetical to education—it is necessary to establish a primary-group type of relation with them. Only after the communicator has been accepted as a trusted member of the group can the school's views make an impact on the family.

Of the mechanisms noted, the detached-worker, the opinion-leader, and the settlement-house approaches permit this type of relation to develop most fully. The opinion-leader approach carries the most intensity because it makes use of existing primary-group relations. The detached-worker and settlement-house approaches develop intensity because the professional roles involve a mandate to develop friendly face-to-face contact. By contrast, formal authority is thought by many to be antithetical to the development of primary-group intensity. The mass-media approach can be expected to achieve hardly any primary-group intensity. Mechanisms high in intensity should be more effective for closing social distance and those low in intensity for increasing or maintaining social distance.

3. *Focused expertise.*—Messages, or contents of communications, can vary in complexity. In general, we would hypothesize that the more complex the message, the greater the need to provide feedback and flexible response if the message is to be communicated. Schools often need to communicate quite complex information, for example, about new approaches to mathematics or reading or about problems of adaptation for rural migrants to the urban community. Other messages are essentially simple, such as giving dates of meetings, school openings and closings, the child's specific academic standing, and so forth. Attempting to change values and per-

ceptions of socially distant families is likely to involve complex communications. The detached-worker, settlement-house, and formal-authority approaches are clearly most likely to provide the informed, flexible responses to face-to-face feedback which we call "focused expertise." In general, we suggest that linking procedures permitting considerable focused expertise will be more useful than those with limited focused expertise for communicating when distance is great and for narrowing the distance.

4. *Scope.*—Although it is not necessarily related directly to social distance between school and families, the capacity of a mechanism of co-ordination to reach many or few families with given resources will always have to be considered as a practical matter. Other things being equal, we should expect the procedure with the greatest scope to be preferred as a matter of economy. With its almost one-to-one relationship, the detached-worker approach is obviously very limited in scope, whereas the mass-media approach has very wide scope.

Recognizing this analysis of dimensions as both tentative and incomplete, it is useful nevertheless to summarize our assessment of the mechanisms of co-ordination empirically identified. Table 1 assigns an arbitrary position along each dimension for the seven mechanisms. These are initial estimates

of how each linking mechanism might fall on some strategic dimensions of communication. Other dimensions of communication may also be relevant, and aspects of linking mechanisms other than communication may need to be considered. This analysis is intended only to suggest a general strategy for approaching the problem of co-ordinating mechanisms between bureaucratic organizations and external primary groups. . . .

Notes

[1] Max Weber, *The Theory of Social and Economic Organization*, trans. A. M. Henderson and Talcott Parsons (New York: Oxford University Press, 1947), pp. 354–58; Talcott Parsons, *The Structure of Social Action* (New York: Free Press, 1949), pp. 542–52.

[2] William F. Ogburn, "The Changing Functions of the Family," in *Selected Readings in Marriage and the Family*, ed. Robert F. Winch and Robert McGinnis (New York: Holt, 1953), pp. 74–76; Joseph A. Schumpeter, *Capitalism, Socialism, and Democracy*, 2nd ed. (New York: Harper, 1947), p. 157; Louis Wirth, "Urbanism as a Way of Life," in *Cities and Society: The Revised Reader in Urban Sociology*, ed.

Table 1—Dimensions of Communication

Mechanisms	Initiative	Intensity	Focused Expertise	Scope
Detached worker	highest	high	highest	lowest
Opinion leader	low	highest	low	moderate
Settlement house	moderate to low	high to moderate	high	moderate
Voluntary association	lowest	moderate to low	moderate	high
Common messenger	moderate	moderate to low	lowest	highest
Mass media	moderate to low	lowest	lowest	highest
Formal authority	high	high to low	high to low	moderate

Paul K. Hatt and Albert J. Reiss, Jr. (New York: Free Press, 1957), pp. 593–94.

[3] Talcott Parsons, "The Social Structure of the Family," in *The Family: Its Function and Destiny*, ed. Ruth N. Anshen, rev. ed. (New York: Harper, 1959), pp. 260–63; George A. Theodorson, "Acceptance of Industrialization and Its Attendant Consequences for the Social Patterns of Non-Western Societies," *American Sociological Review*, 18 (1953), pp. 480–81.

[4] Charles H. Cooley in Paul Hare, Edgar F. Borgatta, and Robert F. Bales, eds., *Small Groups* (New York: Knopf, 1955), pp. 15–20.

[5] H. H. Gerth and C. Wright Mills, trans. and eds., *From Max Weber: Essays in Sociology* (New York: Oxford University Press, 1946), pp. 196–203.

[6] The development of experts might be supported, even when they are no better than the nonexpert, on the grounds that in the long run they will be able to do better. This hope is often fulfilled, as evidenced by the success of some research efforts. However, this should not obscure the issue that for any decision that has to be made at a given time the expert may not have the adequate answers. An excellent illustration of this point is given by Edward C. Banfield, *Political Influence* (New York: Free Press, 1961), pp. 33–36. In attempting to decide where a hospital should be built, they were sharp disagreements by experts on whether new staff could be attracted to a given location and, if it could be attracted, what the quality of the staff would be. Furthermore, to gather the information necessary to answer these questions would be very expensive and unlikely to be conclusive because of insufficient knowledge with which to determine with exactitude what attracts doctors and nurses to a given hospital and what surrounding circumstances are necessary for excellence in practice. Harold L. Wilensky, *Intellectuals in Labor Unions* (New York: Free Press, 1956), pp. 187 ff., has pointed out some of the circumstances when experts may be most profitably used.

[7] Harold L. Wilensky and Charles N. Lebeaux, *Industrial Society and Social Welfare* (New York: Russell Sage Foundation, 1958), pp. 250–57, point out some further defects of premature specialization, such as the problem of communication between specialists and the development of gaps which are handled by no one at all because they do not fit within the prior job definitions.

[8] Peter M. Blau, *Bureaucracy in Modern Society* (New York: Random House, 1956), pp. 58, 62; Robert K. Merton, "Bureaucratic Structure and Personality," in *Reader in Bureaucracy*, ed. R. K. Merton, A. P. Gray, B. Hockey, and H. C. Selvin (New York: Free Press, 1952), p. 364; Philip Selznick, "A Theory of Organizational Commitment," in *ibid.*, pp. 194–202.

[9] Donald I. Warren, "Modes of Conformity and the Character of Formal and Informal Organization Structure: A Comparative Study of Public Schools" (Ph.D. dissertation, University of Michigan, 1964), pp. 122–51.

[10] Peter Blau and W. Richard Scott, *Formal Organizations* (San Francisco: Chandler, 1962), pp. 87–115.

[11] This "balance theory of co-ordination" is elaborated in another paper by Litwak and Meyer, "A Balance Theory of Coordination between Bureaucratic Organizations and Community Primary Groups," *Administrative Science Quarterly*, 11 (1966), pp. 31–58. Our use of the term "balance" should not be confused with the use of psychological theories of balance. These are restricted to cognitive states. One psychological theory of balance which ours possibly overlaps is J. Alan Winter's concept of strategic balance: *Cognitive Balance, Strategic Balance and Discomfort in a Competitive Situation* (Preprint Center for Conflict Resolution, University of Michigan, 1963). Most psychological theories of balance do not deal with the concept of balance where the individual might seek to maximize two or more equally desirable events.

[12] For a description of such a program, see P. L. Crawford, D. I. Malamud, and J. R. Dumpson, *Working with Teenage Gangs* (New York: Welfare Council of New York City, 1950). A detailed consideration of this as well as the following linking mechanisms has been made in Eugene Litwak, Cheryl Mickelson, Henry J. Meyer et al., *Theory and Practice of Local School-Community Relations* (mimeographed, December, 1964).

[13] Katz and Lazarsfeld, *op. cit.*, pp. 1–100.

[14] S. Kobrin, "The Chicago Area Project: A Twenty-Five-Year Assessment," *Annals of*

the American Academy of Political and Social Sciences, 322 (1959), pp. 19–37.

The School and the Family 435

[15] Another term which is commonly used to express the same settlement-house idea is "store-front" services. Thus store-front libraries, store-front welfare services, and so forth are generally embraced in our concept of settlement house.

[16] We do not believe that the use of these mechanisms is the same when initiation is from the primary group rather than the formal organization. There are at least two major sources of difference. First, there is a matter of resources. Most formal organizations have resources to employ any or all of these linking mechanisms. By contrast, few primary groups can employ detached workers or settlement houses. Because of this differential we would suggest that when the primary group initiates linkage procedures, they must generally start with voluntary associations in order to provide a resource base for the other mechanisms.

A second consideration is that formal organizations are more likely than primary groups to be sensitive to public pressure because, in general, they are more exposed and need public support to survive. As a consequence, they can frequently be reached by mechanisms with low initiative like the mass media. Efforts to change the community stance of formal organizations are likely to use different mechanisms, and in different sequences, than organizations seeking to change primary groups.

Such considerations do not exhaust possible factors in the asymmetry of the linking mechanisms, but only point out some bases for it. For a more detailed discussion, see Litwak, Mickelson, Meyer et al., *op. cit.*, ch. 8.

[17] We approach this problem theoretically by analyzing the extent of uniformity and nonuniformity characterizing specified "educational tasks" and hence seek to develop criteria for determining relative contributions of primary-group relations and of organizational expertise necessary for task accomplishment. An empirical approach would seek to determine correlates of some dependent variable (such as high educational achievement) with measures of "social distance" between school and family. An experimental approach would manipulate "social distance" to determine optimum balance by maximizing some dependent variable.

[18] The possibility of inadvertent class bias among teachers was most forcefully made by W. Lloyd Warner, Robert J. Havighurst and Martin B. Loeb, *Who Shall Be Educated?* (New York: Harper, 1944). Also see Albert K. Cohen, *Delinquent Boys: The Culture of the Gang* (New York: Free Press, 1955), pp. 112–20.

[19] Hoyland, *op. cit.*, pp. 1062–1103; Eugene Litwak, "Some Policy Implications in Communications Theory with Emphasis on Group Factors," in *Education for Social Work, Proceedings, Seventh Annual Program Meeting* (New York: Council on Social Work Education, 1959), pp. 96–109; Herbert I. Abelson, *Persuasion: How Opinions and Attitudes Are Changed* (New York: Springer, 1959).

[20] Herbert H. Hyman and Paul Sheatsley, "Some Reasons Why Information Campaigns Fail," *Public Opinion Quarterly*, 11 (1947), 412–23.

[21] *Ibid.*

[22] Katz and Lazarsfeld, *op. cit.*, pp. 48–66.

Part VI
Auxiliary Readings

Ronald G. Corwin, *A Sociology of Education*. New York: Appleton-Century-Crofts, 1965.

The power environment of the school is composed of numerous pressure groups representing both national and local interests. Because the school must mediate between the demands of these various interests, it too acquires the characteristics of a special interest group. The author shows that the question of who runs the school is not a simple one, but depends upon the localism or cosmopolitanism of community leaders and on community features such as size and economic structure. School-community conflict should not be viewed primarily in terms of parents or school boards versus the school, but in the wider context of opposing orientations to the national and local society and of changing local traditions.

John M. Foskett. *The Normative World of the Elementary School Teacher*. Eugene, Oregon: Center for the Advanced Study of Educational Administration, 1966.

Consensus on the teacher's role between teachers, school board members, and parents is explored. It is shown that teachers have no greater agreement on the norms relevant to their job and their position in the community than do their role partners. Teachers tend to overestimate both the consensus and the restrictiveness of parents and school board members while they underestimate the consensus of their principals. The authors conclude that there is a great deal of ambiguity in the definition of the role of the elementary school teacher.

David Wilder, Nathalie S. Friedman, Robert Hill, Eva Sandis, and Sam D. Sieber. *Actual and Perceived Consensus on Educational Goals between School and Community*, Section V. New York: Bureau of Applied Social Research, Columbia University, 1968. (USOE Grant No. OE–5–10–238).

The number of school-structured efforts to provide observability for parents is shown to vary among different types of communities and between elementary and secondary schools. Mother's knowledge of school matters is higher when extensive formal channels between school and home are provided. Parents who have high contact with the school are somewhat less likely to be very satisfied with the school, but more likely to support the school and to vote in bond issue elections.

Robert Herriot and Nancy Hoyt St. John. *Social Class and the Urban School*. New York: Wiley, 1966.

The authors attempt to investigate the impact of the socioeconomic composition of elementary schools on teachers, principals, and pupils. Teachers in low SES schools are younger and less experienced than those in high SES schools. And although they are more satisfied with their occupation, teachers in low SES schools exhibit lower morale, innovativeness, and interest in pupils. Principals do not vary significantly in origins, attitudes, or effectiveness according to the SES of the school. The authors indicate that the quality of the prinicpal's performance is more critical for the teacher's performance in low than in high SES schools.

David Rogers. *110 Livingston Street*, pp. 363–94. New York: Random House, 1968.

The author analyzes the history of problems between local community groups and the central school system in New York City. The school board's unresponsiveness to local feelings produced coalitions between militant left-wing groups and parent associations. Attempts to create local school boards in the early fifties were ineffectiveness in meliorating conditions because the boards lacked sufficient power and were never integrated into the centralized system. Inadequate representation at the local level persisted through the screening out of "troublesome" candidates, while attempts to organize local action groups were regarded as "extremist" tactics.

William H. Sewell and Vimal Shah. "Parents' Education and Children's Educational Aspirations and Achievements." *American Sociological Review*, 33 (1968), pp. 191–209.

The authors attempt to test the theory that a discrepancy in the educational levels attained by parents leads to parental pressure for academic achievement in their children. Educational levels of parents and the intelligence of the child are positively related to parental encouragement, college plans, college attendance, and graduation. A higher proportion of males perceived parental encouragement. The findings cast doubt on the initial hypothesis regarding discrepancies in the educational levels of mother and father.

Index